THE GREAT TV SITCOM BOOK

Expanded Edition

by
Rick Mitz

A PERIGEE BOOK

This book is dedicated to
My parents,
Who told me to turn off the television and get to work, and to
Connie Goldman,
Who told me it was okay to turn it on again and have some fun.

ACKNOWLEDGMENTS

This book wasn't all watching TV and writing about it; sometimes I actually talked to people and, less often, listened to people. From the bottom of my picture tube, I'd like to thank the following friends for their aid, comfort, enlightenment, inspiration and entertainment: Mark Miller of *Broadcasting* Magazine; Julie D'Acci and Maxine Fleckner at the Wisconsin Center for Film and Theater Research; Motion Picture Section of the Library of Congress; Lincoln Center Library (top floor); Larry Gelbart; Norman Lear; Grant Tinker; Jim Brooks; Irving Pincus; Jeff Satkin at Viacom; Leslie Slocum of the Television Information Office; Kathie Berlin at Rogers and Cowan; Marianne Muellerleile; Kathy Matthews; Priscilla Morrill; Randi Schnur; Joan Tarshis; Jerry and Pat Brody; David Sokolow; Andrea Wyatt; Mary Tyler Moore; Robin Mitz; Allan Rich; Helen "Pussycat" Barrow; The Marek Mob: Gypsy da Silva, George Caughlan, Ron Lief, Fred Sawyer, Anne Knauerhase, Bill Parkhurst, and Rupert Holmes, who said, "Life's a constant disappointment when you live on celluloid . . ."

A Special Thank You to the Virginia Center for the Creative Arts, where I was a Fellow and where much of this book was written. And thanks to two people who believe in me nearly as much as I believe in them: Robert Cornfield and Joyce Engelson. Plus love and devotion to Fannie Enzer, who showed me the joy of writing.

Perigee Books are published by
the Putnam Publishing Group, 200 Madison Avenue, New York, New York 10016.

The publisher and author would like to thank the following people and organizations for their assistance
with stills and information related to the preparation of this book:

Jim Brooks; Larry Gelbart; Dick Van Dyke; Danny Thomas; Calvada Productions; Kathie Berlin, Rogers and Cowan; Grant Tinker, MTM Enterprises; Norman Lear, TAT/Tandem Productions; OTB Ltd.; Irving Pincus; Annette Welles; MCA/Universal; Twentieth Century-Fox Television; Can Creek Enterprises; ABC; CBS; NBC; Wisconsin Center for Film and Theater Research; Broadcasting Magazine; TV Guide; Motion Picture Section, Library of Congress; Jeff Satkin, Viacom Enterprises; Witt, Thomas, Harris Productions; Bob Garon, Four D Productions; David Wolper; James Komack and Company; TTC Productions; Warner Bros. Television; Paramount Pictures Corp. (*Taxi, The Odd Couple, Happy Days, Laverne & Shirley, Mork & Mindy,* and *The Associates* photographs reproduced with the permission of Paramount Pictures Corporation. © Paramount Pictures Corporation. All Rights Reserved. All uses restricted without written permission from Paramount Pictures Corporation); Lorimar Productions; Time-Life Films; William Morris Agency; ITC Entertainment; Worldvision Enterprises Inc.; Four Star Entertainment Corp.; Metromedia Producers Corp.; Columbia Pictures Television; TV Cinema Sales; CBS Entertainment; National Television Association; Filmways, Inc.; Columbia Pictures Industries; and Television Information Office.

Library of Congress Cataloging in Publication Data

Mitz, Rick.
　　The great TV sitcom book.

　　Includes index.
　　1. Comedy programs—United States—History and criticism. I. Title.
PN1992.8.C66M5　1983　791.45'75　82-19055
ISBN 0-399-50767-1

THE GREAT TV SITCOM BOOK

Also by Rick Mitz

The Apartment Book

CONTENTS

Contents

Contents

Early Research: The author and his sister Robin getting ready to watch Ozzie and Harriet.

CONFESSIONS OF A SITCOM ADDICT

I am a child of the tube.

I was born on a Wednesday, ten minutes past *The Honeymooners*. I was born on the cusp between Bilko and the Beaver. Lucy is my rising star. My sign is Panasonic.

I was suckled on situation comedies, lullabyed on their laugh-tracks, reared on the Ricardos. I know more about Lucy's relationship with Ricky than I know about anything else—except, possibly, Harriet's relationship with Ozzie.

The sitcom community was my family, my private people, my dearest friends. I was a displaced baby, hatched from a twenty-four-inch Sylvania and fostered out to my parents until the day when Robert Young and Donna Reed—my *true* parents—would come to claim me.

Sitcoms represented the total sphere of my life. They never let me down. Except for being preempted by an occasional Presidential address, sitcoms were always there when they said they would be. They never kept me waiting. I have stayed awake at night imagining new plots for favorite sitcoms that have been canceled. *Car 54, Where Are You?* lives on in my head.

Sitcoms were my babysitters, my guardians, a mini-community within a television chassis, full of magic tricks. Miss Brooks and Mr. Peepers were the teachers. Mr. Ed brought wildlife to the television environs and moved right next door to our country cousins, the Beverly Hillbillies. Susie McNamara, that publicly private secretary, showed us what the world of business was all about. Amos 'n' Andy integrated the television neighborhood and moved in next door to Molly Goldberg, who dispensed chicken soup right through the TV screen. The military? Ernest T. Bilko gave us the right prescription for conscription. And who needed friends when we had chums like Dobie and Maynard, Margie and Mrs. Odettes, Walter Denton and Eddie Haskell? Sitcoms were the neighborhood of the mind for the lonely or alone. We all tuned in to tune out.

But sitcoms aren't an end to themselves. I have tried to integrate them into the rest of my life. From them, I have learned a fractured sense of American ethics. I have learned how to behave; that good conversation is witty and chatty; that funny lines come once every twenty-eight seconds; and that I get two minutes off every thirteen minutes for a commercial break. I have learned about relationships from Pete and Gladys, Sanford and Son, the Hathaways, Patty Duke and her identical cousin. Sitcoms were the literature of my generation.

Sitcoms became my reality. While my parents were across the hall yelling at each other, I hid away in my room, watching my portable black-and-white, playing voyeur to a neighborhood of television families that got along better than we did. When Paul Petersen had a problem, his mother, Donna Reed, and his father, Carl Betz, dealt with him respectfully and lovingly. Donna Reed didn't scream at her kids to clean up their rooms. On the other hand, Donna's kids never gave her the problems I gave my mother. I screamed and ranted and rebelled. "Aw, shucks," was about all the lip Donna got from her kids.

I studied the shows and thought my father should be like Robert Young (before he became a doctor)—kindly, soft-spoken, wise—and on for only a half-hour a week. Why didn't my mother wear pearls and hose when she mopped the kitchen floor, and how come she never greeted me at the door after school with the requisite glass of milk and plateful of brownies (with variations of cookies and fudge)? TV brothers and sisters, although they often fought and scrapped, always came through for one another when the music got mellow at the end of the show. So where was that mellow music? And why weren't our neighbors wacky and fun-loving like Fred and Ethel? Why did we drive an old car when everyone on the sitcom block always had a new car (except, of course, *The Beverly Hillbillies* and *My Mother the Car*)? How come nobody ever sweated on sitcoms? Real Life (everything that went on between sitcoms) was so complicated; my sitcoms were so . . . so innocent.

Today it's different. Today I have conversations with nine-year-olds about Maude's abortion, Walter's vasectomy, Mary Tyler Moore's affairs, Archie Bunker's sex hang-ups. It's amazing to me—not because these kids are so sexually sophisticated, but because their parents allow them to stay up that late. In my day (and night), I had to stuff pillows into the cracks in the door so my parents, across the hall, couldn't see that my light was still on. Then I would cop a quiet look at my friends—Blondie and Bud and Opie and Ethel and all the rest of them who taught me what real friendship was like. Neat and quick relationships that were finished in a half-hour.

And it's still with me. I would rather watch a good sitcom than anything, even now. I have spent years reorganizing my social life, jiggling and juggling dates to be in front of the TV screen for *The Mary Tyler Moore Show* and the rest of the Saturday Night Lineup or the Monday Night Lineup—whatever night was the best that season. I have written to sponsors and networks asking that they move their programs to a better hour and evening for me. I know better. My subscriptions to *The New Yorker* and *Atlantic* have long since lapsed; I have a five-year arrangement with *TV Guide*, which I read nightly like the Gideon. I gear my days around watching reruns of old favorites, some of which I know by heart, like the Gettysburg Address.

I know better. I know the truth. I can see for myself that sitcoms babysat for a generation that didn't grow up like David and Ricky, or Little Ricky, or the Beaver. TV didn't produce fathers who know best. Our favorite Martian only gave birth to a bunch of spaced-out kids, a media-minded mass that marched in protest, smoked in protest, protested in protest—and then ran home to watch themselves do it all over again on the 6 O'Clock news. I know all that. But I still watch them. I watch the reruns of the old shows. And I watch the first runs of new shows.

It's not because they're so good or because they're so funny or because I see in them something deeper and more meaningful than appears on the surface of the celluloid. No. It's just that watching sitcoms is so much easier. It's easier than living, than planning, than preparing. In sitcoms, everybody always says the right thing and they say it cleverly. And for twenty-four minutes—plus commercials—I can be part of that well-timed, evenly paced world where everything has a happy ending and a theme song. I want a life with a laugh-track.

I'm not a freak, I'm not so different. I'm just an average member of a generation that was weaned on the nineteen-inch screen. I was a tube baby. I always will be. I just can't seem to cut the cord.

Owner's Manual

There is a group of people out there who can read on-screen credits at a superhuman speed, but anything written down on paper, ploddingly slow. This book is for you—the people who grew up watching TV, not reading books. I have tried to write the first book that was as easy to read as watching television. Where all you'd have to do was press a button, turn a dial, and the book would read itself to you.

It didn't work out that way (but with any luck, maybe someday they'll make a series out of this book). For now, though, hard as it is to believe, you actually have to *turn pages*. You might even have to use the *Contents* or the *Index* (think of them as supplements to *TV Guide*). And you might want to read the *Appendixes* —the *Tags* (think of them as sort of the Morning Prayer, "Star-Spangled Banner" and station sign-off). It's hard work, I know, reading a book—but at least you didn't have to go through all the labor I did, like putting your fingers to a keyboard and waiting eighteen months to see it in print.

First, though, a word from your sponsor: Me. Is every sitcom that ever aired in this book? Mostly. But maybe not all of them. The archives of television are, unfortunately, incomplete and spotty, and networks, producers, and sponsors would sooner forget their flops than give out data on them. Guess they don't think shows like *Honestly Celeste* or *Lum and Abner* are that historically significant. But be assured that every sitcom I could

get my hands—and/or my eyes—on is in this book.

Some shows, you will see, have been given more emphasis than others. The ones that I write about in great depth are called *The Front Runners*. The other shows are written about to a lesser extent and are called *Also Rans*. How did I decide whether to make a show a Front Runner or an Also Ran? Certain shows (whether I liked them or not) were Significant or Especially Interesting or Important or Popular and I couldn't leave them out. Other shows—things like *Two Girls Named Smith* and *Me and the Chimp*—just didn't seem to warrant major mentions. There are, I'm sure you'll notice, some borderline cases—shows like *Hogan's Heroes* and *That Girl* and *Green Acres*—that might have been Front Runners in popularity. But after writing in depth about *Sergeant Bilko*, *Mary Tyler Moore* and *Beverly Hillbillies*, it seemed redundant to write about the others (not because they were the same, but because parts of them were similar). There were some shows that I simply couldn't stand enough to write about for more than three paragraphs.

So how should you use this book? Well, like your old Philco, this book too comes with its own set of operating instructions. They're listed below. Oh, and if anything goes wrong, do not attempt to remove the back (there are no reader-serviceable parts in there) and be sure to call a qualified service personnel.

Operating Instructions: How to Use This Book

Options, options, options:

1. You can simply read *The Great TV Sitcom Book*, cover to cover.
2. You can just look at the pictures.
3. Pick a TV season, any TV season. Let's say . . . 1955–1956. From *The Honeymooners* to *The People's Choice*, you can find out what was playing, who was in it, how long it ran, and why. All in alphabetical order, even. Just look up 1955–1956 in the Contents section.
4. Want to know who was in what show? Just turn to the Index and look up—oh, say, Jerry Van Dyke. Follow the bouncing page numbers, and you'll discover all of Jerry's sitcoms (lots).
5. Want to find *My Little Margie*, but can't remember the year she debuted? Look her up in the Index.
6. . . . and try out the Appendixes. They'll tell you which sitcoms won Emmies, which won the highest ratings, which ran the longest.
7. If nothing is good on television tonight—as unlikely as that is—or if your TV's busted, read this book. It's not the real thing, but it'll give you something to do until the repairman gets there.

SITCOMMENTS

So What Is a Sitcom, Anyway?

Any good travel guide to Television Land would point out that a sitcom has its own special set of characteristics. For example, a sitcom usually lasts thirty minutes (including commercials), although there've been sitcoms that were only fifteen minutes long, and others that were an hour. Usually laughter—either live or taped—accompanies a sitcom, but several sitcoms have tried to go it without. And, by its very nature, a sitcom is supposed to be funny, but we all know that the funniest thing on many of them is the incessant howling coming from the laugh-track. A sitcom has a basic format, something like this: There's the credits, then a commercial, then the show, then a commercial, then more of the show, then more commercials, then a short "tag," then the closing credits. (Some shows, like *Barney Miller*, open with the tag.) A sitcom has a lot of commercials, some of which are sitcoms in themselves.

Here's how Parke Levy, the writer-producer of *December Bride*, described sitcoms: "A sitcom is a small hunk of life exaggerated for comic purposes. If you play it realistically, it comes out drama because very little in life itself is funny. People want a mirror held up to life, but at an angle so that it's humorous."

Other people have said other things. This 1961 gem came from Newton Minow, the lawyer John Kennedy appointed head of the FCC (he's the one who called television a "vast wasteland"): "Sitcoms are formula comedies about totally unbelievable families," sandwiched between violence and blood and thunder.

Others have called sitcoms human comic strips. "You can't tell them apart." "They are really silly." All those may sound like negatives, but to the true sitcom lover, those are precisely the reason he watches.

But we're getting ahead of ourselves. You should know that in the sitcom, there's the *sit*—the things that happen—and the *com*—the laughs that, hopefully, come out of the sit. Usually the situation (and the comedy) are quite predictable.

For the most part, at the start of each new episode, the characters are back where they were last week. Ralph is still driving a bus. Lucy is still chasing the stars. Ann Marie still can't find an acting job. It's that predictability that's the basis of the humor. People don't change, the shows seem to be telling us. So no matter what the new situation is—no matter how crazy or dizzy—the characters always respond to it as we expect them to. And that's funny. If someone insults Maude, we wait with her pause—in hilarious anticipation—to see how she's going to react (will it be "God'll get you for that" or another put-down?). And of course, the complications in a story are always resolved, and the principal characters are always happy by the tag, usually complete with a nifty moral. (Some shows, like *M*A*S*H*, occasionally break out of the sitcom format and become sitdrams.)

Family is the most important word in sitcoms. Not just Ozzie and Harriet and David and Ricky, or the "Hi, honey, I'm home syndrome," or any of the other familiar familial devices. Every sitcom must have a family—whether it's the real family of the Cleaver or Anderson variety, or the synthetic, temporary family of the *M*A*S*H* unit, or the WJM-TV newsroom of *The Mary Tyler Moore Show. Mork and Mindy* were each other's family, *Mr. Ed* was part of the family, even *All in the Family* was a family (even though it often appeared to come out of the war zone somewhere).

What isn't a sitcom? Well, *The Carol Burnett Show* was a variety show, not a sitcom, even though it had small-scale situations with continuing characters. At best, *The Carol Burnett Show* was a skitcom. *The Jack Benny Program* was not a sitcom; any show that has its host singing folk songs with Peter, Paul and Mary, or playing the violin (albeit badly) on stage in front of a curtain is not a sitcom.

Which shows are sitcoms? On the following pages you'll read about more than 400 of them. Those are sitcoms.

Another thing you should know about sitcoms: They're traditionally about five years behind The Real World (a.k.a. Real Life). Not that America was living with talking horses in 1956, but the sensibility of the 1961 *Mr. Ed* was about five years behind the times. It's not that Hollywood is that backward; it's just that overcautious network people want to go with supersafe concepts. Which is why next season you'll see repeat performances—sitcom clones—of this season's hit show.

Sitcom's roots used to be radio (whose roots were movies, whose roots were vaudeville). Today's sitcom's roots, though, are yesterday's sitcoms. In a 1978 episode of *Diff'rent Strokes*, when Gary Coleman, playing a Harlem kid who'd been adopted by a Park Avenue millionaire, saw his new swank home, he rolled his eyes and said: "This is better than anything I ever saw on *The Brady Bunch*."

Possibly the most apt thing that's ever been said about sitcoms is this, from a network official: "What sitcoms have in common is that they make people feel good, make them feel comfortable."

We feel as if we know the characters in a sort of sitcamaraderie. And that they know us. If, for example, Archie and Lucy and Ted and Margie and a host of others from the sitcommunity would have been on the other side of the tube—watching TV instead of being on it, you

can be sure they would have spent their time watching sitcoms. Can't you just picture Dobie running home to catch the latest episode of *Burns and Allen*—and of course Ted Baxter hoping to catch the last few minutes of himself? "I don't know why they call it *The Mary Tyler Moore Show*," he mutters. "It's *my* show."

The future of sitcoms? Well, certainly more of the same—more shows about space cadets landing on earth, the trials and tribulations of young marrieds, blue-collar workers who shout at their wives (or husbands). And, no doubt, in the next few years, there will be gay sitcoms, sitcoms about incest (with a whole new kind of laugh-track—the gasp-track) and, probably, sitcoms about mass murders, bag ladies, and people who write books about sitcoms.

But one thing for sure: Any minute now, sitcoms are going to become Art. That's right—just like they've done to old Bob Hope movies and other bits of elevated nostalgia, some guy who works for a film society somewhere will come across a faded print of *Mr. Ed* and discover that—yes, yes—the sitcom is the Art Form Of Today. *Laverne and Shirley* an Art Form? *My Three Sons? The Beverly Hillbillies?* Art Forms?

Sure. But we knew that all along.

Some Words About Words

As you read this book, you'll come across some terms that you should know. Here are some informal definitions in no particular order whatsoever:

SYNDICATION What a show goes into, usually after it's finished its prime-time run—i.e., when *I Love Lucy* finished its long stint on CBS, all the episodes (except for one that was a bomb that the producers were embarrassed to release again) were sold to a syndication (not to be confused with a syndicate—that's another kind of organized crime), which then leased it to TV stations around the world, which is why you now see *I Love Lucy* about six times a day on some local stations.

NETWORK There are three of them—ABC and CBS and NBC (there used to be another one, the DuMont Network, but it died). Networks often purchase sitcom "packages" from producers who may or may not be affiliated with the network. For example, one network put up the money for Norman Lear to shoot his pilot of *All in the Family*, then decided it didn't like it, and so CBS bought it. Sometimes networks make mistakes.

NIELSEN RATINGS Somewhere around the country—nobody seems to know them—there are people with boxes attached to their TV sets (a box on a box) that signals the Nielsen people (who tell the networks, who tell the advertisers) what people are—and aren't—watching.

KINESCOPE When series were shot live (i.e., not filmed, but telecast directly around the country), the shows were often filmed right off the set to get a record of the show. Sometimes these kinescopes were then sent to other parts of the country in a different time zone, where they were aired at a later time.

PRIME TIME The big-bucks hours for the sponsors (and the big time to watch TV), usually somewhere between 7 P.M. and 11 P.M.

CANCELLATION What happens to a show when its ratings hit the pits. Sometimes the show is reincarnated as a syndicated rerun—heaven—or sometimes it's reduced to a footnote in television history.

RERUNS When you see an episode that's already been on television before, that's a rerun.

LAUGH-TRACK A tape machine that produces various varieties of laughs—and chuckles and guffaws and groans—that are added to a sitcom after it's been taped or filmed.

MIDSEASON REPLACEMENT When a show has a rotten rating after its initial thirteen-week run, it is replaced in midseason—often January, the middle of the sitcom season—with a new and (hopefully) improved show. This has come to be called "The Second Season," which eager network officials hope will be more like the Second Coming. Some nasty networks often replace a sitcom with another one after only one or two episodes—like baseball.

TV SEASON From September to September—like school.

SUMMER RERUNS When the network airs an episode over again during the summer of the season it's originally aired.

PILOT Like an out-of-town tryout for a Broadway play, production companies often film or tape a sample episode of a sitcom to try to sell it to a network. Often a network will buy a pilot and air it to gauge audience response (see Nielsen). Sometimes, in fact, a network will buy several episodes of a show and run it as a "limited series," in hopes of its becoming popular enough to continue full time.

STUDIO AUDIENCE As in "Taped before a studio audience." Means that the sitcom is more or less run through like a play, complete with a "live" audience, who respond to the show—and also to the applause signs and the person who "warms up" the audience with jokes and gags (Garry Marshall, *Happy Days*, et al, producer, actually throws candy to the audience to keep them from getting restless). Often the audience response is doctored afterward in the privacy of the control booth.

SPONSOR The "product" (i.e., Ovaltine or Chicken of the Sea tuna) whose advertising dollars pay to put the show on (and whose commercial messages interrupt the show at least every fifteen minutes).

Seven Sitcom Species

There are seven types of sitcoms. Some of them overlap, some of them don't. They are:

1. Domcoms—domestic comedies that revolve mostly around family life (*Father Knows Best, Donna Reed, All in the Family*).
2. Kidcoms—comedies about kids (*Dobie Gillis, Happy Days, My Little Margie, Laverne and Shirley, Leave It to Beaver*).
3. Couplecoms—sitcoms that mainly revolve around two people and their relationship (*I Love Lucy, Pete and Gladys, Burns and Allen*).
4. SciFiComs—sitcoms that use magic and fantasy as their situations (*Bewitched, My Mother the Car, Mr. Ed, Mork and Mindy*).
5. Corncom—rural-oriented sitcoms (*Beverly Hillbillies, Real McCoys, Andy Griffith*).
6. Ethnicoms—shows about a particular ethnic group (*Mama, The Goldbergs, Amos 'n' Andy, Sanford and Son*).
7. Careercoms—shows that mainly center around the leading character's work life (*Dick Van Dyke, Private Secretary, Our Miss Brooks, Mary Tyler Moore, Taxi*), and a subdivision, the Servicecom (*Sergeant Bilko, McHale's Navy, M*A*S*H*).

There are, of course, some shows that overlap. *The Real McCoys* is a rural sitcom, but it's about a family. And shows like *Leave It to Beaver* and *Dennis the Menace* basically center around the kids, but within the family structure. Same with *Ozzie and Harriet*. And *My Little Margie*, although it was about a kid, was also about a relationship between a girl and her dad. And of course, the ethnic sitcoms—*The Jeffersons, The Goldbergs, Mama*—were really domestic comedies. Got the picture?

Setcoms

There is an important subdivision of the sitcom called the domestic comedy (or domcom, as it's known in the trade). Some early examples: *The Aldrich Family, Ozzie and Harriet, Father Knows Best, Donna Reed, Leave It to Beaver. All in the Family* was a domestic comedy (although not quite as domesticated).

How to know a domcom when you see one? Well, one of the distinguishing characteristics is that instead of the plain and pure rowdy laugh-track, a domcom has a chuckle-track, filled with oohs and aahs and even an occasional sniffle. A domcom's music is mellower. And—oh, yeah—the most important thing: A domestic comedy takes place in a house—usually comfortable and upper-middle-class and suburban, always in the best of low-key taste, and somehow very Protestant. So are the people. The house, though, is almost more important than the people in it, and perhaps these domestic situation comedies should be called *setcoms*. There's a room for every character—a kitchen for Mom, a den for Dad (with a Favorite Chair), bedrooms for the boys and girls. Around these houses are sidewalks so clean you could eat off them.

Dad comes home from work—"Hi, honeee, I'm home"—every day at the same time, and brings no problems with him. Mom is always in the kitchen, whipping up some fudge or some aphorisms. The kids are cute and precocious and the regulation shaggy dog never messes.

The final clue: The classic domcom family is filled with peace, love, and laughter. Just like Real Life, right?

Stock Sitcom Characters

Television—like any other business—relies on formulas to ensure success. One of the ways to make sure a sitcom has at least a fighting chance is to write in characters who are just like everyone else on every other sitcom—same personality, different dialogue. Here are sixty-seven of the most typical sitcom types and an example or two of each.

1. Cantankerous old geezer—Amos McCoy, Fred Sanford.
2. Man-hungry, self-deprecating secretary/neighbor/associate—Schultzy, Rhoda and Brenda Morgenstern, Sally Rogers, Miss Brooks.
3. Perky, nutty, single girl—Sally Fields, Marlo Thomas, Karen Valentine, Sandy Duncan.
4. Sassy secretary—Carol on *Bob Newhart*.
5. Plain Jane—Miss Jane on *Beverly Hillbillies*, Olive/Vi on the Ann Sothern shows.
6. Dumb sexpot nymphs—Chrissy on *Three's Company* and Elly May on *Beverly Hillbillies*.
7. Extraterrestrial terror—Mork, *My Favorite Martian*, Samantha.
8. Spirited spirits—*My Mother the Car, Topper, I Dream of Jeannie*.
9. Wacky neighbors—Fred and Ethel, Millie and Jerry from *Dick Van Dyke*, Ed and Trixie Norton, *Bewitched*'s the Kravitzes.
10. Cute kids—Beaver, *Donna Reed*'s offspring, *Family Affair*'s gang.
11. Active-but-average adolescents—Dobie, the Sweathogs, the *Good Times* clan, Laverne and Shirley.
12. Tough-but-tender hoodlum—The Fonz, Vinnie Barbarino.
13. Sensible mother—Donna Reed, Margaret Anderson, Harriet Nelson, June Cleaver.
14. Father knows best—Fred MacMurray, Jim Anderson, Ward Cleaver.
15. Bumbling pa—Ozzie Nelson, Riley.
16. Dizzy wife—Gracie, Lucy, Gladys.
17. Patient husband—George, Ricky, Pete.
18. Lovable geriatric—Lilly *December Bride* Ruskin.
19. Nosy oldie—Granny Clampett, Verna Felton as Hilda Crocker on *December Bride*.
20. Nice sensible housewife (who also happens to be a witch or Frankenstein's bride)—Samantha, Morticia Addams, Lilly Munster.
21. Lovable illegal alien—José Jimenez, Latka on *Taxi*.
22. Out-of-the-mouth-of-boobs—Ted Baxter, Lenny and Squiggy, Gomer Pyle, Jethro Bodine, Schneider on *One Day at a Time*.
23. Testy-but-tender boss—Lou Grant, Dick Doyle on *Rhoda*, Mr. Mooney on the Lucy shows, Colonel Potter on *M*A*S*H*.
24. Glandular problems, male variety—Jack Tripper on *Three's Company*, Bob Collins on *Love That Bob*.
25. Straight man to bent single girl—Donald on *That Girl*.
26. Lovable lunatic—Klinger on *M*A*S*H*.
27. Contagious con man—Bilko, Kingfish.
28. Uppity black woman with high ratings—Florida on *Good Times*, Florence on *The Jeffersons*.
29. Child-is-the-father-of-the-man—Lamont on *Sanford and Son*.
30. Sassy and sex-crazed—Sue Ann Nivens on *Mary Tyler Moore*, *Alice*'s Flo, Mrs. Roper.
31. Levelheaded heroine-type—Mary Richards, Ann Romano on *One Day at a Time*, Alice.
32. Daffy sidekick—Buddy Sorrell of *Dick Van Dyke*, Barney Fyfe of *Andy Griffith*.
33. Lovable incompetent—Howard Borden on *Bob Newhart*, Maxwell Smart.
34. Nice-but-nutsy—Georgette on *Mary Tyler Moore*, Edith Bunker.
35. Sex-change artists—Felix Unger, Charles Nelson Reilly, Paul Lynde, *The Ugliest Girl in Town*.
36. Overblown windbags—Ralph Kramden, Don Rickles, Archie Bunker, George Jefferson.

37. Sarcastic-but-sensitive leading man—Hawkeye on *M*A*S*H*.
38. Lovable slob—Oscar, Lou Grant, Doberman.
39. Prig—Charles and Frank on *M*A*S*H*.
40. Putting on airs on the air—Phyllis, Chatsworth Osborne, Jr., *Angie*'s in-laws.
41. They've got a secret—Wilbur and Mr. Ed, Samantha and Darrin, Mork and Mindy, Tim and Uncle Martin, Cosmo and the Kirbys.
42. Innocent foil—Amos, Harry Von Zell, Bilko's brigade.
43. Harried husband—Fred Mertz.
44. Ever-suffering wife—Peg Riley, Alice Kramden, Louise Jefferson.
45. Wise-ass progeny—Mike and Gloria, Chico, Barbara and Julie on *One Day at a Time*, Rusty and Linda on *Make Room for Daddy*.
46. Outcast as "in"—Maynard, The Fonz, the Sweathogs.
47. Rebel with a clause—Maynard—"You Rang?"—and The Fonz—"A-a-a-a-y!"
48. Shy guy—Bob Newhart, Mr. Peepers.
49. Heartwarming immigrant—Mama, Papa Lars, the Goldbergs.
50. Show-biz couple—Mr. Adams and Eve.
51. Surrogate father—*Bachelor Father*, *Diff'rent Strokes*.
52. Surrogate mother—Betty Hutton, *Farmer's Daughter*, Giles on *Family Affair*, Bub and Uncle Charlie on *My Three Sons*, Aunt Bee.
53. Surrogate family—WJM-TV newsroom, *Taxi*, *Gilligan's Island*, *M*A*S*H* unit.
54. Dizzy daughter—His little Margie.
55. Lovable pet—Tramp on *My Three Sons*, Fang in *Get Smart*, Ladadog on *Please Don't Eat the Daisies*.
56. Peculiar pet—Thing on *Addams Family*, Eddie Wolfgang Munster and his pet Spot, *Mr. Ed* himself, Cleo on *The People's Choice*.
57. Frustrated father—Mr. Gidget, Vern Albright, Laverne's pop.
58. Son image—The Fonz, Chico, Howard on *Bob Newhart*.
59. Strange couples—Oscar and Felix, *Mork and Mindy*, *Chico and the Man*, Max and 99.
60. Sarcastic-but-sensible spouse—Emily Hartley on *Bob Newhart*.
61. Domestic who runs the show—Hazel on *Hazel*, Giles on *Family Affair*.
62. Noisy prop—toilet flushing on *All in the Family*.
63. Big-mouthed boss—Honeywell on *Margie*, Larry Tate on *Bewitched*, Mr. Mooney.
64. Big-mouthed bigot with a heart of mold—Archie Bunker, George Jefferson, Fred Sanford.
65. Working woman—*Private Secretary*, *Our Miss Brooks*, Mary Richards.
66. We're in the money—*The Jeffersons*, *The Beverly Hillbillies*.
67. Poor but pure—*Real McCoys*, *Good Times*, *Honeymooners*.

Good for a Laugh

One sure way to get a laugh is to have a running joke that reappears week after week. Or so goes an old adage in sitcomland. Well, apparently, it works, because a lot of those phrases associated with a character on a sitcom stick—i.e., the shtick sticks. Here are some examples of famous phrases over the years (in order of appearance):

E-U-U-U-U Lucille Ball as Lucy Ricardo on *I Love Lucy*, whenever she found herself in trouble (often).

G-R-R-R-R Gale Storm as Margie Albright on *My Little Margie*, whenever she found herself in trouble (often).

WHAT A REVOLTIN' DEVELOPMENT THIS IS William Bendix as Chester A. Riley on *Life of Riley*, whenever he found himself in trouble (often).

SLAM, BANG, TO THE MOON Jackie Gleason as Ralph Kramden in *The Honeymooners* to his wife, Alice, whenever he found her to be trouble.

FORGET IT, RALPH Audrey Meadows as Alice Kramden on *The Honeymooners*, to her husband, Ralph, whenever.

YOU RANG? Bob Denver as Maynard G. Krebs on *The Many Loves of Dobie Gillis*, when anyone said something like "dirty, disgusting, despicable."

YOU RANG? Ted Cassidy as Lurch on *The Addams Family*, whenever anyone rang his bell.

WOULD YOU BELIEVE Don Adams as Maxwell Smart on *Get Smart!*, whenever someone didn't believe him and he was trying to come up with an acceptable alternative.

MEATHEAD, DINGBAT, STIFLE Carroll O'Connor as Archie Bunker on *All in the Family*—epithets he would hurl at various members of his family.

GOD'LL GET YOU FOR THAT Beatrice Arthur as *Maude*, whenever she was angry at someone (usually husband Walter).

A-A-A-A-Y Henry Winkler as The Fonz on *Happy Days*, whenever he would make an entrance (or an exit . . . or anything in-between), said with his thumbs pointing to the sky.

IT'S NOT MY JOB Freddie Prinz as Chico on *Chico and The Man*, whenever anyone asked him to do something that wasn't part of his job description.

DYN-O-MITE Jimmy Walker as J. J. Evans on *Good Times*, whenever anything happened.

KISS MAH GRITS Polly Holliday as Flo on *Alice*, whenever she was angry at someone (usually Mel).

STOW IT   Vic Tayback as Mel on *Alice*, whenever he was angry at someone (usually Flo).

NANOO-NANOO   Robin Williams as Mork on *Mork and Mindy*, whenever.

Canned Laughter

Laugh-tracks are no laughing matter. But from the deafening din of the Norman Lear shows (where the laughs wave across the screen in hyenaesque hilarity) to the low-grade chuckles of the domestic comedies (*My Three Sons* and *Leave It to Beaver*), laugh-tracks are here to stay.

What are they? Originally, laugh-tracks were called "canned laughter"—recordings of different audiences laughing, cackling, chuckling, and "awww"-ing, that are cued over (allegedly) funny sequences and lines so it looks like there's a studio audience howling along (a carryover from radio, when there really was a studio audience howling along). But on television, the purpose of the laugh-track is to let the viewer know what's supposed to be funny, in case they hadn't figured it out.

The 1950 *Hank McCune Show* was the first sitcom to employ the laugh-track. Here's what a prophetic *Variety* said about that: "Although the show is lensed on film without a studio audience, there are chuckles and yuks dubbed in. Whether this induces a jovial mood in home viewers is still to be determined, but the practice may have unlimited possibilities if it's spread to include canned peals of hilarity, thunderous ovations and gasps of sympathy."

Some shows—*I Love Lucy, Dick Van Dyke,* and many others, especially in the seventies—were holdouts for a live studio audience. But that didn't mean the laughter wasn't controlled. There exist machines—part of a whole new technology of audio engineering—that regulate an audience's laughter in the recording studio. A turn of a few knobs can make the laughter rise and fall—and go crazy—beneath the dialogue. Oh, the audience is real. It's just that the sound coming from them is manipulated to become the typical hoots, whoops, chuckles, "aaahhhs," and other assorted sounds, like the Greek chorus that the laugh-track is.

Laugh Insurance

In sitcoms, the comedy usually grows out of the situations. Lucy gets stuck on a ledge, many floors above the street. Phyllis forgets to pick up Rhoda to take her to her wedding, so Rhoda hitches a ride on a subway. Granny Clampett gets involved in Women's Lib. Mr. Ed writes a letter to Dear Abby complaining how unhappy he is and signs Wilbur's name to it (and naturally, Wilbur gets in trouble when his wife intercepts the letter). Archie gets trapped in an elevator full of multiethnic passengers, including a woman who goes into labor.

Here's a list of a few of the things that make for laughs on sitcoms of today and yesterday:

PEOPLE EAVESDROPPING   "Ah, the reason I have this glass held up to the wall is because . . . my ear is . . . thirsty."

PEOPLE SAYING THE TRUTH BY MISTAKE AND THEN COVERING UP   "I hate him . . . I mean, I *date* him."

ALL-IN-GOOD-FUN NARCISSISM   "I told them I was the best darned anchorman in the country. I had to—I was under oath."

MISUNDERSTANDING   "You mean Shirley isn't dead? But I thought . . ."

MISTAKEN IDENTITY   "You mean, you're not the Contessa? But I thought . . ."

COINCIDENCES   "Guess who I saw at the school dance last night who was supposed to be at the library studying for finals . . ."

TOILET HUMOR   Archie Bunker's toilet flushing.

AMNESIA   "Cosmo—it's me, Henrietta."

IRONY   "We've all been fired—except Ted."

RACIAL SLURS   "I don't like no Hebes, spics or coons, y'hear?"

MALAPROPISMS   "It's just a pigment of your imagination."

FUNNY COSTUMES   "Look, that's Laverne dressed as a giant chicken."

SELTZER/PIE IN THE FACE   "Wham!"

BAD SINGING   "Sweet Ad-o-line!"

OUT-OF-THE-MOUTHS-OF-BABES HUMOR   "Mommy, I think Billy's having an identity crisis."

RECURRING LINES OR JOKES   "God'll get you for that, Walter."

PLAYING DUMB   "Gee, I didn't know it was loaded, Mr. Mooney."

GUEST STARS   "Oh, gosh, Ethel—it's William Holden."

PRATFALLS   "Well, you've certainly got the padding for it—only kidding, kid."

The First Sitcoms

The first sitcoms that people still remember took place during the 1949–1950 season—*Mama, The Goldbergs, Life of Riley,* and a couple of others. But actually there were three live sitcoms that ran even before them. In order of appearance, they are:

☐ *Mary Kay and Johnny* (1947–1950). Mary Kay Stearns and Johnny Stearns played themselves (so who else?), young New York newlyweds. Johnny was serious (he worked in a bank) and Mary Kay was simply screwy and pretty. They lived in Greenwich Village. When the real Mrs. Stearns gave birth to a baby boy in 1948, the TV Stearns worked him into the show (forecasting *I Love Lucy* some years later). He appeared in his bassinet a few weeks later (played by the real Christopher William Stearns). Mary Kay's mom was played by Nydia Westman, who would go on to play flighty Aunt Bertha in the 1951 sitcom *Young Mr. Bobbin*. An interesting sidenote to *MK&J*: The sponsor was Anacin (even in 1948, they were using their outline chart of the human body with flashing lights and claims for "Fast, fast, fast relief"). Since there were no ratings at the time, the sponsor had no idea how big their viewing audience was. So several weeks after the show's premiere, the sponsor decided to conduct a giveaway to find out how many people were really watching: a free mirror to the first 200 viewers who wrote in to comment on the show. Just to be safe, Anacin ordered an extra 200 mirrors if more than 200 people should write in. Boy, were they surprised when nearly 9,000 letters poured in. ☐

☐ *The Laytons* (August 1948–November 1948). Not too much is known or remembered about this short-lived ethnicom, starring Amanda Randolph (known at the time as Sapphire's Mama on the radio version of *Amos 'n' Andy*; she would later go on to recreate the part on the TV version, and then get domestic work in the Williams household as Louise on *Make Room for Daddy*). *The Laytons* was the first case of a show that had run on a local station (in New York) for a month before it was transferred to network television (in this case, the now-defunct DuMont network). Another actress named Vera Tatum was also in the cast. ☐

☐ *The Growing Paynes* (1948–1949). This sitcom had a bit of everything that was to come: the "trials and tribulations" (there would be a lot of that going around) of an insurance salesman (shades of Jim Anderson) and his screwball wife (Lucy, Lucy, Lucy) and two young kids (like the many young kids thereafter). Plus a maid who "saved the day" (all TV maids saved the day). Although the show ran only ten months, it had a cast overhaul after only a few. The first set of Mr. and Mrs. Payne was played by someone named John Harvey (a.k.a. John Henry) and Judy Parrish (who'd go on to play a newswoman on the 1948 drama *Barney Blake, Police Reporter*). Then the Paynes were played by Ed Holmes and Elaine Stritch (who'd go on to play Ruth Sherwood, the "my" in *My Sister Eileen* in 1960). Plugs for the sponsor—Wanamaker's Department Store—were often worked into the scripts, a not uncommon practice in the early days of sitcom. ☐

The Sitcom Stork

Sometimes, sitcom stars just seem to hatch—"Where did he come from?" people always ask—because TV most often breeds its own stars, a special kind of celebrity that works better in the living room or at the foot of the bed than on the big screen or stage.

But when many movie stars' careers began to wane, some of them would try TV. Sitcoms, specifically. Some of sitcom's early (and biggest) stars were movie transplants: Eve Arden, Bob Cummings, Ann Sothern, Lucille Ball, Robert Young, Donna Reed, Fred MacMurray, Walter Brennan, and more.

But look at the list of movie stars who tried to become sitcommers but couldn't make it: Ronald Colman, Peter Lawford, Bing Crosby, Gene Kelly, Tab Hunter, Loretta Young, James Stewart, Shirley MacLaine, Jack Lemmon, Jean Arthur, Lee Grant, Ray Bolger, Ann Sheridan, Fay Wray, Red Buttons, Diana Rigg, Hume Cronyn and Jessica Tandy (although they were from the Broadway stage), Mickey Rooney, Ray Milland and many others.

And since the sitcom has its roots in radio series, it was no wonder that so many sitcom stars came from radio: Joan Davis, William Bendix, Ozzie and Harriet Nelson, Burns and Allen, Gertrude Berg, and several others.

A lot of sitcom stars—Mary Tyler Moore, Dick Van Dyke, Henry Winkler, among others—have tried to translate their success to the movie screen. None has made it. With the exception of a guy named John Travolta.

What's in a Name?

Ever wonder how sitcom characters got their names?

Simple—the writers just changed the stars' already-innocuous names to something even more innocuous. Here are a few of the TV stars who changed their names—for business purposes: From Andy Griffith to Andy Taylor (*The Andy Griffith Show*) to Andy Sawyer (*The New Andy Griffith Show*); from Jim Bouton to Jim Barton (*Ball Four*); from Bing Crosby to Bing Collins (*Going My Way*); from Mary Tyler Moore to Mary Richards (*The Mary Tyler Moore Show*); from Robert Cummings to Robert Beanblossom (*My Hero*) to Bob Collins (*Love That Bob*) to Bob Carson (*The Bob Cummings Show*) to Robert McDonald (*My Living Doll*); from Lucille Ball to Lucy Ricardo (*I Love Lucy*) to Lucy Carmichael (*The Lucy Show*) to Lucy Carter (*Here's*

Lucy); from Bob Newhart to Bob Hartley *(The Bob Newhart Show)*; from Cara Williams to Cara Wilton *(The Cara Williams Show)*.

Some names were even less subtle. Consider the list of sitcom stars whose characters' names were the same as their own: Donald O'Connor; Pinky Lee; Ozzie, Harriet, David, Ricky, June and Kris Nelson; Paul Hartman.

Reruns

If you think that episode of *That Girl* looks shorter than when you first saw it in prime time—that's because it is. When a show is sold to a syndication (the people who distribute the shows to local stations—you can see their logo after the episode's over), the local stations want to make more money from the show, so they snip minutes from the episode to fit more commercials in. Sometimes the cuts are done with some sense of continuity; other times, as you've noticed, they just seem to throw in a commercial whenever. Prime-time sitcoms have only a few minutes of commercials; the syndicated reruns usually have about six minutes of advertising.

Sitcom Cycles

First there were the holdovers, leftovers, and overhauls from the radio—things like *Mama, The Goldbergs,* and even *I Love Lucy* (Lucille Ball had been the star of the radio series *My Favorite Wife)*. Then, later in the fifties, were the family shows, full of supposedly stable people *(Ozzie and Harriet, Leave It to Beaver, Father Knows Best,* etc.). In the early sixties, the rural shows began to pollinate *(Beverly Hillbillies, Green Acres, Petticoat Junction,* etc.). The "social" comedies started in 1970, beginning with *All in the Family* and the rest of the Norman Lear shows *(The Jeffersons, Maude, One Day at a Time* and others) as well as *M*A*S*H*.

In the mid-seventies—beginning with *Happy Days* —there was a swing back to the just-for-the-fun-of-it comedies, including *Laverne and Shirley* and *Mork and Mindy*. In the late seventies, there is an inkling— although a very, very small one—that there might be a swing back to the intelligent shows *(The Dick Van Dyke Show* and *The Mary Tyler Moore Show* were smart shows), as indicated by the presence of things like *Taxi* and *The Associates*.

Sitcom Statement

These words from sitcom king Garry Marshall, creator of *Happy Days, Laverne and Shirley, Mork and Mindy* and other hitcoms: "You need about twenty-one million people to make a hit. So we figured you get seven million with laughs, and another seven million with warmth and heart and nice and crying a little, and the third seven with interesting and intelligence and fascinating and things you don't see any other place—that's the hardest seven million. Some people think you can get it all with just laughs—and then they only get seven million people watching and then they go off the air."

1949–1950

The Goldbergs

Mama

OFF-SCREEN

9/29 Mrs. Iva Toguri D'Aquino is found guilty by federal jury of charge of broadcasting for Japan in World War II as "Tokyo Rose."

10/9 Yankees win the twelfth World Series (4–1).

10/12 First woman ambassador in US—Mrs. Eugenie Anderson of Minnesota is nominated for Denmark by Truman.

10/24 Permanent United Nations headquarters dedicated in New York, with Truman as speaker.

12/30 State of Vietnam given large measure of internal sovereignty by France in agreement signed at Saigon.

1/21 Alger Hiss convicted of perjury in federal court in denying giving secret US documents to Whittaker Chambers.

1/24 Amendment to Fair Labor Standards Act raises minimum wage to 75¢ an hour.

1/26 India proclaimed free and independent republic.

5/1 Columbia University announces award of 1950 Pulitzer for best play to Rodgers/Hammerstein for *South Pacific*; best novel to A. B. Guthrie, Jr., for *The Way West*.

5/12 American Bowling Congress votes to repeal rule restricting membership to white males.

5/25 Brooklyn-Battery Tunnel, longest vehicular tunnel in US, formally opened to traffic.

FRONT RUNNERS

THE GOLDBERGS

Without his Sanka decaffeinated coffee, Mr. Goldberg would be grouchy as a bear. I tell you, I tell you truly, really, and I would not lie to you because if I did, would you ever believe me? If Mr. Goldberg did not drink Sanka decaffeinated coffee, I don't know what I would do—I, I don't even know if we'd still have a marriage, I mean it, I really do, I mean, without Sanka I just don't know what we'd do. I'm not saying to you that this Sanka decaffeinated coffee is the greatest product in the world—would I say that to you? No. Why would I say that? All I'm saying is try it, try it once and see how good it tastes and how good you sleep and . . . that's all—just try it once and that's what I'm telling you.
—MOLLY GOLDBERG, leaning out her window, delivering a Sanka commercial

In 1949, Jews moved into the television neighborhood for the first time (not to be seen again until twenty-three years later when Bridget made the intrareligious mistake of loving Bernie) when Molly and Jake Goldberg took to the screen.

Actually, Jews had always been involved in TV—they were the show biz mavens who moved and shaked the television industry: the writers, producers, and directors. But the Goldbergs were the first Jewish people to integrate TV Land (along with other minority neighbors *Amos 'n' Andy* and a Sweedisha *Mama*).

Following the thousand-year tradition of the Wandering Jew, Molly and clan pulled up stakes and moved from radio to TV, the Promised Medium, stopping by their apartment at 1030 East Tremont Ave., Apartment 3-B, in The Bronx, to deposit their shabby furniture. We had heard Molly Goldberg shout "Yoo-hoo, Mrs. Bloom!" to her neighbor across the airshaft on radio since 1932, but this—on Monday, January 10, 1949—was the first

look we got at matriarch Molly and her family; before they had existed only in our imaginations.

We met husband Jake Goldberg and their two kids, Sammy and Rosalie, and also live-in Uncle David . . . ah ha, so *that's* what they looked like.

And we met Molly. Like a long-lost relative, a pen pal finally met in the flesh, Molly looked like Molly talked. Gertrude Berg—with her sad twinkly eyes, her basset hound face, and her potato sack body—*was* Molly Goldberg. But of course! We knew it all the time.

And so we said "Yoo-hoo" to the Goldbergs.

It wasn't an easy reign that the G's had on TV. Gertrude Berg—the star and writer and producer—would be besieged by *tsouris* almost from the start. Molly—homish and haimish—was bound to keep wandering.

The Goldbergs wasn't a soap opera, but a *soup* opera—of the chicken-soup variety. Molly handled her small family crises with a ferocious ethnic energy and

Molly Goldberg	Gertrude Berg
Jake Goldberg	Philip Loeb (1949–1951); Harold Stone (1952); Robert H. Harris (1953–1954)
Rosalie Goldberg	Arlene McQuade
Sammy Goldberg	Larry Robinson (1949–1952); Tom Taylor (1954)
Uncle David	Eli Mintz
Mrs. Bloom	Olga Fabian (1953)

Also: Betty Walker, Dora Weissman, Henry Sharp

humor as though their lives depended on it. And perhaps they did.

With an eloquent shrug, a little fluttering of the hands, and a skillful inflection, she managed to mismanage the English language. Molly would dispense advice the way doctors give out penicillin. Perhaps she'd be trying to find a wife for a widowed neighbor. Maybe her gruff but practical husband, Jake, was working too hard, so she'd attempt to get him to take it easy. Or perhaps Molly—who wears a size 46 dress—would try to lose weight. Her friends at the club needed a show? Molly put on *Die Fledermaus*. Friends, family—they all had problems, and Molly tried to solve them all. Each week Molly turned these folks' foibles into folk fables.

Berg's Molly was generous and self-effacing. Unqualifyingly loving and accepting, no matter what your kink. She was nurturing and nourishing. In her attempt to help others, she fortunately had the capabilities to resolve each dilemma before the final Sanka commercial (which she herself delivered leaning out the back window).

Although Gertrude Berg said she never used a Yiddish accent for the part, the placement and arrangement of words and use of malapropisms—Mollyprop-isms, they came to be called—made everything sound Jewish. Some of Molly's greatest hits (or misses):

"In the pot, put the chicken."

"So who's to know?"

"Enter, whoever. If it's nobody, I'll call back."

"Come will and come may, I must face it."

"We're at the crossroads and the parting of the ways."

"I loved the movie *Southern Boulevard*."

"Answer me, Jake. Is it bad?"

"Give me a swallow the glass."

"It's late, Jake, and time to expire."

The show explored the quiet thrills of neighborhood life—the meat markets, holidays, graduations, recipes, wallpaper patterns.

The action took place in the Goldbergs' cluttered six-room Bronx apartment, where her tenacious sense of humor and tenement sensibility ruled the roost and the roast. If the family seemed downtrodden, they weren't. There was always a way out—even if it meant merely spending the Fourth of July at the family's favorite retreat, Pincus Pines in the Catskill Mountains. And even when the family went away for the summers, they never forgot their friends and acquaintances: Solly the doctor, Tate Elke, Mrs. Herman Across the Hall, Mrs. Kramer Upstairs, Mrs. 5-C, Cousin Simon the Rich One, Sylvia from Jersey and—but of course—Mrs. Bloom in the next apartment.

Molly was ever faithful to her family; blood was thicker than water, and chicken soup was thicker than both. One early episode has daughter Rosalie, fourteen-and-a-half, worried about her own future "inhibitions and emotional scars," determined to free herself from her parents' yoke. Molly is uneasy about her daughter's plans (which include cutting her hair), but realizes that the world has changed since she was a girl. Jake will acknowledge no such thing. "I am the father in the home, or what am I? If I am, I want to know!" he yells.

And more: Rosalie wears lipstick (!) for the first time, and when she goes off babysitting without her homework, a neighbor boy comes to the door to ask where she's babysitting that night so he can join her. It turns out that Rosalie didn't have the nerve to get her hair all cut off. Jake is so relieved, he agrees to let her have a hair trim (the episode ends with the camera aimed at hair snippings as they glide to the floor).

The big question about *The Goldbergs'* transplant: Why television?

"I always felt the Goldbergs were a family that needed to be seen," Berg said when the sitcom became a hit. When asked why Mrs. Bloom—as in "Yoo-hoo, Mrs. Bloom!"—was never seen, Berg said, "I'm afraid that *Goldbergs* fans have decided in their own minds what Mrs. Bloom looks like, and they may be disappointed in her physical appearance." (Only once did Mrs. Bloom utter an "oy" on radio.)

The second season began with the Goldberg family's return from California aboard a transcontinental train. Papa had wanted to move there, but the family was against it. And so they stayed on East Tremont Ave.

Although some of the scripts are around, only a handful of kinescopes seem to have survived. Until the last year of its television existence, *The Goldbergs* was broadcast live from New York, on Mondays after an eighteen-hour rehearsal.

Gertrude Berg wrote *The Goldbergs* every day at 5 A.M. (that's when the city was quiet) from her Upper West Side New York apartment. She would eventually write 10,000 Molly Goldberg scripts, more than fifteen million words. That included the radio series, the television series (plural), several books, a comic strip, a Broadway play, a movie, and a vaudeville routine which had given birth to the Goldbergs in 1925. Molly, said Mrs. Berg (who spoke perfect English), was modeled after her own mother and grandmother.

Everything was going—you should knock wood—great for the Goldbergs. Their ratings were excellent, the show was beloved. And then . . .

In June 1950, out of nowhere, came the publication of a paperback book: *Red Channels*. This was, after all, the Red Scare, and this book was paranoid propaganda about Communists and Communist sympathizers working in the media. Among other things, the book listed names and dossiers of performers who were allegedly Communists or friendly to Communist causes.

One of these names was Philip Loeb.

Loeb (who played Jake Goldberg in the sitcom as he had on the radio) was one of the most visible victims upon whom *Red Channels* had painted a scarlet letter. Gertrude Berg was shocked.

Mealtime (from left): Gertrude Berg, Philip Loeb, Arlene McQuade, Larry Robinson

Take One: Eli Mintz, Gertrude Berg and Assistant Director George Ackerson

So was the sponsor, General Foods, who didn't want to be underwriting a show featuring a "possible Communist." They tried to get rid of him. Loeb was offered $85,000 to quit. He wouldn't take it. But nobody would fire him. They were all afraid of the controversy. Gertrude Berg said repeatedly that she would not fire Loeb.

Finally, General Foods dropped the show, explaining that Loeb was "too controversial." NBC picked it up, which could have been a coup (the sitcom was worth $3,500,000 a year in billings at that time), but no sponsor would touch it with Loeb, who, all the while, protested futilely.

"Philip Loeb has stated categorically that he is not and has never been a Communist," Gertrude Berg told the New York *Times*. "I believe him. There is no dispute between Philip Loeb and myself." Ultimately, though, she felt forced to give in and hire another actor to play Jake Goldberg. She paid Loeb his regular salary, $85,000, for two years. "There are twenty people depending on the show for a living, and their savings are dwindling," Berg said. "It's unfortunate that after doing what I did, waiting for the situation to clear, I have to go along without him. It's too bad. I certainly have tried. I think everybody in the business knows it pretty well." But Loeb's television and radio work ceased after that. When he occasionally appeared in a stage play, audiences harassed him.

Said Loeb's sister: "He's been hurt so terribly. Now see what they did to him. They took his living away."

And perhaps his life. On September 1, 1955, Loeb killed himself by taking an overdose of sleeping pills. Said a tribute in the New York *Times*: "Philip Loeb died of a sickness commonly called 'The Black List.'"

And *The Goldbergs* went on. In February of 1952, the show returned (with Harold Stone as the new Jake) in a three-times-a-week, fifteen-minute format, back-to-back with *Kukla, Fran and Ollie*. It ran at 7:15 P.M., which was a problem; NBC couldn't clear the time with their affiliate stations (many used it locally). One sponsor canceled after the first week. Finally the show was canceled.

The Goldbergs resurfaced in 1954 when they—like so many first generation families—moved to the suburbs. And, finally, moved from live television to film.

"After so many years," Gertrude Berg said, "I felt the series needed a change, so I moved the family out of the city to the mythical Haverville. And from live television to film. Of course, the money from repeat showings was no small consideration."

The new show was shot at New York's Biltmore Theater and on location in the suburbs. The situations were typically suburban, sort of a Jewish precursor to *The Donna Reed Show*. When Molly's cronies from the Old Neighborhood said they were going to miss her, she insisted: "So you could come visit. . . ."

Shows dealt with the beauty parlor, the Girl Scouts, working with the nurse's aide. Once, a Mrs. Van Est analyzed Molly's dreams as representing signs of artistic frustration and domestic misery. So Molly took the interpretations seriously and began piano lessons. When she realized she was neglecting her family, she quit.

But even in the suburbs, Molly had impact. One Michigan viewer whose son had just died of cancer wrote this to Gertrude Berg:

"You are my heroine, my favorite. My only son's lingering, hideously painful cancer death these last twelve months has been unbearable. Time was not a healer to us, unfortunately. But Molly Goldberg is a pleasure. I can lose myself in it at least once a week. Having married into a Scotch clan where outward manifestations of affection are judged as signs of weak character, I especially respond to the warmth of this wonderful, fictitious family."

Only thirty-nine half-hours were filmed. And then Molly—a victim of poor ratings—split, only to return again in 1963 with *Mrs. G. Goes to College* (she was Mrs. Green this time, and she was a widow—she knew better than to press her luck with another Jake—but everything else was the same). "I was finished with the Goldbergs and couldn't sell them again. So what would you do? I had to sell something else. It's the same Molly, just older."

Over the years, many different actors played many different roles on *The Goldbergs*. But there was only one Molly.

In 1966, Gertrude Berg died. From yoo-hoo to boo-hoo, it was as though television's mother had died. Finally, Gertrude Berg, who was always busy, busy, busy—"I'm too busy to be neurotic," she once said—was at rest.

No doubt at Pincus Pines.

MAMA

. . . but most of all, I remember Mama.
—KATRIN

You might not remember *Mama*, but you certainly do remember *I Remember Mama*, from many Sunday afternoons on TV's Big Movie. And you've got to remember the same-named play from so many high school productions. Or even Richard Rodgers' messy musical *I Remember Mama*. For some reason, most of you missed the TV show—probably because your parents wouldn't let you stay up that late. Or maybe you weren't even born yet. And if you missed it in reruns, don't feel bad—there weren't any. *Mama* was shot live. But your local library will certainly have the book upon which all the versions were based: *Mama's Bank Account* by Kathryn Forbes.

Each version seemed to become more and more distilled, although they were all warm and softhearted stories of a Norwegian family living—or trying to live—in San Francisco during the turn of the century. The TV show, its title simply snipped to *Mama*, was more diluted from the original source than either the play or the movie, but it had a small-screen charm that kept it running for eight years, with a patriotic following chasing it all the way. The show was sponsored by Maxwell House (interestingly enough, its Jewish ethnic counterpart, *The Goldbergs*, was sponsored by Sanka; *Mama*, though, was only slightly more caffeine-free). *Mama* was half soft-soap and half soap-opera. It was not sitcom but domcom—domestic comedy. Its humor was gentle and gentile.

Every week the show started the same way: with the older, sentimental daughter Katrin's hand opening the family album, her voice lilting nostalgically: "I remember the big white house on Elm Street, and my little sister Dagmar, and my big brother Nels, and Papa. But most of all, I remember Mama."

And then the action would begin. Here is a typical story line:

Young Dagmar becomes self-conscious about her new braces. When Nels sees her, he aches with laughter and taunts: "You look like you swallowed a mousetrap and it didn't go all the way down." Dagmar is devastated and decides, as she puts it, "to become a hermit"—until her teeth are straight, anyway. Mama enters (complete with her usual warm advice) and saves the day. Or at least the episode.

It was always Mama with her down-to-earthiness and her good humor who would put things back together. She was wise and nurturing—truly inspirational, supportive, and compassionate; she was actually more like a grandmother than a mother. Mama—a.k.a. Marta Hansen—and Papa Lars, a stern carpenter, reeked of Old World Charm; in fact, they still pronounced their j's like y's. "Ya, Yenny," Lars would say when Mama'd give him hints on how to discipline the children. And the three totally Americanized children never made fun of their parents. Nor did the writers and actors; their difficulties with English were never used as a comic device (as, say, Ricky Ricardo's would be two years later). *Mama* was a pioneer in domestic comedies and set the style for all that would follow, including such standards as *My Three Sons* and *Father Knows Best*. In fact, this show was Mother Knows Best. And, boy, did she! If nothing else, *Mama's* moral was that parents in their wisdom could solve all of young people's problems, that family love could lick and heal the wounds of youth.

But the most significant thing about *Mama*—at least today, when everything is pretaped, sliced, spliced together and laugh-tracked—is that, from 1949 until 1956, *Mama* was broadcast live. Each Friday night the actors would give a performance in front of the cameras, and thousands of people would watch at home as it was happening.

Robin Morgan—today a poet and well-known feminist—played Dagmar, the impish little sister. She remembers *Mama* this way: "When, despite the

Marta Hansen (Mama)	Peggy Wood
Lars Hansen (Papa), a carpenter	Judson Laire
Katrin Hansen	Rosemary Rice
Dagmar Hansen	Robin Morgan (1949); Toni Campbell (1950–1956)
Nels Hansen	Dick Van Patten
Aunt Jenny, Mama's older sister	Ruth Gates
Aunt Trina, Mama's younger sister	Alice Frost
Uncle Gunnar	Carl Frank
T. R. Ryan	Kevin Coughlin (1952–1956)
Also: Abby Lewis	

perfectionism of our set designer, the antique player piano went mechanically berserk, snapping its rolls like a Kabuki dancer his fans, there was no reshooting for any such linguistic contradiction as 'live-on-tape': we ad-libbed, live on the air. When one of my wobbly baby teeth fell out in the middle of a show, I worked its loss into the plot. When an adult colleague's eyes glazed over with dialogue amnesia (no TelePrompTers for *us*), one had to rescue the victim and save the continuity. Children, of course, are crazy enough to relish this sort of challenge, and I admit that it does develop a pride in craft which has subsequently served me well as a writer and feminist activist."

It is interesting to note, when wandering through some of the old scripts, how certain provisions were made in stage directions to accommodate the problems of live TV. For example:

(*Fade into—close-up of Katrin's hands grating a cabbage. Note: Hold on this long enough for Katrin to get into scene*)

In other words, they used another actress' hands to substitute for Katrin in a close-up, while she popped off to be in the next scene. Here it happens again in the stage directions:

(*Scene dissolves to: close-up on a hand, presumably Gunnar's, busily figuring on a scratch pad. The pad is covered with arithmetic. Hold on it long enough to cover Gunnar, then—Dissolve to: Gunnar in the Gunnarson parlor, busily figuring*)

The program was ruled by the liveness—and aliveness—of the medium. Those who watched it say there was an excitement, a spontaneous quality of the unexpected and unsuspected that made it like theater.

The program debuted on Friday, July 1, 1949, with a typical situation such as this one, called "Mama and the Library Book," which gives an indication of what the sensibility of the first few years of live television was.

Katrin is reading an adult romance book, Elinor Glyn's *Three Weeks*: ". . . and suddenly she crept close. 'Paul,' she whispered. Paul stood up to his full height. He put his arms around her . . . slowly her red lips melted into his young lips in a long, strange kiss. . . ." She lends the book to her friend Gwen.

Katrin is curious about love. Mama tells her that "Papa was the handsomest man in the village. And the most lively, the most gay . . . he was the life of every party. And his dancing! He could dance for hours and hours and never be tired. . . ." (Papa comes in after a hard day of carpentry, complaining that he "can't take it anymore," that he's tired, that he's just not what he used to be.) Then Gwen comes in and speaks to Katrin alone:

"My mother found the book! She went looking for pickle preserves in that closet under the stairs and she found it—and *burned* it! And that isn't all. I'm being

punished and she's phoning your mother so *you'll* be punished, too!"

The phone rings. The news is spread.

PAPA: I do not wish you to read a book that people say is bad.
KATRIN: Gee whiz, Papa. I don't think it's fair. You're judging a book that you haven't even read—Mama, I'm not a baby.

Mama goes to the library and is so enthralled with the book that she checks the book out and takes it home.

Meanwhile, Papa—who fears he is losing his sex appeal—buys some hair restorer. As he hides it in a closet, he discovers the book Mama's hidden there. He thinks it's Katrin's. She says she gave Mama her library card that morning; Papa realizes it's Mama's and thinks she's reading it because she's dissatisfied with their marriage.

PAPA: Why have you been reading that book? You cannot deny, Marta, that you were hiding it from me.
MAMA: Not from you. From the children. And because I felt so foolish, reading it—
PAPA (*hopefully*):   I guess you just wanted to know about it for Katrin, ja?
MAMA (*sheepishly*):   I think . . . I wanted to know about it for myself, Lars.
PAPA: Mr. Hughes says that women read such things when they are restless—and need romance—
MAMA: Oh. . . ?
PAPA: You know, when their husbands are getting older . . . and . . .
MAMA (*bursts out laughing again*):   I guess this also explains the hair medicine in the closet, ja?
PAPA (*lamely*):   Well . . .
MAMA: Lars Hansen! I think you are losing your mind!
PAPA: My hair—my youth—is what I am losing. Can you blame a man if he don't want his wife to think—
MAMA (*interrupting*):   What? To think what?
PAPA: Well . . . that he is . . . getting different from what he was . . .
MAMA: But of course you are different! Of course, when I look at you, I do not see the same person as in that old picture album. . . .
PAPA: Exactly. And—
MAMA: Thank goodness! You think, after twenty years, I still want to be married to a—a—"Waltz King"? Or to the life of the party? No, thank you! I could not take it! (*Laughs.*)
PAPA: I never thought of that. . . .
MAMA (*Comes close to him, kneels where he is sitting*):   I see the father of my children. My friend. My companion

. . . that I have never been away from—in thousands and thousands of days and nights—

PAPA (*deeply touched*):   You say that so nicely, Marta—

MAMA (*a little surprised at her own eloquence*):   Ja . . . (*She holds up the copy of "Three Weeks."*) I guess it must be this book I have been reading. . . .

(*Fadeout*)

A simple, sentimental ending. Corny. Neat—but not neat enough. The problem with this episode is that a very important issue is taken up—censorship—and then it is just dropped and left totally unresolved. Can Katrin read the book? What does Mama decide? It was as though the writer didn't want to commit himself on this issue. Or perhaps he wrote it one way and then was instructed to obfuscate it—to just leave it dangling so that maybe it would "just go away"; maybe no one would notice. Or

maybe it was just the writer's idea of proper child-rearing. *Mama* was a sentimentally domestic show, not a political one, and should not have dealt with such substantive topics as censorship. It would be another twenty-one years—when Norman Lear's Archie Bunker and his crew hit the screen—before issues such as this would be honestly (or at least openly) dealt with in sitcoms. Even Robert Young—the daddy who knew best—wouldn't have touched that one.

The most famous *Mama* episode—a television classic—was "The Night the Animals Talked," so popular, in fact, that the cast repeated it every year at Christmastime.

It was a Yuletide fantasy. Papa tells Dagmar that each Christmas night animals are given the ability to speak as a reward for the all-night vigil of the beasts that witnessed the birth of the Christ Child in Bethlehem. So,

Remembering (from left): Rosemary Rice, Judson Laire, guest Toni Campbell, Peggy Wood

when everyone else is asleep, Dagmar sneaks out to the barn and awaits the animals' conversation. Eventually she falls asleep out there. When she awakens she hears the animals talking. She tells her family. No one believes her. No one except the viewers, that is.

On July 27, 1956—horror of horrors—CBS canceled *Mama*. Canceling *Mama*, viewers seemed to feel, was like canceling your own mama. There were thousands of letters, wires, petitions, phone calls, newspaper editorials. Okay, okay—CBS relented. And they brought *Mama* back from the dead. This time, in fact, it was taped. This time it flopped. On March 17, 1957, *Mama* coughed up her last "ja" and left the air.

And so, once again, we can only remember *Mama*.

ALSO RANS

The Aldrich Family

This was a big year for TV transplants. *The Goldbergs* had been a radio favorite, *Mama* had many previous incarnations, and typical-American Henry Aldrich had been a radio regular for years. Anyway, here's what this one was all about: The Aldriches lived in their Typical American Household on Elm St. in Centerville, USA (the first of many mythical TV towns). The show centered around young Henry's family, his high school friends (especially best-buddy Homer Brown), and his crushes on schoolgirls. The show was created by Clifford Goldsmith, based on his play *What a Life*. Each week, Henry's mother would call "Henry! Henry Aldrich!" and Henry would wearily respond, "Coming, Mother . . ."

Actor House Jameson was one of the few radio cast members to switch to TV in his same role—Henry's long-suffering father, Sam Aldrich. He remained with the show for its four-year run, but viewers must have been befuddled that Sam went through five different sons, three daughters, and three wives, thanks to a high turnover in actors. One especially tragic turnover was an actress who never even got to play the part of Alice Aldrich, Henry's mother. Jean Muir, a movie and radio actress for more than twenty years, was dropped from the show at the last minute because, like Philip Loeb of *The Goldbergs*, she was listed as a Communist in *Red Channels*, the book put out by proponents of Senator Joseph McCarthy's vicious tactics. Nobody even bothered to ask to hear Muir's side of the story, and she was quickly fired. The sponsor, General Foods (also *The Goldbergs'* sponsor), and the ad agency, Young and Rubicam, canceled the opening episode of the show until they could find a new actress to play the part. (Later, before a Congressional committee, Muir stated that she had never been a member of the Communist party, but nobody really cared. The accusation destroyed her career.)

Here's who played whom: Henry Aldrich was played by Robert Casey until 1950, at which time Richard Tyler took over the part until 1951, when Henry Girard stepped in until the end of the season. Both Kenneth Nelson and Bobby Ellis played Henry during the 1952–1953 season, one right after another. Mother Alice was played by Lois Wilson during the first season, then by Nancy Carroll, who was replaced by Barbara Robbins for the last two seasons. Sister Mary had three actresses:

Charita Bauer, Mary Malone, and June Dayton. Best-friend Homer was played by Jackie Kelk (a holdover from his radio role), and then Robert Barry and Jackie Grimes. His mother (played by Leona Powers) had also had the same role on radio.

Apartment 3-C

John Gay and Barbara Gay played themselves in this series revolving around a couple of young marrieds living in the title apartment at 46 Perry St. in New York City. The allegedly comic adventures of this writer and his scatterbrained wife were apparently less than irresistible, even to the CBS executives who gave them air time; the show lasted through one season, and each episode lasted only fifteen minutes.

The Hartmans

Paul Hartman and Grace Hartman played themselves—a suburban New York family who had many (according to the NBC press releases) "trials and tribulations." They had a brother-in-law (played by Loring Smith) and a handyman (played by Harold Stone, who'd go on to replace the blacklisted Philip Loeb on *The Goldbergs*) and they had a contract that was canceled after one season.

Heavens to Betsy

Not to be confused with *Heaven* (singular) *for Betsy* in 1952, this one-season NBC sitcom starred Elizabeth Cote as Betsy, and Mary Best as her chum. They played two young Broadway hopefuls seeking a career in show business. Russell Nype played the cabdriver.

The Life of Riley

The first time around—with a paucity of success—Jackie Gleason played Chester A. Riley (but only because William Bendix, who had originated the radio Riley, was otherwise engaged). Simply: it was the story of a bumbling riveter with Stevenson Aircraft and Associates, who lived in LA with his wife, Peg (Rosemary DeCamp—later

The Life of Riley

Bob Collins' live-in sister on *Love That Bob*), and two kids, Babs (Gloria Winters) and Chester (Lanny Rees), who was always called Junior. Sid Tomack played Jim Gillis, Riley's co-worker and neighbor. John Brown played the local mortician, Digby "Digger" O'Dell. The show lasted only one season on the old DuMont Network. When it was resurrected in 1953 with Bendix in his original role, the show became a huge success.

Lum and Abner

This had been a popular item on radio. Then someone got the bright idea to move it to TV. CBS housed this series about Lum Edwards (Chester Lauck) and Abner Peabody (Norris Goff), who ran the Jot 'em Down General Store in Pine Ridge, Arkansas.

The Pinky Lee Show

Five years before he would charm the pants off of us after school and on Saturday mornings, Pinky Lee tried to score in this sitcom (he'd try again two years later with *Those Two*). This time, though, it was a semi-sitcom in which Lee—playing someone known as "the Stagehand"—worked in a vaudeville theater, dressed in baggy clothes, ready and willing to fill in for singers and comics who couldn't make it. Also in the show: William Bakewell as "the Stage Manager." The show was shot live from Hollywood (and sent to the rest of the US via kinescope). Incidentally, Pinky Lee's real name was Pincus Leff; he changed it for business purposes.

Wesley

This show has the distinction of being one of TV's first canceled sitcoms—after only three months (and you thought that only happened with the invention of the Nielsen families . . .). It was all about a twelve-year-old kid who was getting ready to become a teenager (played by Donald Devlin for two months, then by Johnny Stewart for the last month). Wesley Eggleston had a good buddy named Alvin (Billie Nevard), who was his surrogate brother, and he had a real teenage sister, Elizabeth (Joy Reese), with whom he'd fight. The show, aired live on CBS, took place in a small rural town, and Wesley's relationship with his mom and dad was basically of the warm-and-loving variety, although they did have some mild disagreements. Mr. Eggleston was played by Frank Thomas; Mrs. Eggleston was played by Mona Thomas, and there was a Grandpa played by Joe Sweeney.

Wren's Nest

In the beginning . . . sitcom characters had many "trials and tribulations," as they were called in the network press releases. That could have meant a lot of things—dire disease, financial wipeouts, unwanted pregnancy—but it didn't. In sitcom lingo, "trials and tribulations" meant that, at worst, She burned the roast when He was bringing home The Big Boss for dinner. Or perhaps Sis was too shy to ask That Boy to the school sock hop. You know, that kind of trials, those kinds of tribulations.

Wren's Nest was one of the first of the T and T genre. It starred Sam and Virginia Wren (Hollywood film stars from the twenties, thirties, and forties) playing themselves on this fifteen-minute, thrice-weekly ABC sitcom set in suburban New York. Well, they might have had trials and tribulations, but they did not have high viewer response (as it was called before the rating system), and so their show lasted less than one season.

Young and Gay/The Girls

Authors Cornelia Otis Skinner and Emily Kimbrough had written an autobiographical novel, *Our Hearts Were Young and Gay*, and CBS bought the rights and shortened the title to *Young and Gay*. But not for long. After two episodes had aired, they changed the title to *The Girls*. But not for long. After several more episodes, they canceled the whole thing. Here's what it was all about, though: Two young Bryn Mawr graduates—Cornelia Otis S. (played, first, by Bethel Leslie, and then by Gloria Stroock) and Emily K. (Mary Malone)—were looking for work in New York, after a fast fling to Europe. They moved to the Village (Greenwich Village, that is), where Cornelia hoped to be discovered as an actress, and Emily wanted work as a writer. (Bethel Leslie, incidentally, left the sitcom to work in a new play—which was considered a much better prospect than TV—and was replaced by Gloria Stroock, who was the sister of Geraldine Brooks.)

1950–1951

The George Burns and Gracie Allen Show   **Beulah**   **Amos 'n' Andy**

OFF-SCREEN

10/7 Yankees win Series again, beat Phillies 4–0.

11/10 1949 Nobel Prize for Literature goes to Faulkner, 1950 prize to Bertrand Russell.

11/19 Last-minute agreement between one station and three networks and five unions averts nationwide strike of TV performers.

12/19 Eisenhower named commander in chief of Allied forces in Europe by North Atlantic Council.

2/26 Twenty-second amendment to Constitution, prohibiting any US President after Truman from serving over two terms, goes into effect.

3/7 House Un-American Activities Committee releases list of 624 organizations and 204 publications cited as subversive by Justice Department, HUAC itself, or other legislative groups.

4/5 Julius and Ethel Rosenberg sentenced to death.

4/7 Ho Chi Minh orders his Indochinese Communist forces to switch from orthodox military tactics to guerrilla warfare.

5/15 AT&T becomes world's first corporation to have one million shareholders.

6/25 First US commercial color telecast—CBS in New York City.

FRONT RUNNERS

AMOS 'N' ANDY

> ANDY: *Kingfish, you mean to say that you is an actual doctor?*
> KINGFISH: *Well, I ain't been blabbin' it around but I been takin' a correspondence course in doctorin' from that, uh, big medical school down dere in, uh, Baltimore. I'm taking a blood count heah—that's four, subtract two. Hmmmm. Dat's the most anemic blood I ever did see.*

Amos 'n' Andy: two dirty words in the history of American television broadcasting (even the *'n'* was not too well received). Not even when Maude Findlay got an abortion was there such controversy surrounding a sitcom. *Amos 'n' Andy* was, in fact, the first show to have been blacklisted or—as they might have said back then—colorlisted. In the mid-sixties, after years of protests, it was yanked off the air because it allegedly showed a degrading and demeaning picture of black people—no, black *folks*. But behind and beyond the controversy lies a program beloved by some, beloathed by others, but either way, a slice of Americana—pasteurized and homogenized, to be sure—that just won't die. It's a classic—not only a classic of prejudice and ethnic stereotyping—but a classic of good writing and great acting. The show (and not just for the wrong reasons) was funny.

Amos 'n' Andy ran until June 11, 1953, when filming was halted—not because it lacked an audience, but because black organizations such as the NAACP objected to it. The sponsor, Blatz Beer, yielded to the organizations' campaigns and withdrew its sponsorship. The reruns continued to be syndicated until 1966 when,

during the Civil Rights Movement, CBS removed all copies of the show from both domestic and overseas markets and, in fact, made it unavailable for any broadcast purpose. Today, however, illegal pirated private prints of the show turn up on college campuses and in off-beat, late-night film festivals.

The characters were the show:

● Amos Jones was an honest, wholesome, intelligent man who was the sole owner and driver of the Fresh-Air Taxicab Company. He was a very "nice" person, and therefore not very exciting; his role in the show was greatly downplayed.

● Andrew "Hog" Brown, on the other hand, was "lazy and shiftless" and dimwitted. He spent his time aiming for (and missing) the fast buck, and roving after the girls, particularly the singer Madame Queen (but he also had the hots for Miss Blue, Abigail Simpson and Señorita Butterfly).

● George "Kingfish" Stevens was a new major addition to the *Amos 'n' Andy* family; he didn't appear much on the long-running radio version, but his part was beefed up on TV because Amos and Andy, frankly, weren't very

Andrew Halt Brown	Spencer Williams, Jr.
George "Kingfish" Stevens	Tim Moore
Amos Jones	Alvin Childress
Sapphire Stevens, George's wife	Ernestine Wade
Mama, Sapphire's mother	Amanda Randolph
Lightnin', the cab company janitor	Horace Stewart
Algonquin J. Calhoun, the inept lawyer	Johnny Lee
Ruby Jones, Amos' wife	Jane Adams
Arabella Jones, Amos and Ruby's daughter	Patty Marie Ellis
Madame Queen, Andy's former romantic interest	Lillian Randolph
The three Old Maid Gribble Sisters	Monnette Moore, Zelda Cleaver, Willa P. Curtis
Miss Genevieve Blue, the cab company secretary	Madaline Lee

Sapphire and Kingfish: Ernestine Wade, Tim Moore

Amos: Alvin Childress

interesting characters. In fact, the show could have been called *Kingfish 'n' Andy*. Kingfish was president of the local Harlem lodge of the Mystic Knights of the Sea. He loved collecting the dues. He was a con man, a black Bilko, who tried to pluck a buck from anyone he could. Usually his target was the ever-gullible Andy.

● There were other characters of note: Lightnin', the slow-motion janitor who cleaned up around the lodge hall; Ruby and Arabella, Amos' wife and daughter; Sapphire, Kingfish's nagging wife, who shrieked nonstop for him to get a job; her mama, who wore huge hats and went into great fits of rage; and Algonquin J. Calhoun, disbarred shyster lawyer, who practiced anyway.

Their interactions were often hilarious, and although they lived in Harlem (on Lenox and 135th Street), it looked like they lived in a clean, small town. Everyone was black—except most authority figures: judges, some doctors, government officials.

Amos 'n' Andy was another of those radio transplants. Done in "black-voice" by white creators Freeman Gosden and Charles Correll since 1925, it was one of radio's most beloved broadcasts. In 1930, the two donned blackface (as they had done in minstrel shows) and made a successful *Amos 'n' Andy* movie called *Check and Double Check*, which also featured "real" Negroes (but of the cockamamie variety).

When TV happened along, Gosden and Correll thought *Amos 'n' Andy* could make it on the new medium

and took two years to prepare for the transition. They decided on one big difference: they would never appear on the show, although they would use their "black" voices to announce each TV episode. They then hired black actors, and so, TV had its first (and nearly last) blackcom. They got busy writing episodes, such as this very typical one:

Trouble. Kingfish has spent his mother-in-law's money that was earmarked for a special vacation. His wife, Sapphire—who doesn't know George has spent the savings—is so excited about the vacation that she's gone out and bought a trailer. Uh-oh.

George sells his car and buys a motor scooter and hitches it up to the trailer. It doesn't work. He doesn't know what to do to get back the money. And then he thinks of Andy.

"Andy's got four hundred dollars and a minus IQ."

He decides to take Andy—"who doesn't know Yellowstone Park from Central Park"—on an "around-the-world" trailer tour—in Central Park, just blocks from their apartment.

He talks Andy into the whirlwind tour, reading him a poem by "Ralph Walnut Emerson. I quote ver-bacon—'See America in a trailer'." Kingfish then goes on to describe the incredible sights that Andy will see, such as North Dakota—"a fisherman's parasite." Andy is convinced. And it will only cost him . . . $400.

In Central Park, outside the trailer, George sets up

deck chairs, flowerpots, and a sign that reads "Welcome to Kentucky."

"This is a lot better than that New York air," Andy exclaims, just as a man with a distressingly thick Brooklyn accent steps into their "Kentucky" and asks for a match. "Did you hear that Kentucky twang?" George exclaims.

George suddenly looks at Andy and tells him he has "Bluegrass fever" and must be blindfolded immediately. Although unable to see, Andy takes a hike, where he passes a babbling brook (water in a pail which George proceeds to step into).

They get in the trailer and drive around the park, until they land in North Dakota—"The State to Unlax in," announces George's latest sign. Then they're off to the Central Park Zoo "to see the mountain lions." But Andy—with blindfold finally off—is disappointed in Wyoming when he reads a sign: "Welcome to Wyoming—Danger—No Trespassing—Indian Uprising."

To make him feel better, George says he'll go scout "some fresh ranch eggs and some fresh ranch pastrami" and leaves. Who should walk by but Mama and Sapphire. They spot the trailer and they spot Andy.

"What are you two doing in Wyoming?" Andy asks them.

"And what are you doing in Central Park?" they answer, blowing the lid off George's latest scheme.

An army of talent scouts traveled 25,000 miles to interview and audition 800 actors for the roles in the show. They finally narrowed it down to fifty screen tests. By the time it debuted in the summer of 1951, it couldn't have had its cast more together.

Amos was played by Alvin Childress, a Broadway and film actor who thought that he just wasn't right for the show; to study up on the accent, he spent months listening to air checks of the radio program and mimicking the voices of the white actors mimicking black people. (Later, Childress would occasionally play the minister on *Sanford and Son*.)

Overweight Spencer Williams played Andy. Little is known about him except for his *Amos 'n' Andy* role. He died in 1969 at the age of seventy-six of a kidney disease. Ernestine Wade (Sapphire) was the only member of the radio show (which she was on from 1939) to carry her radio role to television. On radio, she had also played the roles of Mrs. Henry Van Porter and the old maid Sara "Needlenose" Fletcher.

George "Kingfish" Stevens was brilliantly played by Tim Moore, who had a fifty-year show business background that included medicine shows, vaudeville, and music halls. As a kid, he toured the world as a boxer named Young Klondike. In 1942 he performed in Broadway's *Harlem Cavalcade*. He died in 1958.

Television viewers thought *Amos 'n' Andy* was either the funniest or the most offensive show they'd ever seen.

The Gribble Sisters (from left): Monnette Moore, Zelda Cleaver, Willa P. Curtis

The Handwriting on the Back: Kingfish and Lightnin'

The Christian Science Monitor called the sight gags and slapstick "violent" and said that the laugh-track was "in poor taste." The biggest problem was that, after twenty-six years of listening to the show on the radio, lots of people couldn't get used to *seeing* the characters; they had "seen" them in their minds all those years and had trouble adjusting their images. That was often a special problem in the television translation of radio shows. Audiences had trouble making the transition from something that was so strongly affixed in their mind's eye to a new, fixed picture on television. That's why many radio-to-TV transplants failed.

One episode of *Amos 'n' Andy* contained these bits of dialogue that help illustrate just what the characters were all about:

KINGFISH: Holy Mackerel! Andy has got a nickel worth two hundred and fifty dollars!
SAPPHIRE: George Stevens, it was bad enough openin' Andy's letter. You ain't thinkin' 'bout gyppin' him outa that coin, is you?
KINGFISH: Who, *me?* Innocent Stevens? Ha, ha, ha . . . I'll say I is!

Later in the episode, Kingfish and Andy are caught breaking open a pay telephone in search of the lost coin. They hire the crooked lawyer Calhoun to defend them.

CALHOUN: Your honor, I'd like to enter a plea of not guilty for these two crooks.

JUDGE: On what grounds? According to the report, these two men were caught trying to break into a telephone coin box in the presence of a witness who also was a police officer in this city.
CALHOUN: W-e-l-l, yes, sir, your honor. But they done learned their lesson. They ain't n-e-v-e-r gonna break open nothin' in front of a cop no mo'!
JUDGE: Isn't your name Calhoun?
CALHOUN: That's right, your honor. Algonquin J. Calhoun.
JUDGE: And didn't I disbar you three years ago?
CALHOUN: Woooooooooo . . . So long, boys!

Like so many other situation comedies, *Amos 'n' Andy* was written in a series of exclamation points. Between the punctuation was racist humor; the comedy played on strong ethnic stereotypes. But if Andy and Kingfish had been white, it would have been like any other sitcom. Ernest T. Bilko concocted no less dishonest situations. Yet the *Amos 'n' Andy* characters were well loved in those innocuous times and actually weren't too far removed from their distant and future cousins, Fred Sanford and George Jefferson, both of whom would do their share of deceiving and conniving. The difference was that Sanford and Jefferson didn't try to outwit their "brothers"; they tried to outwit society. But whatever the analysis, from *Julia* to *The Jeffersons*, *Amos 'n' Andy* was the real television roots of black situation comedy.

They didn't look at it that way back in the sixties, though. *Amos 'n' Andy* is probably the only show whose problems started ten years after it had stopped being made. When it was rerun in syndication, it became extremely popular, especially in the South. At one time, it was seen in 218 United States TV markets, as well as Austria, Guam, Bermuda, and England. In 1963, *Amos 'n' Andy* was purchased by African television stations in Kenya and Western Nigeria, where it was a big hit. (In Africa, it was aired in English with subtitles; most of the TV set owners were white settlers.)

And then the trouble really began. In 1964, an Urban League director issued this statement: "The show depicts the Negro as a foot-shuffling handkerchief-head. The station owners who run it are going to catch hell, and the sponsors of the show will not sell to the Negro market."

Dissent came from all over the country, such as this from the president of a Chicago TV station, where *Amos 'n' Andy* was coming into its twelfth rerun: "I'm going to run the show despite the protest. . . . Trying to keep the program off the air is comparable to book-burning in Nazi Germany."

In 1966, CBS—heavily under pressure—acquiesced and withdrew the show from syndication; it hasn't been seen on television since.

Alvin Childress (who played Amos) protested the withdrawal: "What its detractors fail to mention is that it was the very first time we saw a few blacks playing professionals—judges, lawyers, doctors." Ernestine "Sapphire" Wade added this: "I'm proud to have been on

Checking in: Mr. Kingfish and Ms. Andy

the show. I know there were those people who felt offended by it, but I still have people stop me on the street to tell me how much they enjoyed it—and many of those people are black members of the NAACP."

Looked at today, the *Amos 'n' Andy* episodes might seem innocent enough, but back in the fifties and even the early sixties, it was virtually the only image we had of the black person on television at all. Archie Bunker could have said the same things Kingfish did—a line such as George's "These kids is smarter than they was in my degeneration"—but the origin of the line is more important than the line itself. Archie Bunker's oppression is different from George Stevens'. Of course, were Fred Sanford to utter the line . . . well, the difference there is the difference of twenty-three years.

But back in 1950, Kingfish—who didn't pay his taxes and who tried to get out of the military by dodging the draft—was, indeed, shiftless. The clue to it all, the key to *Amos 'n' Andy*, was its laugh-track: it was *white* laughs we were hearing. And that's the difference. *Amos 'n' Andy* was a show about black people for white people; *The Jeffersons* is for black people—although it's okay if white people want to listen in.

At the start of each episode, angelic voices sang out over the popular theme called "The Perfect Song," as hands turned the pages of the book while a voice announced the show. We've turned the pages of our book too, but it sure would be nice to have *Amos 'n' Andy* back, to see how far we have—or haven't—come.

Fitness: Kingfish measures Calhoun as Andy looks on.

THE GEORGE BURNS AND GRACIE ALLEN SHOW

GEORGE: *Gracie, what do you think of television?*
GRACIE: *I think it's wonderful—I hardly ever watch*
radio anymore.

This sitcom was the original in cockamamie comedy— all about a dazzlingly dizzy housewife involved in domestic schemes, often waged against her tolerant and knowing husband. George Burns played straight man to a very bent woman.

GEORGE: Gracie, how's your Uncle Harvey?
GRACIE: Oh, last night he fell down the stairs with a bottle of scotch and never spilled a drop.
GEORGE: Really?
GRACIE: Yeah, he kept his mouth closed . . . The world lost a great man when my Uncle Harvey was born.

And then George would take a slow puff on his cigar and say, "Say goodnight, Gracie." And, with a little bow, Gracie would say "Goodnight."

And it was always a good night when Burns and Allen were on television. On Wednesday nights, all of us—all 30,000,000 of us—watched them.

Following the same format they had originated in vaudeville in the twenties and later in movies and radio, Burns and Allen had their act together so tightly that the public really believed their goofball goings on. They were married (since 1926, after four years together as a vaudeville team), and people naturally assumed that Gracie was . . . *Gracie.* It didn't help anything (except ratings) when George would say things like: "Gracie's the kind of girl who shortens the cord on the electric iron to save electricity." But mainly the fantasy rang of reality because here were two married people (sometimes appearing with their own son) involved in a comedic cross-breed of situation and domestic comedy. They didn't pretend they were anyone but themselves—not George and Gracie Ricardo. George, who played himself, would frequently break up the show's action to give porchside monologues.

GEORGE: For the benefit of those who have never seen

George Burns	Himself
Gracie Allen	Herself
Harry Von Zell, George's Announcer	Himself
Ronnie Burns, George and Gracie's son	Himself
Blanche Morton, Gracie's friend and neighbor	Bea Benaderet
Harry Morton, Blanche's husband, a CPA	Hal March (1950–1951); John Brown (1951); Fred Clark (1951–1953); Larry Keating (1953–1958)
Bonnie Sue McAfee, Ronnie's girlfriend	Judi Meredith
Ralph Grainger, Ronnie's friend	Robert Ellis
Imogene Reynolds, Ralph's girlfriend	Carol Lee
Jane Adams, Gracie's wardrobe girl	Elva Allman
Frank Adams, her husband	James Flavan
Edie Westlip, president of the Ronnie Burns Fan Club	Anna Maria NaNasse
Malcolm Rogers, Edie's boyfriend	Stevie Tursman
Verna Mason, an aspiring actress	Valerie Allen
Vickie Donavan, the Hat Check Girl at the MaCombo Club	Jackie Loughery
Al Simon, the Burns' business manager	Lyle Talbot
Professor Ainsworth, Ronnie's instructor at UCLA	Howard Guendell
Gloria Gallagher, one of Harry Von Zell's girlfriends	Barbara Stuart
Mr. Jentzen, the plumber	Howard McNair
His daughters	Yvonne Lime, Mary Ellen Kay, Jody Warner,
Mr. Beasley, the mailman	Ralph Seadan
Chester Vanderlip, a society friend	Brandon Rhodes
Detective Soyer, a Los Angeles cop plagued by Gracie	James Flavan
Clara Bagley, a friend of Gracie's	Irene Hervey
Joey Bagley, her son	Garry Marshall
Announcers:	Bill Goodwin (early, not syndicated episodes); Harry Von Zell

Neighbors: Bea Benaderet, Larry Keating, George, Gracie

me, I am what is known in the business as a straight man. If you don't know what a straight man does, I'll tell you. The comedian gets a laugh. Then I look at the comedian. Then I look at the audience—like this. *(looks)* That is known as a pause. And when I'm really rolling, this is one of my ad libs. *(surprised look with mouth open)*

Another duty of a straight man is to repeat what the comedian says. For example, if Gracie should say, "A funny thing happened on the streetcar today." Then I say, "A funny thing happened on the streetcar today?" And naturally her answer gets a scream. Then I throw in one of my famous pauses. *(looks)*

I've been a straight man for so many years that from force of habit I repeat everything. I went out fishing with a fellow the other day and he fell overboard. He yelled, "Help! Help! Help!" so I said, "Help? Help? Help?" And while I was waiting for him to get his laugh, he drowned.

After many successful years on the stage, movies, and radio, when television became TV, George Burns

and Gracie Allen—who had simply become Burns and Allen—a partnership as well known as Dun and Bradstreet or Sears and Roebuck—wanted in. Or, at least, George did. Gracie was scared. "This is one thing that I will not be pushed into," she announced. But he talked her into making one TV screen test. Said George afterward: "Gracie looked so pretty, she couldn't help but okay it, and we were in business."

And what a business it was. Carnation shared the sponsorship with B. F. Goodrich, and for two years the show was shot live every other week from the Mansfield Theater in New York, and then moved to Los Angeles.

Ralph Levy was resting in Mexico in 1951 when he got a call to return to take charge of the new *Burns and Allen* TV program. Said Levy: "George had some cock-eyed idea for a show . . . in very bad taste." What ultimately evolved was a cross between sitcom and vaudeville. There was a set of the Burns house, another one for their neighbors (Harry and Blanche Morton) and, downstage, an area for George to stand and talk directly to the audience about Gracie, predict the rest of the show, and comment on daily life in and around the neighborhood.

Burns—as the "reality" figure—kept the show in human context for us. He reminded us that we were watching TV. One episode had him finishing one of his monologues by telling the audience that his time was up—but he promised to wave to us after he walked back into the scene. And he did. In later episodes, George had a magic all-seeing TV set in his upstairs office—he could turn it on and see what Gracie, Blanche, and the rest were up to. He would turn from the set, face the camera, and say: "According to my calculations, Harry Von Zell should be over at the Mortons' and by now Gracie should have him mixed up in this too. . . . Let's take a look. . . ." It added a surrealistic element to the show; George was doing what we were doing—watching his show on TV.

One week, Burns was talking about how sometimes his writers couldn't think of any way to end the show. As he spoke, the camera did a slow fade until the picture was only a tiny dot and then disappeared totally into blackness. The next week on the show, a character was complimenting George on how clever that gimmick was. Burns replied that it would probably never happen again—and as he said this, the picture began to disappear from left to right, with Burns (on the left) wiped out at the end.

Burns, Levy says, was not an ad libber, and used to walk down Sunset Boulevard (when the show was later filmed in Hollywood), talking to himself, rehearsing monologues and perfecting every word and nuance.

Television was frightening. Many performers—including the invincible Fred Allen—had failed on TV. Burns and Allen became an even bigger success. But they had a lot to learn. George played to the audience, but Gracie didn't; she considered herself to be a "method" actress of sorts. Once during those first two live years, Gracie, midshow, peeked at the camera and stopped dead in her tracks, and then went on. Later she wanted to know what that little light on the camera was. "I never want to see it again," she said. "It scares me."

The show wasn't all Burns and Allen. There was a stable of supporting players who helped make up one of TV's best repertory companies. Harry Von Zell played Harry Von Zell, who was a straight man to the straight man, George, who heaped much abuse upon him. Von Zell (the real one) had been a radio announcer in the thirties and forties for such performers as Phil Baker, Paul Whiteman, Lawrence Tibbett, Ed Wynn, and Fred Allen, for whom he was known for his tongue-twisting introductions: "Presenting that lackadaisical leviathan of laconic lampoon . . ."

On *Burns and Allen,* he played George's foil. He was goofy, an overstuffed teddy bear who was always worried about his job security (George, the character, fired and rehired him regularly). And Von Zell worried whether his shoulders were broad enough to win the attention of some nubile teenaged girl (played by one in an interminable series of starlets who inevitably preferred his boss' son, Ronnie Burns). And, somehow, Harry Von Zell always got messed up in Gracie's schemes. Once she dressed him up as a witch doctor to chase away unwanted guests. Poor Harry (almost one word) always raced in and made a fool of himself. And he always tried to be so helpful.

HARRY VON ZELL (*thinking George is crazy*):   We can't handle this. George needs somebody who understands these cases, and I know just the man . . . he has hundreds of nervous patients. . . .
GRACIE: He can't be so good if he makes all his patients nervous.

Blanche and Harry Morton were the television Burns' neighbors. Golden-haired (and hearted) Blanche was the perfect pal for Gracie. She tolerated her in a loving, nurturing way; you always got the feeling that Gracie relieved the boredom in her humdrum life. But she was, oh, so patient.

BLANCHE: Wait till you hear this! I just got a phone call from Lucille Vanderlip and she told me Margie Bates got a beautiful diamond bracelet from her husband.
GRACIE: I can't believe it.
BLANCHE: Why not?
GRACIE: If Lucille's husband gave another woman a diamond bracelet, you'd think she'd be the last one to mention it.
BLANCHE: Er . . . Gracie . . . you misunderstood me.

Or this exchange:

GRACIE: Blanche, I heard some gossip about you from a woman.

Pre-Von Zell: George talks to announcer Bill Goodwin

Kids: Ronnie and Sandra

BLANCHE: Oh—what was it?
GRACIE: I don't remember—I forgot it the minute I told it to her.

Bea Benaderet had been around. Before Blanche, she had played scores of radio shrews on shows such as *Jack Benny, Ozzie and Harriet*—and even the *Burns and Allen Show*. Her own favorite radio roles: Amber Lipscott in *My Friend Irma*, Gloria the Maid on *Ozzie and Harriet*, Mrs. Carstairs on *Fibber McGee and Molly*, and Mama on *Meet Millie*.

"When TV began," she later said, "I think there was some doubt as to whether I could walk or not."

She could and did. And TV's Blanche Morton—a carryover from her role on the radio show—kept her in the public eye (and ear—she had a laugh that you thought would shatter your TV screen).

With Blanche and Gracie, it was definitely the women versus the men, and Blanche had the perfect enemy in husband Harry Morton—"a person of perpetual pomposity," as he might himself say it. Blanche and Harry had a running battle; they were Fred and Ethel to George's and Gracie's Lucy and Ricky and, according to Harry, Blanche was the battleax.

BLANCHE: Oh, I wish I was a man! I'd knock some of that pompousness out of you.
HARRY: Yes, it's too bad you're not a man. We might have been good friends.

Harry was originally played by actor Fred Clark, who left the program to do a Broadway show. He had also asked Burns for a high salary—$1,500 an episode—$350 more than George himself was getting—so George had replaced him with Larry Keating at $750 a show.

This is how the switch was handled:

On Fred Clark's last show, Blanche was waiting by the door to hit him over the head with a vase because she didn't like the iron deer he had bought for the front door. When Clark entered, Burns walked into the scene and said, "Hold it!" and then explained to the audience about Clark leaving the show. George introduced Larry Keating—the new Harry—to the audience, then to Bea Benaderet. They bowed, and George said, "Now let's get back to the story." Keating exited and then reentered—and Blanche hit him over the head with the vase. (Burns has disappointedly said he never received one letter about the episode.)

Keating had been on radio for seven years in *This Is Your FBI*, and had made forty movies, including *Daddy Long Legs, Monkey Business, The Buster Keaton Story* and *The Eddie Duchin Story*. He had entertained during World War II with the Bob Hope troupe.

When the two couples got together—with Harry Von Zell running an ineffectual interference—the result was a merry mayhem, a kooky bedlam so typical of fifties sitcoms. Just a glance at two *Burns and Allen* plot lines bears out the possibilities of these improbable situations:

"Gracie Buys a Boat for George": Harry Morton tries to induce George to play golf, and when this fails, Gracie recruits Harry Von Zell to buy a boat for George.

"Gracie Thinks Harry Morton Is in Love with Her": Gracie, convinced of neighbor Harry's passion, cools his ardor by giving him a sandwich spiced with chopped shoelaces.

These stories were dreamed up by a team of writers, including George's brother Willie Burns, about whom George said: "My brother Willie hasn't got an easy life. If the rating is down, it's Willie's fault. If it's up, I'm wearing a red tie."

Gracie had nothing to do with the writing, although she would edit out certain lines, particularly anything about physical afflictions.

It was a hectic shooting schedule for her. On Mondays, she had to be fitted for clothes for four hours and then studied her script (forty-three pages of dialogue) for three hours after dinner. At 9 A.M. on Tuesdays, rehearsals began. The shooting was Wednesday. Thursday was a day off. Friday was spent picking clothes, Saturday meeting with the directors, and Sunday studying the script.

The show was taped and—instead of using canned laughter—it was run before a live audience. That laughter was recorded—although they would add a laugh if a joke laid an egg or cut out laughter if it was too big. The film was shot with two cameras—one focused on the person making the joke, another on the other person's reaction. If the joke got a laugh, the shot used was the reaction; if no laugh, the camera stayed on the joker and followed his or her exit.

In 1955—after the show had been on the air for many years—George had a talk with his twenty-year-old adopted son, Ronnie, then a student at the University of Southern California. "Ronnie, have you ever thought about acting? . . . Well, start thinking about it!"—and from then on, Ronnie Burns was playing Ronnie Burns— a regular. (He had had one brief TV stint on *The*

Honeymooners, for which he was paid a new Buick convertible.)

It was odd when Ronnie joined the show. As a sophisticated college student with his constant giggling gaggle of girlfriends and his down-to-earth manner, he somehow seemed older than his parents. He was taller, anyway. His salary was $285 a week (Fred Clark would not have been happy) and, almost at once, 5,000 viewers joined his fan club. His presence added a domestic dimension that heretofore hadn't been on the show. George and Gracie now had to be responsible parents, a role viewers hadn't imagined them in. Especially Gracie. But as zanily zapped out as she was, people could actually relate to her. Unfortunately, she couldn't relate to it— and she wanted out.

In 1958, Gracie decided to retire from show business. After dozens of years (she started at three as a dancing colleen in an Irish vaudeville act), she was ready to hang up her tutu. Her last episode aired June 11, 1958, and the show—with the rest of the cast intact— went on for another year until it fizzled out without her.

In 1961, Gracie had a severe heart attack and, thereafter, heart flutters. When she retired she spent her time with her family and grandchildren. On August 27, 1964, Gracie died. For a long time after, George could not get to sleep unless he slept in Gracie's bed.

Somewhere it came out after her death that Gracie had one blue eye and one brown eye. Maybe that explains the dizziness.

Burns tried another sitcom and tried working with Connie Stevens and Carol Channing—but it didn't work. He needed Gracie.

We all did. Gracie Allen had a way of scrambling up the pieces of the puzzle and putting them back together in a way that fit only to her. We understood her jigsaw madness—like travelers in a foreign country who've had a weekly half-hour lesson of Allen Berlitz—and we loved her.

There was a running gag on the show. A closet in the living room was filled with men's hats, neatly organized and labeled by Gracie with the names of their owners—

men who had hastily left the Burns' house—too much in a hurry to retrieve their hats as they escaped Gracie's loony bin. They weren't able to grasp the fifth dimension of Gracie like we could. When we left the Burns house every week, we were in no hurry to leave. We always remembered to take our hats.

George put it this way: "Gracie isn't really crazy. She makes sense in an illogical sort of way. She's off-center. Not quite right, but nearly right."

Or, as Gracie once said in a classic bit of explanation:

"The reason I put the salt in the pepper shaker and the pepper in the salt shaker is that people are always getting them mixed up. Now when they get mixed up, they'll be all right."

Say goodnight, Gracie.

ALSO RANS

Beulah

This early "race sitcom" was—like its black brother *Amos 'n' Andy*—withdrawn from syndication via NAACP protests in the fifties and sixties. Taking place in New York, it was all about the Henderson family, an attorney, his wife, and son. Mostly, though, it was about their maid Beulah, the Queen of the Kitchen. Beulah worked hard to solve all the problems that arose from the family—sort of a *Hazel* in blackface. Her girlfriend Oriole was played by Butterfly McQueen (Miss Prissy in *Gone With the Wind*) and she had a shiftless beau named Bill Jackson, a fix-it-shop owner.

Three of the country's greatest black actresses tried their hands at the role of Beulah: first, singer/actress Ethel Waters, who was replaced in 1951 by Hattie McDaniel, who fell ill. In 1952, Louise Beavers was Beulah. CBS aired the show, which ceased being filmed on September 22, 1953, when Beavers decided she'd had enough.

Beulah started life as a character on radio's *Fibber McGee and Molly* in 1944. She got her own radio series when Marlin Hurt, a white actor, created a separate show for her. "Somebody bawl fo' Beulah?" was her catchphrase, and something that contributed to making her one of radio's and TV's most beloved characters.

Beulah Number 3: (From left) Louise Beavers with guest Ruby Dandridge

The Hank McCune Show

How does this official NBC plot description sound to you? "The misadventures of Hank McCune (played by himself), a kind-hearted bumbler who seeks but inevitably fails to achieve success." Also in the cast of this one-season sitcom (one of the first) was Larry Keating, who would go on to play Harry Morton on the *Burns and Allen Show*. The show was pure slapstick. On the first episode, for example, Hank went to a convention (supposedly the convention of his sponsor, Peter Paul candy bars) where he screwed up all the reservations and disrupted a neighboring convention of a mystical fraternal order. He even managed to anger several lifeguards. This was, incidentally, the first sitcom to have a laugh-track. And one of the first shows to be canceled after only three months.

Meet Corliss Archer

The long-running radio version (since 1943) of this show was still on the air when it hit TV in June of 1951. As on radio, it was still the story of a "typical high school girl" (played by Lugene Sanders, who'd go on to play Riley's daughter Babs in 1953) who had a boyfriend named Dexter Franklin (Bobby Ellis, who would go on to play Henry Aldrich on TV in *The Aldrich Family* in 1952). Corliss also had two parents (well, really three, if you count Irene Tedrow, who took over the part from Frieda Inescort in 1952; Tedrow, incidentally, had played Mrs. Archer on radio; Fred Shields, who played Mr. Archer, was also a radio leftover).

Aired live from New York, the sitcom had a strange viewing history. During its first summer, it was seen in the Midwest on Thursday nights (the rest of the country was watching *Your Esso Reporter*). Then, on Friday nights, the cast would reassemble and perform the show for the rest of the country.

In 1954, CBS started to film the show, starring Ann Baker as Corliss. So the show went from live to film . . . to dead, when the network dropped the show in 1955 .

Menasha the Magnificent

Menasha Skulnik played himself (so who else?) in this live NBC sitcom, in which he was manager of a decrepit restaurant. A Yiddish comedian, Skulnik began each show singing "Oh, What a Beautiful Morning," but ended up singing other songs, because his days were usually filled with troubles. Some of those problems revolved around his domineering boss, Mrs. Davis (played by Jean Cleveland in the first telecast, then Zanah Cunningham the next week). Skulnik/Menasha was a little guy who didn't so much walk as hop. The show hopped off NBC after only three months. Vinton Hayworth and Danny Leane also appeared on the show.

The Peter and Mary Show

Peter and Mary were, respectively, Peter Lind Hayes and Mary Healy, who played themselves on this unusual sitcom with a very pat format: At the start of each episode on NBC each week, we'd see the guest star (or stars) on the phone, explaining that they were sorry, but they couldn't have dinner that night because they had a previous commitment to have dinner with Peter and Mary. When they got to P and M's house in New Rochelle (in a near-exact replica of the married-together stars' real home in New Rochelle), we could be sure we'd see a lot of singing, dancing, jokes (but little eating, though). One of the guests, Claude Stroud, came for dinner and never left until the end of December, as did their housekeeper, Mary Wickes. Also in December, the name of the show was changed to *The Peter Lind Hayes Show* (which wasn't a very nice thing to do to Mary), but, by March of 1951, the whole thing was canceled anyway.

The Ruggles

Charlie Ruggles starred as himself in this three-month sitcom on ABC. As his wife "Mrs." was Erin O'Brien Moore (later played by Irene Tedrow), and as his daughter Sharon: Margaret Kerry.

The Stu Erwin Show: The Trouble with Father

Dagwood, Riley—none of TV's bumbling daddies had anything over Stu Erwin, who was the king of the incompetents. Stu Erwin had played the same kind of character in the movies and on radio, and his translation to television was successful. He played a man named Stu Erwin (odd for TV, which would have ordinarily renamed him something like Stu Erickson), who was principal of Hamilton High School (located—where else?—in the town of Hamilton). Most of the action, however, took place around his house, where everything he touched turned to trouble. Oh, he had good intentions—he wanted to fix something, he wanted to surprise someone, he wanted to help his kids. But it never worked. Thankfully, there was the required levelheaded, sensible, down-to-earth Mom played by June Collyer (Erwin's Real Life wife), who'd come to the rescue. Plus the kids could take care of themselves: Jackie, a tomboy (played by Sheila James, who would become Zelda on *Dobie Gillis* some years later) and teenaged Joyce (played, from 1950 to 1954 by Ann Todd, and then by Merry Anders, who'd go on to play Val, the aspiring model on *It's Always Jan* in 1955). The Erwins also had a handyman named Willie (played by Willie Best, best remembered as yet another handyman on *My Little Margie*). In 1954, Joyce began going steady with Harry (played by Harry Hayden) and in December they were married (so Stu got to botch up the ceremony). That same year, though, Stu became a little less bumbling (but just a little) in the network's attempt to clean up Erwin's image—something he'd been hoping for for some seasons. The show had several aliases: *Life with the Erwins* (the original title), *The Trouble with Father* (which continued as its subtitle) and—during its final season on ABC in 1954–1955—*The New Stu Erwin Show*.

That Wonderful Guy

Jack Lemmon hit sitcomdom (but not stardom) this year with this one, about a would-be actor who's employed as a valet by a pompous, sophisticated drama critic (played by Neil Hamilton). Harold/Lemmon's girlfriend was played by Cynthia Stone (Lemmon's wife). The stories (and there weren't many of them; the show lasted only a few episodes on ABC) revolved around Harold's romantic and business misadventures in New York City.

1951–1952

I Love Lucy

Mr. Peepers

My Little Margie

OFF-SCREEN

9/4   Millionth US soldier to die in battle since 1775 reported killed in Korea.

10/10   Yankees win third straight Series, defeating NY Giants.

10/26   Winston Churchill designated Prime Minister by George VI.

11/10   Personal transcontinental dial phone service inaugurated on experimental basis in Englewood, NJ.

2/6   King George VI dies unexpectedly; elder daughter, Elizabeth II, named queen by Privy Council.

3/3   Puerto Ricans overwhelmingly ratify constitution giving self-government under US control.

3/20   Oscars go to Humphrey Bogart *(African Queen)* and Vivien Leigh *(A Streetcar Named Desire).*

4/13   FCC ends prohibition against construction of new TV stations and assigns 2,053 new stations to 1,291 communities in US.

5/3   First scheduled jet airliner flight completed by British jet landing in Johannesburg after flying from London (6,724 miles) in 23 hours, 38 minutes.

5/26   US Supreme Court, reversing NY ban on *The Miracle,* unanimously holds that films are entitled to First Amendment guarantees of free speech and free press.

FRONT RUNNERS

I LOVE LUCY

I loved playing Lucy Ricardo—I got to act out all my childhood fantasies.
        —LUCILLE BALL, talking about *I Love Lucy*, 1979

Reams—books, articles, speculations—have been written about *I Love Lucy* and its impact on everything from attitudes toward American humor to American pregnancy to Cuban immigration. So what is there left to say about the most popular sitcom in the history of television?

Plenty.

In one form or another, Lucille Ball kicked around (and kicked up) TV comedy in a regular series for twenty-three years (with several seasons off for such vacations as TV specials and divorce from Desi). You can still, in some cities, see Lucy—in various incarnations—aired as many as five times a day. Says Lucille Ball: "I don't like it—every time you turn on the water tap, you get me." She should complain? She was lucky she even got on the air.

Suppose you were a network programming official back in 1950 and someone called you up and said they had a hot idea for a weekly wacky situation comedy about the antics of the stagestruck wife of—get this—a Cuban band leader. The redhead was that former brunette from movies, Lucille Ball, and her husband was conga-player Desi Arnaz. Big deal. Would you have put it on the air? Could anybody have been interested in such a show?

The answer is implicit in the fact that the following "facts" actually mean something to so many people:
● The Ricardos' babysitter was Mrs. Trumbull from upstairs.
● Ricky Keith (the child actor who played Little Ricky) was six years old when he signed on, he earned $300 a week; his real name was Keith Thibodeaux; he says he hasn't heard from Lucy or Desi in years.
● Lucy and Ricky and their landlords, the Mertzes, lived at 623 East 68th St. in Manhattan.

People cared—and cared—about the adventures of Fred and Ethel and Ricky and Lucy. From Ricky's theme song (Ba-ba-lu) to Lucy's maiden name (MacGillicuddy), this whole country—even thirty years later—still knows—and loves—*Lucy*.

The show began—not in an effort to give Americans a truly funny show—but as a way to save the Arnaz marriage. It didn't save their marriage (they were divorced in 1960), but it did give America a truly funny show. It seems to have been more than worth the casualty.

I Love Lucy gave birth to at least three generations of sitcoms in which one couple interacted zanily with another couple (*The Honeymooners* and the Bunkers and the Stivicks went on to do it in later years). *I Love Lucy* was the supreme sitcom, the godmother of them all.

Here's how it did—or almost didn't—start: Lucille Ball was unhappy with her film career, and so had been starring with Richard Denning on radio's *My Favorite Husband*, on which she played Liz, wife of a Midwestern banker. In 1950, CBS-TV offered to bring the show to television, but Ball insisted that her real-life husband, Cuban Desi Arnaz, play opposite her. The networks did not think, for some reason, that the viewing public would

Lucy Ricardo	Lucille Ball
Ricky Ricardo	Desi Arnaz
Fred Mertz, their friend, the landlord	William Frawley
Ethel Mertz, his wife	Vivian Vance
Little Ricky Ricardo, Lucy and Ricky's son	The Mayer Twins; Richard Keith
Betty Ramsey, their neighbor (Connecticut-based episodes)	Mary Jane Croft (1957)
Ralph Ramsey, her husband	Frank Nelson (1957)
Mrs. Trumbull, the Ricardos' neighbor	Elizabeth Patterson

accept a thick-accented Latin as the husband of a typical American wife. Ball was, at the time, thirty-eight years old. She remained adamant and said she wouldn't do the show unless Desi costarred.

They had been married since 1940, and it was no surprise to anybody that their marriage was in trouble. They had been separated by their work—he toured with his band, she stayed at home and made radio programs—plus they argued all the time; Ball thought that it might help their relationship if they could work together. The networks and advertisers were against the idea. So Arnaz and Ball decided they'd let the public decide.

They formed Desilu Productions and took a twenty-minute comedy act cross-country. They were a hit. But still, no TV show. Lucille went back to radio. Desi hit the road. By late 1950, CBS said they would "okay air time" for the Arnazes, but would not financially underwrite any test film of any proposed series starring the two.

Says Lucy: "Everyone warned Desi and me that we were committing career suicide by giving up highly paid movie and band commitments to go for broke on TV, but it was either working together or good-bye marriage." Then, she has said, she had a dream about her friend Carole Lombard, who said to her, "Honey, go ahead. Take a chance. Give it a whirl." They raised the money themselves and made a pilot script, about the real-life Arnazes, not Ricky and Lucy, but a successful orchestra leader and his movie-star wife. It didn't have Fred and Ethel Mertz, but did have "Jerry the Agent" (who was dropped but then popped up in many segments years later). They tried to find a sponsor to underwrite it so they could buy time from CBS. They couldn't find anyone who was interested. And so *I Love Lucy* almost didn't happen.

The problem was that the pilot was mostly like the vaudeville show the Arnazes had toured with; lyricist Oscar Hammerstein II gave his friends the idea of making the couple ordinary and wholesome, but dizzy, sort of like radio's *Fibber McGee and Molly* (which itself would hit TV in 1959, but only lasted out the season).

And a new format was born.

Said the head of the ad agency that handled Philip Morris: "If you can create characters for yourselves with whom the average person can associate—everyday people, not Lucille Ball, the movie star, and Desi Arnaz, the $150,000-a-year bandleader—I'll make a commitment here and now."

The results: Lucy and Ricky Ricardo. Married. Living in Apartment 4-A at 623 East 68th St. He worked at the Tropicana (pay: $150 a week). She was a housewife who hungered for a career in show business.

The title of the series created a problem. CBS wanted to call it *The Lucille Ball Show*, because, well, who knew who Desi Arnaz was, anyway? Lucy got upset and told CBS to forget the whole thing. She didn't even want to call it *The Lucille Ball and Desi Arnaz Show* because his name was listed last. Finally, someone from

the ad agency came up with an offbeat title: *I Love Lucy*. She agreed, because "I" referred to Desi, and so he was mentioned first. That settled, the agency asked the Arnazes when they would be moving to New York to begin shooting the show live. Desi was stunned. They loved Los Angeles and didn't want to move.

Problem: Doing the show live from LA would mean that New York audiences would get inferior quality kinescopes (films from TV monitors; there was no videotape or filming of TV shows then), and since "more potential Philip Morris smokers" lived in New York, they wanted that market to get the best reception.

Solution: Desi had an outlandish brainstorm: filming the show in California on 35mm film, like a movie. The budget for each show was only $19,500 (filming would cost much more), but the quality would be better for everyone; instead of kinescopes, they'd send the films around—just like the motion picture studios did.

Lucy's and Desi's salary was, together, $5,000 a week; they took a $1,000 cut to allow for the extra expense of film. Desi then demanded that he and Lucy own 100 percent of the shows. CBS said yes. It may have been the most expensive yes the network ever uttered; years later Desilu sold the shows for syndication for many millions of dollars.

They had to figure out how to film a half-hour TV show; no one had ever tried before. They hired cinematographer Karl Freund (he had filmed Garbo in *Camille*, and won a 1937 Oscar for *The Good Earth*). They decided to film the show like a play, in front of a live audience (Lucille Ball insisted she needed an audience to perform best), with four cameras running simultaneously, each picking up a different angle.

Gale Gordon and Bea Benaderet were the Arnazes' first choice to play neighbors Fred and Ethel Mertz; as everybody knows, it didn't happen: Gordon was committed to do the CBS radio show *Our Miss Brooks*; Benaderet was already playing Blanche Morton on the Burns and Allen television program.

William Frawley, who had worked with Ball in 1946 on *Ziegfeld Follies*, called her and asked her for the part of Fred Mertz. She and Desi were hesitant; Frawley was sixty-four at the time and was rumored to be unstable and an alcoholic. Frawley, who was having hard times getting work, was told by Desi that if he were ever late to the set or couldn't perform except because of illness more than once, he'd be bounced out of the show. He agreed. And then they set off to find an Ethel.

Marc Daniels, who was picked to direct the show, was familiar with the work of an actress named Vivian Vance. He took the Arnazes—who'd never heard of her—to watch her perform in a summer theater where she was playing the nasty Other Woman in *The Voice of the Turtle*. Daniels went backstage and got Vance to agree, quite reluctantly, to be in the series. But the problems were not over.

They had to get a studio. They had to develop a new

lighting system for the show. They had to create exit doors and a sprinkler system. And they had to put in a new floor that could accommodate all the dollies and cameras.

They did it all, including renting a seven-and-one-half acre Hollywood lot, which they renamed The Desilu Playhouse. Ninety-five people were hired to put together the show—from producer to janitor.

There were many changes at the last minute.

They installed the famous louvred shutter between the Ricardos' kitchen and living room; it had been just a dead wall before and they wanted more mobility to be able to shoot through the opening.

Just as the audience was filing into the theater past the No Smoking signs (the Philip Morris folks weren't too pleased about that touch), the Department of Health and Welfare inspector told Arnaz that there wouldn't be any show that night—because there was no women's bath-

room, only a men's. Lucy gave up her bathroom, and the women tramped backstage to her dressing room.

So far, $250,000 had been spent—quite a sum of money back then—and nothing had even been filmed yet.

Nine P.M., Monday, October 15, 1951. The first episode of *I Love Lucy*, "The Girls Want to Go to a Nightclub," airs. That's the one in which Fred and Ricky plot to go to the boxing matches, even though their wives have made plans to go to a nightclub for the Mertzes' anniversary that night. Lucy and Ethel refuse to go to the fights with them. When Fred and Ricky arrange for blind dates for themselves, Ethel and Lucy dress up as hillbillies to substitute for the blind dates.

The show was a hit with the critics, who flung around adjectives like: "the very best," "refreshing," "high-level," "high-quality," "spirited." *Variety* predicted that the show "should sell a lot of cigarettes."

One critic dissented, and, quickly, Philip Morris tried to get out of their contract. They were talked out of it and *Lucy* lived on. And on and on. Even that first season, it was a huge hit, winning twenty-five awards and plaques.

The show was shot in a prototypical manner that is being used by most sitcoms even today.

TUESDAY Production people, actors, and writers sat around and did a read-through of that week's script. The cast spent the day rehearsing, making changes. Writers rewrote when necessary—sometimes only single lines, other times entire pages or scenes.

WEDNESDAY Cast rehearsed on the set, not around a table. There were about fifty pages of dialogue, and usually, by then, they had been memorized. By the end of the day, the cast ran through the show with cinematographer Freund, who studied the players and planned his camera moves.

THURSDAY Freund and the electrical crew began lighting the set, finishing usually by noon, when camera crew members were instructed on camera movements. With all the crews, the cast rehearsed until 6. A dress rehearsal

In Hollywood: Lucy and William Holden

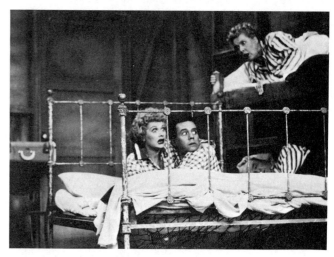

Night Out: The clan visits Bent Fork, Tennessee

Lighting Lucy: Head Cameraman Karl Freund and (far right) Director Marc Daniels

was held at 7 P.M. Meanwhile, the writers were working on next week's show. From 8 until at least 10 P.M., they got together and dissected that week's show, making cuts and changes, trying to tighten up the show.

FRIDAY By 9 A.M., the cameramen were onstage, blocking out their chalk lines. The lighting men used stand-ins to mark cues. By 1 P.M., the entire cast and crew rehearsed again, until a final dress rehearsal at 4:30. Close to 8 P.M.—after Lucy had acted as headmistress to the cast and crew at their weekly communal dinner and then they all "talked through" the show for any last-minute problems—the audience filed in. Nothing was left to chance. The audience members were given cues for laughter, groans, cheers, applause. Then Desi would come on, and do a "warm-up" for the audience, introducing everyone including the stagehands. All scenes were shot in order, and the show went on for twenty-four and a half minutes (added later were the minute of opening titles and the minute for closing titles). The episode was processed, and prints—costing $30 each—were made and sent to CBS outlets across the country in time for airing.

During the course of *I Love Lucy* several things occurred that would make history:

Prior to filming one of the last episodes of that first successful season, Desi announced that Lucy was pregnant (their daughter, Lucie, had been born some years earlier). Said Desi: "We could have filmed enough shows in advance to tide us through until the baby came, but I wanted to talk about my son. I didn't want to put Lucille in a closet for nine months. Having a baby is a perfectly natural happening." Apparently CBS didn't think so. Later, a CBS official said: "When Lucille Ball announced that she was going to have a baby, all we could think of at first was complete disaster. As it turned out, it was the best thing that ever happened to *I Love Lucy*. It gave the show a change of pace, a change of perspective." Philip Morris urged Desi to hide Lucy behind chairs or, better, not feature her at all during her period of pregnancy. Desi got angry. Desi got his way.

They started filming immediately, so that all the episodes wouldn't be "pregnancy" episodes. When word leaked out (via Louella Parsons), there was widespread worry that the show would be canceled. After all, no one had been pregnant on television before. "Lucille Ball's pregnancy won't keep her off TV," wrote *TV Guide*. "The approach of the stork will be written into *I Love Lucy*."

They got a minister, they got a priest, they got a rabbi, all to look over and approve the scripts. The company had decided there would be seven episodes that dealt with the pregnancy—except they couldn't call it pregnancy. Said Desi: "CBS didn't like that word, so we used 'expectant.' CBS thought it was a nicer word."

In the first "expectancy" episode, Lucy has the classic problem of how to tell Ricky.

RICKY: Oh, what a business. Sometimes I think I go back to Cuba and work in a sugar plantation. Just the two of us.
LUCY: Just the two of us?
RICKY: Yeah. I don't mean to get you all involved in my affairs, but you should be happy you're a woman.
LUCY: Oh, I am, I am!
RICKY: You think you know how tough my job is, but believe me, if you traded places with me . . . you'd be surprised.
LUCY: Believe me, if I traded places with you, *you'd* be surprised.

Finally, in the last scene, she manages to tell him. The script called for him to be excited. Instead, Arnaz broke down and cried. Some of the audience cried right along. The director, thinking this had ruined the scene, ordered a retake. They ended up liking the crying version better and went with it.

A major publicity campaign got started. At first, since Ball was really going to have her baby (by cesarean section) the same day the birth episode would be telecast, they thought they'd insert the baby's sex when they knew the real baby's gender. They discarded that idea; they decided to make the baby a boy so their daughter Lucie Arnaz wouldn't feel she'd been left out. Plus, Desi wanted a boy.

Long memos went out—under the heading of "Various Aspects of the Ricardo Baby in the *I Love Lucy* Publicity and Promotional Campaign"—that went into intricate detail about how the baby's sex would be kept a secret.

When the episode "Lucy Goes to the Hospital" was broadcast, 44,000,000 tuned in to watch. Eisenhower was sworn in the next day; 20,000,000 people watched that. "How about that," mused Desi. "She's as important as Ike. I wonder if we could run her for President in fifty-six?"

In the hospital the day of the airing, the real Lucy gave birth to a boy, Desi, Jr. Said Walter Winchell: "This was a banner week—the nation got a man and Lucy got a boy."

Said Desi: "That's Lucy for you. Always does her best to cooperate."

Said writer Jess Oppenheimer when he found out

that Lucy "followed his script": "That makes me the greatest writer in the world. Tell Lucy she can take the rest of the day off." She did.

In 1953, something else was born, that nobody was expecting: Walter Winchell announced that "America's top comedienne has been confronted with her membership in the Communist party." It meant big trouble: it was the heyday of the McCarthy Era and its Red Scare. The House Un-American Activities Committee was holding hearings. The publicity could ruin *I Love Lucy*.

Newspapers were full of items, including a front-page headline with four-inch-high red letters LUCILLE BALL NAMED RED. It seems that Ball had registered Communist in 1936, intent on voting Communist party "to please my grandfather," she had told the committee the year before when they had cleared her.

Lucy and Desi were worried. Desi was prepared to buy television time to "tell our story." Lucille Ball was a nervous wreck; she was certain that all of America hated her. They feared that Philip Morris—whom they had not heard from—would pull their sponsorship from the show. The empire was in danger of collapsing.

The sponsor said they'd support Lucy. And, just minutes before the broadcast that Friday, the Committee had issued a statement saying they had cleared Lucy.

In his preshow warm-up, Desi Arnaz cried out to the studio audience: "Lucille Ball is no Communist! Lucy has never been a Communist, not now and never will be. I was kicked out of Cuba because of Communism. We both despise the Communists for everything they stand for. Lucille is one hundred percent American. She's as American as Barney Baruch and Ike Eisenhower. Please, ladies and gentlemen, don't believe every piece of bunk you read in today's papers." The audience rose and cheered. Lucy stood in the wings, sobbing. He called her out to introduce her. "And now I want you to meet my favorite wife—my favorite redhead—in fact, that's the only thing red about her, and even *that's* not legitimate." End of crisis.

In *Roman Scandals*, a villain came at Eddie Cantor and threw a handful of mud at him. Cantor bent over and the mud landed in the face of one of the Goldwyn Girls. During rehearsals, Busby Berkeley had asked one of the girls to volunteer. Everyone had backed off, except one—Lucille Ball. Cantor shouted: "Get that girl's name! That's the one who will make it."

She made it, she made it. Lucille Ball was always the golden Goldwyn Girl with mud on her face. She was an actress who could play comedy (not the other way around), and the key to her comic persona was that she was totally believable. Sure, her antics were far-fetched, but the basic personality was realistic. She could get dressed up and go out, and we would believe that Lucy Ricardo was a real person. Partly because of Ball's acting ability, but also because the things she wanted—to get over her money problems, to become well known, and to pull down the pants of some authority figure—were universal. She was goofy, she was nutty, she was zany and wild, involved in unbelievable situations—but she was a believable person involved in unbelievable situations. And that's why the show worked.

Desi Arnaz—a popular nightclub performer in this country when *Lucy* started broadcasting—has never been taken seriously as a performer. He's always been considered strictly a straight man to Ball's funny-lady; his reputation grew as a producer and director, as the man behind the genius of *Lucy*. As Ricky Ricardo, though, Arnaz brought a great deal to the role. He wasn't funny, per se, but he did have a certain charm—a certain cuteness—that worked well with Lucy. In fact, many people felt, when the two got divorced and Lucy went on her own, the reason those subsequent shows didn't work as well as *I Love Lucy* was because the chemistry between the two was missing. Alone, Desi Arnaz was not spectacular; with Lucille Ball, it was like playing tennis. Alone, you're still a good tennis player, but without the game, who cares?

Vivian Vance seemed to *be* Ethel Mertz. She wasn't—proof of what a good actress she was. Ethel was the prototypical "best friend," the gal-next-door, grown up and grown out. She was frumpy, but never dumpy. With her long "Ohhhhhs" and "Weeeellls" that she uttered whenever Lucy was about to boil the water they were about to get in, Vance was the perfect foil for Ball. Lucy brought adventure into Ethel's life, as she did to all of ours.

William Frawley—a former song-and-dance man and movie character actor—also seemed to *be* Fred Mertz. Frawley knew about a lot of things—among them barbershop quartets and drinking—and spent his *Lucy* years being antagonistic and bitter toward Vance, whom he didn't like. Several years after *Lucy* stopped filming, he had this to say about his "honey-bunch": "She's one of the finest gals to come out of Kansas, but I often wish she'd go back there. I don't know exactly where she is now and she doesn't know where I am and that's exactly the way I like it." On the set, though, he was known to be easygoing and foulmouthed. He was as acid and foultempered as Fred Mertz often was. Frawley was also a great gossip. About *Lucy* he said: "I just took the money and ran."

Over the years, several actors played the part of the Ricardo's Little Ricky. Twins Richard Lee and Ronald Lee Simmons were the first Little Rickies. (Because of California child labor laws, actors under six months old could pose only two hours each day, so they needed two.) Their stand-ins, for rehearsals, were a pair of dolls. The Simmonses were paid $25 per show and were accompanied on the set by a nurse and a Welfare Department social worker.

The second older Rickies were Michael and Joseph Mayer, who were quickly retired from show biz by their skeptical mother when they were four. The bigger Little

Albuquerque: Ethel gets upstaged in her home town

Ricky (there was only one of him by this time) was five-year-old Keith Thibodeaux, who had been billed as "The World's Tiniest Professional Drummer" when Desi caught his act and signed him to a seven-year contract starting at $300 a week. He looked like a mini-Desi. Thibodeaux's name was changed to Ricky Keith and he was immediately given Spanish lessons. Later, he was featured in a couple of "drumming" episodes.

Over the six seasons, several changes were made, none of which altered the basic format or changed the basic characters. When the show got started, it was the basic story of a man in show business and a wife wanting to get into the act. Then they did more husband-and-wife humor. Then they had a baby in 1953. Desi was sent to California in 1954–1955, and the entire cast came along, including Lucy's mother, Mrs. MacGillicuddy (Kathryn Card), who always called Ricky "Mickey." For the 1955–1956 season, the Ricardos and the Mertzes were to travel to Europe; that year and the following saw the addition of many guest stars including Tennessee Ernie Ford, John Wayne, Bob Hope, Charles Boyer, Tallulah Bankhead, Harpo Marx, Orson Welles, and others. In 1956–1957, the two couples (and Little Ricky) went to Florida, and then on to Cuba. At the end of that season, the Ricardos and the Mertzes left Manhattan for a house in Connecticut.

The show also worked, thanks to the writing of Bob

Carroll, Jr., Madelyn Pugh, Jess Oppenheimer and others. Says Lucille Ball: "We had wonderful writers. They wrote understandable comedy that you could follow even if you didn't know the language. They wrote structured plays, with a beginning, middle, and end. When they wrote a stunt for me to do, they went down on stage and did it. Walking on stilts or roller-skating or doing a flip on skis or anything.

"The believability of all our unbelievable situations is what made it funny. People could identify with my problems, my zaniness, my wanting to do everything, my scheming and plotting, the way I cajoled my husband. People identified with the Ricardos because we had the same problems they had. Paying the rent, getting a new dress, getting a stale fur collar on an old cloth coat, or buying a piece of furniture were all worth a story."

There was never a *Lucy* episode that was truly bad. Some were better than others, and some were great. Some were even classics, and sitcom classics seldom happen. Archie Bunker gets kissed by Sammy Davis, Jr., and—bam—you know that's going to be a classic. Chuckles the Clown dies. Instant classic. *I Love Lucy* garnered itself several classic episodes—acknowledged so by legions of fans:

☐ "Lucy's Italian Movie" (first aired April 16, 1956), in which Lucy, en route to Rome, is spotted by famous Italian film director Vittorio Fellipi for a role in his new movie, *Bitter Grapes*. Lucy goes out to "soak up some local color," as she puts it, and visits a winery where the supervisor, impressed with her feet (which one of the local women compares to "big pizzas"), puts her to work stomping grapes into chianti with one of the local women (in real life, a California grape-stomper). With her dress pulled up between her legs, diaper-style, Lucy starts stomping and then tires. Her co-worker becomes angry and they get into a grape-throwing fight that eventually turns into a wrestling match—right in the vat. Lucy, stained and drained, returns to the hotel to find out that the role she was to play was that of a typical American tourist. "Can't I be an American who's so homesick, she's blue?" No, she can't, and Ethel gets the part. ☐

☐ "Job Switching" (first aired on September 15, 1952), in which Lucy, after writing a rubber check (she writes on the back: "Dear Teller, be a lamb and don't put this through until next month") goes out with Ethel to get jobs as candymakers at Kramer's Candy Kitchen. First, Lucy gets into a fight with a co-worker; Lucy and Ethel are then transferred to the "wrapping" department, where they have to wrap each piece of candy as it goes by on a conveyor belt. The machine moves too quickly and, in order to keep up with it, they end up stuffing the excess candies into their blouses, mouths, hats. ☐

☐ "Lucy Goes to the Hospital" (first aired on January 19, 1953), in which Lucy does just what the title suggests—but not without confusion. "Ricky keeps staring at me like I'm going to explode," Lucy tells the Mertzes. So they "rehearse" what's going to happen when Lucy's ready. Naturally, when the time comes, they get it all mixed up. In the hospital waiting room, Ricky realizes it's nearly time to go to the club to do his act, and, getting ready for his "voodoo number," applies full witch doctor makeup and costume. He leaves for the club and then races back for his first look at Ricky Ricardo, Jr. ☐

There were other favorites: when Lucy does a TV commercial, she gets drunk on the product—Vitameatavegamin—because it contains 23 percent alcohol and she can't deliver the commercial properly; Harpo Marx and Lucy (dressed as the silent clown) think they're one another in a mirror; Lucy dresses as Superman for Little Ricky's birthday party—and then the real Superman flies over; Ethel goes home with the Ricardos and everyone thinks *she's* the star, not Ricky; Lucy gets a loving cup stuck on her head and gets lost in the subway; in Connecticut, the Mertzes and Ricardos become chicken farmers, but the baby chicks get loose in the house. In fact, practically any episode of *I Love Lucy* could be considered a classic.

Overworked, overwrought, overtired, Lucille Ball and Desi Arnaz decided that their 1956–1957 sitcom season would be their last. Not, however, before selling all the *Lucy* episodes to CBS Films for $5 million. (On May 6, 1957, "The Ricardos Dedicate a Statue," the last *Lucy* episode, was aired.) Then they decided to institute *The Lucille Ball-Desi Arnaz Show*. (By this time, Ball didn't mind her name going before Arnaz's; in fact, she probably wouldn't have minded his name being omitted totally. Their marriage was at its rockiest. Said Ball some years later: "Desi drank and I knew he went out with other women, but I didn't worry about it soon enough. The last five years were the same old booze and broads, the only change being that he was rarely at home anymore. And that was a blessing. . . .") The regular cast starred in the comedy hour (which once ran sixty-five minutes because Desi liked the script).

The Arnazes—and therefore the Ricardos—broke up when Lucy won a no-fault divorce in 1960. "It wasn't the industry and our working together that broke us up," she said. "The pressure had a lot to do with it. He was a very sick man. And I was living with hope for many years."

She immediately left for New York to star in a musical called *Wildcat!*, which was commercially very successful. There she met comedian Gary Morton, whom she later married. He urged her to go back into television. She did: first, with *The Lucy Show* (1962–1968), which featured Vance and Gale Gordon (she finally got him). From 1968 to 1974, the show was retitled *Here's Lucy*, and featured Gordon and Lucy's real-life children—Desi, Jr., and Lucie. Vance made only guest appearances, and Desi, Jr., left the show after three seasons. All *Lucy* shows aired at 9 P.M. (e.s.t.) Monday nights on CBS, giving the network dominance of the night virtually every season Ball was on TV.

Arnaz continued running the massive Desilu studios. In 1962, he asked Lucy to buy him out, and she did,

Going West: Packing the convertible with Mother MacGillicuddy

giving him $2,552,975 for his 300,350 shares of Desilu stock. He retired to his horse-breeding ranch. He remarried (a redhead) and returned to TV as an independent producer (he produced *The Mothers-in-Law* in 1967). He made occasional guest appearances, such as a 1976–1977 episode of *Saturday Night Live*, which included playing a marvelous send-up of *I Love Lucy*, with Gilda Radner playing Lucy.

Vivian Vance tried her hand at a TV pilot that didn't sell. Instead, she moved to Connecticut (just as she had done on *Lucy*) with her husband and started gardening and becoming active in civic projects. In 1976, she appeared on *Rhoda* as the upstairs neighbor, but it never became a regular part. She appeared in commercials and, occasionally, on a Lucille Ball TV special. She died of cancer in 1979.

In 1960, Frawley appeared as a regular on *My Three Sons* in the role of Bub, a part not unlike Fred Mertz in temperament. He said that he loved getting the *Lucy* residual checks. He continued in the role for five years and retired due to poor health. He died of a sudden heart attack on March 3, 1966; his last TV role had been a guest appearance on *The Lucy Show*. When he died, pallbearer Desi Arnaz took out a full-page ad in the Hollywood *Reporter*; underneath Fred/Frawley's picture it said "¡Buenas Noches, Amigo!"

Today, you can see *I Love Lucy* on TV, at all times and all hours, sliced up and diced up by commercials for devices that slice up and dice up vegetables. Still, they always seem to get Number One ratings in their time periods, and three generations of people are now watching them.

Lucille Ball has an analysis that's probably as good as any: "We just took ordinary situations and exaggerated them. I don't think people would buy it now. Too tame. If we were starting out now, how could we compete with all the sex and explicit language now on the air? Still, I could be wrong."

Could be. Several years ago, Ball—after trying her hand at a number of Lucy-unrelated projects (including a disastrous movie musical version of *Mame*)—said she saw the handwriting on the wall. At sixty-five, she said, she thought she was too old to play Lucy, and had been "trying a lot of other things lately, trying to play my age, trying to do something they would believe and buy. Well, they didn't buy it. What the people seem to want is Lucy. So I'm doing Lucy." And so she made several TV specials playing Lucy.

It didn't matter, though. Because *Lucy* is still with us. Maybe because she represents a respite in these feminist times. Maybe because she gives us a dose of fantasy in our days of reality. Maybe because it's a deep-rooted psychological thing, our suppressed notions of the child fighting back against the father-figure of society. Or maybe—and you know this is the one—maybe just because *I Love Lucy* was—and is—so very, very funny.

I Love Lucy Leftovers

• Desi Arnaz's fractured English—"Frat Mers" for Fred Mertz, "wunt" for won't and "ever thin" for everything— was not written into the scripts. It just happened naturally. One wag put a sign on Arnaz's dressing room door: "English Broken Here." "¡Miraquetienecosalamujeresta!" he used to babble on-screen to Lucy.

• Lucille Ball's mother, De-De, never missed a filming. Once, when Ball flubbed a line nine times in a row, she broke the tension by shouting into the audience, "Don't worry, Mom, I'll get it!"

• There were numerous similarities between Lucy and Ricky and Lucy and Desi, besides the obvious ones. Both Lucies went to high school in Celeron, New York. Both couples were married at the Byram River Beagle Club in Greenwich, Connecticut, in 1949. Both couples repeated their wedding vows. Marion Strong, an occasional character on the show, was one of Lucy's (and Lucy's) best friends.

• In her contract it was stipulated that Vivian Vance must wear frowsy housedresses and must remain twenty pounds overweight in order to appear frumpier than Ball (who's one year older than Vance).

• Although 179 episodes were made of *I Love Lucy*, only 178 are ever aired. One has not been aired since December 24, 1956, when it was originally broadcast. According to those who saw it (and made it), it wasn't very funny. *TV Guide*'s capsule description said: "It was Christmas and Fred Mertz grudgingly buys a tree for Lucy Ricardo, then Lucy decides to improve on its looks by cutting off branches here and there."

MY LITTLE MARGIE

MAN: *How do you and your father get along?*
MARGIE: *Oh, fine—although there were those eighteen months I didn't speak to him.*
MAN: *When were those?*
MARGIE: *From the time I was born till the time I could talk.*

Like *can't-stop-eating-'em* potato chips and Hostess cupcakes, *My Little Margie* was the junk food of a generation. The critics of the day thought the show was the worst, the ultimate in television trash. The New York *Herald Tribune*—which went the way of *Margie* and was itself eventually canceled—had this to say: "*My Little Margie* may not be the worst television show in all creation, but it is trying hard."

Trouble with *My Little Margie* (which the *Herald Tribune* critic obviously didn't understand) is that it wasn't television. It was TV. *Playhouse 90* and anything with Alistair Cooke in it were all television. Even shows like *Bonanza* and *Our Miss Brooks* were, on occasion, television. *The Flintstones, Mr. Ed, The Munsters,* and *My Little Margie* were all TV. Maybe even Tee Vee. It was the difference between taking yourself seriously and deliriously.

The point was: Margie was perky and cute and friendly and schemed up wild shenanigans. What more could you ask for?

She was a grown-up Eloise, playing games and creating harmless havoc in an apartment building in New York—the Carlton Arms on East 57th St., Apartment 10-A—with a complete cast of characters: her widower father, Vern Albright; eighty-three-year-old Mrs. Odettes; Charlie, the elevator operator; and others: Vern's boss, George Honeywell (of Honeywell and Todd); Margie's impoverished boyfriend, Freddy; and Roberta, her dad's lady friend.

Margie and her pop would have this voice-over exchange at the start of every episode:

VERN: I've been both mother and father to her since she was born. She's grown up now. . . . When she was a little girl, I could spank her and make her mind me. I had control over her. . . . When she disobeyed, I took her roller skates away for a week. What can you do when a girl reaches this age? She's completely out of hand. I've got a problem, believe me, I've got a problem.

MARGIE: I've raised him from . . . my childhood. He's nearly fifty now and you'd think he'd settle down, wouldn't you. Today, he looks better in shorts on a tennis court than fellows twenty-five. Girls wink at him and—what's worse—he winks back at them. I want a nice old comfortable father. I try to look after him, but he just won't settle down. I've got a problem, believe me, I've got a problem.

Margie spent a lot of time intervening in Vern's romantic life; Vern spent a lot of time intervening in all other areas of Margie's life. What was so socially significant back then about the program—something that really got us thinking—is how when she was in a jam, Margie would turn directly to the camera and trill, "G-g-g-r-r-r-r . . ." It always sounded like she had a mouthful of saliva.

How could the critics not love this show? It was the kind of program that had episodes like this: Margie tries to give her dad a portrait of him on his birthday to replace the one accidentally shot to pieces by a neighbor. This episode also included a phony love affair, two fistfights, and general confusion.

That confusion—general and otherwise—was the

Margie Albright	Gale Storm
Vern Albright	Charles Farrell
Freddy Wilson, Margie's impoverished boyfriend	Don Hayden
George Honeywell, Vern's employer	Clarence Kolb
Roberta Townsend, Vern's romantic interest	Hillary Brooke
Mrs. Odettes, the Albrights' eighty-three-year-old neighbor	Gertrude Hoffman
Charlie, the elevator operator	Willie Best

rule, not the exception, in *My Little Margie*. Margie's antics caused great pains to Vern. Weekly, Vern's boss, the pompous Mr. Honeywell, would get in a snit and puff: "Albright, this is the last straw. You're *fired!*"

Margie was a dime store Lucy Ricardo, and nearly as loony. She hatched her schemes in her mind, sometimes with the aid of dear Mrs. Odettes (Gertrude Hoffman), who lived down the hall.

MRS. ODETTES: Yoo-hoo! Margie!
MARGIE: Come on in, Mrs. Odettes.
MRS. ODETTES: *(entering):* Hi, honey.
MARGIE: Hi, Mrs. Odettes.
MRS. ODETTES: I thought I'd just drop over and see what you were doing that your father says you shouldn't.
MARGIE: Mrs. Odettes, I told you I'm not disobeying my father anymore.
MRS. ODETTES: You're not really serious? If you're going to be obedient, what are we going to do for *kicks* around here?

She need not have worried. Margie quickly changed her mind and we—the viewer—looked at Margie with the same fascinated amusement that Mrs. Odettes did. That was the thing about Margie—and Lucy and Gracie and all the other TV zanies: they were exciting. Now maybe the New York *Herald Tribune* critic's life was exciting. Maybe he got to go to a lot of fancy cocktail parties with some fancy network executives. But our lives were not exciting; our lives were routine: toilet training, puberty, pimples, prom, college, and then the Predictable Adult Crises. Our lives didn't have any Antics. But there was Margie—a nice kid from a nice family who knew how to have fun and how to rattle her cage. Sure, she caused lots of confusion—but it was all wrapped up snappily and happily by the conclusion of each episode. Each show finished with Margie's and her dad's photographs appearing in a frame. Then, like magic, their pictures would come to life and Margie would explain her reasons for her bizarre behavior. Vern would conclude with a smile and sigh, "Well, that's my little Margie." Pretty exciting stuff for us kids.

The show premiered on June 16, 1952, as a last-minute summer replacement for *I Love Lucy*. Gale Storm—a princess of B movies—was approached by Philip Morris to star in the show. No pilot film was ever made, and the program was slapped together in two weeks. The critics blanched and deemed that the show was a supreme insult to the audience's intelligence. Yeah—the audience's intelligence was so insulted that, for 128 episodes, they couldn't get enough of *My Little Margie*. So offended were they that they helped pop the show up to third place in the national ratings. In fact, in a switch from the normal pattern, *Margie* was made into a radio show after it had debuted on TV; it reached the Top Ten on radio, bypassing such standards as *Fibber McGee*

and Molly, Jack Benny, and *Bob Hope;* the radio program lasted two seasons.

On TV, Margie's father was played by former silent film star Charles Farrell. He had been half of the talkies' first and most popular "screen lovers" in the late 1920s and early 1930s with Janet Gaynor. His popularity slipped in the mid-1930s, and he took lesser roles. By 1941, he worked in B movies and then on Broadway. Later he would become mayor of Palm Springs, a tennis club manager and the star of his own sitcom.

As Vern, he played an aging wolf who, as one critic put it, "made eyes at women in order to land an account" for his advertising firm. His boss, the apoplectic George Honeywell (Clarence Kolb), spent a lot of time leering at all the girls. Freddy (Don Hayden), Margie's penniless boyfriend, just couldn't seem to hang on to a job. Vern's girlfriend—the high-class Roberta Townsend, who spoke like a Britisher—was played by Hillary Brooke . . . who was born in Astoria, Queens.

The gal (and she was a *gal*—not a girl or woman or lady) who held it all together was Gale Storm. Besides her gurgly tongue, she possessed a pair of cute and crinkly eyes. She was thirty-one when the show debuted (Margie was supposed to be twenty-one) and her real name had been Josephine Owaissa Cottle. Born in Bloomington, Texas, she won the name Gale Storm in Jesse Lasky's "Gateway to Hollywood" talent search. She also won an RKO contract, but was dropped after six months. Then she moved to Monogram and Universal studios, where she made little impact. Although she made such B pictures as *Where Are the Children* (1943) with Patricia Morrison, and *The Kid from Texas* (1950) with Audie Murphy, she was best known in westerns as Roy Rogers' leading lady.

Several months after *My Little Margie* premiered, Philip Morris dropped the program on CBS. Little Johnny, attired in a bellhop's uniform, had opened the show with his famous "Call . . . for . . . Philip . . . Morraaaaiiisss!" No more. Now Scott Paper (complete with Manners the Butler and his famous falling napkins that didn't *cling*) would open the show on NBC after the sponsor's *Music Hall* fizzled. Between the two seasons, Gale Storm sang in nightclubs. In 1955, in fact, she had two hits on Dot Records—"Teen-Age Prayer" (on the Hit Parade for fifteen straight weeks) and "I Hear You Knocking" (which soared up to the Number Two position). By the time she had finished her singing career, Storm had sold more than 4,000,000 records—which doesn't exactly make her a Linda Ronstadt, but back in the fifties, 4,000,000 was quite respectable.

In the late seventies, Gale Storm publicly acknowledged that she had been an alcoholic for years—and even took to TV again to promote an alcoholic rehabilitation center in the Northwest.

When *Margie* fizzled out—in 1955 after three years—Gale Storm went on to star in another Margiesque sitcom, *Oh! Susanna* (also called *The Gale Storm Show*), in which she played the singing social director on the SS *Ocean Queen*, who could make a loud whistle by placing two fingers in her mouth (no more "G-g-g-r-r-r-r-r"). She could do other things as well—such as create trouble for Captain Huxley (Roy Roberts) with her man-hungry friend, beauty salon operator Miss "Nugey" Nugent (ZaSu Pitts). "We're trying to make the jokes more motivated," Storm said about the program, "and we're trying to make Susanna more intelligent." Those two ingredients—motivation and intelligence—apparently were the kiss of death, and the show just didn't work. And—for a long time—neither did Gale Storm.

Margie isn't rerun much. And it's probably a good thing. After a diet of Laura Petrie, Mary Richards, and Edith Bunker—even *That Girl's* Ann Marie—Margie's mindless madness probably wouldn't seem too thrilling anymore. Maybe it's because our lives—like that of the newspaper critic's—have become more exciting (after all, we lived through the sixties). We created our own Antics. Or perhaps it's because we got older and more discerning and can now tell the difference between the good and the grotesque.

One dissenting note from a September 1953 edition of *Variety:* "*My Little Margie* is quality programming."

Quality programming? No way. But it sure was fun. *G-g-g-r-r-r-r.*

MR. PEEPERS

I keep a gumball on me for recess period. It helps pass the time away.

—ROBINSON PEEPERS

It wasn't Mr. Wizard who first brought science to the small screen, it was another mister—Mr. Peepers—who also brought laughter and lightness as he tiptoed into the TV every week from 1952 until 1955. The series was created around the talents of then young comedian Wally Cox—unfortunately better known to younger TV audiences as a Hollywood Square and underwearer of Jockey Shorts ("Outside I might look like Wally Cox, but inside, I feel like Tyrone Power"). As a science teacher at Jefferson High, a typical American school, Mr. Peepers was soft-spoken and shy, frail and diffident. He was the little fellow—a fifties hybrid of a whitebread Woody Allen and well-bred Bob Newhart. He was a wimp, a nebbish. *Mr. Peepers* didn't contain any jokes, and the show was built around the gentle humor that radiated from Cox's gentle characterization. Robinson Peepers wasn't a man—he was a chap. He was Walter Mitty—without the Secret Life.

Mr. Peepers had his problems—a student who didn't share his love of biology; a jammed locker door; a beautiful female teacher who preferred a young man with a snappy car. Somehow he lived through it all. Once a pushy used car dealer tried to sell him a wreck. "I have a deal for you—she's ready to roll," the man told Mr. Peepers, who believed him. But everything worked out anyway. "When I see something I like," Peepers said in an ironic tone, "I snap it right up." Peepers was the type who would say, "Now, class, who can give me some examples of how ornithology is helpful in the real estate business?"

Every morning—on weekdays only—Mr. Peepers had breakfast at the counter of the local drugstore. In one of the early episodes, he sat down at the counter, started studying the menu, and then suddenly looked up and discovered us, the viewers, watching him. And so he introduced himself.

"I'm Robinson Peepers. I teach general science at the little junior high school across the street. Being a single bachelor-type, I commonly eat breakfast here in the drugstore. I have the same thing every morning: prune juice and two scrambled eggs. Sometimes on paydays I get a little wild and get a side order of sausages. They have specials here for those of us who like to watch our pennies. Here, for example, is the businessman's luncheon—appetizer, main course, coffee and dessert for only forty cents. Sometimes I have that at noon—they don't know I'm not a businessman. Course I don't have that every noon; there's no sense running a good thing in the ground . . ." And then he lifted his fork and started eating.

Wally Cox and Robinson Peepers got mixed up a lot. Cox once said, "There isn't the slightest doubt in my mind that Robinson J. Peepers and I look alike. But it seems a little unfair that he must assume responsibility for my actions." Throughout his career, Cox—who looked like a Charles Atlas ad—the *before* photo—was forever typecast as the Mr. Peepers character—something that crippled his career. Said Cox: "Mr. Peepers put me on the map and I love him." But it was definitely a love/hate relationship. Cox never worked much after the show—

Robinson J. Peepers	Wally Cox
Harvey Weskitt, his friend, the English teacher	Tony Randall
Nancy Remington, the school nurse, Robinson's girlfriend	Patricia Benoit
Marge Weskitt, Harvey's wife	Georgianna Johnson
Mrs. Gurney, a friend	Marion Lorne
Mr. Remington, Nancy's father	Ernest Truex
Mrs. Remington, Nancy's mother	Sylvia Field (1953–1955)
Mr. Bascom, the principal	George Clark; also David Tyrell
Frank Whip	Jack Warden (1953–1955)
Mom Peepers	Ruth McDevitt (1953–1955)
Agnes Peepers	Jenny Egan (1953–1955)

"But I didn't suffer and tear my hair if I didn't work"— and he spent much of his time (as Peepers might have) bird-watching.

But that—and so much more—was to come later. In its prime, *Mr. Peepers* was *the* show to watch. But it almost never happened. NBC couldn't figure out quite what to do with this strange bird of a comedian. They had seen him perform, and quickly starred him in David Swift's *The Copper*—about a mousy little policeman—for *Philco TV Playhouse*. It was such a success that the network wanted it to be made into a series, but it didn't work out. They decided, instead, on the story of a science teacher in a small town. *Mr. Peepers*, they'd call it.

In pre-programming preparation, Cox didn't like the scripts. Although the character was basically the same as the one that would evolve, the first Mr. Peepers was involved in slapstick routines and sight gags—with Peepers being tossed around in the school's ventilating chutes, or getting his head stuck in a basketball hoop. Cox—as Peepers would not have—complained; none of that broad humor, he begged, but slight exaggerations of real-life problems. That's just what the show became. In one episode, for example, Peepers was unwrapping a new shirt and took dozens and dozens of pins out of it. That was funny when Cox did it. In another show, he was trying to impress his girlfriend, but unwittingly unraveled a partially completed hooked rug dear to her mother's heart. Cox's humor wasn't broad, and so Peepers became diminutive and introspective, vague, and wistful. Cox didn't need the big stuff; he was funny cocking an eyebrow, shrugging a shoulder, pulling his upper lip down over his lower lip and looking bewildered and toothless. As Steve Allen once said: "He is the mouse in us all; we want to protect him and feel tender toward him." He could have been talking about both Mr. Peepers and Mr. Cox.

In a pilot script written early in 1952, Robinson Peepers arrives early for his new teaching post—about six months early, in fact—because he has forgotten to read the starting date on his letter of acceptance. So they put him to work co-teaching (i.e., sharpening pencils and washing test tubes) for a nasty science teacher who is threatened by Peepers and who tries to get him fired. In the climactic slapstick scene, Peepers accidentally gets his sleeve caught on the teacher's toupee in the school cafeteria, thinks it's a funny-looking salad, and puts catsup on it. The teacher is mortified (he always bragged about his hair) and leaves his job—which Peepers gets. This episode was never aired and all the characters were changed, but it shows some of Peepers' basic characteristics.

The people were replaced by a staple of regulars who delighted television audiences for three years. Best known today (for his work on *The Odd Couple*) is Tony Randall, who played Harvey Weskitt (called Wes), Peepers' brash, aggressive friend, a show-off, know-it-all teacher. Marion Lorne played Mrs. Gurney, a trembly,

Live from New York: Cox and Benoit

befuddled middle-aged English teacher who was well known for her long and funny double takes. (She was later to portray Aunt Clara, an old bumbling witch, on *Bewitched*.) Jack Warden played the Jefferson High athletic coach.

Pat Benoit played the high school nurse, Nancy Remington, the show's lovely ingenue with the liquid voice. She eventually became *Mrs.* Peepers on May 23, 1954. Others in the cast included Ernest Truex (Mr. Remington, Nancy's father), Sylvia Field (her mother), Reta Shaw, George Clark (Mr. Bascom, the principal) and several others.

In one episode—before nurse Nancy became Mrs. Peepers—she invites Robinson over to meet her parents. She explains to him that an old boyfriend of hers will also be there. Mr. Peepers is flustered but of course tries to be helpful.

MR. PEEPERS:　I don't want to get in the way. You want me to bring some ice cream?
NANCY:　No, just bring your own charming self.

Weskitt discovers that Peepers is nervous and suggests that he learn to tell jokes and perform card tricks so that Mr. and Mrs. Remington like him.

MR. PEEPERS:　That's not like me. I don't do jokes and card tricks. That's not my personality. I'm just going to stand on my own two personalized feet. If they don't like me . . . well, they just won't like me.

Wedding Daze: Ernest Truex, Marion Lorne, Pat Benoit

He almost backs out when he remembers that the Other Man will be there.

MR. PEEPERS: To tell the truth, I never do very well at those social gatherings where there are other men present. It always turns into a competition to see who can say the brightest thing. Well, in a word, I just don't have *dash*. I'm not peppy. I don't think I'll go tonight.

He goes. He's greeted at the door by Nancy and sees her for the first time not dressed in her nurse's uniform. "You look wonderful in your civvies," he says to her. And when asked what he does, he says, "I'm in the teaching game." He tells them all about his older sister in Satuba, Ohio, whose husband owns a restaurant/gas station—while the other man tells jokes and performs card tricks. But of course the parents like Peepers better and ask him to stay way past the other man. Finally, Robinson says, "I have to go—it's past my bedtime."

The program was shot live in New York in NBC's large Center Theater before an audience of 2,500 people. The Ford Motor Company agreed to sponsor the show for an eight-week summer run. Critics loved the show and heralded Cox as a new comic star. Even before the eight episodes had been aired, NBC ordered another five. The show was a success—NBC had Wally Cox postcards printed, which it gave out to tourists.

But the pressures of doing the weekly live show were too demanding and NBC decided not to renew the program. On the last airing, NBC had nearly 2,000 phone calls complaining about *Peepers* going off the air, and more than 15,000 letters of protest. But it was too late because the fall schedule had already been locked up.

Then something happened: *Doc Corkle* (starring Eddie Mayehoff) bombed after two weeks and opened up a prime-time slot. So they threw *Peepers* on again. Since one of the writers had quit after the summer, they found a new one (Everett Greenbaum, a writer who had been working at Macy's, selling toy frogs). After a close call, Cox was once again a star.

Cox's stardom came as quite a surprise to everyone—especially himself. With his glasses, hesitant smile, and soft voice, Cox had started out as a stand-up comedian—in the living room of his cold-water flat doing routines for friends who thought he was funny. His roommate back then was a struggling Marlon Brando. "I started going around with Brando to meet girls," Cox later said, but they had been best friends since childhood. By day, Cox taught the Lindy Hop at a dancing school for $1.50 a lesson. He had come to New York from Omena, Michigan; his mother and grandmother were writers and his father was in the advertising business. "I used to consider myself insignificant and anonymous-looking," Cox had said. In 1946—after an industrial arts course—he started making cufflinks and tie clasps to sell in Manhattan shops, earning about $40 a week. Living in the Village with Brando, Cox was coaxed to recite his little narratives based on real-life characters he'd known. Word got around that this guy was good, and he got bookings at the Village Vanguard and the Blue Angel,

Odd Couple: Tony Randall's head peeks out on right

where he was an instant hit, doing offbeat routines such as a monologue about his school pal Dufo, who played around during recess doing tricks. It was at one of these engagements that NBC discovered him.

Because the show was live, you'll probably never see it again. Back in the fifties, in order for *Mr. Peepers* to play on the West Coast as well as the East Coast, where it was shot, kinescopes (actual films made of a TV screen while the show was aired) had to be shipped out. The scenery on the show was flimsy, the lighting was crude, and the actors had to run from set to set, changing their clothes behind the scenery in a mad dash to make it to the next scene. Plus, the writers had to make sure that the show ran exactly on time when an audience and its laughs were added. So cuts always had to be made. Cox couldn't handle cuts because, Tony Randall has said, he

didn't know his lines that well anyway. Marion Lorne— "dear old Marion Lorne," Randall called her—couldn't be given cuts because they'd ruin her timing. And so, Randall said, it was always *his* lines and business that were dropped.

Said writer Greenbaum: "We once went eight months without a day off. Saturdays, Sundays, anything. In those days, nobody ever thought that you might have several teams writing one situation comedy series. They might have been doing that out in Hollywood, but in New York they hadn't heard about anything so efficient."

All along, Mr. Peepers had become more and more involved with Miss Remington, the school nurse. NBC wondered if perhaps they should marry the two of them off. After a lot of talk, they decided to do it. Urged on by his pal Weskitt, Peepers mustered up the courage to ask her. When the wedding finally took place on the air, it was a big event—even Milton Berle told everybody at a party he was at to be quiet so he could watch the nuptials. Greenbaum feels the wedding idea was a bad one—"changed the whole emphasis of the show. Turned it into a husband and wife series, the same as dozens of other shows."

Many thought that was what killed the show—which finally ended its run the next year in 1955. Others say that the pace of doing a live show just exhausted everybody. Of course, its low ratings opposite *The Jack Benny Program* didn't help matters much.

And so *Mr. Peepers* was dead. But Mr. Peepers lived on. Wally Cox was continually being offered Peeperesque parts—and the die was cast for the rest of his life. After the show, Cox went back to nightclub work, but in Las Vegas he was heckled off the stage and finally bowed out of the engagement after a few days. In 1956, he went back on the air with another sitcom—*The Adventures of Hiram Holiday*—the saga of a meek and mild-mannered proofreader who goes around the world and has many adventures foiling unscrupulous characters. The show lasted four months.

Besides that program, Cox guested on many sitcoms —*Ozzie and Harriet; Car 54, Where Are You?; Dick Van Dyke; Mister Roberts; Beverly Hillbillies; Jean Arthur Show* and *Here's Lucy.* In 1958, NBC gave him an unusual seven-year, $50,000-a-year contract and a figurehead position working on special projects. Cox felt bad about taking the money—but he took it anyway and spent most of his time watching birds and reading *Scientific American.* He also wrote several books and a play—*Moonbirds*—which opened (and closed) in 1959 after three performances.

On February 15, 1973, Wally Cox died of a heart attack. He was forty-eight. His friend Brando flew from Tahiti to Los Angeles to handle the cremation. It was ironic that Cox had died in Los Angeles—even more ironic that he had lived there. He had loved New York and when NBC asked him to move the *Peepers* show to LA—in an attempt to save its life—Cox said no. He wouldn't leave his beloved New York. Finally he did—to appear on *Hollywood Squares* and to do underwear commercials.

Mr. Peepers lives on—not, unfortunately, on tape or film as other sitcoms do—but in the minds and hearts of those who remember it. It was one of the last live shows—and this show was *alive*—that, like so many experiences we have, will just have to be rewound and played back in our heads.

ALSO RANS

Boss Lady

This series was something of a rarity among 1950s television programs—one which starred a woman in a very nontraditional role. Lynn Bari—the undisputed "Queen of the Bs" at Twentieth Century-Fox a decade earlier (nearly always playing The Other Woman)— finally strode into the small-screen spotlight as Gwen F. Allen, owner and operator of the Hillendale Homes Construction Company. Until 1954, Gwen leaped the hurdles her male-dominated field placed in her way each week, first on the DuMont network and then on NBC.

A Date with Judy

Based on the popular radio program of the same name, this show featured teenaged and bobbysoxed Judy Foster (played first by Patricia Crowley, then by Mary Lynn Beller) of Santa Barbara, California. Her general unpredictability and relations with her family and her boyfriend, Oogie Pringle (Jimmy Sommers), were the basis for Judy's half-hours, which ABC featured through 1953. It was first seen as a Saturday daytime series starting in June. In the fall, it moved to prime time.

The Egg and I

This 1951 sitcom—one of the few that ran for only fifteen minutes each day—was a comedy serial about two chicken farmers, Betty and Bob MacDonald (Patricia Kirkland and Frank Craven). Their chicken farm was somewhat run-down, and so was the program, which laid an egg and crossed the road to oblivion in 1952. Based on the popular autobiographical novel by Betty MacDonald, and the movie (which, incidentally, introduced Ma and Pa Kettle).

It's a Business?

Dorothy Loudon, Leo DeLyon and Bob Haymes starred (but for only two months) in this Victorian sitcom, all about music publishers who spent their time (and ours) demonstrating their songs (ditties like "After the Ball Is Over"). Sometimes there were guest stars (visiting vaudevillians), who joined the partners (the men, naturally) and their secretary (the woman, naturally).

Those Two

One of the two was Pinky Lee, in his second sitcom attempt (his first was the short-lived 1949 *Pinky Lee Show*). The other of the two was Vivian Blaine (later replaced by Martha Stewart at the beginning of the second season on NBC), who played a nightclub singer Pinky had the hots for. She loved another man, but that didn't stop them from singing together. But only until April 24, 1953, when Pinky started to think about going on to other things.

Two Girls Named Smith

This ABC midseason entry was about two small-town aspiring models—sisters Babs and Peggy Smith—who moved to New York to pursue fame and fortune. Peggy Ann Garner (and later Marcia Henderson) played Babs; Peggy French played Peggy. Each had a boyfriend and a shared landlady.

Young Mr. Bobbin

Jackie Kelk played eighteen-year-old Alexander Bobbin, a determined (and of course trouble-prone) young businessman. Pat Holsey played his girlfriend, Nancy, who happened to live next door. Alexander lived in an old house with his two maiden aunts: the reliable and organized Aunt Clara (played by Jane Seymour) and the flaky Aunt Bertha (played by Nydia Westman). Nancy's tomboy sister Susie (Laura Weber) was Alex's buddy, although she teased him a lot. The show ran live on NBC from August 26, 1951, until May 18, 1952.

1952–1953

The Adventures of Ozzie and Harriet

The Life of Riley

Our Miss Brooks

OFF-SCREEN

9/23   Rocky Marciano knocks out Jersey Joe Walcott in Philadelphia to win heavyweight championship.

10/7   Yankees win fourth straight Series; beat Brooklyn Dodgers in seventh game.

11/4   General Eisenhower and Senator Nixon win thirty-nine states and 442 electoral votes to win presidential election; Republicans also win control of both houses of Congress by narrow margin.

12/30   Tuskegee Institute reports that 1952 was the first year without a lynching since 1882, when records were first kept.

1/14   Marshal Tito elected first President of Yugoslavia under new constitution.

2/21   Truman announces sale of memoirs to *Life* magazine.

3/5   Joseph Stalin, Soviet dictator for twenty-nine years, dies in Moscow.

4/25   Senator Wayne Morse breaks all Senatorial records by speech lasting twenty-two hours, twenty-six minutes, in opposition to bill on offshore lands.

5/29   Mount Everest scaled for first time by Edmund P. Hillary and Tensing Norkay, members of British expedition headed by Colonel John Hunt.

6/19   Rosenbergs executed at Sing Sing.

FRONT RUNNERS

THE ADVENTURES OF OZZIE AND HARRIET

Well, uh, gosh, what do you think, Harriet?
—OZZIE NELSON

Back in the fifties, we grew up with the Nelsons. And they grew up with us. And yet, somehow managed to stay the same. David was pleasant and Harriet was nice and Ozzie didn't work (at least he never seemed to go anywhere or do anything except hang around the house in his alpaca cardigan; he must have married rich)—but Ricky was *the one*. There was something about him: a glimmer to his eyes, an impishness, all giving us a sneak preview of what the next strange decade would be. He had a subdued rebelliousness that even the restraints of TV sitcomdom couldn't hold back. We all could have guessed that Beaver Cleaver would end up selling insurance, that Betty and Kathy Anderson would end up divorced and unhappy, that His Three Sons would end up traditionally married and traditionally boring—but not Ricky. Even though he was trapped in the middle of a stagnant format (his parents' program), he somehow rose above it all. Ricky was a survivor.

Anyway, there didn't seem to be any other reason to watch *The Adventures of Ozzie and Harriet*, as it was called during its fourteen-year run. Fourteen years! That's longer than most real families run. But maybe that's because the Nelsons' adventures weren't very adventurous. Or very real.

It all began on Friday, October 10, 1952, when ABC launched the series, describing it as "the pleasures and trials of raising a couple of boys." The New York *Times* called it "fine family fun." And if there was any built-in significance to the show, it was that it was supposed to be a realistic portrayal of a family, not a caricature. Ozzie was less bumbling than he was fumbling. Harriet was Capable. And the boys were Basically Good Kids. If TV sitcoms at that time were cheesy, *Ozzie and Harriet* was definitely Velveeta. Processed and refined. With lots of chemicals added.

But it all actually began somewhat earlier—Sunday, October 8, 1944—when a golden-throated radio voice announced:

"From Hollywood—International Silver Company presents *The Adventures of Ozzie and Harriet*! Starring young America's favorite couple—Ozzie Nelson and Harriet Hilliard!"

The show, which became a hot item on radio for many years, was different from the TV show. On radio, Ozzie had a job (he was a bandleader and Harriet was a vocalist, as they had been in Real Life before they became Ozzie and Harriet). Plus, the radio show had more jokes—one of the best-remembered was Ozzie's

Ozzie Nelson	Himself
Harriet Nelson	Herself
David Nelson	Himself
Ricky Nelson	Himself
June Nelson (David's wife)	Herself (1961–1966)
Kris Nelson (Ricky's wife)	Herself (1964–1966)
Mr. Thornberry, the Nelsons' neighbor	Don DeFore (1952–1958)
Joe Randolph, Ozzie's friend	Lyle Talbot
Clara Randolph, his wife	Mary Jane Croft
Darby, a friend	Parley Baer (1955–1961)
Doc Williams, a friend	Frank Cady
Wally, David and Ricky's friend	Skip Young (1957–1966)
Ginger, Wally's girlfriend	Charlene Salern
Melinda, a friend	Diane Sayer
Sally, Kris' friend	Kathy Davies
Miss Edwards, David and Ricky's secretary (in law firm)	Connie Harper
Dean Hopkins	Ivan Bonar
Also:	Barry Livingston, Kent Smith, James Stacy

comment that his "mother-in-law was bowlegged because she hitchhiked out here from the East on oil trucks." The TV show would never have had a line like that; the humor on the TV *Ozzie and Harriet* grew out of the situations. It was gently domesticated, and overtly housebroken. The radio show had Characters (including Bea Benaderet, who played whining, adenoidal Gloria, the maid, as well as the domineering Mrs. Waddington). But these characters were eventually eliminated on television because Ozzie thought they were too exaggerated to match him and Harriet. They decided to hire an actor—Joel Davis, age thirteen—to play David, age eight. But in 1949, Ozzie acquiesced under the pressure of his kids to let them play themselves on the radio show.

The radio Nelsons flourished. David—and especially Ricky—were immediate hits. Ricky (who was eight years old) would say things like "I don't mess around, boy," and had a habit of mispronouncing words—"unusural" instead of "unusual"; after a few months of mispronunciation, the writers finally wrote his special way of speaking into the radio scripts, since it was getting so much attention. Poor David, though. He was a twelve-year-old straight man to a little brother who was getting all the laughs. Harriet used to say, "It'll be a wonder if David doesn't murder Ricky in his bed some night." He hasn't yet (so far).

That same year, Ozzie had an idea—putting the Nelsons on television. He negotiated carefully and worked out a deal with ABC that gave him complete artistic control of both radio and TV programs. And then he got busy writing—not a TV script, but a script for a movie to be called *Here Come the Nelsons*, which would be the show's pilot. It was filmed in 1951 and, although Ozzie and Harriet had been in movies before, it was the first for Ricky and David—also a first for Ozzie, who had a *job* as an executive for the H. J. Bellows and Company Advertising Agency. Never again. (Also in the movie was a young actor named Roy Fitzgerald, who later changed his name to Rock Hudson.) The movie was a success and the following October, in 1952, *The Adventures of Ozzie and Harriet* hit the small screen. America was ready for it.

Ozzie—who, in character, seemed unable to handle anything on the show—actually handled everything. He was the program's producer, director, story editor, and head writer. Harriet supervised the kids' wardrobes and designed much of the set decoration. And everyone was busy: not only were they doing a weekly TV series, but they were all also taping the weekly radio show with a totally different script. Ricky and David went to school. But somehow those stolid Nelsons withstood it all.

At that time all the networks felt that the only way to get an acceptable TV picture was through "flat" photography—which meant filming the background brightly lighted so there wouldn't be much contrast and to minimize shadows or dark areas. Ozzie wasn't happy with this. Therefore he hired a *movie* photographer—just as *I Love Lucy* had done—an Academy Award-winning cin-

ematographer even: William Mellor. Ozzie offered him $1000 a week ($250 more than he'd been getting) and Mellor accepted—and brought along his own crew. They decided to just ignore the flat lighting and to go with "movie lighting."

However, Ozzie was disappointed when the show still looked rotten on the screen. He discovered that the trouble was with the inept operator who was running the transmitter at the TV studio—so while the program was being broadcast, one of the producers would go down and talk to the operator—while someone else would fiddle with the knobs, bringing the picture into better focus. But that was only in LA; for the rest of the country, the picture still looked bad.

The set of the Nelson house was an exact replica of their own home, including the kitsch eagle over their fireplace that became the Nelsons' mascot, the family pet. Often they would use their real house for long shots.

It was 1952. The Nelsons had their own TV show. America had the Nelsons. And Ricky and David were each making more money than the President. Not of ABC. Of the United States.

The TV show was mellow. There was no evidence of the frenetic sight gags of *I Love Lucy*. Or even the clever humor of *Mr. Peepers*. In its own way, *The Adventures of Ozzie and Harriet* was a landmark—a precursor to shows like *My Three Sons* and *The Brady Bunch* as well as many of the domestic comedies in between. Nothing serious ever went on. It followed—reinforced, in fact—the old TV formula of misunderstood situations. And family battles were never evident, of course; just gentle misunderstandings. The show always focused on the most trivial elements of family life: perhaps there was a mixup in having a new chair delivered; perhaps the kids were trying to raise money for the frat house swimming pool building fund. But Harriet never had an identity crisis as even Margaret Anderson once had. Ozzie couldn't counsel his kids, and he certainly did not know best. Just by watching the show, you could tell everything about the characters: Ozzie and Harriet were Republicans; she bought frozen vegetables; they made love (they did not Have Sex) in the missionary position only; Ozzie never cheated on Harriet. She never drank (although, the one time Harriet took a glass of sherry—viewers' protests poured in).

Harriet was always there with a pot of coffee and a plate of freshly baked brownies. She smiled wanly through every situation. And yet there was something appealing about it all, because it took family life—a hotspot of American insecurity—and trivialized it to the point of innocuousness, while squeezing out all the humor like puerile pulp. *Ozzie and Harriet* was the ultimate in home movies—with an annoying laugh-track.

And the plots were simple. Some samples:

☐ Two large chairs are delivered to the Nelsons by mistake. Ozzie phones the department store and the

clerk thinks it's her girlfriend Mabel trying to kid her. So, rather than the first two chairs being picked up from the Nelsons', two more chairs are delivered. Ozzie decides to keep two and return two—also to give the two old chairs to his bowling club. By mistake, the four new chairs are picked up by the bowlers, and the store driver picks up the two old chairs. No, Ozzie does not have a nervous breakdown and spend the rest of the season in Menninger's Clinic. The situation, of course, is straightened out. □

□ It's Ozzie and Harriet's nineteenth anniversary (married, not on the air) and Ozzie wants to take Harriet out—but fourteen-year-old Ricky is having a party that night and Ozzie and Harriet have to stay home and chaperone. The parents stay upstairs until out of curiosity they come downstairs and discover—a surprise party for them. □

□ Ricky is on a date with a coed (as they were called back in 1963, when this episode first aired). He spills a malted milk on her dress and tears it while closing the car door. So he buys her a new dress. Harriet finds it and assumes it's a gift from Ozzie. Eventually the situation is straightened out. (Today, of course, if a sitcom mother found a dress in her son's closet, she would assume that *he* was in the closet. No such sophistication back then—thank God.) □

There was no sex on the Nelsons' show. In fact, except for Ricky's onstage gyrations, the Nelsons were all strangely sexless. But, then, so were the fifties.

Although most of the show's humor centered around Ricky and David (especially Ricky), Ozzie and Harriet were an important part of *Ozzie and Harriet*. Everything bounced off them. Not only did they play straight men to

their sons, they played straight men to each other.

Here's an example of some of the show's early dialogue. David is having dinner with a girl—and the family, which is also having dinner, thinks it might be serious.

HARRIET: He's eating dinner at her house tonight.
OZZIE: I know—you said so. That doesn't mean he's going to marry her. After all, I ate dinner at your house lots of times . . .
HARRIET: Well?
OZZIE: Well, it was just that your mother was such a good cook.
HARRIET: You didn't marry her.
OZZIE: Well, no—she wasn't available at the time. . . . I was engaged to you. . . . Well, I don't think there's anything to worry about. David's too young to get married.
HARRIET: We were pretty young when we got married. In fact, we get younger every time you tell about it.

(Ricky enters.)

RICKY: Is this all right?
OZZIE: What's that supposed to be?
RICKY: Mom told me to put on a tie.
OZZIE: Yeah, I know—but she told you to put on a shirt, too.

HARRIET: Where are you eating dinner—at the gym?
OZZIE: You see, Harriet, you're worried about the boys getting married and they can't even dress themselves.
RICKY: Who's getting married?
OZZIE: David . . . that is, your mother is worried about his getting married.
RICKY: What's the matter, Mom? Don't you like Susan?
HARRIET: Who told you about Susan?
RICKY: David.
HARRIET: Oh?
RICKY: I wouldn't mind having her for a sister-in-law. Sure—then if they had any children, they'd be my nephews and nieces. I think Uncle Ricky'll put on a shirt after all.

Today sponsors buy "spot" advertising time. Back in the fifties, one sponsor would buy all the commercial time on a show. In 1956—after a couple of seasons with Hotpoint and Listerine—Eastman Kodak became the Nelsons' sole sponsor. If you remember a lot of scenes shot in the Nelsons' kitchen prior to fifty-six, that's because they wanted to show their Hotpoint kitchen and please the sponsor. (They did not gargle and make the Listerine people happy—although, Ozzie said, the Listerine folks did try to coax him to write in some gargling scenes.) When Kodak clicked on, a representative from its advertising agency would hang around the set with a bunch of cameras to place around the necks of cast

members—picnics, parties—although Ozzie said "No" to mowing the lawn with a camera around his neck. "A few years later," Ozzie said, "I had to convince the Aunt Jemima people that we didn't eat pancakes for dinner, and the Coca-Cola people that we didn't drink Cokes for breakfast. . . ." Beginning in fifty-six, also to accommodate the Kodak people, many of the scenes were filmed outdoors.

That same year, Wally Plumstead (Skip Young) joined the cast, playing David's happy-go-lucky, chubby fraternity brother. Later that season, Lyle Talbot and Mary Jane Croft joined the cast as Joe and Clara Randolph. But basically the show stayed the same and the formula was not to be broken. The kids were still cute. Ozzie dispensed advice from his den, while Harriet dispensed coffee from her pot.

Nineteen fifty-seven brought the biggest change yet, and on April 10, America got a look at an episode called "Ricky the Drummer." The seventeen-year-old Ricky (the real one) had been pestering his father to let him sing on the show and to make a record (because, he later admitted, he wanted to impress a girl he'd been dating). That episode, he sang the Fats Domino hit "I'm Walkin'," and it immediately went to the top of the charts. A fan club was started and Ricky became a rock 'n' roll star. David was busy with movie roles (*Peyton Place, The Big Circus, The Remarkable Mr. Pennypacker*) and the episodes had to be filmed around them, with Ozzie and Harriet getting weeks ahead of the sons in shooting. Other titles for the year: "David and the Stewardess," "Fixing Up the Fraternity House," "A Picture in Ricky's Notebook," "Harriet's Dancing Partner," and "Tutti-Frutti Ice Cream"—in which Ozzie and Harriet get a craving for tutti-frutti ice cream and drive all over town to find some. Immediately after, ice cream stores all over the country were besieged with requests for tutti-frutti.

In 1959, the Nelson event of the year was a show called "The Circus," built around Ricky and David's trapeze act. They put up a full-sized circus tent and hired hundreds of extras. David had taught his brother the flying tricks while he had filmed *The Big Circus*. The episode was a sensation.

In 1960, on the show, David, twenty-three, had graduated from college, enrolled in law school, and begun clerking in a law office. Joe Flynn played David's boss, Donald Kelley (the name of the Nelsons' real attorney). Flynn left later to costar in *McHale's Navy*.

Throughout the boys' TV college years, there were many girls on the show—with first names like Joi, Venetia, Brooke, Mikki, Andra and Tuesday (yes—Ms. Weld). The fraternity brothers were often played by Ricky and David's real-life pals. Barry and Stanley Livingston played kids' roles on the show before they became regulars on *My Three Sons*. One actress whom they hired—June Blair—married David the following year (1961). She was immediately written into the show, first as David's girlfriend, then as his wife. They had a

Neighbors: Nelson and Nelson with Lyle Talbot

baby and so—in the show—they had a baby. It all worked
out niftily. When Rick married an old family friend's
daughter, Kris Harmon, in 1964, she too joined the
program. Once again it was a case of TV reflecting life,
which reflected TV. Everything that happened to the
Nelsons—short of conception—was recorded on film.
How bizarrely appropriate that the show was sponsored
by Kodak.

The program was canceled at the end of the
1965–1966 season—although the Nelsons lived on. It
seemed that they had lived in front of the cameras so
many years that when they lost their show, they didn't
know how to function.

Ricky went on singing, but was never able—except
for his "Garden Party" hit in 1971—to repeat his hits of
the fifties: "Hello, Mary Lou" and "I'm Walkin'." David
had directed several *Ozzie and Harriet* and *O. K.
Crackerby* episodes and started his own TV production
company. Ozzie and Harriet tried a syndicated series—
Ozzie's Girls—in which they rented out Ricky's and
David's old rooms to two college girls, Susan Hamilton
(Susan Sennett) and Brenda MacKenzie (Brenda Sykes).
The show was canceled after one season.

When they started building the set for the new
show—a replica of the same house (at 522 Sycamore Rd.,
Hillsdale)—Harriet said, "Don't let them put that eagle
over the fireplace. If there's one thing I got sick of
looking at after fourteen years, it's that goddamn eagle."
And so it was removed. The Nelsons without their *eagle?*
No wonder the show flopped.

But the question still remains in the minds of

America—what did Ozzie do for a living?

Once, on *The Johnny Carson Show,* Harriet turned
to Ozzie: "Would you mind answering a personal question? It's something that's been bothering me for years."

"Of course not," Ozzie replied. "You know we have
no secrets from each other. What is it?"

"What do you do for a living?"

(Ozzie once explained, "by not designating the kind
of work I did, people were able to identify with me more
readily.")

A while back, Richard Decker drew a cartoon in *The
New Yorker* that showed a middle-class couple seated in
their living room, watching television. She turns to him
and says, "I'll make a deal with you. I'll try to be more
like Harriet if you'll try to be more like Ozzie."

We all tried to be more like Ozzie and Harriet . . .
and Ricky and maybe even David, too. They gave us
fourteen years of their lives—a lot of half-hours—not
counting radio. And now? Harriet's a grandmother—
somehow she always was, even before she was—and still
pouring coffee somewhere. Ricky is trying to make it
again as a musician. In an interview, David said that his
life "really began when I accepted Jesus Christ as my
savior." Obviously, Ozzie wasn't enough for him.

And Ozzie is dead. He died in 1975. But his reruns
live on.

Ozzie—and the rest of the Nelsons—gave us something that the rest of the TV families never did: hope.
After watching their meek and mild-mannered "adventures," we realized how much more interesting our own
family lives really were.

I MARRIED JOAN

*I married Joan / What a girl, what a whirl, what a
life . . .*
                                        —from the show's theme song

In the *I Love Lucy* tradition, *I Married Joan* centered around the life of another zany wife. She was full of dreams and schemes. Her straight man was her husband, a judge. Years before *Laugh-In* brought the phrase to television, on this show, "Here comes the judge" always meant trouble. Whether she was boiling a live turtle in the living room to make turtle soup or just giving a simple surprise party for what she thought was her husband's birthday (when it was really her own), Joan was always causing crises.

Joan Davis (the marvelous comedienne who played Joan Stevens) was a clown, a buffoon. In the movies she was always dressed in strange clothes, rushing around, falling, mugging. From one of her early films, a manic Mack Sennett hillbilly piece called *Way Up That,* to her spots on the popular Rudy Vallee radio program (which she inherited when Vallee entered the Coast Guard in 1943), Joan Davis was one of America's favorites. For ten years, she made six movies a year. By 1937, she was voted the most popular screen comedienne. In 1950, Davis moved from NBC to CBS radio to do her show *Leave It to Joan.* Davis was the woman, Fanny Brice once said, whom she wanted to play her in the movies.

A typical Joan Davis radio routine went like this:

"I never win anything. With me, everything has been like a horse race. Why, in the middle of life, I was left at the post. In the race for love, I was scratched, and in the race for matrimony, huh! I can't even get out of the stable for that one."

Strictly vaudeville kind of routine. But that's what she did. Until she took the leap and plunged into television.

I Married Joan premiered on Wednesday, October 15, 1952. *Time* hated it: "It might have been better left on the shelf." But *Variety* praised her "comic zest and vitality." Joan Stevens, true to the then-current sitcom genre, was as scatterbrained as the rest, but with her own set of outrageous gestures, hard falls, raucous vocal tricks, and muscle-straining grimaces. Said Davis: "I'm the gal who has fallen twenty thousand times." She was proud of it.

So was NBC. The show did well and, one year later, was the third most popular network comedy show. Davis had had many offers to appear on television, but she always said no. "I knew exactly what I wanted to do in television, and this series just about spells it," she had said. "Television is a new medium, and should be treated as such by entertainers. Every show wanted me to do my old man-chasing act, complete with screams, pratfalls, and 'Love That Boy' lines.

"But after watching TV, I began to see that it was the more relaxed characters who were successful. You can't forget for one minute that this show is going into people's living rooms, where the atmosphere is relaxed and people don't want to feel ill at ease by your trying to high-pressure them. And they don't want to be shocked out of their living room chairs."

It wasn't all terrific. "Two a week in vaudeville was beautiful. Radio? What a breeze. It was stealing money. But this—I've never worked so hard in my life. I'm glad I took care of myself as a little girl."

Jim Backus was cast as her husband, Bradley Stevens, a sophisticated domestic-relations court judge. Davis had worked with him on radio. His voice was

Joan Stevens	Joan Davis
Judge Bradley Stevens	Jim Backus
Charlie, their neighbor	Hal Smith
Mabel, his wife	Geraldine Carr
Janet Tobin, Joan's friend	Sheila Bromley
Kerwin Tobin, her husband	Dan Tobin
Mildred Webster, Joan's friend	Sandra Gould
Minerva Parker	Hope Emerson (1952–1953)
Beverly Grossman, Joan's sister	Beverly Wills (1953–1955)
Alan Grossman, her husband	Himself
Helen, Joan's friend	Mary Jane Croft

already familiar as *Mr. Magoo* on the popular cartoon.

The show was a departure for Davis. Every situation was not milked to the bitter end, although they all were outlandish. Once Joan went into a dress shop, tried on dresses that were too large for her, and then tried to sell them to a stranger. She couldn't cope with a checking account, so her husband cut off all her charge accounts. In many ways, her relationship to "the judge" was more father-daughter than husband-wife. And it was the perfect career culmination for Joan Davis (real name: Josephine Davis), who, at age six, did a serious song recital in her native St. Paul—and the audience broke out into laughter.

Reminisced Davis: "I read *Variety* before the first-grade primer. Later on I approached algebra as a shortcut method of determining a year's income, at, say fifty dollars a week." She said, later in life, "I have no desire to do Shakespeare. I'm well adjusted."

She gave this advice to her daughter Beverly Wills (who played Joan's sister on the sitcom; they talked exactly alike): "There are thousands of young, beautiful girls who each year flock to Hollywood and New York, all of them thinking themselves potential Bette Davises. The woods are full of dramatic actresses—but try and find a good comedienne. They're as scarce as men."

Davis, however, had her share of men. One—a real estate salesman to whom she was engaged for two years—was eleven years younger. One night she had her realtor Romeo arrested for assault and battery (later she decided not to prosecute) and broke off the relationship. It was in all the papers. "A woman's place is in the home, even an actress," Davis had said after her divorce. "But when there isn't much of a home left, a woman who has been as active all her life as I have has to have another outlet." She had plenty of outlets. She was president of Joan Davis Productions and worked all the time. "I don't go to

sleep," she said. "I fall down unconscious." As a producer, she was always called "JD." Off-screen she was shy and quiet, a woman who liked to go fishing, play golf, go to boxing matches, or just stay home and read through her file of gags—which filled more than twelve large volumes.

The show took three cameras to film, and Joan—unlike other TV stars—decided to memorize her lines. "I don't use a TelePrompTer. I never sit still long enough to look at it."

Toward the end of the show's run, in 1955, the ratings had slipped. The show had never done well in New York, an important market that was holding back the ratings. "If I had time," Davis said, "I'd go from door to door."

She didn't have much time. For anything. After ninety-eight episodes, she retired from the show, saying she was "worn out." "If show business has been good to me, it has robbed me of many things." The show went into reruns, from May 1956 through March 1957, as a replacement for *Howdy Doody*. It did phenomenally well, tying with *Queen for a Day* as the highest-rated daytime show.

Joan Davis tried selling several TV sitcom pilots—including one about the first woman astronaut to train and condition for a flight to the moon—but they never took off.

Discouraged, she went into virtual retirement in 1959. In 1961, she died of a heart attack.

"The films," she had said, referring to her sitcom, "have to be good. They are my legacy both as a comedienne and a businesswoman. The pictures will be playing when I'm in a wheelchair and after that it'll be great for my daughter. I'll leave her with a cracked voice and a lot of negatives." And a lot of positives as well.

THE LIFE OF RILEY

Oh, Riley!—
PEG RILEY

Fathers seem to have always gotten the short end of the sitcom stick on television. They weren't lovable and didn't say clever things like their young children. Their wives were usually sensible, practical, patient, and nurturing. Their dogs were cute and never messed. But from the household head in *Father Knows Best*—who had to maintain perfection for six years—to the clan leader of *All in the Family*—who had to maintain imperfection for nine years—it was basically bad to be a dad. At least on TV.

The original idiot father was Chester A. Riley. The life of Riley was an existence of stupidity. He was a bumbling bimbo—prototypically typical of a feast of fathers who would follow in his pratfalls. True, Riley was likable . . . but *so* stupid. How he ever managed to Bring Home the Bacon was a mystery to everyone.

The show had had an unsuccessful one-season TV run in 1949 on the old DuMont network, where it was one of television's first sitcoms. A very static (and thin) Jackie Gleason starred in this one-camera, no-laugh-track show with interactions like this one between Riley and his wife, Peg (Rosemary DeCamp).

RILEY: Oh, Peg, give me a kiss. . . .
PEG: Well, it's not your birthday and you're not leavin' for work. . . . *(She gives him a perfunctory kiss.)*
RILEY: *(seriously)* Say, that was quite a kiss. . . .

That was not quite a show.

The only reason Gleason was offered the part, anyway, was because William Bendix—who had starred as radio's Riley beginning in 1944—had other commitments. Gleason's Riley was a flop. But in fifty-three, NBC decided to try a *Riley* again, this time with Bendix in his own role. "Riley's for the little guy," Bendix announced and proceeded to play him the way he knew how: as an oafish, ordinary working stiff. The resurrected show was an instant success and in fact was one of the few radio-to-television transplants that worked.

Those were the days when Communists—called "reds"—were hiding under every blond oak dining room table, the days when Dwight Eisenhower and Richard Nixon (the first time around) ruled the land. Riley fitted right in. He dealt with all the troubles of the world by watching the ball game and drinking beer.

Riley was considered to be the Average Joe Amer-

DuMont Version (October 4, 1949–March 28, 1950)

Chester A. Riley	Jackie Gleason
Peggy Riley	Rosemary DeCamp
Babs Riley	Gloria Winters
Chester Riley, Jr. (Junior)	Lanny Rees
Jim Gillis, Riley's neighbor	Sid Tomack
Digby "Digger" O'Dell, the mortician	John Brown

NBC Version (January 2, 1953–August 22, 1958)

Chester A. Riley	William Bendix
Peggy Riley	Marjorie Reynolds
Babs Riley	Lugene Sanders
Chester Riley, Jr.	Wesley Morgan
Jim Gillis	Tom D'Andrea (1953–1955, 1956–1958)
Honeybee Gillis, Jim's wife	Gloria Blondell (1953–1955, 1956–1958)
Don Marshall, Babs' boyfriend	Martin Milner (1957–1958)
Carl Stevenson, Riley's employer	Douglas Dumbrille
Waldo Binny, Riley's friend	Sterling Holloway
Millicent, Waldo's girlfriend	Stanja Lowe
Otto Schmidlap, Riley's friend	Henry Kulky
Calvin Dudley, Riley's neighbor	George O'Hanlon (1955–1956)
Belle Dudley, Calvin's wife	Florence Sundstrom (1955–1956)
Cissy Riley, Chester's sister	Mary Jane Croft
Anne Riley, Chester's sister	Larraine Bendix
Moose, Junior's friend	Denny Miller

ican. He made $110 a week as a riveter at Stevenson Aircraft and Associates. He lived in a modest home at 1313 Blue View Terrace in Los Angeles. He was married to an ever-suffering woman, Peg. Like every other good American, they would have had the 2.3 children, but because that would have been difficult to portray on television, they settled for an even two: a daughter, Babs (age seventeen), and a son, Chester Riley, Jr. (age twelve). They also had a dog named Rex.

Riley always managed to create gentle havoc wherever he went, whatever he did. Not because he had bad luck. But because he had bad brains. The show wasn't a sitcom, it was a sitfarce. When he botched things up, Riley would throw up his arms and mutter his most famous line: "What a revoltin' development *this* is!"

After the first season, audiences and critics started complaining about Riley being so cretinesque. "No one that dumb could support a family," many viewers said. And so, in response to audience reaction, the producers brightened up Riley a bit. But just a bit. They cut down on his double takes and his mugging. Before, he had just fallen down a lot; now they gave him a motivation—like a pair of roller skates—to fall over. Method Falling.

Either way, 8,000,000 American families weekly tuned into Riley's preposterous predicaments, usually aided by Riley's neighbor Jim Gillis (they were both riveters), who was always helping "Rile" get into trouble. "That rat is my best friend!" Riley exclaimed.

In one episode, peering over the fence, Riley was eavesdropping on an argument between Gillis and his wife, Honeybee. When Riley peeked over the fence for a better look, he got a wad of wet clothes thrown in his face, originally intended for Gillis.

RILEY: What an arm on that Honeybee. She ought to be pitchin' for the Dodgers!
PEG: It serves you right for being so nosy.
RILEY: You want to know what they were fighting about?
PEG: Definitely not. What goes on between the Gillises is none of our business whatsoever.
RILEY: (*can't stand it any longer*)   Y'sure you don't want to know what they were fightin' about?
PEG: Absolutely not.
RILEY: Okay—then I won't tell you.
PEG: (*after pause*)   Riley—what were they fighting about?

The Gillises had been fighting about a trip they were going to take to Portland. After they were finished arguing, they popped over to ask Riley to guard their house while they were on vacation.

GILLIS: Just take care of our mail, Rile, that's all.
RILEY: Leave it to me. I'll take as good care of your house as I do my own.

HONEYBEE: That does it. Let's call off the trip.
GILLIS: Now, Honeybee! What could Riley possibly do to our house?
HONEYBEE: You wouldn't think a couple of termites could eat half our porch, but they did. And Riley's bigger than they are.

The comedy is preposterous. Sometimes the situations were even more moronic, like the time when Riley takes his family on a vacation to a friend's cabin—which happens to be in the middle of the state penitentiary (it turns out his "pal" was the groundskeeper there).

When Junior goes off to college, Riley is depressed (no, not depressed—unhappy; depression didn't hit television until 1976 when *Maude* turned fifty). Riley was even more upset in later years when Junior brings his girlfriend home. "I really got her trained, huh, Pa? She'd make a perfect wife," Junior says after his girlfriend takes off Riley's boots. But Riley's afraid that he's lost his son:

RILEY: (*whining*)   I think I'll go lie down.
PEG: Can I get you anything, dear?
RILEY: Yeah . . . get me my little boy. . . .

Of course it ends up happily, with the girl announcing that "Going steady has nothing to do with marriage. I've gone steady nine times and I haven't been married once." Riley then develops a silly and benign crush on the girl. All very chaste for 1956; today it would have broader implications.

Life of Riley was television in its ultimate age of innocence. The point was that Riley was *average*—the way Ralph Kramden was later average. It was un-American not to like Riley. Said Bendix: "Riley and his

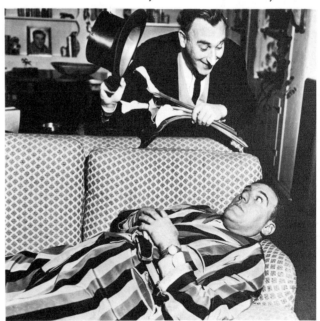

"Guess I'd better be shoveling off": Digger O'Dell (John Brown) visits Riley

Neighbors (from left): Marjorie Reynolds, Gloria Blondell, Tom D'Andrea, William Bendix

family are appealing because they portray the average American family. They have no prestige or polish. They are just good middle-class Americans. Of course they're somewhat exaggerated. Otherwise they wouldn't be funny."

Riley was an emotional person. He cried, he whimpered, he acted weak—all the things that only women on television were allowed to do (how many times did Lucy Ricardo do the same things?). Part of what made Riley funny was that here was this "big lunk of a guy" doing something that only women were supposed to do: show emotions. The other thing that made Riley work so well was William Bendix, radio's Riley who had been acting since the Depression, making $21 a week (even less than Riley took home) with the Federal Theater.

Bendix grew up in a New York tenement on Third Ave. and 45th St. He appeared in six Broadway flops before his success as Krupp in *The Time of Your Life*. In 1939, he headed for Hollywood, where he appeared in numerous movies as the tough, all-American guy. When he became TV's Riley, he gave up everything to devote all his energy to the role. He had a "ten percent off-the-top piece" of *Riley* and, together, he and Riley made 217 episodes, many of which are now being rerun on local late-night television. In 1958, the series was canceled; Bendix was canceled in 1964 at age fifty-eight when he died of pneumonia, complicated by a stomach ailment.

Bendix's wife, Teresa, said that much of his fan mail had come from wives who said that their husbands liked to identify with Riley because it helped them feel better about their occasional stupidity.

In one episode Riley's father comes to visit, after not having seen his son for twenty years. Riley, of course, has botched things up—"but good"—and at the show's end, Riley Senior looks at Riley Junior and says:

"What a revoltin' development *he* is!"

OUR MISS BROOKS

> MR. BOYNTON: *Tell me, Miss Brooks—did you or did*
> *Miss Davis make these ribs?*
> MISS BROOKS: *Do you like them, Mr. Boynton?*
> MR. BOYNTON: *Very much.*
> MISS BROOKS: *Then I made them!*

Beginning on Friday, October 3, 1952, and running for 154 episodes—that adds up to practically a whole semester—Connie Brooks with her crisp, mordant wit was the matron saint of the television schoolyard. Miss Brooks was the man-hungry schoolmarm—but with a difference. Her good looks and tart-tongued humor made her a sexy woman—not just another woe-is-me, Olive Oyl character who chased but remained chaste. Sure, Connie Brooks wanted her man—and the unlikely object of her affections was a dense and dull bumbling biology teacher named Philip Boynton—and we always suspected that she could teach him a few things about biology. Unfortunately, he was more interested in his frog, Mac.

That was okay, too, because it left Miss Brooks more time for us and the other characters on the show—Osgood Conklin, the dictatorial principal at Madison High School in Los Angeles; Walter Denton, a squeaky-voiced student; Bones, the class dunce; and Mrs. Davis, her silly ninny of a landlady.

But it was Miss Brooks' relationship with her students that was so special. They "talked back" to her—not disrespectfully but personally. They thought of her as their friend and took appropriate liberties.

WALTER: I'd say you were in your late twenties or early thirties or—
MISS BROOKS: Quit now. Teeth become you.

It was her upper lip that became Eve Arden, the actress who played Miss Brooks and a dozen characters like her in movies. She had a magic mouth that she would curl up as she rolled her eyes and bit into a line.

WALTER (*scheming to break into principal's office*): How does the idea sound to you, Miss Brooks?

MISS BROOKS: It sounds risky, far-fetched, and impractical—and we'll get started right after school.

When she would crack her wises, she threw her comments to the corner of the TV screen, as if that's where we, her intimates, were sitting, waiting to catch them. Her one-liners and throwaways were meant exclusively for us—no one else seemed to understand them. But the person who understood Miss Brooks the least was the person she wanted the most understanding from—Mr. Boynton.

Format One (1952–1955)

Connie Brooks	Eve Arden
Osgood Conklin	Gale Gordon
Philip Boynton	Robert Rockwell
Walter Denton, the main problem student	Richard Crenna
Harriet Conklin, Osgood's daughter	Gloria McMillan
Mrs. Davis, Connie's landlady	Jane Morgan
Mrs. Davis' cat: Minerva	

Format Two (1955–1956)

Connie Brooks	Eve Arden
Osgood Conklin	Gale Gordon
Gene Talbot	Gene Barry (1955–1956)
Clint Albright	William Ching (1955–1956)
Angela Nestor, the owner of the school	Nana Bryant (1955–1956)
Oliver Munsey, Angela's eccentric brother	Bob Sweeney (1955–1956)
Mrs. Nestor, Angela's sister	Isobel Randolph (1955–1956)
Benny Romero, ten-year-old problem child	Ricky Vera (1955–1956)

MR. BOYNTON (*in his classroom, looking at his frog*): Mac's been kind of lethargic lately; just mopes around in his cage.

MISS BROOKS: Maybe he's tired of being in there all by himself—some creatures get pretty lonesome (*hopefully*), don't they, Mr. Boynton?

MR. BOYNTON: Yes, indeed. That's why I spend as much time with my frog as possible.

MISS BROOKS (*dryly*): Maybe he's got a friend for me?

MR. BOYNTON: What's that, Miss Brooks?

MISS BROOKS: Ah . . . skip it.

And he did skip it. But we didn't. We understood Miss Brooks and felt that if she could know us, if she could communicate with us, she'd be much happier.

Once she invited an aloof Mr. Boynton to her house:

MISS BROOKS: Anything special you want for dinner?

MR. BOYNTON: I'm not fussy. I'll love whatever you put on my plate. I'll be there at seven.

MISS BROOKS: Fine—I'll be on your plate.

Connie Brooks was the precursor of some of TV's lovable, lonely ladies like *Dick Van Dyke*'s Rose Marie and *Mary Tyler Moore*'s Rhoda. All used laughter to cover up their pain and, with their obvious vulnerability (that only we seemed insightful and sensitive enough to appreciate), these were the original undiscovered women. All were pals—misfits in a society that dictated you had to get married and have children. Well, Miss Brooks had children—a classroom full of them—but she wanted marriage. Badly.

MRS. DAVIS: Give Mr. Boynton a subtle hint or two.

MISS BROOKS: Like what, for instance?

MRS. DAVIS: Tell him you're sick and tired of being single.

MISS BROOKS: Oh, that's fine—or maybe I could dump a bowl of rice over his head and whistle the wedding march.

If Miss Brooks had ever gotten married, it would have destroyed the show. (Look what it did for *Rhoda*—and back in those days you couldn't take it back with a quickie TV divorce.) "Our Mrs. Boynton" wouldn't have been anybody's anything. In 1956, Warner Brothers released a one-and-a-half-hour movie version of the show—also called *Our Miss Brooks*—with the complete TV cast. It dragged on for a long time—because we knew all along that Miss Brooks was going to snatch Mr. Boynton. Within the first fifteen minutes of the movie, they were already going steady—and the movie even included a dream sequence of what it would be like to be Mrs. Boynton. By the end, of course, they did get married. But there was none of the sardonic tension and suspense that the sitcom had. Miss Brooks wasn't ours—she was Mr. Boynton's. We couldn't relate to that.

Before premiering on TV, the show was popular on radio for four years (and, in fact, the fifth year of radio overlapped with the first year of the TV program). (On the radio show, Jeff Chandler played Mr. Boynton. Although his voice was right for the part, he looked wrong, so the producers persuaded him to stick with movies, in which he became a star.)

The TV show was produced by Desilu—short for Desi Arnaz and Lucille Ball—who were taking some of their tremendous *I Love Lucy* profits and investing in other shows (later, *Make Room for Daddy* and *December Bride*).

As soon as the show hit the screen, it had its criticism—not from the critics, but from schoolteachers saying, as one wrote, that the show "sets the teaching profession back 100 years," mostly because it "undermines the profession by presenting undignified caricatures of teachers and a devastating portrait of a bullying principal."

Countered Eve Arden: "Would you like your real-life school to be reproduced on TV? I wouldn't." Later she would say that she based her Miss Brooks character on two of her own teachers—Lizzie Kaiser, "a slightly unorthodox teacher who had a way of making things

Biology: Miss B. helps Mr. B. on with his costume for the masquerade party.

interesting," and Ruth Waterman, "who had warmth and sweetness." Miss Brooks had all of those qualities. "I tried to play Miss Brooks as a loving person who cared about the kids and kept trying to keep them out of trouble, but kept getting herself in trouble. We tried to wipe out the notion that all teachers were fuddy-duddies."

Eve Arden was also criticized for wearing fancy clothes on a teacher's salary. (Her own salary was about $4,000 a week.) Arden actually purchased her own costumes—and in Miss Brooks' price bracket. Once when she was told to forget Mr. Boynton, that there were other fish in the sea, Miss Brooks shrugged: "Yes, but on my salary I can't make the bait as attractive as it should be."

Of course Miss Brooks had her fans. The mail kept pouring in. A Chicago teacher she hadn't met wrote and asked Arden to be maid of honor in her June 1953 wedding. She did. Offers came in to join school boards. She didn't. One letter from a teacher—which Eve Arden calls her "diploma" and hangs framed in her home—reads: "Thank you for recording the fact that we are not all pokerfaced leftovers."

In 1955, Miss Brooks moved. Not to another network. But to another school. She went off to become a dramatics instructor at Mrs. Nestor's Private School. Madison High, her alma mater for three seasons, had fallen victim to a convenient TV *deus ex machina*—it had been torn down to make room for a state road. And when she arrived for that first day at the new school—guess who was there: crusty Mr. Conklin. Missing from action, though, were Walter Denton (Richard Crenna's voice had changed so much the season before that he had taken to simulating his squeak), Mrs. Davis (although they brought her back at midseason), and particularly Mr.

Boynton. Whom would Miss Brooks chase?

No one. Starting with the new format, she would *be* chased—by a string of admiring beaus:

● Mr. Munsey (Bob Sweeney), an eccentric inventor who announced in the third script that he was a confirmed bachelor

● Clint Albright, a wolf (played by William Ching)

● Maharajah of Boongaddy (Hy Averback) who teased (but not tempted) Miss Brooks with lines like: "If you come to Boongaddy, I could be your sugar daddy."

● Gene Talbot (Gene Barry), a musclebound gym teacher

Mrs. Nestor's Private Elementary School: Gale Gordon, Nana Bryant, Eve Arden

. . . and at midseason—guess who came back? Mr. Boynton. But somehow it wasn't the same and, the following season, the cast made only seven new episodes before CBS started running repeats.

Said Eve Arden at the time: "I do love Miss Brooks, but enough of a good thing can be too much."

It was in reruns that *Miss Brooks* achieved its all-time popularity—and it was rerun everywhere. "People are going to have to go to Siberia to escape me," Arden said. Four years later she told a reporter: "A woman came up to me in Hollywood recently. She held up her year-old baby to me and said, 'Marvin sees you every morning. Marvin, say da-da for Miss Brooks.' Porters on trains, Chinese in San Francisco, lobstermen in Maine—one and all, they come up to me and say something nice about Miss Brooks."

The role was the highlight of a career that had consisted of playing wiseacre best friends of leading ladies in movies. She's best known for being Mildred Pierce's buddy in that Joan Crawford movie.

In the 1930s, Eunice Quedons was reading a book—she doesn't remember its title—about a girl named Eve, and immediately changed her first name. She picked up Arden from a jar of cosmetics she was using. Her big break came in 1934, when Florenz Ziegfeld cast her in his Follies as Fanny Brice's mother in a Baby Snooks skit. And then she made her movies. In 1941, she starred in

"Hi ya, honey": Gene Barry visits Eve Arden and Jane Morgan

Let's Face It with Vivian Vance.

In the early fifties she said, "No more Eve Arden parts"—the star's brash, brittle girlfriend whose caustic comments got her laughs—but then someone sent her the *Our Miss Brooks* script. "I did it because I found her warmhearted, sympathetic and thoroughly likable." She named her daughter Connie, after Miss Brooks. But when her *Our Miss Brooks* experience was over, Eve Arden vowed: "No more TV," and moved to Europe.

In 1962 she broke her vow and did *The Eve Arden Show*—"Fifteen writers tried to bail us out," she sighed—but it fizzled out after six months. (Her hairdresser didn't like the show and refused to watch it.) In 1967, she made *The Mothers-in-Law* with Kaye Ballard, which lasted two seasons.

Miss Brooks taught us that teachers are people too, and that they have a private life. Miss Brooks made that private life public.

So where is Connie Brooks now? Is she doing any substitute teaching? How has the women's movement affected her? Is she now our *Ms.* Brooks? Did she manage to keep her sense of humor through Watergate and Vietnam? Did she ever get a promotion?

In 1978, Miss Brooks—Eve Arden—returned to the screen in *Grease,* playing, of all things, the school principal.

Mr. Conklin would have been proud.

PRIVATE SECRETARY

This program has been selected to be shown to our armed forces overseas.

—announcement that ran on a 1953 episode

The TV critics slaughtered this show when it hit the airwaves. *Variety* said it was of "dubious merit" and pointed to its "stock and broad characters," and its deafening laugh-track. Said the New York *Times* of this situation comedy: "It's all situation and no comedy." Another reviewer deemed it "featherweight comedy" with "transparent situations." And those were the *good* reviews.

Oh, well. More than twenty years later it all seems rather harsh; today in reruns, *Private Secretary*'s worst offense is innocence. Even in these sophisticated TV times, Susie McNamara—for that was her name—gives us thirty minutes of amusing entertainment, albeit scatterbrained and zany. A lot of viewers were grateful that *Private Secretary* went public.

If the series worked—and it worked—it was because of the charm of the actress who carried the show: Ann Sothern, just another in the fifties string of movie actors and actresses who traded in the silver for the small screen. Sothern's Susan Camille McNamara was the alert and sharp-tongued secretary to Peter Sands, a stern theatrical agent; she—like her sitcom sisters—created schemes and scams, but was always able to rescue her boss from trouble. By the closing credits, Susie always got her way. It helped that she was armed with a quick wit and an able assistant, Vi Praskins, the dizzy office receptionist. "Oh, to be liberated from the tentacles of the switchboard," Vi would moan.

Ann Sothern was no newcomer to the Susie character; she'd been playing her for years, especially as Maisie, a dumb blonde, in a series of movies. In real life, Sothern wasn't dumb (or blonde, for that matter). By the time *Private Secretary* went off the air, Sothern was president of five corporations and had nearly $1 million invested in an Idaho cattle ranch. She was a smart cookie, a stubborn lady who got what she wanted. Once she reportedly had her appendix unnecessarily removed in order to get out of an MGM picture she didn't like.

Two years before Sothern took the job as *Private Secretary*, she was near death with hepatitis. According to some reports, this shot her weight up from her glamour-girl status to heavyweight; from the waist down, she was fat. As Susie, she always wore black (more flattering to the figure) and was never shot below the belt, the view often obstructed by file cabinets, typewriters, and desks.

Ann Sothern—and Susie McNamara—was relaxed and poised and smooth, even in the most outrageous of situations. She had a voice (later to be used when she actually played the title voice in *My Mother the Car*) like a hot knife going through butter.

"Cat on a Hot Tin File" (a name-play on the then popular Tennessee Williams play *Cat on a Hot Tin Roof*) is as typical an episode as any. Violet comes in to Susie's office to tell Susie she's found a cat that came in through the office window and wants to keep her. Susie—dressed in black, as usual, with a white tie—tells her not to bother Mr. Sands about it today. "He's in his Simon Legree mood this morning." But Susie will see what she can do.

She brings Mr. Sands his coffee into his office, paneled, with a philodendron on his desk. She calls him Mr. Sands. He calls her Susie. She flirts with him, bubbling over; it is evident even this early on who the boss really is. He sees the cat sleeping in a file cabinet and says that it must go.

So Susie puts holes in Mr. Sands' (new) suitcase and takes the cat around, seeing if she can find it a home. She gives the cat to a restaurant owner, but it comes back. She decides to keep the cat in the office.

Mr. Sands announces that an important client is coming to the office—and she's allergic to cats. What to

Susie McNamara	Ann Sothern
Peter Sands	Don Porter
Vi Praskins, the office receptionist	Ann Tyrrell
Cagey Calhoun, a rival talent agent	Jesse White
Sylvia, Susie's secretarial friend	Joan Banks
The drugstore boy	Joseph Nartocana

The Competition: Ann Tyrrell, Ann Sothern, Jesse White

Sothern was born Henrietta Lake in Valley City, North Dakota. A student of the violin, she played an original composition with the Minneapolis Symphony Orchestra when she was thirteen. Her mother became a vocal coach for Warner Bros., and Henrietta was discovered singing with her mother. She was in two notable Broadway shows—*Smiles* and *Hotcha*—before she was brought to Hollywood in 1936. She was well known for living beyond her means (even though her means were beyond most people's) and each day she'd ride to work in a chauffeured limousine.

In 1957, when *Private Secretary* went off the air, Sothern filed suit against the producer to get more than $93,000 that she claimed was owed to her in distribution profits. Finally she relinquished control of the series; another producer tried to resurrect the show starring Don Porter without Ann Sothern, but he couldn't find a suitable actress to replace her.

Porter—a former movie heavy—was an Oklahoma businessman who went to Hollywood in his twenties. After his appearances on Ann Sothern's shows, he went on to play *Gidget*'s father on that sitcom in 1965.

do? Susie and Vi scheme to get rid of the cat, but the haughty and overdramatic actress comes early and starts sneezing. No one can imagine why. But when Susie is sitting in on the meeting, the cat creeps in and goes near the actress, who jumps into Mr. Sands' arms. There is a great deal of screaming and mugging and carrying on. The actress says she's going to sue.

"*Missssss* McNamara!" Mr. Sands calls her, as he does whenever he's angry. He berates her when he discovers she's let the cat in. "There's not room in this office for the three of us. Now start counting."

Susie has a talk with Vi, who has a hunch. She thinks that the actress' allergy is psychosomatic and wants to send her to a psychiatrist. But they know she won't go. They have a psychiatrist, a friend of Susie's, meet them in a restaurant—The Black Cat Café. As it turns out, the actress once lost a part "to a catty rival," and has been allergic to cats ever since. The doctor and the actress hit it off and it looks like they might be seeing more of one another. And—as a kicker—the actress takes a part in a play about cats and wants to use the cat in the play.

After the Lucky Strike cigarette packs have danced around during the commercial, there's this tag: The cat—which they had thought was a male—has had kittens, right in the office. "Susie!" Vi squeals. "We're grandmothers!" The Kittens even melt the cold, cold heart of Mr. Sands. And the show is over.

After she lost her job as *Private Secretary*, Sothern started a new sitcom in 1958 and called it *The Ann Sothern Show*, in which she played the assistant manager of The Bartley Hotel. Lucille Ball, Sothern's good friend, was the guest on the first show, playing (so who else?) Lucy Ricardo, who checks into the hotel because Ricky has gone fishing for the weekend. The two go through a zany scheme to get Katy O'Connor—that was Susie's new name—romantically linked to an eligible bachelor. (There was a small hassle on the set because Lucille Ball wouldn't buy a new dress for the part.)

Katy's boss that first season was hotel manager Jason Maculey (Ernest Truex) and there was a whole slew of new characters (including Joel Grey as the bellboy) plus Vi (called Olive Smith in this incarnation). All were fired (except Olive) and replaced by Don Porter as hotel manager James Devery. "No use fighting it," Katy said knowingly to her new boss, "the two of us are inseparable."

Katy, of course, was still Susie, and the shows had similar situations—Olive, for example, is wooed by the hotel dentist, who falls in love with her dentures—and basically, *The Ann Sothern Show* was just a continuation of *Private Secretary*.

In 1961, *The Ann Sothern Show* went off the air, and Susie, Katy, Maisie, and Ann in the character of the dumb-but-shrewd blonde haven't been heard from since. Sothern went on as an infrequent guest on *The Lucy Show* (playing the Countess) and as the auto's voice in *My Mother the Car*.

As hemlines have dropped, consciousnesses have raised. Secretaries have let it be known that they want to be treated like people, not like pieces of office machinery. Susie McNamara knew all that years ago. She was her boss' boss. She was independent and self-assured and had dignity and—even when she brought Mr. Sands in his coffee—you knew that if he didn't treat her well, she just might dump the pot over his head "by accident."

ALSO RANS

Dave and Charley

At least as far as his one friend was concerned, Charley Weaver (Cliff Arquette) got funnier as he got older. His senility somehow endeared him to crony Dave Willock (played by himself), an unemployed clerk. Their misadventures appeared on NBC in fifteen-minute segments for one season. Then the show croaked.

Doc Corkle

Doc (Eddie Mayehoff) is the friendly neighborhood dentist—a character everybody knows, but no one wants to think about too often. The Corkle clan, which includes a daughter (Connie Marshall) and old Pop Corkle (Chester Conklin), found this out the hard way: NBC ran their series for only one month and then extracted them all.

Duffy's Tavern

No one ever sees Mr. Duffy, the elusive owner of this run-down restaurant and bar on Third Avenue in New York City "where the elite meet to eat." That's just fine with Archie (Ed Gardner), the con man who runs the place for the absentee boss. After all, if the owner showed up to watch, how long could Archie get away with charging 15¢ for the "free lunch" that's served with every beer? But Duffy's influence is not entirely unfelt. His spinster daughter (Patte Chapman), known locally as "Nature's Revenge on Peeping Toms," sits hopefully in front of the bar every week. NBC kept the tavern (based on an old radio show of the same name) open for five months in 1954, proving once again that there's no such thing as a free lunch—even one you have to pay for.

Ethel and Albert

One of America's most favorite forties radio programs was *Ethel and Albert* that, like so many others, was transplanted to TV in the fifties. Basically, it's the story of middle-aged Ethel and Albert Arbuckle (Peg Lynch and Alan Bunce), a happily married couple living in the small town of Sandy Harbor. Margaret Hamilton (best known as the Wicked Witch in *The Wizard of Oz*) played Aunt Eva. The situations were simple: disaster meant a ruined dinner, a blown fuse, a burnt-out bulb. *E and A* debuted in April on NBC, then ran on CBS during the summer of 1955, and then finally popped over to ABC for the following season. The TV sitcom debuted as a sketch on *The Kate Smith Hour*.

Heaven for Betsy

Jack Lemmon—yes, Jack Lemmon—played Peter Bell, an impulsive, trouble-prone buyer in a toy store, in this CBS sitcom that lasted three months. Cynthia Stone played his wife, Betsy (and was, in fact, Lemmon's wife); she had also played his girlfriend on *That Wonderful Guy* in 1950. The premise: the struggles of newlyweds living in New York. The show was unusual in that it ran only for 15 minutes each episode.

Leave It to Larry

Not to be confused with *Hello, Larry* (this one only preceded it by about twenty-six years), or even *Leave It to Beaver* (that was a whole different sitcom), the Larry that everyone left it to here was played by Eddie Albert (years later he'd be grazing in *Green Acres*). This time, though, Eddie played Larry Tucker, a pleasant guy who had the bad luck to be living with his father-in-law (Ed Begley) and working with him too in his shoestore. Plus, Larry's family—his wife, Amy (Betty Kean), and his kids, Stevie (Glenn Walkin) and Harriet (Lydia Schaeffer)—always was filled with confusion (not serious) and trouble (nothing serious). Poor Larry. Plus—as if that weren't enough—CBS canceled him after only eight episodes.

Life with Luigi

This CBS sitcom was yet another transplant from radio. It all took place at 221 North Halstead St., in Chicago, the home and business of Luigi Basco (J. Carroll Naish, who'd originated the role on radio in 1948, and later Vito

Scotti), who was an antique dealer. He was brought to Chicago from Italy by his friend Pasquale (Alan Reed, who would go on to play the studio boss in 1957 on *Mr. Adams and Eve*), who owned the Spaghetti Palace. Luigi was just trying to adjust; Pasquale was just trying to get Luigi to marry his daughter Rosa. The show went off the air in 1953. Apparently the reason for its short TV run was that many Italian-Americans found the extreme Italian ethnic stereotyping distasteful.

Meet Millie

In Manhattan, Millie Bronson (played by Elena Verdugo in her pre-*Marcus Welby* days) worked as a secretary who was secretly in love with her boss' son, Johnny Boone (Ross Ford). It was no secret to us, though, and it was no secret to her mother (played by Florence Halop), who was always introducing her to Eligible Young Men. Also on the show: Isabel Randolph as her boss' wife and Marvin Kaplan as Alfred Prinzmetal, Millie's friend who was an aspiring poet-author-composer.

Meet Millie (from left): Florence Halop, Marvin Kaplan, Elena Verdugo

Meet Millie had been a radio favorite since 1951 (starring Audrey Totter, who'd later become a cast member of the 1962 *Our Man Higgins*). But her movie studio wouldn't let her do the TV version, so Verdugo won the part (and, in fact, eventually took over the radio role as well before it went off the air in 1954). Earl Ross had also played the boss on radio, but was replaced by Roland Winters (who'd go on to play the Smothers Brothers' publisher boss on their 1965 sitcom). In March of 1956, CBS had Millie meet her maker.

My Friend Irma

My Friend Irma

This show had two formats during the two seasons (1952–1954) it was on CBS. Irma Peterson (Marie Wilson) lives at Mrs. O'Reilly's (Gloria Gordon) Boarding House, 185 West 73rd St., Apartment 3-B, in New York. Irma—a dumb but beautiful blonde secretary—lives with Jane Stacey (Cathy Lewis), a levelheaded secretary who's constantly bothered by Irma's scatterbrained antics.

The show revolves around their romantic heart-throbs: Irma and her boyfriend, the poor and jobless Al (Sid Tomack), a con artist who calls her "Chicken." He sees Irma only as a means to further his crazy moneymak-

ing schemes. Jane's boyfriend is her multimillionaire boss Richard Rhinelander III (Brooks West, Eve Arden's husband), an investment counselor whom Jane wants to impress and marry. Jane often speaks directly to the camera and establishes scenes, a narrative device that was carried over from the show's radio roots.

During the opening curtain speech of the second season, Irma informed viewers that Jane had been transferred to Panama, and that she's acquired a new roommate, Kay Foster (Mary Shipp), a newspaperwoman, whom Irma found by placing an ad in the classified section of the newspaper. Stories also revolved around a later boyfriend, Joe Vance (Hal March), and Irma's dumb schemes to help others. John Carradine played the neighbor and Margaret Dumont (of Marx Brothers movie fame) played Rich Rhinelander's socialite mother. *My Friend Irma* was the first show to be broadcast from the new CBS Television Center in Hollywood.

My Hero

For one season on NBC, Bob Cummings—soon to become the love-object on *Love That Bob*—played Robert S. Beanblossom, a carefree and easygoing real estate salesman who worked at the Thackery Realty Company in LA, got in jams, but always made the sale. His secretary, Julie Marshall, was played by Julie Bishop; John Litel was the big boss Willis Thackery, who often took his wrath out on Beanblossom. The show was also called *The Robert Cummings Show*.

My Son Jeep

Not to be confused with *My Mother the Car*, this sitcom was an ABC summer replacement all about Doc Allison (Jeffrey Lynn) and his attempts to get his life back together after the death of his wife. All episodes centered around the antics of his ten-year-old son, Jeep (Martin Huston), who was a person, not a vehicle. This show was not a great vehicle for anyone involved.

1953–1954

Colonel Flack

Make Room for Daddy/The Danny Thomas Show

Topper

OFF-SCREEN

9/13 Election of Khrushchev as First Secretary of Soviet Communist party Central Committee reported.

10/5 Yankees win fifth series in row, defeating Brooklyn Dodgers.

10/30 Nobel Peace prizes announced for George C. Marshall (1953) and Albert Schweitzer (1952).

1/3 Fourteen major companies announce formation of tobacco industry committee to investigate charges that cigarette smoking contributes to lung cancer.

2/2 Ike confirms in report to Congress that US had produced first full-scale thermonuclear (H-bomb) explosion at Eniwetok in 1952.

2/23 Inoculation of school children with Jonas Salk's antipolio serum begins in Pittsburgh.

3/10 Ike states at press conference that US wouldn't get involved in war in Indochina unless Congress authorized declaration of war.

4/1 Senate votes 57-28 to grant statehood to both Alaska and Hawaii simultaneously.

4/22 Army-McCarthy hearings begin.

5/29 Pope Pius X (d.1914) canonized in Rome by Pius XII.

FRONT RUNNERS

MAKE ROOM FOR DADDY/ THE DANNY THOMAS SHOW

You should be a very happy woman—you're beautiful, you got a nice home, three great kids, a husband who adores you. That oughta be enough for any gal.
—DANNY WILLIAMS to his wife, Kathy

Make Room for Daddy was one of the first sitcoms about a father who wasn't stupid. Danny Williams—played by Danny Thomas—was a nightclub entertainer, but he was just like everyone else. Danny Thomas was such a warm and endearing performer that he managed to inject his small-screen alter ego with the same dimensions. Without Thomas' sarcasm, vulnerability, self-mockery, insecurity, and hot-fuse temper, the show would have collapsed. Instead, it inflated and the balloon took off—not to come down for eleven years.

Format One (1953–1957)

Danny Williams	Danny Thomas
Margaret Williams	Jean Hagen
Teresa Williams (Terry)	Sherry Jackson
Russell Williams (Rusty)	Rusty Hamer
Louise, their maid	Amanda Randolph
Jesse Leeds, Danny's agent	Jesse White
Elizabeth Margaret O'Neal (Liz), Danny's press agent	Mary Wickes
Ben Lessy, Danny's piano player	Himself
Frank Jenks, Danny's tailor	Himself
Phil Arnold, Danny's agent (later episodes)	Horace McMahon
Charlie Helper, the owner of the Copa Club	Sid Melton
Williams family dog, a terrier:	Laddie

Format Two (1957–1964)

Danny Williams	Danny Thomas
Kathy Williams (also referred to by the maiden name, Kathleen Daly)	Marjorie Lord
Terry Williams	Sherry Jackson, Penny Parker
Rusty Williams	Rusty Hamer
Patty Williams (O'Hara)	Lelani Sorenson
Linda Williams	Angela Cartwright
Louise, their maid	Amanda Randolph
Elizabeth Margaret O'Neal	Mary Wickes
Charlie Helper	Sid Melton
Bunny Helper, Charlie's wife	Pat Carroll
Phil Arnold, Danny's agent	Sheldon Leonard
Uncle Tonoose, the head of the Williams family	Hans Conried
Pat Hannegan, comedian, Terry's boyfriend; then husband (1960)	Pat Harrington, Jr.
Harry Ruby, Danny's songwriter	Himself
Gina Minelli, Italian exchange student living with the Williamses	Annette Funicello
Piccola Pupa, a young Italian singer discovered by Danny	Herself
Buck, Gina's boyfriend	Richard Tyler
Jose Jiminez, the elevator operator	Bill Dana
Alfie, a Copa Club waiter	Bernard Fox
Mr. Heckendorn, the building landlord	Gale Gordon
Mr. Svenson, the building janitor	John Qualen
Mr. Daly, Kathy's father	William Demarest

The premiere episode of the show—aired on ABC on September 29, 1953—was titled "Uncle Daddy," and set the pace for the next eleven years of the program.

Danny Williams is headlining at the Café Paree in Chicago. He gets a rousing hand as he finishes a song. (To show how good he is, the camera zooms in on a couple, clapping wildly and nodding approvingly to one another.) Then he launches into his routine. He lives in New York and hasn't seen his wife and kids in three months. "My wife doesn't work—she just has babies. I haven't seen 'em so long—my kids call me Uncle Daddy!" This gets a big laugh from the café and studio audience (we can, in fact, hear the inimitable guffaw of Desi Arnaz, who produced the series).

Finally, he is home on vacation—in Apartment 803. But no one is there. Finally the family returns. His wife tells him to wipe his feet. The dog barks at him. His kids play with their toys. All of the presents he's bought for them are too small. The phone rings. He has to leave unexpectedly for Vegas the next morning to fill in for an ailing headliner. The kids are full of smartalec remarks. Suddenly the house is filled with tailors and jokewriters and songwriters and Danny gives all his attention to them. Finally his wife, Margaret, interrupts: "I haven't seen my husband in three months and tomorrow he's leaving. Give a girl a break."

She seduces him (in a very 1953 on-screen manner) to cancel the engagement. They sing and kiss until their daughter comes in. "Where's the peanut butter?" she interrupts. He and Margaret decide to go away the next day.

DANNY: We're going to Atlantic City tomorrow.
RUSTY: Why?
DANNY: Well, it's been a long time since I've had salt water taffy.

But his daughter Terry wants him to stay home and participate in her school show, reciting "The Children's Hour" by Longfellow. Danny thinks it's "dumb and silly" to read that to kids and, anyway, he wants to go away.

Margaret speaks: "This is home and these are your kids and they need more than a pat on the head and an armload of toys." He stays. But he won't do the show. "But our friends don't believe I have a father. They think I was hatched." Okay, okay, he'll do the show.

On stage in front of the class, he comes off very Vegas, high-powered and busily show-bizzy. The class stares at him blankly.

"Mommy," Terry says, "Daddy's laying an egg."

"No, dear, an omelette."

Danny switches tacks. "A funny thing happened on the way to recess. . . ." Still no laughs. So, in desperation, he recites the Longfellow poem, and suddenly—but of course—the kids sit up and listen.

The next day Danny announces to his family that he's booked the honeymoon suite—"finally"—in Atlantic City—but his son Rusty informs him that he's booked him for his class show. The end—and theme song—an uptempoed "Danny Boy"—lilts over the credits.

Not a particularly amusing episode, but it illustrates the foundation upon which the show was built. As Danny Thomas said when he made the first show: "It's about the private life of a man who has no private life."

But as the series went on, it became more sophisticated (it was, after all, about show business) and the kids grew into real New York kids.

DANNY: Let's play horsey.
TERRY: Okay, Daddy. Here's two dollars—put it on Count Flash in the seventh.

The fifties was the era of Togetherness. *McCall's* Magazine came out with a famous special that heralded Family Togetherness. Danny Williams strove for that togetherness, but never seemed to make it. His family was together, but he was separate. Our families all strove for closeness back then, and it was heartening to see that Danny Williams had as much difficulty as we did.

Girl Scouts: Guests Katie Sweet and Buddy Hackett

The Williamses were different from their TV neighbors. Danny was often the target of a three-person attack by his wife and children. The show's formula was domestic discord and then sentimental reconciliation. And the children were brats, snotty kids who were quick with their wise remarks and—like the rest of us—were easily bought off, as in this exchange:

MARGARET: Victor is not just a hairdresser. He's an artist. Haven't you noticed what he's done with my hair?
DANNY: It looks the same to me.
MARGARET: Everbody talks about it. They say it's never looked lovelier. People say to me, "Margaret, I've never seen your hair so beautiful."
DANNY: Name me one people who said that. (*Terry enters from the living room.*) Hi, sweetheart.
TERRY: Mother!
MARGARET: What?
TERRY: I've never seen your hair looking so beautiful.
(*Rusty walks in.*)
RUSTY: Mother, I've never seen your hair looking so lovely.

MARGARET: Thank you, thank you very much.
RUSTY: It's a regular knockout.
MARGARET: That's sweet of you to say so. Run along, dear.
RUSTY: No, really, I've never seen your hair look so lovely.
(*Margaret looks uncomfortable at this.*)
MARGARET: Run along, dear. Help your sister set the table.
(*Terry enters.*)
TERRY: Mother, I just can't get over the way your hair looks. It's beautiful.
RUSTY: Yeah, it's so chic.
DANNY: All right. All right. That's enough. Now, what's with this hair routine?
RUSTY: Haven't you tried to swing it yet, Mother?
DANNY: If there's going to be any swinging, I'm the one that's going to do it. All right, kids, get lost. I want to talk to your mother.
RUSTY: Do you think you can handle this alone, Mother?
MARGARET: I have a feeling I should have handled it

Portrait (from left): Rusty Hamer, Angela Cartwright, Danny Thomas, Marjorie Lord and (top) Sherry Jackson

alone from the beginning. You overplayed your parts.

TERRY: What did you expect for fifty cents—Lunt and Fontanne?

MARGARET: Get lost!

Jean Hagen was wonderful as Margaret. Her delivery was broad, her comedy sharp, and she'd dig at Danny and cut him down to size. She was best known for her 1952 Oscar-winning role of the screechy-voiced silent star in *Singin' in the Rain*. In those black-and-white days, the New York *Herald Tribune* television critic described Hagen as "a pretty young woman with reddish-blonde hair that will be sensational in color television."

She thought her role on *Make Room for Daddy* was "thankless." She felt she played fourth fiddle to Danny Thomas and the two kids. Even though she received 7 percent of the series' profits and was nominated for Emmies in 1954 and 1955, after three seasons, she quit.

The producers didn't know quite what to do. Divorce was out of the question on television. They could have just replaced Hagen with another Margaret. They decided, instead, to kill her off.

When Hagen left the show, a wet-eyed Danny Williams explained to his kids that "Mommy has gone to heaven." That was the end of Jean Hagen . . . and of the 1955 season.

The following year, 1956–1957, the program got a new name: *The Danny Thomas Show*. In the last four episodes, widower Williams met Kathy O'Hara, a pretty Irish widow with soft red hair and slate-blue eyes. By the next fall they were married. (They would have been married sooner, but Marjorie Lord was superstitious and wanted to wait until the following season because she was already getting married off-screen that year; she thought "two weddings" in one year was bad luck.) Marjorie Lord was insecure and paranoid, given to walking off the set crying. Her Kathy, unlike Margaret, didn't bark at Danny—she just teased him. His Lebanese personality contrasted with her fiery Irish temperament.

There were other changes as well. Sherry Jackson left the show to "go off to school." She was replaced by Kathy's young daughter Linda (Angela Cartwright), who inherited Terry's sarcasm. Seven-year-old Angela, with her bobbing pony tail, had to be conned into crying with threats that she wouldn't get the pony she had been dreaming of. Before her *Danny Thomas* stint, she'd been in MGM's *Somebody Up There Likes Me*. As Linda, she got 200 fan letters a week and, at one time, had more than 100 fan clubs in the U.S.

In 1957, *The Danny Thomas Show* was transplanted to CBS, where it played out its long run.

Show biz was a recurring theme of the show—not with Danny Williams so much but with his two wives. Three examples:

☐ Margaret, catching Danny's act at a nightclub, draws an accidental laugh from his audience and promptly envisions herself a potential star. Danny isn't

At the Copa: Sid Melton, Pat Carroll

amused. A theatrical agent persuades her to accept a one-night engagement in Altoona, Pennsylvania. She buys a dress for $150; her salary is $30. ☐

☐ Four years later, Kathy—who had once sung with a band—gets the show biz bug. She confides in her kids that she plans to return to her career and asks Rusty not to tell anyone.

RUSTY: I don't know, Kathy. I'd like to keep your secret, but you know what a blabbermouth I am. Of course, fifty cents might unblab me. *(no reaction)* Thirty-five . . . thirty . . . twenty-five, and that's my last bribe. But that's just for today. Tomorrow we have to renegotiate.

Finally, Kathy gets a gig at her daughter's school dance. Rusty gives it away, explaining: "My bribe ran out yesterday and you didn't pick up my option." Kathy tries to sing, but has a psychological block—"the Puckers"—in which she opens her mouth to sing and nothing comes out. She screams and runs offstage. ☐

☐ Things worked out better for Kathy in another episode where she decided to try a show business career.

DANNY: But you have no talent!

KATHY: *What?!*

DANNY: I didn't mean that! Don't get excited now. I just meant you have no theatrical talent.

KATHY: Well, let me tell you something, Mr. Smarty. You're skating on very thin ice. I haven't told you this before, but I've had offers to go into show business.
DANNY: To do what? Be the new Lassie? What offers have you had to go into show business? What a silly statement to make.
KATHY: I suppose you don't remember the party we went to with the people from the television agency last month?
DANNY: I remember it quite well, yes.
KATHY: Well, Stanley Cooper, the television producer, told me that I ought to be in television.
DANNY: Pure parlor talk, that's all.
KATHY: It was not parlor talk. You remember I was playing charades.
DANNY: I remember you playing charades.
KATHY: Well, when I acted out "see no evil, speak no evil," everyone was very impressed.
DANNY: How come nobody guessed it?

Danny dares her to try and attempts to teach her "a lesson." Using connections, he arranges a screen test for her in which Kathy is subjected to every physical inconvenience the director can concoct. Kathy catches on and is furious with Danny. She does land a small part in a television commercial, which inflates her ego and acting ambitions. We see Danny put on Kathy's apron, accepting defeat. □

Brother and Sister: Guests Joey Bishop and Marlo Thomas

The program was filmed before a studio audience of 400, and ran an hour with stops and starts. If they flubbed a scene, they would occasionally redo it. Danny Thomas felt he couldn't work without an audience and did the pretaping audience "warm-ups" himself with songs and routines.

Throughout the show, there were many memorable characters, now considered to be television "legends"; everyone's favorite was Danny's boisterous Uncle Tonoose (Hans Conried), from Toledo. Originally cast as the cousin of Danny Williams' first wife, he would arrive unexpectedly and check up on his favorite nephew. He was steeped in Lebanese tradition and took charge of everything.

The family's housekeeper was Louise (Amanda Randolph). The owner of the Copa, where Danny Williams performed, was a hyper Charley Helper (Sid Milton), who appeared more often than his wife, Bunny (Pat Carroll). Gale Gordon (veteran of *The Brothers*, *Our Miss Brooks* and, later, *The Lucy Show*) played Mr. Heckendorn, Danny Williams' complaining landlord. Jose Jiminez (Bill Dana) played the Latino elevator operator in Danny Williams' building ("My name ees Jose Jiminez"), and later got his own show. Sheldon Leonard (ex-movie heavy and television producer) played Phil Brokaw, yet another of Danny's agents. Jesse White—today the "lonely Maytag repairman"—played press agent and close friend "Uncle Jesse." Danny's piano accompanist was Benny (Ben Lessy).

Once, on a trip, Danny ran through a stop sign in an out-of-the-way rural Southern community. The town—Mayberry—and the sheriff—Andy Taylor—eventually became their own show: *The Andy Griffith Show*.

When Terry (Sherry Jackson) went overseas to college, they hired former Mouseketeer Annette Funicello to play Italian foreign exchange student Gina Minelli, who lived with the family. But then Terry returned (magically reappearing in the persona of actress Penney Parker). She immediately fell in love and was courted by a young comedian who was appearing on the same nightclub bill as her father. His name was Pat Hannigan—and Uncle Tonoose insisted they have a traditional Lebanese wedding. Hannigan was played by comic Pat Harrington, Jr., who had created the role of golf pro Guido Panzini on *The Jack Paar Show* (and would go on to play Schneider on *One Day at a Time*). Harrington, the *Danny Thomas Show* producers had hoped, would take over the show when Thomas eventually retired—but because the format lacked popularity with the viewers, that idea was dropped.

Retirement? For Danny Thomas? No way. But for Danny Williams—there was a way. "I'm tired of the grind," Thomas announced, and he stopped the show in 1964—after eleven years of high ratings. Thomas later tried two other shows (*Make Room for Granddaddy* and *The Practice*), but they didn't come near his success on the original. His daughter, Marlo, had luck with her show, *That Girl*.

of family show that was about realistic families—complete with cantankerous husbands and kvetching wives—people who had problems, kids who got in trouble, parents who got upset.

True, each week *The Danny Thomas Show* had a happy ending, but it got there through human humor and lifelike foibles. It brought reality to the small screen. It showed parents hollering at their kids and the kids yelling right back at them—just like we all did. And it gave a generation of mouthy kids an excuse that would last a lifetime: "But they do that on television. . . ."

Singing: Dinah, Danny, Marjorie

But for a trip back, *The Danny Thomas Show* is a wonderful vehicle. It has a veneer of age that makes it a period piece, good secondhand information about an era long gone. Even more than twenty-five years later—could it be that long?—the jokes are still sprightly, the acting is tight, the plot is believable. *Make Room for Daddy* made room—twenty years later—for a new style

TOPPER

THE SOCIALITES: When Henrietta Topper lures Cosmo into a bridge game with some dull guests, George and Marian Kirby, the gay ghosts, spookily stack the deck to save Topper from boredom and bankruptcy.
—from a 1953 TV listing

When Amos McCoy moved into his house, he found Pepino, a Mexican farmhand, living there. When Wilbur Post inhabited his home, he inherited a talking horse named Ed. Mrs. Muir found herself living with Captain Daniel Gregg. And when Cosmo Topper moved into his new house, he discovered it was haunted by two live-in (but blithe) spirits, George and Marian Kirby, who used to reside there before they died. Of the four choices, most people would go with the talking horse.

Cosmo Topper didn't have such luck (but what can you expect from someone named Cosmo?). His new home, with its three live-in ghosts (including a brandy-guzzling Saint Bernard named Neil)—who were killed in a Swiss avalanche on a skiing trip on their fifth wedding anniversary—became a haunted house, with doors opening arbitrarily and sofas floating around the room. And like Wilbur on *Mr. Ed*, no one could see or hear the Kirbys except Cosmo. Or, as the voice announced at the start of each show: "Anne Jeffreys as Marian Kirby, the ghostess with the mostess; Robert Sterling as George Kirby, that most sporting spirit; and Leo G. Carroll, host of said ghosts as Topper."

And that's *Topper*: a one-joke show with a loud laugh-track.

MARIAN (*upon seeing a man admire a woman*): What has she got that I haven't got?
GEORGE: Visibility.

Topper was TV's first fantasy sitcom. Based on two successful stories by Thorne Smith—*Topper* and *Topper Returns* from the early thirties—the TV series also has its roots in three Topper movies (also in the thirties), the first of which starred Cary Grant, Constance Bennett, and Roland Young (as Topper in all three), produced by Hal Roach, Sr.

In 1953, Topper took to the tube. With his wacked-out wife, Henrietta, and comical ghosts who used to sit on top of picture frames, *Topper* moved right into our homes. There we were, every week, looking at a small box with a glass screen, thinking how silly it was that Topper was seeing ghosts. What were we seeing as we looked at the magical flickering figures on the little screen—chopped liver?

The humor of the show came from the ghosts' unseen interaction with people of dubious character—fraudulent insurance salesmen, bad-taste interior decorators, snobby rich people, con men and crooks—and Topper himself. When Topper makes out his usual $5 pledge to the Alumni Fund, the Kirbys increase the pledge to $5,000 by adding a few zeros, and Cosmo is elected the school's Most Famous Old Grad. Neil (the dog) steals Topper's leather portfolio, containing his important bank papers. The Kirbys sabotage an important chess game. . . .

And on it went. Stuffy Topper was a terrific target for their schemes. He was a silly but likable middle-aged

Cosmo Topper	Leo G. Carroll
Marian Kirby	Anne Jeffreys
George Kirby	Robert Sterling
Henrietta Topper, Cosmo's wife	Lee Patrick
Mr. Schuyler, the bank president	Thurston Hall
Katie, the Toppers' maid	Kathleen Freeman (1953–1954)
Maggie, the cook	Edna Skinner (1954–1955)
Neil	Buck

man who was vice-president of the National Security Bank in New York. Leo G. Carroll played Topper, and the New York *Times* called his performance "in questionable taste" because he seemed to imitate the voice, manner and appearance of Roland Young, the movie's Topper, who had recently died. Seems that Young's ghost was haunting the new Topper. Jeffreys and Sterling—the husband-and-wife-ghosts—were married off-screen too.

The reviews were not terrific. Again the *Times*, unimpressed with the slapstick goings-on and the disappearing acts, said that "the evening's chief honors seemed to fall to the International Brotherhood of Electrical Workers." It wasn't so much electronics, though, that made the magic. When furniture floated around, it was wires that moved them. When George got Marian a cigarette, it was a tiny wire that wafted it to her lips. It was all done with mirrors—and a substance called ectoplasm which made the screen images appear invisible and made forms fade in and out. When a sofa seemed to be moving through a room and then—wham—George would suddenly be perched on it, it happened because the camera stopped and Sterling got in place, and then the camera started rolling again.

Many of us thought they were real ghosts and hoped that our own homes might be haunted by such lovable spirits instead of the real folks who lived with us. Especially beloved was Neil, the alcoholic Saint Bernard (he drank—not brandy—but something called "attar of beef marrow" from that lifesaving container around his furry neck). Weighing in at 165 pounds, he was billed by the show's producers as the grandson of the canine who costarred with Clark Gable in *Call of the Wild*. Whatever his theatrical roots, he rehearsed each scene three or four times and seemed to enjoy wearing an ice bag on his head for those weekly hangovers. Once the ghosts were giving Neil an invisible bath in the backyard. Emotional and naive Henrietta saw all the water splashing around (she couldn't see the ghosts or the dog) and beckoned Topper who—used to always quickly coming up with some explanation—described the situation as "our new sprinkling system." Later:

MARIAN: He's got fleas.
TOPPER: Fleas don't live on dead dogs.
MARIAN: They're dead fleas.

Topper itself seemed to do some quick disappearing acts on the air and, during its four-year run, appeared on all three national networks.

In March 1953, a pilot was made of the show and was quickly sold to the R. J. Reynolds Co., which aired it on CBS, Friday nights at 8:30. It became a hit—one of CBS's highest ratings for that time period. During the second season, Reynolds sold half of the sponsorship to Procter and Gamble, but Reynolds backed out and went with another program instead. In 1955, the series was

Cosmo and Henrietta: Leo G. Carroll, Lee Patrick

sold to Standard Brands and telecast at 7:30 P.M., Mondays, on ABC. *Topper* hit NBC the next year when it was sold to General Foods as a replacement for *Lives of the Bengal Lancers* on Sunday nights at 7. Later that year it bounced back to NBC, and in 1957 was put out to pasture—into the meadows of syndication.

Today *Topper* looks old and dark and dated—a true period piece of a period piece (fifties sitcom masqueraded as thirties screwball comedy). There is a musty quality to the program, like an old faded print of a movie. Other shows of the era twenty-five years ago—*Danny Thomas*, say, or *Bilko*—do not have that patina of age that hasn't worn well. *Topper* appears to have been darkly filmed, as if the Toppers' drapes were always drawn.

But still . . . the magic shines through in the persons of Marian and George. They were every kid's fantasy (they were invisible and could get away with anything). In a way, they saved Topper—they were the children he never had. They were the only ones on the program who had any sense of humor or zest for life—yes, *life*, even though they were dead (they had no zest for death). They seemed to take the helpless Topper in on their identity simply because they wanted to have some fun and because he seemed to be a "decent sort," as Topper himself might have said. Without the Kirbys, Topper's life was boring. Certainly his marriage to Henrietta was no fun; you could tell by the way he always kissed her on the cheek, sideways, without his lips ever touching her. Hardly a hot romance. Why didn't they undraw the drapes and look at each other?

A favorite *Topper* episode is one in which Marian wants to celebrate her birthday in grand style in Topper's house. Henrietta is in the hospital, so Marian picks a date, thinking that all is clear. She and George send out invitations to all their old living friends and sign Topper's name. The guests—who can't see George or Marian—arrive to Topper's surprise. The women start making a fuss over Cosmo, who goes along with the party but looks perplexed. Of course, Henrietta returns from the hospital unexpectedly and finds her husband entertaining a big drinking crowd.

George and Marian are naughty—they poke fun at sham, they continually tease and cajole, and they are constantly unbuttoning somebody's stuffed shirt. They have nothing to lose—such as their lives—and so they aren't afraid to do anything. That's why we like them so much—they're immortal because they're already dead, and therefore immune to the distresses, fears, and anxieties that we have to live with. "Death's not so bad," they seem to whisper to us. And they might be right. Not nearly so bad as cancellation.

In the Beginning: Marian, George and Neil get killed in an avalanche

ALSO RANS

Bonino

Babbo Bonino (played by basso Ezio Pinza) realizes one day that, as a busy opera singer, he has been giving dismal performances in the role of father (shades of Danny Thomas . . .). Son Andrew (Van Dyke Parks . . . later a cult-figure rock singer) and his seven brothers and sisters are motherless. Not wanting them to feel orphaned altogether, Bonino suddenly abandons his career and becomes a full-time father, much to the chagrin of his manager and his valet. The problems which followed this decision were the basis of this one-season live NBC series. Pinza sang one song on each episode of the show—before its swan song.

Colonel Flack

Retired Colonel Humphrey Flack (B-movie actor Alan Mowbray) and his partner in crime Uthas P. Garvey, also known as Patsy (Frank Jenks), teamed up to play modern-day Robin Hoods around the world. Conning the con men wherever they found them, the two men change their clever tactics as often as they change locales, giving their proceeds to the needy as they gave a few laughs to

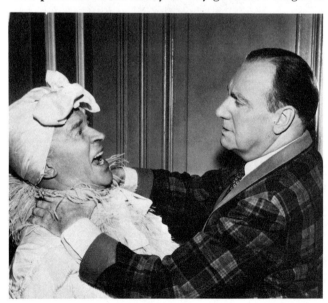

Colonel Flack *(from left)*: Frank Jenks, Alan Mowbray

the rest of us. Appropriately, the show itself ran through several aliases—*Colonel Humphrey Flack*, *Fabulous Fraud*, and *The Impostor*. Whatever its names, though, it was shown live on the DuMont network, and then filmed for syndication in 1958. The show was based on a series of *Saturday Evening Post* articles.

The Duke

Duke London (Paul Gilbert) firmly believes that old fighters never die—they just move on to ritzier rings. Suddenly discovering a love of the arts, the prizefighter opens a nightclub with his friend Rudy Cromwell (Claude Stroud). But there at ringside is Duke's old trainer, Johnny (Allen Jenkins, later cabdriver Al on the 1956 sitcom *Hey Jeannie!*) who wants Duke to box again, as does fight promoter Sam Morco (Sheldon Leonard, who went on to play one of Danny's several agents on *Make Room for Daddy*, and to produce *The Dick Van Dyke Show*, among others. In 1975, he played the title role in the short-lived *Big Eddie*). Anyway, Duke finds himself lined up for a new fight as he struggles each week to foil Johnny's schemes to get him back in the ring. NBC settled the question after three months—by throwing them both off the air.

Jamie

Jamison John Francis McHummer—Jamie (played by child star Brandon De Wilde)—was an orphan who came to live with his relatives (by way of ABC) after the death of his parents. The series focused around his relationship with his grandfather (Ernest Truex—better remembered as Mr. Remington on *Mr. Peepers*). Also on the show: Kathleen Nolan (later Kate McCoy on *The Real McCoys*) as cousin Liz McHummer. *Jamie* ran for two seasons.

But the Brandon De Wilde story is much more interesting than the Jamie saga. De Wilde—hot off his eight-year-old success in Broadway's *The Member of the Wedding*—started off to sitcomland to star in his own sitcom, *Jamie*, a weekly live series. There was much concern for the eleven-year-old De Wilde (a kid being totally immersed in a grown-up business, etc.), and his parents drew up a special contract that he could exit the show any time he wanted to, or if his parents thought the show was wrecking his emotional health. Two weeks into the second season, De Wilde was pulled off the show—in a business dispute between the network and the sponsor. They tried to relocate the show to another time slot, but it didn't work. Footnote: De Wilde—who was never able to sustain the success he had as a child star—died at age thirty in a car accident in 1972.

Life With Elizabeth

Long before she played bittersweet Sue Ann Nivens on *The Mary Tyler Moore Show*, Betty White starred as Elizabeth White, a sweet-sweet young married. She and her TV husband, Alvin (Del Moore), played a San Francisco couple trying to survive the first difficult years of marriage. In 1955, the DuMont Network canceled both their marriage and this show.

Life With Father

This double period piece—*from* the fifties *about* the turn-of-the-century—was all about the Day family, who lived on West 48th St. in New York. Head of the family was stern-but-fair Clarence Day (Leon Ames) a Victorian Wall Street banker. His wife, Vinnie (Lurene Tuttle), took care of their redheaded children: Clarence, Jr. (played first by Ralph Reed, later by Steve Terrell),

Life With Father: *Leon Ames and the Day clan*

Whitney (Ronald Keith first, then B. G. Norman, then Freddy Ridgeway), John (first Freddie Leiston, then Malcolm Cossell) and Harlan (Harvey Grant). It was based on the long-running Broadway play by Lindsay and Crouse, which was based on the book about his own family by Clarence Day. The sitcom version ran on CBS through the 1954–1955 season. It was the first live color network series airing from Hollywood.

Marge and Jeff

This one—a daily fifteen-minute broadcast over the now-defunct DuMont Network—ran one year and starred Marge Greene and Jeff Cain as newlyweds in New York. Also in the show: a cocker spaniel named Paisley. Strange-but-true: Cain changed his first name from Jess to Jeff so his name would be the same as the character he played.

The Marriage

Jessica Tandy and Hume Cronyn—Hot Shots on the American Theater Scene—went Sitcom in this summer show (actually, Hume and Jessica had done the same show on radio until earlier that year). In this live show (one of the first network series to be telecast in color), he was New York lawyer Ben Marriott, and she was his housewife, Liz (the Cronyns were married in Real Life as well). She had had a job before (as a department store buyer) and she got antsy—so she'd get involved in all sorts of Projects (including their two children: ten-year-old Pete (Malcolm Broderick) and fifteen-year-old Emily (Susan Strasberg, daughter of Lee Strasberg, head of the Actors Studio). NBC sent the Tandy-Cronyn's back to Broadway after a month.

Meet Mr. McNulty/The Ray Milland Show

This show had two formats, both starring Ray Milland as Professor Ray McNulty, an English professor. For the first season, he taught at Lynnhaven, an all-girls' college (as they were called back then; today they are all-women's colleges). For the second season, he got a new school: coeducational Comstock College in LA—and a name change to *The Ray Milland Show*. Phyllis Avery starred as his wife, Peggy. In 1955, CBS expelled the show.

My Favorite Husband

Lucille Ball starred in this one on the radio in 1948 (the networks wanted her to star in it on TV too, but she said no unless husband Desi could be in it too; producers would not take him seriously as a young American bank executive so she went off and started her own sitcom—something called *I Love Lucy*). Anyway, on TV, Joan Caulfield played Liz Cooper, a beautiful but scatterbrained wife. She is married to George (Barry Nelson) and, once again, they have a lot of "trials and tribulations," as the CBS network press releases liked to call them. Also in the cast: Bob Sweeney as Gilmore Cobb, a neighbor who is a peanut manufacturer (who did not run for President) and his snobby wife, Myra. During the second season, Vanessa Brown stepped into the role of Liz (complete with new next-door neighbors). The show ran until September 1957.

Pride of the Family

Paul Hartman and Fay Wray (of *King Kong* fame) and Natalie Wood—that's right: Natalie Wood—starred in this ABC sitcom that was also known as *The Paul Hartman Show*. (It was also known as unsuccessful; the network gave it the ax after one season.) It was all about the Morrison family: Albie (Hartman), the advertising head of a small-town newspaper; his wife, Catherine (Fay Wray), their teenage daughter Ann (Natalie) and son Albie, Jr. (Bobby Hyatt). Like so many TV daddies of the era, Albie bumbled and fumbled and, though well-intentioned, made a mess of everything he got involved in. Somehow, his wife and kids loved him all the same.

Take It from Me

This one—a.k.a. *The Jean Carroll Show*—starred that stand-up comedienne as an "average American housewife," living in The Bronx. Others in the cast: Alan Carney as her bumbling husband; Lynn Loring as their daughter; Alice Pearce (eleven years later to become Gladys Kravitz on *Bewitched*) as their neighbor. Each episode began with one of Carroll's monologues, and she made continual comic asides to the viewer during the course of each episode (which often consisted of her trying to trick hubby Herb). Two months later, they moved out of the neighborhood, courtesy of ABC.

Where's Raymond?

This was possibly TV's first—and last—musical sitcom. Its title was a play on *Where's Charley?*, Ray Bolger's big Broadway hit. And singer-dancer Bolger starred in this one too (also called *The Ray Bolger Show*), all about a song-and-dance man in Pelham, New York, who was called Raymond Wallace. He had a girlfriend Susan (Margie Millar) and a partner Peter Morrisey (Richard Erdman). Verna Felton (Hilda Crocker in both *December Bride* and *Pete and Gladys*) played—are you ready for this—his understudy's wife's mother. Poor Ray—he always got to the theater at the last minute (that was the show's premise, but Bolger got to sing and dance a lot).

The next season, Ray apparently got amnesia, because he'd forgotten about the first season. He was still a Broadway Star, but now in love with a girl from Iowa who wanted to be a writer. Plus, Ray had new friends and foibles. The show ran on ABC until June of 1955.

1954–1955

December Bride

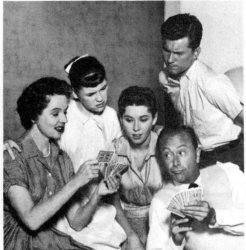
Father Knows Best

Love That Bob

OFF-SCREEN

9/7 FCC orders TV and radio stations to give equal treatment to all legally qualified opponents for public office.
10/2 NY Giants beat Cleveland Indians to win Series in four games.
10/7 Contralto Marian Anderson becomes first black engaged by Metropolitan Opera.
10/18 US Air Force announces production of first US supersonic bomber (B-58).
10/28 Nobel prize for literature goes to Ernest Hemingway.
11/3 Linus Pauling of California Technical Institute wins Nobel prize for chemistry.
12/9 Lawrence (Yogi) Berra of Yankees named MVP in American League in poll of Baseball Writers Association of America; Willie Mays of Giants voted MVP in National League.
12/16 USSR threatens to break off diplomatic relations with France.
12/20 USSR threatens to break off diplomatic relations with Britain.
4/6 Churchill resigns.

1954—1955

FRONT RUNNERS

DECEMBER BRIDE

*This show makes every dame over forty-five think she's
still desirable.*

—producer of *December Bride*

Besides their own two children, Lucille Ball and Desi
Arnaz—a.k.a. Desilu—produced a lot of offspring: *The
Danny Thomas Show, Our Miss Brooks*—and this vener-
able family program: *December Bride*. It was a one-joke
show—the old mother-in-law cliché turned inside out—
and audiences loved it because it was funny and, more
importantly, because it directly followed *I Love Lucy*
each week. What more could any program ask for?

They made 154 episodes of the show—all about a
sweet fluttery old lady who moves in with her daughter
and son-in-law. In a way, Lily Ruskin (as she was called)
was a video Mary Worth—she was always on some do-
good project—meddling and managing—saving the marriage of a wrestler and his wife (in about ten minutes),
rescuing her son-in-law from some financial disaster, or
just tying up some loose ends that she and her crony
Hilda helped untie. She was a nice lady.

No, *nice* is an understatement. Lily was the perfect
old person. She was never sick. She never complained
about anything. She was self-sufficient. She was always
cheerful. She was more openminded than her children
and she loved trying new things. She adored a good
adventure. Lily was a young kid in old person's drag. She
was never a burden. She was bubbly and sweet and
nurturing and a lot of fun. So was the program.

To add a balance to all that wonderfulness, the
producers wisely drew two more characters: cynical
neighbor Pete Porter, said nasty things about his wife
Gladys, and wasn't especially wild about mothers-in-
law—especially his own. "When my mother-in-law was in
San Diego, she walked out on the pier and the fleet
refused to come in." Wisecracking Hilda Crocker was

Lily's willing accomplice (i.e., her "Ethel") and when
they plotted a new scheme, they would lock arms and
dance a spirited jig. Hilda was interested in snaring a rich
husband, and her lines often set the laugh-track going at
top volume.

December Bride debuted on October 4, 1954—but
that was its second incarnation. With Spring Byington at
the helm, *December Bride* had first been a successful
radio series in the early fifties. Comedy writer Parke
Levy had created the show and based it on his own
mother-in-law. Before that, he had worked on *The Joe
Penner Show* and *My Friend Irma* on TV. But he ran into
trouble with the networks: nobody wanted Spring Byington to repeat her original role as Lily.

It's hard to believe now. Born in 1893, Byington had
been acting since high school, where she set up a theater
company on inheritance money from her father and
toured mining camps in Colorado, where she grew up.
She appeared in several Broadway shows, and made
many movies, including the 1935 *Mutiny on the Bounty,
Jezebel* (1938), and *You Can't Take It With You* (1938).
Sweet and gentle Lily Ruskin was a role made for her. To
not let Spring Byington play Lily Ruskin was almost like
having someone other than Ozzie play Ozzie. Unthinka-
ble.

Unsinkable, Levy took his idea to Desi Arnaz, who
was having quite a success with *I Love Lucy*. Desi
shrugged and told Levy: "I think Spring would be great
in it." And that was that.

And so they started casting. As Lily's daughter, Ruth
Henshaw, they found Frances Rafferty, a redhead who
had done some pictures at MGM (she was the sister of

Lily Ruskin	Spring Byington
Matt Henshaw	Dean Miller
Ruth Henshaw	Frances Rafferty
Hilda Crocker, Lily's Friend	Verna Felton
Pete Porter, the Henshaws' next-door neighbor	Harry Morgan

Age Before . . .: Verna Felton eyes chorine Joi Lansing.

Max Rafferty, a right-wing California politician). Ruth's husband, Matt, was played by Dean Miller, considered by the press to be a "second-rate Cary Grant." Verna Felton, a leading radio and movie comedienne, played Lily's best friend and neighbor, Hilda. Harry Morgan, a top character actor and comedian, played caustic Pete. And they were ready to roll.

An early episode was called "The Texas Show," and showed all the characters interacting in a typical manner.

Pete—an amateur magician—walks in carrying a padlock, chains, and a straitjacket—"symbols of my seven-year marriage," he tells Lily, who twitters. She is incredibly sweet and wide-eyed, with a voice like a bird. She wears her hair in curls behind her head. She announces that she has met a "handsome Texas millionaire," Bill Jeffries (Lyle Talbot), who's loud, pretty obnoxious and is, he has told her, "in the oil business." Also, he has given Lily a costly diamond. *And* he wants her to invest money in his oil company. "I want to do nice things for you," he says, but nobody—except Lily—believes he's for real. And so, she invests $1,000 in a new oil well.

The family assumes that this man—who has taken her out six nights in a row and sent her forty pounds of chocolate one morning—is a deadbeat. Says Pete: "Mrs. Ruskin, you have just made the worst investment since I paid two bucks for a marriage license."

Matt and Pete, unbeknownst to anyone, go to pay a little visit on Mr. Jeffries. After they retrieve Lily's check, Pete informs him that "it's guys like you that give crooks a bad name."

Hilda—dressed in a wild hat and a black dress—comes zooming in the next morning with a newspaper article. "Lily, you struck oil! Beautiful, black, gooey, smelly oil!" In fact, she announces, Jeffries has called the new well "The Lily Ruskin."

When Lily finds out that Matt rescued her check and lost all her investment, she isn't mad. Instead, she beams: "Oh, Matt, dear, you were just trying to help me. . . ."

Mr. Jeffries comes in and says that—of course—he had made out another $1,000 check and invested it in Lily's name, so all is well. He then invites them all to spend a couple of weeks with him in Texas. They accept.

Said Spring Byington: "Lily hasn't lost her appetite for life and is now free to do ridiculous things. She can play with life much more because she is mature of heart. She isn't stopped because other people aren't doing it. She drives to Mexico alone. If something appeals to the mature person, if there is really no cogent reason for not doing it—let us do it, let us not be bound by homebound convention." And Byington herself seemed to be much like Lily: "TV keeps me young because it keeps me busy, keeps my mind alert, my senses sharp and my interest up." Also her ratings.

Audiences adored the show and wrote love letters to Lily by the hundreds every day. (One episode, however, drew the viewers' wrath, as they wrote in to complain about a scene in which Frances Rafferty and Dean Miller were in their fifties' sitcom twin beds. He had gotten out of bed and had gone over to her, although he never touched her. "Keep the show out of the bedroom!" the letters roared.)

The show was a pleasant switch. The in-laws were not outlaws. There was a real warmth among the characters. But—still—it was sitcom, as these plot descriptions bear out:

☐ "Skid Row"—Lily Ruskin's family believes she has fallen under the spell of a bookmaker, and they contrive to keep her in the house "until the fever dies down." Believing Lily to be safely upstairs, they turn on the television set and see her during a news broadcast lined up with Skid Row characters at a soup kitchen. ☐

☐ "Wrestler Show"—Repentant over her various misadventures, Lily promises her family she will not meddle in other people's affairs in the future. Lily tries, but when a 200-pound singing wrestler with movie aspirations asks her to be his manager, it proves one challenge she cannot ignore. ☐

☐ "Family Quarrel"—Lily believes her family doesn't love her anymore, so she tries to get them to ask her to move out. She burns the food, ruins the laundry, and turns the house into a menagerie—but nothing works. ☐

☐ "Post Office Show"—Chaos occurs when Lily and Hilda try to retrieve a letter of resignation that Matt has written to his boss. Postal authorities get on their necks when the two women raid the mails. ☐

It was a nice show. Lily was a flower—sweet and

perfumed—and we could almost smell her in our living rooms. She was one of those TV people who never went to the bathroom. (Her friend Hilda definitely went.) How interesting, too, that someone named Spring had a show called *December Bride*.

When the show left the air after five years, *December Bride* had one of the most unusual afterlives of any sitcom—until *Mary Tyler Moore* started spinning off. For years, Pete had bemoaned his wife, Gladys, who had never appeared on camera. When *December Bride* was married off to obscurity, another show was created: *Pete and Gladys*, starring Morgan and Cara Williams. Gladys wasn't the nitwit Pete had made her out to be on *December Bride*, but together they were goofy enough to continue the screwball tradition for two seasons, joined by Verna Felton as a regular and Frances Rafferty as an irregular (Rafferty later concentrated her modest talents on TV commercials). Afterward, Harry Morgan appeared in *Dragnet* and achieved his biggest success playing Colonel Sherman Potter on *M*A*S*H*.

Leaving her own show at age sixty-six, Spring Byington made a pilot called *Here Comes Melinda*. It didn't sell. For two years, she appeared in the series

Without Gladys: Spring Byington, Pete and baby

Trick Photography: Frances Rafferty and guest Ed Wynn

Family Argument: Dean Miller threatens to leave Frances Rafferty

Fan Club: Lily and Hilda butter up guest Desi Arnaz after wrecking his rumpus room

Laramie and then free-lanced on other programs such as *Dennis the Menace*, *Blondie*, and *The Flying Nun*. She never repeated her tremendous success of *December Bride*, and to television audiences she will always be Lily Ruskin.

Sure, its laugh-track was too loud and its jokes were sometimes obvious and its situations were of the fill-in-the-blank variety. And they often had to resort to guest stars—Ed Wynn, Zsa Zsa Gabor, Rudy Vallee, Edgar Bergen, Rory Calhoun—to add zest to lifeless plots. But . . .

But it was the only sitcom in TV history to show an old person who wasn't decrepit and the object of either everyone's pity or jokes. We aren't so comfortable with old age in this country, and *December Bride*, smack-pat in the mid-fifties, marked the transition between the time the American family took in its aged, and now—when we put our old people—calling them Senior Citizens—in homes. True, Lily Ruskin was hardly convalescent, but even in black and white, we could clearly see that her hair was gray.

And then one day—just as we learned they would do—*December Bride* faded into January, and the networks came along and canceled the program.

FATHER KNOWS BEST

> BUD: *Hi, mom, I'm home.*
> MARGARET: *Is that you, Bud?*

There was an episode, a few years back, of *Marcus Welby, M.D.*—a dramatic doctor show—in which Jane Wyatt, who played a sick patient (Welby had only terminally sick patients; you never saw them past one episode), fell in love with Marcus, played by Robert Young. But when they saw each other for the first time, they didn't recognize each other. They didn't seem to remember that they had been married for eight years as Jim and Margaret Anderson, that they had lived at 607 South Maple St., in Springfield, USA, for all those years, that they had three perfect children together. How soon they forget. Were they pretending (Jane Wyatt was not a patient suffering from amnesia; that was the week before) or did they truly not remember? Or was it all a lie—all a joke—anyway? *Father Knows Best* was so real to us. Why wasn't it real to them?

Father Knows Best was the American Gothic of the fifties—with a pitchfork exchanged for a fishing rod and a Hoover Power-Vac hoovering somewhere in the background. It was the era of Family Togetherness, and *Father Knows Best* seemed to both epitomize and exploit the mood that prevailed throughout the country. Eisenhower was President and Robert Young was Father. They could have traded jobs at any time and no one would have noticed the difference.

Except the Hearns. They were a Real Life set of suburban parents, living outside of Milwaukee, who—like other Good Parents around the country—forced their daughter Susie (at allowance-point) to watch *Father Knows Best* every week. When the violin music would seep through the plotline at the end, they would weep through it. And each week Mrs. Hearn would turn to her daughter and say, "Susie, why can't you help make our family be like that?" To this day, Sue has a chemical aversion to Robert Young and Jane Wyatt.

Also to Billy Gray, Elinor Donahue, and Lauren Chapin, who played the three Anderson kids, James, Jr., Betty, and Kathy. Betty was also known as Princess; young Kathy's alias was Kitten. And James, Jr., was always called Bud. The way it should be.

When the show was a radio program in the early fifties, the title had been a joke; it originally had a question mark at the end, because this father wasn't supposed to have known any better than any of the other radio or TV fathers from Dagwood to Riley. The title was meant to be sarcastic. But the show didn't turn out that way. Robert Young—who used to play the nice guy in movies—played the nice guy in this series too, both on radio and TV. As Jim Anderson, manager of the General Insurance Company, he took out an emotional insurance policy on his family—insuring them against insecurity and an unhappy ending. So did a lot of fathers, but Young

Jim Anderson	Robert Young
Margaret Anderson	Jane Wyatt
Betty Anderson (Princess)	Elinor Donahue
Bud Anderson (James Anderson, Jr.)	Billy Gray
Kathy Anderson (Kitten)	Lauren Chapin
Miss Thomas, Jim's secretary	Sarah Selby
Claude Messner, Bud's friend	Jimmy Bates (1954–1959)
Kippy Watkins, Bud's girlfriend	Roberta Shore (1958–1959)
Ralph Little, Betty's boyfriend	Robert Chapman (1957–1958)
Ed Davis, the Andersons' neighbor	Robert Foulk (1955–1959)
Myrtle Davis, his wife	Vivi Jannis (1955–1959)
Dotty Snow, Betty's friend	Yvonne Lime (1954–1957)
Patty Davis, Kathy's friend	Tina Thompson; Reba Waters
April Adams, Bud's girlfriend	Sue George (1957–1958)
Burgess Vale, Kathy's boyfriend (later episodes)	Richard Eyer
Hubert Armstead, the high school principal	Sam Flint
Emily Vale, Margaret's friend	Lenore Kingston
Joe Phillips, Bud's friend	Peter Heisser

The Girls (from left): Elinor Donahue, Jane Wyatt, Lauren Chapin

was the only one who had his own sitcom and 25,000,000 people watching him do it each week.

America got to meet the Andersons on October 3, 1954, when CBS gave TV its first real father-figure. He was a superdaddy who could—and would—do anything. He made anyone who was feeling worse feel better. He was the ideal father—whether he was counseling Bud about running away from home, advising Betty about her prom plans, or chatting with Kathy about a school paper. (How strange that today it would be Bud and VD, Betty and her drug problem, and Kathy about her first period. But back then there was an innocence to television, a naiveté—not so much a reflection of the way things were, but a refraction. And declared in such a positive, that's-the-way-it-is way. Refractions with no retractions.) Daddy was never wrong.

Neither were the producers, obviously. *Father Knows Best* ran—trotted—forever, even though there were a few faulty steps at the beginning. In 1955, after two years on the air, CBS canceled the series. The public was outraged and, in one of the first examples of how you *can* talk back to your television, letters came pouring in asking for the show's reinstatement. And so NBC ran the program the next year. By 1958, it was back on CBS. In 1960, Young decided that he had "had enough," and that was the end of *Father Knows Best*.

The end? Hardly. You can still see it—and see it and see it—through various reruns all over the channels. And not just in this country; it's been dubbed into many languages. (In Japan, for example, one man reads everyone's voices—Jim's and Margaret's, Bud's and Kitten's.)

Along with Robert Young's Jim Anderson, it was the program's theme music that held it together. The lilting theme played confidently at the beginning of the show, then turned despairing as problems occurred, then took on a minor key as the show took on a typically mellow note at the end. "Recently," said one fan, "I saw some *Father Knows Bests* and found myself crying in the same places I had twenty years ago; my head knows better, but my heart didn't. It's the music; I am conditioned and programmed to react to it. I can hear its plaintive chords over the Muzak at the A & P, and there I am, sobbing in Produce."

The *New York Times*—which knows even better than Father—had this to say about the show when it debuted: "Robert Young and Jane Wyatt have restored parental prestige on TV." And it was true. Here was a show where the characters were not comic book zombies. Even though they constantly reaffirmed old values, they did carry with them a certain credibility. Mother Margaret was a perfect and dignified housekeeper. Jim Anderson was rational and wise and warm and understanding—and the first TV father you never laughed at, creating a new wave of TV fathers (which finally waved goodbye, with the seventies' advent of Archie Bunker and a slew of other Norman Lear daddies). Reviewing its competition today, it's no wonder that *Father Knows Best* was considered the most appealing and domestic sitcom on TV. Part of that was because the show never resorted to slapstick; it was often gooey, warm, and enragingly engaging—but it never gagged it up; the humor came directly from the story. Which is why some of the story lines appear just that: story lines.

Consider this one that ran in 1959—"Good Joke on Mom"—typical of the *Father Knows Best* syndrome:

Margaret is vacuuming (in heels and button earrings). It's been a bad day for her. She's had an argument with Kathy, who tells her she thinks Mom's ignorant. Then Jim walks in, mail in hand.

JIM: Doesn't anyone bring in the mail anymore?
MARGARET: Who has the time? By the time I've finished the dishes and picked up after all of you and repaired the vacuum cleaner which you broke again accidentally . . .

The phone rings in the middle of all this. Margaret is asked to be "chairman" of a building project in town.

JIM: They should know better than to throw all that responsibility on one small woman with no experience—it's pretty stupid.
MARGARET: To hear you people talk, you'd think I was the dumbest person in the world.
BETTY: No, it's nothing against you, Mom. It's the Women's Aid League—for making such an utterly stupid error.
MARGARET: I see.
JIM: Those women should realize that washing dishes, making beds, and cooking beans hardly qualifies a person as a building contractor.

Angry, Margaret takes the job, only to find out from her neighbor Myrtle that "All the work's been done; all you have to do is look pretty." You see, Margaret got the job because she's the most photogenic of the ladies in the League, and will look best in the newspaper pictures.

But Margaret is too embarrassed to tell her family that the job's just a ruse. So she and Myrtle cook up a scheme so she can fool her family into thinking she's really doing all the work. Myrtle calls and Margaret "talks to" the "contractor" and the "mayor." But it all falls through when, at a business luncheon, Jim meets the contractor, who has no idea who Margaret is.

Meanwhile, Kathy has written a report for school all about how her mother is doing all the work and giving orders to the mayor. And still, Margaret acts desperately and quietly, as she continues to cheat her family.

After school, Kathy gets in a fight with some kids who said that her mother is a fake. Finally, Margaret tries to admit to Kathy's friends that she is a fraud. She vacillates, stumbling and stammering her way through the explanation. Jim saves the day by going to a phone and making calls and stories to impress the schoolkids—that Margaret is important in the project. When the schoolchildren leave, Margaret is moved and crying—as are we, the viewers. She says to her family:

MARGARET: Oh, you knew what a fraud I was—what you people must think of me . . .
JIM: Mrs. Anderson, we think you're the importantest woman we've ever known (*violin music rises*), and even though you are the prettiest clinic builder in the world (*chuckle on laugh-track*), don't build anymore—we need you too much right here. . . . (*He smiles, she smiles, they embrace, the music comes up, and there is applause.*)

The series is loaded with object lessons. In fact, *Father Knows Best* was one of the first sitcoms to have a moral, a precedent that has been faithfully followed.

That same year (1960), Kathy had her own lie in a program episode entitled "Kathy's Big Deception." Short, chubby, awkward (but cute as hell, thanks to a pair of crinkly eyes), Kathy (who is twelve) needs a date for the picnic. All the other girls have boyfriends, but all Kathy has is a crush on a schoolboy named George. All this is explained while Mother is arranging flowers. Kathy wants romance in her seventh-grade life; everyone in the family is busy with their own lives (or flowers). The interaction between the kids is not smartass—just slightly irreverent. Kathy—now that Bud has grown up—is the misfit in the family. And everyone is concerned—especially Kathy. She rushes up to her room (the kids have their own rooms) and throws a TV tantrum as she looks into the mirror, sobbing: "I just hate you—you're ugly, fat, and stupid. Nobody likes you. You're just a big mess."

Kathy lets everyone assume that George—who doesn't give Kathy the time of day, much less a tumble—is her boyfriend, and that they are going to the picnic together. In a priceless sequence, in which Bud comes home and announces that George barely knows Kathy, we see the family's framed reactions: Father raises his eyebrows and purses his lips in his knowing-yet-unknowing expression; Margaret and Betty look at each other, concerned. Margaret says, "Kathy would never tell us anything that wasn't true." Kathy looks on, guilty.

On the day of the picnic—Kathy has told everyone that she's going with George—she is sobbing in her room as Bud comes to comfort her—to the accompaniment of violins stirring, of course. Bud tells Kathy how proud he is of her, and urges her to be honest. He is so understanding and supportive. They are all so understanding and supportive. It might be better for mental health to grow up in a family like the Andersons'—but it certainly seems to be boring.

Anyway, the doorbell rings and, of course, it is George; Bud has arranged the whole thing, to save Kathy's pride.

They do everything but write "THIS WEEK'S MORAL" in subtitles on the screen: Don't Lie (or Robert Young will find out . . .).

The basic premise of *Father Knows Best* is that one member of the family is always isolated from the rest—playing into the Number One American fear: rejection and resultant loneliness. Usually the plot revolves around something that's been misplaced—usually it's a value that's been lost and Daddy tries to put it back. But sometimes it's a school paper or a pocketbook. *Father Knows Best* is a self-righteous portrayal of a family, and there was always something smug about the Andersons—but it was really only that their family had better scripts than ours. For example, when Bud was feeling alienated, Father advised Betty to pretend to need him, to make him feel like a part of the family again. And so, when Bud had "run away," Betty called him: "Bud, could you spare the time to come over and fix my radio?" Bud came running back.

Today, the only running that Bud does is off the mouth. Billy Gray is now a race car driver and, after years of being Bud-the-misfit, he still has a lot to say about the program's detrimental effects on society.

Runaway: Jim stops Princess just in time.

All in the Family (from left): Billy Gray, Elinor Donahue, Lauren Chapin, Jane Wyatt, Robert Young

"I wish there was some way I could tell kids not to believe it—the dialogue, the situations, the characters— they were all totally false. The show did everybody a disservice. The girls were always trained to use their feminine wiles, to pretend to be helpless to attract men. The show contributed to a lot of problems between men and women that we see today.

"And it gave everyone a bad comparison with their own lives. People said to themselves, 'If my mother and father aren't like that, they must be really bad people.' I think we were all well motivated, but what we did was run a hoax. *Father Knows Best* purported to be a reasonable facsimile of life. And the bad thing is that the model is so deceitful. It usually revolved around not wanting to tell the truth, either out of embarrassment, or not wanting to hurt someone, or . . . Looked at from a certain slant, it's an incredibly destructive pattern for emulation. . . ."

Gray went on to talk about a certain episode he particularly remembers:

"Jim teaching Margaret how to drive, for example— an authentic, identifiable situation and source of real argument in many households, I'd imagine. When she fails to do everything just right, he becomes short-tempered and starts fuming—normal stuff. Then they get into almost a scream-out in the living room where we kids are all standing watching open-mouthed. They notice us and go through this little façade, or rather, wait. . . . Betty, my older sister, takes them off the hook, that's it. Evidently we'd never seen our parents argue before—our parents don't argue—which is pretty interesting. But Betty applauded and said, 'Oh, isn't that nice. You're making believe you're arguing, to show us what it would be like if we didn't have such wonderful parents who got along so well.' And they agreed. Later, Margaret

and Betty drive off and I'm standing with Jim and I say, 'Gee, you know I saw you guys arguing and it . . . Are you *sure* you weren't arguing?' I really put it to him, and he said, 'Nope.' Just looked me in the eye and fuckin' lied right at me. Now you might not think that's so awful, but a more helpful thing to say would have been, 'Everybody argues at times. It's not the end of the world. We don't enjoy it, but sometimes our frustrations outweigh our restraint and common sense, and we get carried away. It'll happen to you, too. We don't encourage it. We're not proud of it. But it happens.' That's a real approach to living."

But what about back then? "All along I protested. I was never able to change a word, though. The writers knew best. I tried to make the character as human as possible in my approaches and responses to things.

"I'm so ashamed that I had any part in it," Gray says—but obviously not too ashamed to appear in a 1976 *Father Knows Best* reunion—called, appropriately, *Father Knows Best Reunion*—in which the family was reunited for ninety minutes of insipidity. They didn't exactly update the program, but, in a way, froze the old values of the fifties and clothed them in seventies' drag.

A favorite *Father Knows Best* episode is one called "Betty's Double."

The show opens, of course, with Margaret, cleaning and vacuuming, this time in a little smock. She has sent Betty's picture in for the singing movie star Donna Stewart's Double Contest, and Betty has won. In fact, Betty and Donna (both played by Elinor Donahue) look exactly alike. Betty wins a trip to Hollywood, sponsored by the women's club. Jim is angry and doesn't want Betty to go.

"For a change," Betty cries, "I'll be something other than plain old Betty Anderson of Springfield. For two whole days, I'll be sort of important."

Jim's objection is that "just because you look like somebody famous doesn't make you famous or impor-tant." But he lets her go if she "thinks it's just for fun."

And so, Betty and Margaret fly to LA. Betty has publicity photos taken, rides in a limousine, is hounded for autographs, meets Donna Stewart at the studio, becomes smitten with the leading man, and gets a glamorous wardrobe. (Actually, the most significant thing about this scene is that Betty wears short white gloves and Margaret wears a hat with a veil—showing how sensible, at heart, they really are.)

That day, Miss Stewart, the star, telephones the family in Springfield to say hello; Bud and Kitten comb their hair in preparation for the call. Jim talks to Margaret: "When are you coming home? We're running out of dishes!"

Betty looks glamorous. Margaret looks dubious (but sensible). Betty signs Donna Stewart's name in some-one's autograph book. In a nightclub that evening, they announce that Betty is Donna Stewart. A drunk comes up and calls her a phony. He wants Betty to sing and gets "ugly" with her (in a TV sitcom way, that is). Betty is upset and wants to go home. Then Betty gets a long-distance call. Father calls to wish her luck on a live TV interview she's going to do. On the phone she's distraught and becomes hysterical. She's too embarrassed to go on because she has made a fool of herself and "tried to be somebody else."

Jim: "To your friends and family, you are a celebrity."

In Springfield, Jim, Bud, and Kathy sit around the TV, watching Betty. As Betty gives all the right answers to the interviewer's questions, the camera shoots to Margaret's proud reactions—with, of course, ample violin music under. The interview is about to wind up when Betty says:

"May I say goodnight to my fan club?" She does: "Good night, Father. Good night, Bud; good night, Kathy." And as she does, each member of the family says goodnight to the TV screen at home. Fade out to more music.

The moral, of course, is that you should be yourself. But maybe you shouldn't. In fact, that moral—Be Yourself—is what typified the whole *Father Knows Best* experience. Here were these actors from Hollywood, acting at being *our*selves—maybe not what we really were, but what we wanted to be. Or what they thought we wanted to be. Or were told we wanted to be. *Father*

1955 Award: "For Constructive Portrayal of American Family Life"

Knows Best reinforced American mythology in the fifties. It was the same reality that forced Jane Wyatt, in one bedroom scene with Robert Young, to wear a brassiere under her nightgown. That seemed to typify the program, which was about as realistic as a bra under a nightie.

On the other hand—if we wanted reality, we could have turned the TV off and watched our own family—fuming and fussing and fighting and doing what everyone else on the block was doing. No—everyone else on the block was exactly where we were: sitting in front of the set, watching the Andersons.

But maybe the Andersons weren't supposed to be a Typical American Family. Maybe they were just supposed to be the Ideal—a family who did good things (and they did do good things)—and maybe we were supposed to look up to and emulate them. But—in the process—boy, did they sell a lot of cornflakes!

Father Knows Best was the apotheosis of the Morality Age, and people like Jim and Margaret Anderson were its pioneers, their early-American house being their covered wagon. The morals it fed us weren't bad—keeping one's word, honor, finishing a job and doing it well, working regularly at something and earning the reward of leisure—it was just that the spoon with which those maxims were fed to us was tarnished.

So who knows best? Billy Gray knows the answer: "If I could say anything to make up for all the years I lent myself to that kind of bullshit, it would be:

"*'You* know best.'"

LOVE THAT BOB

CHUCK: My, Uncle Bob sounds cheerful this morning. He's singing in the shower. What happened?
MARGARET: He thinks he found a new girl. We'll just overcook his eggs.

More than any other sitcom in the fifties, *Love That Bob* showed how we looked at women. And that was it: we looked at them. Although the show got less than enthusiastic reviews, viewers tuned in every week to watch Bob Cummings as a perennial rover—a Don Giovanni in modern dress, whose High F had nothing to do with singing.

The show was about a man named Bob Collins and his sex life—the story of a boy and his penis. It wasn't so much where he put it as where he didn't put it. Usually his romances were foiled.

He was a bachelor photographer, but we always suspected that he dabbled in pornography on the side. Cummings played Wolf Man to a bevy of beautiful models, but they could take care of themselves. It was literally tit for tat: he treated his photographic subjects as objects, they treated him as an object.

Besides the sitcom-sexy goings-on between Bob and the girls, there were two other significant women on the program: Bob's put-upon widowed sister who played wife/mother to her helpless brother, and his Bob-hungry scrawny secretary, Schultzy.

The program debuted on January 2, 1955, on NBC, where it ran one-half season. Then it shot over to CBS for two years—and then back to NBC for two more years. At last, it ended up at ABC until 1959 when it finally petered out and left the air. Throughout the years, the show always opened with Cummings and his camera. "Hold it!" he would say, "I think you're going to like this picture."

One episode—"Bob Gets Out-Uncled"—is a perfect example of the show's setup. Bob gets out of bed. His widowed sister, Margaret (Rosemary DeCamp), reminds him that he promised to play tennis with her teenaged son, Chuck MacDonald (Dwayne Hickman) at 7 A.M. But both Bob and Chuck have been out carousing and are exhausted. She thinks that Bob is a bad example to Chuck, and she has a scheme: she wants her friend, football star "Crazy Legs" Hersh, to pretend to be Chuck's other uncle to teach Bob a lesson.

In the next scene—a sexy non sequitur in the script—Bob is giving a "tennis lesson" to a voluptuous girl, whom he has his arm around. He asks Chuck to go get them some balls and then swings his racket.

Bob Collins	Bob Cummings
Margaret MacDonald, his widowed sister	Rosemary DeCamp
Chuck MacDonald, her son	Dwayne Hickman
Charmaine Schultz ("Schultzy") Bob's secretary-assistant	Ann B. Davis
Harvey Helm, Bob's friend	King Donovan
Ruth Helm, Harvey's wife	Mary Lawrence
Shirley Swanson, the beautiful blonde model determined to marry Bob	Joi Lansing (1956–1959)
Paul Fonda, Margaret's romantic interest	Lyle Talbot
Francine Williams, Chuck's girlfriend	Diane Jergens (1955–1956)
Joe DePew, Chuck's friend	Jeff Silver
Pamela Livingston, Bob's friend, a bird-watcher	Nancy Kulp
Frank Crenshaw, Schultzy's friend	Dick Wesson
Josh Collins (Grandpa), Bob's father, a semiretired photographer	Bob Cummings
The models:	Tammy Lea Marihugh, Dona Foster, Gloria Marshall, Julie Bennett, Penny Edwards, Jean Moorhead, Katherine Hughes, Barbara Wilson, Lisa Davis, Carole Conn, Shirley Boone, Carole Le Vegue, Jeanne Vaughn, Jan Harrison, June Kirby, Leigh Snowden, Patricia Blake, Jeanne Evans, Patricia Murlin, Gloria Robertson, Valerie Allen, Kathy Marlowe, Elaine Edwards, Rose Beaumont, Sylvia Lewis, Marjorie Tenny, Gloria Marshall, Suzanne Alexander, Barbara Long
Also:	Rose Marie
Announcer:	Bill Baldwin

Spies (from left): Ann B. Davis, Bob Cummings, unidentified starlet

BOB: Did you observe how that was done?
GIRL: Yes—you got rid of him very smoothly.
BOB: Now we can settle down to a nice serious lesson. . . . *(He hands her a racket.)*
GIRL: Is this *still* tennis?
BOB: If it weren't would I put a weapon in your hand?
GIRL: I guess I can trust you. *(Bob gives her a sarcastic "oh-sure-you-can" look, leers, and touches her.)*

Finally, "Uncle" Roy ("Crazy Legs") arrives. He is an all-around athlete and a perfect role model for Chuck, as Margaret explains to Bob.

MARGARET: He's an excellent example of good living—"early to bed and early to rise—"
BOB: "—and your girl goes out with the other guys!"

Bob bucks up for an athletic competition with Uncle Roy—he does chin-ups (but we see when the door is closed that he has really been standing on a chair) and we see him playing catch with a very forceful off-camera catcher. "Beautiful—what a pass. Let's take a little rest," Bob calls out. The pitcher, of course, turns out to be Schultzy, who is very strong.

Bob and Uncle Roy are in a fierce all-sports competition. Bob keeps losing; Chuck keeps winning more and more respect for his new "uncle." But Bob's ace in the hole—he keeps telling everyone—will be tennis, and he brags that he once beat Pancho Gonzalez. Pancho, of course, turns out to be a seven-year-old Mexican kid from the neighborhood. So Bob is exposed as a windbag and cut down to size. The end.

As Bob, Cummings brought a soft-spoken charm to the role. He was so obviously an insecure male that we couldn't help liking him. Everyone seemed to like him. Shirley Swanson was a beautiful blonde model who was hot for Bob. The role was played by Joi Lansing, so curvaceous that she almost looked like a caricature of a woman. Lansing was a small-screen version of Marilyn Monroe—family-room sexy as opposed to bedroom sen-

suous. Other pals of Bob's were Harvey Helm (played by King Donovan, Imogene Coca's husband) and the wonderful, tight-lipped, small-hipped and tall Nancy Kulp (she went on to become better known playing Miss Jane in *The Beverly Hillbillies*) as Bob's bird-watching friend Pamela Livingston. Then, of course, there was the never-ending bouquet of curvy models—Donna, Gloria, Sylvia, Jan, Lisa, and so many others—who loved that Bob. Lyle Talbot (veteran of dozens of sitcoms) played sister Margaret's boyfriend, Paul Fonda. Even Rose Marie (Sally on *Dick Van Dyke*) made a few guest appearances. The most unusual guest star was—Bob Cummings, playing Josh Collins (a.k.a. Grandpa), Bob's father, a semiretired photographer. For the role, Cummings whitened his hair, hunched over, and acted aged.

For all his roving, we always knew that he would end up with a Nice Sensible Girl—someone like his sister or Schultzy. Schultzy! She was the one we truly cared about. She had unending energy and a lust for—well, lust. With her hair tied up in a little kerchief and her body hidden in baggy clothes, she was the down-to-earth counterpart to all the girls who sashayed into the office. She was substantial—not boringly sensible like sister Margaret—but someone you could talk to, laugh with, have a good time with. You knew that without a doubt Schultzy was the best lover on the show. And the wisest. In one episode she quits her job to work in a missile factory—in order to meet men. When she sees that her replacement is a voluptuous, bubble-brained blonde, she decides not to quit. She was a friendly scarecrow. We knew—as we know about our friends in these matters—that she shouldn't waste her time pining away for a cad like Bob. She was too good for him. But there was nothing that could keep her away from Bob—except network cancellation.

That came in 1959. The show ended right where it started. Schultzy was still single. All those girls were still eligible. Sister Margaret was still alone. Nephew Chuck had skipped town and changed his name to Dobie Gillis. Schultzy went on to keep house for *The Brady Bunch*. And Bob was still horny.

TV sex in the fifties was all tight sweaters, winks, leers, and allusions to the back seats of girls and cars. Women—sorry: gals, dames, broads—were pursued by men according to the Base System, and no one ever got past first base.

Bob Cummings was our first sex-ed teacher. True, we didn't learn very much about prophylactics or social diseases, but we did learn some very enlightening stuff about relationships between men and women. Of course, it all turned out to be wrong.

Bob Collins was a sexual Ralph Kramden. Bob looked better, but underneath they were chasing the same rainbow—Ralph with his organizing, Bob with his organ. For seven years, Bob ran from network to network, until his rating finally dropped. He just couldn't get it up.

ALSO RANS

Dear Phoebe

When ex-college professor Bill Hastings (Peter Lawford) decides he'd prefer to try his hand at the more dramatic profession of journalism, he's assigned a whole new identity to go with his job. The Los Angeles *Daily Blade* hires him as Phoebe Goodheart, it's advice-to-the-lovelorn columnist. He also acquires a new girlfriend, "Mickey" Riley (Marcia Henderson, the paper's sportswriter), who gives him more problems each week than any of Phoebe's correspondents. Added to that were eager-beaver copyboy, Humphrey Humpsteader (Joe Corey) and Mr. Fosdick (Charles Lane), the crusty managing editor. NBC gave them office space for one season.

The Donald O'Connor Texaco Show: Here Comes Donald

This show was nothing more than an excuse for song-and-prance man Donald O'Connor (playing a character named Donald O'Connor) to sing and prance on the small screen (just as he had on screens considerably larger). With him, playing his songwriting partner, was Sid Miller (playing a guy named Sid Miller). They spent their half-hours trying to find people to buy their songs, and they always seemed to end up in situations where they'd jump around and try to be funny. Joyce Smight played their secretary Doreen. And NBC housed them all for one season of song.

Halls of Ivy

This show—about the problems of a small college—starred movie great Ronald Colman as Dr. William Todhunter Hall, smart, witty president of Ivy College in Ivy, USA. The other Halls of Ivy were his wife, Vicky (Benita Hume, Colman's real wife), who was former stage performer Victoria Cromwell; their housekeeper Alice (Mary Wickes, veteran of many sitcoms and commercials); Clarence Wellman (Herb Butterfield), chairman of the board of Ivy College; his wife (Sarah Selby); and Professor Warren (Arthur Q. Bryan). There were also many students who would visit the Halls at their residence at Number One Faculty Row. The program ran on CBS for one season. A male chorus sang the theme song ("We love the Halls of Ivy/That surround us here today") that became a hit. The show was another radio transplant.

Hey Mulligan

Mickey Rooney starred in this NBC show (also known as *The Mickey Rooney Show*, not to be confused with the 1964 ABC sitcom of the same name) about Mickey Mulligan, a page at IBC (International Broadcasting Company) in LA. His mother (Claire Carleton) is a former burlesque star and his father is a policeman. His girlfriend is a secretary at IBC, and, when he wasn't getting in misadventures with them, he'd get into them at acting school or any of a number of his part-time jobs. No one encouraged him in his pursuit of acting except his father, the cop (played by Regis Toomey), and his girlfriend Pat (Carla Balenda). Both Mulligan and Rooney were canceled in June 1955.

The Mickey Rooney Show

Honestly Celeste!

Known for her great success as Ado Annie in *Oklahoma!*, Celeste Holm hooked her wagon to the wrong star with this one: the show lasted only three months. During that time, she played Celeste Anders, a Minnesota college teacher living in Manhattan, who tries to get journalism experience by working on the New York *Express*. She also got some other kind of experience by dating the publisher's son, Bob Wallace (Scott McKay), with whom she pursued some hot stories. But CBS killed the story.

It's a Great Life

This show didn't have a great life, but it did have a not-bad life; it ran two seasons on NBC.

The action took place in Hollywood, where two recently discharged GIs answer an ad for a furnished room at the Morgan Boarding House. The men are Denny David (Michael O'Shea) and Steve Connors (William Bishop). Widow Amy Morgan (Frances Bavier—later Aunt Bee on *Andy Griffith*) runs the boarding house. The two men become pals with Mrs. Morgan's unemployed and conniving brother Uncle Earl (James Dunn). The plots: all three men need money and they go about trying to come up with ways to make it. They didn't. The show didn't.

It's a Great Life: *William Bishop and wife*

The Joe Palooka Story

This short-running syndicated sitcom (based on the character created by Ham Fisher) starred Joe Kirkwood, Jr., as the heavyweight boxer who's clean-living, moral, and actually pretty stupid. He is continuously confronted with gambling, fixed fights, blonde sirens, and nightclubs—but he plays it clean with his girlfriend Ann Howe (Cathy Downs) and his trainer Humphrey Pennyworth (Maxie Rosenbloom).

Mayor of the Town

Springdale was the residence of this syndicated series, which revolved around the home and working life of Thomas Russell (played by Thomas Mitchell) who just happened to be mayor of the town. Like so many of TV's elder statesmen, he was a widower who had a secretary, a nephew, a housekeeper—he even had an enemy named Joe Ainsley (played by Tudor Owen).

Norby

The Norby family, who lived in Pearl River, New York: Pearson (David Wayne), vice-president of small loans at the First National Bank; his wife, Helen (Joan Lorring), and their children, Diane (Susan Hallaran) and Hank (Evan Elliot). Paul Ford (later on *Phil Silvers* and *The Baileys of Balboa*) played the bank president, but only until April when the show ended its three-month run on NBC. Sponsored by Kodak, *Norby* was the first sitcom filmed in color (earlier color sitcoms were shot live).

Professional Father

Notable mostly for the appearance of Barbara Billingsley (later *Beaver*'s mother) as Helen Wilson, the mother and wife of Thomas Wilson (Steve Dunne), a child psychologist. A precursor of Bob Hartley on *The Bob Newhart Show* nearly twenty years later, Wilson was a whiz in the office, but floundered at home. The Wilsons had two mischievous children—sort of in preparation for Wally and the Beaver—named Kit and Twig. Like so many other sitcom families, they had a housekeeper named Nana and a neighbor named Fred and a handy-man named Mr. Boggs.

So This Is Hollywood

So this is television. This early entry was all about Kim Tracy (Virginia Gibson) and her roommate, Queenie Dugan (Mitzi Green), who live in a place called the LaPaloma Courts. Kim's an aspiring starlet. Queenie's a wise, weathered stunt lady. Both are trying to make it in the movies. They didn't do so hot in television, either. NBC sent them packing after half a season.

The Soldiers

Hal March and Tom D'Andrea had often teamed up on variety shows over the years playing two trouble-prone GIs who complained about everything—the food, the officers, everything. So NBC gave them a shot at a live summer sitcom, each episode of which focused on a different aspect of army life—letters from home, passes, special assignments, adjusting to civilian life after being discharged. What's probably more interesting than this, though, is the other projects March and D'Andrea were involved in. In 1950, March had been the first Harry Morton on *Burns and Allen*, when the show was still being shown live. In 1953, he did a stint as the leading lady's boyfriend on *My Friend Irma*. But he was probably most famous for his role as "emcee" starting in 1955 on *The $64,000 Question*. D'Andrea's only claim to fame in the wonderful world of sitcoms (but it was a big claim) was as his next-door neighbor's best buddy, Gillis, on *Life of Riley* with William Bendix.

That's My Boy

Eddie Mayehoff starred as Jack Jackson, Sr., an ex-college athlete, now a junior partner with Patterson and Jackson. Rochelle Hudson played his wife, Alice, a former Olympic swimming champion. Of course, their son, Jack Jackson, Jr. (Gil Stratton, Jr.), is a total klutz—nearsighted, a bookworm, prone to hayfever and sinus attacks. The parents try to relive their youth through the kid by instilling him with the sports spirit. But Junior wants to do his own thing, and enrolls at Rossmore College in Rossmore, Ohio. Jack, Sr., makes life lousy for everyone by treating the world like an overgrown football game. The whole thing was based on the movie of the same name (in which Jerry Lewis played the son) which didn't run much longer than the sitcom. *That's My Boy* was canceled by CBS in January of 1955 (although the network later rebroadcast it in 1959).

Those Whiting Girls

This CBS show, which was a summer replacement for *I Love Lucy* in 1955 and 1957, starred sisters Barbara and Margaret Whiting (playing themselves) as two girls (Barbara was a student at UCLA; Margaret, a singer) who had many romantic misadventures in Hollywood. Also on board: Mabel Albertson as their mother, and Jerry Paris ("Jerry" on *Dick Van Dyke* and much later producer-director of *Happy Days*) as Margaret's accompanist, Artie, during their second (and final) summer.

Willy

June Havoc (Gypsy Rose Lee's younger sister—remember Baby June?) played Willa Dodger, a woman lawyer in a town that mistrusts women lawyers. The show had two formats: the first (through March, 1955) had Willy practicing law in Renfrew, New Hampshire, with a cast highlighted by a dog named Rags. In April 1955, Willy moved to Manhattan (sans Rags) and became the legal counsel for the Bannister Vaudeville Company. Sterling Holloway played her pal Harvey Evelyn, the owner of the company. And then came the third format change: Willy moved off the air in July 1955. Courtesy of CBS.

The World of Mr. Sweeney

This daily sitcom (that's right: fifteen minutes each day) starred Charlie Ruggles as Cicero P. Sweeney, a general store owner who involves himself in the problems of others. Some of those others: his grandson Kippy Sweeney (Kippy Franklin), his daughter, Marge (Helen Wagner), and several friends. Also in the cast: Lydia Reed as Little Eva, "the refugee girl." NBC gave us Mr. Sweeney's world for only two summer months (its roots were as a regular segment on *The Kate Smith Evening Hour*) and then as a fourteen-month daytime show on NBC. In all, 345 installments were presented, giving it the all-time record (so far) for the largest number of episodes of an NBC sitcom.

1955–1956

The Honeymooners

The Phil Silvers Show: *You'll Never Get Rich*

OFF-SCREEN

9/26 Heaviest single-day dollar loss in NY Stock Exchange in history, totaling $14 billion.
10/4 Brooklyn Dodgers defeat Yankees in Series.
10/7 World's most powerful warship, USS *Saratoga,* launched at Brooklyn Naval Shipyard.
12/5 AFL and CIO formally merged to produce American Federation of Labor and Congress of Industrial Organizations, headed by George Meany.
4/19 Actress Grace Kelly married in Monte Carlo to Prince Rainier III of Monaco.
4/28 The New York Coliseum, world's largest exhibition building, opens in New York City.
6/23 Nasser elected President of Egypt.

FRONT RUNNERS

THE HONEYMOONERS

Forget it, Ralph.
—ALICE KRAMDEN

There is a corps of fanatics—hanging out in the appliance sections of department stores, leaving parties early to run home for reruns, insisting on changing channels at the corner bar—who wouldn't miss an episode of *The Honeymooners* for anything. And they know everything—*everything*—about the show. They know, for example, that Ed Norton and Ralph Kramden both make $62 a week. They know that Ralph's social security number is 105-36-22. That Ralph and Ed bowl on alley number three. That the initiation fee for the Raccoons is $1.50. And that, when a sewer explosion on Hudson St. landed Norton in the hospital, he was put in Room 317.

These people call themselves Honeymoonies.

But there are others (they call themselves fans) who have a gentle, less enthusiastic appreciation for the thirty-nine—that's right, only thirty-nine—filmed episodes of one of the greatest sitcoms ever made. Genius Jackie Gleason and his band of fine writers and actors have created characters that have forever changed the course of comedy.

It's the story of a little man who happens to be big: in size and in dreams. And in schemes. Ralph Kramden, a Madison Ave. bus driver, tries to improve his lot a lot. His foil is his upstairs neighbor Ed Norton, who gets involved in his ploys. Waiting at home in a small Brooklyn apartment is his wife, Alice, who tries to put some sense into her husband's fat head. It's not easy. Alice Kramden's only relief and release is visiting Ed's wife, Trixie, upstairs.

Sounds like a premise with promise. When they get going—when people actually move into these parts—there's no stopping them.

Their two-room, "modestly furnished" (very modestly) apartment at 328 Chauncey St. in the Bensonhurst section of Brooklyn is the key to it all. An ice box with a pan for drippings is on the right, next to an old stove and a beat-up sink. Next to it is a window, from which Alice "phones" Trixie upstairs. At left is a battered dresser on which sits a lunch pail and an oriental candy dish. Center sits a round wood table with a red and white checked tablecloth on it. Through the door at left is the Kramdens' bedroom (which we never saw). These things never changed.

Neither did the people who lived there.

Ralph is a loser—which is why he was a winner to us. He's a guy who makes mistakes but, fortunately, never learns from them; if he did, he wouldn't be back on the next episode making the same mistakes again. And giving us so much pleasure.

Ralph is a fighter, a Don Quixote, whose windmill is the circumstances of life. He complains about his poverty—but he tries to do something about it. He growls instead of groaning. He is an Everyman, always after that pot of gold. His vehicle? He has dozens of moneymaking miracle ideas: diet pizza, Day-Glo wallpaper, his famous KranMar Mystery Appetizer, which turns out to be dog food that he feeds to his boss.

Ralph is the irritable bus driver who always turns out to be a nice guy if you ever get the chance to actually talk to him. Ralph's rages—his lashing out in frustration, his innocent lies, his bogus behavior, his incompetence—are all his defenses against a world that has placed him in the wrong neighborhood (physically and psychologically). What makes Ralph different from the rest of us is that he's willing to fail, to recover and try again. He is a

---

Ralph Kramden	Jackie Gleason
Alice Kramden	Audrey Meadows (1955–1956); Sheila MacRae (1971)
Ed Norton	Art Carney
Trixie Norton	Joyce Randolph (1955–1956); Jane Kean (1971)

Additional characters (not given screen credit): Mrs. Gibson, Alice's mother; Mrs. Manicotti, a tenant; Mr. Marshall, Ralph's employer; Mr. Johnson, the landlord; Morris Fink, the Grand High Exalted Ruler of the Raccoon Lodge, Ralph and Norton's fraternity; Mr. Monahan, the president of the bus company

toughie—a survivor—who takes swings, always gets knocked down, and gets up fighting. He is adventurous, not in a *Sea Hunt* way, but in the real-life, day-to-day adventure of living with verve and nerve.

Ralph is the fat kid in school who grows up to be the fat kid out of school. Hiding beneath those layers of fat are more layers of fat. Ralph eats and eats to counteract the nourishment he isn't getting from life; the layers of fat protect him against the bruises he knows he's going to receive. Everyone had something to say about Ralph's girth:

ALICE'S MOTHER (*at their wedding*): I'm not losing a daughter, I'm gaining a ton.

RALPH: I promise you this, Norton. I'm gonna learn. I'm gonna learn from here on in how to swallow my pride.
ED: That ought not to be too hard. You've learned how to swallow everything else.

RALPH (*bragging about another surefire scheme*): This is probably the biggest thing I ever got into.
ALICE: The biggest thing you ever got into was your pants.

ED: Boy oh boy, how could anyone so round be so square?

Ralph had a good buddy, his relaxed and easygoing crony Ed Norton from upstairs, who spent his days downstairs—way downstairs—cleaning sewers. He referred to himself as an "underground engineer," and he knew his business.

RALPH: It's rush hour. We'll never be able to get across town in this traffic.
ED: Trust me. We'll go by sewer.

Ed Norton played Stan Laurel to Ralph Kramden's Oliver Hardy. They feuded and fought and fussed and always made up. In his uniform of T-shirt, vest, and shapeless felt hat, Ed sauntered around waving his arms and hands. He tried to be the perfect pal to Ralph; he tried to be supportive and encouraging to Ralph, but his good heart and clumsy tongue did not often work in unison, were not always perfectly coordinated. "You're the stupidest man I ever knew," Ralph would bellow to Ed, the innocent.

When Norton would write something, he would prepare with an elaborate series of hand gestures and flourishes that would leave Ralph in a fury. "Will you cut that out, Norton?!" Ralph would howl.

When a dejected Ralph loses his job (on a live episode aired in 1954) Ed tries as best he can to cheer up his good buddy.

ED: Come on, boy, let's have a little smile. (*Ralph tries to smile.*) There, that's my boy. Bigger, bigger, that's it! That's the way you gotta stay even if it takes a whole year to get a job. Even if you never get another job!
RALPH (*bitterly*): A fat lot I've got to smile about. Nine years on the job. Today I'm fired and by tomorrow I'm forgotten. They won't even remember what I look like.
ED: That's great . . . go right back tomorrow morning and ask for a job.

Ralph's wife, Alice, is the voice of resigned reason. "Baby, you're the greatest," Ralph would say to her after she had once again been right in proving him wrong. He wasn't being sarcastic. He meant it—the "greatest" for putting up with him and probably for marrying him in the first place. Her barbed-wire tongue and sarcastic wit could match his carryings-on any day.

When Ralph loses his job . . .

ALICE: Look, Ralph, maybe until you get something for yourself I could get a job and help out.
RALPH: Oh, no, you don't. When I married you, I promised you'd never have to work again.
ALICE: But it won't be for long.
RALPH: I don't care, Alice, I've got my pride. Before I'd let you go to work, I'd rather see you starve. We'll just have to live on our savings.
ALICE: That'll carry us through the night, but what'll we do in the morning?

Alice was often the object of Ralph's ravings. "Oh, you're a regular riot, Alice! Har-de-*har*-de-har-har!" When provoked, Ralph would threaten with "You're askin' for a knuckle sandwich, Alice. . . ."

And when Alice squelches Ralph, he gets all puffy and winds up, ready to explode.

RALPH: Alice, I'm gonna belt you one.
ALICE: Oh, you are, are you? Well, go ahead and belt me, Ralph.
RALPH (*backing down*): One of these days, Alice. One of these days—POW—right to the moon!

Alice always told-him-so, but Ralph never listened to her until it was too late. When Ralph wants to buy 2,000 Handy Housewife Helpers and go into business selling them, Alice reminds him of all his other surefire schemes that have failed, such as the uranium field in Asbury Park. ("You don't love me, you never loved me," Ralph wails. "You married me because you were in love with my uniform.")

Or, the night before the company physical, Alice warns Ralph not to go bowling because he might ruin his back. He goes and can't stand up straight. When Alice finds out the next night, she gives Ralph dinner—his bowling trophy.

Why did Alice, a sensible, attractive, intelligent woman, marry a loudmouth lout like Ralph? It wasn't for his money or the excitement—she spent her days emptying the tray under the ice box (the iceman kept complaining about traveling across town in the hot summer to deliver one melting block of ice). They didn't have a phone or a television. They lived in a shabby two-room Brooklyn flat. (Alice's mother once said to her: "Just because you married a horse doesn't mean you have to live in a stable.") They had a maid once, but only because Alice went out to get a job so she could afford one. And Ralph always seemed to prefer bowling or lodge meetings to being with Alice.

So why did she marry him? It had to be love (TV in the fifties was too naive for self-destructive motives). And Ralph did have his socially redeeming values. Once, he got angry and took Alice's dog to the pound. When he got there and found out they were going to put the dog to sleep, he took the dog back home—and several others as well. Another time when Ralph thought Alice wanted him to act young again by dancing and roller-skating, he failed and said to her: "Acting young isn't what keeps you young, but if you've got some memories, some good memories, of when you were young, that's what keeps you young." Alice can't resist his sincerity and his affection. Who could?

But Alice had an outlet. It was Trixie, the whining woman upstairs, Ed's wife and accomplice in various neighborly crimes. She was basically a fill-in-the-blank character; she acted as Alice's one friend, which gave Alice someone to talk to during the day, and Trixie provided a suitable motivation for Alice to leave the apartment so Ralph could cook up his schemes with Ed.

The filmed episodes—the ones we see on reruns today—were full of laughs and fun, but also had an existential note to them, with O. Henry twists: a sureness that, somehow, you can't win. It wasn't all that negative. The moral was more like: accept your lot. Ralph was deceitful, and he won the Olympics in Conclusion Jumping.

In one episode, Ed needs Ralph to be a credit reference for him. Ralph needs Ed to vote for him as the Raccoons' next convention manager. When Ralph loses the election by one vote, he assumes it's Ed. When the credit request arrives, Ralph writes "The applicant is a bum." It turns out that Ed *did* vote for Ralph, and he confesses about the credit reference to Ed, who forgives him, explaining that if he had gotten the loan, he was going to buy furniture for Ralph and Alice's anniversary. And, once again, Ralph would be shamed.

Friends said that Gleason wasn't totally unlike Ralph. At least they both grew up in Brooklyn. Born in 1915, Gleason had had a tough childhood, as Ralph might have had. His thirteen-year-old brother died when he was three. Five years later, his father disappeared. His mother died a few years later. The family was very poor, but Gleason had great determination and energy. "In school," he said, "I was irritating. Why, I don't know."

He struggled professionally for many years as a carnival barker, a nightclub MC, a revue comic, and a movie bit player. In 1949, he got the chance to star in *The Life of Riley* (radio's Riley, William Bendix, had other commitments, so they cast Gleason). It bombed and Gleason swore off TV. But then, two years later, he was the third choice to star in *The Cavalcade of Stars*, broadcast over the now-deceased DuMont Television Network. It was on this show that *The Honeymooners* was born.

The idea was for a quiet (but shrewd) wife and a big-mouth husband. They were going to call it "The Beast." Or "The Lovers." Or "The Couple Next Door." They finally decided on "The Honeymooners." Their mission: to make it real, to make it the way people really live.

With Pert Kelton playing his "long-suffering wife, Alice," the honeymoon was just beginning.

The first episode was just a few minutes long and was between only Ralph and Alice. There were no other characters, except a policeman played by an actor named Art Carney. Gleason was so impressed with Carney's work that he wrote him into the script. He became Ed Norton.

Carney had been around. On radio's *Report to the Nation*, Carney did impersonations of President Roosevelt, Churchill, and Wendell Willkie. He had also been on Morey Amsterdam's *Silver Swan Café* radio, and then television, show.

The DuMont show was such a success that CBS signed Gleason to do his own live-from-New York Saturday night show the following year (weekly salary: a neat $10,000). And the honeymoon went on.

At CBS, Gleason brought his troupe with him: Carney and, as his wife, Trixie (an ex-burlesque queen), actress Joyce Randolph, but Pert Kelton got sick and they needed a new Alice.

Audrey Meadows wanted the part. Gleason said no; she was too well known as one of the most beautiful women in New York; he wanted someone briny and

The Cast (from left): Jackie Gleason, Art Carney, Audrey Meadows, Joyce Randolph

frumpy. Meadows hired a photographer to wake her up first thing in the morning and take her photo. When Gleason saw the prints, he gave her the part. "The Honeymooners," then still a feature on Gleason's variety show, went on twice a month. This would soon change.

Rehearsals were strange. Gleason had a photographic memory and would never bother to rehearse. Plus, he liked to be spontaneous, he liked to ad-lib. But the other cast members didn't have the gift of being able to memorize sixty pages of script in one morning. But it always worked out.

"The Honeymooners"—by 1954, up to a half-hour, sometimes even an hour—was a sensation. Kramden's glossary of phrases—"One of these days, POW, right on the kisser" and "bang-zoom, right to the moon"—were recited like the Pledge of Allegiance. Viewers sent Alice curtains and aprons. Gleason's walk and Gleason's talk were now famous. Ralph Kramden had turned into a folk hero.

It was time to turn a TV sketch called "The Honeymooners" into a TV show called *The Honeymooners*—television's first spin-off.

Up until that time, the show had been shot live. Gleason signed an agreement to film seventy-eight episodes—two years' worth—with a new process called Electronicam, something that would make the shows seem "live on film" by shooting with a studio audience there.

"The excellence of the material could not be maintained," Gleason claimed, and pulled out of the contract after filming thirty-nine episodes. The result: the Classic 39—the same shows you see over and over again on TV.

Gleason called all the shots (and, often, shot all the shots—he had his hands in everything). And he ruled with a clenched iron fist. The show went through writers like popcorn; they were afraid of the autocratic Gleason who, when in a bad mood, just didn't think anything was funny. Including their work.

Producing, writing, directing, conducting, compos-

ing, acting—Gleason did it all. He had boundless energy. He was an insomniac and called himself what Ralph called Alice: "the Greatest." He spent frantic energy trying to justify that insistence.

Steve Allen (who is Audrey Meadows' brother-in-law) called Gleason "one of the most neurotic comedians." He's a compulsive eater, Allen said, who eats when he worries. "TV makes him worry." Several times a year, Gleason would check himself into Doctors Hospital in New York to go on a strict weight-reducing diet.

Said show business restaurateur Toots Shor: "He was always crazy—the only difference is he can afford it now."

And Gleason could make decisions to stop filming *The Honeymooners*. But he could also change his mind as well.

On September 29, 1956—seven days after the last filmed *Honeymooners*—*The Jackie Gleason Show* was back on the air—live. *The Honeymooners*, which had spun off on its own, now rolled back home and was once again "The Honeymooners." Little did Gleason know that this would be the last season of his variety show to feature the Nortons and the Kramdens. Art Carney had decided to leave the show to devote more time to acting.

But in 1962, with Sue Ann Langdon as Alice and Patricia Wilson as Trixie, *The Honeymooners* was back, when Art Carney returned for several guest appearances. Langdon had trouble getting along. "Who needs her?" Gleason snapped when she quit. In 1966, the last black-and-white episode of *The Honeymooners* reunited Carney, Meadows, and Gleason; it was an hour-long special called "The Adoption," in which Ralph and Alice try to adopt a baby.

For the 1966–1967 season, *The Honeymooners*

The New Cast: Jackie Gleason, Art Carney, Sheila MacRae, Jane Kean

From Glad to Sad: Jackie Gleason in conference

returned on a regular basis with Carney and Sheila MacRae (as Alice) and Jane Kean as Trixie (that season, Pert Kelton, who played the original Alice, was back—as Alice's mother, Mrs. Gibson). During the 1970–1971 season, CBS canceled *The Jackie Gleason Show*, and the Kramdens and the Nortons went down with it.

In 1976, *The Honeymooners* celebrated their twenty-fifth anniversary when Carney, Gleason, Meadows, and Kean got together for a special; they did it again at Christmas the following year, and again with a 1978 Valentine's Day special.

Over the years, hundreds of episodes were made. There have been four Alices, four Trixies—but only one Norton. And certainly only one Ralph.

Even without a psychological readout, we knew Ralph inside out (certainly better than he knew himself). Each week, over that same checkered tablecloth, Ralph would plot his checkered plans to make millions and become Someone. We knew his schemes wouldn't work out—if they ever did, the Kramdens would have moved to the suburbs and turned into Donna Reed and Carl Betz. And the honeymoon would have been over.

They didn't know it, but the Kramdens and the Nortons *were* rich—rich in energy and enthusiasm and humor and love for one another. And that's why, with only thirty-nine episodes, we can still—week after week and night after night—play house with Ed and Trixie and Alice and Ralph.

THE PHIL SILVERS SHOW: YOU'LL NEVER GET RICH

Fifty cents a ball, boys?
—ERNIE BILKO, approaching a pool table, after which the men scurry like roaches when a light's been turned on.

Y*ou'll Never Get Rich, Sergeant Bilko, The Phil Silvers Show*—whatever it was called (and it was called all three, as well as being called "brilliant," "hilarious" and, simply, "the best"), this sitcom was a classic. Not many were. Lucy, Van Dyke, Gleason, Moore, Benny, Burns and Allen—all had classic shows. Silvers—who could outtalk and outholler any of them—was right up there at the top.

Ernest T. Bilko (serial number 15042699) had a big smile and a big mouth, out of which emerged a phony line of chatter and patter touched with a tad of larceny. He was a likable (even lovable) con man, out to pick up a quick buck and knock down authority. Even in those days when we were only trying to confuse our dads into thinking they hadn't given us our allowances yet, we knew that there was a bit of Bilko in all of us.

As staff sergeant of the motor pool at Fort Baxter, Kansas (a nearly forgotten outpost of the US Army), like his sitcom comrade, Ralph Kramden, Bilko spent his time dreaming up schemes; week after week, he organized his get-rich-quick master plans, hoping to make a killing.

PRIVATE ZIMMERMAN: Imagine, Bilko's doing something without making a profit.
PRIVATE PAPARELLI: Even the chaplain is stunned. He's using it for the subject of next Sunday's sermon.

Bilko was perfectly played by silver-tongued Phil Silvers; every little line, every little movement was perfectly honed to Silvers' comic temperament. There was a bubbling chemistry about the program—test tubes carefully poured back and forth—that made this show explode. But with an ounce less luck and a lot less chutzpah, *You'll Never Get Rich* might never have gotten on the air. Ernie Bilko almost never saw the light of the picture tube.

Writer-producer-director Nat Hiken was looking for a suitable sitcom format for Silvers, a veteran of clubs, vaudeville, movies, and Broadway. At first, Hiken thought Silvers should hit sitcomdom as a wise-guy brother-in-law . . . or a Little League team manager . . . or a phony-stock peddler . . . a bellboy . . . an attendant in a Turkish bath. Hiken nixed them all because the roles seemed too limiting.

Then they hit upon Ernest T. Bilko: an eternal

Sergeant Ernie Bilko	Phil Silvers
Colonel John T. Hall	Paul Ford
Master Sergeant Joan Hogan, WAC, Bilko's girlfriend	Elizabeth Fraser (1955–1958)
Private Duane Doberman	Maurice Gosfield
Corporal Henshaw	Alan Melvin
Private Dino Paparelli	Billy Sands
Private Fender	Herbie Faye
Private Zimmerman	Mickey Freeman
Corporal Rocco Barbella	Harvey Lembeck
Mess Sergeant Rupert Ritzik	Joe E. Ross
Sergeant Francis Grover	Jimmy Little
Private Mullin	Jack Healy
Private Lester Mendelsohn	Gerald Hiken
Private Greg Chickeriny	Bruce Kirby
Captain Hodges	Nelson Olmsted
The chaplain	John Gilson
Nell Hall, the colonel's wife	Hope Sansberry
Edna, a nurse	Barbara Barry
Mrs. Ritzik, Rupert's wife	Beatrice Pons

Also: Tige Andrews, Walter Cartier, Skippy Colby, Bill Hickey, Jack Davis
Announcer: Bern Bennett

1955–1956

dreamer, a brash shyster, a loser who acted like a winner, a con man who cooked up elaborate strategies to bamboozle the system, but who always failed because he was a softy. People could relate to Bilko, Silvers said, because "inside everyone is a con man wiggling to sneak out."

They called him "Bilko," after someone "bilking" you—but mostly after Steve Bilko, a minor-league player who hit sixty-one homers. Hiken and Silvers were great sports fans and filled out the supporting cast of the platoon with sports-world figures, which gave the show an earthy army-private realism. Walter Cartier, a middleweight fighter who began as a stand-in, became a series regular. Private Paparelli was played by former umpire Billy Sands. Over the years, Yogi Berra, Whitey Ford, and Gil McDougald made their TV debuts on the show. There were many ex-boxers in the cast: Lou Nova, Maxie Shapiro, Mike O'Dowd. With an assemblage like that you'd think that Rocky Graziano must have been the casting director. And he was. In fact, Graziano's old manager, Jack Healy, played Private Mullin. Said Silvers: "Sometimes I felt like Rocky was using our show as a training camp."

Comic Buddy Hackett was immediately signed to play Bilko's assistant corporal, Rocco Barbella. But Hackett left the cast to be in a Broadway loser called *Lunatics and Lovers* (in those days, Broadway was considered a much better bet than TV). It was a good thing, too, because, as Hiken said, "Silvers threw every line Hackett's way" and wasn't as effective playing Bilko. Instead they hired an actor named Harvey Lembeck (later to become seaman Gabby Di Julio on *Ensign O'Toole*).

They put out an open call for an actor to play the part of a fat, sloppy private. When Maurice Gosfield waddled in, they knew they'd found their schlepper. With his sadsack, Doberman pinscher puss, they immediately named the character Private Duane (for a touch of class) Doberman.

These stalwarts of Bilko's provided four seasons of headaches and heartaches for Commanding Officer Colo-

Silvers and Gosfield: An uncharacteristically affectionate moment

nel John T. Hall, played by Paul Ford, a Baltimore insurance man who, at forty, moved to New York to look for work in radio and television. Hall knew to steer clear of Bilko and his boys; they were the ones who really ran Fort Baxter. As Bilko bellowed to his platoon: "When are you gonna learn: who runs this post—me or the colonel?"

CBS loved the show and bought it even before finding a sponsor, which was unheard of back then. Silvers' friend Jackie Gleason had just signed an $11-million contract, so Silvers called him and asked *him* to sponsor the show. Said Silvers: "We'll just say that Jackie Gleason is good for you." Gleason didn't have to make a decision, because Camel Cigarettes—which had even more money than Gleason—picked up sponsorship of the show.

At 8:30 P.M., Tuesday, September 20, 1955, *You'll Never Get Rich* premiered, unfortunately opposite the second half of TV king Milton Berle's hour-long comedy smash show. The ratings were disastrous for Silvers, who said, "I had a hot flash in my stomach as if I'd swallowed a pack of Camels—already lit."

Camel wanted to cancel, but the network took mercy and switched the show's time slot to 8 P.M., so it wouldn't have to compete with Berle's second half-hour. That year, the show went on to win five Emmies, many other awards, 23,000,000 viewers, and—the biggest prize of all: knocking Berle off the air after an eight-year reign as Mr. Television. Needless to say, Camel didn't extinguish the show. (Writers and directors were, in fact, always working the cigarettes into the action by having someone always steal Bilko's pack of Camels. Silvers did the commercials himself; the Camel people really liked them because "he really bit into the cigarettes," they said.)

The show began each week with marching music over an animated cartoon of Bilko hooting out hut-twos. Finally Doberman's figure plops across the screen, carrying an upside-down placard reading STARRING PHIL SILVERS.

In one well-remembered episode, an eager captain devises a scheme to cut army induction time in half, making the platoon into an assembly line. A young man appears at the train platform for induction . . . with a chimp, which he was to turn over to his brother, who never shows up. In a panic, he stuffs the chimp into his duffle bag. When the chimp climbs out, the assembly line inducts the monkey. The harried WAC, typing out his name, can't hear his name. She calls out, "Harry, speak up!"—the chimp nods agreeably, and that becomes his name.

For the psychological test, the monkey leaps up on the doctor's desk and spins around on his skates (the chimp could skate and ride a bike), while the shrink mouths all the cliches: "rejected by his mother . . . violence under control. . . ." The chimp places fourth highest in the intelligence test; a visiting general congratulates him—after Harry is sworn in and is officially inducted into the US Army.

Harry bites a sergeant. When the army finds out, a court-martial is held. Bilko is assigned as defense attorney. In the courtroom scene, the chimp sits at a table next to Bilko. Whenever Phil Silvers goes *tsk-tsk-tsk*, Harry leans toward him, as if consulting. Silvers ad-libs: "Don't worry, I'll bring that up."

A prop man by mistake left a phone on a stand near the courtroom. In the midst of Bilko's impassioned plea to the panel, the chimp spots the phone, leaves his seat, and picks it up. "I plead for adjournment," Silvers ad-libs. "My client is calling for a new attorney."

Ad-libbed remarks often helped give the show a spontaneous sparkle. Once, Silvers got so caught up dancing during a scene that he forgot his cue to answer a ringing phone. A soldier who'd gone AWOL (played by Pat Hingle in his TV debut) waltzed by and yelled: "The phone, Sarge! It must be for you!"

Induction: Harry passes his intelligence exam.

Introduction: Bilko meets Doberman's sister.

Paul Ford always had a hard time with his lines; Silvers said he could always tell when Ford was about to flub a line in the midst of filming because two beads of sweat always broke out on the left side of his upper lip just before he went blank. Silvers would then shoot him the line in the form of a question—"You mean to tell me . . . ?"—and Ford would pick it up.

Through his impersonation of Doberman, Maurice Gosfield became a celebrity. "He never accepted the realities of his appearance. And talent," said Silvers, who evidently didn't think much of him. "Offstage, he thought of himself as Cary Grant playing a short, plump man," Silvers said, adding that Gosfield had no professional discipline and came late for rehearsals with such exotic excuses as having tripped on a piece of paper and hurt his leg. Gosfield appeared on the *Ed Sullivan Show* once and bombed. Said Silvers: "He began to have delusions. He believed he was a comedian." (Although Silvers may not have liked Gosfield, Harry the Chimp did, and would leap into his arms. The writers wrote Gosfield out of the episode and kept him off-camera since the chimp would respond to his directions.)

Gosfield, Silvers said, had stained ties, drooping pants, rotten table manners, and varicose veins on his stomach. Between seasons one year, Silvers and his troupe played the Riviera Hotel in Las Vegas; they always kept a running bet on how many fly buttons on Gosfield's GI uniform would be open.

Still, the audience loved Doberman and couldn't get enough of him. So the writers kept making him the center of the scripts, as in this classic called "The Face on the Recruiting Poster."

Because of a computer error (Bilko continually pointed up the inefficiency of the Army), Doberman is chosen as the All-American GI, and because of this honor his face will appear on all the recruiting posters. Nobody

The Platoon: Maurice Gosfield, Phil Silvers and (at right) Harvey Lembeck, Herbie Faye

has the heart to tell him that it is a mistake. Finally, they call in General "Iron Guts" Kramer—the toughest officer in the army—to tell Doberman the truth. The general, it turns out, looks exactly like Doberman. "Nice-looking officer," the general says. "He should be on all the posters." (The show's producers found Doberman's look-alike on Staten Island one day when they saw Jim Williams, a sailor.)

The show was shot at the old DuMont Studios in New York on East 67th St., right above a delicatessen where the cast used to hang out. Except for major scenery changes or mechanical breakdowns, the show was filmed nonstop. Three cameras were used; if one ran out of film, they used the other two. At first, they filmed it with a live studio audience; later, they filmed the show without an audience, edited it, and then ran it in front of an audience of GIs and recorded their laughs. The show never used canned laughter.

New scripts were written each week. The cast would rehearse three days, and on Friday would run through the show and then film it. Hiken did all the work—writing, directing, and producing. The first year it was on the air, a young writer friend of his died of a heart attack. Hiken, forty-one, got scared and turned over the head writing responsibilities to his assistant. A young writer named Neil Simon was one of the staff writers.

After one year on the air, *You'll Never Get Rich*, in a tribute to the talents of Phil Silvers, had its name changed to *The Phil Silvers Show*. Silvers was not at all like Bilko. Where Bilko was loud, brash, overconfident, a con man and a backslapper, Silvers was gentle, considerate, sensitive, and most important: soft-spoken (although not on the subject of Gosfield).

Brooklyn-born in 1911 of poor Russian-Jewish parents, Silvers started his career as a boy soprano, and then on to vaudeville and the Borscht Belt when his voice

cracked. He was in many Broadway shows and movies. Said Silvers: "I always seemed to play the same part—Blinky, the hero's friend who in the last reel told Betty Grable that the guy really loved her." After a musical flop in 1951, Silvers is credited with uttering the classic show-biz line: "This show is so bad that people will go out of the theater humming the costumes." He was a funny man. *Bilko* made him a star.

The show was innovative in a number of ways. It was the first sitcom to use black actors without calling attention to them. They were just there. Silvers tells a story of how he was mugged by a black man in New York—until the man realized it was Silvers he was mugging. "You're okay," the man said, and let him go.

The show was also the important debut for many future TV stars. Fred Gwynne (later on *Car 54, Where Are You?* and *The Munsters*), gaunt and thin, was an advertising man when he was cast as a compulsive eater in an eating-contest episode (Hiken always liked to cast against physical type) and was in another sequence that was a satire of *The $64,000 Question*. Joe E. Ross, who became Gwynne's *Car 54* costar, got his start on *Bilko* playing Sergeant Ritzik, "the Lucretia Borgia of Company B."

Dick Van Dyke played a boy from the Southern mountains who could hit the bull's-eye on a firing range with rocks. Bilko decided he should play baseball and tried to sell him to the New York Yankees for $125,000. Dick Cavett once answered a phone in an episode. Dina Merrill made her TV debut on *Bilko*. Guests on one 1958 show included Peggy Cass, Orson Bean, and a twenty-two-year-old Alan Alda. The clapper holder on the set—the man who yelled "Take One"—was a young Bill Dana.

Over the years, the show has not lost one ounce of its urbane humor and extraordinary energy. The boys in the platoon—the malingerers, the ragpickers, the sharp-

he doesn't mean it. "As a sergeant," Silvers said, "I can play the middle ground and attack those above and below me." And that's what Bilko did. Before it was acceptable to protest the army, Bilko poked holes in authority.

In early 1959, four years after *Bilko*'s premiere, Silvers was surprised—and appalled—to hear that CBS had canceled his show. Without telling him. Two years before, Hiken had sold his interest in the show to CBS, and the network wanted to syndicate the now-called *Sergeant Bilko* while it was still hot. The show played in Australia, the British Isles (over the BBC), Argentina, and France (where it was titled *Pepe le Bilko*).

Hiken went on to create, produce, and direct *Car 54*, a Bilkoesque sitcom that never achieved *Bilko*'s popularity or success. He died in 1968.

Silvers tried another show—*The New Phil Silvers Show*—on which he played another con man named Harry Grafton. The 1963 show didn't last more than one season; audiences, it seemed, just couldn't accept Silvers as anyone else but Bilko.

ies, the anathemas of authorities—still ring true every time. And Bilko—Bilko, that conceited ham, the neighborhood kid whom we felt superior to and tolerated. And, played by Silvers with that bogus air about him, we know

PRIVATE ONE: Bilko'll get his.
PRIVATE TWO: Oh, he's already got his—and he's got yours too.

ALSO RANS

The Charlie Farrell Show

Charlie Farrell (formerly Vern Albright, Margie's dad) played himself playing host to vacationing Hollywooders in this series, which made two separate bids for success on CBS. It was a true story, all based on things that really happened to Farrell. As a retired film actor who now owns and operates the Racquet Club resort in Palm Springs, California, Charlie coped in each episode with the difficulties of entertaining his guest-star clientele. The resort opened its doors to the public for three months in 1956 (when it was summer replacement for *I Love Lucy*). Richard Deacon (Mel on *Dick Van Dyke*) played the resort's manager, Sherman Hull.

The Great Gildersleeve

During the 1955–1956 season, interested viewers could tune into NBC to watch this sitcom about—are you ready?—the antics of a water commissioner and his orphaned niece and nephew. Throckmorton P. "the Great" Gildersleeve (played by Willard Waterman . . . *Waterman?* Is that why they made him the water commissioner?) lived at 217 Elm St. in Summerfield with his wards: Marjorie and Leroy Forrestor (Stephanie Griffin and Ronald Keith). Of course there was also the obligatory housekeeper (Birdie Lee Coggins, played by Lillian Randolph) and Lois, Gildersleeve's girlfriend (Doris Singleton). *The Great Gildersleeve* was based on the radio program of the same name.

It's Always Jan

This CBS sitcom revolved around the home and working lives of three girls: Janis Stewart (musical comedy star Janis Paige), a widow, nightclub owner, and Broadway hopeful; Valerie Malone (Merry Anders, who'd played the daughter on the 1950 *Stu Erwin* show) a curvaceous blonde secretary; and Patricia Murphy (Patricia Bright), a secretary with a heart of gold. They all share a Manhattan apartment, but Jan is the star, as she tries to raise her ten-year-old daughter, Josie (Jeri Lou James), and make it in the big city. The show only made it on the big network for one season. (Sid Melton—later Danny Williams' agent on *The Danny Thomas Show*—began his agenting career on this show). Paige sang in nearly every episode.

Joe and Mabel

New York City. Two lovers: Joe Sparton (Larry Blyden), a cabbie who feels he isn't ready for the responsibilities of marriage, and Mabel Spooner (Nita Talbot), who feels that he is. In the meantime she remains a manicurist, but doesn't give up trying to change his mind while he remains adamant in his determination to remain single. Joe's best buddy is Mike, a cabbie (played by Norman Fell, later Mr. Roper on *Three's Company*). The relationship took place on CBS until they broke up after one season.

The People's Choice

Living in New City, California, Socrates "Sock" Miller is a Bureau of Fish and Wildlife Ornithologist studying to become a lawyer. Once, when he's stranded on a country road in a broken-down car, he is befriended by Amanda "Mandy" Peoples, the mayor's daughter. She thinks he might be just the right man for the city council vacancy, and she delivers a television speech and urges a write-in vote for Sock. He is elected and becomes head of Barkerville, a housing development.

They want to get married, but the mayor says no, because Sock's not a lawyer yet. So they elope and spend their time trying to conceal their marriage during the 1956–1957 season. Several months into the 1957–1958 season, the mayor (played by Paul Maxey) discovers their marriage. He is bitter but finally accepts it. The rest of the series depicts Sock's attempts to sell real estate in Barkerville and to work out his marriage. (Sock was played by Jackie Cooper; Amanda was played by Patricia Breslin.) Soon a freeloading buddy, Rollo (Dick Wesson), moves in with them.

Commenting on all situations is Sock's bassett hound named Cleo (voice provided by Mary Jane Croft, an irregular on *I Love Lucy*.) Cleo could do tricks like pulling herself from the front legs (you had to be there) and, in the closing credits, flapping her ears up.

The show ran on NBC through 1958.

1956–1957

OFF-SCREEN

9/25 World's first transatlantic telephone cable system begins operating.
9/26 Electricity from nuclear power produced for first time at Marcoule, France.
10/29 Metropolitan Opera season opens with Met debut of Maria Callas.
10/29 Israel invades Sinai Desert.
11/6 Eisenhower wins Presidency by landslide.
11/13 US Supreme Court holds segregation on buses to be violation of 14th Amendment.
11/30 Floyd Patterson becomes youngest man to win the heavyweight championship.
1/5 Eisenhower proposes Eisenhower Doctrine to protect Middle Eastern nations against Communist aggression.

WHATEVER HAPPENED TO 1956–1957?

When they talk about the Golden Age of Television, this is the age they mean. The list of sitcoms celebrating their return engagements of successful runs is enviable: *Private Secretary, Burns and Allen, Danny Thomas, I Love Lucy, December Bride, Phil Silvers, Ozzie and Harriet, People's Choice, Father Knows Best, Bob Cummings, Life of Riley*—and those were just the sitcoms (it's hard to believe but, yes, America did watch other things besides sitcoms). But the only new sitcom that was truly popular was Gale Storm's *Oh! Susanna*, a retread of her *My Little Margie*.

This was also the year of *Ted Mack's Original Amateur Hour, GE Theater, Ed Sullivan, Steve Allen,*

Alfred Hitchcock, Loretta Young, The $64,000 Question (and its Sunday-night neighbor, *The $64,000 Challenge*), *Wyatt Earp, Arthur Godfrey, I've Got a Secret, The Millionaire, Kraft Television Theatre, US Steel Hour, Wednesday Night Fights, This Is Your Life, Eddie Fisher, My Friend Flicka, Kukla, Fran and Ollie* (five nights a week), *Walter Winchell, Jackie Gleason, George Gobel, Caesar's Hour* (Sid Caesar's follow-up to *Your Show of Shows*), *Your Hit Parade*, Groucho's *You Bet Your Life, Name That Tune, Rin Tin Tin, Dick Powell's Zane Grey Theater, The Lineup, Dragnet, Playhouse 90*—all in all, not a bad season. Not a bad season.

ALSO RANS

The Adventures of Hiram Holliday

After he corrects a newspaper story and heads off what would have been a multimillion-dollar libel suit, mild-mannered proofreader Hiram Holliday (played by meek Wally "Mr. Peepers" Cox in his second-chance sitcom) is given a year-long trip around the world by his grateful publisher (and NBC). Never one to miss a potential story, the publisher sends along reporter Joel Smith (Ainslie Pryor) to be on hand for whatever news Holliday happens to make. And they're not disappointed—Hiram stumbles onto a season's worth of unscrupulous guest stars whose evil doings he attempts to foil each week—taming lions, piloting jet planes, saving men at sea, and once, in his spare time, performing an emergency tracheotomy with a carpenter's brace and bit. Conveniently, this series stayed on the air for just one season, after which time Hiram's ticket ran out.

Blondie

This first version of the sitcom based on Chic Young's bumbling father and levelheaded wife starred Pamela Britton as Blondie and Arthur Lake as Dagwood (he had played Dagwood in the movies too). With their kids, Alexander and Cookie, and Dagwood's tightwad boss Julius Caesar Dithers (Florenz Ames), they recreated the comic strip. And, of course, they had Daisy the family dog—"the purebred mongrel." As you may recall, Dagwood was an architect with the Dithers Construction Company. He was simpleminded and just tried to cope with life. NBC ran the show from January 1957 through September. With a cast headed by Patricia Harty and Will Hutchins, and Jim Backus (later on *Gilligan's Island*) as Mr. Dithers, a CBS version ran a half-season in 1968.

Blondie: Will Hutchins, Pat Harty

The Brothers

Strong-willed Harvey and quiet Gilmore Box, down and out in San Francisco, are desperate for money and equally at a loss for experience in making and keeping any. When an opportunity to purchase a photography studio presents itself, the brothers (played by Gale Gordon and Bob Sweeney) pool all their resources and begin their dash toward an ever-elusive success in the bewildering business world. During their single CBS season, the Boxes developed more complications than they did photographs. During the summer of 1958, reruns of the series alternated with *Bachelor Father*.

A Date with the Angels

Gus (Bill Williams)—another of TV's stable of bright-go-getting-young-insurance-salesmen—has just married his pretty and sensible sweetheart, Vicki (Betty White, later Sue Ann on *The Mary Tyler Moore Show*). These are the Angels, and the series introduced viewers to their friends and neighbors while tamely exploring the complications of young married life in the Los Angeles of the 1950s. The honeymoon began on ABC in 1957 and ended early the following year. Once again, Richard Deacon turned up on this show, playing neighbor Roger Finley.

Hey Jeannie!

Hey Jeannie! Your show was canceled after only one season! This slight sitcom on CBS was about Scottish immigrant Jeannie MacLennan (Jeannie Carson), who hit New York and had a lot of misadventures. She moved in with her sponsor, Al Murray (Allen Jenkins), and his sister Liz (Jane Dulo) and spent her time trying to find a job and adjust to the American way of life. Americans had trouble adjusting to Jeannie and, when ABC rebroadcast the shows during the summer of 1960, under the title of *The Jeannie Carson Show*, she didn't fare much better.

His Honor, Homer Bell

It all took place in Spring City. Homer Bell (played by Gene Lockhart—not to be confused with his daughter *June* Lockhart, Ruth Martin on *Lassie*), was an understanding and respected justice of the peace. He had a wife and a housekeeper and a show that was syndicated for one season only.

The Marge and Gower Champion Show

Marge and Gower Champion played Marge and Gower Champion on this short-lived sitcom all about a husband and wife dance team who try to make a normal life for themselves outside of the hectic demands of show biz. Their sidekick: Cozy (played by drummer Buddy Rich). Jack Whiting played their agent and business manager, as well as Marge's father. The catch: Marge and Gower danced at least once each week. This show switched off with *The Jack Benny Program* on Sunday nights. The show hit the air on March 31 and hit the skids on June 9 of the same year.

Mr. Adams and Eve

Mr. Adams and Eve: *Howard Duff and Ida Lupino*

Movie star spouses Howard Duff and Ida Lupino (she directed many of the episodes) starred as a husband-and-wife show business couple in this sitcom which ran for one season on CBS. She is overdramatic. He likes to watch the football games on TV. The point: they were supposed to be like every other couple. The show was produced by Fred de Cordova, who worked on *Burns and Allen*, *Jack Benny*, and *Tonight* shows. Many of the episodes were supposedly based on the real-life adventures of Duff and Lupino.

Oh! Susanna

This one took off where her *My Little Margie* left off. This time around Gale Storm played the trouble-prone social director of the luxury liner *SS Ocean Queen*. Her sidekick was Miss Esmerelda "Nugey" Nugent, who operated the ship's beauty salon, played deftly by ZaSu Pitts. Roy Roberts played Susanna Pomeroy's boss, Captain Huxley, who acted as her adversary. On and off ship would come attractive young men, whom Gale Storm would often sing to. Instead of going "Gr-r-r-r-r-r," as she had done in *Margie*, she had a new characteristic here: she gave off a loud whistle by placing her fingers in her mouth. After three seasons on CBS, it shipped out to ABC; the whole thing died of seasickness in 1960 when the SS *ABC* made it walk the plank.

Stanley

Years before she achieved stardom on her own show (or even recognition on *The Gary Moore Show*), Carol Burnett popped up on this oddity, all about Stanley, the sloppy, outgoing manager of a New York City hotel-lobby newsstand. She played his girlfriend, Celia. Horace Fenton (played by Paul Lynde) owned the hotel chain. And hapless Stanley was played by Buddy Hackett. It didn't work out well, and NBC took it off the air in March 1957. Before its demise, it was live from New York.

Stanley: *Buddy Hackett*

1957–1958

Leave It to Beaver

The Real McCoys

OFF-SCREEN

9/4 Arkansas National Guardsmen, on orders of Governor Orval E. Faubus, bar nine black students from Little Rock Central High School.

10/4 James R. Hoffa elected Teamsters president in Miami Beach.

10/5 USSR announces successful launching of manmade satellite into space.

10/17 Albert Camus wins Nobel Prize for literature.

1/3 New Zealand group led by Sir Edmund Hillary reaches South Pole after 1200-mile overland trip.

1/31 US Army "Explorer I," first successful US satellite, launched at Cape Canaveral.

3/22 Mike Todd killed in plane crash in New Mexico.

3/27 Khrushchev chosen Premier of USSR.

4/4 Cheryl Crane, daughter of Lana Turner, kills hoodlum Johnny Stompanato.

6/1 Charles de Gaulle elected Prime Minister of France.

FRONT RUNNERS

LEAVE IT TO BEAVER

Wally, if your dumb brother tags along, I'm gonna— Oh, good afternoon, Mrs. Cleaver! I was just telling Wallace how pleasant it would be for Theodore to accompany us to the movies.

—EDDIE HASKELL

Suzi Lee, a typical young TV addict who is about Beaver Cleaver's age, lives in Hopkins, Minnesota, and has this to say:

"Leave It to Beaver turns me off. First of all, no one person can be as ignorant as Beaver. Even a dumb kid. Second, Wally could not possibly get along with his parents. Next, Ward is just the opposite of a real father. He never seems to have business meetings or something too important to take his time away from home. Also, June, lovely June (who wears a chiffon dress while she stands on a chair to clean the tops of the curtain rods), always has time to get her children some cookies and milk after school. And have you noticed that the Cleavers never, ever, ever go to any parties? Or that they never have just one too many glasses to drink? *Beaver* is so revolting that it should have about a dozen Pepto-Bismol commercials at each break."

So says Suzi Lee. What she doesn't say is that she keeps watching the show in reruns day after day. She is an electronically dependent child. She needs treatment. Her parents are thinking of putting her in a halfway house on a cessation therapy program of something called radio.

But back in 1957, an eight-year-old Beaver Cleaver (Beaver was short for Theodore—Cleaver wasn't short for anything) emerged on the TV screen at 7:30 one Friday night. The first episode, "Beaver Gets Spelled," had Beaver's teacher giving him a note to take home. He's sure he's being expelled (or "Spelled," in his language) and loses the note. He runs away and hides in a tree. His parents coax him out and all ends happily.

OK, Suzi: it may not have been a realistic show—but it was *reasonable*. There was no cantankerous father, no bungling wife, no babbling mother-in-law. The kids got in trouble and talked like kids. The difference between their life and ours is that their life only lasted a half-hour each week.

The show was about kids growing up—and as they

Ward Cleaver	Hugh Beaumont
June Cleaver	Barbara Billingsley
Wally Cleaver	Tony Dow
Theodore "Beaver" Cleaver	Jerry Mathers
Eddie Haskell	Ken Osmond
Clarence "Lumpy" Rutherford	Frank Bank (1960–1963)
Julie Foster, Wally's girlfriend	Cheryl Holdridge
Larry Mondello	Rusty Stevens (1958–1959)
Gilbert Bates	Stephen Talbot (1960–1963)
Whitey Whitney	Stanley Fafara (1960–1962)
Fred Rutherford	Richard Deacon (1961–1963)
Gwen Rutherford	Majel Barrett
Violet Rutherford	Veronica Cartwright
Miss Landers	Sue Randall (1959–1962)
Mrs. Rayburn, the school principal	Doris Packer
Gus, the fire chief	Burt Mustin
Judy Hessler	Jeri Vale
Mrs. Mondello	Madge Blake

did, so did we. It wasn't an uproarious comedy like *Lucy,* or a spoof show like *Get Smart!* There were no gimmicks. It was full of "WWW"—Warmth, Wit, and Wisdom.

For six years, *Leave It to Beaver* was a kids' show with an adult laugh-track. Here's an early typical episode of the show, called "The State vs. Beaver."

The credits are drawn in wet cement. We enter the two-story suburban house to find Super Mother June Cleaver cleaning a closet. She is wearing an apron, pearls, and earrings. Beaver and his older brother Wally then go out to work on their go-cart. The dirt on Beaver's face has been cleanly applied. Super Father Ward Cleaver (wearing a cardigan over a sports shirt) is delighted to help the kids, who have total respect, love, and admiration for their dad (they treat their mom like a den mother; the show was written and produced by men). When Ward comes back into the house, June queries him: "Are you sure they're all right in that thing alone?"

"Of course they are," Ward says. "What's there to worry about?"

"Of course! They're just our children, that's all," June sighs.

They call each other "dear" all the time.

But Ward decides to give the boys a serious safety talk and tells them they can only drive the cart when he's with them.

WARD: It's for your own good.
WALLY: Sure, Dad, every time you bawl us out, it's for our own good.
BEAVER: I sure wish there was somebody in this family for *me* to yell at.
WALLY: That's your tough luck.

In the next scene, Larry Mondello—a fat kid who's always eating—tries to talk Beaver into driving the go-cart. "I bet you don't even know how to drive it," Larry taunts. So Beaver and Larry take it out onto the street. A policeman spots them, stops them, and asks Beaver to see his license. Beaver doesn't have one, he says, because he's only "seven-and-three-quarters years old." The officer writes him out a ticket.

That night, after the family all pitch in with the dishes (June washes, Ward dries the front of the plates, Wally dries the back, and Beaver puts them away), it's dessert time. Beaver says he doesn't want ice cream, and in fact, wants to go right to bed.

"Uh, Mom, could I be 'scused?"

"Ah . . . yes, of course, dear." Then: "Ward, you don't think they're up to anything, do you?"

In their bedroom, Beaver confesses to his brother: "Dad told me not to never touch the car," he explains.

The next day June is talking to Ward while he reads the paper.

JUNE: Oh, what a day—my broiler caught on fire this afternoon.
WARD (*still reading paper*):   That's fine.
JUNE: You're ignoring me.
WARD: Good, dear—I'll take care of it tomorrow.
JUNE: You're not paying a bit of attention to me.
WARD: Yes I am. You said the vacuum cleaner caught on fire.
JUNE: . . . and I thought you weren't listening.

Later, Beaver and Wally go to court.

Beaver tells Wally: "No matter what happens, I'm not going to cry."

Beaver tells the judge that his parents work on a ship and are also sick. He finally confesses, explaining that he was scared to bring his parents. He cries. The judge wipes Beaver's tears.

JUDGE: I think Theodore has learned his lesson—haven't you, Theodore?
BEAVER: Yes, sir. I'm not gonna take no vehicle no place.

The judge lets them go, saying he will "expunge it from the records," and tells them to get rid of the go-cart.

BEAVER: Do I have to tell my father?
JUDGE: I'll leave that up to you . . .

But of course he does.

When Beaver informs his father, Ward is only angry that he didn't come to him right away when he got into trouble.

BEAVER: I guess I was a-scared to, Dad.
WARD (*delivering this episode's moral*):   I don't care what kind of trouble you may get into in life—you don't ever need to be afraid to come to your parents and tell them.

Beaver goes to his room as Wally delivers the clincher: "Dad, he didn't want to hurt your feelings, because you were so nice in helping us build the car and everything. He didn't want to make you feel bad 'cause you've got a kid like him."

Music . . . tears . . . applause . . . end of show.

Leave It to Beaver was not really a kids' show; it was an adult version of what kids were like. The writers (some of the same people who wrote *Amos 'n' Andy,* incidentally) got the ideas and speech patterns from their own kids just as, perhaps, the ideas for *Amos 'n' Andy* came from their own cleaning ladies. It wasn't so much that *Beaver* wasn't real, but that it was based on the memory of being a child, rather than being a child.

Nobody had any problems. They only had foibles. Girls were girls and—most important—boys were boys.

Beaver and Wally prided themselves in being messy, in not wanting to take a bath, in throwing their towels and clothes around. Once Beaver and Wally took a four-day trip and never once changed their clothes. As if a can opener had been applied, the canned laughter ripped forth.

Mr. Cleaver was an accountant. Mrs. Cleaver was a housewife. They lived at 211 Pine St. in Mayfield, USA, a suburb of Utopia.

The show—along with its uncle, *Father Knows Best*, and its aunt, *The Donna Reed Show*—broke the stereotypes of the cantankerous father and the bumbling mother—but replaced them with Perfect Parents. Mrs. Cleaver's only fault was that she was overprotective. But she was always ready with fudge and cookies, which seemed to be her most important function after childbirth. Mr. Cleaver was the perfect father, always coming to the rescue, always ready with an ounce of advice and an anecdote from his own childhood. There was always a moral.

In a way, the show was the *Amos 'n' Andy* of childhood. It played on cultural, rather than ethnic, stereotypes. Beaver hated homework, fidgeted in his classroom seat, and liked recess. "Good gosh!" Ward would say when he was astonished. Whenever Beaver was scolded, older brother Wally liked to hang around and listen.

Beaver's and Wally's friends were far more interesting than they were. One of them was Eddie Haskell, Wally's two-faced sneaky pal who irritated Beaver by calling him "Squirt." "Wally, if your gunky brother comes with us, I'm gonna . . . Oh, hello, Mrs. Cleaver, I was just telling Wallace how pleasant it would be for Theodore to accompany us to the movies." Conboy Eddie was the show's Bilko and Kingfish.

Clarence "Lumpy" Rutherford, Wally's oafish, jelly-belly buddy, had an overprotective father (who happened to work in Ward's office). Whenever Lumpy went home whimpering, his father always made Clarence "march straight over" to the Cleavers' and apologize. "Gee, that's okay, Lumpy," Wally would say.

Beaver's buddies were of a different variety. His best friend, Larry Mondello, was loaded down with baby fat and was always munching on something high in saturated fat. His other friends from school were Whitey Whitney and Gilbert Bates. On his way home from school, Beaver occasionally stopped by the firehouse to chat with his friend Gus, an old-time fire-fighter. One person who was not his friend was Judy Hessler, an overgrown, pigtailed girl who sat in the "smart row" and teased him. Overseeing it all was—sigh—the Grant Avenue Grammar School's own lovely Miss Landers, whom little Beaver had a big crush on.

For the most part, it wasn't a funny show—"humorous realism" is how its producers described it—and, in the TV trade, it was considered, not a big laugh

Mother Knows Best: Barbara Billingsley, Jerry Mathers

show, but "a chuckle show." They probably had to go out and buy a whole new laugh-track for it.

At the end of his audition for the role of Beaver, eight-year-old Jerry Mathers fidgeted and said: "I gotta go now, I got a Cub Scout meeting." They hired him right away, because he seemed "so real."

He was no newcomer to the screen, large or small. In 1950, when Mathers was two years old, an advertising director of a department store approached his mother and asked if Jerry could model for their Christmas calendar. Yes. The photographer who took the pictures suggested Jerry be signed to an agent who specialized in children performers.

At two and a half, Mathers debuted on Ed Wynn's television show and, in 1954 (along with his sister Susie), played a child on *This Is My Love*. Alfred Hitchcock saw him on a Lux Video Theater Show and signed him for his 1955 film *The Trouble with Harry*. Shortly after that, he appeared in two Bob Hope movies, *The Seven Little Foys* and *That Certain Feeling*. In 1957: *Beaver*. Said *Variety*: "Beaver was played with fetching naturalness by little Jerry Mathers." *Beaver* made him a star.

Mathers idolized his on-screen brother, Tony Dow, because he was a champion swimmer and diver, not because he was a champion actor. Dow (twelve when he got the part of Wally) was such a bad actor, in fact, that they had to administer massive doses of private coaching to him. The son of *Our Gang*'s silent screen bathing beauty Muriel Montrose, Dow had agreed to help a friend audition for a part at Screen Gems. His friend didn't get the part, but Dow did. Screen Gems put him in a series (which bombed) and that led to *Beaver*.

Barbara Billingsley was, off-screen, the mother of two sons who, she said, "are both like Beaver." And she was like June—mild-mannered and soft-spoken. Also insecure. She always thought she got the part because the producers felt sorry for her. Before *Beaver*, she had appeared on two sitcoms: *Professional Father* (1955) and *The Brothers* (1956).

Sometimes she felt the writers were "too harsh" on Beaver, that she was required to scold him for things that weren't so bad. And so she rewrote the scripts to make her character "more realistic."

In one episode, Beaver wouldn't eat his brussels sprouts. "I just don't like them," he tells his mother. She punishes him by making him stay home while the rest of the family goes to the football game. In the near future Beaver relents and says that he will eat them the next time they are served (which just happens to be the night of the Big Game). In a restaurant that night, Beaver eats them and discovers that he likes them after all. He apologizes for "being a kid" and his parents apologize for pushing the matter too hard.

In 1962—when Mathers was fourteen and pushing puberty—he was still talking and acting like a seven-year-old. "Beaver the Bunny" had him walking to a school pageant dressed in a bunny suit. It was all about being embarrassed. The truly embarrassing thing was that the producers didn't let Beaver grow up.

Because that's what the show was all about: growing up. In the suburbs, true. (Beaver wasn't very street-wise. He was very living-room-wise, as were the rest of us; strangely enough, the educator in our living rooms was Mr. Television, who taught us lessons like Beaver 101.)

Beaver always said "Yes, sir" and "Yes, ma'am" to his parents. The kids always came up with cogent comments—"I'd rather go look at a skunk than look at a girl," Beaver once said—and set examples for the rest of us. Beaver and Wally always came through for one another. You could tell because of the show's closing credits, when they were walking home from school, and Wally had his arm around Beaver.

Brothers: Jerry Mathers, Tony Dow

In 1963—after six seasons and 234 episodes—*Leave It to Beaver* left. By this time, *Beaver* had been traded to ABC (back in 1958 after one unsuccessful season on CBS) and had scored high in the ratings race. We knew, somehow, that without the benefit of a prepared script, Beaver and Wally and Eddie and Lumpy and Larry and the other kids in Mayfield would grow up on their own.

Lately—with Archie and Edith going at it, and Mary Richards teaching life's facts to the little girl next door—*Leave It to Beaver* is camp—summer camp, to be sure, but classic camp, complete with its own set of media myths. For example: Somewhere in Los Angeles there's a policeman named Ken Osmond who once played Eddie Haskell. A fable grew around him that he grew up to become rock star Alice Cooper.

And Jerry Mathers, another rumor tells us, died in the Vietnam War. There had been a wire service story reporting that Mathers had been killed in action, and actress Shelley Winters spread the word on a talk show that night. Even though Mathers' parents sent out a retraction, "People sent letters of condolence and flowers to my family," Mathers—quite alive—says. In fact, Mathers finally did get out of Miss Landers' classroom, enrolled in the University of California at Berkeley (in philosophy, yet), and went on to TV selling real estate. Starting in the late seventies, Mathers and his TV brother Tony Dow started touring the country, performing together in dinner theater plays. (Barbara Billingsley, incidentally, retired to southern California. Hugh Beaumont moved to Minnesota, where he began raising and selling Christmas trees.)

Mathers gets no residuals from the show's reruns (he was only paid for the first seven showings), although the distributing company makes hundreds of thousands a year—for only the cost of shipping the program.

"I don't even watch it anymore. It's boring for me," Mathers says. "My little brother likes it. And my mother. But I'm sick of it."

Sick of it? But surely he must get a little misty, a few goosebumps—just as we do—when we hear the credits where they say: ". . . and Jerry Mathers as the Beaver."

THE REAL McCOYS

*Want you to meet the family/Known as the Real Mc-
Coys . . .*

—opening lines of theme song

*T*he *Real McCoys* was the real McCoy when it came to countrified sitcoms. It hit the screen several years before the rating-racing *Beverly Hillbillies,* and although its impact was slighter, *The Real McCoys* was a resident-in-good-standing of Sitcom City for six years. Week in, week out, Amos and Luke and Kate (and Pepino) spun enough yarns to make sweaters, mufflers, and mittens for the city of Los Angeles, from where the show originated. True, the people in that warm climate didn't need sweaters, mufflers, and mittens. Neither did they need *The Real McCoys.* But, like the rest of us, that's what they got.

Like *Ozzie and Harriet* and *My Three Sons,* the show didn't seem to be anybody's favorite (the way, say, *Lucy* and *Topper* were) but in its innocuous Wonder Bread way, it hung on forever and everyone watched. Like brushing your teeth and getting your hair cut, watching *The Real McCoys* was just one of those things you had to do when you were growing up in late-fifties America. (The term "the real McCoy," incidentally, refers to an eighteenth-century sewing machine manufacturer named McCoy who advertised his product as "the Real McCoy.")

Unlike *The Beverly Hillbillies,* it didn't poke fun at itself or at its genre of rural sitcoms. *The Real McCoys* was gentle and believable—not about what we knew to be true, but about what we imagined to be true. It was a country show for city people, a man's show for women. It wasn't a spoof or satire, it just was what it was: a simple comedy show about simple people who cared about simple things.

And then there was Grandpappy Amos, an incorrigible codger who was against anything anyone else was for: hot rodders, air force jets flying over his head, talkative old ladies, even television. Amos McCoy was a cross between Archie Bunker and Mr. Ed. He had the regulation Heart of Gold stuck away somewhere, but he was as cantankerous as all get out.

KATE *(pleading)*: But, Grandpa, there're two sides to everything.
AMOS: Yeah, and I'm on the right side!

With his shoulders and arms jumping, Amos walked like a chicken with a limp. He was the grandpa—but he was really the child. He was stubborn and ornery and had to be taken care of by his grandchildren, Luke and Hassie and Little Luke, and Luke's wife, Kate (whom Luke called "sugar babe"), as well as their Mexican farmhand—who "came with the house"—named Pepino.

In the first episode—aired on October 3, 1957—the family has had a hard trip from their old West Virginia farm to their new ranch in Los Angeles' San Fernando Valley. The small, run-down house seems beautiful to the family, but Grandpa hates it all. He misses his old cronies. Finally he has a fight with a neighbor that restores his good humor.

Amos McCoy	Walter Brennan
Luke McCoy	Richard Crenna
Kate McCoy	Kathy Nolan (1957–1962)
Hassie McCoy	Lydia Reed
Little Luke McCoy	Michael Winkleman (1957–1962)
Pepino Garcia	Tony Martinez
George MacMichael, Amos' friend	Andy Clyde
Flora MacMichael, George's sister	Madge Blake
Mac Maginnis, Amos' friend	Willard Waterman
Lela Maginnis	Shirley Mitchell
Mrs. Jensen, the McCoy housekeeper	Connie Gilchrist
Helga (replaced Ms. Jensen)	Eva Norde
Frank Grant, Helga's boyfriend	James Lydon
Louise Howard, owner of ranch next to the McCoys (CBS episodes)	Janet De Gore
Gregg Howard, her son	Butch Patrick
Frank, their handyman	John Qualen
Winifred Jordan, Louise's aunt	Joan Blondell
Hank Johnson, Amos' friend	Lloyd Corrigan
Harry Purvis, Amos' partner in the roadside egg business	Charles Lane

Grandpa Amos was the type who, when someone tried to get him to trade in his horse for a tractor, said, "I ain't a-gonna plow with anything I can't yell at."

And yell he did; six years' worth. He bullied, he blustered, he cajoled, he did everything he could to get his own way. From getting rehitched (he was a widower) to learning to read (he was illiterate), he put up a fuss and a fight.

The day after the show's premiere, the New York *Times* said it was "for anyone who wants his corn as high as an elephant's eye." *Variety* called it "cornball, hillbilly comedy, strictly *Ma and Pa Kettle* stuff."

Critics aside, the public liked the show (or at least watched it) and after a couple of weeks, *The Real McCoys* was giving its competition—*Climax* and *Playhouse 90*—a run for their ratings. Down-home humor helped it climb up the ratings.

In one of the first episodes, Luke McCoy is locked out of his bedroom by his wife, who is trying to force him to learn how to read, which he considers "sissy." Grandpa advises his son to stick it out and curb any yearnings he may have for his wife with "willpower and cold water applied to the back of the neck."

Sound country advice, perhaps, but of course Luke becomes literate and the show ends happily.

But it didn't end there. The show was full of preaching; the moral tone was a tad louder than most other sitcoms. Once when Grandpa almost gets involved in a shady land deal, Kate tells him that "the Lord is warning you what's gonna happen iffen you go through with that deal," adding that "the only way to live is by the Golden Rule."

Like the other sitcoms of the time, *The Real McCoys* was often infected with a bad Case of the Cutes, as when Little Luke is watching Big Luke kiss his wife: "Gee whiz, she's makin' him kiss her again."

Says sister Hassie, "She's not making him. He likes it."

Little Luke snorts: "He likes it! Bubble gum tastes better and lasts longer."

A lot of the shows revolved around what was then called the Battle of the Sexes, usually between Luke and Kate, with Grandpa decidedly on Luke's side. When Kate wants to wear a low-cut dress to a dance, Luke and Amos are in a snit. She insists and all is forgiven when it is discovered that the bare-shouldered blonde ogling Gramps is the new minister's wife.

Sexism seemed to waltz through like it was a barndance. On "The Mrs. Homemaker Contest," Luke and Amos want to buy a gun at the General Store. But it costs $48.50, and they don't have the money. Then they get an idea: to enter Kate in the "Mrs. Homemaker Contest"—prize: $50. Says Amos: "Think of the honor . . . and the gun."

They enter Kate's name without telling her. They come home, and Kate is cooking.

AMOS: Just take a whiff of that soup she's makin' . . . um-um. . . .
KATE: I'm boilin' Little Luke's overalls. . . .
AMOS: How do you like that? She makes everything smell good.

Kate says she doesn't want to be entered in the contest. "As long as my family knows that I'm a good homemaker, that's good enough for me." Luke tries to talk her into it: "Imagine, walking into the next PTA meeting as Mrs. Homemaker. . . ." "It does sound kinda nice," Kate muses.

She says Okay. Grandpa and Luke are like two little boys. Now they have to go out and talk the judges into voting for Kate. They wine and dine one of them. Another is Amanda Comstock, "who used to be sweet on me," Amos says. The problem: he called her Old Flap Jaw at the last Grange Dance and she isn't speaking to him.

So Amos dusts off his Sunday suit (which he wears with white socks) and tells Luke to "Pick me some flowers—but don't get nothin' that'll make her sneeze, because I don't want her to open her mouth more than she has to." Amos gets in his jalopy and drives over to court her. "Don't flash that dazzling smile on me," he woos her, "have pity on an old man." When he lets slip the real reason for his visit, she gets angry. Then Amos tries to bribe the other two judges. Nothing works.

Days later: Kate's not home. A telegram arrives for her. Luke opens it: Kate's won the contest and the $50. "Now we can go get the gun before Kate finds out," Amos says. Too late: Kate has already found out and has bought a carpet sweeper and a toaster. Bellows Amos: "But it don't shoot nothin' but toast." And the episode is over.

Kathy Nolan (Kate) first received national attention when she appeared as Wendy in Mary Martin's Broadway and TV *Peter Pan*. She played Cousin Liz on the

Order of Mystic Nile Convention: In L.A., Grandpappy and bellboy (Billy Curtis)

Where's Pepino? (from left): Richard Crenna, Walter Brennan, Kathy Nolan

1953–1954 sitcom *Jamie*, on which she was billed as Kathleen Nolan. When *The Real McCoys* ended its run, she went back to using Kathleen Nolan. She started her career as an usher on Broadway at the Palace Theater when Judy Garland performed there. At an audition, she said to a producer: "I met you at the Palace when I was with Judy Garland." Her real name: Joycelyn Joan Schrum. She was "killed off" on the show after the 1961–1962 season when she demanded more money and script consideration.

Luke was played by Richard Crenna, who was known on radio and early TV for his high, squeaky voice. On radio, he was Oogie Pringle on *A Date With Judy*, Andy Hardy's next-door neighbor Breezie, among other high-pitched Henry Aldrich-type kids. He made more than 6,000 radio shows. He was best known, though, as the pubescent Walter Denton on *Our Miss Brooks*, both the radio and TV versions. Crenna went on to direct some episodes of *The Real McCoys* and became the star of *Slattery's People* in 1964, and Norman Lear's *All's Fair*. He had trouble getting his part on *The Real McCoys*. Said the producer when Crenna asked for the role: "I want a tall, manly guy, not a simpering boy." Fortunately, Crenna was not so typecast that he couldn't effectively make the transition.

"Luckiest thing ever happened to me was a kick in the face," said Walter Brennan, the three-time Academy Award winner who played Grandpappy Amos. The kick he was referring to was an accident in a movie scene where he lost all his teeth. Since that time, he started to play old men.

Brennan was sixty-one when *The Real McCoys* hit

the airwaves, and the character he played was similar to his film roles. Throughout the show's run, Brennan continually threatened to quit, claiming he couldn't do comedy.

In 1962, CBS bought *The Real McCoys* from ABC for a reported $7,500,000. Brennan, however, was getting tired and wanted to star in only sixteen of the year's twenty-six episodes. And so Kate and Luke were on their own more. Even though the show was pitted against *Bonanza* and *The Sunday Night Movie*, it still managed to pull 30 percent of the audience. Then CBS announced that *The Real McCoys* was penciled in for a seventh season, to appear right before a new CBS sitcom called *The Beverly Hillbillies*, which some considered an imitation of *The Real McCoys*.

And then, as if out of nowhere, at the end of the sixth season, *The Real McCoys* got canceled. "It's because of the fatigue factor," explained a CBS vice-president. "If a show begins to wear thin on the ear and eye, you don't just say, 'Well, the tread is thin, but I'll wait till next year to buy new tires.' You change now and avoid a blowout."

Walter Brennan would move on to a new series—back on ABC—called *Tycoon*, in 1964. It didn't do well. Neither did he. Brennan died in 1974. Television had been good to him.

Not to Grandpappy Amos, though, who hated the dad-burn thing. "Why," he squawked, "it's just pure foolishness, squattin' all day in front of a little black box, starin' bleary-eyed at people who ain't no more than two inches high. It's a passing fancy, I tell you, like buggy whips and high-button shoes. . . ."

ALSO RANS

Bachelor Father

This popular sitcom went through many changes, so listen carefully:

The basic premise: at 1163 Rexford Dr., Beverly Hills, California, bachelor-attorney Bentley Gregg (John Forsythe) lived with his Chinese houseboy, Peter Tong (Sammee Tong), who ran the house, and orphaned thirteen-year-old niece, Kelly (Noreen Corcoran), who became his ward after her parents were killed in an automobile accident (dead sitcom parents seemed to be always either killed in a car accident or something bizarre like an avalanche). There was also the requisite shaggy dog, here named Jasper.

Anyway, the stories revolved around Bentley's attempts to adjust to being a Bachelor Father while maintaining his persona as womanizer.

Here are the changes: Kelly's girlfriend Ginger (always played by Bernadette Withers) went through three unaccountable name switches. In 1957, she was

Bachelor Father: *John Forsythe and guest Gisele MacKenzie*

called Ginger Farrell. She had a mother named Louise Farrell. In 1958, she became Ginger Loomis. Her "mother" was dropped, and she was given a new set of parents (the actor who played her father, Whit Bissel, had previously played Steve Gibson, the father of a friend of Kelly's). Then, in 1960, Ginger got a new last name: Mitchell. Then both her parents were dropped, and she got a new set. The family dog, Jasper, however, stayed the same through the show's run, although we never found out about *his* parents.

As if that weren't enough confusion for the viewers, Kelly went—within a two-week period—from high school to college (without even a summer break or a trip to Fort Lauderdale) and, suddenly thereafter she got a new love in her life—Warren Dawson (Aron Kincaid), a young lawyer who became Bentley's junior partner and Kelly's groom-to-be (they went off the air before they could get married). During this time, stable old Bentley went through five different secretaries: Vickie (Alice Backus), Kitty (Shirley Mitchell), another Kitty (Sue Ann Langdon—later *Arnie's* wife), Suzanne (Jeanne Bal), and Connie (Sally Mansfield). Others appearing in the show: Sid Melton (who played Danny Thomas' agent and pal), Mary Tyler Moore (pre-*The Dick Van Dyke Show*), and Harry Von Zell (post-*Burns and Allen*).

Perhaps, though, the show's main distinction was its unusual network history: from 1957 until 1959, it was on CBS; then, until 1961, it was housed by NBC; it was on ABC through 1962. Forsythe, nearly 20 years later, achieved vocal distinction when he played the voice of the invisible Charlie Townsend on *Charlie's Angels*.

Dick and the Duchess

CBS decided to brighten up the mundane—and probably not very funny—world of the insurance claims investigator by dropping off Dick Starrett (Patrick O'Neal) in London. In what must be the weirdest accident of his career, Dick runs into Jane (Hazel Court), a real live British duchess. He makes her both his wife and his assistant. Her family is upper-crust, but that doesn't stop her meddling in his job. For one season, curious Americans were allowed to follow as Dick and his duchess snooped around the city. While we weren't looking, they sneaked right off the air.

The Eve Arden Show

This show was not a success in its attempt to bring the comedienne back to the small screen after her triumph as *Our Miss Brooks*. In this series, Arden played Liza Hammond, a mother, widow, and traveling lecturer. She had twin daughters—Jenny (Gail Stone) and Mary (Karen Greene)—and her share of *tsouris*. Frances Bavier ("Aint Bee" on *Andy Griffith*) played housekeeper Nora and George Howell (played by Allyn Joslyn) booked her tours. CBS gave the program the ax in March of 1958.

Love That Jill

Since America had loved *Love That Bob* three years before, ABC decided to rip off two-thirds of the title and try their luck at a sitcom all about the heads of rival Manhattan model agencies (played by real-life marrieds Anne Jeffreys and Robert Sterling, who came back to life after being ghosts on *Topper*). Jack wanted Jill (yes, those were their names), and there were plenty of beautiful models with names like Melody and Peaches and Ginger. Jack and Jill's ratings slid down the hill, and they lost their jobs after three months.

Sally

Joan Caulfield (*My Favorite Husband* exile) and Marion Lorne (*Mr. Peepers* alumna) starred as Sally Truesdale and Myrtle Banford, who travel around together. Myrtle is a rich, elderly widow who's young at heart. Sally's her young, pretty, and single traveling companion. Together they journeyed—via NBC—until February 1958, when their format changed. After that (but not for long) Sally and Myrtle Banford spent most of their time running the Banford-Bleacher Department Store (of which Mrs. B. was part-owner). And there were three notable new cast members: other owner Bascomb Bleacher (played by Gale Gordon, post-*Our Miss Brooks*, pre-*Lucy Show*) and his incompetent son Bascomb, Jr. (played by Arte Johnson, pre-*Laugh-In*), and Sally got a new love interest, played by singer Johnny Desmond. But even with those added attractions, the show lasted only another month.

Tugboat Annie

Marie Dressler made Annie famous in the movie, and in the television version, Minerva Urecal played Annie Brennan, a middle-aged skipper of the tugboat *Narcissus*. Also with her were Walter Sande as Horatio Bullwinkle, Annie's employer, and Stan Francis as Murdoch McArdle, the *Narcissus'* owner. The show was syndicated and filmed for one year only. It was also called *The Adventures of Tugboat Annie*.

1958—1959

The Donna Reed Show

The Ann Sothern Show: *Sothern and fifteen-year-old daughter, Patricia*

OFF-SCREEN

10/6 The atomic-powered submarine *Seawolf* sets undersea endurance record when it surfaces after sixty days.
10/1 John Joseph Scanlon, thirty-eight, notorious hoodlum, is fatally shot.
10/23 Opening of Broadway comedy about television, *Make a Million,* with Sam Levene.
2/17 Fidel Castro becomes Premier of Cuba.
2/1 Zachariah Davis Wheat designated for Baseball Hall of Fame.
2/17 Vanguard satellite achieves orbit after Cape Canaveral launch.
4/7 Lorraine Hansberry first black to receive NY Drama Critics Circle Award for *A Raisin in the Sun.*
6/19 Governor Earl Long of Louisiana committed to state mental institution.

FRONT RUNNER

THE DONNA REED SHOW

There are cookies in the jar and milk in the refrigerator.
—DONNA STONE to son Jeff when he'd arrive home
from school.

The show opened the way—for sure—no family you ever knew opened their day: the phone rings and Mother—in her stylish housedress and obligatory string pearls—comes down the stairs of her upper-middle-class-traditionally-furnished home and picks up the phone on—of course—the second ring. She smiles as she answers and, as her handsome Husband walks in—in conservative business suit—smiles as she hands the phone to him. Her two kids—a well-dressed older Daughter and a squeaky-clean younger Son—come in to see what's going on. She gives the children their books and lunches—the husband takes his black bag (for he is a physician)—they all kiss her and leave. After they are gone, she leans against the door and smiles contentedly.

And then she has an affair with the milkman.

No way. This is 1958 and it wasn't until at least 1978 that wives had on-camera affairs with their milkmen. Actually, Donna Stone—the mother in question—never had an affair with anyone—but—for five years—America had a one-night-a-week stand with her on *The Donna Reed Show.*

The Donna Reed Show was one of those domestic comedies designed specifically to make you feel inadequate. Nobody ever yelled in that household. Dinner was always on time, everything somehow got done—and Donna never was seen doing a thing. She looked like she came right out of the Mommy Mold, and her corners never crumbled.

And who could compete with the pre- and later-pubescent perfection of Paul Petersen? If you were a daughter, you couldn't come out ahead of Shelley Fabares, who always said, did, and—most important—wore the right thing. Carl Betz as Alex Stone—Dr. Alex Stone—was different from other physician fathers; he never worked late and was always home for dinner, he never was exhausted from overwork, none of his patients—God forbid—ever got sick.

And Donna—short for Madonna, no doubt—was the *best*. Pretty, prim, precise, proper, and all the other Ps—especially perfect—that made good sitcom mothers. She was TV's first Sitmom. As one mother has said: "Donna Reed set back a whole generation of mothers. None of us could be like Donna Reed. Donna Reed was a myth for mothers. Even Donna Reed couldn't be like Donna Reed. One thing for sure, though—Donna Reed would never have let her kids watch *The Donna Reed Show.*"

None of the sitcom families (until *All in the Family*) ever watched TV. It was not considered a part of sit-community life. Maybe they watched TV the other 167½ hours of the week they weren't on TV—but not while we were watching. And we were watching.

So were millions of Americans. They were viewing

Donna Stone	Donna Reed
Alex Stone	Carl Betz
Mary Stone	Shelley Fabares (1958–1963)
Jeff Stone	Paul Petersen
Midge Kelsey	Ann McCrea (1963–1965)
Dr. David Kelsey	Bob Crane (1963–1965)
Smitty, Jeff's friend	Darryl Richard (1965–1966)
Herbie Bailey, Mary's boyfriend (early episodes)	Tommy Ivo
Scotty Simpson, Mary's boyfriend (later episodes)	Jerry Hawkins
Karen Holmby, Jeff's girlfriend	Janet Langard (1964–1965)
Bibi, Jeff's girlfriend	Candy Moore
Susanna, Smitty's girlfriend	Sandy Descher (1965–1966)
Trisha	Patty Petersen (1963–1966)

Hubby and The Little Woman: Donna Reed and Carl Betz

typical episodes such as this one: "The Football Uniform"—aired in 1958—as only Swanson TV Dinners could sponsor it.

ALEX: If anyone wants me, I'll be at the hospital having a consultation.
DONNA *(oven timer rings):* Oh—there's my oven—I better have a consultation with my chocolate cake.
ALEX *(grins):*   Need the help of a specialist?
DONNA *(lovingly reprimanding):*   No, thank you. There are no complications. *(He exits.)*

A conversation ensues between Donna and her daughter. Donna wants to get rid of an ugly vase that they got for a wedding present—but she's sure that Alex is crazy about it and sentimental over it. (Later, Alex tells his son the same thing, that he hates it but is sure Donna loves it.)

Their son, Jeff, is seen with some buddies saying how mothers are pushovers. "My mom's always telling me to clean up my room," he boasts, "but by the time I get around to it, she's already done it." He heads home to try to con his mother into buying a football uniform for $22. "Did you wipe your feet?" she asks him as he comes into the kitchen. Of course he did. He goes into his uniform routine and Donna says sweetly: "Jeff, it's about time you learn you're not going to get everything you ask for."

(A commercial here: a family is smiling and eating Swanson TV Dinners. They too have no TV and look much like the Stones.)

Next scene: the family has decided that in order to get a uniform, young Jeff must work for it—and he only has two weeks. He comes in from walking a mean dog and announces that he has only until Thursday because the team picture is being taken for the local paper. This is tearing Donna apart and she looks very sad. When Alex enters, Donna backs down and tries to talk him into giving Jeff the money. "No." Then Donna finds a used uniform at an auction (she is resourceful). Jeff wants to bid on it but he's only earned $2.50. Donna matches him,

but tells him not to tell his father, who does the same thing. They all bid on the uniform, not knowing the others have bid (since they can't see one another). Mutters Alex to himself: "Some female is trying to outbid me on that uniform." But in the end, Jeff gets the uniform and everyone embraces. They also decide to keep the ugly vase.

When Dr. and Mrs. Stone and family debuted at 9 P.M. in 1958 on a Wednesday night (Wednesday? How appropriate—doctors' day off), *Variety* called the show, in which the family attempted to get away for a weekend, a "pleasant family situation comedy"—and the key word there is *pleasant*. The comedy was low-keyed and the situations were sober, sensible, and plausible. The Stone family was just that—also solid and upright, not daffy or silly like so many of their TV neighbors. It was definitely a comedy of recognition—not so much of the way we were, but of the way we wished we were. *The Donna Reed Show* held up a funhouse mirror to American family life and called it reality. But—as Donna Reed said and so many viewers obviously believed—"We've worked very hard to put together a believable family and a realistic picture of family life." She was later to revoke those words.

Donna Belle Mullenger was an even-tempered Iowa farmgirl who came to Hollywood and got her name from an MGM press agent who wanted to name her Donna Adams or Donna Drake—but both were taken by other actresses, so he settled on Donna Reed. "Donna," one friend said about her, "is not prettier or more talented. She has character." By the time she started her series, she had been in more than forty movies, winning, in fact, an Academy Award for her 1953 role in *From Here to Eternity*, in which she played a whore "who longed for a man of her own"—a role she hoped would change her goody-goody wholesome image—but obviously didn't. Five years later, she and her husband, Tony Owen, coproduced the show, forming TODON Productions.

The show was not an instant success. Its first-season ratings were low—playing opposite the popular *The Millionaire* and the invulnerable *Milton Berle Show* (actually, Berle hosting the *Kraft Music Hall*) which had been running forever and was seemingly immune to rating drops. Not for long.

"I'm fed up to here with stories about kooky, amoral, or sick women," Reed proclaimed.

But it wasn't all Donna Reed. One young woman cried when she heard that Carl Betz—who played Alex Stone—had died at fifty-six in 1978. "He was so decent, so clean, so good-looking—so boring—and I've been looking for my Carl Betz ever since I saw the show." A former radio DJ, Betz came to New York to work in the theater, which he did. He later appeared on many TV shows, including *Playhouse 90, Alfred Hitchcock Presents, Love of Life,* and *Gunsmoke.* After he left *The Donna Reed Show,* he starred as a high-powered Texas attorney in the dramatic series *Judd, for the Defense.*

Ponytailed, pedal-pushered, and popular (more Ps), Shelley Fabares as Mary Stone always walked about the house with her shirttail out (very chic in the late fifties). Episodes sometimes revolved around trying to think of ways to enhance her popularity at school. She was boy-crazy—except about one boy, her precocious brother, Jeff (played by Paul Petersen), with whom she often argued. In 1963, Mary "went off to college" (in other words, was written out of the show) when Fabares left to concentrate on her singing career. (Both Fabares and Petersen had hit singles—hers: "Johnny Angel," his: "My Dad." When Fabares left *Donna Reed*, the first thing she did was cut off her ponytail. Mary was replaced by Trisha, an adopted daughter who followed them home one day. The part was played by Patty Petersen.

The show was a hit, with episodes such as this from 1959:

☐ Alex takes a "rate-your-wife" quiz and scores Donna near-perfect. But she's not flattered, because he rated her 100 percent in thrift and she doesn't want people to think she's frugal (although she is). So Donna threatens to go on a shopping spree—but is thwarted by her true nature. ☐

Or this episode:

☐ Mary accidentally meets and dates a young man (James Darren, who also sang two songs on the show) who is about to be inducted into the army. She behaves romantically and innocently—but learns through her brother's research in a fan magazine that he's really a teen idol from Hollywood. Mary is crushed. Donna soothes the hurt with an understanding woman-to-woman talk, and Mary sees her dreamboat off without letting him know that she knows who he really is. But it ends happily when he tells her that he found her simplicity refreshing and that he appreciated his date with her more than she realized. Sentimental happy ending. ☐

One more:

☐ Jeff saves a rich widow's life. She offers him a blank check. After a visit to a crowded ward in his father's hospital, he wants to use the money to build a new children's wing. ☐

By 1962, the show had run four seasons and Donna Reed announced she was going to retire from the still-popular series. This was later revealed as an idle threat, made just in time for negotiations—and it worked: production was cut down, her salary was raised, and she received a bonus. Still she complained; she was a perfectionist and it took her two hours to get made up each morning. Plus—someone announced—she had "hard hair to work with." What's more: Donna Reed did not enjoy her success.

That year, a reporter asked an increasingly more cynical Donna Reed what television had given her.

"Money," she emphatically answered.

She grew bitter. In 1966, she called it quits and dropped out, taking, of course, her millions with her.

She divorced her husband and began speaking out

Cleanup: Neighbors Donna Stone and Midge Kelsey

against the Vietnam War; she became chairperson of Another Mother for Peace. Both of her sons became conscientious objectors. She started speaking out on feminist issues.

Donna Stone?

She announced that she had "contempt for the two-dimensional, stereotyped woman" she had played and that she had "disdain for the male mentalities that control TV programming." She vowed that if she returned to the screen, it would probably be with a woman producer, because she felt that the TV and movie image of women was a male fantasy.

Donna Stone?

"I'd never go through that ordeal again," she said recently, referring to her show.

Donna Reed—an antiwar feminist, burning—not her bra—but many celluloid bridges behind her. And Carl Betz dead of lung cancer at fifty-six. . . . And what are we left with?

Reruns. About 100 hours of *The Donna Reed Show* to remind ourselves and to remind our children what life was—and wasn't—like when we were growing up.

Years later and still addicted, we watch *Donna Reed* today—and we do watch it, transfixed, the way we watch an accident on the street—for *Donna Reed* is an accident of our youth, a mythical mutation that affected the way many of us will forever feel about parents and children. The *Donna Reed* experience taught us that no one is consistent. Donna Stone—with her louvre doors, ugly vase, two all-American kids, happy hubby, home in the suburbs, and a tasteful string of pearls that seem to be Elmer's-glued onto her neck—and Donna Reed—with her divorce, "anti-American" kids, and outspoken feminist politics—just couldn't compete with each other. Donna Stone made Donna Reed rich—and both of them made us American kids a little bit poorer as we grew up to the disappointment that life on our lane wasn't like life in the Stone household.

Maybe that's it: we had houses and they had a household. True, the show was canceled after eight years, but in the reruns of our minds, the better-homes-and-gardens mythology that *The Donna Reed Show* planted and cultivated plays on.

ALSO RANS

The Ann Sothern Show

This was another of those fill-in-the-blank sitcoms. It was just like Ann Sothern's first show, *Private Secretary*, except in this one, she was Katy O'Connor instead of Susie MacNamara, and she worked in a hotel (the Bartley House in New York) instead of a Manhattan theatrical agency.

During the first part of the season, she played opposite Ernest Truex as Jason Maculey, the hotel manager, whose wife was Flora (Reta Shaw). Olive (that was Violet in the new incarnation) remained and was still played by a fluttery Ann Tyrrell.

But all was not well. The format didn't work, and so they transferred Mr. Maculey to Calcutta. Katy had hoped to get his job, but, instead, they brought back Don Porter as her "new" boss James Devery, the hotel manager (he had been Mr. Sands on *Private Secretary*). Also of note: Louis Nye played Dr. Delbert Gray, the hotel dentist who falls in love with Olive's teeth; Ken Berry played Woody the bellboy. CBS said there was no more room at the inn in September 1961.

The Ed Wynn Show

Comedian Ed Wynn flopped in this NBC show—his second attempt on the network (his first was a variety program in 1949)—about the troubles of John Beamer (Wynn), who is a retired businessman in a small Midwestern town. He also—as if that weren't enough—has two orphaned young granddaughters, Midge (Sherry Alberoni) and Laurie (Jacklyn O'Donnell), whom he was trying to raise. If that weren't enough, he even manages to get elected to the city council. The program bit the dust early in 1959.

The George Burns Show

This sitcom lasted only six months, and included the cast of the original *Burns and Allen Show* (minus Gracie, who had retired)—Harry Von Zell, Bea Benaderet, Larry Keating, and Ronnie Burns—all playing their original characters. In this show, George once again played himself—this time as a comedian who decided to become a theatrical producer. The stories revolved around George's attempts to bring sanity to such chaotic situations as auditions; performer tantrums; son Ronnie's romance with Judi Meredith, his steady girlfriend; George's secretary (Blanche Morton) and her antics; and Harry Von Zell and his insistence that he was right for any part.

Gracie was referred to a lot, especially when Blanche tried to keep George's eye from straying to the sexy starlets he met. In December, the series switched to a sitcom/variety format, à la *The Jack Benny Program*.

How to Marry a Millionaire

Based on the movie of the same title, this syndicated situation comedy was the old yarn about three "gals" living in a Manhattan apartment, all trying to snare a rich husband. The most famous of the bunch was Barbara Eden, who played Loco Jones, a model, who might not have married rich here, but later became a rich genie on *I Dream of Jeannie*. Merry Anders and Lori Nelson played secretaries Michele (Mike) Page and Greta Lindquist. Later, Lisa Gaye replaced Nelson and the character's name was changed to Gwen Laurel.

Peck's Bad Girl

Child star Patty McCormack starred in this one as twelve-year-old Torey Peck who seemed to get into a lot of trouble. Her father, lawyer Steve Peck, was played by Wendell Corey; her mother, Jennifer, was portrayed by Marsha Hunt. The Pecks were a "typical middle-class" U.S. family with a daughter who was part prepubescent and part tomboy. *Peck's Bad Girl* did badly, and CBS canceled this summer replacement show in August of 1959.

1959–1960

The Many Loves of Dobie Gillis

Dennis the Menace

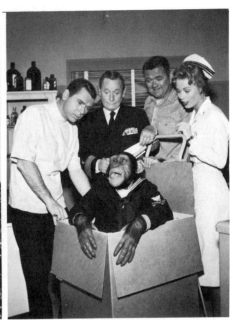

Hennessey

OFF-SCREEN

10/10   Initiation of first passenger service circling the globe introduced by Pan American World Airways.

10/19   *The Miracle Worker* opens on Broadway with Anne Bancroft.

12/19   Last veteran of American Civil War dies at age of 117.

1/2   Sixteen-year-old Bobby Fischer wins US chess championship.

1/18   Japan and US sign mutual security treaty.

2/11   Jack Paar walks off his show in protest of NBC censorship of his jokes of the previous night.

3/25   Wilt Chamberlain retires from basketball.

5/5   Announcement is made that a US spy plane has been downed over Russian territory.

5/19   Alan Freed, originator of the term ''rock and roll,'' arrested on charges of commercial bribery.

6/2–13   All twenty-two legitimate Broadway theaters close after Actors' Equity strike against one theater.

FRONT RUNNER

THE MANY LOVES OF DOBIE GILLIS

Hi, poopsie!
—ZELDA GILROY to Dobie Gillis

In the first episode of *The Many Loves of Dobie Gillis*, in 1959, the color of Dwayne Hickman's hair changed from light brown (at the beginning of the show) to blond by the show's end. Throughout the years—and the show ran for four of them—his crew cut grew out and the color would eventually change back to brown. And with each color change would be a format change—Dobie in high school, Dobie in the army, Dobie in college, until—finally—Dobie off the air.

But while *Dobie Gillis* was on the air—it was terrific. Finally American teenagers had a show of their own—not *Father* this or *Mama* that or a career girl named Suzy or a pair of stuck-up ghosts. We had *Dobie*. No, *no*, we kept telling our dads—*Dobie*, not *Dopie*!

Dobie was TV's first teenager—first *real* teenager. He hit puberty, he ran away from his father (who did not know best), he disliked school, he hung around with weird kids as we did, he hated school and he schemed for money—and he talked to himself just like the rest of us did.

Actually, Dobie didn't talk to *himself*—he talked to Rodin's *The Thinker* in the park, often imitating the statue's crouching pose. This is how a very blond Dobie introduced himself on the first show as he put his fist up to his chin: "My name is Dobie Gillis and I love girls. I'm not a wolf, mind you. A wolf wants lots of girls. I just want one—one beautiful, gorgeous, soft, round, creamy girl for my own—one lousy girl! But to get a girl you need money, and standing between me and money is a powerful obstacle—"

And the camera swept to Dobie's father scowling in his grocery store under a "Ham—53¢/lb." sign. After all, it was 1959. And this was Central City—you know Central City—at 285 Norwood St., where Mr. Gillis had his store and the family had its home above the store. And the camera swept back and forth from school to the park to home to the store. That sweep of the camera—called a "swish-pan" by photographers—was highly innovative for television, and it gave the program a jerky and spontaneous snap-crackle-pop quality that helped make

Dobie Gillis	Dwayne Hickman
Maynard G. Krebs	Bob Denver
Thalia Menninger	Tuesday Weld (1959–1960)
Herbert T. Gillis	Frank Faylen
Winifred Gillis (Winnie)	Florida Friebus
Zelda Gilroy	Sheila James
Chatsworth Osborne, Jr.	Steve Franken (1960–1963)
Mrs. Chatsworth Osborne, Jr.	Doris Packer (1960–1963)
Davey Gillis, Dobie's brother	Darryl Hickman (1959–1960)
Ruth Adams, the high school math teacher	Jean Byron (1959–1960)
Charlie Wong, the owner of Charlie Wong's Ice Cream Parlor	John Lee
Mrs. Blossom Kenney, a member of the school board	Marjorie Bennett (1959–1961)
Milton Armitage, Dobie's rival for Thalia	Warren Beatty (1959–1960)
Clarice Armitage, Milton's mother	Doris Packer (1959–1960)
Miss Burkhart, the college anthropology instructor	Jean Byron (1961–1963)
Mr. Promfritt, the college biology teacher	William Schallert (1961–1963)
Duncan Krebs, Maynard's cousin	Michael J. Pollard
Dean Magruder	Raymond Bailey (1961–1963)
The Osborne chauffeur	Angelo De Meo (1960–1963)
Lieutenant Merriweather, Dobie's commanding officer	Richard Claire (1961)
Also: Diana Millay, Ronny Howard, Jack Albertson, Jo Anne Worley	

the show sparkle. On *Dobie Gillis*, the unexpected was always to be expected. People would pop up from bushes and from behind trees. "Hi, poopsie!" Zelda Gilroy—the pesty girl who sat next to Dobie in class (Gillis, Gilroy) would say as she sprang from a bush. It was crazy. When Dobie would say that something Zelda did was "low-down disgusting and despicable," from out of nowhere would pop beatnik best buddy Maynard G. Krebs with a "You rang?" Or Maynard would utter a terrified and screechy "WORK?!" when anyone brought up the subject (usually Mr. Gillis). Flustered, Dobie would spit out "Just a darn minute" whenever Zelda or Maynard (who was constantly badgering "Dob, good buddy") showed up. All of the Dobie Gillisisms became pet classroom jokes at school the next day.

They all had a daffy way of talking—not clever like *Dick Van Dyke*, not domestically warm like *Donna Reed*, not cute like the Beaver—but twisted around just enough to refract reality with an illogical logic. For example:

MAYNARD　*(trying to talk his high school teacher, Mr. Promfritt, out of quitting)*:　Don't go, Mr. P. Central High needs you—like who else could learn me English so good?
DOBIE:　Maynard, you're killing the point and sit down.
MAYNARD:　Think how bad I'd talk if he didn't learn me so good.

Or when Maynard brought frogs—"14 of them—almost a dozen"—to class. Or how Maynard, at the end of a particularly sentimental segment, would say, "Gee, Dob, I'm getting like all misty," adding lemon to cut the sweetness.

This was the shtick that the show did over and over, expected pieces of comedic ritual that the viewers waited for.

In one episode, Dobie is sitting in the park and finds an abandoned baby with a note attached. "Look," he says to Maynard, "here's a note." Maynard sees it and is crestfallen as he looks at the baby. "Ooh, Dob—it writes better'n me." And probably talks better, too.

Mrs. Winifred Gillis was the sweet, suffering sort who often sided with Dobie and, in fact, would sometimes slip him some money (for dates) behind his father's back. Her husband, Herbert T., was a grumbly grocer and could contain himself only with his wife's persuasion. He wore old clothes and hated to part with a nickel. He was sure everyone was trying to exploit him. In Dobie's case, he was right. Dobie irked him (he wanted Dobie to work in his store), and Mr. Gillis hated Maynard—but he loved him too, in a very ambivalent way. Perhaps his best remark—when referring to The Lettermen singing group, who once guested on the show—was: "Those kids have so much loot, they're the only college kids putting their fathers through business." Maynard always endearingly called him Mr. G.

Dobie was an affable, straight-ahead guy just trying to do his job—which was chasing girls. He wasn't a sex maniac—he just liked girls and did anything he could to go out with them. He was—it has been categorized—of dull-normal intelligence and a "good guy." He was the foil for others' escapades—Maynard's adventures, Zelda's aggressiveness, his father's work demands—as well as the demands of the girls he wanted. There was always some action, some adventure—and it usually had something to do with Dobie getting what he wanted (usually a girl), the obstacles standing in his way, and then his not getting her. But on *Dobie Gillis* it was okay that boy did *not* get girl—because the girls Dobie wanted were most often pretty silly. We liked Zelda much better.

But the one we liked the best—possibly America's first nubile fantasy—was Thalia Menninger. Played by Tuesday Weld (and no one else could have played her), she was stacked and so was her hair. When he first sees Thalia at the movies, Dobie walks up to her and introduces himself:

DOBIE:　I'm Dobie Gillis. I think I love you.
THALIA:　I'm getting nauseous.

She was affected and talked in a breathy voice. She was interested in Dobie only if he had money—she was interested in security and often referred to her father's kidney ailment. "Dobie," she says, "you're cute and kind of helpless and I could fall for you with no trouble at all—but where would I be? My father's sixty years old and has a kidney condition." Thalia wants Dobie to be a doctor "so you can make ten dollars on a house call and make a call every fifteen minutes. . . ."

Blunt Zelda with her ponytail, impish face, her smarts in tact and her formal vocabulary, always streaks in, hoping to snatch Dobie for her own catch. "Dobie, with your negative face and inoffensive personality, and my brains, drive and ambition—you could go right to the top," she'd caw. Whenever she sees Dobie, she twitches her nose at him as a mating call and, in automatic reaction, he twitches back at her—then gets angry at himself with an "Oh, Zelda, stop wrinkling." We know that, even with all the beautiful girls Dobie chases, Zelda is going to win him in the end. And of course she does. In a 1977 "reunion" show, Zelda and Dobie are married, and, unfortunately, have turned into Ozzie and Harriet—but that's another book.

Zelda tries to save Dobie from himself—for herself. She wears sensible skirts, white blouses with button-down collars. A little imp, she calls him "Poopsie."

In one episode, Dobie is smitten with a girl named Phyllis and announces that they're going to be married (Phyllis Gillis) in the morning—except that he has to study at Zelda's house.

PHYLLIS:　That's okay—I don't care if I never see you—as long as we can be together.

Zelda tries to prove to Phyllis that Gillis is not a good marriage prospect. She displays his report card, a sample of his handwriting, the results of his intelligence test, a photo of his father (whom he will grow to look like), and a set of Dobie's X rays in which everything is upside down.

"Zelda!" Dobie exclaims. "That was unprincipled, treacherous, foul, mean, contemptible and low!"

"Sure was, Poopsie," Zelda says. "But I forgive you."

One young beauty figures that if Zelda—who is the smartest person in the class—"sees something in Dobie," there must be something to it—"because Zelda wants the best."

Zelda even tries to make Dobie jealous by "flirting" with Maynard.

ZELDA: Kiss me or I'll break your neck.
MAYNARD: Break the neck, break the neck!

Zelda always outmaneuvers Dobie through sheer brain power, and even though she is always rebuffed, Zelda wins in the end—if not Dobie's affections, at least she helps win the loss of Dobie's latest flame—and announces: "Halt! Dobie, we are a fact, a verity. Dobie, you and I are simply a thing that exists."

But the loved one was Maynard—Maynard G. Krebs, lovable, sappy, sad—a devoted puppy dog of a friend to Dobie—who acted dumb, went around beating his bongos and was the butt of everyone's jokes, including his own. He was scraggly and spinach-bearded and wore a dirty sweatshirt with the sleeves cut off. He was once described as a one-man slum. Maynard was scared of girls and thought that Dobie was the greatest. He was an outcast, television's first rebel. He had a pet iguana. He loved jazz. Once Maynard got picked up for vagrancy. He was TV's first space-man, but he always made perfect sense:

MR. GILLIS (*after hearing that Maynard's father has been transferred*): When are you moving?
MAYNARD: Either tonight or October.

And:

MR. GILLIS: Maynard—take these groceries and I'll give you a quarter.
MAYNARD: A quarter?! Joy for joy—that's almost fifteen cents.

Or:

DOBIE: You bet.
MAYNARD: Like, ditto.

When Maynard cries, he says, "Sniff."

Maynard is almost like a male Gracie Allen in that he knows no malice; he is an innocent . . . but with a tinge of self-pity. "I'm nothing but a poor miserable shnook," he says.

Once, Dobie was dictating a letter to Maynard for a class reunion:

DOBIE: Write "Dear Alumni."
MAYNARD: How do you spell it?
DOBIE: A-l-u-m-n-i.
MAYNARD: No . . . ! "Dear."
DOBIE: *I'll* write it . . . !

Bob Denver, who played Maynard, was drafted after four episodes. Art imitated life by having him also drafted on the show. He was immediately replaced by Michael J. Pollard as Maynard's cousin. However, it turned out that Denver was classified 4-F due to a neck injury and so, after two episodes, Pollard was out and Maynard was back in—discharged from the army as a hardship case—hardship on the army, that is. And anyway, Maynard was allergic to khaki. (Denver was a former athletic coach, history and math teacher.)

The show was full of changes throughout its four-year run. *Dobie Gillis* was based on Max Schulman's book, *The Many Loves of Dobie Gillis*. In 1953, it was made into a movie starring Bobby Van and Debbie Reynolds. For two years, Schulman—best known for having written *Rally Round the Flag, Boys*—tried to get Dobie on television. Finally, Dobie was changed from a

In the Army: Chatsworth Osborne, Jr., and Dobie

Filing: Dobie, Maynard and Kilroy

college kid to a high-school kid—making him a teenager to appeal to the TV audience, full of teenaged kids.

Signed to play eighteen-year-old Dobie was Dwayne Hickman, about whom *TV Guide* said, "He's so clean-cut, you could slice roast beef with him." Hickman was familiar to TV viewers as Bob Cummings' nephew Chuck MacDonald in the early 1950s on *Love That Bob,* in which he studied Womanizing 101 from Uncle Bob. Seems that it paid off when he graduated to girl-chasing Dobie.

While playing Dobie, Hickman recorded songs for Capitol Records, including one which opened the second season in 1960, "I'm a Lover, Not a Fighter," which later appeared on his first LP, *Dobie. Variety* called the song "a cutie of a tune." In one episode, Zelda writes a song for Dobie called "Who Needs Elvis?" which he sings to woo gorgeous, six-foot Esme Lauterbach away from trumpet-player Maynard.

At the time when *Dobie Gillis* began shooting, Hickman announced that he was "a leading boy," adding that "I have almost no natural talent in acting . . . but I have worked until I've surpassed those with more natural talent." A professional actor since the age of ten (complete with a jealous, look-alike brother, Darryl, also an actor), Dwayne Hickman lived with his parents and sister while making the show. "I have no close friends," he said. One of the least close was Tuesday Weld, who played Thalia Menninger. Hickman once said that he was glad that there was a different girl in the show each week. "I can't get along with the same girl for very long, especially actresses. They're a pain in the neck." And, about Tuesday, he said, "She just wasn't a professional, that's all," to which Tuesday replied, "If I haven't anything kind to say of a person, I prefer to say nothing."

In her column, Louella Parsons called Weld a "disgrace to Hollywood"—and, indeed, she was unconventional. She would come onto the set with a ferocious white German shepherd which would bite the director. At first her feud with Dwayne Hickman was only a publicity stunt; later, it exploded into reality when she left the show after the first season.

Warren Beatty got his acting start on the show playing Milton Armitage, the school's stuffy but talented man-of-distinction. Beatty thought the role was "absurd" and quit, and was replaced by Stephen Franken as Chatsworth Osborne, Jr., the richest kid in town, who spoke with a Darien accent and referred to his mother (Doris Packer) as "Mumsie." "What if Mumsie hears? She'd pack me off to military school quicker than one can say 'Federal Reserve Note.'" The Osborne, Jrs., lived in a palatial house with a stone fence and iron gate, dollar-sign-shaped pool, Louis XIV furniture, a blue sports car and a mother who snapped at him, "Chatsworth, you *nasty* boy!"

Chatsworth is a well-heeled heel, Dobie's flamboyant classmate and rival—and his complete opposite. Chatsworth is in love with Chatsworth. He's a chess genius, an expert and master of languages (even in a Mandarin dialect found only on some vases). At age six he was elected to the state legislature, at age eleven he performed a successful appendectomy, and at age fourteen he wrote a bestseller. When he and Maynard and Dobie were drafted in the 1960 season, Chatsworth wore a solid gold dogtag and blue suede combat boots lined in mink. He always had a pained look on his face (ostensibly because of an ulcer Franken had). Franken was in about one episode out of four, but he later said he was so typecast that *Dobie Gillis* ruined his acting career in Hollywood.

Although all these actors formed an ensemble company that clicked, the characters couldn't sustain themselves. All were character parts—all Ethels and Mrs. Odetteses and Walter Dentons and Schultzies. They were all the wacky-next-door-neighbor types written in for comic relief, and after two seasons, the substance of the show—a teenager, undecided about life, in search of some answers—ran out of clever words; Dobie became another rebel without a clause. As the years went on, the producers had to place Dobie in some extraordinary circumstances—in the army, in a spoof on *Ben Casey,* in a junior college. In 1963, Dobie quietly sneaked off the air. There was talk of a spin-off—*Zelda*—but it never spun off.

We don't have a Dobie anymore. We've had other kids, but they too went away—Beaver grew up, Vinnie came down with Saturday Night Fever, and Dennis didn't seem so menacing anymore. But none was as special as Dobie. The pace and feel of the show—its texture—were like fingers snapping in time to the early sixties, coupled with an innocence that died when Kennedy was shot.

For a generation that went from Coke to coke, from drive-ins to sit-ins, from proms to promiscuity, Dobie was Everykid.

ALSO RANS

The Betty Hutton Show

Goldie Appleby (Betty Hutton) is a lowly but outspoken New York manicurist whose claim to fame is a one-time career as a showgirl. Then one day she files the nails of lonely (but wealthy) Mr. Strickland. She accepts his invitation to dinner. Then he dies, and soon, inexplicably, she finds herself the beneficiary of his will and executrix of his $60-million estate—and guardian of his three orphaned children. Episodes of this CBS series dealt with the problems faced by Goldie, the bewildered new director of the Strickland Foundation (not all the complications of incredible wealth are fun) during the show's two seasons.

The Dennis O'Keefe Show

As though life as a columnist for a Los Angeles newspaper couldn't get complicated enough by itself, the writers who dreamed up columnist Hal Towne (Dennis O'Keefe) made him a widower. And *then* saddled him with a young son named Randy (Rickey Kelman), on top of everything else. Plus, Towne had to get his column—"All Around Towne"—written. Without the military discipline of Sarge—the housekeeper, played by Hope Emerson—the Townehouse could never have held itself together. Even with her help, though, CBS maintained this ménage for one season only.

Dennis the Menace

This show changed the word "menace" from meaning something bad to meaning something cute. And cute it was. And cute he was. As played by blond, all-American seven-year-old, forty-nine-pound Jay North, Dennis Mitchell was incredibly lovable . . . mischievous, at worst. He tried to be helpful, but he always made things worse. He lived at 627 Elm St., in Hillsdale, with, of course, his parents: Henry (Herbert Anderson), an engineer with Trask Engineering; and his mother Alice (Gloria Henry). The prime target of Dennis' carryings-on

Dennis the Menace: *Dennis Mitchell and George Wilson*

was neighbor George Wilson (Joseph Kearns), who just wanted to be left alone to work in his garden and to watch birds. When Kearns died, he was replaced by Mr. Wilson's brother, John (Gale Gordon). Dennis also had a dog named Ruff. After several seasons, when North started aging a bit, one of the producers cracked: "Maybe we'll change the title to *Mr. Dennis the Menace.*"

The show went off the air in 1963 when CBS got a little mischievous itself and went and canceled Dennis. Based on Hank Ketcham's popular comic strip of the same name.

Fibber McGee and Molly

Fibber McGee and Molly had been one of the most popular of all radio shows, running twenty-two years. When it hit TV, its stars were also alumni of radio-turned-TV shows: Cathy Lewis was Irma's roommate on the TV version of *My Friend Irma;* Bob Sweeney had been on *My Favorite Husband* (the TV remake of the Lucille Ball radio show), and *Our Miss Brooks,* which had been a radio favorite. Their Fibber and Molly didn't fare so well (the show was canceled after thirteen episodes). The McGees lived (as they had on radio) at 79 Wistful Vista, and had a lot of friends and neighbors to cope with. Fibber seemed to overstate things (i.e., fib) and was always in trouble. Molly was filled with common sense and seemed to always be able to repair any troubles Fibber had caused. She wasn't a great housekeeper, though, because Fibber brought along his famous filled closet from radio (all its contents always fell out in a crash when he opened it). Many viewers thought that seeing the closet on TV wasn't as funny as hearing it on radio. The only actor-holdover from the radio days was Harold Peary, who played Mayor La Trivia; he had played a different part on radio—Throckmorton P. Gildersleeve, and he eventually got his own radio (and TV) spin-off called *The Great Gildersleeve*.

Happy

So this is what happened to sons of former sitcom stars who have nothing else to do. Ronnie Burns (progeny of George and Gracie) played half of a young married couple (Yvonne Lime played the other half) who managed and partially owned the Desert Palm Motel, a ritzy resort. With them were meddlesome Uncle Charlie (Lloyd Corrigan) and also-owner Clara Mason (Doris Packer, who, at the same time, was playing Chatsworth Osborne, Jr.'s, mama on *Dobie Gillis*). Happy, however, was not what they were. Happy was the name of Charlie (Ronnie) and Yvonne (Chris's) kid. And he was definitely George's grandson: he often voiced (that's right, voiced) his reactions to the goings-on at the motel even though he was a mere tot (sort of reminiscent of Cleo in *People's Choice*). *Happy* ran as a summer entry in 1960, then returned, briefly, for nearly nine months in 1961—after which NBC gave birth to a cancellation.

Hennessey

Another in the series of "service" sitcoms, this one starred Jackie Cooper (post-*People's Choice*) as Lieutenant Chick Hennessey, who enlisted for two seasons on CBS. This navy doctor's romantic interest was Nurse Martha Hale (played by Abby Dalton) and their misadventures took place around their San Diego Naval Base. James Komack played Harvey Spencer Blair III, a ladies' man dentist waiting out a million-dollar inheritance. Hennessey married Martha on May 7, 1962, with the

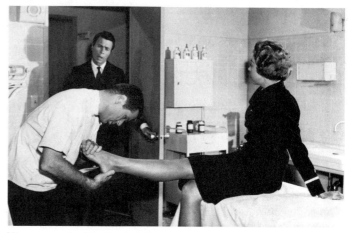

Hennessey: Jackie Cooper examines an obviously sick patient's foot

blessings of Captain (later to become Admiral) Shafer (played by Roscoe Karns). *Laugh-In's* Arte Johnson played a seaman named Shatz.

Love and Marriage

This one should have been called *Love, Marriage and Divorce*—because NBC sent it to Reno after only four months. The story: A man (William Demarest—later Uncle Charlie on *My Three Sons*) owns a bankrupt music publishing company in LA. His daughter tries to acquire rock and roll personalities in order to save the company. Too bad she couldn't do the same for the show. Murray Hamilton and Stubby Kaye also starred.

Too Young to Go Steady

Read what the press release said about this one: "The innocent romantic misadventures of fifteen-year-old Pamela Blake, a tomboy who suddenly discovers the opposite sex and is endowed with an urge to date." Anyway, Brigid Bazlen played this well-endowed girl. Her parents—lawyer Tom Blake, and his housewife, Mary—were played by Don Ameche and Joan Bennett. Pamela also had an older brother, Martin. Pam and her girlfriend Timmy (Lorna Gillam) were obsessive about Love. Much ado about not much; NBC canceled this one after only one month.

1960–1961

The Andy Griffith Show

My Three Sons

Harrigan and Son

OFF-SCREEN

9/3–9/12   One hundred forty-eight persons killed in US; heavy damage done by Hurricane Donna.

10/29   Sixteen members of California State Polytechnic College football team killed in plane crash; twenty-two killed in all.

11/3   Professor Willard Frank Libby and Professor Donald A. Glaser win Nobel prizes in chemistry and physics, respectively.

11/8   John F. Kennedy elected President of United States.

1/3   US breaks off diplomatic relations with Cuba.

2/1   Poll of 276 newspapers votes NY *Times* as best daily paper.

3/1   President Kennedy institutes Peace Corps.

4/12   Major Yuri Gagarin first man to travel in space around the Earth.

5/5   Kennedy raises minimum wage to $1.25.

5/9   Newton Minow, Chairman of FCC, calls TV "a vast wasteland."

FRONT RUNNERS

THE ANDY GRIFFITH SHOW

We're goin' to a picnic at Meyers Lake.
—ANDY TAYLOR

The Andy Griffith Show was civilized country. It wasn't prone toward cornpone like such shows as *The Beverly Hillbillies* and *Green Acres*. It was a show that seemed more influenced by Jimmy Carter (who wouldn't be President for another eighteen years) than by John Kennedy, who was elected President when the show went on the air in 1960.

Andy Taylor was sheriff of sleepy Mayberry, North Carolina (pop. 1,200), a crimefree hamlet that he ran with his fists unclenched. For nearly a decade, Mayberry thrived as TV's top town and Andy (as played by Griffith) was the ruler of the ratings. Not only was Andy sheriff, he was also justice of the peace, newspaper editor and—most important—crackerbarrel philosopher. He wasn't a comic-book character, and although he had funny-book people surrounding him (most notably his bumbling cousin deputy Barney Fife), Andy remained serious and substantial and sympathetic—the kind of person you might meet and chat with on a long busride from Chapel Hill to Fort Worth.

Andy Taylor	Andy Griffith
Barney Fife	Don Knotts (1960–1965)
Opie Taylor	Ronny Howard
Bee Taylor	Frances Bavier
Ellie Walker	Elinor Donahue (1960–1961)
Mary Simpson, the county nurse	Sue Ann Langdon; Julie Adams
Irene Fairchild, the county nurse (later episodes)	Nina Shipman
Helen Crump, later Andy's wife	Anita Corsaut (1964–1968)
Thelma Lou, Barney's girlfriend	Betty Lynn
Otis Campbell	Hal Smith (1965–1967)
Howard Sprague	Jack Dodson (1967–1968)
Briscoe Darling	Denver Pyle
Charlene Darling, his daughter	Margaret Ann Peterson
Briscoe Darling's Boys	The Dillard Brothers
Ernest T. Bass	Howard Morris
Gomer Pyle	Jim Nabors (1963–1964)
Malcolm Merriweather, a friend of the Taylors'	Bernard Fox
Goober Pyle	George Lindsey (1965–1968)
Clara Edwards, Bee's friend	Hope Summers
Floyd Lawson	Howard McNair (1965–1968)
Deputy Warren Ferguson, Barney's replacement	Jack Burns
Mayor Pike (early episodes)	Dick Elliot
Mayor Stoner (later episodes)	Parley Baer
Jim Lindsey, a friend of Andy's	James Best
Captain Barker, the state police chief	Ken Lynch
Emma Brand, the town hypochondriac	Cheerio Meredith
Sam Jones	Ken Berry
Millie Swanson	Arlene Golonka
Mike Jones	Buddy Foster
Emmet Clark	Paul Hartman
Skippy, a fun-loving girl from Raleigh, sweet on Barney	Joyce Jameson
Daphne, her girlfriend, sweet on Andy	Jean Carson

Buddies: Barney, Gomer, Andy

*New Man in Town: George Nader woos Andy's girl,
Elinor Donahue*

Every Monday night, Andy and an entanglement of characters who peopled the town (or people who charactered the town, rather), would get into some down-home dilemma: perhaps Aunt Bee felt unappreciated and wanted to take flying lessons; maybe Barney wanted to use third-degree techniques on town drunk, Otis; a promising guitar player wanted a job; an aging spinster needed some medication; the town hillbilly would keep courting lovely Charlene Darling, even though she was married. And Andy Taylor—with his soft-spoken sensibility, his country logic and his bright insight—would, like maple syrup seeping from the bottle, dispense a few words of advice to make it all better. (Later Griffith would request that the script writer "make Andy wrong once in a while," and they obliged occasionally; but even when he was wrong, Andy was always right.)

Like Dorothy in Oz, Andy was like a real person who landed in the middle of a sitcom.

Barney Fife—whose body looked as fragile as his ego was—was a lovable incompetent. Barney—the 97-pound weakling personified—wanted to be Paladin, but Andy never allowed him to carry more than one bullet, and not in his gun. So Barney carried his bullet in his left breast pocket. A descendent of Ralph Kramden (from the thin side of his family), Barney was childish (certainly more childish than Andy's son Opie). Barney was goofy. Sometimes he did things that were so infuriating that we wanted to give him a swift kick in the county seat; Andy—bastion of patience—always reasoned with him, calmly. Often Barney's interaction with Andy was like something from Burns and Allen that ended up on the cutting room floor.

BARNEY: The last big buy I made was my mom's and dad's anniversary present.
ANDY: What'd ya get 'em?
BARNEY: A septic tank.
ANDY: For their anniversary?
BARNEY: They're awful hard to buy for. Besides, it was something they can use. They were really thrilled. It had two tons of concrete in it. All steel reinforced.
ANDY: You're a fine son, Barn.
BARNEY: I try.

Andy often helped Barney save face, as when he'd lay the groundwork for an arrest and then let Barney accept the praise. And Barney would accept the praise. All of it.

Barney was part of Andy's huge extended family, which also included members of his real family: fluttery Aunt (pronounced Ain't) Bee, the kind of woman who, if Andy put somebody in jail (he never "threw" anybody in jail), would bring a home-cooked meal at night for the inmate; Andy's son Opie was a mini-Andy and a very good kid who didn't like to clean his room and didn't suffer from a case of the cutes like some of his TV neighbors like Beaver and Dennis. Andy (who was a widower) and Aunt Bee played mother and father. Opie and Barney were the kids, although Opie was clearly the older brother.

Others in the cast were like family. Scatterbrained and busybody Floyd the Barber was always so awed by the world that went on around him. Emmet Clark, operator of the Fix-It-Shop, tried to keep pace with his younger companions. The town drunk, Otis Campbell, served time in the very minimum security jail (usually unlocked), where he voluntarily committed himself for his regular Saturday night visit. Millie Hutchins, by day, dispensed creampuffs and rum cake at Boysinger's Bakers; by night, she dated county clerk Howard Sprague. He was straitlaced and catered to his over-protective mother's every wish. Ernest T. Bass, the naughty hillbilly, would throw rocks in his neighbor's windows. And there was Barney's girlfriend Thelma Lou, whose phone number—rung up by Sarah, the sole phone operator—was 596. Good-natured Gomer Pyle worked at Wally's Service Station.

Andy—from his home, from his office, sometimes even from the local diner—peddled advice the way other sitcoms of the day peddled puns. He was steady and deliberate in his efforts to bring his cronies through hard times. He never pushed; he just got people together and set up circumstances, so it seemed that people worked their troubles out themselves. Perhaps he arranged for a couple to have a quiet talk on the front porch. Or taught his son Opie something by setting up a situation for him to observe. As a sheriff, Andy never carried a gun, never took fingerprints, and left the cell keys hanging on the wall within easy reach of escape. Using country logic, he cornered a fugitive by leaving a pie cooling on the windowsill—nobody, Andy figured, could resist the smell of a pie cooling on the windowsill.

Andy was the protective Big Daddy. We never knew about his parents, and, actually, he wasn't the type to have them; he just seemed to have hatched somewhere, perhaps in a churchyard. Andy Griffith was the perfect

person to play the part. Said executive producer Sheldon Leonard: "For the first time, Andy Griffith will be playing something he is—a semiintellectual with a wry sense of humor." Indeed both Andys were rather Will Rogersyesque.

Griffith started his career as a stand-up comic doing monologues in small nightclubs, and eventually on *The Ed Sullivan Show*. In the mid-fifties, Griffith appeared on Broadway in *No Time for Sergeants* (cast as his sidekick: Don Knotts, alumnus of *The Steve Allen Show*). Both repeated their roles in the *U.S. Steel Hour* version, and Griffith in the movie. By this time, he was getting a reputation as being "another Jimmy Stewart," and, in the late fifties, starred as the sheriff of Bottleneck in *Destry Rides Again*. All the time, however, Griffith owned Nags Head Supermarket in Greensboro, North Carolina, which eventually expanded to sell clothing too. Griffith (a music major at the University of North Carolina) also owned a record store and two music companies.

He was a guest on *The Danny Thomas Show* (February 15, 1960) playing Andy, mayor of a small town, Mayberry. Griffith's rich drawl drew rich ratings, and a spin-off was ordered by Thomas. When Griffith's friend Knotts saw that *Danny Thomas* episode, he asked to be written into the show. So the part of Barney Fife was added to the scripts. Also, in the pilot, Frances Bavier was cast as townsperson Henrietta Perkins; her role in the house was taken by a housekeeper named Rose. Rose was let go, and Henrietta (changing her name to Aunt Bee) got the job.

Griffith—then thirty-three—owned 50 percent of

Tender Moment: Aunt Bee, Opie, Andy

Drunk: Andy, Barney, Otis

Andy's Wedding: Barney, Andy, Helen Crump

the show, and worked sixteen hours each day, thirty-nine weeks a year, on it. He edited scripts, set policy, superseded directors and, incidentally, became a millionaire. Each week, the entire cast, producers, and director held story conferences. By the time each episode was filmed, six different scripts would have been turned out. Griffith took part in story ideas as well: "We thought we had a real original plot the other day," Griffith said one afternoon in 1960, "but darn it if that night we didn't see the same story on *Lassie*."

The show's scripts were much shorter than the average sitcom—perhaps thirty pages, as compared to Bilko's forty-five-page scripts. The reason: the cast's Southern comfortable way of talking was slower than the more citified shows.

Said Griffith: "If ah was to lose mah accent, ah'd have to compete with actors and ah wouldn't do that for a hundred dollah bill." Griffith did not want to call his character Andy Taylor. He wanted to use his own name. "Why cay-an't ah use mah own nayame? They tole me because ah'm a married mayan. Been married ten years and had two children. On the show ah'm a widower with

one child an' it wouldn't do for me to be makin' eyes at a girl if I was married ten years."

By mid-1963, 36,000,000 folks were watching the show. Griffith got more than 1,000 fan letters each month. Even in its eighth year, the show was Number One in the ratings.

The show opened with Andy and Opie going fishing, with the theme tune—bright and bouncy—whistled over the credits. In one episode, Aunt Bee is going away to Mt. Pilot, the "big city." She is concerned that Andy and Opie won't take care of themselves while she is gone. "She's wured about us, Opie," Andy says, "while she's on her tri-ap." So they start to clean the house when she leaves. Opie's in charge of wiping the dishes. He heaves them in the air, and then uses his sleeve, then a handkerchief, to finish the job, finally dropping some. Then Andy realizes something: Aunt Bee doesn't really want them to get along so well without her; she wants to feel needed. So they quickly tear apart the house. While Andy and Opie are out "fetching" Aunt Bee, a busybody neighbor, Clara Edwards, lets herself in and sees that the place is a mess. She cleans it up. When Aunt Bee

returns, she is crestfallen and the boys are confused. Opie quickly runs upstairs and messes up his room, and Andy holes up in the kitchen and messes it up. Aunt Bee is delighted. The neighbor is confused. The episode is over.

Another poignant show revolving around Aunt Bee had her wanting to do one important thing in her life— and so she signs up to take flying classes. Everyone laughs at her. But she does it. When it comes time to fly solo, she's afraid to do it, but she does it. And then quits flying forever and goes back to her domestic life. She only, she says, wanted to do one great thing.

The episodes were more like gossip than stories— tales (both short and tall) about people we knew and wanted information about. Whether it was Floyd the barber, or Howard Sprague the county clerk, or Emmet, the owner of the Fix-It Shop, everyone had his yarns to spin. It seems appropriate that television should have had a show about a small town; television *is* a small town, with a few families running on it—at that time it was the Douglases, the Petries, the Munsters and the Addamses, the Stevenses, and several others, all linked by a common electrical cord.

Like any show that ran as long as *Andy Griffith* did, many changes occurred over the years. After the 1964–1965 season, Don Knotts left the show to make movies. He was "replaced" by Warren Ferguson (Jack Burns of Burns and Schreiber), who never managed to achieve Barney's popularity or lovability. Jim Nabors was so popular as gas station attendant/village idiot Gomer Pyle that he eventually spun off to his own show—going

Briscoe Loves Bee: Andy Griffith, Frances Bavier, Denver Pyle

on an active duty tour in the Marine Corps in 1964— leaving behind his sappy-looking cousin Goober Pyle (he had been called Goober Beasley before he became Gomer's cousin). George Lindsey played Goober with a crown-shaped hat on his head.

Andy had a number of girlfriends. The first was folksy Ellie Walker (who ran the drugstore), played by Elinor Donahue (formerly Betty/Princess on *Father Knows Best*). That bashful romance didn't last long, and he started dating the town nurse, played by Joanna Moore (Steve McQueen's costar in *The Blob*). Then it was time for Andy to settle down and get a wife, and so Helen Crump, the fifth-grade teacher, married Andy during the eighth season.

Some things stayed the same. The family always lived at 14 Maple St. Aunt Bee stayed right where she was. And Ronnie Howard—from age six to fourteen— continued playing Opie. Most important: the theme music stayed the same.

In the spring of 1968, Universal Pictures offered Andy Griffith a five-year, ten-movie contract. So he quit the show (which was Number One on the Nielsen charts) and left to make movies (or movie—he broke the contract after one year and one picture, *Angel in My Pocket*).

Ken Berry—who had been playing widower Sam Jones, (along with Frances Bavier, Jack Dodson, George Lindsey, and several others), the town councilman—took over the series. The show got a name transplant to *Mayberry, RFD*, debuted on September 23, 1968, and ran through 1971, when Mayberry finally became a ghost town. Although Sheriff Andy was often referred to, he was never seen.

Griffith tried television again, but never had any success (what he did have, though, was a CBS contract for $3.5 million a year). His series *The Headmaster* (which was "Andy Goes to School") flopped, as did *The New Andy Griffith Show* ("new" shows never seem to do well), in which he played "Andy Sawyer, former sheriff and justice-of-the-peace-turned-mayor, in Greenwood, North Carolina." Andy Taylor should have never left Mayberry.

Andy Taylor was a good sheriff—a gentle mayor who taught us to trust, who taught us to amble through life, who taught us some wisdom about the world in our small town. He was the last mayor we had when innocence ruled prime time TV.

MY THREE SONS

UNCLE CHARLEY: This is California—the land of milk and money.
STEVE: You mean milk and honey.
UNCLE CHARLEY: I'm too old for honey—I'll take money.

The premise of *My Three Sons* was to show an all-male family who did all-American things. This show—in its simplicity and naiveté—was definitely rated G—Gee-whiz.

My Three Sons was an innocent, leisurely domestic situation comedy—half dom, half sit—that was a hybrid between two popular shows of the time, sort of *Bachelor Father Knows Best. My Three Sons* starred Fred Mac-Murray, who had played the nice guy in so many movies. Here, he played Super Dad.

This widower father and his boys—products of a broken home (death, not divorce, God forbid)—ran twelve years. They lived in a disorderly (but clean) house in a town called Bryant Park. They, like their TV neighbors, had "a lot of trials and tribulations." The three sons—Mike and Robbie and Chip—all loved each other and would do anything for each other and always fought with each other. No, they wouldn't fight; they would spat. Once one of them called the other "bean brain."

The woman in their life was a man named Michael Francis "Bub" O'Casey (played by William "Fred Mertz" Frawley), who was actually the boys' grandfather and did all the cooking, cleaning, and chores. He was the Mother

(back when Mother still meant Mother), and he was a Mother in the later sense of the word too—crusty but (we were sure) with a heart of gold.

On one of the very first episodes of the series—"Chip's Composition"—Chip gets an assignment to find the best mother in the neighborhood and write about her. Chip talks to all the mothers in the neighborhood and decides that Bub (his grandfather) is the most maternal.

Bub (and later his successor, Uncle Charley) was the producers' way of flirting with sixties' sexual boundaries: here was an obviously virile man (after all, he had been married to Ethel all those years) doing Woman's Work. They could never have cast more sexually ambiguous actors like Paul Lynde or Charles Nelson Reilly to play the role.

Over the years, *My Three Sons* wouldn't change much in style—only in structure when, in 1970, it became a truly different show with Steve and his kids married.

The problems were always there, though—

Mike wanted a new car . . .

Rob was unjustly accused of stealing hubcaps . . .

Steve Douglas	Fred MacMurray
Michael Francis "Bub" O'Casey	William Frawley (1960–1964)
Charley O'Casey (Uncle Charley)	William Demarest (1965–1972)
Mike Douglas	Tim Considine (1960–1965)
Robbie Douglas	Don Grady
Chip (Richard) Douglas	Stanley Livingston
Sally Ann Douglas (Morrison)	Meredith MacRae (1963–1965)
Barbara Douglas (Harper)	Beverly Garland (1969–1972)
Katie Douglas (Miller)	Tina Cole (1967–1972)
Ernie Douglas (Thompson)	Barry Livingston (1963–1972)
Polly Douglas (Thompson, unrelated to Ernie)	Ronnie Troup (1970–1972)
Dodie Douglas (Harper)	Dawn Lyn (1969–1972)
Steve Douglas, Jr.	Joseph Todd (1970–1972)
Charley Douglas	Michael Todd (1970–1972)
Robbie Douglas II	Daniel Todd (1970–1972)
Terri Dowling	Anne Francis (1971–1972)
Fergus McBain Douglas (enacted by)	Fred MacMurray (1971–1972)
Fergus McBain Douglas (voiced by)	Alan Caillou
Bob Walters, Steve's employer	Russ Conway; John Gallaudet
Sylvia Walters, his wife	Irene Hervey
Also	Jodie Foster
The Douglas family dog: Tramp	

Ceremony (from left): Fred MacMurray, Meredith MacRae, Tim Considine

Chip had a crush on a girl who he thinks isn't interested in him . . .

—and Father Steve, an aeronautical engineer, would always come through with a batch of wholesome, sensible, down-to-earth advice dispensed from his study.

Perhaps the most interesting thing about *My Three Sons* is that "my"—Fred MacMurray—never wanted to be in the show. The producers had originally wanted to call it *The Fred MacMurray Show*, but he objected: "If your name is on it, you have to be on the show all the time," he said, and MacMurray didn't want to be on the show all of the time. He hardly wanted to be on the show some of the time.

While most sitcoms shoot at least seven months out of the year, all the season's episodes of *My Three Sons* were filmed in three months because that's the way MacMurray wanted it. The scripts were all written in advance so that MacMurray could shoot his scenes for the year in sixty-five days. And so, all of the scenes from all of the scripts that took place in the upstairs hallway, for example, were shot in an afternoon, out of sequence, one right after the other. (Frawley—used to years of shooting *I Love Lucy* in sequence—couldn't get comfortable with this schizophrenic method of filming.) All MacMurray had to do was change his cardigan and (maybe) his expression. He was so low-keyed most of the time that he looked like he was napping. Hardly Method Acting.

Said MacMurray: "Working on that show was like working long weekends, that's all. I always went from year to year. You can get canceled, you know."

In Real Life (although, what has this or any other sitcom got to do with Real Life, anyway?) a single father like Steve Douglas, someone who was "just there," dispensing advice but nothing more, would have raised three really screwed-up kids. They would have become delinquents and/or acquired severe sexual disorders. Not here. These kids were Good Kids. Yeah, they had problems (once Steve was worried because Robbie had been reading too many mystery novels), but their prob-

lems were always resolved by the end of each episode (Robbie gave all his mystery novels to Chip, who started reading them, much to his father's concern).

In the very first episode (on ABC, sponsored by Chevrolet), Steve is trapped by a "wily and predatory" female at just about the same time he has told his youngest (precocious) son, Chip, not to give the brush-off to the little girl who's been chasing him. Chip is able to politely escape his girl, but his father can't seem to talk his way out of the situation.

The show went along predictably for four and a half seasons, and suddenly, the first of the format changes hit it (actually, the show changed formats so many times that it was like different sitcoms with the same title): in 1965, William Frawley retired due to ill health (he died in 1966) and was replaced by William Demarest, who played Charley O'Casey (a.k.a. Uncle Charley), a retired sailor who is hired by Steve to replace Bub. Demarest was the veteran of over thirty years in vaudeville and had been in more than 100 movies.

Once again, Uncle Charley was the "female" in the house (even after there were real females in the house). As a former sailor, he was used to cooking "mess" (and cleaning messes, too) for a bunch of guys. Like Bub, he was rough and tough and bitched at the kids all the time. Underneath—but of course—another golden heart.

During the 1965–1966 season, Mike (Tim Considine, a Walt Disney veteran) marries Sally Ann Morrison (Meredith MacRae, daughter of movie actor Gordon MacRae). They leave Bryant Park and move east, where Mike gets a job as a psychology instructor. Meanwhile, Chip (Stanley Livingston) becomes friends with an orphan, Ernie Thompson (played by Barry Livingston,

Beatles' Haircut: Uncle Charley chews out Chip.

Stanley's brother), whom Steve later adopts (once again: three sons).

Two years later (the 1967–1968 season) and more changes: Steve is transferred to North Hollywood and the family goes with him. Robbie (Don Grady), by this time, is nineteen and is going to college. He meets and marries Kathleen Miller (Tina Cole) and they go on to have three sons—triplets, yet—named: Steve Douglas, Jr. (after Dad), Charley Douglas (after Uncle C.), and Robbie Douglas II (after Robbie).

Tina Cole (as Katie) had troubles looking pregnant. Three different types of foam, over the months, were used to simulate her increasing pregnancy. In the later segments, weights had to be strapped onto the foam to give the semblance of heaviness. A stand-in took Cole's place under the hot lights every day until they were ready to shoot.

Having triplets on the set caused real problems for the casting people involved with the show. The requirements were that they had to be twin boys, of fair complexion, with light hair and blue eyes, born between June 17 and 24. They also had to be California residents. Finally, after a long search, it was narrowed down to twelve sets of twins. Then they went on to pare it down to the final sets of twins who looked as much alike as possible to use three at a time and, in the words of the producers, "keep the fourth on reserve." Under California law, babies that young can only be on the set two hours a day, and can only be in front of the camera for twenty minutes, and each exposure, because of the bright lights, can last only thirty seconds (really twenty, as it takes the camera at least ten seconds to start and stop). There was always a nurse, a welfare worker, and a couple

Off-camera: MacMurray with Director Peter Tewkesbury

of mothers in attendance. It took three solid days which were devoted to shooting enough footage to last four segments. Finally, they "skipped" six months between two episodes and hired two sets of older twins.

In 1970, Ernie—now in high school—starts having some troubles with a new teacher, Barbara Harper (Beverly Garland), a widow and mother of a young daughter, Dodie (Dawn Lyn). Trying to help his son, Steve arranges a meeting with the teacher. Soon they—you guessed it—get married. (MacMurray's wife, June Haver, said she helped pick Garland for the part.) And then—perhaps because the writers couldn't think of anything else to do—Chip, now in college, marries Polly Thompson (Ronnie Troup). For some reason, her last name was the same as Ernie's before he got adopted, although they were not related.

This episode—"The First Anniversary"—opens in the California house. There are lots of people around. Tramp is barking. Uncle Charley is playing the cello. Katie and Rob (who don't live at home) are visiting (Rob now works with his dad). Steve and Barbara are getting ready to celebrate their first anniversary soon. Seven-year-old Dodie comes in and says something clever. The laugh-track chuckles maniacally. She decides to throw a party for her mom and dad's "university," as she calls it. No one takes her seriously and, anyway, everyone is planning to do something else that night. Steve finally enters and asks everyone to come to the party. "I don't want that little girl hurt," he says about his adopted daughter. She gives the party, and everyone exchanges presents—except Dodie, who runs up to her room, crying. Why are you crying? everyone asks. "Because," she sobs, "my present is rotten." Well, let's just see about that, someone says. Steve opens the present as sad violin music rises to the occasion. It's Dodie's handprint with a message: "To my Mommy and my Daddy—my left hand nearest my heart." It's a weepy moment. Also the end.

New Arrival: Barry Livingston, checking out his new family.

The Wrong Robbie: Don Grady plays himself and look-alike rival for Melinda Plowman's affections.

Stray Dog: They decide to keep Harry.

In 1972, as sort of a change of pace—sort of—Fred MacMurray played "Laird" (Lord) Fergus McBain Douglas, who arrived from Scotland looking for a first lady. (MacMurray played the lord; Alan Caillou played his voice.) He meets Terri Dowling (Anne Francis), a cocktail waitress at the Blue Berry Bowling Alley. He—but what else?—marries her and she becomes Lady Douglas.

On August 24, 1972, the show was dropped—finally—by CBS. Nobody was too surprised or disappointed. The show had been running twelve years, and in reruns would continue to run countless more. In 1977—in a joint venture with *The Partridge Family*—there was a TV reunion of all the sons, all the daughters and daughters-in-law, Uncle Charley and Tramp.

Even Fred MacMurray managed to find time to show up.

ALSO RANS

Angel

"Angel" is the French-born Angel Smith (Annie Farge), newly married to architect John Smith (Marshall Thompson) and settled in an anonymous New York City suburb. For one CBS season, this transplanted housewife struggled to cope with her bewildering new lifestyle and the problems and perils of married life—not the least of which was cancellation in the fall of 1961.

Bringing Up Buddy

Buddy Flower (Frank Aletter) is contented with his life as a successful Los Angeles investment broker. He's also perfectly happy with his status as eligible bachelor—but his meddling spinster aunts Iris (Doro Merande) and Violet (Enid Markey) decide that two unplucked Flowers are enough for one family. His upbringing will remain incomplete, they feel sure, until they find him a wife.

Buddy's weekly efforts to extricate himself from their match-making schemes formed the nucleus of this one-season entry in the CBS lineup.

Guestward Ho!

Advertising executive Bill Hooten (Mark Miller) is fed up with life in New York and decides to purchase, sight-unseen, Guestward Ho, a dude ranch in New Mexico. And so he moves there with his wife Babs (Joanne Dru), and their son, Brook (Flip Mark). When they arrive, they find their dude ranch is a dud ranch: run-down. The episodes revolve around their adjustments to their new

Guestward Ho!

life—and how they are trying to round up some paying customers for the ranch. J. Carroll Naish played Chief Hawkeye, the owner of the local trading post, an Indian trying to win back the American continent for his people, but who, in the meantime, reads *The Wall Street Journal* and sells authentic Indian trinkets (made in Japan). The show ran for one year on ABC.

Harrigan and Son

The only reason that America knows how to spell the name of this show is because of the theme song: "H-A-double-R-I-G-A-N spells Harrigan . . ." (from the old George M. Cohan ditty). Also because Pat O'Brien starred in this sitcom about a father and son law firm in New York, Harrigan and Harrigan. The other Harrigan, James, Jr., was played by Roger Perry, and the stories revolved around their conflicts as lawyers: Dad thought there was a human angle in defending clients; Son felt they should be defended according to the book. Another plot twist: Senior had a glamorous secretary, Gypsy (Georgine Darcy), and Junior had a "sedate" secretary, Miss Claridge (Helen Kleeb). This ABC sitcom was thrown out of court after only one season.

The Jim Backus Show: Hot Off the Wire

Jim Backus started his sitcom career as the judge husband on *I Married Joan;* after *Hot Off the Wire,* he was a favorite on *Gilligan's Island,* and, always, he was the voice of *Mr. Magoo.* This ABC show however was not his greatest moment. He portrayed John Michael O'Toole, an editor-reporter at the Headline Press Service, a newspaper in financial trouble. From week to week, he dodged creditors, tried to acquire major stories and improve circulation. Nita Talbot played his assistant, Nora.

My Sister Eileen

This sitcom (based on the book by and two movies about Ruth McKenney) gave us two sisters from Ohio who come to Greenwich Village to make their way. Ruth (Elaine Stritch) and her sister Eileen (Shirley Boone) want to be a writer and actress, respectively. Also in the cast: Jack Weston (as Eileen's agent) and both Richard Deacon and Rose Marie (who would appear the following year in *The Dick Van Dyke Show*). Ruth got a job working for a publisher and Eileen spent her days (and nights) fending off con men and boyfriends. CBS sent everyone back to Ohio in 1961.

Pete and Gladys

After hearing about Pete's wife, Gladys, on *December Bride* for six years, we finally got to meet her on their own series, which ran on CBS through September 10, 1962. And—for all his wisecracking—it turned out that Pete was an affectionate and caring husband, and that Gladys was a nice—albeit daffy—person. Anyway, the

Pete and Gladys: And Hilda

story takes place in LA. Pete is an insurance salesman and Gladys is a scatterbrained housewife. Verna Felton (playing nosy pal Hilda Crocker, a holdover from the *December* days) was also on the show, as was Gale Gordon (Mr. Conklin on *Our Miss Brooks* and later Uncle Harry on Lucille Ball's shows) who played Pete's Uncle Paul Porter. Ernest Truex played Gladys' dad and, during the last season, Frances Rafferty (Ruth Henshaw on *December Bride*) appeared as Gladys' buddy Nancy.

Peter Loves Mary

Peter Lind Hayes and Mary Healy—married in Real Life—played Peter and Mary Lindsey, a show business couple living in Connecticut. They tried hard to divide their time between their Broadway careers and their home life (which included two children—Leslie and Steve). Helping to hold it all together was their housekeeper, Wilma (played by Bea Benaderet, who had been Blanche on the *Burns and Allen Show* and would move on to her own *Petticoat Junction*). The catch was that Peter loved the excitement of the city; Mary wanted the

still of suburbia. The show played for one season on NBC, about the same length as Hayes' and Healy's 1950 sitcom, *The Peter and Mary Show*.

The Tab Hunter Show

Glamour-boy Tab Hunter played playboy Paul Morgan, the creator and artist of the comic strip "Bachelor at Large," which Paul also happened to be. He had a long stream of beautiful women. He had a disapproving housekeeper (Reta Shaw). He had a friend, Peter Fairfield III (Richard Erdman), and a publisher, John Larsen (Jerome Cowan). And he had a network, NBC—but only until September 10, 1961.

The Tom Ewell Show

Tom Ewell played Tom Potter, a family man who sold real estate in LA to support his habit: a clan that included his wife, Fran (Marilyn Erskine); his three daughters, Debbie, Carol, and Cissy (Sherry Alberoni, Cindy Robbins, and Eileen Chesis)—and, as a bonus, a live-in mother-in-law, Irene Brady (Mabel Albertson). The show was also known as *The Trouble With Tom*, and, apparently, the trouble with the show was that no one was watching. CBS bid it adieu after one season.

Yes Yes Nanette

The Mama Syndrome: Nanette Fabray (who would later play Mary's mama on *The Mary Tyler Moore Show* as well as, later, Anne Romano's mother on *One Day at a Time*) played the stepmama of two rude kids in this one. She was a former actress named Nanette McGovern, married to Dan McGovern (played by Wendell Corey). They lived in LA. (The episodes, incidentally, were based on the lives of Fabray and her husband, writer Ronald MacDougall.) At midseason she replaced her own show with a renovated model called *The Nanette Fabray Show*. It was canceled by NBC, who said No No to Nanette after six months.

1961–1962

Hazel

The Lucy Show

The Dick Van Dyke Show

OFF-SCREEN

9/1 Seventy-eight die in US commercial aviation's worst plane crash in Hinsdale, Illinois.

11/19 Michael Rockefeller, son of New York governor, reported missing off coast of New Guinea.

12/5 President Kennedy calls for "broad participation in exercise" by American people.

12/29 *West Side Story* named best film by NY film critics.

1/– Contessa Christina Paolozzi appears in the nude in a full-page photograph by Richard Avedon for *Harper's Bazaar.*

2/14 Kennedy says US troops in Vietnam are on training missions and are instructed to fire when fired upon, but are not combat troops.

2/14 Mrs. John F. Kennedy leads 46.5 million TV viewers on tour of the White House.

4/19 Skybolt, 1st US airborne ballistic missile, launched.

5/7 *How to Succeed in Business Without Really Trying* wins Pulitzer Prize for drama.

5/14 Astronaut M. Scott Carpenter launched by Atlas rocket, orbits earth three times in Aurora 7.

FRONT RUNNERS

CAR 54, WHERE ARE YOU?

There's a holdup in the Bronx/Brooklyn's broken out in fights . . .
—opening of *Car 54* theme song

On Tremont Ave. in The Bronx—where the Goldbergs had lived twelve years before—the 53rd Precinct opened its doors to America every Sunday night. There was a corps of cops in that place—Officer Rodrequez, Officer O'Hara, Officer Reilly, Officer Nelson—but the two that we cared about were Gunther Toody and Francis Muldoon, two patrol officers assigned to Car 54.

They were also assigned to NBC for two seasons, when Nat Hiken—the mastermind behind the great *Sergeant Bilko* series that went off the air in 1959—gave us *Car 54, Where Are You?* (It had been first called *The Snowwhites* for the pilot episode.) One day Hiken was visiting the New York City police department precinct office. "These police sounded and acted just like any other group of men at work," Hiken said, and decided—as he had done with the army—to give the airwaves a new breed of TV cops, unlike the straight and rugged

bunch on *The New Breed* and *Naked City*. These would be cops without robbers, without violence. These would be cops with comedy. It was almost as though Hiken had discharged the boys from Fort Baxter and transplanted them to the streets of New York.

They were funny, they were funny. "Ooh!-ooh!-ooh!" Toody would exclaim in a staccato that sounded like a cow singing bel canto. When someone got in his way, he'd sputter: "Do you mind? Do—you—Mind!?" He chattered and chattered on and on. "Am I boring you, Francis?" he'd ask his partner, Muldoon. "You, Gunther? *Never*," Muldoon would respond. And he meant it.

Once, Toody and Muldoon were assigned to escort the President from Idlewild Airport to the United Nations. Muldoon faints at the word "President" because, as a kid, he had met Truman on the street and it had been a traumatic experience for him. So the FBI

Gunther Toody	Joe E. Ross
Francis Muldoon	Fred Gwynne
Captain Martin Block	Paul Reed
Lucille Toody	Beatrice Pons
Patrolman Leo Schnauzer	Al Lewis
Sylvia Schnauzer	Charlotte Rae
Patrolman Ed Nicholson	Hank Garrett
Desk Sergeant Sol Abrams	Nathaniel Frey
Officer Rodrequez	Jack Healy
Officer O'Hara	Al Henderson
Officer Anderson	Nipsey Russell (1961–1962)
Officer Steinmetz	Joe Warren
Officer Wallace	Fred O'Neal (1962–1963)
Officer Murdock	Shelly Burton
Officer Nelson	Jim Gromley
Officer Reilly	Duke Farley
Officer Kissel	Bruce Kirby
Officer Antonnucci	Jerry Guardino (1961–1962)
Mrs. Bronson, the Bronx troublemaker	Molly Picon
Mrs. Muldoon, Francis' mother	Ruth Masters
Peggy Muldoon, his sister	Helen Parker
Al, a friend of Toody and Muldoon's	Carl Ballantine
Rose, his wife	Martha Greenhouse
Bonnie Kalsheim, Muldoon's occasional date	Alice Ghostley
Mrs. Block, the captain's wife	Patricia Bright
Charlie the drunk	Larry Storch

training officers start referring to the President as "you-know-who" and "that certain party from Washington." Muldoon is so scared he munches tranquilizers and ends up falling asleep during the test drive.

In another episode, a police captain tries to split up Toody and Muldoon after nine years of sharing the front seat of Car 54 (Muldoon always drove). They aren't happy about the switch.

MULDOON: I guess most of the men are smarter than Gunther and less trouble than Gunther, but . . . well, I'm so *used* to Gunther. When he chatters away, the days just fly by. I'd just be *lost* without Gunther.

TOODY: You mean ride around with someone next to me that's not Muldoon? Francis is a quiet man. He doesn't say a word. He just sits there all day thinking. It's very comforting for a man like me to know there's someone next to him doing the thinking for both of us.

But the change went through. No one, however, could endure Muldoon's funereal silence or Toody's garrulity, so they got back together again.

There was also another threat to their relationship: the captain assigned a third man to the patrol car, a Harvard graduate who spoke Intellectualese with Muldoon while Toody sat there—in silence. So Toody went home and started to memorize the encyclopedia, starting with the letter A. The next day, midconversation, Toody sprang into action: "Did anyone mention 'aardvark'?"

It was a friendship based on the fact that they had absolutely nothing in common. Muldoon was intellectual, calm, and quiet. Toody was innocent, excitable, and talkative. Muldoon was tall and gaunt, Toody was short and squat. Toody was the kind of guy who would say that he thought he should get a police citation "for having the cleanest locker." Muldoon was the kind of guy who would say nothing.

The critics, however, said plenty. Most objected to the farcical situations (in the first episode, the cops go through the typical tangle with their wives to let them go fishing) and, in fact, some critics thought the show was "disrespectful to the police." True, the police in the 53rd Precinct were silly and bumbling and ridiculous, but what critics didn't seem to realize was that the show was a parody of TV cops, not of real policemen.

That didn't stop the nation's police forces from taking offense. Said Deputy Police Commissioner Walter Arm: ". . . it gives a poor and inaccurate picture of a New York policeman in the sixties. I can tell you for a fact that police chiefs around the country are saddened to see a couple of buffoons masquerading as policemen." Added another dissenter: "Being a policeman is a grim and humorless business, not at all funny." In San Antonio, Texas, policemen passed a resolution saying that *Car 54* "makes us look stupid." In Dayton, Ohio, the department dropped #54 from their fleet; in Akron, Ohio, the two drivers of Car 54 quickly got fed up with all the teasing they got.

But some policemen liked it. One station bought TV sets so everyone could watch the program while at work. New York City policemen seemed to love the show, saying that Toody and Muldoon were just like their fellow officers. Ross (who played Toody) was happy the way the cops were treating him. "They often lead me to the front of the movie lines," he said. "And I get less traffic tickets now than I used to."

Acquiescing to the criticism, Hiken made some changes in the scripts. The satires became more believable, and Toody and Muldoon did more "goodwill" missions like giving rides to residents and delivering groceries.

The show wasn't filmed on a backlot in Hollywood, as most sitcoms are, but in The Bronx at the old Biograph Studio (the one where D. W. Griffith had made his silent movies) on West 175th St. The exterior was made to look like a police station. All was going fine until one morning, in the middle of a scene, in ran a housewife screaming: "Help, police! My husband is beating me!" They quickly removed the Police Station sign and replaced the old Biograph banner.

But the East Bronx neighbors knew that something was up across the street, and many would hang out of their tenement windows and watch Toody and Muldoon "riding around" in their wheelless car (painted red and white, so people wouldn't think it was the regulation green and white New York police car). Once, word got out that the director needed a dog for a scene. Dozens of neighbors brought in their pets for auditions.

In the Biograph building, thirteen permanent sets were built and ready for weekly use, while other sets were built each week as the need arose. Exterior shots were often filmed on City Island. Hiken had hired a technical adviser (a retired detective) to look over the scripts to make sure they had some accuracy—or at least plausibility—to them. One note of authenticity: all these sitcom cops wore real police uniforms, except for the insignia on the collars which read "53" for the fictional 53rd Precinct.

Not all of the action, however, centered around the precinct headquarters. Some of it was domestic—of a very undomesticated nature—comedy. Francis was a bachelor who sometimes dated Bonnie Kalsheim (Alice Ghostley). But Toody had his wife, Lucille, who continually nagged him.

TOODY: When we got married, every morning Lucille would ask me what I want for dinner. Now, not only does she not ask me what I want for dinner, she won't even tell me what I ate. I turn over my paycheck to her and she criticizes my handwriting. She thinks everything is my fault. When I got drafted into the army, she accused me of starting World War II just to get out of the house . . .

Often they would get together with Patrolman Leo Schnauzer (who looked like a Schnauzer; Hiken had first given us a Doberman who looked like a Doberman on *Bilko*) and his wife, Sylvia.

The casting was brilliant. Joe E. Ross (Toody) was a much-beloved veteran of Hiken's *Bilko* show, where he played Sergeant Ritzik. At sixteen, he had debuted as a singing waiter in The Bronx. "I used to sing heartbreaking songs to hoodlums," he said. "They'd cry in their beer. With a voice like mine, I guess I was lucky they didn't shoot me." He went on to do nightclubs and work in burlesque, until he ran into Hiken and found his way onto *Bilko*.

Fred Gwynne (Muldoon) was a somber-faced Harvard English graduate who got a job as a copywriter at the J. Walter Thompson advertising agency. He had once, in fact, wanted to be a policeman, but flunked out of the training course. At Groton, where he went to prep school, he made his debut as Henry the Fifth, and he was in *Irma La Douce* on Broadway. He had appeared in two *Bilko* episodes, and Hiken wanted to star him in *Car 54* (after which he went on to do *The Munsters* and more Broadway).

Lucille was played by Beatrice Pons—one of Hiken's favorite character actresses—(she had played Ross' wife on *Bilko*) who seemed to specialize in the curlers-and-sloppy-bathrobe roles. On one episode, Toody's craziness finally gets to her and she flings open the window and shouts: "*Listen*, America! My husband is a *NUT!*" On another episode, when Toody is caught dancing with a blonde woman at the Policemen's Ball, Lucille gets jealous, bleaches her hair, and puts on fake big eyelashes

and a black sequined dress. She was smarter than Toody (she went to Hunter College) and spent her time (1) desperately trying to achieve culture, elegance, and status, and (2) saving Toody from the situations he got himself into.

Car 54 didn't last long—only two seasons—but it was a show of such crackerjack intensity and such wiseacre energy that it just finally fizzed out because it couldn't sustain itself. It's got a claque of admirers who, even today, can remember favorite episodes: the time that Sylvia Schnauzer tries to publish a book about her love life, the one where Toody makes a plaster cast of Sergeant Abrams' feet to give him orthopedic shoes for his twenty-fifth year as a cop, the episode where the precinct enters the barbershop quartet contest, the time that Toody sees *The Taming of the Shrew* in Central Park and tries to tame Lucille . . . and many more.

To others, the individiual episodes all blur together, and they remember nothing but the show's theme song (with the title sung over police horns beeping) and the opening scene (in which Toody salutes and drops the ice cream out of the cone he's been trying to hide, or, when Toody and Muldoon mix up their hats and trade back).

Still others remember only the news stories about the show, like the one from Nyack, New York, when a police car was stolen from its parking place in front of the station. The townspeople immediately dubbed it Car 54.

It was a great show, all about two patrol car partners—stuck somewhere in time between the Keystone Kops and *Barney Miller*—lovable lunatics driving around in the ever-errant Car 54.

Ooh! Ooh! Ooh!

THE DICK VAN DYKE SHOW

Oh, Ro-o-o-b!
—LAURA PETRIE when she is upset

There was one classic episode of *The Dick Van Dyke Show*—but weren't they all classics?—in which Sally, the ugly-duckling, man-hungry staff writer, was on a talk show asking eligible men to send her a postcard because she was looking for a husband. That was nearly twenty years ago, but you can be sure that Rose Marie's still looking.

Because nothing changes in the sitcom kingdom. Through the magic of reruns, Sally—and Buddy and Laura and Rob and, yes, even Mel—are still up to their old tricks so that new and newer generations of TV addicts can get hooked on the disarming charms of *The Dick Van Dyke Show*, just like we did. We had to wait every week for Monday nights. They're lucky; they get it every day.

Dick Van Dyke was the first sitcom that was rated A—for Adult. Rob and Laura Petrie were sensible, grown-up people. They were funny and they did funny things. They were not the Burnses, who were zany and did zany things. Nor were they madcap Margie and her foolish father or the warbling Partridges. Laura and Rob Petrie were not silly people. They didn't act; they behaved. They were substantial—more so than Donna and the rest of the Stones. That's just it: the Petries weren't stone, they were . . . clay. They were like real people. Real people who made jokes, but *weren't* jokes. They even—yes—they even had a television set and, once in a while, they even—gasp—watched it. Just like we watched them.

And did we ever watch them—35,000,000 of us.

The Dick Van Dyke Show was the *other* Camelot family. It was 1961 and the Petries and that other family,

the Kennedys, were reigning supreme in the country. There was a first-family magic to the Van Dyke show, a sparkle that twinkles on even today through the faded black and white images on the small screen.

The Dick Van Dyke Show was a lot of people's favorite because—just like the Kennedys—it gave the country a sense of family and unity and community. John Kennedy and Dick Van Dyke started serving their country the same season. In a way, it was the same show (although Van Dyke's term lasted longer). Rob and Laura (she and Jackie had practically the same hairdo) ruled televisionland together; both families had great ratings. *Dick Van Dyke* was a much-appreciated relief after the madcap antics of fifties sitcoms; the Kennedys were a welcome relief after similar Presidential antics. Both families exchanged prattle and pratfalls for grown-up goings-on. *The Dick Van Dyke Show* and the John F. Kennedy Show both ushered in the sixties. These were believable people. Both had vigor (and vigah).

Dick Van Dyke was a show about a man who lived in the suburbs with his wife and son. Most of all, it showed him at work.

And it was his work that really set this show apart from the others. Because Rob Petrie was a TV writer and, for the first time, television gave us a look at television. The show deglamorized TV and poked fun at it. But it wasn't just a television show about television, the way *The Beverly Hillbillies* was a TV show about hillbillies. *The Dick Van Dyke Show* was about the foibles and fallacies of "good people." On this show, the truth was stretched; on the others, truth was abandoned for freak-show stylizations and fun-house mirror effects.

Rob Petrie	Dick Van Dyke
Laura Petrie	Mary Tyler Moore
Buddy Sorrell	Morey Amsterdam
Sally Rogers	Rose Marie
Millie Helper	Ann Morgan Guilbert
Jerry Helper	Jerry Paris
Mel Cooley	Richard Deacon
Alan Brady	Carl Reiner
Richie Petrie	Larry Matthews
Pickles Sorrell, Buddy's wife	Joan Shawlee
Freddie Helper	Peter Oliphant; David Fresco
Sam Petrie, Rob's father	Tom Tully; J. Pat O'Malley
Clara Petrie, his wife	Isabel Randolph
Ben Meehan, Laura's father	Carl Benton Reid
Mrs. Meehan	Geraldine Wall
Herman Gilmcher	Bill Idelson
Stacy Petrie	Jerry Van Dyke

This episode—"Coast-to-Coast Big Mouth"—was typical of the fine quality of writing of the show, and also shows what *The Dick Van Dyke Show* was all about:

Rob has gotten Laura and their neighbor Millie tickets to sit in the studio audience of the *Pay as You Go* game show. Millie's name is picked out of a bowl to be a contestant, but she's too scared to go on. "I'll die . . . Laura . . . I'll die." So Laura hesitantly agrees to go in her place. Johnny Patrick, the show's host, is a sneaky rat who traps his guests into telling him—and America—embarrassing things.

LAURA: My husband is . . . the head writer of *The Alan Brady Show*.
PATRICK: Tell me, Mrs. Petrie . . . is the show any better than it used to be?
LAURA: Oh, yes—*(caught)*—I mean, no.

Boss Alan Brady and Rob are watching the show as this is going on.

ALAN: It's not really important what she wins. The important thing is . . . she didn't lose.
ROB::   Hunh?
ALAN: Your job.
ROB *(nodding)*:   Yeah. Right.

Alan and Rob leave for lunch (Alan trips and twists his ankle, blaming it on Laura because her show made him late, which made him run, which made him fall, which made him twist his ankle). Meanwhile, Laura and Johnny Patrick are still on nationwide television.

PATRICK: Oh . . . I meant to ask you.
LAURA: Yes?
PATRICK: Have you ever been to Alan Brady's house?
LAURA: Oh, yes . . . many times.
PATRICK: Does he wear his toupee at home?
LAURA: Oh, yes. He wears it all the time. *(Her eyes widen in horrible realization.)*
PATRICK: You mean Alan Brady is bald!
LAURA: Well, no.
PATRICK: Then why does he wear a toupee? *(laughs)*
LAURA: Well, well . . .
PATRICK *(laughs—to audience)*:   Well, gals, the secret is out. She said it and she knows. Alan Brady is bald and you learned it here! How about that, folks? Aren't we devils?!

Later that night, Laura tells Rob what she has done. He is dumbfounded.

LAURA: He tricked me.
ROB: I'm surprised you didn't tell him about Alan's nose job!
LAURA: I didn't know Alan had a nose job.

ROB: Oh. Yeah. It used to be a secret.
LAURA: I thought we had no secrets.

In the middle of this, Buddy calls to tell Rob that an item in that evening's paper said that "The wife of the future ex-writer of *The Alan Brady Show* announced that Brady was bald."

The next morning at work:

ROB: He won't fire me. It'll look bad in the papers.
BUDDY: Yeah . . . it looks bad to fire a guy the same day you kill him.
ROB: He's not gonna kill me.
BUDDY: Well, he ain't gonna give you a raise.

In his office, Alan Brady—with his hurt feet elevated on his desk—is wearing a hat, surrounded by a series of his toupees on mannequin heads. Laura walks in.

LAURA: I just wanted to see you personally to apologize . . . and . . . uh . . . try to explain.
ALAN: What's to explain, you have a big mouth.
LAURA: Alan . . . please . . . you don't have to do that. May I say something?
ALAN: You have *more* to say?
LAURA: Well, I've been thinking about it . . . and, well, for instance, I think you look very nice . . . uh . . . without . . . your . . . uh . . .
ALAN: It's hair! *(takes hat off, puts it on again)*
LAURA: Well, yes . . . I've . . . I've . . . now believe me, I'm not saying this because I'm in trouble . . . although goodness, I am.
ALAN: Oh, no.
LAURA: But, sincerely . . . really sincerely, and you can ask anybody . . . I've always liked you better without your . . .
ALAN: It's hair . . . hair . . . ! *(throws hat on desk)* You didn't have any trouble saying it yesterday! *(then)* When did you ever see me without my hair?
LAURA: Well . . . uh . . . a couple of times. Remember that time on your boat when you fell overboard . . .
ALAN *(accusingly)*:   The time you bumped into me.
LAURA *(weakly)*:   No . . . *(He stares at her.)* I really like your hair . . . not on . . . uh . . . you without it.
ALAN: If this is so, then why didn't you tell me in private?
LAURA: I didn't feel it was my place.
ALAN: No, your place is on network television.

Rob comes storming in. Alan forgives them both: "The fact is . . . this incident took a big strain off my brain. It's tough keeping a secret like this. But now that it's out I feel better."

ROB: Boy, how about that, honey. I bet you never thought this would work out so well.
LAURA: *(blithely trying to maintain the good mood)*:

Art Expert: Howard Morris appraises "The Masterpiece."

The Producers: Mary Tyler Moore, Richard Deacon

Never! *(to Alan)* Maybe I ought to go on television and tell about your nose.
(Rob stiffens.)
ALAN *(getting steamed—to Rob):* You told her about my . . .
LAURA: I don't know anything. Ask Rob. I always said I liked you without your nose.
ROB: She loves it, she loves it!
ALAN: Did you tell her about my capped teeth, too?
ROB: Do you have capped teeth?
ALAN: No!
ROB: See how easy it is to blurt something out when you get excited?
ALAN *(starts chasing Rob and Laura out):* Get out of here, both of you! Out! Why don't you come to my house? Then you can tell all about my wife's . . .

And they're all out the door.

We loved—literally loved—the characters on this show:

Sally Rogers (Rose Marie) was a good guy. Her mama-pecked boyfriend was Herman Gilmcher. He wasn't-good-enough-for-her, but there didn't seem to be anyone else around. Sally had Been Around (she used to be in vaudeville, just like the Mertzes; in fact, on this show she and Buddy *were* the Mertzes) and wore her heart on her tongue. Sally's female persona fell somewhere in between Schultzy and Rhoda; she was the charter member of TV's ladies' lonely hearts club, eager to snatch an eligible man as her romantic prey. She used mannish mannerisms to hide her womanly desires. Once when Rob was in a staff meeting, his son called.

ROB: Yes . . . I'm working . . . I'm in an important meeting. Rich, what . . . *(sighs)* Uncle Alan, Uncle Mel, and Uncle Buddy.
(Sally gets his attention.)
ROB: And Uncle Sally.

Sally was a wiseacre, ranking right up there with the best of them.

ROB *(looking for Laura):* Where's Laura?
SALLY: I saw her get in the elevator.
ROB: The elevator?
SALLY: Yeah, that little room in the lobby that goes up and down.

Buddy Sorrell (Morey Amsterdam) was TV's first real American Jew (the Goldbergs didn't count; they were TV's first Jewish immigrants—from radio). He even got bar mitzvahed on the show once. Another vaudeville alumnus, Buddy was wry and spoke as you'd expect an uneducated New Yorker to speak: he said "Ain't" and said things like "She don't do anything wrong . . . because she don't do anything." He was faintly irresponsible and always picked on producer Mel Cooley (who was star Alan Brady's brother-in-law/coolie) with his biting bald jokes. He often complained about his wife, Pickles, a bleached-blonde former showgirl. We heard so much about her and how incompetent she was that when we met her, it was a disappointment. The writers must have known that, because they never brought her back on again. Anyway, we all knew that Buddy was in love with Sally even if he didn't know it. It was that simple.

Charades (from left): Mary Tyler Moore, Ann Morgan Guilbert, Rose Marie, Morey Amsterdam, Jerry Paris, Dick Van Dyke

Also that simple was Mel Cooley (Richard Deacon) who was a toad, and a sneaky rat. He was "in charge" of Rob's writing unit, and harassed them whenever he could. He was a groveler when it came to Alan Brady, who was a scourge—also a bully: vain, powerful, successful, detestable, and ruthless. He treated Mel in a satanic way. Check out the following:

ALAN *(to Sally):*   If I need any help, I'll ask for it.
MEL: Right, if Alan needs any help, he'll—
ALAN: Shut up, Mel.
MEL: Yessir.

Or:

MEL *(answering phone):*   Hello?
ALAN: Shut up, Mel . . .
MEL *(whispers):*   Rob, it's for you.
ALAN: Speak up, Mel.
MEL: It's for—*(louder)*—the phone is for Rob.
ALAN: So shut up and give it to him. Come on, dress me.

Or:

ALAN: I know his wife. She's crazy.
MEL: I've always felt . . .
ALAN: You never felt anything, Mel.

Squashing Mel was an Alan Brady reflex, and Mel lived in perpetual humiliation from Alan. But most of the time, on most of the shows, Alan wasn't around, and Mel

bullied the writing staff. Mel was a worm. Alan was a terror.

Alan was also a creator. Or at least Carl Reiner (the man who played Alan) was. *The Dick Van Dyke Show* was Carl Reiner's baby (so, incidentally, was Rob Reiner, who played Mike/Meathead on *All in the Family*, but not for another nine years). You see, Reiner had originally conceived the show to star himself.

In October of 1958, Reiner, a veteran of both the Broadway stage and the *Sid Caesar* and *Dinah Shore* shows, announced that he was putting together a pilot for a situation comedy in which he would star. "It's a wonderful idea," he announced at the time, "but if I tell people what it's about now, somebody with better facilities will make one just like it and then where will I be?"

In 1959, Reiner announced that, indeed, he had just finished a pilot about writers for a variety show. It was called *Head of the Family* and, along with Reiner, starred Barbara Britton as Reiner's wife, and Morty Gunty and Sylvia Miles as Reiner's assistant writers on the show.

But things didn't work out so well. He couldn't find a sponsor.

1959: "I'm angry," Reiner said. "I don't know who to be angry with, but I'm angry. All the tradesmen agree that I have a quality product, but nobody buys it. It's too late to work a private eye or Western theme into the show. . . ."

Sheldon Leonard (who played gangsters in movies and eventually went on to become an eminent TV comedy surgeon and big-time TV comedy producer) saw Reiner's pilot and liked everything in it—except Reiner.

"I liked the idea," Leonard said, "but Carl wasn't right playing the lead."

"Who have you got in mind?" Reiner asked him.

"Dick Van Dyke."

"Great."

Dick Van Dyke had had a great deal of television experience, including starring in a 1955 New Orleans local TV variety show called *The Dick Van Dyke Show*. Van Dyke moved to New York and appeared in many New York TV programs and had starred in both the Broadway and movie versions of the musical *Bye Bye Birdie*. He was rubber-faced and rubber-everything-else, for that matter. When he stood up, he could make his body look like it was swaying in the breeze. He had a vast repertoire of mannerisms—looks of wild surprise, hand gestures that, with a whisk through the air, indicated the futility of it all. Most of all, Van Dyke—and Rob Petrie—were cute. Cute without being cloying.

Van Dyke's Rob was important in the development of the male on TV. He was the first man on television to admit that he wasn't always strong, that he had problems, that he was insecure. He was television's first neurotic. Van Dyke was a tall, gangling, Silly-Putty person who oozed charm, warmth, and lovability—and a certain irresistible goofiness. Dick Van Dyke needed a very special actress to be his TV wife.

Laura Petrie was played by a young actress named Mary Tyler Moore (once "Happy Hotpoint," the dancing elf on that commercial), who had, previous to *The Dick Van Dyke Show*, played Sam the switchboard girl on the *Richard Diamond* detective show (only her legs showed). Reiner said he hired her to play Laura Petrie because "she could say 'hello' for real." She had, some time before, auditioned for the role of Danny Thomas' daughter on *Make Room for Daddy*. Although he liked her,

Thomas didn't give her the part because he felt she just wasn't quite right for the role of his daughter. Thomas turned up later as the coproducer of the *Van Dyke Show* and remembered her in a most unusual way. They had been trying unsuccessfully to fill the role of Laura. One day, a casting person asked Thomas, "Can you think of any more actresses?" The wore "more" touched something off and he thought of Moore, Mary Tyler. She got the part.

Laura was the program's updated housewife. She wore pants. It was her modern sense of early sixties taste that picked out the atrocious flower wallpaper over their beds (twins, of course) and the princess phone next to them—but not without asking Rob how he felt about it first. She was full of insecurities—not as a mother or a wife, but as a person. She questioned her role as an independent person. Although she was often childish and dependent, she was basically at ease with herself. She was shy and kind and had a vagueness about her—as though what she really wanted to do was bust out of there and go work in a television newsroom in Minneapolis. She acted like a real person (although in one episode she got her toe stuck in the bathtub faucet) and behaved like the rest of us do.

Debuting in 1961, *The Dick Van Dyke Show*—the comedy saga of a TV scriptwriter, his family and friends in suburbia—got some pretty mixed reviews. *Variety* said the show was "about par" as situation comedies went. The New York *Post* called the show "flimsy," but added that it was the best situation comedy on the air. The first season started slowly, and the sponsors nearly dropped the show. But when the program won an Emmy award for best comedy program, the sponsors reconsidered and the show never left the Neilsen Top Twenty until it went off the air.

Wholesale: Laura and Millie vie for the same fur.

Pet Duck: Rob and Richie

The comedy always grew out of the characters. The show was filmed before a live audience (no laugh-track here) and sometimes the sound editors had to delete some of the laughs; TV audiences had gotten too used to canned laughter and didn't believe the real thing.

That laughter didn't always come directly from the scripts; sometimes the routines were improvised on the spot. In one scene, Laura and Rob were talking and Rob was supposed to be preoccupied with worry. But the director decided that the scene needed some extra "business," something that Van Dyke could do to perk things up. Neither Van Dyke nor the director could come up with anything. Suddenly, Carl Reiner lept to his feet.

"How about this?" Reiner said, and picked up a necktie. "All through the scene, Rob makes and remakes a tie, without getting the ends to come out even. Then, for the tag, Laura says, 'You're really not that nervous, are you?' Rob rips off his tie and he starts across for the bathroom and says, 'Oh, no? When was the last time you saw me put on a tie to take a shower?'"

On September 7, 1966—after 157 episodes—*The Dick Van Dyke Show* went off the air. But it wasn't because the network was killing it. CBS, in fact, did everything it could to make them change their mind. But, no, Reiner and Van Dyke were adamant. "We want to quit while we're still proud of it," Van Dyke said. And there was lots to be proud of: by the time the show had ended, it had received Emmy nominations in every possible comedy category: best show, best direction, best writing, best supporting actress and actor, best leading actress and actor. In fact, many people feel that the show was—quite simply—the best sitcom that had been on TV.

Dick Van Dyke tried again in 1971 with *The New Dick Van Dyke Show*, a funny show which just couldn't live up to the old. He went on to become a costar on *The Carol Burnett Show* in its final season, but it didn't work out and he left the cast. After a couple of TV dramas, Van Dyke started turning up on electronic toy commercials, as well as the movie *The Runner Stumbles*. Mary Tyler Moore, of course, got her own show with her own name on it in 1970 and, in 1978, bombed with *Mary* and *The Mary Tyler Moore Program*, both variety shows. Both Rose Marie and Morey Amsterdam have been playing around on various comedy shows (Rose Marie was a secretary on *The Doris Day Show* in 1968). Except for Mary Tyler Moore, none has ever achieved the excellence or success they did on *The Dick Van Dyke Show*.

We have the reruns, and for that we are truly fortunate. But even though it's on every day, we miss it.

Nepotism: Sleepwalking Jerry Van Dyke

MR. ED

MR. ED: (impatiently)   *Come on, let's go, Wilbur!*
WILBUR: You're *on the bottom.*
MR. ED: *Sorry.*

And that's the way this one-joke show—a shaggy-horse story—went. And went. And went. For six years. Until finally—and thankfully—it trotted off the air.

The situation—very simple: a young architect buys a house that comes with a horse who turns out to be able to talk—but only to the man. Sort of *Topper,* equestrian-style. The stories depict the misadventures of the man, as he struggles to conceal his possession of the talking horse from his newly wedded wife, neighbors, and anyone else.

The comedy was very strained and obvious. Yet the show won two Emmies and at least three or four times that many fans.

Mr. Ed was very successful. But there was something almost racist about the show. The talking horse took on an ethnicity of his own, and it was embarrassing to listen to him telling horsey jokes—"You heard it from the horse's mouth," he'd say—almost like blacks doing watermelon routines or Jews making money jokes. But there was no antidefamation organization for palominos.

It all began in 1954 (actually, it all began years earlier with the successful "Francis, the Talking Mule" movies), when producer Arthur Luben (who had directed the "Francis" flicks) tried to peddle the Mr. Ed idea to Alan Young, a former stand-up comic who had never been on a horse before. Young had been on radio and TV, the star of his own *Alan Young Show.* He had urged CBS to start taping his live show, and they suspended him. Angry, he left for England, where he made twenty-five TV shows. He wanted no part of *Mr. Ed.* "It's not the sort of thing I want to do," he said simply. The networks didn't think it was the sort of thing they wanted to do either.

In 1957, Luben tried Young again. Young—again—said no. So Luben went ahead and produced a pilot for the show—starring Scott McKay and Sandra White (Ed was played by a different horse in the pilot, but the show was essentially the same). The pilot didn't sell.

By 1960, Young hadn't been working much and reluctantly agreed to do the show. But the networks still wouldn't buy *Mr. Ed.* So Luben and executive producer Al Simon put the show in syndication, and it was an instant hit.

Shortly afterward, CBS was in need of a children's show for their 6:30 P.M. Sunday time slot. So they bought *Mr. Ed,* one of the first shows fo go from syndication to network, which set immediate track records with a 20 Neilsen rating.

Ed—with his deep baritone voice and flaxen hair—was a typical sitcom character. He was cranky and ornery, or, as Young described him: "Ed is a terrible slob who is good to his mother." Ed was also a hypochondriac and a voracious reader. He had definite opinions: he loved Leonard Bernstein, he deplored violence on TV. He wanted his stall to be furnished in Chinese Modern, and he demanded the right to vote.

Each week, the show began with Ed popping his head through the stable door, whinnying and announcing: "Hello, I'm Mr. Ed," followed by the show's theme song, singing that a horse was a horse, "of course, of course."

Here is a typical 1964 episode—complete with a guest star (they had many, from Zsa Zsa Gabor to Mae West)—called "Mr. Ed Writes Dear Abby."

It is morning. Ed isn't in his stable and Wilbur is worried: "His hay hasn't been slept in." Then a disheveled Ed walks in, in party hat and streamers. Wilbur is angry that he's been out partying all night. Ed says that he wants to run away and have his own "swingin' pad—a bachelor apartment." Wilbur reminds Ed that he's only eight years old.

Ed—who is a smartass horse (as opposed to Wilbur, who is a horse's ass)—types a letter to Dear Abby, signs Wilbur's name, and mails it—but forgets to stamp it. His wife, Carol, reads the letter when the mailman returns it

Wilbur Post	Alan Young
Carol Post	Connie Hines
Roger Addison, their neighbor	Larry Keating (1961–1963)
Kay Addison, his wife	Edna Skinner (1961–1964)
Gordon Kirkwood, their neighbor	Leon Ames (1963–1965)
Winnie Kirkwood, his wife	Florence MacMichael (1963–1965)
Mr. Carlisle, Carol's father	Barry Kelly

(actually, in true sitcom form, she is "too honest" to open and read her husband's mail, and has to have her neighbor open it for her and read it), and discovers that "Wilbur" wants to leave home. "You fought to win him," the neighbor says, "now fight to keep him."

Says Carol: "I'm gonna be the best little wife . . ."

On his own, Wilbur calls Dear Abby to tell her about his horse, who wants to move out. She thinks he's playing a game and tells him that Ed should be able to come and go as he pleases. Wilbur is crestfallen, but helps Ed pack up his comic books, glasses, shower cap, and other paraphernalia.

"I guess I'll get another horse," Wilbur laments.

Replies Ed: "Why not get a dog or a cat? Everybody's going in for compacts these days."

But—suddenly—Ed changes his mind and says he'll need "a year or two" to think it over—and all is happy again as Ed lies in the sun with his sunglasses on, trying to get a tan.

A tall-horse story, critics argued. But not really. For example, wife Carol had every reason to be worried, because, in a sense, Wilbur was married to Ed, and their relationship had an intimacy that most couples never achieved. And, anyway, Mr. Ed had much more dimension than Carol, who was a half-dimensional character. In fact, actress Connie Hines considered her stint on the show "a steady paycheck," nothing more.

Years after the show left the air in 1970, The Big Secret was finally revealed: the baritone voice of Ed was supplied by a man who made Westerns—Allan "Rocky" Lane. That information had been guarded for years.

Mr. Ed and its apparent frivolity was all part of the wave of early 1960s fantasy shows—*Gilligan's Island, Bewitched, My Living Doll, My Favorite Martian* were others—all of which served as escapes from the realities of American life as the country was in the early stages of national turbulence. Rocket ships with Martians, sexy robots, domestic witches, and talking horses all took us away from the truths we were about to face as a nation. When we couldn't avoid them anymore, the shows were canceled; we didn't need them.

But back then we weren't so analytical. Every week, we watched the wagging tale of this flipped-out Fury who took bubble baths with Mae West, learned to dance the twist, and longed for the patter of four hooves.

Cramming: Mr. Ed brushes up on some lines.

Mr. Ed is now seen in fifty-seven countries, although not in too many American cities. Today, the show could never be made as a sitcom; instead, they'd give Ed his own late-night talk show. Zsa Zsa, Charles Nelson Reilly, and Dr. Joyce Brothers would all exchange witty patter with him, and he would no doubt come out with the "Mr. Ed" line of clothing. Not to mention the Las Vegas appearances and the county fairs and the record albums and autobiography and posters. . . .

We were lucky and we didn't even know it.

But, alas, fate took a tricky turn toward tragedy, and Mr. Ed died on February 28, 1979, about 15 years after his last on-screen speech. He was 33. For the last five years, he'd been touring the country making personal appearances (on the lecture circuit, no doubt). But, said his owner, "he had lost all his teeth and he just couldn't eat any more, even though we had him on a special baby beef formula for the past few months."

There was no funeral. No memorial service. Just reruns.

ALSO RANS

The Bob Cummings Show

Bob's third comedy series—his first was *My Hero* and his second was *Love That Bob*—saw the perennial bachelor cast as pilot Bob Carson. Assisted by sidekick Lionel (Murvyn Vye), Bob spent each episode trying to round up charter flight parties and solve his financial problems, which remained unresolved when his ill-fated plane disappeared from CBS's airwaves in 1962 after one season aloft.

Father of the Bride

Elizabeth Taylor and Spencer Tracy had done it in the movies, so now it was televison's turn. *Father of the*

Father of the Bride: *Myrna Fahey*

Bride had been a movie smash, so CBS figured: Why not TV? Better question: Why? Either way, here's what the story was: Stanley Banks (Leon Ames, who'd played another father on *Life with Father*, and would later play *Mr. Ed's* neighbor) and Ellie Banks (Ruth Warrick) were having a tough time adjusting to the engagement of their daughter Kay (Myrna Fahey). Everyone was enthusiastic about the wedding—including their son Tommy (Rickie Sorensen) and their housekeeper Delilah (Ruby Dandridge)—everybody, that is, except for Stanley. And so the episodes revolved around his getting used to his son-in-law-to-be, Buckley (Burt Metcalfe), and Buckley's father, Herbert Dunston (played by former radio emcee and comic Ransom Sherman). But Father should have had no trouble getting used to Mrs. Doris Dunston—she was played by Lurene Tuttle, who had played Ames' wife, Vinnie, on *Life with Father*. And here she was playing his in-law. Small world. But only for one season.

The Hathaways

The thing about this show, you see, is that this family had three wards—Enoch, Charlie, and Cindy—who were chimpanzees (played by the Marquis Chimps). Ha ha.

The Hathaways: *Peggy Cass, Jack Weston and a Marquis Chimp*

Anyway, Jack Weston played Walter Hathaway, a real estate salesman. Peggy Cass played his wife, Elinore. Harvey Lembeck played Jerry Roper the chimps' agent (yes, they worked for a living riding bikes and making faces). Naturally, the neighbors were wondering what was going on next door. ABC cut out the monkey business after one season.

Hazel

This sitcom, based on the beloved *Saturday Evening Post* cartoon about a daffy domestic, was almost as dearly loved as its source. The show had two formats. The first (from 1961 to 1965) was about Hazel's attempts to solve crises—legal and domestic—as she meddled in her boss' business affairs. She lived with the Baxters at 123 Marshall Rd., in Hydsberg, New York—George, an attorney with Butterworth, Hatch, and Noell; his wife, Dorothy; and their very blond son, Harold.

The second format (1965–1966) took place at the home of Steve Baxter, George's brother, at 325 Sycamore St., also in Hydsberg. He was a real estate salesman with a wife, Barbara, and a daughter named Susie. George, you see, had been transferred to the Middle East on business (doing legal work for Arabs?) and left Harold with Steve and Barbara so that the kid's education wouldn't be interrupted—or the program. Hazel became the Baxter II's maid.

Shirley Booth played Hazel Burke, the know-it-all maid. The Baxter family was portrayed by: Don DeFore

Hazel's Second Family (clockwise): Bobby Buntrock, Julia Benjamin, Shirley Booth, Ray Fulmer, Lynn Borden

(George), Whitney Blake (Dorothy), Bobby Buntrock (Harold), Ray Fulmer (Steve), Lynn Borden (Barbara), and Julia Benjamin (Susie). Smiley was the name of the Baxters' dog. The show ran on NBC for four seasons, and then crawled on to CBS for one season.

Holiday Lodge

This CBS summer replacement starred Canadian comedy team Johnny Wayne and Frank Shuster as Johnny Miller and Frank Boone, social directors in a New York State hotel. They tried to provide fascinating entertainment (which is more than the show did), but they always ran into trouble with the hotel's varied assortment of guests, as well as the management.

Ichabod and Me

Ichabod was George Chandler; Me was Robert Sterling (he had been George Kirby in *Topper*). This CBS show was about Bob Major (Sterling), who left New York to purchase the Phippsboro *Bulletin* in a small New England community. He became editor and was assisted by the former owner Ichabod Adams, who was now the traffic commissioner. Bob also had a six-year-old son, Benjie (played by Jimmy Mathers, not to be confused with Jerry Mathers, the Beaver). The show continued on for one year.

Hazel (from left): Shirley Booth, Bobby Buntrock, Don DeFore, Whitney Blake

The Joey Bishop Show

There were two *Joey Bishop Shows*, really, because the show changed formats in the middle.

First, as a spin-off from *The Danny Thomas Show*, Bishop played Joey Barnes, a Hollywood PR man who had nothing but troubles working with the ad agency of Wellington, Willoughby and Jones. His stage-struck sister, Stella Barnes (Marlo Thomas—Danny's daughter and later *That Girl*), added plenty of trouble too.

The next season, the show switched: Joey became a talk-show host living in New York. He no longer had a sister, but a wife, Ellie Barnes (Abby Dalton), as well as a manager named Freddie (Guy Marks, later replaced by comic Corbett Monica as Larry Corbett). In 1963, they got a baby (played by Abby Dalton's son Matthew Smith). The show was dropped by NBC after three seasons, but was picked up by CBS for its final season, until it went off the air in 1965.

The Lucy Show

After she divorced Desi and starred in a Broadway musical (*Wildcat*), Lucille Ball returned to sitcomland, where she belonged, and settled in for a long run as Lucy Carmichael, a scatterbrained continuation of Lucy Ricardo, whose format changes were as schizophrenic as she was. First: she lived at 132 Post Rd. in Danfield, Connecticut, with her two kids, Chris (Candy Moore) and Jerry (Jimmy Garrett)—*sans* a husband (she was a widow). What she did have, however, was a buddy: Vivian Bagley, a divorcée (certainly television's first divorced woman) played by Vivian Vance (who, of course, had been Lucy's sidekick, Ethel Mertz). Also on hand: Gale Gordon as Theodore J. Mooney, the president of the Danfield First National Bank. She always called him "Mr. Mooney." Dick Martin (as in "Rowan and . . .") played Lucy's friend Harry.

In 1965, Lucy moved to San Francisco (708 Gower St.) without Viv, who went somewhere else. Now she was Mr. Mooney's secretary at the Westland Bank, of which he was vice-president. This time Mr. Mooney had a boss too—Harrison Cheever (played by Roy Roberts). Lucy's buddy this time was Mary Jane Lewis (played by Mary Jane Croft), a secretary employed at Mammouth Studios. And this time Lucy didn't have any children. It didn't matter, just as long as she didn't have any brains (and she didn't), because that's what the people wanted. And that's what the people got. Until 1968, when the show went off the air to become *Here's Lucy* that same year.

The Lucy Show: *Lucille Ball, Gale Gordon*

Margie

No relation to *My Little Margie*, this one was about another girl with a penchant for trouble: Margie Clayton (Cynthia Pepper), who lived in the small New England town of Madison during the twenties. Life in the twenties, apparently, was the same as in the sixties (with the exceptions of rumble seats and bathtub gin). As a clever touch: silent film slides—"Please Pay Attention," "The Plot Thickens," etc.—flashed across the screen.

Margie *(from left): Wesley Tackitt, Cynthia Pepper, Dave Willock*

Margie had a father, a mother, a sophisticated aunt, and a boyfriend. She also had a network (ABC) who canceled her show after ten months. Based on a popular forties movie.

Mrs. G. Goes to College

After so much *tsouris* with *The Goldbergs* during the Red Scare of the fifties, Gertrude Berg tried TV again. This time, though, she didn't mess around with Molly Goldberg anymore. She created a new name and persona for Molly: this time around she was Sarah Green, a middle-aged widow who enrolls at the University of Southern California to pursue a long-sought dream—a college education. Along the way, this Nice Jewish Lady runs into Professor Clayton (Sir Cedric Hardwicke), a visiting instructor from England. They become fast—although cross-cultural, to be sure—buddies. Mrs. G. lives in Winona Maxfield's (Mary Wickes) boarding house, where she dispenses advice like chicken soup. CBS canceled this show in 1962.

Oh, Those Bells!

The Wiere Brothers—Herbert, Harry, Sylvester—played the Bell Brothers—Herbert, Harry, and Sylves-

Oh, Those Bells: *The Wiere Brothers*

ter—in this show about three zanies who run the Hollywood Prop Shop. They were always in financial trouble and stayed solvent on CBS only two months. The show brought slapstick to sitcoms—very Three Stooges-esque—but briefly.

One Happy Family

Three years before he became Darrin on *Bewitched*, Dick Sargent played Dick Cooper in this midseason replacement on NBC. With his wife, Penny (Jody Warner), Dick moved in with her parents and her grandparents for a night, but ended up staying until cancellation. The generations gapped, but not much else happened.

Room for One More

This family loved children and, besides their own two, ended up adopting two more. In LA, engineer George Rose (Andrew Duggan) lived with his wife, Anna (Peggy McCay), and their two kids, Laurie and Flip. Along the way they pick up Mary and Jeff, played by Anna Carri and Timmy Rooney (Mickey's son). Jack Albertson (later "the Man" with *Chico*) played a friend of the family. They also had a dog named Tramp (which they perhaps borrowed from *My Three Sons*?). The show ran on ABC from January until September 1962. Based on Anna Perrott Rose's memoirs, which were made into a 1952 Cary Grant movie called *Room for One More* (later retitled *The Easy Way*).

Window on Main Street

Between being a father who knew best and playing *Marcus Welby, MD*, Robert Young starred in this—well, not exactly a sitcom. More like a sitdram. Anyway, in the small town of Millsburg (Robert Young was never the type who could live in a big city), Cameron Garrett Brooks (that's what Jim Anderson had changed his name to) had come to live after the deaths of his wife and son. It's his hometown and he, a novelist, had come to write. Better he should have stayed in Springfield. CBS sent him off to medical school in 1962.

1962–1963

The Beverly Hillbillies

McHale's Navy

OFF-SCREEN

9/23 Philharmonic Hall, first building completed of New York's Lincoln Center for the Performing Arts, opens with gala concert.

9/27 New York Mets finish first season as a National League baseball team losing three out of every four games played.

9/29 *My Fair Lady,* longest-running musical in Broadway history, closes.

10/18 Watson, Wilkins, and Crick win Nobel prize for discovery of DNA.

11/15 Twenty-year-old Cassius Clay knocks out Archie Moore in fourth round.

11/20 President Kennedy signs executive order prohibiting racial discrimination in federally funded housing.

12/23 Cuba begins releasing prisoners captured in 1961 invasion for supplies and food.

2/21 Medicare program submitted to Congress by President Kennedy.

4/9 Winston Churchill proclaimed honorary US citizen in ceremony televised from White House.

6/10 President Kennedy signs bill for equal pay for equal work, regardless of sex.

FRONT RUNNER

THE BEVERLY HILLBILLIES

*We can use some fresh meat—try and get a possum or
some squirrel.*

—Granny's shopping list

The critics hated it. *Hated* it. But the audiences loved it. *Loved* it. When the Clampetts moved from the Ozarks to television (via Beverly Hills, California), they changed the nature of sitcoms—from suburban to nature. For the next ten years, television was overcrowded with rural blight, as *The Beverly Hillbillies* spun off such knock-offs as *Green Acres, Petticoat Junction, Here Come the Brides,* and a number of others—all high on the hog and high on the ratings—until an executive at CBS said Enough Already and canceled them all.

On September 26, 1962, *The Beverly Hillbillies* debuted and ran to the top of the ratings as if the police were after it (and some say they should have been—arrested for dumbness). The show was all about an Ozark mountain clan who had struck oil, and it rich, and moved to Beverly Hills on an old flatbed truck loaded with jugs of corn liquor—and $25,000,000.

Throughout the show's nine-year run, the family remain true to their old environment. Jed longs for life the way it was. Granny is miserable—she can't practice her unlicensed mountain doctoring (a Dr. Roy Clyburn threatens to press charges if she does), she finds that her lye soap pollutes the air, and can't find her favorite ingredients (such as possum innards) in city stores. Elly May tries to prove that she's superior to any man and wonders why she can't find a steady beau. She spends time, instead, with her many critters. Jethro, with his sixth-grade education, loves the big city and tries hard to "find a sweetheart."

Living in their mansion at 518 Crestview Dr., the

Jed Clampett	Buddy Ebsen
Daisy Moses (Granny)	Irene Ryan
Elly May Clampett	Donna Douglas
Jethro Bodine	Max Baer, Jr.
Jethrene Bodine	Max Baer, Jr.
Milburn Drysdale	Raymond Bailey
Jane Hathaway	Nancy Kulp
Margaret Drysdale	Harriet MacGibbon
Pearl Bodine, Jethro's mother	Bea Benaderet (1962–1963)
John Brewster, president of the OK Oil Company	Frank Wilcox
Isabel Brewster	Lisa Seagram
Lester Flatt	Himself
Earl Scruggs	Himself
Gladys Flatt, Lester's wife	Joi Lansing
Louise Scruggs, Earl's wife	Midge Ware
Homer Winch	Paul Winchell
Jasper DePew, Jethrene's boyfriend	Phil Gordon
Ravenscott, the Drysdales' butler	Arthur Gould Porter
Marie, the Drysdales' maid	Shirry Steffin
Dash Riprock (Homer Noodleman), a movie star	Larry Pennell
Mark Templeton, Elly May's beau (later episodes)	Roger Torrey
Homer Cratchit, the bank bookkeeper	Percy Helton
Elverna Bradshaw, Granny's nemesis	Elvia Allman
Sonny Drysdale, Milburn's son, in his 19th year in college	Louis Nye
Janet Trego, a bank secretary	Sharon Tate
Dr. Roy Clyburn, Granny's nemesis	Fred Clark
The psychiatrist	Richard Deacon
Harry Chapman, a movie producer at Mammoth Studios	Milton Frome

simple backwoods family wish they were back in Sibly (where the OK Oil Company bought their Ozark land), but do their best to adjust—or, rather, not so much adjust to their new surroundings, but make their new surroundings adjust to them. There is a luxurious laundry room, for example, but Granny prefers to use her scrub board when washing overhauls. They serve their "vittles" in what they call their "fancy eatin' room"—the billiard room. They call their swimming pool "the cement pond" and use it as a communal trough for all the family's critters, including their hound dog Duke.

Granny (who is ornery and crotchety and also Jed's mother-in-law) didn't "cotton" to leaving the mountains in the first place. And so she had to be transported to Beverly Hills in her rocking chair, with one jar of moonshine and another of mountain medicine. This cantankerous old coot, even in the Beverly Hills mansion, sticks to her old ways: she cooks hog jowls, fatback, mustard greens, salted-down possum belly, squirrel shanks, cow gizzards, boiled toad, and even golf balls (as you soon shall see).

The show was pure and flaky country corn (appropriately sponsored by Kellogg's). The episodes were more yarns than situations. But *The Beverly Hillbillies* did accomplish something significant: they had been complaining for years about too much violence on prime-time programming. *Beverly Hillbillies* had none of that.

What it had was happy people with happy problems. It was a farce, the ultimate fantasy—a cross between *Ma and Pa Kettle* and *Cinderella*. It was about class differences, how you could still keep your simple, honest beliefs and get along in the big-bad-world. Said Director Richard Whorf: "You know that no one will be killed, no one will have a brain tumor." Nobody ever got hurt on *The Beverly Hillbillies*. Except, said some, the viewers' intelligence.

Every week the show opened with a Johnny Cash sing-alike voice talking these cornpone lyrics over film credits of the cast acting out words about "a man named Jed" who "kept his family fed." All to music by Flatt and Scruggs. And what would follow would be a typical episode, such as this one from 1963, "The Beverly Hillbillies vs. The Dodgers."

Granny and Elly May are cooking in their huge kitchen, but Granny's not happy; she wishes she had some fresh squirrel to make for dinner. Jed pops in and announces that he's going out with Mr. Drysdale from the Commerce Bank of Beverly Hills (where they stash their cash).

JED: We're gonna be shooting some game called golf.
GRANNY: What in tarnation is a golf?
JED: I don't know, but they must be thicker'n crows in a corn patch around here because everybody in Beverly Hills shoots 'em.
GRANNY: Never seen 'em around. They must live in holes in the ground like a gopher.

Christmas at the Clampetts: Granny thinks the TV set is really a fancy washing machine.

JED: Reckin maybe you're right. Mr. Drysdale says he shot nine holes of golf and got fifty-seven.

Curvaceous Elly May brings in the golf bag, which Jed assumes is for putting the game in after it's been shot. Then she sees the golf shoes. "First you shoot 'em, then you club 'em, then you stomp 'em with spikes—I can't wait to tangle with golfs!"

"Well, dogie!" caws Jethro, as Elly May picks up the clubs and puts them in the golf bag. Everyone thinks that's a great idea. "Funny nobody ever thought of that before," she muses. Granny then picks up a putter and discovers it's "dandy for stirrin' greens" in her kettle cooking on the stove.

When Jed and Jethro arrive at the Wilshire Country Club, the doorman thinks they're the gardeners. "You here to take care of the greens?"

"As a matter of fact," Jed said, "we did promise to cut some greens for Granny." They're told to park their jalopy in the back and ask for the greenskeeper. Then Jed gets his first look at the people playing golf.

JED: Those people take two little white eggs outa that hole down yonder. When a golf comes out of the hole to get his eggs back, you shoot him.

They run into Leo Durocher, the manager of the Dodgers and their fourth in golf, who thinks they're caddies. "I've seen seedy caddies in my day, but . . ."

Suddenly a golf ball gets caught in a tree. Brawny

Actors Studio: Donna Douglas watches as bear's trainer holds pop bottle over his head as incentive to perform.

Jethro throws a baseball to get it out. Durocher is so impressed with his throwing skills he wants to sign Jethro to the Dodgers.

When Jed and Jethro return home with the "golf eggs"—Granny: They're hard to crack; I'll have to boil 'em—they announce that Jethro's going to be a baseball pitcher. Elly May's upset. "I can throw as good as Jethro." Then the doorbell chimes.

JETHRO: There goes that spook, playin' music in the walls again.
JED: Reckon I better get out front. Somebody always comes to the door when that music plays.

It's the Dodgers' general manager, who thinks the Clampetts are the caretakers.

JETHRO: All baseball teams need a big, strong pitcher.
GRANNY *(goes to cupboard and gets a ceramic pitcher)*: If he don't mind one that's chipped a mite . . .

They talk about baseball. Jethro describes the plate that's made of wood, set in the ground. Mugs Granny: "Well, you wouldn't get *me* to eat offa it . . ."

The double meanings go on for some time (swinging a "bat," playing on a "diamond," etc.) and then Jethro throws a ball to Mr. Durocher—so hard that Mr. Durocher falls in the pond. Granny gives him some soup (chicken hawk with boiled golf eggs) and Elly May announces (in front of the electric dryer) that he will dry his clothes by running around the block with them trailing in the wind.

It is discovered that Jethro has used possum fat to throw straight, and that's illegal. So he can't join the Dodgers. Plus, Jethro says, he doesn't want money; he does it just for the fun of it. Elly May says that she can throw a ball just as well as Jethro—and she too tosses a

ball to Mr. Durocher, who falls into the pond again. The end.

And that was a very typical episode. Clever. But cloying. It may not seem like much on paper (and, in fact, it may not seem like much on television,) but *The Beverly Hillbillies*—like a swift kick in the Neilsen's rear—shot up to the top of the ratings faster than any other show in television history. In fact, it even killed off the invincible *Perry Como Show*, and overwhelmed *The Lucy Show* and *Dick Van Dyke*, which wasn't very nice of it.

The show's theme, as they say, was as old as the hills: the comical mountain dweller and his moonshine and his family—the ultimate prime-time farmer's daughter joke.

Thirty-five million people laughed at that joke each week, a cross between cornpone and comic strip. Each episode the bucolic bumblings gave viewers the same message: people have more material goods than they need; people should live more simply. The critics— "those critic-critters," Granny would have called them— were once again outraged by the humor; they saw it as an exploitation of the old hillbilly stereotypes, and made all Southerners look like dim-wits. The show won admirers among sophisticates, who saw it as a lampoon on a money-mania society. And because the Clampetts wouldn't change, they were incorruptible.

This exchange typified the show's viewpoint:

JED *(looks at his sweeping lawn)*:   Fine, we'll commence plowing tomorrow.
BANKER: But this is Beverly Hills.
JED: Dirt is dirt.

You couldn't fault the casting. Audiences were already familiar with Buddy Ebsen when he was Davey Crockett's TV companion, as well as Holly Golightly's estranged hillbilly husband in the film *Breakfast at*

Birds of a Feather: Guest Wally Cox with Nancy Kulp and Donna Douglas

Tiffany's. Ebsen began his career as a song-and-dance man—boy—performing with his sister Vilma. He had come to New York (after working at his father's dancing school) in 1928 with $26.65 in his sock. He quickly landed in the chorus of Eddie Cantor's *Whoopie*. In 1954, Walt Disney chose him to play George Russell (Fess Parker's sidekick) in the *Crockett* series; many collectors still covet the dancing doll that Disney modeled after Ebsen and marketed. He later appeared in the one-season TV flop *Northwest Passage*.

At 6'1", with a rugged strength and air of simplicity, Ebsen was the only choice for his role in *Beverly Hillbillies*, although he didn't want the part. He had sworn off hillbilly parts. But he reluctantly put on his battered hat and painted-on mustache for the role of Jed Clampett, the itinerant mountaineer.

By the seventies, the series started to fall flat, and the Clampetts really should have moved back to the Ozarks to dig for some more material. One particularly tasteless 1971 episode—"Women's Lib"—has Granny and Elly May making a jolly joke out of the women's movement as they picketed for their organization GRUN (Girls Resist Unfair Neglect). Never would sitcomdom have parodied the NAACP the way it took shots at NOW and other feminist organizations. Here's how it began:

JED: Coffee smells good.
GRANNY: Would you like me to pour it for you?
JED: That would be nice. *(She pours it into the sink.)*

The episode ends up being the inevitable men-and-women-switch-roles-routine, seventies-style. Jethro tries to cook breakfast and can't. Jed darns socks together—all the while, the women (including, by this time, a live-in chimp named Bessie—anything to improve the ratings) are outdoors picketing for women's rights.

Cousin Pearl: Bea Benaderet with Irene Ryan

The episode becomes very complicated—an attempt to increase the sit and therefore improve the com (it didn't work)—and Japanese karate experts and Geishas are brought in to stretch things out a bit. It ends when the women move into Miss Jane's apartment (where Granny gets rolled up in a hideaway bed) and where everything is eventually straightened out—in other words, everyone goes back to his or her old roles.

Eventually the writers started to think that the show was getting as monotonous as the critics had thought it was. So they had the family buy a motion picture studio, complete with Gloria Swanson. The ratings dropped instantly. Within a few weeks the Clampetts were out of show business—and the ratings went up instantly.

In 1972, someone at CBS thought—even though the ratings were still high—that *The Beverly Hillbillies* (and its sitcom country cousins, *Green Acres, Petticoat Junction*, et al) might be alienating the more sophisticated urban and suburban audiences. And so—wham—down came the ax. And—bam—*The Beverly Hillbillies* went to rerun heaven.

And all that's left?

Reruns.

And lines like these:

"Do you like Kipling?"

"I don't know—I ain't never kippled."

The only advantage the Clampetts seemed to have over us is that they didn't have to watch themselves on television each week. But then, neither did we.

Con Man: Guest Phil Silvers and Buddy Ebsen

ALSO RANS

Don't Call Me Charlie

Private Judson McKay (Josh Peine), a country veterinarian from one of Iowa's more obscure corners, wasn't bargaining for anything more than a few cases of hoof-and-mouth disease when he joined the army. But what he got was a post in Paris—a fact that was never allowed to interfere with his simple backwoods style. He also got a colonel named U. Charles Baker (John Hubbard), who didn't mind a little camaraderie with the boys—but couldn't stand being called "Charlie," which probably explains why everybody kept doing it, and certainly clears up the question of the title. One of Charlie's boys during his single season on NBC, Corporal Lefkowitz, was played by Arte Johnson, who had to wait until *Laugh-In* before the world got a chance to salute him. The show was discharged—dishonorably—after four months.

Ensign O'Toole

This NBC sitcom is still fondly remembered by many old fans. Based in the South Pacific, it's the story of the misadventures of a group of officers of the US Navy destroyer USS *Appleby*. Morale Officer Ensign O'Toole (played by Disney movie star Dean Jones) was constantly bickering with C.P.O. Homer Nelson (Jay C. Flippen), who believed in following the rules. O'Toole liked to live spontaneously—and there was conflict between the two. The crew liked Ensign, didn't like Nelson—and they followed the former's leadership. Harvey Lembeck and Beau Bridges both played seamen in the show. Also on the show, Lt. Cdr. Virgil Stoner (Jack Albertson) received orders on the "squawk box" from an unseen captain. Bill Lederer—author of the books *All the Ships at Sea* and *Ensign O'Toole*—was the show's consultant.

Fair Exchange

In the age of "teenagers," this show featured an American and an English family who decided to exchange their

Fair Exchange: *daughters Judy Carne (top) and Lynn Loring with Victor Maddern, Diana Chesney, Dennis Waterman*

teenage daughters for a year—and the program lasted as long as the concept. Each episode seemed to emphasize the girls' difficulties in adjusting to their new countries and new families—as well as their fathers' struggles to adjust to their new daughters (the mothers, being good TV Mommies, apparently had no such troubles).

Anyway: the American family consisted of Eddie Walker (Eddie Foy, Jr., comedian and musical actor), a World War II veteran; his wife, Dorothy (Audrey Christie); their daughter, Patty (Lynn Loring), who wanted to study acting at London's Royal Academy of Dramatic Arts.

In England, daddy is Tommy Finch (Victor Maddern), who also happened to be a World War II veteran (that's how he and Walker met); his wife, Sybil (Diana Chesney); their son, Neville (Dennis Waterman); and their daughter, Heather (Judy Carne, best known now for her stint on *Laugh-In*). The show was shot in both New York and London.

Fair Exchange began as an experiment—the first hour-long sitcom. But it didn't fare well, so CBS canceled it after three months. Barrels of mail poured in, and CBS decided to try the show again—this time trimmed to a half-hour—and it failed to pick up in the ratings again. It finally went off the air in September of 1963.

Going My Way

Gene Kelly was yet another movie exile who tried to make it big in sitcoms. And, just to play it safe, he borrowed his buddy Bing Crosby's vehicle—*Going My Way*, in which Bing was King in 1944. But nearly twenty years later, the translation to TV didn't work so well. This clerical comedy was all about Father Chuck O'Malley, a progressive young priest who was assigned to a parish in the slums of New York, helping to aid a crotchety old pastor, Father Fitzgibbon (played by Leo G. Carroll, who'd played Cosmo on *Topper* nearly ten years before). Also in the cast: Dick York (soon to be married to Samantha on *Bewitched*) as boyhood pal Tom Colwell, who ran the local community center. Mrs. Featherstone (Nydia Westman) was the rectory's housekeeper. Father Chuck—and brother Gene—stayed on ABC a single season only.

I'm Dickens . . . He's Fenster

This show, which took place in LA, was all about the crazed goings-on of two carpenters, Harry Dickens (played by John Astin, who'd later join the *Addams Family* and marry Patty Duke), and Arch Fenster (comedian Marty Ingels). Responsible Harry was married and henpecked; scatterbrained Arch was single and swinging. Frank De Vol played Myron Bannister, the shiny-headed building contractor. This ABC show ran for one year on ABC and then went into syndication.

It's a Man's World

This one took place in an Ohio rivertown called Cordella. It revolved around the experiences and "their attempt to prove it's a man's world" (according to a 1962 NBC press release) of three recently orphaned friends: Wes Macauley (Glenn Corbett), Vern Hodges (Randy Boone) and Tom-Tom DeWitt (Ted Bessell—later Donald on *That Girl*, "me" in *Me and the Chimp*, and, for a while, Mary's beau on *The Mary Tyler Moore Show*). They were college students who lived in a houseboat docked at the water's edge. Their parents were killed in a car accident and Wes' younger brother, Howie (Michael Burns), also lived with them. They all dropped out halfway through the season in January 1963.

McHale's Navy

This sitcom—ever-popular and still rerunning all over the place—had two formats.

McHale's Navy *(top row from left):* **Carl Ballantine, John Wright, Gary Vinson, Edson Stroll, Gavin MacLeod;** *(bottom row):* **Billy Sands, Ernest Borgnine, Tim Conway**

The first: In the South Pacific, on the island of Taratupa during World War II, Lieutenant Quinton McHale (Ernest Borgnine) has a bickering relationship with Captain Wallace B. Binghamton ("Old Lead Bottom," played by Joe Flynn). McHale is the commander of Squadron 19 and PT Boat 73; Binghamton is the commanding officer who feels that his life is plagued by McHale and his crew of "pirates" who have turned the island into "the Las Vegas of the Pacific." Binghamton feels that the war provides him with serenity that he can enjoy between naggings from his wife, and he spends his—and our—time trying to expose McHale's gambling activities. With no luck. All Binghamton wants is a court-martial and a transfer for McHale. That's all.

In 1965, enter format two: Voltafiore, a small town in southern Italy, is the place that McHale—in 1944—and his Squadron 19—are transferred. Guess who else is there? Captain Binghamton. Same old story. Also in both formats: Gavin MacLeod (later Murray on *The Mary Tyler Moore Show*) as Seaman Happy Haines (he practiced sailing here before taking over on *The Love Boat*), and Tim Conway as Ensign Charles Parker. The show went off the air in 1966, after four seasons on ABC.

Novelist Joseph Heller (*Catch-22, Something Happened* and *Good as Gold*) wrote an episode of the show, but had his name removed from the credits after a squabble with the producers. Said Heller: "At the time, I was willing to do anything new. I still get residuals—maybe a couple of hundred bucks a year."

McKeever and the Colonel (*from left*): *Allyn Joslyn, Keith Taylor, Scott Lane*

(played by Jackie Coogan, former child star, later the *Addams Family*'s Uncle Fester). Everyone was expelled after one academic year.

The New Loretta Young Show

This wasn't the one in which Loretta Young would fling herself through the French doors (that was *The Loretta Young Theater* on NBC from 1954 until 1961). In this CBS sitcom, Young played Christine Massey, a Connecticut children's book writer, widow, and mother of seven. She tries to get a job as staff writer on *Manhattan Magazine*, and she submits a story to the editor. Editor Paul Belzer (played by James Philbrook) says he'll hire her if she'll start writing in a more sophisticated manner. She says okay and, after one dinner, they—guess what—fall in love, marry, and set up housekeeping (today it might not be in that order). But, true to life, the couple—and the show—went on the rocks after only six months.

McKeever and the Colonel

NBC enlisted this one about the adventures of Gary McKeever (Scott Lane) a mischievous cadet at the Westfield Military Academy for Boys. His youthful cronies were Tubby (Keith Taylor) and Monk (Johnny Eimen). McKeever's commander was Colonel Harvey Blackwell (Allyn Joslyn), whose aide is Sergeant Barnes

1963–1964

My Favorite Martian

The Patty Duke Show

Petticoat Junction

OFF-SCREEN

9/14 Quintuplets born to Mrs. A. Fischer in South Dakota.

10/2 White House states that aid to South Vietnam to be continued; war might be over by 1965.

10/9 President Kennedy approves wheat sale to USSR.

11/22 John F. Kennedy assassinated in Dallas; Lyndon B. Johnson takes presidential oath.

11/24 Lee Harvey Oswald is shot and killed by Jack Ruby while millions watch on TV.

12/8 Frank Sinatra, Jr., kidnapped at Lake Tahoe; released December 11 on payment of ransom.

1/11 Surgeon General reports that cigarettes contribute to mortality from certain specific diseases.

1/25 Echo II, first joint USSR-US space program, launched.

4/22 New York World's Fair opens.

6/21 Jim Bunning pitches first perfect game in a regular season since 1922.

FRONT RUNNER

MY FAVORITE MARTIAN

PROFESSOR: *Where were you born?*
UNCLE MARTIN: *In a hospital.*

Like a bat out of heck—as they might say in sitcomdom—Martin the Martian splashed down on the tube one Sunday night in 1963. There was a whimsical quality to this show about a "stranger in a strange land" who, it turned out, was a lot less strange than most of the Earthtypes he encountered. Uncle Martin was like the rest of us kids: he and we were "different" from everyone else but, due to circumstances beyond our control (his because he crashed here, ours because we were born here), we were all stranded on Earth.

In the very first episode, when Martin meets a young reporter who befriends him, Martin gives him an impatient look and says: "What are you waiting for me to say—'Take me to your leader'?"

He was an amazing Martian. Martin could make himself disappear, and had antennae on his head that could go up and down. He could do anything—*anything*—like read minds and fly and make dogs salute and plants grow and safes open. He even seemed to make ratings rise. He had no fingerprints. He was a magic Martian. And he knew it all. "I was there when George Washington tried it and Alexander Hamilton before him," he once said, referring to a "new" idea someone had. He was sophisticated and arrogant and always had a whimsical disdain for this planet. "Earth's all right for a visit," he said, "but I wouldn't want to live here."

For three seasons, *My Favorite Martian* did live here, and quite successfully. A cross between *Mr. Ed*, *Topper*, and *The Beverly Hillbillies*, *My Favorite Martian* was another one-joke show that yukked on a little longer than it should have. The most predictable "element" (for he was hardly a character) was Bill Bixby as a young reporter (Harrison Salisbury could rest easy) who reluctantly befriended Uncle Martin when he landed and, in fact, was the only one who knew his true identity. A talking horse? A husband and wife set of ghosts? Fill in your own blanks. Bixby—Tim O'Hara—lived, of course, in LA (as did many in sitcom land) where everything looks sunny and funny and there is no snow or gray. We didn't see Tim at work much—usually he was sitting around complaining how Uncle Martin was complicating his life and playing straight man to Uncle Martin (Ray Walston). Often, Uncle Martin actually did Tim's work for him, as in this scene when he types by telepathy.

TIM: I thought you could give my article—on ESP—a special slant.
MARTIN: Yes, I could. (*Via telepathy, he makes Tim stand at an angle.*)
TIM: Come on, Uncle Martin. I'm serious.
MARTIN: I'm Uncle Martin.

Tim and Martin posed as uncle and nephew, but they were really best friends—almost husband and wife. They were as much a married couple as George and Gracie, Ricky and Lucy, or any of the other sitcom couples in which one is a bit wacky and the other spends his or her time trying to keep the other under control. Martin and Tim never displayed much physical affection (although neither did Burns and Allen). But they bickered just like *The Honeymooners*.

In one 1964 episode, the two nearly split up. In "Hitchhike to Mars," Uncle Martin finds out that scien-

Martin O'Hara (Uncle Martin)	Ray Walston
Tim O'Hara	Bill Bixby
Lorelei Brown, Tim's landlady	Pamela Britton
Angela Brown	Ann Marshall (1963–1964)
Detective Bill Brennan, LAPD, Martin's rival for Lorelei's affections	Alan Hewitt (1964–1966)
Mr. Burns, Tim's employer	J. Pat O'Malley (1963–1964)
The police chief	Roy Engle (1965–1966)

tists have created a rocket to Mars. "A way to get home for my parents' five-hundredth anniversary!" he exclaims. He goes through all kinds of shenanigans—with Tim posing as a reporter on a phony assignment—to interview the head of Inter-Galaxy Corp. to find out final flight plans.

In the next twenty minutes—to get those flight plans—Martin opens safes by telepathy, does magic tricks, extends his antennae, disappears, and has an extended conversation with a cat.

Finally he gets ready to leave for Mars (which, he says, has green, blue, and orange snow). He wears a new beret—"I'll be the sharpest Martian on Galaxy Boulevard." He says goodbye to Tim in a sappy, sloppy, and sentimental scene. Tim goes to watch the launching and sees the doors open and nobody (an invisible Uncle Martin) gets in.

Tim goes home. He is brooding and lonely. And then suddenly—Uncle Martin is back. He decided not to go after all. In another sentimental scene, Tim tells Martin: "Mars's loss is my gain," and the episode ends.

The show's dialogue ran the gamut from sophisticated to comic-book humor. The special effects were some of the best TV audiences had seen. Ray Walston's antennae weren't photographic tricks, but actually activated by a transistor device that rested under his collar. He could push a button to operate it. If a scene was shot from the rear, he wore a wig with wires attached. If Uncle Martin was required to fly, they would pull him up in a harness (just like Mary Martin's TV *Peter Pan*). Often, Walston had to work with animals. In one scene he was mauled by a chimp in a car. Shooting for the day was suspended so Walston could undergo three hours of plastic surgery. When he healed, he came back to work.

Walston had had a long career of playing Uncle Martins. In the stage and motion picture productions of *Damn Yankees* (about a man who sells his soul to Satan to become a great baseball player), Walston played the devil. His dry, irritable—"bitchy," it would be called today—style was a trademark throughout his career.

After playing Tim, Bill Bixby went on to star in *The*

Paper Trained: Ray Walston, Bill Bixby

Courtship of Eddie's Father, The Magician, and *The Incredible Hulk.*

My Favorite Martian was an anti-ecology show—but back in 1963, who even knew what ecology was? Uncle Martin had a disdain for Earth—"this primitive planet," he'd call it—and it had to do with more than separating cans and glass, recycling cardboard and using white toilet paper. Martin couldn't wait to leave Earth. Maybe it was just LA he hated so much? No, it was the whole place.

On September 4, 1966, *My Favorite Martian* flew off the air. Beginning in 1973, CBS aired an animated spin-off of the show called *My Favorite Martians*—in addition to Uncle Martin, Tim also ended up befriending Martin's nephew Andy, and their dog Oakie Doakie. That show departed in 1975.

Throughout it all, Martin the Martian—who could live forever—learned that on Earth, we have something more mysterious than anything on Mars: cancellation.

ALSO RANS

The Bill Dana Show

Jose Jiminez, the Latin American bellhop whose characteristic nasal whine made his creator's career, was the central character in this NBC series, a spin-off from *The*

Danny Thomas Show. Writer-comedian Dana created his Jose Jiminez character on *The Steve Allen Show* and went on to play him in nightclubs and on LPs. Jiminez tried to give aid and advice to the guests of New York City's Park Central Hotel, and also tried to adjust to his adopted lifestyle north of the border. Sometimes dream sequences took Jose away from the hotel and into other—though no less bizarre—situations. Incidentally, Don

Adams, later star of the spy series *Get Smart!*, got his start as a crime buster on this show playing the Metropolitan's lame-brained house dick, Byron Glick.

The Farmer's Daughter

Based on the Oscar-winning 1947 Loretta Young movie of the same name, this sitcom was a watered-down version. It all takes place at 307 Marshall Rd. in Washington, D.C., when Katy Holstrum, a Minnesota farmgirl (played by Inger Stevens), comes to Congressman Glen Morley (William Windom) and asks him for help: she wants to get a government job teaching underprivileged children in the Congo and she needs his endorsement. He tries to help her, but they both get tangled up in red tape and Katy ends up staying on—for three seasons. She finds a home at the Morleys' (also at ABC) and with widower Glen's two kids: Steven (Mickey Sholdar) and Danny (Rory O'Brien). Morley's mother, Agatha (Cathleen Nesbitt), also lives in their home. Things go along so swimmingly that Morley offers her the position of governess. She accepts. Later in the series he offers her the position of wife. She accepts and they wed on November 5, 1965. The episodes basically revolved around the home and working life of Congressman Morley, as well as Katy's attempt to adjust to political and city life. Inger Stevens—who always seemed so happy—killed herself shortly after (though not necessarily because) the series went off the air.

The Farmer's Daughter: *Inger Stevens and William Windom*

Glynis

This sitcom about the pranks and misadventures of mystery writer and amateur sleuth Glynis Granville (Glynis Johns) lasted only three months on CBS in 1963. While Glynis tries to solve crimes in order to get some material to write about, her husband, Keith (Keith Andes), goes to work as a lawyer and naturally they are

Glynis: *Glynis Johns with Keith Andes*

quite a daffy duo. Chick Rogers (George Mathews), a retired policeman, is her consultant. In 1965, CBS rebroadcast the show as a summer replacement series.

Grindl

This goofy little show starred *Your Show of Shows'* Imogene Coca as a domestic affiliated with the Foster Employment Agency, who worked around and got herself in a lot of trouble. James Millhollin played her harried boss, Anson Foster, and the rest of the cast changed each week, depending on whom Grindl was working for. Sometimes she played maid, other times laundress, babysitter, ticket taker, and more. NBC hired her for one season only.

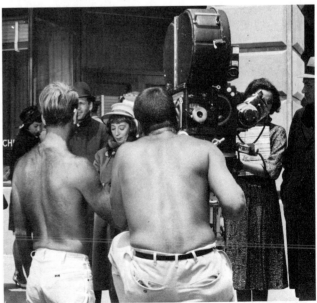

Grindl: *Take One with Imogene Coca*

Harry's Girls

Larry Blyden played Harry Burns, star and manager of a vaudeville song-and-dance act that tours Europe (mainly because it's too hokey for the sophisticated USA). The show was, in fact, filmed on location in Europe, and sometimes the act was even shown. Dawn Nickerson, Susan Silo and Diahn Williams played Lois, Rusty, and Terry, Harry's troupe—all of whom were canceled in midseason by NBC. For all we know, they just might still be touring.

Mack and Myer for Hire

Funny rhyme. Not such a funny show. This one—fifteen minutes long and syndicated—starred Mickey Deems annd Joey Faye as M. and M., two craftsmen who tried to make it in the business world. Also the television world. No dice.

Mr. Smith Goes to Washington

Jimmy Stewart starred in the 1939 movie, and here was Fess Parker (Davey Crockett!) playing the part in this ABC sitcom all about Eugene Smith, a country politician who was elected to replace a senator who died suddenly. He had mature wisdom, boyish charm, warmth, and dignity—a regular Andy Griffith, except . . . Eugene had a wife (Patricia, played by Sandra Warner). Red Foley played Eugene's guitar-playing uncle, Cooter Smith, a rural philosopher, and Stan Irwin played Arnie the butler. On March 30, 1963, Mr. Smith went back home.

The New Phil Silvers Show

This follow-up to Silvers' wonderful *You'll Never Get Rich* never got anywhere (it lasted one season on CBS). In this one, Silvers was cast as Harry Grafton, a factory foreman for Osborne Enterprises—a con artist (for a change) who manipulated men and machines for his own benefit—he hated work and loved loot. He never should have left Fort Baxter. Stafford Repp played the boss, Mr. Brink, who could only look on with dismay.

Our Man Higgins

Stanley Holloway (hot off the path from playing Alfred Doolittle in *My Fair Lady*) played Higgins (not Henry), a high-tone English Butler who was inherited by the MacRoberts family, who had to keep him if they wanted to keep their inherited silver service. Both Higgins and the MacRobertses adjusted to one another. And, fortunately, Higgins saved the family from fates not worse than death. ABC let them all go in September 1963. The show was based on the radio program, *It's Higgins, Sir*.

The Patty Duke Show

Herein lies a strange genetic twist: identical cousins, Patty and Cathy Lane (both played by teenage Oscar-winning actress Patty Duke, who came to fame as Helen Keller in both the Broadway and film versions of *The Miracle Worker*).

The story: The Lane family lives at 8 Remsen Dr., Brooklyn Heights, New York. Martin (William Schallert) is managing editor of the New York *Chronicle;* he has a wife, Natalie (Jean Byron), a son, Ross (Paul O'Keefe),

The Patty Duke Show *(from left): Patty Duke and Patty Duke*

and a daughter with straight hair, Patty, who chews bubblegum and listens to bubblegum music. Also with them is their glamorous Scottish cousin, Cathy Lane (she's the one with the wavy hair), who's completing her high school education until she can rejoin her father, Kenneth Lane (William Schallert), who's a foreign correspondent for the *Chronicle*. Their housekeeper is Mrs. MacDonald, played by Margaret Hamilton of *Wizard of Oz* Wicked Witch fame (and later Maxwell House Coffee commercials). Patty has a boyfriend named Richard (Eddie Applegate), a part-time Western Union messenger.

The show revolved around the lives of these sixteen-year-old girls and their differences: Patty is average and seems to get into offbeat situations; Cathy is shy, warm, and sensitive. She treasures her European upbringing and sometimes has difficulty adjusting to the American way of life. Sounds like two sitcoms in one. Frankie Avalon, Bobby Vinton, et al made guest appearances.

A young woman named Rita McLaughlin played Patty Duke's stand-in (she was Cathy when Duke was Patty, and vice versa). The show ran on ABC from September 18, 1963, until August 31, 1966.

Petticoat Junction

This *Beverly Hillbillies* spin-off reigned supreme for the seven seasons it played on CBS. Here's the poop:

In Hooterville (a farm valley), life revolves around the Shady Rest Hotel, run by widow Kate Bradley, who has three beautiful daughters: Bobbie Jo (Pat Woodell), Billie Jo (Jeannine Riley), and Betty Jo (Linda Kaye). The hotel's self-proclaimed manager is Uncle Joe Carson (Edgar Buchanan).

Background: Discovering a long-abandoned but working railroad branch line in Hooterville, Homer Bedloe (the vice-president of the C.F. & W. Railroad) intends to scrap the Cannonball (an 1890s steam engine, coal car, and mail/passenger coach) and discharge its engineers, Charlie Pratt (Smiley Burnette) and Floyd Smoot (Rufe Davis). Though Kate objects, Bedloe keeps trying to become a big shot in the company.

Things change: After crash-landing near the hotel, pilot Steve Elliott (Mike Minor) is rescued and nursed back to health by the Bradley girls. It seems he's in love with Billie Jo, although he ends up marrying Betty Jo, with whom he sets up housekeeping not far from the hotel. They have a daughter, Kathy Jo.

In 1968, Bea Benaderet (who played Kate and is well known as *Burns and Allen*'s Blanche Morton) died. Her character was an understanding and comforting mother, and she was replaced by the same type of person: Janet Craig (June Lockhart—remember her from *Lassie*?), a doctor who takes over from the valley's retiring physician, Barton Stuart (Regis Toomey).

The stories depict the struggles of the married couple; Janet's attempts to acquire the trust of people who are wary of a woman doctor; Joe's endless moneymaking ventures, and the romantic troubles of Billie Jo and Bobbie Jo.

Petticoat Junction: *Kate with Billie Jo, Bobbie Jo, Betty Jo and Uncle Joe*

1964–1965

The Addams Family

Bewitched

OFF-SCREEN

10/14 1964 Nobel Peace Prize is awarded to Reverend Martin Luther King, Jr.
10/20 Herbert Hoover dies in New York at age of 90.
11/3 Lyndon B. Johnson elected president.
11/21 Verrazano-Narrows Bridge formally opened; world's longest suspension bridge.
12/5 President Johnson gives Medal of Honor to Captain Roger H. C. Donlon for service in South Vietnam.
2/13 Sixteen-year-old Peggy Fleming wins US women's senior figure-skating title.
2/21 Malcolm X shot to death in Harlem.
2/23 Stan Laurel dies at 74.
4/11 Thirty-seven tornadoes sweeping through six states kill 242, injure 5,000.
6/12 Discovery of new celestial objects known as blue galaxies lends support to Big Bang theory of the birth of the universe.

FRONT RUNNERS

THE ADDAMS FAMILY / THE MUNSTERS

They're creepy and they're kooky . . .
—theme song from *The Addams Family*

Devotees of *The Munsters* or strong supporters of *The Addams Family* will tell you (and tell you and tell you) that the two shows were simply not the same.

"Ha!" laughs a *Munster* maniac. "*The Addams Family* were just poor relatives from down the block!"

"Oh, yeah?" challenges an *Addams* aficionado. "The Addamses could outghoul *The Munsters* any day—and any night! So there."

So there—actually—wasn't much difference between the two shows. At the time, yes. Now, naw.

The Addamses, based on Charles Addams' marvelously macabre eccentrics from his *New Yorker* cartoons, were different from *The Munsters,* a mob of monsters who obviously couldn't spell very well. But in the race between the two shows, both started and stopped on the same week. *The Addams Family* went into an animated version in 1973—but it was different: their haunted house was converted into a camper and they took a motor tour of America—sort of like when the Ricardos and the Mertzes drove cross-country to get to Hollywood.

The Addams Family, who lived in a funereal world, thought they were normal.

The show's musical theme said that they were "creepy" and "kooky" and "ooky"—an understatement.

Members of the family included: Gomez, a wealthy lawyer; his beautiful wife, Morticia; their children, Pugsley and Wednesday; and a variety of relatives and

---

Cast for The Addams Family

Morticia Addams	Carolyn Jones
Gomez Addams	John Astin
Uncle Fester, Morticia's relative	Jackie Coogan
Lurch, the zombielike butler	Ted Cassidy
Wednesday Addams	Lisa Loring
Pugsley Addams	Ken Weatherwax
Grandmama Addams, Gomez's mother	Blossom Rock
Ophelia Frump, Morticia's sister	Carolyn Jones
Cousin Itt	Felix Silla
Mr. Briggs, the postman	Rolf Sedan
Esther Frump, Morticia's mother	Margaret Hamilton
Thing, the family's servant, a human right hand	Itself

Addams Family pets: Kit Kat, a lion; Cleopatra, Morticia's African Strangler (a man-eating plant); Aristotle, Pugsley's octopus; Homer, Wednesday's Black Widow Spider

---

Cast for The Munsters

Herman Munster	Fred Gwynne
Lily Munster	Yvonne DeCarlo
Grandpa	Al Lewis
Marilyn Munster	Beverly Owen (1964); Pat Priest (1964–1966)
Edward Wolfgang Munster ("Eddie")	Butch Patrick
Mr. Gateman, Herman's employer	John Carradine
Clyde Thornton, Herman's co-worker	Chet Stratton
Dr. Edward Dudley, the Munster family physician	Paul Lynde
Munster family pets:	Spot, Igor the Bat, Raven

The Addams Family: *John Astin and Lisa Loring*

other assorteds: Uncle Fester, Morticia's relative; six-foot-nine-inch Lurch, their zombielike butler; four-foot-tall Cousin Itt (completely covered with blond hair); Morticia's mother, Esther Frump; and Thing—the family's servant, a human right hand. They also had a variety of pets: Kit Kat (a grown lion); Cleopatra (Morticia's African strangler—a man-eating plant); Pugsley's octopus, Aristotle; and Homer (Wednesday's black widow spider).

Yes. Just like the Nelsons, the Andersons, the Cleavers—another typical American family.

At the end of the first episode, Gomez says, "It's

The Munsters: *Paul Lynde visits Fred Gwynne.*

possible we've saved the world." Morticia answers, "I wonder if we've done the right thing."

Their house—surrounded by a huge hedge and an iron fence—was quite unusual, to put it mildly. The living room was dominated by a huge stuffed bear; there was a giant tortoise in the center, along with a rococo harpsichord below the noose with which to ring for Lurch. There was also a large hookah (remember, this was back in 1963; when hashish wasn't fashionable yet) and black roses next to Morticia's peacock chair. On the walls hung a swordfish head and a giant moose head with its antlers drooping. Gomez's steer-horn armchair was flanked by a ticker-tape machine (his passion) and an elephant foot filled with popcorn. The walls were blood red, and the carpets were Oriental. Thing was housed in a nail-studded golden box next to an old-fashioned phone, which he answered.

The playroom was just as interesting. It was brick-walled and contained a bed of nails and stocks labeled "hers." There was a full suit of armor with a dead soldier inside. And a rocking unicorn for the kids.

The fantastic makeup for the show took two hours for Morticia (Carolyn Jones) each day. Her wig was made of human hair (so what else?).

More tidbits:

● Uncle Fester (who was toothless and hairless) loved to fish—with dynamite. (Fester, incidentally, was played by Jackie Coogan, best known for playing the title role in Chaplin's movie *The Kid*. He had earned $4 million in films, which made another $4 million; by the time he played Uncle Fester he was fifty years old and nearly broke. Everyone thought he must be dead. *The Addams Family* proved that he wasn't.)

● The identity of Thing was never revealed. A Boston paper said it had discovered that it was Ted Cassidy (the actor who played Lurch), but Cassidy denied it.

● Gomez played with electric trains—getting them into wrecks. Pugsley played with a disintegrator gun that made things disappear.

● When visiting Russians opened a phone book at random and stuck a pin into it, picking the Addams Family as the "typically American family," Morticia felt the pin prick her.

● A typical hors d'oeuvre: eye of tadpole (instead of caviar). And breast of alligator as the main course.

● Lurch—in his inimitable low voice—always entered a room with "You Rang?" Uncle Fester wore a lightbulb in his mouth and rode a motorcycle around the house.

● Once Uncle Fester fell in love with a bearded lady: "I just can't resist a pretty face." He told time with his hourglass watch.

In the second (and last) season of the show, some new characters were added: Morticia's older sister, Ophelia Frump (also played by Carolyn Jones); Gomez's mother, Grandmama Addams, who lived in a separate cottage with a large broom parked in front; and Woodrow, the kids' invisible eight-year-old playmate.

In 1973, there was a musical remake of *The Addams*

Family. But it was dropped because forty-two underwriting stations saw the pilot and thought it was terrible.

The Munsters was written and produced by the same people who wrote and produced *Leave It to Beaver*, who were the same people who wrote *Amos 'n' Andy*. Somewhere, there, this is a direct line that means something—although it's not exactly clear what.

Here's the poop:

The Munster family lived at 1313 (unlucky numbers; get it?) Mockingbird Lane in Mockingbird Heights, in a creepy, spiderweb-covered mansion. The residents all looked like movie monsters of the thirties: Herman was a Frankenstein type who worked as a funeral director at Gateman, Goodbury and Graves; Lilly, his wife, was a vampire; their ten-year-old son, Edward "Eddie" Wolfgang, was a werewolf; Lilly's father—Grandpa—was Count Dracula, a 378-year-old mad scientist; their young niece, Marilyn, was the black sheep of the family. And, of course, there were the inevitable family pets: Spot (a prehistoric creature found by Grandpa while digging in the backyard); Igor the bat; and an unnamed raven that constantly uttered Poe's immortal word, "Nevermore."

Even if it was bright and sunny everywhere else, there were usually rain and howling winds around the Munster house. Son Eddie brayed at the full moon. The show was, its star Fred Gwynne once said, "*The Donna Reed Show* with monsters."

The show opened with Herman bursting through the door and the rest of the cast walking through the opening he had made, to the accompaniment of rock 'n' roll music. They drank bat's milk. Books moved by themselves. Breakfast was cooked in a steaming caldron. When Herman blew a kiss, it shattered glss.

On the show's first episode, there was a masquerade party at Marilyn's date's house. (Poor Marilyn, the pretty, normal-looking niece who lived with the Munsters. The family pitied her because she looked so different and couldn't hold on to a boyfriend. Wonder why. . . .) Anyway, at the costume party, Herman ran into somebody else dressed as Frankenstein.

Some *Munsters* tidbits:

● The makeup took two hours each day per character to apply, and nearly as long to get off. According to Al Lewis (Grandpa), the show took more time to film than any other in the history of TV. Gwynne's costume (foam rubber and Orlon) weighed four pounds (Boris Karloff's original Frankenstein weighed thirty-five pounds and his makeup took four hours). There was a harness inside Gwynne's suit and the bolts were glued to his neck. He couldn't blow his nose with makeup on—and he was allergic to all the oils and acids that the special effects people used.

● The first year, the show received a 13 Nielsen rating; the cast thought this was very lucky.

● Gwynne was 6' 7"; Lewis, at 6' 1", looked short next to him.

● In November 1964, Gwynne and Lewis rode in the Macy's Thanksgiving Day Parade—on top of a coffin in a hearse.

● Al Lewis decided to do the show because he thought it was "the first original idea to hit television in fifteen years."

● Although the show was shot in black and white, the makeup was in color. Gray-green was used on Yvonne DeCarlo's eyes and cheeks. The actors said they performed better with green makeup because they felt closer to the parts they played. Lilly had long black fingernails. Herman had a rubber headpiece and a wig and black grease on his lips. Eddie wore a special headpiece with pointed ears, as well as big, bushy eyebrows. The special effects were equally eerie: Grandpa, for example, could roast a marshmallow stuck on his fingertip.

● They had a specially built car for the show—a $20,000 coach-type machine with red plush upholstery and a footman's seat. It was made of stretched fiberglass, a version of a 1927 touring car. It was built by the same man who made the Batmobile. For the second season, Grandpa got his own car—a 160-mph coffin on wheels called "The Dragula." Although his other car had a lab inside, this one was fancier, with gold-leaf paint, silver spiders for hubcaps, purple silk-velvet upholstery, chrome pipes for exhaust—all costing $10,800 to construct.

In 1979, many years after *The Munsters'* demise, Gwynne said: "Funny thing, yesterday morning I found my youngest son and daughter watching the rerun of an old episode and I said, 'My God, *that's* not still on, is it?' Well, even so, I was very lucky and it was great fun to be as much of a household product as something like Rinso. I almost wish I could do it all over again." He did complain, though, that playing Herman had, for some time, type-cast him as a gold-hearted ghoul and got in his way of getting other kinds of roles.

But what could he expect? *The Munsters* lived forever. Being monsters, they never died.

Except on television. They were canceled in September of 1966—as were their neighbors, *The Addams Family*.

The Munsters: *Al Lewis and lady guest*

BEWITCHED

Abner, I'm going over to the Stevens' to return the cookie cutters.

—MRS. KRAVITZ

It was a simple enough premise: a show about a man married to a woman who, it turned out, was a witch. Not so unusual. After all, Topper had a houseful of ghosts, and Tim O'Hara had an "uncle" who was a Martian. Wilbur had a talking horse, and later Dave Crabtree had a mother who was a car. So why not a witch?

From 1964 until 1972, American audiences answered that question every week by tuning into ABC and taking part in Samantha Stevens' benign witchcraft antics—whether it was finding a way to get a stoplight put up at a busy intersection, foiling her husband's boss, or simply waving her hands to clean up the kitchen when unexpected company arrived. On her wedding night, she confessed her talents to her husband, Darrin, who wasn't very happy about it. He wanted her to stop practicing witchcraft and to settle into being a nice suburban housewife . . . just another case of the witch who sits around the house all day doing nothing because her husband won't let her use her skills.

And so, Samantha became the Suburban Everywitch, sort of the Donna Reed of Sorcery, or, as *Life* Magazine put it, she was a witch "with her cauldron hooked to the rotisserie."

She was the kind of witch who used her broom for cleaning, not flying. But every once in a while (at least a few times each episode) she couldn't struggle any longer to contain her powers. She couldn't suppress the urge to make a flower grow or throw her voice so it sounded like her baby was talking. Samantha was never unkind; she was just occasionally naughty.

Bewitched was fantasy with its feet firmly planted in reality, in which two myths collided—the myth of witchcraft and the myth of the suburban idyll. Lucy and Ricky took reality and bent it out of shape to fit a special fantasy. Samantha and Darrin took fantasy and bent it *into* shape to fit a certain reality. The main comic appeal of *Bewitched* was the possibility of dominion over environment. It was a one-joke show with a built-in situation.

It was all as simple as Samantha's upper lip, which she wriggled quite frequently to conjure up a spell or spirit (much like Lucy had conjured up an antic). Sam was mischievous and did all the things we wanted to. We didn't realize it, but, of course, we could do magic tricks with Samantha, making her appear and disappear simply by turning a knob on our magic boxes at home. Maybe it wasn't so mysterious after all.

Elizabeth Montgomery was on her third marriage, to producer/director William Asher. At thirty-two, she didn't want any part of television (her father was actor Robert Montgomery), and she agreed to star in the show only to work with her husband, who directed the pilot and the first fourteen episodes (he had previously di-

Samantha Stevens	Elizabeth Montgomery
Serena	Elizabeth Montgomery (credited: Pandora Sparks)
Darrin Stevens	Dick York (1964–1969); Dick Sargent (1969–1972)
Endora	Agnes Moorehead
Larry Tate	David White
Louise Tate	Irene Vernon (1964–1966); Kasey Rogers (1966–1972)
Gladys Kravitz	Alice Pearce (1964–1966); Sandra Gould (1966–1972)
Abner Kravitz	George Tobias
Maurice, Samantha's father	Maurice Evans
Uncle Arthur, a warlock, Samantha's relative	Paul Lynde (1965–1972)
Dr. Bombay, Samantha's family physician	Bernard Fox
Aunt Clara, an aging, bumbling witch	Marion Lorne (1964–1968)
Tabitha Stevens	Erin and Diane Murphy (1966–1972)
Frank Stevens, Darrin's father	Robert F. Simon; Roy Roberts
Phyllis Stevens	Mabel Albertson
Esmeralda, a shy witch	Alice Ghostley (1969–1972)
Adam Stevens	David and Greg Lawrence (1971–1972)
Betty, Darrin's secretary	Marcia Wallace

The Stevens: Darrin (Dick Sargent), Samantha, Tabitha, Adam

rected *I Love Lucy*, the *Danny Thomas* and *Patty Duke* shows). She became pregnant right after the pilot was filmed. When the show was sold to ABC, twenty-four days after giving birth, she filmed twelve shows in three months, working fourteen-hour days. It wasn't all bad; she ended up earning nearly $6 million from the show.

The first episode had the newlyweds invited to what they were promised was "a very casual" dinner party at Darrin's former girlfriend's house. Naturally, when they arrived, everyone was dressed formally. Samantha was angry and ready to raise hell. She tried to control herself, but gave in to her temptation to sabotage the party and humiliate her well-dressed hostess by putting her elbow in the soup and giving her a black tooth.

Starring in the show with Montgomery was Dick York as Darrin and David White as his boss, Larry Tate. Right away, the show was a hit, beating out *Bonanza* in a thirty-city Nielsen survey. *Bewitched* was not particularly funny. It was silly and fantastic. The most masterful thing about it was its special effects, which took a lot of time to devise and film. Dick Albain was the true star of the show; he was the special effects man. He was, under law, responsible if anyone got hurt on the set, and he always had about six assistants running around.

This is how it was done. When things appeared or disappeared from Samantha's hand, Montgomery would freeze at the proper point and Albain would come onto the set and take the object away. The footage of him

would be cut away, and it would look like the object vanished. Said Montgomery: "It took a lot of practice before I learned how to hold my hands perfectly still. But even that's much easier than the scene in which I was supposed to clean up the kitchen by witchery. I sort of went 'Swoosh' with my arms raised, then had to leave them up in the air—aching—while the crew rushed in and swept and dusted to get the kitchen immaculate before the scene resumed. I'm getting better at it, I guess," she said in 1964. "I almost never flinch or recoil anymore, no matter what happens."

Other tricks: the Stevens' magic vacuum cleaner (which seemed to work by itself) actually did work by itself. It was run by a reversible motor underneath, controlled by switches off-set.

Once, when Sam decided to leave Darrin, she first became invisible so that the suitcases seemed to pack and leave home on their own. This was done by having a special effects man standing on planks above the set, working wires attached to everything, like puppets.

As ratings declined, *Bewitched* viewers saw a number of changes—none of them invisible. First, Darrin and Samantha became parents of Tabitha, who turned out to be (on the first show of the third season) a witch just like her mommy. Samantha's mother, Endora (played by Agnes Moorehead, most famous as Orson Welles' mother in *Citizen Kane*), added an elegant element—the old my-mother-in-law-the-witch routine—to the show. Then they added Samantha's twin cousin, Serena (also played by Montgomery), a naughty, fun-loving witch. In 1969, the Stevens had another kid—Adam, a warlock.

There was another big change in the show: at the end of the 1968–1969 season, Dick York left and was replaced by another Dick—Dick Sargent, who looked a lot like him. There was no announcement about the switch. It just happened. One week York was Darrin, the next week Sargent was Darrin. It was like witchcraft.

Said Sargent: "I don't know why York quit the show. I just thank God that he did." Sargent had been considered for the role of Darrin when the show was originally cast, but he was under contract to Universal. He had played Kathy Nolan's boyfriend in *Broadside*, Tammy Grimes' twin brother on her short-lived (four episodes) series, and had appeared in a number of movies.

Sargent (his real name was Cox, but he changed it when Wally Cox got hot) became a father after five episodes with the birth of Adam (whose sexual identity, until the "birth," was kept a secret, a precedent started on *I Love Lucy* years before when Ricky, Jr., was born).

On Sargent's first show, Tabitha decides that Samantha and Darrin like boys better, so she runs away by changing places with Jack (played by *Family Affair*'s Johnny Whitaker) and climbing his beanstalk, with Sam following her. (LA Rams' defensive end Deacon Jones made his TV debut in this episode as the guardian of the giant's castle.)

Samantha's mother, Endora, was one of the most popular characters of the program, counterbalancing Sam's own golden goodness. Said Moorehead about her role: "I am quite a sophisticated gal. Endora is a very attractive and charming witch with a supernatural philosophy all her own. The humans in the script do plenty of very foolish things, and she loves showing up their foolishness."

When she would teleport in for tea, one of the objects of her scorn was her son-inlaw. "Oh, Darrin!" Endora would say, "it's impossible to carry on a successful relationship with something that is ninety percent water, six percent potash, and four percent mohair."

Other character actors made occasional appearances on the show: Paul Lynde sometimes appeared as Samantha's Uncle Arthur, a warlock in the mold of Lynde's typical snide characterizations. Marion Lorne (Mrs. Gurney from *Mr. Peepers*) was hilarious as Aunt Clara, a senile witch. Alice Ghostley played a retiring wallflower witch named Esmeralda.

Cousin Serena: Elizabeth Montgomery with guest Peter Lawford

Tabitha was played by three sets of twins (California law dictated that babies could work only two hours a day, and *Bewitched* had a long shooting schedule). Although she looked different each time, it was hard to tell which witch was which.

Once, in 1970, Darrin was turned into a toad when he refused to accompany Samantha to a witches' convention in Salem, Massachusetts, home of the famous 1692 witch hunts, in which nineteen men and women were hanged for allegedly being witches.

DARRIN: Sam, I've been thinking . . . I mean, Salem, Mass.—isn't that kind of a dumb place for a witches' convention?
SAM: Not when you consider that one of the items on the agenda is to install a new resident. . . . We've had one living there secretly ever since the witch hunts of 1692—just to make sure it doesn't happen again.

The Salem locations were the first exterior shots ever done on *Bewitched;* the rest was done on Hollywood back lots. However, during the show's last season, when the situations (and the comedy) were really running dry,

The Hex: Marion Lorne and Elizabeth Montgomery

the cast went off to Europe and filmed episodes such as the one in which Samantha and Darrin were transported back to Henry VIII's court, where she was stripped of her powers and her memory. Endora—noticing that Henry seemed to be taking a fancy to Sam—sent Darrin back home. Guess if it ended happily or not. . . .

Probably the happiest ending the show could have had was when it finally ended on July 1, 1972, after eight seasons. It had become stale and tired—not because anyone had cast a spell over it—but just because it had run its course. Its gimmick had lost its glow.

In 1977, ABC tried a spin-off called *Tabitha*, about the Stevens' now-grown daughter who worked for a TV talk-show host. The show—and Tabitha—vanished after a few episodes. All we have left of *Bewitched* is reruns—hundreds of them—as the show continues to be popular. Why?

Agnes Moorehead answered the question best when she responded to a writer who wanted her to write the introduction to a book on witchcraft. "But you *are* a witch, aren't you?" the writer asked her.

"No," she said, "I'm just a fantasy witch."

At the Office: Dick York and David White

ALSO RANS

The Baileys of Balboa

Bailey's Landing, Balboa Beach, California, was the setting of the weekly arguments between Sam Bailey (Paul Ford, alumnus of *Sergeant Bilko*) and Cecil Wyntoon (John Dehner), archrivals for local dock space. Sam's decrepit charter boat, *The Island Princess*, is the splinter in Cecil's side; as commodore of the ritzy Balboa Yachting Club, Cecil demands a higher class of vessel (although apparently not of comedy) from Sam and shipmate Buck Singleton (Sterling Holloway). They made waves on CBS and finally sank after one season.

The Baileys of Balboa: *Les Brown, Jr., and Judy Carne*

The Bing Crosby Show

For a single season, Bing Crosby temporarily gave up crooning to play Bing Collins, a former singer who changed his tune rather late in life. Now an electrical engineer (although he'd occasionally sneak in a song), Bing lived with wife, Ellie (Beverly Garland), and their two young daughters in Los Angeles. Janice (Carol Faylen) was fifteen years old and boy-crazy; ten-year-old Joyce (Diane Sherry) had an IQ about 112 times higher than this show's ratings. Their half-hour ABC series brought the Collins family's problems onto our sets. Then Bing—and Bing—went back to singing.

Broadside

This spin-off from *McHale's Navy* focused on four WAVES—Lieutenant Anne Morgan (Kathleen Nolan) and Privates Selma Kowalski (Sheila James), Molly McGuire (Lois Roberts), and Roberta Love (Joan Staley)—assigned to the motor pool at a navy supply depot on tranquil Ranakai Island, a place that just wasn't used to the presence of Women. Plus it was commanded by an officer who wanted it kept Pure: Rogers Adrian (Edward Andrews), who couldn't have the women's orders rescinded—after all, there would have been no show if he could—so he spent each episode plotting to discredit the WAVES in his futile effort to get rid of them (such as cutting off their lipstick supply). The women managed to avert exile avery week. Other regulars on this year-long ABC series included Dick (*Bewitched*) Sargent as Anne's boyfriend, Lieutenant Maxwell Trotter, and Jimmy Boyd as Marion Botnick, victim of an embarrassing clerical error which made him the navy's only male WAVE. Arnold Stang played world-famous chef to Ranakai, Stanley Stubbs. At the end of the one ABC season, they were all sent home.

The Cara Williams Show

Cara Wilton works as a file clerk for Fenwick Diversified Industries, Incorporated, where she meets Frank Bridges (Frank Aletter), a fellow employee. Her good looks persuade him to ignore both Fenwick's policy against employing married couples and Cara's own scattered brains. As the company's efficiency expert, he hits on a plan that provided plots for this series throughout its first five months: in order to keep their jobs, the newlyweds must keep their secret safe.

Once the show's writers had exhausted the possibilities of this format, they turned to a new one: tired of living in dread of discovery, Cara and Frank finally reveal their secret to boss Damon Burkhardt (Paul Reed). Burkhardt is not amused (nor were most of the viewers)—but Cara uses her incomprehensible but essential filing system to browbeat Mr. Fenwick, the company's president (Edward Everett Horton), into letting both spouses stay on. Both formats together ran for a total of two seasons on CBS.

Gilligan's Island

This sappy show lasted three seasons—the average lifespan of a successful sitcom—and can be seen daily in many cities, where it is still a favorite. It was, in 1974, made into an animated cartoon series, with most of the cast intact. And in the late seventies, there was even a 90-minute *Gilligan's Island* reunion. Now rerun constantly, *Gilligan's Island* is a big hit with the prepubescent set.

The story: Seven members of a sight-seeing boat are shipwrecked on an unchartered South Pacific island after a tropical storm. The travelers on the SS *Minnow* develop a community after they realize that they are stranded on the island. Episodes revolve around their humorous struggles for survival and their endless attempts to be rescued, despite the bumbling actions of the first mate, Gilligan (Bob Denver, formerly Maynard G. Krebs on *Dobie Gillis*). Others in the cast: Alan Hale, Jr. (who played Jonas Grumby, the skipper); Tina Louise (as beautiful movie actress Ginger Grant); Jim Backus (the judge in *I Married Joan* and the voice of Mr. Magoo) as millionaire Thurston Howell III; his wife, Lovey (played by Natalie Schafer); Mary Ann Summers, a pretty clerk who had worked in a general store in Kansas (Dawn Wells); and Professor Roy Hinkley, a brilliant research scientist (Russell Johnson).

The show was a *Wizard of Oz* without the wizard. *Island* stayed afloat on CBS until September 3, 1967.

Gilligan's Island: *Bob Denver with guest Hans Conried*

Gomer Pyle, USMC

Gomer Pyle, USMC: *Frank Sutton and Jim Nabors*

This popular, long-running spin-off of *The Andy Griffith Show* featured the bumbling hayseed Gomer Pyle (Jim Nabors) as a marine private at Camp Henderson in LA. Pyle creates chaos when he unconsciously diverges from the rules of the Second Platoon, B Company, and complicates everything he comes near—because he is simpleminded and very naive. Pyle's superior, Sergeant Vincent Carter (Frank Sutton), is continually plagued by Gomer, and tries to resolve the situations. Also in the cast was Ted Bessell (Don Hollinger in *That Girl,* one of Mary Tyler Moore's beaus in the program of that name, and a veteran of other sitcoms). Gomer—who had been a gas station attendant in Mayberry before enlisting—always said "Shazam" when he was excited. The program ran on CBS until September of 1969, and reran in prime time during the summer of 1970.

Harris Against the World

Jack Klugman—pre-*Odd Couple* days—starred—albeit briefly—as Alan Harris, a superintendent at a large movie studio plant. He lived at 90 Bristol Court (along with *Karen* and *Tom, Dick and Mary,* who were also part of this weekly sitcom trilogy). So did his wife, Kate (Patricia Barry), and his two kids, Deedee (Claire Wilcox) and Billy (David Macklin). But life wasn't always so rosy for Alan Harris—he had debts, taxes, a boss or two, and a wife who spent money in order, it seemed, that he'd have to work harder and harder at the part-time jobs she managed to find for him. But it was all okay, 'cause Alan was a real softy at heart. After three months, NBC decided it was time for the Harrises to relocate. And so they did.

Karen

Not to be confused with Karen Valentine's short-lived *Karen* during the 1974–1975 season, this *Karen* starred Debbie Watson, and was yet another part of *90 Bristol Court*, along with *Harris Against the World* and *Tom, Dick and Mary*. All were canceled at midseason, except for *Karen*, which got a stay of execution and lived on (on NBC) until the following September. Here's the story. Karen was a cute high school girl who always got herself into a lot of mischief. Her parents (in the personas of Richard Denning and Mary LaRoche) were always amazed (and amused) by her. Her tomboy sister (played by Gina Gillespie) also created a few problems of her own. Their handyman, Cliff Murdock, was the only character to appear in all three components of *90 Bristol Court*. (*The Bob Newhart Show*, years later, borrowed the name Cliff Murdock for Bob's buddy, the Peeper). Also on the show: a young Richard Dreyfuss, who played Karen's friend David. The theme music was by the Beach Boys.

Many Happy Returns

Widower Walter Burnley (John McGiver) was the manager of the complaint department of Krockmeyer's Department Store in LA. He had a married daughter (Elinor Donahue, fresh from *Andy Griffith* and *Father Knows Best*) and a staff member named Lynn Hall (Elena Verdugo, TV's *Meet Millie* and later nurse Consuelo Lopez on *Marcus Welby, MD*). The hitch: Burnley's boss, J. L. Fox (Jerome Cowan), didn't like him to accept any returns, so Burnley had to resolve complaints in a manner that would please his boss. CBS returned the show to where it belonged—on the shelf—in April of 1965.

Mickey

Mickey Rooney didn't make it in this sitcom (or any other), in which he played a retired businessman living

Mickey: *Mickey Rooney shakes with Sammee Tong*

with his wife, Nora (Emmaline Henry), and children at the Newport Arms Hotel in Newport Beach, California. There were money troubles at the hotel, including shyster lawyers and high-interest mortgages. Timmy Rooney (Mickey's son) played Timmy Grady, and Brian Nash played eight-year-old Buddy Grady. Sammee Tong (remember him as Peter on *Bachelor Father*?) played the hotel's manager, who had "a lifetime contract." ABC kicked them all out of their rooms on January 13, 1965. Fourteen years later, a 59-year-old Rooney—then a big Broadway star in *Sugar Babies*—had this to say about television: "You know, I always thought in show business you had to have certain credentials to qualify you to run something. Not so TV. They're businessmen who have no business in the business. They're eighth-rate citizens who treat actors like so much meat."

My Living Doll

This time around, Bob Cummings—"oh, *him* again?"—played a psychiatrist who gets custody of a shapely robot named Rhoda (Julie Newmar). It all takes place in LA at the US Space Project AF 709. Bob McDonald (Cummings) lives with his sister (Doris Dowling) named Irene (remember how Cummings lived with his sister on *Love That Bob?*). He tells her that Rhoda's a patient who requires constant care and attention. In a real switch from his other shows, Bob tries to develop the robot's mind and character for science—while his roving playboy buddy, Dr. Peter Robinson (Jack Mullaney), has the hots for her. Bob, ever sexist, wants Rhoda to be "the perfect woman" who does what she is told and speaks only when spoken to. Betty Friedan, where were you? Well, it all ended on September 8, 1965, anyway, when CBS canceled the show.

No Time for Sergeants

Andy Griffith starred in the Broadway (1955) and movie (1958) versions, upon which this sitcom was based. It was all about a Georgia hillbilly farmboy (pre-Jimmy Carter) who is naive and reluctant and who is drafted into the air force (Andrews Air Force Base, specifically). He tries hard to adjust to military life and spends time plaguing his superiors with his philosophies of kindness. Once, for example, he trades military equipment for good food for the mess hall. Sammy Jackson starred as Private Will Stockdale. The whole platoon was discharged after one season by Commanding Officer ABC.

Tom, Dick and Mary

Another part of the *90 Bristol Court* trio, *T, D and M* was most notable for its cast. Don Galloway (Tom) would become Raymond Burr's assistant Ed Brown on *Ironside;* Steve Franken (Dick), was hot off the *Dobie Gillis* trail, where he played Chatsworth Osborne, Jr.; Joyce Bulifant (Mary) would go on to play the guidance counselor on *The Bill Cosby Show,* before becoming Mrs. Murray on *Mary Tyler Moore.* On this show, however, the situation went like this: Tom, a doctor, lived with his wife, Mary— but they also lived with Dick (all to save money, of course; nothing naughty). Actually, Tom was only an intern, and Mary was a mere medical secretary, so they didn't have the loot to live alone—and that wouldn't have made a very interesting sitcom, anyway. Although neither did this one. After three months, they called it splitsville and left 90 Bristol Court (not to mention NBC).

The Tycoon

Post-*The Real McCoys,* Walter Brennan tried it again with this one: all about a sixty-five-year-old industrialist millionaire who tried to operate his company in accord with his own fair standards. He was called Walter Andrews and his company was the Thunder Holding Corporation in LA. Naturally, Walter was cantankerous and eccentric, softened by his granddaughter Martha Keane (Pat McNulty) and his housekeeper Una Fields (Monty Margetts). Van Williams played his aide, Pat Burns. Brennan ruled for one season only on ABC.

Valentine's Day

Tony Franciosa starred in this ABC sitcom as Valentine Farrow, the playboy nonfiction editor for the Park Avenue publishing house of Brackett and Dunstall. He had a valet, Rocky Sin (Jack Soo, later Nick Yemana on *Barney Miller),* and a secretary named Libby (Janet Waldo). He had one meaningful relationship: his mother (played by opera singer Helen Traubel). And he had poor ratings. He lasted only one season.

Wendy and Me

George Burns did this one somewhere between the time when he played with Gracie and when he played God. It starred Connie Stevens and Ron Harper as a husband and wife team. He was a pilot. She was a scatterbrained person. There was also a Best Buddy, Danny Adams (James Callahan) who was never without his Little Black and Red books. J. Pat O'Malley (Mrs. Naugatuck's beau and eventual husband on *Maude)* played the building's super, Mr. Bundy. Burns was their landlord. Every once in a while he'd step forward and speak directly to us, giving us clues to what was going on, relating monologues and complicating the complications. Sound familiar? The show lasted one year on ABC until Burns said, "Say goodnight, Wendy."

1965–1966

Get Smart!

Green Acres

I Dream of Jeannie

OFF-SCREEN

10/17 New York World's Fair closes after two years.
11/2 John V. Lindsay elected mayor in closest race in New York City in twenty-five years.
12/24 Engagement of Luci Baines Johnson to Airman Patrick Nugent.
1/29–31 Worst blizzard in seventy years hits eastern coast.
1/31 President Johnson announces resuming of US bombing raids on North Vietnam.
3/16 First successful space docking of Gemini VIII.
4/6 Cesar Chavez' National Farm Workers Association recognized as bargaining agent for farm workers of Schenley Industries.
4/24 Longest newspaper strike in a major city of the nation begins as Newspaper Guild walks out on World-Journal-Tribune, Inc.
5/15 Over 10,000 picket White House to protest war.
6/11 McNamara announces escalation of troops in Vietnam, bringing total to 285,000.

FRONT RUNNER

GET SMART!

If you don't mind, 99, I'd like to handle this myself.
—MAXWELL SMART

Would you believe that *Get Smart!* was the most popular TV sitcom of all time?

Well, then, would you believe that *Get Smart!* was the *second* most popular TV sitcom of all time?

Hmmm . . . the *third* most popular?

How 'bout most popular *new show* of the 1965–1966 season. . . ?

Sorry about that. But *Get Smart!* was really amazing. From its weekly opener, we all knew we were in for something different: Maxwell Smart drives through the opening credits in a small sports car, walks through a series of doors and then into a phone booth where, after dialing the phone and receiving a busy signal, he drops through the floor to his spy agency headquarters. Another quiet trip to work.

Maxwell Smart never managed to live up to his name. A distant cousin to Robinson Peepers and a long line of other TV dingdongs, Max was a brash braggart with a heart as big as all indoors. He wasn't dumb—just myopic, and he went through life with blinders on. He was the antecedent of Ted Baxter and other celebrated second bananas who slipped on their own peels.

Over the years, Maxwell Smart gave us a whole slew of new expressions that we got to try out on the kids in class the next day:

"Would you believe?"

"Let me handle it, 99" (and then he does and botches it up).

"Sorry about that, Chief" (when he botched something up).

"And I'll be loving it" (on threat of unspeakable torture).

"I find that hard to believe. . . ."

. . . and a few others that now seem to be clichés, but back then were fresh. They all just seemed to tumble out of Max's mouth.

Don Adams, who played Max, was insistent on having the show's predicaments built around those few repeated punchlines, which had worked for him when he had answered mild insults on *The Perry Como Show* with "You sure know how to hurt a guy" and with his "would you believe" routine on *The Bill Dana Show*. They lifted "Sorry about that" from Ernie Kovacs' right-hand man, Joe Mikalos, who heard the phrase used by GIs. After

Maxwell Smart	Don Adams
Agent 99	Barbara Feldon
The Chief	Edward Platt
Conrad Siegfried, the head of KAOS	Bernie Kopell (1966–1969)
Larrabee, a CONTROL agent	Robert Karvelas (1967–1970)
CONTROL Agent 44	Victor French
Admiral Harold Harmon Hargrade, the former CONTROL Chief	William Schallert
Dr. Steele, head of CONTROL's lab (located in a burlesque theater)	Ellen Weston
Hymie, a CONTROL robot	Dick Gautier (1966–1969)
Charlie Watkins, shapely CONTROL agent ("a man in disguise")	Angelique
Professor Windish, a CONTROL scientist	Robert Cornthwaite
Carlson, a CONTROL scientist	Stacy Keach (1966–1967)
Dr. Bascomb, the head of CONTROL's crime lab	George Ives
Agent 13	Dave Ketchum (1966–1967)
Starker, Siegfried's aide	King Moody (1966–1969)
99's mother	Jane Dulo (1968–1969)
CONTROL's dog agent:	Fang (Agent K-13)

Get Smart! became so popular, "Sorry about that" was picked up and used by NASA ground control when urine bags burst on the Gemini 7.

Maxwell Smart was a secret agent based at 123 Main St. in Washington, DC, with CONTROL, an international spy organization (it seemed more like a club, actually) dedicated to destroying the diabolical KAOS, an international organization of evil. It was the good guys against the bad guys.

The show was a bent spoof of the James Bond movies which, unfortunately, have lasted longer than their TV parody. The title, *Get Smart!*, had two meanings: (1) as a command to Max to become more intelligent (no easy task), and (2) as a command to the enemy to "Get Max"—and they always tried to.

Max was also known as Agent 86 (bartenders' code for cutting off service to a drunk). His apartment—with its booby-traps of locks, guns, and an invisible wall—was also Number 86. He "posed" as Maxwell Smart, salesman for the Pontiac Greeting Card Company.

Max was clumsy and couldn't seem to hold anything—but week after week, he held the show together. He was the hero—the TV triumph for a country that was just about to exit the innocent age. Kennedy was killed in 1963 and Max emerged onto the screen in 1965—in the Johnson era before Vietnam and Cambodia, before hippies and hashish, before America got its first kick in the teeth with a major counterculture explosion. Maxwell—although he didn't know it—was the last of the innocents. And in 1970—when being a spy for the USA and saving the country from the bad guys was no longer a spoof—*Get Smart!* left the airwaves. We weren't so sure who the bad guys were anymore.

It was a clever show, full of ingenious gimmicks and sensational sight gags. Max was the Gracie Allen of the sixties—complete with a jigsaw puzzle personality, illogical logic, and quavering idealism. Consider these snatches of Smart dialogue:

SIEGFRIED (*the bad guy from KAOS*): Your chief has been silenced by a pistol butt.
MAX: That's a little drastic—couldn't you have just shushed him?

Or:

CHIEF: Once you get through customs, you will be met by our San Saludos agent—numero cinco y ocho y quatro y seis y nuevo y uno y tres.
MAX: Gee, that's a long number, Chief. I'll never be able to remember it. Couldn't I just call him Lopez?
CHIEF (*surprised*): You know his name?
MAX: Naturally. Who else is numero cinco y ocho y quatro y seis y nuevo y uno y tres?

Or:

CHIEF: Max, this is a difficult assignment in San Saludos and your lives will be in constant jeopardy. But there's one supreme danger you've got to be on guard against every moment.
MAX: What's that, Chief?
CHIEF: The entire time you're there—don't drink the water.

And:

SANCHEZ (*putting Max before an angry firing squad*): Would you like a blindfold? A last cigarette?
MAX: No, I'm trying to break the habit.

If this TV dialogue sounds like it's something out of Mel Brooks—that's because it is. Back in the mid-sixties, comedian/director Mike Nichols was asked to write the show, but he refused, claiming he was busy until 1970. So Brooks, who'd been writing around for some time and dabbled in comedy as the creator of the famous 2000-Year-Old Man routine, became the next choice. The co-creator of the show was Buck Henry.

The series was built around the unique talents of Don Adams, a reformed stand-up comic who had first come to sitcom attention with his portrayal of Glick, the house detective, on *The Bill Dana Show*. (Dana had previously played the elevator operator on *The Danny Thomas Show*, who—well, this could go on forever.) Adams and Dana had been New York advertising executives in their firm, Adams-Dana-Silverstein, Inc., located on Madison Avenue.

Smart talk: Max and their Chief

ABC put up the money for the pilot (filmed in black and white; actual episodes were in color), but didn't like it and turned it down. NBC bought it and on the air it went.

Hired as Adams' costar was velvet-voiced Barbara Feldon—hot off the Revlon Tiger Girl commercials (she had also won on *The $64,000 Question* as a Shakespeare expert)—to play 99, Max's levelheaded first assistant (and, four years later, his wife). 99's mother (Jane Dulo) was unaware of her daughter's spy activities and thought she was the Chief's secretary. Max's other assistant was a shaggy dog named Fang, a.k.a. K-13.

There was also the Chief, played by Edward Platt. The only other name he had was Harold Clark, when he was posing as a greeting card salesman. The Chief was always befuddled, although he certainly was a better administrator than Max. His superior was Zebra 642.

Max called into work with a dial phone on the sole of

86 Meets Mr. Big: Don Adams and Michael Dunn

his shoe (this was before touch tones), and he often got a wrong number. Another device was the Cone of Silence—a clear dual-helmet contraption with a connecting tube which Max insisted on using when he talked to the Chief—and then, of course, neither could hear when it was on. Max also wore jet shoes that shot him up (often hitting the roof), and he was so security-minded that he'd often swallow secret messages before reading them. In one famous episode, Max and 99 are in a phone booth, trying to escape evil Dr. Braam. "I've got a feeling this is no ordinary phone booth," Max says as it starts to fill up with water. (That gimmick cost $950 to construct. It used heated water. Don Adams couldn't swim.)

Many of the characters were also gimmicks: there was a guy called Secret Agent 13 who hid in mailboxes, water fountains, and clocks. There was Hymie, an android who sometimes teamed up with Max—TV's real first bionic man. And there was Admiral Hargrade, the former spy agency chief who often toppled over into a comalike sleep at unexpected moments. Once—in 1969—Max, the other agents and Chief all had a meeting on the moon.

Then there were the bad guys who made up KAOS. Mr. Big (played, of course, by a dwarf), Siegfried (the KAOS mastermind), and his brawny assistant Starker.

Once, Mr. Big cornered Max and was ready to kill him. Max thought fast.

MAX: At the moment, seven coast guard cutters are converging on us. Would you believe it?
MR. BIG: I find that hard to believe.
MAX: Hmmm . . . would you believe *six*?
MR. BIG: I don't think so.
MAX: How about two cops in a rowboat?

Max was a square—a boor—with absolutely no sense of humor. 99—who loved him for years—was always treated by him like a piece of office furniture—not because he didn't like her, but because he was all business and never noticed how warm and lovable she really was. He was smug and stuffy and vain—and we liked him anyway, because we knew that inside he was soft and vulnerable. Max never talked to people; he talked to the action and the circumstances. He would interrupt the reality that the audience saw and interject the reality he saw up there. He wasn't unkind, he was unshakable. Nothing jarred him. He lived inside of his head, not in the real world.

After four seasons, romance was added to Max's life—in an effort to pick up ratings. We always knew that Max and pussycat 99 would someday get together and—in 1968—86 married 99 and they lived happily together as 185. In 1969, they had twins—a boy and a girl—and the show became more like a domestic family sitcom than the zany farce it had been.

There was an innocence to *Get Smart!*— a taco delivery boy is stabbed in the back, but he doesn't bleed. The violence is never frightening and somehow comes off less angry than Saturday morning cartoons. Even the showdowns are strictly show biz:

SIEGFRIED: And now—a little magic trick. (*He pulls a rabbit out of his hat, opens the rabbit, and pulls out a gun.*)
MAX: The old gun-in-the-rabbit trick—and I fell for it. (*Siegfried pulls the trigger—the gun turns out to be a cigarette lighter.*)
MAX: Ah . . . it's the old lighter-gun-in-the-rabbit trick—and I fell for it.

In one episode, 99 is held captive by KAOS in a lovers' lane. Max—to the rescue—carries an inflatable girl in his glove compartment so he won't look conspicuous on lovers' lane alone. Naturally, the girl deflates at the critical moment.

A Nielsen Wedding: Max and 99 and the Chief

In 1969, because of bad ratings, NBC canceled the show. CBS picked it up for another season—and then dropped it.

Today, we watch *Get Smart!*, and the show still works. Its pace—like the screwball comedies of the thirties—and its fractured humor still crackle along. It seems dated only in that the commercials that now interrupt it in reruns advertise devices more sophisticated than the ones either CONTROL or KAOS used—technological marvels that "slice, dice and chop. . . ." And, of course, today government officials have proven themselves to be even more inept than Max.

But somewhere in Rerun Heaven, Max is up there, taking abuse, botching everything up, and getting in trouble. And you know what? He's loving it.

ALSO RANS

Camp Runamuck

Once there were two summer camps—Runamuck for boys and Divine for girls. The boys' camp was operated by Commander Wivenhoe (Arch Johnson) in a slipshod fashion. He was a child-hater and had a staff of lamebrains: Spiffy (Dave Ketchum), Pruett (Dave Madden), Malden (Mike Wagner), and Doc (Leonard Stone, later replaced by Frank DeVol). Divine, however, was impeccably maintained under the care of Counselor Mahalia May Gruenecker (Alice Nunn) and her gorgeous assistant, Caprice Yeudleman (Nina Wayne). Eulalia Divine (Hermione Baddeley) owns the camp. The situation: Wivenhoe attempted to cope with the kids, and the women manipulated his counselors into performing bur-

Camp Runamuck

densome tasks for Camp Divine. The show—which did not fare so divinely—ran only one season on NBC and then quietly went away for the summer.

The Double Life of Henry Phyfe

Mild-mannered Henry Wadsworth Phyfe (Red Buttons) never asked to lead the thrilling, dangerous, important life of an international spy for Central Intelligence. In fact, he was perfectly happy as an accountant. But when Agent U-31 died in a hit-and-run accident before he could reveal his vital secrets, Sub Chief Gerald B. Hannahan (Fred Clark) found out that only one man could take his place. Henry turned out to be U-31's exact double—so when the call from Washington arrived, he reluctantly stumbled into the dead spy's identity and his job. As things worked out, Henry was right to have resisted the sub chief's orders. ABC released him from active duty after only one season, leaving the forces of democracy much better off.

F Troop

A lot of people loved this show, which, at the outset, took place in a Union camp during the closing months of the Civil War. The plot was complicated, so pay attention: Wilton Parmenter (Ken Berry) of the Quarter

Masters Corps (he was a private in charge of officers' laundry) had an allergy that caused him to sneeze. Once, when he did, the sneeze sounded like "CHARGE!"—and that's just what the troopers did, foiling Confederate soldiers and causing the final Union victory. Parmenter was promoted to captain, given the Medal of Honor, and assigned to command F Troop at Fort Courage.

When he arrived, he met an assortment of characters: Sergeant Morgan O'Rourke (Forrest Tucker), president of the illegal O'Rourke Enterprises, a company that dealt in Indian souvenirs manufactured by the friendly Hekawi (pronounced Ha-cow-we) Indians in conjunction with the town saloon; Corporal Randolph Agarn (Larry Storch), the business' vice-president; Private Hannibal Dobbs (James Hampton), the inept company bugler; Trooper Duffy (Bob Steele), survivor of the Alamo; and Trooper Vanderbilt (Joe Brooks), the almost blind lookout.

After dismissing the troops, Parmenter met and befriended the beautiful, marriage-minded Jane Angelica Thrift—Wrangler Jane (Melody Patterson)—who was the proprietress of the fort's general store and the post office.

Guest stars included Edward Everett Horton as Roaring Chicken, Phil Harris as the 147-year-old Flaming Arrow, Milton Berle as Wise Owl, Paul Lynde as Sergeant Ramsden (a singing Mountie), and Henry Gibson as jinxed cavalry trooper Wrongo Starr. Two Indian favorites on the show were Chief Wild Eagle (Frank deKova) and Crazy Cat (Don Diamond).

Stories related the misadventures of Parmenter—"the scourge of the West"—as he struggled to maintain the peace, adjust to frontier life, and escape the matrimonial plans of his girlfriend. O'Rourke and Agarn complicated matters as they constantly devised schemes to conceal and expand their illegal enterprises. ABC discharged everyone in August of 1967.

Gidget

It was a California story about—so what else?—surfing, based on the Sandra Dee movies. The sitcom had this as its premise: Fifteen-and-a-half-year-old Francine Lawrence was swimming near Santa Monica when she began to suffer from a cramp. She was rescued by surfer Jeff Mathews, called Moon Doogie by his pals. He immediately nicknamed her "Gidget," his name for a girl who is about 5'2"—not tall, but not a midget) and through Jeff she discovered "the exciting world of surfing."

Gidget was played by Sally Field (later to become the flying nun and even later Burt Reynolds' girlfriend and Norma Rae). Her father, an English professor and a widower, was played by Don Porter, who for years was Ann Sothern's boss. Gidget also had a lot of friends

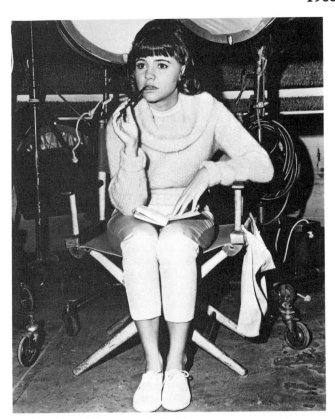

Gidget: *On the set with Sally Field*

Green Acres: *Eva Gabor and Eddie Albert*

besides Doogie (Steven Miles); they had names like Larue, Treasure, Becky, Mel, Siddo, and Ken. The series did not make a great splash and went under, after one season on ABC, when Gidget uttered her last "toodles."

Green Acres

Eddie Albert and Eva Gabor starred in this popular countrycom—in the tradition of *The Beverly Hillbillies*—about a couple, Attorney Oliver Wendell Douglas and his wife, Lisa, who decide to live in the country. They purchase, sight unseen, a 160-acre farm in Hooterville (*Petticoat Junction* also lives there) and give up their gay and glittering life of luxury in Manhattan, to live in a shabby, run-down unfurnished shack—"Oliver's Green Acres Dream." Lisa reluctantly says she'll try it—but only for six months. Being bighearted, however, she relents when she discovers that their cow, Elinor, and their chicken, Alice, will be killed when they leave. So they stay on CBS. Sort of a *Gilligan's Island* in country drag, the stories show two city dwellers trying to adjust to farming and country life. Others in the cast: Tom Lester as Eb Dawson, their handyman; Pat Buttram as Mr. Haney, a conniving salesman; Hank Patterson as Fred Ziffel, a pig farmer; Frank Cady as Sam Drucker, the general store owner; Sid Melton (remember him on *The Danny Thomas Show*?) as Alvy Monroe, a carpenter

Oliver hires to repair their house; and Edgar Buchanan as Joe Carson, manager of the Shady Rest Hotel. And let's not forget Arnold the Pig (Fred Ziffel's smart pet pig—the animal considered to be his son). The show was canceled in 1971, when CBS purged itself of rural sitcoms.

Hank

This one was about a college drop-in who's trying to achieve his life-long dream: to get a college education. Hank Dearborn (Dick Kallman) is an enterprising young businessman who is determined to get the college education denied to him when his parents were killed in a car crash and he was forced to drop out of high school and work to support his younger sister, Tina (Katie Sweet). So he supports himself by operating several concessions on campus. He also attends classes without registering (i.e., without paying tuition), under several aliases. To make money, he takes in laundry, repairs watches and shoes, and even starts a dating service. His girlfriend, Doris Royal, was played by Linda Foster. Doris' father, Dr. Lewis Royal, just so happens to be the registrar of the college. The show was bumped off the NBC schedule after one season and, once again, Hank was a dropout.

Hogan's Heroes

This popular sitcom took place in Stalag 13, a prisoner-of-war camp officially run by the naive and inept Colonel Wilhelm Klink (Werner Klemperer) and his obese, bumbling assistant, Sergeant Hans Schultz (John Banner). Unofficially, events and camp life are manipulated by Colonel Robert Hogan (Bob Crane), of the US Air Force, and a senior officer in the camp.

Hogan's Heroes: *Bob Crane massages Werner Klemperer's neck; John Banner watches.*

He is assisted by inmates Louis LeBeau (Robert Clary), the French corporal; Newkirk (Richard Dawson), the English corporal; Andrew Carter (Larry Hovis), the American sergeant; and James Kinchloe (Kenneth Washington), the American corporal. Hogan uses the code name Papa Bear and conducts vital missions for the Allies. Through phone taps, underground escape routes, radio contacts, and custom tailoring, the prisoners assist Allied fugitives and secure top-secret information for their superiors.

Often Schultz becomes an unwitting and reluctant accomplice to their schemes. Fear of betrayal and transfer to the Russian front keeps him silent. "I know nothing!" he says.

Others who lived the good (but dangerous) life in Stalag 13: Colonel Crittendon (Bernard Fox), the commander of Stalag 13 and Hogan's nemesis; Gestapo commander Major Hockstedder (Howard Caine) and Marya (Nita Talbot), the beautiful Russian spy.

Because it was so similar to the play, *Stalag 17*, there was a plagiarism suit (which the playwright won). But the whole thing ended when Hogan and his heroes ended their imprisonment on CBS on July 4, 1971.

Post Script: In 1978, Bob Crane was brutally bludgeoned to death. John Banner died in 1973 of a hemorrhage on his 63rd birthday. Richard Dawson went on to host TV's game show *Family Feud*.

I Dream of Jeannie

This popular show (it ran for five seasons on NBC and seems to be in a perpetual state of rerun) was all about a Jeannie who was a genie. She was born in 64 B.C. (TV's first older woman/younger man romance) in Baghdad.

Blue Djin, a powerful and feared genie, wanted her to marry him. She said Nope. He said: Okay, then, spend the rest of your life as a genie in a bottle. She was then sentenced to life on a desert island.

Centuries passed. Neither Jeannie's bottle nor her body were affected by the passing of time.

And then, one day in 1965, Captain Tony Nelson, an astronaut on a flight from the NASA Space Center in Cape Kennedy, crash-landed on a desert island in the South Pacific. And guess what he found? The bottle. When he opened it, pink smoke emerged—and so did a curvaceous girl dressed as a harem dancer.

She talked too: "Thou may ask anything of thy slave, Master," she told him, and crossed her hands over her chest, blinked her eyes, and conjured up a rescue helicopter. She blinked herself back into the bottle and sneaked off into his survival kit, without his knowledge.

When he got home (1020 Palm Dr.) and discovered her, he realized he'd better keep quiet or there would be problems at NASA. He even tried to get rid of her, but she wouldn't go; she was eternally grateful to him for setting her free. But he made her promise three things: to keep her identity a secret, to not use her magic powers,* and to grant him no special wishes. She said Sure.

However, astronaut Roger Healey (Bill Daily, later Howard on *The Bob Newhart Show*) found out about Jeannie and was the only other person to know. But Jeannie used her magic, and Roger and Tony became the object of fascination by Dr. Alfred Bellows (Hayden Rorke), the NASA psychiatrist who observed, pondered, and recorded their activities.

During the first season, Jeannie tried (and succeeded) to break up Tony's relationship with his fiancée, General Stone's daughter Melissa (Karen Sharpe).

The show—which ran until 1970—revolved around the jealous genie and her attempts to protect her master from harm and from other female admirers, and the master's attempt to control and conceal the presence of this fun-loving genie. She wooed him and pursued him until, finally, he married her on December 2, 1969.

Barbara Eden played Jeannie (also her sister, Jean-

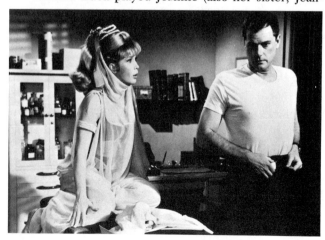

I Dream of Jeannie: *Barbara Eden and Larry Hagman*

nie II, who wanted Tony for herself). Larry Hagman (Mary Martin's son, who'd go on to stardom in the late-seventies' *Dallas*) played Captain Tony Nelson (later promoted to major). Ted Cassidy played Habib, Jeannie II's master.

One of the show's special effects mysteries that still lingers on in viewers' minds today: How come Barbara Eden—who always had a bare midriff—had no navel? Was it a network cover-up, or did she just not have one?

The John Forsythe Show

Like so many other sitcom stars who retired from a hit series, John Forsythe graduated to a sitcom bearing his own name. In this one he was no longer the *Bachelor Father*, but the bachelor headmaster at the Foster School for Girls in California. A former US Air Force major, he inherited the school from its founder, his late aunt. The episodes related his attempts to adjust to new responsibilities and to try to solve the problems that stemmed from being around 120 teenage girls, among them Forsythe's own Real Life daughters, Brooke and Page. John Foster (as Forsythe was called) had many misunderstandings with Ed Robbins (Guy Marks), a former air force crony who was now helping John run the school.

Also in the cast: Elsa Lanchester as Miss Culver, the principal; Peggy Lipton (later on *Mod Squad*) as Joanna; and Ann B. Davis (née Schultzy from *Love That Bob*) as Miss Wilson, the gym teacher.

In the spring of 1966, the writers sent John and Ed on a world tour as US undercover agents, using the school as their base.

NBC expelled them all after one season.

Mr. Roberts

Roger Smith (now Ann-Margret's husband/manager) played Lieutenant JG Douglas Roberts, a cargo officer of the *Reluctance*, a US Navy cargo ship nicknamed "the Bucket" by its reluctant-to-serve crew. Feeling he's displaced and because he longs to serve aboard a fighting vessel, Roberts seeks to acquire a transfer, but, by shouldering the antics of the men, he encounters hostility from the ship's commander, Captain John Morton (Richard X. Slattery), who won't forward Roberts' letters to the proper authorities. The show presented a sentimental version of World War II in the South Pacific. However, they were all discharged by NBC after serving only one season. *Mister Roberts* was based on the successful Broadway play (1948) and movie (1955), both starring Henry Fonda and both based on Thomas Heggen's book.

Mona McCluskey

Six-foot-three dancer Juliet Prowse played Mona, a movie star who's married to an air force sergeant. She earns $5,000 a week; he makes $500 a month. They live in Hollywood in a modest two-room furnished apartment. His name is Mike McCluskey; her stage name is Mona Jackson, but she uses his name in married life, and spends her time trying to supplement the tight budget without Mike catching on. Definitely a pre-Liberation show, Mona and Mike divorced themselves from NBC on April 4, 1966.

My Mother the Car

This one is a classic favorite sitcom flop. Its only redeeming feature was Ann Sothern as the mellifluous voice of the car—or the mother, depending on your point of view. Here's the story: In LA Dave Crabtree (Jerry Van Dyke, Dick's brother) is looking to buy a car. He becomes fascinated with a 1928 Porter. Then he hears a female voice coming from the radio. It's Mother—reincarnated as a car.

So he buys her and returns home, where his family raises a stink about the jalopy. They wanted a station wagon. Even after he overhauls the car (license plate PZR 317) the family still isn't happy. (Of course they don't know it's his mother.) Then, of course, there is a devious antique car collector, Captain Bernard Mancini (Avery Schreiber), who is determined to add the Touring

My Mother the Car: *Jerry Van Dyke and Ann Sothern*

Mobile to his collection. NBC sent the whole mess to the junkyard in September of 1966.

lawyer. They had a 150-pound sheep dog named Ladadog. NBC canceled this show in 1967.

O. K. Crackerby!

This short-lived ABC show (it popped off after only a half season) starred Burl Ives as Mr. O. K. Crackerby, an Oklahoma widower with three children (one played by now-movie star Brooke Adams). O.K. was, incidentally, the world's richest man. Even so, he was not accepted by the genteel people in society (or by the television audience, for that matter), and so he hired a penniless Harvard grad, St. John Quincy (Hal Buckley), to teach his kids some Culture so they could "get into polite society." The rest of the time, O.K. fought unrelentlessly against snobbery. The show was the brainchild of Cleveland Amory, former *TV Guide* chief critic, and dramatist Abe Burrows.

Please Don't Eat the Daisies

Based on Jean Kerr's book (as well as the Doris Day movie version), this one was all about the suburban Nash Family: James (Mark Miller), an English professor at Ridgemont College; his wife, Joan (Patricia Crowley), a freelance magazine writer (her pen name is Joan Holliday); and their kids: Kyle and Joel, and Trevor and Tracy (who are twins). Also in the show: Ellen Corby (who would, in 1972, play Grandma on *The Waltons*), who here played Martha O'Reilly, the maid; and King Donovan (Imogene Coca's husband), who played their neighbor Herb Thornton, a

Please Don't Eat the Daisies *(front, from left): Jeff Fithian, Kim Tyler, Brian Nash, Joe Fithian and (back, from left): Patricia Crowley and Mark Miller*

The Smothers Brothers Show

Not to be confused with the controversial *Smothers Brothers Comedy Hour* two years later, this sitcom had (but of course) an unusual premise: Tommy Smothers (played by Tommy Smothers) had been drowned at sea. He returns to earth (specifically LA) as an apprentice angel and sets up shop with his brother Dick (Dick Smothers) in Dick's bachelor pad. Tom—inept—is supposed to help people in trouble. Dick reluctantly helps him complete his assignments so that he can become a full-fledged angel. It didn't work out so well. At least CBS didn't think so, and sent them all in the other direction in September 1966.

Tammy

Debbie Reynolds scored big with the 1957 movie *Tammy and the Bachelor*. Sandra Dee made it with *Tammy Tell Me True*. The ABC sitcom version starred Debbie Watson. Debbie *who?* Oh, well. This continuing saga of the Tales of Tammy didn't last long anyway.

It was all about Tammy Tarleton, a young, lonely riverboat girl who was raised in the desolate Bayou country in Louisiana by her grandfather (Denver Pyle) after her parents' death. She enrolled in secretarial school after completing special education courses at nearby Seminola College. After completing school, she got a job as a secretary to a wealthy widower, John Brent (played by Donald Woods). It should be noted that Tammy could type nearly 200 words per minute.

One day Tammy was milking her goat, Nan, when she received a telegram at the *Ellen B.* (the name of her houseboat) that she had gotten the job with Mr. Brent at Brentwood Hall. She was delighted.

Not so delighted was Lavinia Tate (Dorothy Green), an attractive (but nasty) widow who wanted the job for her daughter Gloria (Linda Marshall). Also: Lavinia had the hots for Brent. Lavinia was mad that Tammy got the job, and spent the episodes trying to sabotage it so Tammy'd be fired. But Tammy believed in Love and Understanding, and somehow managed to overcome Lavinia's creepiness. But not entirely: they all lost their jobs after one season. However, in 1967 Watson and crew made a movie: *Tammy and the Millionaire*.

1966–1967

WHATEVER HAPPENED TO 1966–1967?

What can you say about a television season in which the big new sitcom hits were shows like *That Girl, The Monkees,* and *Family Affair*—quite a disparate (and desperate) crop, to be sure. Even the leftover successes from the seasons before were nothing to write home about (or write a book about, for that matter): *Gilligan's Island* continued to float along; *The Lucy Show* was more-of-the-same; *I Dream of Jeannie* was a nightmare; *Petticoat Junction* and *Beverly Hillbillies* and *Green Acres* were polluting the airwaves with their clean air and down-home humor. The season before, *Hazel* had hung up her apron, *Donna Reed* gave up television for politics, *McHale's Navy* was finally discharged and—one of the worst tragedies in television history—Dick Van Dyke had given up his show. What we were left with was latter-day *Andy Griffith,* worn-out witchery on *Bewitched,* and more oldies like *F Troop, Gomer Pyle,* and *My Three Sons* (which had expanded to Nielsen-knows how many offspring). As for the new shows—well, read on and you'll remember why you didn't watch television in 1966–1967.

ALSO RANS

Family Affair

This show—a favorite among young kids—was a family program that was about as domestic and housebroken as you could get. It was heartwarming, sentimental, and sometimes even realistic. Brian Keith played Bill Davis, president of the Davis and Gaynor Construction Company. Davis had agreed to raise his brother's children after his brother and sister-in-law were killed in a car crash. The other relatives, you see, didn't want them—so Bill took them in.

Also there was Giles French (Sebastian Cabot) a "gentleman's gentleman," who played nanny to the three

OFF-SCREEN

9/18 Valerie Jeanne Percy killed by intruder in her father's (Republican Senate candidate Charles Percy) home.
1/3 Jack Ruby dies in Dallas prison.
1/18 Albert DeSalvo, the "Boston Strangler," given life sentence.
1/27 Astronauts Grissom, White, and Chaffee killed in fire in their Apollo I capsule during ground tests.
3/31 President Johnson signs first US-USSR consular treaty since Russian Revolution.
4/15 Richard Speck found guilty of murder of eight nurses.
5/10-11 One man killed, two wounded on campus of Jackson State College during riots.
5/14 Mickey Mantle hits five hundredth home run.
6/5 Six Days War breaks out between Israel and Arab neighbors.
6/20 Cassius Clay (Muhammad Ali) given five-year sentence for draft evasion.

Family Affair *(from left): Brian Keith, Kathy Garver, Sebastian Cabot, Anissa Jones and Johnnie Whitaker*

kids—Catherine/Cissy (Kathy Garver) and twins Jody and Buffy (Johnnie Whitaker and Anissa Jones). Giles tried to provide love and security to the kids, who were often lonely and disillusioned because their uncle was often away working. Giles was anal-compulsive (the kids weren't), and so they negotiated everything from neatness to noise. Nancy Walker (later Rhoda's mother and *McMillan and Wife*'s maid) got her sitcom start as a part-time domestic on this show, playing Emily Turner, Bill's inept housekeeper, during the show's last season. (During the first season, Cabot took ill—called to duty by the Queen, was the excuse for Giles' disappearance—and his brother Niles (John Williams) took over for nine episodes.) This long-runner played on CBS until September 9, 1971.

The Hero

This show pooped out after only four months and starred Richard Mulligan (later Burt on *Soap*) as Sam Garret, a bumbler at home, but at work a fearless law enforcer: Jed Clayton, US marshal. Not really, though, because Sam was actually a TV actor with his own Western—but he was afraid of horses, allergic to sagebrush, and a total klutz. Episodes—and there weren't many of them—dealt with his attempts to hide his real persona from his fans. NBC had the honor of hosting this one.

Hey, Landlord!

An aspiring writer and an aspiring comedian became landlords of a ten-room Manhattan brownstone. They were evicted by NBC after one season. Woodrow "Woody" Banner (the writer) was played by Will Hutchins (he'd been *Sugarfoot* in 1957 and would go on to play Dagwood on sitcom's second incarnation of *Blondie* in 1968); Sandy Baron played comedian Chuck Hookstratten. Other notables in the cast were Michael Constantine, Pamela Rodgers, and Ann Morgan Guilbert (Milly from *Dick Van Dyke*), who all played tenants. Sally Field (pre-*Flying Nun*) played Woody's sister. Movie actor Tom Tully played his father. Woody was a trusting kid from Ohio; Chuck was a native New Yorker. Everyone was always looking for the landlords. Except the TV viewers.

It's About Time

In one short season this show went through a major format change, but the basic fantasy principle stayed the same. The first format: A NASA rocket launched from the Florida Space Center penetrated a turbulence area and broke the time barrier. After a crash landing in a swamp, the astronauts Mac (Frank Aletter) and Hector (Jack Mullaney) escape unharmed. Then their adventures begin. (Although they'd had adventures before: Aletter had been married to Cara Williams on her 1964 show, and in 1960 he was Buddy on *Bringing Up Buddy*. Mullaney got his sitcom start in 1958 as Johnny on *The Ann Sothern Show* and went on to play Lieutenant St. John on *Ensign O'Toole* in 1962; in 1964, he was lecherous neighbor Peter on *My Living Doll*.)

First, while exploring the surrounding area, Mac and Hector discover and rescue a young boy, Breer (Pat Cardi), who's been trapped on a ledge. And that's when they find out: they have landed in the Prehistoric Era. They meet the boy's family: his father, Gronk (Joe E. Ross), his mother, Shad (Imogene Coca), and his sister, Mlor (Mary Grace). Because the astronauts look, dress, and act strangely to the cave dwellers, they are thought to be evil spirits and are ordered to be killed. They are saved because, as they explain to the Cave Boss (Cliff Norton), they saved Breer's life. They spend the rest of the first part of the TV season trying to relate to the past era and to find copper to repair their disabled spacecraft.

The second format (starting January 22, 1967) has Mac and Hector repairing their rocket (after they've discovered a copper mine). The Cave Boss doesn't like the looks of things—he thinks they're evil spirits after all and orders them and the cave family killed. Mac and Hector learn of the plans and, after they have taken off in the rocket, discover that the cave family, with nowhere else to go, has sneaked aboard. They rebreak the time barrier and land in LA of 1966, and the cave family is hidden in Mac's apartment. And then the gimmick is switched: the cave family has to adjust and master the ways of modern society, and Mac and Hector spend their time trying to conceal the family's presence from NASA officials.

Whichever format they used, neither worked very well, and CBS canceled the show in 1967.

The Jean Arthur Show

Movie great Jean Arthur reluctantly agreed to star in this sitcom as the female half of a mother-and-son legal team, Marshall & Marshall. She needn't have bothered; the show went off CBS after three months. Arthur played a widow who got involved in antics with her clients. Her twenty-five-year-old son, Paul, was played by Ron Harper (who'd been Detective Bert Kling on *87th Precinct* in 1961, Jeff Conway on *Wendy and Me* in 1964, and would grow up to play Lieutenant Garrison on *Garrison's Guerrillas* in 1967 and astronaut Alan Virdon on *Planet of the Apes* in 1974). One of the gimmicks was that Jean Arthur never shut up on the show—so no one else did much talking, including her chauffeur, Morton (Leonard Stone).

Love on a Rooftop

Judy Carne (remember her from *Laugh-In*?) and Rich Little starred in this ABC sitcom about a young couple

Love on a Rooftop: Judy Carne and Peter Deuel

(Little played the next-door neighbor; Peter Deuel played the husband) who live at 1400 McDoogal St., in San Francisco, in a rooftop apartment. He is an apprentice architect earning $85.37 a week. She is an art student (but her dad is rich and she gave up wealth for love). The network gave it all up for money and canceled this show in August of 1967, which is too bad, because good apartments (not to mention sitcoms—which this one was not) are hard to find: it may have been a walk-up, but it had a terrific view of the San Francisco Bay. However, the show was rerun during the summer of 1971. Incidentally. Rich Little's character, Stan Parker, was an "idea man" who composed menus for a living.

The Monkees

The Beatles' *A Hard Day's Night* was clearly the inspiration for this rock 'n' roll sitcom that starred Davy Jones, Mike Nesmith, Mickey Dolenz, and Peter Tork, as themselves: The Monkees. They wrote and performed all the music and rollicked through slapstick routines in this most unrealistic show. Notable was the photography, which often sped ahead on fast-forward and other surrealistic techniques. As is well known, the group was "manufactured" by music mogul Don Kirshner, who picked the Not-So-Fab Four from more than 500 applicants. Although not really all musicians, they did have three hits—"Last Train to Clarksville," "I'm a Believer," and "Words." In 1967, The Monkees made headlines when Nesmith ("Wool Hat") disclosed that "We're being passed off as something we aren't." The group broke up after NBC dropped the show in 1968, later to pop up as a Saturday-morning rerun on CBS.

Mr. Terrific

Mr. Peepers, Mr. Ed, Mr. Smith (who went to Washington, *Mr. Deeds* (who went to town)—now there was another Mr. in sitcom city: *Mr. Terrific*. This was all about Stanley Beamish (played by Stephen Strimpell), who roomed with his best buddy, Hal Walters (Dick Gautier). They had no secrets—except one: Stan had a secret power pill that enabled him to become the crimebuster, Mr. Terrific. The pills weren't your ordinary over-the-counter drugstore variety; they were supplied to Stan by Barton J. Reed (John McGiver) from the Bureau of Special Projects, and Reed sent Stanley on all kinds of missions (but the pills lasted only one hour; in a pinch he could take two and get an extra twenty minutes—although why that made any difference in a half-hour sitcom doesn't make sense). Anyway, Stanley didn't always do such a hotshot job, because he was very shy and timid and naive and gullible, and he'd often return to normal at the worst times. After seven months it didn't matter anyway, for that's when CBS canceled them. And sitcom watchers had to wait ten years for another Mr.—*Mr. T. and Tina*—which, itself, turned into a failure (obviously hadn't been taking their pills).

My Name's McGooley, What's Yours?

This show sounds like it's the forerunner to something (although exactly what is uncertain). It's all about the bickering relationship between a scheming father-in-law (played by Gordon Chates) and his beer-swilling son-in-law (John Meillon) who's married to his daughter (Judy Farr). The syndicated show lasted only one season.

Occasional Wife

This one-season entrant took place in New York and was another of those shows about a company that was offering an executive position only to a married man. (*The Cara Williams Show* had the opposite premise.) And so Peter Christopher (played by Michael Callan) proposed to his girlfriend Greta (Patricia Harty), a beautiful hatcheck girl: "Greta, I want you to be my wife . . . occasionally." And so she posed as his spouse whenever he needed one (he also paid for her rent, her contact lenses, and her art lessons; today, this would be considered a very risqué show). They lived in the same apartment building (he on the seventh floor, she on the ninth) and, of course, there was lots of chaos. Jack Collins played the employer, Mr. Brahms, who owned a baby-food company.

Pistols 'n' Petticoats

Film star Ann Sheridan starred in this Western comedy, rooted in 1871, in a town called Wretched, Colorado. It was all about the gun-slinging Hangs family (Sheridan played Henrietta—a.k.a. Hank). Others were her father, Andrew (Douglas Fowley), his wife, Grandma (Ruth McDevitt), and Henrietta's twenty-one-year-old, city-

bred daughter Lucy (Carole Wells), who is opposed to violence. Meanwhile, they spend their time trying to keep law and order in a very restless territory. Bumbling, incompetent, Sheriff Sikes (Gary Vinson) stood back and watched. CBS gave them only one season in which to do it. And then: BANG.

The Pruitts of Southhampton

Phyllis Diller, Louis Nye, John Astin, Reginald Gardiner, Paul Lynde, Gypsy Rose Lee, Billy De Wolfe, John McGiver, Richard Deacon, Marty Ingels—what a cast. Unfortunately, not what a show. It was all about a formerly rich family, living in Southhampton on Long Island, which has to reduce its living standards when the IRS investigates them and discovers that they owe $10 million in back taxes. Society matron Phyllis Pruitt tries to put on a front and look like she's still loaded, but she also has to adjust to a life of squalor with a small house (only eight rooms), one car, and a butler. This ABC sitcom kicked around for one season. After the first half, it got its name changed to *The Phyllis Diller Show*, and Phyllis rented out her mansion as a boarding house to try to raise money (and ratings). Based on the Patrick Dennis book *House Party*.

Rango

Before he became a "regular" on *The Carol Burnett Show*, Tim Conway starred in this Western sitcom that lasted half a season on ABC. Conway played a lawman named Rango, who was a bumbling idiot. "They" (the authorities, no doubt) wanted to keep him out of trouble, so they assigned him to rule Deep Wells Ranger Station, the quietest post they could find. But somehow he managed to find trouble. The town had been peaceful for twenty years; after Rango got there, a crime wave broke out. He was assisted by an Indian named Pink Cloud (played by Guy Marks, alumnus of both the *Joey Bishop* and *John Forsythe* shows), who was much more interested in living "like the white man" than like the Indian. Said Pink Cloud once: "Rango say him return when sun high over teepee. By that, I presume, he meant he would return back by noon." There was one other character— Captain Horton (Norman Alden), who wanted to have Rango transferred, but there was one hitch: Rango's daddy was head of the Texas Rangers. TV's first nepotism sitcom.

The Rounders

ABC gave this sitcom a chance—but only for four months. It was about two dimwitted contemporary cowboys, Ben Jones (Ron Hayes) and Howdy Lewis (Patrick Wayne—John's son) who are hired hands at the JL Cattle Ranch. Also on the show: J. Pat O'Malley as Vince, the ranch owner's righthand man. Every Saturday night they tore up the Longhorn Café in nearby Hi Lo. Based on the Max Evans novel and the 1965 movie costarring Chill Wills as Jim Ed Love, a role he played on this sitcom.

Run Buddy Run

This sitcom starred Jack Sheldon as Buddy Overstreet, a mild-mannered Los Angeles accountant who's got quite a chase on his hands . . . feet. In a steamroom, Buddy overhears a group of gangland hoods plotting the murder of "the Man in Chicago" and the secret words "Chicken Little." When they discover that Buddy's overheard all this—boy, are they sore! Sore enough to chase Buddy all over the place. So Buddy (hounded by a Mr. Devere) struggles to avoid being captured and to resolve the differences between him and Devere. In January 1967— only four months after he started running—CBS finally apprehended him.

The Tammy Grimes Show

Broadway actress Tammy Grimes turned to TV (a mistake) when she played Tammy Ward, a young heiress who's restricted to a tight budget by her miserly uncle, Simon Ward (Hiram Sherman). She can't claim her multimillion-dollar inheritance—and so she just has to make do until she reaches thirty. Dick Sargent (*Bewitched*) played Terrence Ward, her square twin brother. Episodes depict Tammy's misadventures as she struggles to finance her expensive tastes through elaborate schemes. Not something you'd want to see every week? You needn't have worried: the show only lasted about three of them. Then ABC gave Tammy her inheritance and told her to get lost.

That Girl

This popular sitcom (it aired on ABC through 1971) starred Danny Thomas' daughter Marlo Thomas as Ann Marie (that was her last name: Marie) a "talented, young, and beautiful" hopeful actress in New York. Ann Marie was also a dip. Even back then. For a while she lived at 344 West 78th St., Apartment 4-D; later, she moved to the East Side at 627 East 54th St.

After she left home in Brewster, New York, she got involved with her boyfriend, Don Hollinger (she called him Donald) played by Ted Bessell. Also involved in her life was her father, Lou Marie (Lew Parker), owner of La Parisienne restaurant. Others in the cast: Rosemary DeCamp as Ann's mother; Billy De Wolfe as her drama coach, Jules Benedict; Bonnie Scott as Ann's neighbor Judy Bessemer (Dabney Coleman played her doctor husband); Ruth Buzzi played Ann's friend, and George Carlin was among her many agents on the show. Daddy Danny even made a few cameo appearances.

She wasn't a very liberated woman; in fact, she seemed to always spend her time sharing Don's interests and interacting with her father. She didn't work much, except for TV commercials and bit parts in plays. Somehow, though, she managed to maintain a fantastic wardrobe and a fabulous apartment—but that's because Sugar Daddy ABC was keeping her. In September of 1970, Donald finally popped the question, but Ann Marie was canceled before the ceremony.

That Girl: *Ted Bessell and Marlo Thomas*

1967–1968

WHATEVER HAPPENED TO 1967–1968?

Oh, boy. If you thought the 1966–1967 sitcom season was a wasteland, wait'll you hear about this one. But, actually, you're in luck: there's not much to say (and, therefore, there wasn't much to see back then). Rural sitcoms—*Andy Griffith*, *Green Acres*, *Petticoat Junction*, *Beverly Hillbillies*—were still feeding us corn. So much for that trend. Some of the other by-now old standards were still around (and around and around): *The Lucy Show*, *I Dream of Jeannie*, *Bewitched*, *Gomer Pyle*, *Get Smart!*, *Hogan's Heroes*, and last season's hits were still with us: *That Girl*, *The Monkees*, and *Family Affair*. But it was a troubled time—Vietnam and urban unrest—and the networks didn't know how to respond. So—true to form—they gave us *The Flying Nun* and—one ray of bright light—*The Mothers-in-Law*. Still, another lifeless season.

OFF-SCREEN

9/10 Surveyor V launched from Cape Kennedy soft-lands on moon.
9/28 Walter E. Washington sworn in as commissioner of D.C., first Black to head major city government in nation.
11/20 US population reaches 200 million.
12/5 More than 100 antiwar protesters attempt to close New York induction center; among 264 arrested are Dr. Benjamin Spock and poet Allen Ginsberg.
1/23 *Pueblo*, US Navy intelligence ship, captured by North Korea.
4/4 Martin Luther King, Jr., assassinated in Memphis, Tennessee.
4/23 Students at Columbia University begin sit-in leading to closing of the university on 4/26.
5/7 Dancer's Image disqualified as Kentucky Derby winner when pain killer discovered in his system.
5/10 Peace talks open in Paris.
6/6 Senator Robert Kennedy dies of gunshot wounds.

ALSO RANS

Accidental Family

This sitcom (which lasted one-half season on NBC) was about Jerry Webster, a widower and Las Vegas nightclub performer, played by Jerry Van Dyke, Dick's brother. (Jerry had quite an illustrious TV career. Besides playing Dick's brother on *The Dick Van Dyke Show*, Jerry'd been a regular on the 1963 *Judy Garland Show*, emcee of *Picture This* quiz show the same year, and, in 1965, had a

Accidental Family: *Jerry Van Dyke and Lois Nettleton with kids Teddy Quinn and Susan Benjamin*

mother who was a car. In 1970, he played a physical education teacher on Andy Griffith's *The Headmaster*, and later went on to become a down-and-out comic on *The Mary Tyler Moore Show*.) On this show, Jerry is awarded custody of his son, eight-year-old Sandy (Teddy Quinn)—but only if the kid doesn't live in Vegas. So Jerry relocates to a farm in the San Fernando Valley—and finds that he's unable to evict his tenants: Susan Kramer (Lois Nettleton), a divorcée; her daughter Tracy (Susan Benjamin), and her uncle Ben McGrath (Ben Blue), an ex-vaudevillian. And so they all decide to share the house, with Jerry and Sandy living there on weekends, and Susan living there rent-free and taking care of Sandy.

Captain Nice

After the *Batman* boom, TV decided to put parody in sitcom land—look how well it had worked on *Get Smart!*—and took a shot at the super-heroes with this show and *Mr. Terrific* over on CBS. Nice and Terrific were just slightly different—Mr. T. glided when he flew, and Captain N. flapped his arms. Carter Nash (a.k.a. Captain Nice) was a shy, quiet, hen-pecked chemist whose mother seemed to have a thing for him. His alter ego—Captain Nice—well, he was the same way. It's just that he could fly. It was his mother, in fact, who talked him into waging war on the evil forces; she also made his baggy leotards for him to fly in. He didn't exactly terrify the evil doers, and it didn't help that he was scared of heights. William Daniels played the captain; Alice Ghostley played his mama. Together, they lived in Bigtown. His girlfriend, a police sergeant named Candy Kane, was played by Ann Prentiss. The show was created and written by Buck Henry, who had co-created *Get Smart!*, which this show resembled. A mid-season replacement, Captain Nice flew for only a few months on the NBC airwaves.

The Flying Nun

Nobody will believe this series in 100 years—but, actually, nobody believed it in 1967 either, when the show debuted on ABC: the story of a flighty nun who got into the habit of flying.

It all started when, impressed by the mission work of her aunt, Sister Jacqueline (Marge Redmond, Jack Weston's wife), Elsie Ethington decides to become Sister Bertrille. She is assigned to the Convent San Tanco, near San Juan, Puerto Rico.

As a nun, she has to wear coronets—headgear which has sides that look like wings. These, coupled with the San Juan trade winds, help ninety-pound Elsie soar around town. But being a nice nun, she decides to put her talent to good use to help the poor community. Her landings, however, are a bit bumpy, because she does not have control over her flight patterns. A cross between *The Sound of Music* (without the music) and *Superman* (without the man), Sister Bertrille flew in—and on—the air for two seasons and finally landed in countless reruns.

Sister Bertrille, of course, was played by Sally Field, who, just two seasons before had gushed as Gidget, and, in 1973 would leave the Church to get married to John Davidson on *The Girl with Something Extra*, in which she suffered from ESP. Later, Field went on to play *Norma Rae* and the role of Burt Reynolds' girlfriend.

The show was based on the book *The Fifteenth Pelican* by Tere Rios. At first, the network was afraid of insulting Catholics with the show, but it went on to become Approved, and actually received the blessings of a religious order who thought it "humanized" nuns. Well, well . . .

Good Morning, World

In Los Angeles—again?—Dave Lewis (Joby Baker) and Larry Clarke (Ronnie Schell—he played Private Duke Slater on *Gomer Pyle*) are hosts of small-time radio program *The Lewis and Clarke Show*, aired from 6 to 10 A.M. Lewis is married, shy, and retiring; Clarke is a swinging single. Billy De Wolfe played Roland B. Hutton, Jr., the station manager; Goldie Hawn—pre-*Laugh-In*—played the Lewises' gossipy neighbor Sandy. The program finally said Goodbye World after one season on CBS.

He and She

Richard Benjamin and Paula Prentiss (married in what is commonly called Real Life) played sitcom spouses Richard and Paula Hollister. He was a cartoonist who created the comic-strip-cum-TV-series *Jetman*. She—"beautiful but scatterbrained"—was a traveler's-company aide. Dick spent his half-hours helping Paula untangle the messes when she tried to help others. The show also dealt with the pressures of working in a computerized society. Others on the show: Jack Cassidy as Oscar North, the egocentric, arrogant star of *Jetman*; Hamilton Camp as Andrew Hummel, the building's not-very-handyman; Kenneth Mars as fireman Harry, the Hollis-

He and She: *Paula Prentiss, Richard Benjamin and him—Jack Cassidy*

ters' friend; and Harold Gould (later Rhoda's father) as Dick's employer, Norman Nugent. The whole thing was modeled after *The Dick Van Dyke Show,* and was aired on CBS for one season in 1967–1968, and was later rebroadcast in the summer of 1970.

The Mothers-in-Law

Desi Arnaz produced this show, which aired Sunday nights on NBC for two seasons. Eve Arden and Kaye

The Mothers-in-Law: *Eve Arden and Herb Rudley*

Ballard starred as Eve Hubbard and Kaye Buell, fifteen-year next-door neighbors whose daughter (Eve's) and son (Kaye's) get married and set up housekeeping in the converted Hubbard garage, on Ridgewood Dr. in Hollywood. The two mothers-in-law are constantly bickering and meddling in their kids' lives. Also in the show: Herbert Rudley as attorney Herb Hubbard; Richard Deacon as Roger Buell (a TV scriptwriter—remember when he also produced The Alan Brady Show on *The Dick Van Dyke Show*?); and—yes, indeed—Desi Arnaz as Raphael del Gado, a friendly Mexican bullfighter. The kids eventually gave birth to twins Hildy and Joey. The show, of course, was more about the parents than the kids, anyway. The Hubbards were straight-as-an-arrow, while the Buells were quite unconventional (Roger tested his scripts, which he wrote at home, on anyone who'd listen, and Kaye was a rotten housekeeper and quite overbearing—well, unconventional for TV in the late sixties, anyway). Before Deacon joined the show, actor Roger Carmel had played Roger Buell, but left after the first season over a contractual (read: money) dispute, and was replaced by Deacon—another example of The Total Sitcom Transplant.

The Second Hundred Years

This one had an interesting twist. Here goes. In Alaska in 1900, thirty-three-year-old Luke Carpenter is prospecting for gold. He is buried and frozen alive in an avalanche.

In Woodland Oaks, California, in 1967, his son, Edwin—now sixty-seven—is informed of a recent avalanche in Alaska and of a recent find: his father—alive. Although dad's one hundred years old, he's still thirty-three in looks and outlook. The whole thing, of course, is Top Secret. Hundred-year-old Luke is put in the custody of his sixty-seven-year-old son Edwin and Edwin's thirty-three-year-old son Ken (Luke's exact double, it turns out).

It was a strange, generational-gap show in which Grandpa (age 100) is "younger" than his thirty-three-year-old grandson. Plus, Luke had to adjust to the modern world, as well as make sure he kept his true identity a secret (a military doctor, Colonel Garroway—played by Frank Maxwell—was assigned to look after him). In the first episode, for example, Luke discovered television, and couldn't understand why there were little men pointing guns at him. One thing he couldn't get used to, though, was having a job.

Monte Markham played both Luke and Ken; Arthur O'Connell played Edwin. The show ran on ABC until September 1968, at which time ABC froze the whole thing.

1968–1969

WHATEVER HAPPENED TO 1968–1969?

And so, the drought continued. The old shows were getting older *(Family Affair, That Girl, Bewitched, Flying Nun, Hogan's Heroes, My Three Sons* [still?], *Get Smart!, I Dream of Jeannie, Petticoat Junction,* more *Gomer Pyle, Green Acres,* and *Beverly Hillbillies)* and the new shows seemed a little déjà vu-esque: *Here's Lucy* (we'd had *The Lucy Show* the season before), *Mayberry, RFD* (an update of *The Andy Griffith Show* without, alas, Griffith), and a new rendition of *Blondie,* which had been on before in 1957). So what was new this season? Well,

you had quite a pick—on Tuesday nights you could watch *Doris Day* and *Julia.* Or, on Saturday nights, you could watch *The Ghost and Mrs. Muir.* If they locked you up in your room on, say, a Thursday night, you could watch something called *The Ugliest Girl in Town* (not to be confused with *The Beautiful Phyllis Diller Show,* which was on Sunday nights and was not a sitcom). Or, you had another choice: you could watch the evening news to find out how the war was doing. Either way, it was all about the same number of laughs that season.

OFF-SCREEN

10/12–27 US wins forty-five gold medals in Olympic Games in Mexico City; USSR wins twenty-nine, Hungary, ten.
10/20 Jacqueline Kennedy marries Aristotle Onassis.
11/5 Richard M. Nixon elected President of the United States.
11/15 Roman Catholic bishops defend Pope Paul VI's condemnation of artificial methods of birth control.
12/4 American Medical Association sets new standard of death known as "brain death"; death is reached when it is irreversible.
3/1 Mickey Mantle announces retirement.
3/28 Former President Eisenhower dies of heart disease.
4/23 Sirhan Sirhan sentenced to death for murder of Robert Kennedy.
5/17 Students and members of Berkeley community attacked by police and national guardsmen.
7/20 Neil A. Armstrong becomes first man to walk on moon.

ALSO RANS

The Doris Day Show

After confusing a whole generation of fifties adolescents in the movies, Doris Day went on to do it again, but on TV. Only this time it was not confusion about love and sex; this time it was confusion about format. You'll see why.

During the 1968 season on CBS, she played Doris Martin, the widow and mother of two kids. She's dissatisfied with the big city, and moves to Mill Valley, California, where she lives on her father's ranch and raises her two kids and gets involved in local community affairs. Apparently, Doris became nearly as bored as the viewers did, for in the next season she decided to get a job, and she lands one as executive secretary to Michael Nicholson (McLean Stevenson, later of *M*A*S*H* fame), editor of *Today's World* Magazine. And through that season, the episodes showed her home and working life. (Also in the cast: Rose Marie as Myrna Gibbons, Nicholson's secretary, and Denver Pyle as Buck Webb, Doris' father.)

In 1970—just about when Mary Richards was moving to Minneapolis—Doris and her kids pick up and move back to San Francisco. Her father and handyman Leroy B. Simpson (James Hampton) continue to operate the ranch. Doris now lives at 965 North Parkway (Apartment 207), right over Pallucci's Italian Restaurant (with Kaye Ballard and Bernie Kopell as the Palluccis). Also: Billy De Wolfe played Willard Jarvis, Doris' hot-tempered neighbor. The family also had a sheep dog named Lord Martin.

In September of 1971, Doris must have had amnesia. Suddenly she was single. Suddenly she was a general news reporter for the magazine. Suddenly she had a new boss, Cy Bennett (John Dehner). Suddenly she had a boyfriend (played by Peter Lawford) and later she had another boyfriend (played by Patrick O'Neal). Suddenly she didn't live above—below or beside—an Italian restaurant. And suddenly—on September 10, 1973—Doris went off the air.

The Doris Day Show: *Doris with McLean Stevenson*

The Ghost and Mrs. Muir

Τhis fantasy show—in the tradition of *Topper* and *Mr. Ed*—took place in a haunted house on Schooner Bay, in New England, where Carolyn Muir (Hope Lange) is trying to reconstruct her life after the death of her husband. She is a free-lance magazine writer, and the cottage she's moved into is inhabited by the spirit of its 19th-century owner, Captain Daniel Gregg (Edward Mulhare). The problem, you see, is that Captain Gregg died too soon and didn't get to complete his plans for the cottage. Mrs. Muir and her two cute kids, Jonathan

The Ghost and Mrs. Muir: *Hope Lange*

(Harlen Carraher) and Candy (Kellie Flanagan), and their dog Scruffy disturb Gregg's privacy. The captain tries to scare them off (especially Candy, who's sleeping in his bedroom), but they soon develop an amicable coexistence. Others in the show: Charles Nelson Reilly as Claymore Gregg, the captain's nephew and owner of the cottage; Reta Shaw as Martha, the Muirs' housekeeper; and Dabbs Greer as Noorie Coolidge, owner of the town lobster restaurant. The show ran on NBC until 1969, when it was transplanted to ABC, where it ran another year. Based on the Gene Tierney-Rex Harrison movie of the same name.

The Good Guys

Τhis was yet another sitcom set in Los Angeles, and it ran until January 1970 on CBS. The plot: Bert Gamus (Herb Edelman) and cabdriver Rufus Butterworth (Bob Denver, hot off *Gilligan's Island*, and nine years after *Dobie's* Maynard G. Krebs) were two life-long buddies who pool their resources and buy a diner—"Bert's Place." They are assisted by Bert's wife, Claudia (Joyce Van Patten), and hope for success. Also in the cast: Alan Hale as Big Tom, a truck driver; Toni Gilman as Tom's girlfriend Gertie; and actor/playwright George Furth as Hal.

Here's Lucy *(from left): Lucie Arnaz, Desi Arnaz, Jr., Gale Gordon and Lucille Ball*

Here's Lucy

This was the third and (so far) the last of the Lucy incarnations (*I Love Lucy* and *The Lucy Show* preceded it). This time she was Lucille Carter and she lived at 4863 Valley Lawn Dr. in LA. And she had a job: she was the overzealous secretary to Harrison Otis Carter (she called him Uncle Harry) played by Gale Gordon. He was also her brother-in-law, which made for some madcap situations where they worked—at the Unique Employment Agency ("Unusual Jobs for Unusual People"). None of them could have been more unusual than Lucy herself, whose antics center around the office and her home life with her two kids, Kim and Craig (played by Lucy's Real Life children Lucie Arnaz and Desi Arnaz, Jr.). The show ran on CBS until September 2, 1974, when Lucille Ball retired from sitcomland (in 1979, though, she went to work for NBC as a sitcom scout).

Julia

Not since *Amos 'n' Andy* back in the early fifties had there been a sitcom in which a black person—who wasn't a domestic—played a central character. Then came *Julia*. Starring actress/singer Diahann Carroll, the show was surrounded with controversy when it debuted, but, when audiences became used to new colors on their TV screens, the show settled down to predictable sitcom fare. Here's the story line. In LA, Julia Baker, a nurse with the Astrospace Industries (an industrial-health office), has become a widow when her husband is killed in Vietnam (all this happened before the first episode). She settles down—with a beautiful apartment and an even more beautiful wardrobe—to raise her young son, Corey (Marc Copage). Julia has a part-time mother's helper, a number of boyfriends (including actor Paul Winfield, later star of the film *Sounder*), and even a funny uncle (Uncle Lou, an ex-vaudevillian played by Eugene Jackson.) At work she has to put up with the bark (but not the bite) of Dr. Morton Chegley (Lloyd Nolan, who played the lead role in *Martin Kane, Private Eye*, back in 1951) and fellow nurse Hannah Yarby (Lurene Tuttle, who played Mrs. Clarence Day—Vinnie—on 1953's *Life with Father* and, on another father-show, played the mother of the groom on the 1961 *Father of the Bride*).

Some sample dialogue from the show's first episode—Julia and her soon-to-be boss have this pre-job interview conversation over the telephone:

JULIA: I'm colored. I'm a Negro.

Julia: *Diahann Carroll*

DR. CHEGLEY: Have you always been a Negro, or are you just trying to be fashionable?

Julia lost her job—on NBC, that is—in May of 1971.

Mayberry, RFD: *Ken Berry, Arlene Golonka and Buddy Foster*

Mayberry, RFD

When Andy Griffith left his own series, Ken Berry (playing friendly widower Sam Jones) moseyed into Andy's post in the same show with a new title. His housekeeper, in fact, was Aunt Bee Taylor (Frances Bavier), and Emmet Clark (the fix-it-shop owner played by Paul Hartman) and county clerk Howard Sprague (Jack Dodson) were all back. The producers even gave Sam a son: Mike Jones (played by Buddy Foster). Sam was just like Andy, 'ceptin' he was a full-time farmer and part-time city councilman. In later episodes, Alice Ghostley took over housekeeping duties when Aunt Bee split in 1970. *Mayberry, RFD*, was, for a couple seasons, as popular as *Andy Griffith* (which had been *very* popular), and was still in the Top Twenty when it was canceled as part of CBS's rural-show housecleaning. The show moseyed along until 1971, at which time it went into syndication.

The Queen and I

Funnymen Billy De Wolfe and Larry Storch (Storch had played the assistant schemer, Corporal Randolph Agarn, on *F Troop* three seasons earlier) teamed up to play Oliver Nelson and Charles Duffy in this CBS sitcom all about an aging ocean liner, *The Amsterdam Queen*, whose owners were going to sell her for scrap. But the ship's purser, Duffy, tried to do anything he could to save the boat (not to mention his job). You see, before, he'd done some rather . . . well, unorthodox things to earn a little extra money (like holding Bar Mitzvahs and weddings on the boat when it was docked in port) and so he was quite eager to save it. All of the crew was with him—except First Mate Nelson, who didn't like Duffy, although he never could quite catch him at anything. This midseason entry lasted less than four months before it pulled anchor.

The Ugliest Girl in Town

Listen carefully, because this one takes some explaining: Tim Blair is suffering from a broken heart after his heartthrob, actress Julie Renfield (Patricia Blake) returns to London following the completion of her movie, for which Tim was a talent scout. Then Tim's brother Gene (Gary Marshall), who is a photographer, asks Tim to pose as a girl for some hippie photos he needs. The photos somehow manage to end up in a London ad agency. Mr. Courtney (Nicholas Parsons) is impressed with the photos and wants to do a whole layout with his discovery "Timmie Blair"—Tim dressed as a woman.

So, Tim has finally found a way to be with Julie.

(Why he couldn't be with her dressed as a man is never explained; but it was only 1968, and kinky relationships didn't hit TV until—well, they still haven't). Anyway, Tim goes to London where he finds he's still deeply in love with Julie. He can't leave her. Plus, Gene is in trouble: he's lost 11,000 pounds gambling and he has to pay or else. Tim says he'll stay and help. And so, by day he's Tim; by night he's Timmie. And, by January, ABC canceled the whole thing. Can you blame them?

The Queen and I: *Larry Storch and Billy De Wolfe*

1969–1970

WHATEVER HAPPENED TO 1969–1970?

Well, this is the last season of that disease called Bad TV— for awhile, anyway. We had *Mary Tyler Moore* and *All in the Family* to look forward to, but not for another year. Until then, we could look at the debuts of *The Courtship of Eddie's Father* and *The Brady Bunch*, both of which would be kicking around for a bit. But for the main part, we sat back and watched TV do the strangest things to women in retread shows like more *Julia*, more *Doris*, more *That Girl*, more *Flying Nun*. Plus continuations of *Mayberry*, *RFD*, *Beverly Hillbillies*, *Hogan's Heroes*, and the last of *Get Smart!*, *Petticoat Junction*, *Green Acres*, and—well, you know the rest by heart. The only terrific new entry did rotten in the ratings: *My World and Welcome to It*, loosely based on the life of James Thurber. For the most part, though, it was smarter to watch out for—rather than watch—this year's shows.

OFF-SCREEN

9/22 Willie Mays hits his 600th home run.
10/8 Department of Health, Education and Welfare, it is reported, has blacklisted hundreds of scientists from its advisory panels for offenses such as antiwar statements.
10/15 Millions observe the first Vietnam Moratorium Day.
10/18 HEW bans use of cyclamates in diet foods; later lifts ban for all but soft drinks.
11/26 President signs bill providing for draft lottery.
12/2 Boeing 747 makes first public flight.
2/18 Five of Chicago Seven defendants found guilty.
3/23 National Guard alleviates delays caused by postal workers' strike.
4/7 *Midnight Cowboy* wins Oscar for best film, John Wayne for best actor, Maggie Smith for best actress.
6/13 President Nixon names nine-member commission on campus unrest.

ALSO RANS

The Bill Cosby Show

Richard Allen Holmes High School in Los Angeles didn't have the greatest athletic teams in its league, but it certainly had the best-known and funniest coach—Bill Cosby, post-*I Spy*, who, as gym teacher Chet Kincaid, turned the school's physical education department into the setting for his longest stand-up routine, which ran through 1971 on NBC. Others in the cast: Lillian Randolph (formerly Madame Queen on *Amos 'n' Andy*, and later Sister Sara on *Roots*) as Cosby's mother (replaced the next season by Beah Richards), Lee Weaver as Cosby's brother Brian; Olga James as his sister Verna, and the folks at the school—Sid McCoy as principal Mr. Langford, and Joyce Bulifant (eventually Murray's wife on *Mary Tyler Moore*) as Mrs. Peterson, the guidance counselor. There were also lots of kids, to which Cosby spoon-fed his gentle urban philosophy.

The Brady Bunch

This sitcom preceded its musical neighbors, the Partridges, by one season. It was all about a Los Angeles architect, Michael Brady (Robert Reed), who has three sons: Greg (Barry Williams), Peter (Christopher Knight), and Bobby (Michael Lookinland). He meets (and marries) Carol Martin (Florence Henderson), who has three daughters (see how neatly these things work out on TV?): Marcia (Maureen McCormack), Janice (Eve Plumb), and Cindy (Susan Olsen). Plus a family cat and a shaggy dog named Tiger. They were all wholesome and all-American. They also were crowded; they lived in a four-bedroom, two-bathroom house with their housekeeper, Alice (Ann B. Davis, who was beloved as Schultzy on *Love That Bob*).

Being a typically well-scrubbed family, the situations never became more complicated than Dad becoming upset over the use of the bathroom or the phone (once, he had a pay telephone installed—though never a pay toilet). There were also family camping trips, discussions about Going Steady, and other family fun like Who Broke Mom's Favorite Vase? As a result of all these on-screen scrimmages, the oldest of the child actors, Barry Williams, became a teen idol, receiving about 6,500 fan letters each week in 1971 (he later went on to try out his mouth at a singing career, but failed). Florence Hender-

The Brady Bunch *(from left); Robert Reed, Florence Henderson, Barry Williams*

son later hit the heights of fame with her Wessonality commercial.

They lived on ABC through August 1974. In 1972, that same network made an animated version of the show called *The Brady Kids*. In late 1976, there was a *Brady Bunch* reunion, so well received that ABC installed a *Brady Bunch Hour* on Monday nights in January 1977. It lasted only four months.

The Brady Bunch: *The Brady Bunch, minus mom*

The Courtship of Eddie's Father: *Brandon Cruz and Bill Bixby*

The Courtship of Eddie's Father

Eddie Corbett (Brandon Cruz) may be only seven years old, but he's sophisticated enough to become convinced that his widowed father, Tom (Bill Bixby, pre-*Hulk*), needs a new wife in order to be truly happy. Tom's job as editor of the Los Angeles-based magazine *Tomorrow* keeps him as busy as he cares to be, but Eddie's weekly attempts at matchmaking enmesh his dad in ever more embarrassing situations, all involving beautiful women of Eddie's choice (all somewhat over the age of six). During the show's three years on ABC, Academy-Award-winning actress Miyoshi Umeki appeared regularly as responsible but confused Mrs. Livingston, keeper of the Corbett household; James Komack played "mod" magazine photographer Norman Tinker; and Jodie Foster (lately of *Taxi Driver, Alice Doesn't Live Here Anymore,* and other movies) played Eddie's friend Joey Kelly, while Harry Nilsson contributed the featured song, "Best Friend." Based on the novel by Mark Toby, and a movie, this ABC show left the air in June of 1972.

The Debbie Reynolds Show

They lived at 804 Devon Lane in the suburbs of Los Angeles—he: Jim Thompson (Don Chastain), a sportswriter for the Los Angeles *Sun*—and she: his beautiful and unpredictable wife, Debbie (Miss Reynolds), who longs for a career as a newspaper feature writer. Jim, however, is reluctant to have two newspaper writers in the family, and wants his wife to remain "a loving and beautiful housewife, devoting herself to making her lord and master happy." (Was this 1969 or 1869 . . .?) The screwball stories involve Debbie trying to prove her abilities and achieve her goal, and Jim's attempts to discourage her. It was all very *I Love Lucy*-esque. Instead of Fred and Ethel, though, there was Debbie's sister Charlotte (Patricia Smith, who would go on to play Margaret Hoover on *The Bob Newhart Show* during the 1972–1973 season) and Charlotte's husband, Bob (played by yet-to-become *Happy Days* daddy Tom Bosley). Someone named Bobby Riha played Charlotte and Bob's kid Bruce. This NBC show lasted one season.

The Governor and J.J.

The Governor was William Drinkwater (Dan Dailey, star of many movie musicals) and J.J. was Jennifer Jo

The Governor and J.J.: *Julie Sommars and Dan Dailey*

Drinkwater (Julie Sommars), his twenty-three-year-old daughter and "first lady," who ruled CBS for one-and-a-half terms (through January 1971). J.J. was the curator of the local children's zoo in this unidentified Midwestern town, and spent a lot of time getting her widower father in and out of political hot water. CBS rebroadcast the show as a summer replacement in 1972.

Mr. Deeds Goes to Town

Country hits the city: Longfellow Deeds (Monte Markham), a philosophical country newspaper editor, inherits the multimillion-dollar Deeds Enterprises (after his Uncle Alonzo pops off) and moves to New York. His assistant, whom he has inherited from his uncle, is Tony Lawrence (played by Pat Harrington, Jr., from *Make Room for Daddy* and *One Day at a Time*). Mr. D. spends his time—at least a half-hour each week—adjusting to Manhattan and running his big, powerful business, which, under the helm of unscrupulous Uncle Alonzo, did a lot of Bad; Mr. Deeds tries to get the company to do Good. Longfellow moved back to the country after only four months on ABC. The whole thing was—loosely—based on the 1936 Gary Cooper movie.

My World . . . And Welcome to It

This show—based on "drawings, stories, inspirational pieces and things that go bump in the night" by James Thurber—was a real gem. It had a dedicated audience, but not enough to warrant its success. It took place in Westport, Connecticut, where John Monroe (William Windom) lived in the real and the dream world. He was a cartoonist for *Manhattanite* Magazine and didn't like his job. He was also intimidated by his wife, Ellen (Joan Hotchkiss), and tired of the smartness of kids in general (he was irked by his own, played by Lisa Gerritsen, later Bess on *Mary Tyler Moore* and *Phyllis*). Basically, he was scared to death of life. So he'd retreat to his secret world, where his cartoons would become real and life was great—and he was the king: irresistible to women and a tower of strength in the eyes of men. The show always had John walking into an animated, fantasy world. NBC canceled the show after one season, but CBS bought it and aired it from May 1972 until that September.

The Tim Conway Show

Before he went off and became part of the *Carol Burnett* family, Tim Conway starred in his own sitcom about a pilot (no, not a television pilot—an airline pilot). As oafish, bumbling Timothy "Spud" Barrett, he owned the *Lucky Linda*, a decrepit plane that comprised Triple-A Airlines (Anywhere, Anytime Airline)—along with his cranky partner, Herbert Kenworth (played by Joe Flynn). Located at Crawford Airport in LA, the two are unable to pay their creditors and, with the constant threat of eviction, they try to acquire passengers and maintain their business. This midseason entry was soon replaced itself by CBS.

To Rome with Love

Walter Brennan and John Forsythe both starred in this one, which lasted two big seasons on CBS. Here's the poop: Widower Michael Endicott (Forsythe), is hired to teach at the American Overseas School in Rome. He brings along his daughters—Alison, Penny, and Pokey, and, during the second season, their crotchety farmer-grandfather, Andy Pruitt (Brennan). Aunt Harriet (Kay Medford) lived with them for a while (thirteen weeks during the first season, to be exact), all the while begging them to return to Iowa. They all end up living in Mama Vitale's (Peggy Mondo) boarding house. The series spent time showing us how they adjusted to Rome before it was deported.

To Rome with Love: *Joyce Menges with guest Vito Scotti*

1970–1971

All in the Family

The Mary Tyler Moore Show

The Odd Couple

OFF-SCREEN

9/18 Jimi Hendrix dies of drug overdose at age twenty-seven.

10/4 Janis Joplin dies at age twenty-seven.

10/13 Angela Davis seized on charges of kidnapping, murder and conspiracy.

1/12 Reverend Philip F. Berrigan and five others indicted on charges of conspiracy.

1/25 Charles M. Manson and three women convicted in California of Tate murders of 1969.

3/23 Frank Sinatra announces decision to retire.

3/29 Lieutenant William L. Calley, Jr., convicted of premeditated murder of at least twenty-two Vietnamese at Mylai.

5/3–5 Police arrest over 12,000 in antiwar protests in Washington, D.C., most charges dropped.

6/12 Patricia Nixon marries Edward Finch Cox at White House.

6/30 Twenty-sixth Amendment lowering voting age to eighteen for all elections becomes law.

FRONT RUNNERS

ALL IN THE FAMILY

Aw, chee whiz . . .
—ARCHIE BUNKER

When *All in the Family* finally hit the screen in January 1971—with its surprising repertoire of racial slurs, bedroom humor, and bathroom jokes—the network and the producers expected, as Archie Bunker himself might have said, "The manure to hit the sewer." Instead, nothing happened. Dozens of operators were on duty at CBS headquarters to field the angry calls. They didn't field; they filed their nails. It was almost as though no one were watching.

Almost no one was watching. The Bunker bunch didn't make an impact until the summer reruns—almost unheard of since, during the summer of 1971, everybody was either at the beach or burning down the ghettos. Obviously a few of them stayed home to watch *All in the Family*.

Whether you liked the show or not, you couldn't deny that it was probably the most revolutionary and influential sitcom ever on television. Besides spawning two successful spin-offs *(Maude* and *The Jeffersons), All in the Family* brought subjects and issues into the family that had never been mentioned on television before (and sometimes not even at home in Real Life). After years of silly, spaced-out humor on sitcoms, *All in the Family* came along and dealt with relevant issues from women's liberation to wife swapping. And it didn't just talk about them (the way the news shows had been doing), it *did* them. Or didn't do them, depending on the moral tone of the episode.

The Bunkers were a new kind of sitcom family: they didn't spend twenty-four minutes worrying about getting Edith's misplaced wedding ring out of the PTA bake-off cake before the judges tasted it and swallowed it. No: *All in the Family* had more important things to deal with as it took a swing at (and sometimes hit us over the head or below the belt with) moral issues specific to the seventies: revolution and revelations, liberation and libation, and a range of sexual problems from impotency to too much potency. *All in the Family* was the first sitcom that, through comedy, forced the audience to re-evaluate some of its own situations.

While Dick and Pat were running the White House, Archie and Edith gave America a new—and much more

Archie Bunker	Carroll O'Connor
Edith Bunker	Jean Stapleton (1971–1979)
Gloria Stivic	Sally Struthers (1971–1978)
Mike Stivic	Rob Reiner (1971–1978)
Lionel Jefferson	Mike Evans (1971–1975)
George Jefferson	Sherman Hemsley (1973–1975)
Louise Jefferson	Isabel Sanford (1971–1975)
Henry Jefferson	Mel Stewart (1971–1973)
Irene Lorenzo	Betty Garrett (1973–1975)
Frank Lorenzo, Irene's husband	Vincent Gardenia (1973–1974)
Bert Munson, Archie's friend	Billy Halop (1972–1977)
Tommy Kelsey, the owner of Kelsey's Bar	Brendon Dillon (1972–1973); Bob Hastings (1973–1977)
Justin Quigley, a friend of the Bunkers'	Bert Mustin (1973–1976)
Jo Nelson, Justin's girlfriend	Ruth McDevitt (1973–1974)
Stretch Cunningham	James Cromwell (1974)
Stephanie Mills	Danielle Brisebois (1978–)
Harry	Jason Wingreen (1977–)
Hank Pivnik	Danny Dayton (1977–)
Murray Klein (on *Archie Bunker's Place)*	Martin Balsam (1979–)
Veronica	Anne Meara (1979–)
Mr. Van Ranseleer	Bill Quinn (1979–)
Barney	Allan Melvin

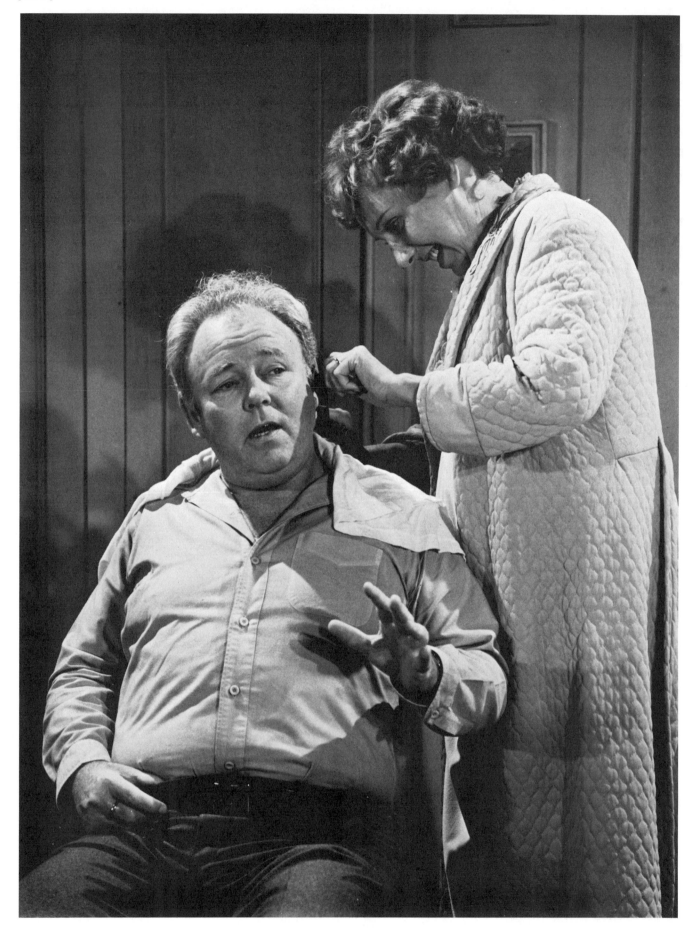

realistic—First Family. It had the perfect postrevolution formula: a fifty-year-old bigoted blue-collar father (Archie Bunker) pitted against a Polish perpetual liberal student (son-in-law Michael Stivic), Archie's "dingbat" gold-hearted wife (Edith Bunker), and his modern-minded daughter (Gloria Bunker Stivic). The comedic clashes revolved around the generational and political differences between the four of them.

They didn't get into madcap situations so much as play verbal (and sometimes physical) Ping-Pong off one another, using the Issues of the Day as a ball. And just as in the world surrounding our TV sets, no one ever really won.

We knew, right at that first episode, that this show was going to be something very different . . . when we heard that flushing sound coming from the second floor of their Queens home. No one went to the bathroom during the first twenty years of television. On *All in the Family*, the Bunkers had a toilet with a very forceful flush that we heard often. That was only the start of ripping open the boundaries. Through the years . . . Edith goes through menopause (several years before an attempted rape). Mike gets a vasectomy. Gloria (who has a miscarriage) makes friends with a transvestite ("She was a nice fella," Archie says) who is killed (after which Edith gives up religion). Mike carries a purse. Mike becomes impotent. A Jewish activist is blown up in his car outside the Bunkers'. Sammy Davis, Jr., kisses Archie in the living room, a year or so after a black family moves in next door. Archie nearly has an affair. Archie is exposed as a compulsive gambler. Edith leaves Archie. Gloria poses in the nude. A relative is revealed to be a lesbian. Gloria gives birth. Gloria suspects Mike of being unfaithful. Archie gets mugged. A guest dies in the bedroom. And everyone grows older.

Based on a British television comedy, *Till Death Do Us Part*, starring Alf Garnett, *All in the Family* took a long time coming. The brainchild of producer Norman Lear, Archie Bunker—who started TV life as a hard-hat portrait of the Agnew era—was modeled after Lear's own father. Fred Silverman (then a CBS vice-president) believed in the show and quietly placed it on the air as a midseason replacement.

The premiere episode contained the following spirited exchange between Archie and son-in-law, Mike:

ARCHIE: You are the laziest white boy I ever met.
MIKE: You wanna call me lazy, okay. But you don't have to put down a whole race just to do it!
ARCHIE: I wasn't putting down a whole race.
MIKE: Yes you were. You said I was the laziest white boy you ever met.
ARCHIE: That's right. You.
MIKE: Meaning that the blacks are even lazier.
ARCHIE: Wait a second, wise guy. I didn't say that. You're the one who said that. I never said your blacks were lazy. I never said that at all . . . of course, their systems is geared a little slower than ours, that's all.

That first show also included black neighbor Lionel Jefferson's confrontation with Archie, in which Lionel tells him their long friendship will continue "in spite of racial differences."

A disclaimer preceded the show: ". . . it seeks to throw a humorous spotlight on our frailties, prejudices, and concerns." Ratings were poor the first time out—"a flop," the New York *Post* deemed it—and there was some question as to whether it would be renewed. But Silverman insisted on rerunning it during the summer, where it picked up a sizable audience. It had been pitted against two movies and followed *Hee Haw*; then, for its second season, it was moved to the coveted spot leading into *The Mary Tyler Moore Show*. Fireworks.

Schoolteachers began writing to CBS, requesting *All in the Family* study guides. A whole new collection of words called Archie Bunkerisms (including the term "Archie Bunker," which has become a prototype for the pigheaded reactionary) invaded our language: "Dingbat" (which Archie called Edith), "Meathead" (which he called Mike), and "Stifle yourself" (which Archie would shout at anyone who was saying something he didn't like).

Not since *Amos 'n' Andy* had so many malapropisms blasted across the screen as Archie would yell, "You're taking it out of contest," "It's just a pigment of your imagination" and "Smells like a house of ill refute, if you ask me." Most startling, though, was that Archie's conversation was spattered with references to Hebes, Japs, fags, coons, polaks, chinks, micks, spicks, and others. He called a spade a spade.

It was for that reason that the show became controversial. In September 1971, during the start of its second season, liberal Laura Z. Hobson, who authored the novel *Gentlemen's Agreement*, wrote an article in the New York *Times* lambasting Lear and his show for a number of indiscretions, among them it's "dishonesty" in using terms like "hebe" and "coon" instead of the "real slanders" of "kike" and "nigger." Plus, she said, the show fosters and shows approval for bigotry and racism. The *Times* received a huge bundle of mail, agreeing with Hobson by a 4-to-1 margin.

All this bickering would have been lost on Archie and Edith who, you can be sure, did not read the Sunday *Times*. If he had heard the controversy about the show, down at Kelsey's bar, Archie would have never watched *All in the Family*, and he wouldn't have allowed Edith to watch either.

If she had watched, Edith would have liked Edith. Archie would have loved the Archie character—"Now there's a fellow with his head glued on straight," he might have said. In fact, that personal identification was the show's major appeal: it was a show with someone for every one. The key to its success was that it took topics

Trapped: Archie in an elevator with assorted "ethnics"

that had been too hot, and it tickled and teased us with them. Poverty, war, sex (even death and taxes, the Two Unmentionables)—these were not subjects we were used to laughing at. *All in the Family* gave us permission to laugh, which took some of the pressure off. Plus, the show reflected Real Life. Watergate happened and—wham!—within several weeks, Mike and Archie were arguing about it. Many of the episodes were typically topical.

But the show was fun too. Carroll O'Connor and Jean Stapleton were marvelous actors, and could evoke an audience response through the raise of an eyebrow or the droop of a lower lip. They seemed to practically dance through their characterizations each week, as if Archie and Edith's spirits had been tattooed onto the actors' souls.

The show also created a whole new inside-out logic based on Archie's absurdisms. Some examples:

☐ "Goddamn it, I don't want to hear any more!" Archie yells about Mike's Watergate taunts. Edith becomes upset at his use of "Goddamn it," so Archie explains: "God—that is your most popular word in the Bible. And dam—like you dam your rivers or something, you know, when somebody does something bad, God dams it. So there it is: Goddamit. A great word in the Bible." ☐

☐ Edith is having a very difficult time going through menopause, something which Archie doesn't understand and doesn't want to hear about. So he shouts at her: "If you're gonna have your change of life, have it right now! You got exactly thirty seconds . . . change!" ☐

☐ When Edith gives up religion, Archie reminisces about how church always produced "a beautiful, peaceful look on your face—like you was chloroformed or something." ☐

☐ In an early episode, Archie gets all dressed up to write a letter to Nixon, which he begins, "Dear Mr. President, your honor, sir:" ☐

☐ Another time—one of many—Archie defends Nixon. "Well, I'll tell you one thing about President Nixon. He keeps Pat home. Which was where Roosevelt should have kept Eleanor. Instead, he let her run around loose

until one day she discovered the colored. We never knew they were there. She told them they were gettin' the short end of the stick and we been having trouble ever since." ☐

The show's impact seemed to go on and on. Two Atlantic Records albums of excerpts from the program's soundtrack were released, followed by an LP of Archie and Edith singing together. Popular Library published *The Wit and Wisdom of Archie Bunker* and, among other books, one was marketed by a religious publishing company all about how "Christian" Edith Bunker was. Five episodes of the TV show were published as plays.

In 1974, German TV came out with a similar show called *One Heart and One Soul;* the Archie character was a Hitler-like man named Adolf Tetzlaff. The show was run on the BBC. But the biggest accolade came in 1972 when Archie was run for President—commercially, at least. Mugs, T-shirts, posters, and stickers were all manufactured and sold. Many people still feel that Archie would have been a better President than the man who won.

Over the years, all was not always love, peace, and harmony off-screen either. Sometimes it looked like the *Family* might be splitting up. Carroll O'Connor and Sally Struthers both went through much-publicized strikes for

Neighborly hula-hooping: The Jeffersons, Irene Lorenzo and Edith

The Family: Mike and Archie, Edith and Gloria

more money and at one point it looked like they each might be written out of the script. In fact, at the beginning of one season, several episodes in which Archie was missing at a convention were written because the writers weren't sure if contract negotiations would ever go through and O'Connor would come back to the show. If not, they might have just had him murdered at the convention and the show would have gone on.

In 1974, there were more problems when O'Connor wouldn't cross a picket line (of air conditioner maintenance men), and the shooting schedule had to be changed until the strike was ended. The next year, Struthers missed four episodes of the show because of contractual squabbles, when she sued to get out of her contract. "I was terrible," Struthers later said. "I was not happy at the time and dumped all my anxieties, hostilities, and frustrations on everyone else." There was a well-publicized blow-up between her and O'Connor when he told her off on the set. She fled the set, weeping. "Did you hear what he said?" Struthers said at the time. "I thought of him as my father." Father or not, Struthers ended up making about $10,000 per episode. O'Connor won out with a yearly $2 million contract. "But I don't make nearly as much as stars on some other, less highly rated shows," he said.

Stapleton and Rob Reiner (son of *Dick Van Dyke's* Carl Reiner) didn't have such troubles. Except, said Stapleton: "The show causes me to behave like a dingbat in real life." Reiner used to walk down the street and hear shouts of "Meathead." "I hated that," he said.

Other problems: In 1973, a writer sued for $6.5 million in damages, saying that *All in the Family* was his idea. The case was quietly (and probably expensively) settled out of court. A man who drew a cartoon show called *All in the Family* took CBS to court to try to enjoin the network from using the title. In 1972, the show's cast wanted to perform at the Ohio State Fair; they were turned down for their booking. The reason: they were "the wrong type." Archie would have liked that one. In 1976, when The Family Hour viewing practices were going into effect, Lear switched *All in the Family* from Saturday nights because he refused to tone it down. Lear

then became the plaintiff in a lawsuit against the family viewing hour.

At the end of the 1974 season, Gloria announced that she was pregnant (the commercials for that episode were Geritol and Preparation H). The baby, Joey Stivic, was born around Christmas of 1975 (a year after the Stivics had moved out of Archie's house and into their own, next door). Right away, The Joey Stivic Doll ("the first physically correct male doll") was manufactured and sold. A police officer's twins, Jason and Justin Draeger, were chosen to play Joey when they were nine days old. Their parents sued the production company, and their salary was upped to $225 for each appearance (and a share of the Joey doll). The boys were always driven to the studio in a limousine.

But childbirth wasn't a big enough event in the Bunker household to put Archie's and Mike's bickering on hold. At the show's start, it was the liberal against the conservative. As the seventies wore on and the factions weren't so clearly defined, neither were Archie and Mike. Archie stayed the same, but Mike changed. He got his hair cut, he graduated from college, he got a job—in a sense he "straightened out" and became more like Archie, so Archie had to look harder to find ways to antagonize him.

In one touching sequence, Mike can't stand it

Man to man: Archie talks to a retarded delivery boy (guest Richard Masur)

anymore. He's just had an ugly fight with Archie and runs into the kitchen, complaining to Edith—always the rock of truth—that Archie mistreats him.

"Do you wanna know why Archie yells at you? Archie yells at you because Archie is jealous of you. You're going to college. Archie had to quit school to support his family. He ain't never going to be any more than he is right now. Now you think that over."

The audience applauded.

One episode of the program got a standing ovation—a special hour-long edition in which Edith is attacked by a rapist (David Dukes) in her living room, a sitcom first and a truly moving and frightening episode.

EDITH: *(as rapist tugs at her zipper):*   Wouldn't you like some coffee?
RAPIST: I don't drink coffee.
EDITH: I've got Sanka.
RAPIST: I want you *(starts to kiss her).*
EDITH *(resigned):*   But couldn't we do this without kissing?

Edith's character changed over the years. Said Jean Stapleton: "The show mirrors the times, and people do change. Edith has changed because the world comes in and touches her. She's smarter and more aware of women's rights and she even stands up to Archie now. The part of Gloria has changed drastically. Who would have dreamed in the early days that she would force Mike, her husband, to have a vasectomy? If we were still doing the same things we used to do in the show, we'd look ridiculous. Archie still *talks* bigotry, but he gets slapped down more and more. That's the way life progresses."

The way TV life progresses is that shows get canceled. At the end of the 1977–1978 season, Lear tried to cancel the show because he wanted Out to make movies. Rob Reiner went off to ABC to work on projects; Sally Struthers to work up some new series ideas for

Church Social: Archie tries to con Father Majeskie (Barnard Hughes) when Edith drops a can of peaches on his car

Stephanie Mills: Archie meets his new "daughter," who's been abandoned on his doorstep

CBS. Carroll O'Connor and Jean Stapleton decided they didn't want to quit, but rather, would stay on and go it alone. Said O'Connor: "I didn't want to be the one to kill the show—my image has never been that good in the press."

At first, Lear wouldn't let them use the name *All in the Family.* "The entity we call *All in the Family,* the song that leads into it, that particular location in Queens, will be gone. But if Carroll and Jean want to do a show called Archie and Edith Bunker, I wish them a long and happy life." And so, for the 1978–1979 season, the duo reappeared—but Lear had backed down for, even though his name was no longer connected to the show, the song, location, and the title were all back with Archie and Edith—as well as an eight-year-old abandoned girl, Stephanie Mills, who was now living with them.

That last show with the entire family was a particularly hard one to shoot. Mike and Gloria were moving to California, where he had a job waiting as an associate professor. Said one writer: "That last scene of the show required one hundred rehearsals because the stars weren't in any shape to do it. Carroll O'Connor finally broke down and Rob Reiner had to leave." Lear got so upset, he had to wear dark glasses to cover his reddened eyes. The laugh-track on that show is not so much chuckles as sobs, sniffs, and handkerchief-rustling.

At the end of that season, the Smithsonian Institution immortalized the program by putting Archie's and Edith's armchairs in their archives of national treasures. It was the least they could have done. With an unequaled five-year rating as Number One, *All in the Family* was television's most popular sitcom.

On Thursday, December 21, 1978, Jean Stapleton announced that, finally, she'd had enough. "I think I've managed to keep my identity pretty well separate from Edith's, but if I keep on in the role, people will never think of me as anyone else. It's time for me to move on."

And so she did. But unlike the season before (when Mike and Gloria left the show and Archie and Edith went on alone), Edith's departure meant that it really was the end of *All in the Family*.

But not quite. It was the old *All in the Family*-is-dead; long-live-*All in the Family*. Because the show got a name transplant. In the 1979–1980 season, Archie came back—without Edith and Mike and Gloria (although they did make an occasional guest visit)—in *Archie Bunker's Place*. More—and less—of the same. You see, two seasons before, Archie finagled Edith into letting him mortgage their house to buy up his favorite haunt, Kelsey's Bar. He had re-named it Archie Bunker's Place. In 1979, he added on a restaurant, but his partner Harry wanted no part of the scheme, so he's bought out by Murray Klein—who happens to be Jewish. "A Jew and a Gentile don't have a Chinaman's chance," Archie fumes. Many viewers thought that *AITF*—without the supporting cast—wouldn't have a chance either. But, even opposite the Nielsen-happy *Mork and Mindy*, it did quite well, pushing *M&M* right off the Sunday night schedule and back to Thursdays.

Shortly afterward, the writers pushed Edith Bunker right off the show. Even though Jean Stapleton was no longer a regular cast member, Archie was still married to Edith and her presence lingered over each episode. In April 1980 Norman Lear announced that he was killing Edith—literally (but only off-camera; Stapleton said she refused to have anything to do with recording the occasion for posterity). The reason for her demise: the writers wanted to invent some new love interest for Archie in order to add some life to the decade-old sitcom. In anticipation of a feminist outrage for killing off Edith, Lear donated $500,000 to promote the Equal Rights Amendment.

But even after *All in the Family* wasn't called *All in the Family* anymore, the show continued to live on, even besides the countless reruns. Why? It was more than the new vocabulary—"Meathead," "Dingbat," and the rest—and it was more than the resurrection of the old vocabulary—"mick," "spick," "coon," and the rest. It was a whole new consciousness that the show brought to television. It taught us that even comedy could be taken seriously, that sitcoms didn't just have to be about a zany couple who gets trapped in elevators (even when Archie was trapped in an elevator, you can be sure it wasn't with a nice bunch of white middle-class Protestants). *All in the Family* brought television viewers their first substantial comedy. That small screen which we looked into for years finally looked back at us and became a mirror. Thanks to *All in the Family*, television will never be the same.

Territorial Imperative: The Smithsonian gets His and Her Chairs, plus Rob Reiner, Sally Struthers, Norman Lear, Jean Stapleton

THE MARY TYLER MOORE SHOW

LOU: *Call me Lou.*
MARY: *Okay, Mr. . . . Lou-u.*

Before the actual filming had begun, the producers were scouting locations in Minneapolis for their heroine's house. Finally they came across one they liked—a white wooden gingerbread Victorian mansion—owned by a humanities professor at the University of Minnesota. They asked her if they could film the exterior for a new program CBS was doing. Thinking it was for a documentary, the teacher agreed. The program turned out to be *The Mary Tyler Moore Show,* such a big hit that Twin Cities tour buses began driving past the professor's home each day, with binoculared spectators gawking and shouting. And presently people, spotting the famous house, started ringing the doorbell at all hours of the day and night, asking for Mary, Rhoda, and sometimes even Phyllis.

Several years later, the *MTM* folks returned to Minneapolis to shoot some more exterior shots of Mary's house. Bug off, said the professor. And so, when they returned the next day to shoot anyway, she had hung banners out of the windows that said "Impeach Nixon." Right, in fact, out of Mary's window.

So they used old footage of the house, and eventually, Mary moved to a high-rise.

No matter that the professor didn't like the program. Her students did. *The Mary Tyler Moore Show,* in fact marked the return to TV of a generation who had given up after *The Flying Nun* flew off and Beaver left it to someone else. These kids had given up on TV for rock and roll and relevance. A generation reared on the tiny tube had discovered movies—Films—for the first time. And then, suddenly one Saturday night in 1970: *The Mary Tyler Moore Show,* starring Dick Van Dyke's ex-wife. It was funny, it was intelligent, it was moving. What a relief from the sixties.

MTM (as it came to be called) didn't so much give us a new set of characters as it gave us a new set of friends: Mary, Rhoda, Ted, Lou, Murray, Phyllis, Georgette, Sue Ann—these were people we not only spent time with on Saturday nights, but thought about during the week. *The Mary Tyler Moore Show* made it respectable to stay at home on Saturday nights.

In its gentle way the show created a quiet revolution. You see, Mary Richards was single. And she didn't mind. She didn't chase after men. In fact, she'd often rather spend a night in with best buddy Rhoda than go out on another boring date (she once calculated that 90 percent of all her dates were bad). And when Mary did date, she *dated.* (One night, she didn't even come home.) "Don't forget to take your pill," her mother once told her father. "I won't," Mary answered by mistake.

It would have been as easy for Mary to have become a pill as to take one. The producers had originally wanted to make her a divorcée—a TV first—a woman with a past. No way, said CBS. "Americans don't like New Yorkers, divorced people, and Jews." (The show went on to give them all three.)

Mary Richards	Mary Tyler Moore
Rhoda Morgenstern	Valerie Harper (1970–1974)
Lou Grant	Edward Asner
Ted Baxter	Ted Knight
Murray Slaughter	Gavin MacLeod
Phyllis Lindstrom	Cloris Leachman (1970–1975)
Bess Lindstrom	Lisa Gerritsen (1970–1975)
Gordon Howard (Gordie), the station weatherman	John Amos (1970–1973)
Ida Morgenstern, Rhoda's mother	Nancy Walker (1970–1974)
Martin Morgenstern, Rhoda's father	Harold Gould (1970–1974)
Georgette Franklin Baxter	Georgia Engel (1973–1977)
Sue Ann Nivens	Betty White (1973–1977)
Dotty Richards, Mary's mother	Nanette Fabray
Walter Reed Richards, Mary's father	Bill Quinn
Marie Slaughter	Joyce Bulifant (1971–1977)
Pete, a news team staff member	Benjamin Chuley
Edie Grant, Lou's ex-wife	Priscilla Morrill (1973–1974)
David Baxter	Robbie Rist (1976–1977)

They thought to make Mary a widow (like *Julia* and Doris Day) but, as one of the producers said, "We don't want to kill off another man to get Mary on the air."

And so she became single. CBS wanted to give her the obligatory boyfriend, to make another *That Girl*. Said the producer: "You know, where they had Ted Bessell hanging around to prove that Marlo wasn't a dyke." (Ironically, Ted Bessell would appear in several episodes as Mary's boyfriend; he didn't last long.)

The producers got their way because Mary became a Possible Person. She was not dopey or zany. She wasn't even young. She was in her thirties and there was, on that first episode, the suggestion that she had lived with a medical student back home. Nobody on television had lived with' a medical student back home. Not even Marcus Welby.

Mary was like someone you met and liked. She cared about her job (which eventually grew into a career) at the WJM-TV newsroom, where she started as associate producer. She cared about her friends and family. She was nonthreatening and vulnerable. It was nice having her over on Saturday nights. If only she could have stayed longer than thirty minutes.

And the people on the show—they didn't talk at each other like on the other sitcoms; they had conversations. And none of them ever got involved in Antics. The com was still there, the sit was what was different. On an early episode, Mary invited some people over for cocktails. They thought they had been invited for dinner. Mary started to panic. What to do? There was nothing in the refrigerator except a carrot. (*Flashback:* Lucy would have climbed down the fire escape, broken into a restaurant, and stolen a turkey.) Not Mary. She simply apologized to her guests and explained that, sorry, but there must have been some sort of misunderstanding. And that was that. Sitcom's first moment of truth.

The first episode of the show introduced the characters and set up the format for years to come.

Mary has just moved to Minneapolis, and Phyllis, an old friend, is showing her an apartment in Phyllis' building. Mary loves it. Phyllis opens the drapes to show her the view—and there is Rhoda Morgenstern—"that dumb awful girl who lives upstairs"—cleaning the windows. "This is my apartment! get out!" Rhoda hollers.

MARY: You think I'm some kind of a pushover, don't you?
RHODA: Right.
MARY (*halfheartedly mustering strength*):   Well, if you push, I might just have to push back—hard.
RHODA: Come on—you can't carry that off.
Mary (*shrugs sheepishly*): I know.

The next day, Mary goes to WJM-TV to apply for a secretarial job, which she discovers is filled. So she applies for associate producer. During the job interview,

Rhoda and Phyllis: Valerie Harper and Cloris Leachman

gruff Lou Grant, the producer, asks her if she wants a drink as he pulls a bottle from his lower desk drawer.

MARY: No, thanks.
LOU: Oh, come on . . .
MARY: Well, all right. I'll have a Brandy Alexander.
LOU: How old are you?
MARY: Thirty.
LOU: What religion are you?
MARY (*hesitates*):   Mr. Grant . . . I don't know how to say this: you're not allowed to ask that when someone's applying for a job. It's against the law.
LOU: Wanna call a cop? Are you married?
MARY: Presbyterian.

At the end of the interview, Mr. Grant smiles at Mary: "You got spunk."

She beams: "Well . . . yes . . ."

He growls: "I hate spunk."

He offers her the associate producer job (which pays $10 a week less than secretary). "If you can get by on fifteen dollars less a week, I'll make you a producer."

"No," Mary smiles, widening her eyes and pointing a finger at him. "Associate producer is all I can afford."

The next morning there is a knock at the door. It's Rhoda (who left New York City because she couldn't find an apartment).

"How do you come off looking that good in the morning? Who'd you get that nightie from—Tricia Nixon?"

That night, Mary's boyfriend—who has strung her along all those years—comes to town. She hopes he'll propose. There is a knock on the door, and it's Mr. Grant, drunk. "Ah *ha*," she says, so that's why she got the job; he's here to make a pass at her.

No he isn't. His wife is out of town and he misses her. He wants to type a letter to her. Mary's boyfriend comes in. They talk and Mary realizes that their relationship is all over. She's got to start a new life for herself. She tells him goodbye.

"That was Rhoda": Ida Morgenstern and Mary

In the Bronx: Mary and Rhoda visit New York for sister Debby Morgenstern's wedding.

"Take good care of yourself," he says.

She pauses and says softly: "I think I just did."

A bittersweet ending for a sitcom. And different from anything anyone had seen on TV: a single woman, frankly-thirty, who wanted her independence, and, in fact, "took care of herself" by eliminating her boyfriend from her life. Plus: a bitchy landlady, a gruff, hard-drinking boss, a "Jewish and New Yorker" neighbor (whom she would become best friends with). Funny people with heart. All very new for TV sitcoms.

But *MTM* wasn't really situation comedy anyway; it was character comedy. The humor grew out of the way people dealt with the situations, and out of the characters' distinct personalities. Mary Richards, for example, was not very funny; her reactions were funny: a shrug, a tentative finger pointed, a special stance that looked like she was the Tower of Pisa, her gentle indignation that took a long time to develop, sizzling and steeping, finally erupting in a tiny, "Oh, Mr. Grant!"

She always called him Mr. Grant, even though everyone else called him Lou. But she couldn't; it was like calling your father by his first name. Lou Grant was a gruff grizzly bear with a golden-soft core. He had a special rapport with Mary that spanned more than the father-daughter relationship. Once toward the end of the show they tried having an affair. Mary even called him Lou. It didn't work out, and Mary went right back to calling him Mr. Grant.

Once when Lou spotted his son-in-law out with another woman, he beckoned Mary into his office (the only private office WJM had) because he was dejected and needed someone to talk to.

LOU: Oh . . . Mary . . .
MARY: I know . . .
LOU: Oh, Mary, Mary, Mary . . .
MARY: I know, I know, I know.
LOU: Oh, boy . . .
MARY: Umph . . .
LOU: Brother . . .

MARY: I know, I know, I know.
LOU (*relaxed now*):   Thanks, Mary. That should do it.

Together, Mary and Lou headed the "family" that was *The Mary Tyler Moore Show*. Rhoda is like Mary's sister; Murray like the mother-hen, clucking over Mary; Lou is the authoritarian, often tyrannical (but golden-hearted) father. Ted is the child. He is vulnerable and needs the most protection. Even though they all make fun of him, there is a bond of affection among them that includes Ted.

Earnest and amiable, Murray is Mary's buddy, her confidant. He thinks she is terrific—or "Ta-*riff*ik," as he would say. He is the scarecrow to her Dorothy. (Murray had been in love with her right from the first season.) For the most part, Murray's function around the newsroom (besides writing the copy for the Six O'Clock News) is to hurl one-liners at Ted and Sue Ann, and to be supersupportive of Mary. But occasionally he has his own situations: once he becomes attracted to another woman and nearly gets involved with her. Another time he is depressed when he discovers that his dreams of being a literary giant are over and he is destined to be just a hack writer. Another time he sells his services to Ted and ghost-writes what turns out to be an award-winning article that Ted gets credit for.

Silver-haired and golden-voiced Ted Baxter—"the silver fox"—wears too much cologne. You can smell it right through the TV screen. Ted is a pompous ass. Ted doesn't walk—he struts, just like a rooster. Ted is selfish and stupid and bumbling and humorless, but we like him (mainly because we know we're going to laugh when he's around; unlike the other characters on the show, we laugh *at* Ted, not *with* Ted). His dressing room is filled with photos of himself, as well as videotapes of his newscasts for instant and not-so-instant replays. He's too insecure to take a vacation for fear his replacement will be better than he is (and, of course, the replacement is). Ted makes a million bloopers. As Rhoda once said: "I take a shower during the Six O'Clock News, or sometimes I vacuum or go to the store. That's the best thing about Ted Baxter—you can do all those things and not feel you're missing anything."

"Hi, guys," Ted would say, and then saunter into his dressing room to get ready for the newscast. Ted's the type of anchorman who reads a news story on the air about an impending strike and then, off the air the next minute, hears Murray talking about the same strike. "Strike—what strike?" Ted asks.

Once Ted has to testify in court.

TED: It's a great experience to appear before a federal grand jury. I told them I was the best newsman in the country.
MURRAY: You didn't!
TED: I had to. I was under oath.

Ted is certain that Albania is the capital of New York State.

"It all started," Ted would say (anytime, anywhere), "in a five-thousand-watt radio station in Fresno, California, a sixty-five-dollar paycheck, and a crazy dream. . . ."

Once Ted was summing up his life: "I'm a lucky guy—I mean, life has been good to me. I've got a good job, good health, a good wife, and a fantastic barber."

Ted's girlfriend (and later his gently dizzy wife) is Georgette Franklin. They meet at one of Mary's disastrous parties (Mary was renowned for her bad parties; once she had secured Johnny Carson to what she was sure would finally be a great party—but there was a power failure and all the lights went out). At the party, Georgette (who was then a window dresser at Hempel's Department Store with Rhoda) meets anchorman Ted. "Are you covering this?" she asked in that tiny voice of hers.

The party was for Rhoda, who was going to move to New York, but had changed her mind. In 1973, she

The Single Life: Murray moves in with Ted when his wife won't have another baby.

would eventually move to New York with her own show, get married, divorced, and canceled. But before she made the transfer and transformation, Rhoda was a schlepper, a pudgy girl, an unmarried misfit who was oral compulsive—food went in her mouth, wisecracks came out. "I've got to lose ten pounds by eight-thirty," she once said before a date. Rhoda had a mother named Ida, whom she always had trouble getting along with. Rhoda would constantly mimic the advice her parents gave her. She became confused about sex from reading the books her parents gave her. "I ended up thinking I had to swim up the Columbia River. . . ." Where Mary was a Gamma Gamma Delta, Rhoda was a "Sharkette" (the ladies' auxiliary of the Sharks, she explained) back in The Bronx. She moved to Minneapolis "because I figured in this weather I'd keep longer." She was man-crazy. When Phyllis' daughter Bess tells Rhoda that she's got a crush on Howie, captain of the eighth-grade soccer team, Rhoda snaps: "Is he married? Sorry—force of habit. . . ."

Says Rhoda: "When we used to play Mommy and Daddy when I was a kid, I always played Mommy's unmarried sister." Once after looking through Mary's family album, Rhoda says: "Could I have it? I'd like to leave it in my apartment and have people think it was *my* life."

Rhoda was on a perpetual diet. Once she picked up a piece of candy on Mary's desk: "I don't know why I'm putting this in my mouth—I should just apply it directly to my hips." (This was something that Valerie Harper actually said when she was dieting and it eventually ended up in the show.)

Rhoda and Valerie Harper started losing weight together. "Want any fruit?" Mary asks her. "Naw," Rhoda responds. "I'm still on my diet—got any wax fruit?"

Mary confronts Rhoda about her self-effacing attitude. "I don't say that *I* am nothing." Retorts Rhoda: "Sure, but you don't have to worry about someone beating you to it."

And then came Rhoda's transformation, in which she stopped joking about herself and started joking about the losers—"the feebs," she called them—that she's dated (like the exterminator who picked her up in his van with a huge roach on the outside).

Even after Rhoda turned into a swan, landlady Phyllis was always there to cut Rhoda down. Once, Mary had been complaining to Phyllis about receiving obscene phone calls—and then the phone rings. "Would you answer that, Phyl?" Mary asks. Phyllis picks up the phone.

"You're right," she says, "it *is* an obscene phone call—it's Rhoda." Phyllis went on to explain her feelings toward Rhoda: "We really like each other—except as people."

And that's exactly how we felt about Phyllis. She's selfish, affected, pretentious, a pseudo-intellectual. Once she's rummaging through her closet and she tries on an old fur coat. "Ah, I miss this," Phyllis sighs, "but ecology is more important than vanity." Responds Mary: "I guess I never realized that Orlon was an endangered species."

When Rhoda and Phyllis were getting ready to leave the show to start up their own respective series, a new character was written in (at first they thought they'd give Mary a steady boyfriend to replace Rhoda, but it didn't work out). Instead, Mary got an adversary in the newsroom: Sue Ann Nivens, the toxic, tart-tongued (with the emphasis on the "tart") Happy Homemaker who had come to WJM thirteen years before when she replaced Chef LeRoy. Her shows had themes like "What's All This Fuss About Famine?" and "Salute to Fruit." She had a smile that seemed to be tattooed to her face, and could switch moods faster than she could fricassee a chicken.

She was man-crazy and always had the hots for Lou. Once they are watching a documentary on Mary's television set.

SUE ANN: There's something wrong with the picture.
LOU: Try the vertical hold.
SUE ANN: Later, Lou, later.

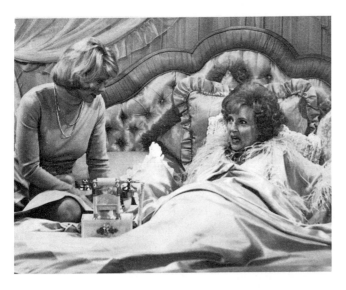

Sister Act: Sue Ann's sister visits The Happy Homemaker, in her vibrating bed.

Once Sue Ann is chatting away to Mary's new good-looking date and, without missing a beat, she adds, matter-of-factly, "Incidentally, you are the most gorgeous hunk of flesh I have ever seen."

She is always poking fun at Mary's apparent purity. Once Sue Ann gives Mary a food sculpture. "I know!" Sue Ann says sweetly, "Why don't you put it in your bedroom? I'm sure you must need something in there to relieve the tedium."

Before she presents the sculpture, she tells Mary to close her eyes. Says Murray: "It's all right, Sue Ann. She's seen you without makeup before." Sue Ann gives a low chuckle, fondles Murray's bald head, and coos: "Oh

"Oh, no, Lou!": Ed Asner and Ted Knight

Murray, I just hope *my* mind's still active when I'm your age. . . ."

Another time, after Murray has zinged her with a remark, she simply laughs and strokes his head: "Oh, Murray, you're so lucky—other men get dandruff. You get waxy yellow build-up." Once at a party: "Oh, Murray—where did you ever find a party hat made of skin?"

The remarks that Murray made (and everybody else thought) were comebacks to things Sue Ann would say, such as: "I was lying in bed last night and I couldn't sleep, and I came up with an idea—so I went right home and wrote it down."

It's when all these people get together to interact that the show blasts off. A classic episode is "Chuckles Bites the Dust," by David Lloyd, a 1975 show that has gone on to become the best-known of the 168 episodes that were filmed.

The scene opens in the newsroom. The circus is in town and Ted wants to be grand marshal. But Lou says no.

LOU: My anchorman isn't marching down the street with a chimp. It tends to give him an undignified image.
TED: Lou, please! It won't give me an undignified image.
LOU: I was talking about the chimp.

Lou sticks to his decision, and Chuckles the Clown, who hosts the kiddie show, gets the job. One night while Ted is doing the newscast Lou comes in, stricken. Says a dazed Lou: "Chuckles . . . Chuckles the Clown is dead. It was a freak accident. He went to the parade dressed as Peter Peanut—and a rogue elephant tried to shell him."

TED: Stop trying to cheer me up, Lou. I mean, it's funny, but it's in bad taste.

Ted "wings" an obituary on the air.

TED: Chuckles the Clown died today of . . . um, died today a broken man . . . I'd like to think that somewhere up there tonight . . . behind those pearly gates . . . a celestial choir of angels . . . is sitting on whoopie cushions. . . .

The next few days disintegrate into bad jokes about Chuckles' death:

LOU: Lucky more people weren't hurt. Lucky that elephant didn't go after anybody else.
MURRAY: That's right. After all, you know how hard it is to stop after just one peanut. . . .
MARY (annoyed): Why is everybody being so callous about this? The man is dead. And it seems to me that Mr. Grant and I are the only ones in this whole place who are showing any reverence.

At this point Mr. Grant comes out of his office laughing hysterically at Murray's joke. "Can't you imagine the insurance claim: 'Cause of death: a busted goober.'"

Lou explains that "It's a release, Mary. People need that when dealing with a tragedy. Everybody does it."

"I don't," she replies.

MURRAY: Aw, come on, Mair. We're not laughing at his death. We all liked him and we're sorry.
SUE ANN: Mary, dear—don't the circumstances strike you as being the least little bit . . . bizarre?
LOU: After all, the guy died wearing a peanut suit, killed by an elephant.
MURRAY: Yeah—born in a trunk, died in a trunk.
MARY: Okay. Forget what he was wearing! Suppose he hadn't been dressed as a peanut—would it still be funny?
MURRAY: It could have been worse—he could have gone as Billy Banana—and had a gorilla peel him to death.

At the funeral the next day, the whole clan assembles in the mortuary chapel.

LOU: Not much of a crowd here.
TED: I know. If it were my funeral, this place would be packed.
MURRAY: That's right, Ted. It's just a matter of giving the public what they want.
LOU: I wonder which ones are the other clowns.
MURRAY: You'll know soon. They're all going to jump out of a little hearse.
MARY: Murray—enough is enough. This a funeral. Somebody has died. It's not something to make jokes about. We came here to show respect—not to laugh.
MURRAY: I'm sorry, Mary. You're right. No more jokes.

And with that, Reverend Burke stands up to deliver his eulogy. Everybody is very solemn as he starts his sermon. But when the Reverend mentions Aunt Yoo-Hoo, Mary has to stifle a laugh. And then the reverend goes on: "Mr. Fee-Fi-Fo would always pick himself up, dust himself off, and say: 'I hurt my foo-foo," Mary again stifles a laugh; the others in the row glare at her.

Once again, Reverend Burke speaks: "From time to time we all fall down and hurt our foo-foos." Mary tries to hide her hysteria. The other people in the chapel turn to look at her.

REVEREND: And what did Chuckles ask in return? Not much—in his own words: "A little song, a little dance, a little seltzer down your pants."

(Mary bursts out into embarrassing laughter. Everyone turns to look, including the minister.)
REVEREND: Excuse me, young lady . . . yes, you . . . would you stand up, please? (Mary reluctantly rises.) You feel like laughing, don't you? (Mary gestures futilely.) Don't try to stop yourself. Go ahead, laugh out loud. Don't you see? Nothing could have made Chuckles happier. He lived to make people laugh. He found tears offensive, deeply offensive. He hated to see people cry. Go ahead, my dear—laugh.

And, of course, Mary bursts into tears.

The casting of *MTM* was as brilliant as the writing. Instead of comics, actors were hired for the roles. Ed Asner, for example, had been respected for his work on the New York stage and for his Brecht and Shakespearean roles in particular. Cloris Leachman went on to win an Academy Award for her role in *The Last Picture Show*, as the coach's lonely wife. Valerie Harper had been in Paul Sills' Story Theater and was an alumna of Chicago's famed improvisational theater company, Second City. Ted Knight (his real name: Tadewurz Wladzin Konopka) was known for his voice-over work. (During the show's peak, Knight threatened to quit. Over money? No. He'd grown weary of playing a one-dimensional bozo. So the producers made him a multi-dimensional bozo—they enlarged his role and gave his character more texture, as well as a girlfriend who seemed to help humanize him.)

But, obviously, they even could—and did—play comedy. Because they were skilled actors, they brought reality and believability to characters who could have become mere caricatures (characters like Ted and Georgette emerged so lifelike because of the tenderness the actors and writers put into them).

Mary Tyler Moore, of course, had been best known prior to her own show as Laura Petrie, the wife of Dick Van Dyke on his beloved sitcom. After that, she made a number of unsuccessful movies (among them one in which she played a nun opposite Elvis Presley, and *Thoroughly Modern Millie*). Then she tried to star in a musical version of Truman Capote's *Breakfast at Tiffany's* called *Holly Golightly*, which producer David Merrick closed out of town "to spare the audience enormous boredom." After a special with Dick Van Dyke, CBS asked her to develop a special of her own. She formed a production company (MTM Productions, with a meowing cat as its mascot) which came up with *The Mary Tyler Moore Show*, vindicating Moore, who had been humiliated after the flop of *Holly Golightly*. (MTM went on to produce other shows beside *MTM*, among them *The Bob Newhart Show, Paul Sand in Friends and Lovers, We've Got Each Other, The Tony Randall Show*, as well as the four *Mary Tyler Moore Show* spin-offs, *Rhoda, Phyllis, The Betty White Show*, and *Lou Grant*.) After *MTM* went off the air, Moore returned in two ill-fated variety shows in 1978–1979. In 1980, she scored a huge personal success in the Broadway play, *Whose Life Is It, Anyway?*

According to the cast members, it was Mary Tyler Moore who held the show together. She never hid out in her dressing room, but was always on the set dispensing encouragement and support, just as Mary Richards would have done. "I'm not an actress who can create a character," she once said during the run of her sitcom. "I play me. I'm scared that if I tamper with it, I might ruin it. My forte is not being funny, but reacting in a funny way to those around me."

Moore kept her private life private. She was neat and always punctual (nearly always; she was late for a rehearsal once in 1974). Said Valerie Harper: "Mary Tyler Moore's wholesome, but not too wholesome. I mean, for example, she likes a great big glass of cold milk—to wash down her birth control pill."

It was only after reading articles about the significance of her show in its realistic depiction of a modern woman "that I've really begun to have a sense of how important the show's been."

Four months after *MTM*'s premiere, a new and radical sitcom called *All in the Family* came on CBS. That show is credited with "revolutionizing" television (and indeed it did make enormous headway for progressiveness on the tube). But *MTM* is not to be slighted. It was the first adult program (that's right; it was really a *program*, whereas *All in the Family* was a *show*). Whereas *All in the Family* painted pictures of its characters in black and white and dealt with moral issues, *MTM* concerned itself not with issues at all, but with the problems of being a person living with other people in living color. *MTM* was the first television program that told the truth. It was the first sitcom in which the characters lived in the Real World, not a dream world. *The Mary Tyler Moore Show* raised sitcoms to an art form. *MTM* was the first sitcom that was also literature.

And it was the first show in which the characters changed just like the audience did. Lou gets divorced and watches his wife remarry. Phyllis' husband has an affair, and she discovers her brother's gay. Rhoda goes from fat to thin, from sad to glad. Mary herself becomes more assertive and confident. And everyone gets older.

After seven seasons—with 43,000,000 people watching it (that's a fifth of the American population)—Mary

Midwives: Georgette gives birth in Mary's apartment.

Tyler Moore (and *Mary Tyler Moore*) decided on a little mercy killing. The show could have run for years more, but she had learned something from the way Dick Van Dyke had ended his show: leave while you're on top. Plus, there was the little matter of making more money when the show was sold to syndication and transcended to rerun heaven.

In that last season, after Chuckles' funeral, the gang all got together (sans Rhoda and Phyllis, who had split for their own shows) and pondered their own funerals.

Here was Ted's vision:

TED: I'd like a real fancy funeral if I were going to die.
LOU: What do you mean "if"?
TED: I'm not going to die.
MURRAY: Why not? How else are you going to be reunited with your brain?
TED: No, I'm not going to die. See, I'm into this thing where if I ever get sick—real sick—like I'm about to go—they take me away and freeze me. Then, two or three hundred years from now when they find a cure for whatever it was that was wrong with me, then they'll just unfreeze me.
GEORGETTE: That's terrific, Ted. Maybe when you come back, you won't complain so much about my cold feet.

Said Sue Ann about her death: "I want to be cremated and have my ashes thrown on Robert Redford."

Lou had a little different picture: "I don't want anybody to make a fuss. When I go, I just want to be stood outside in the garbage with my hat on."

And Mary added this wistful note: "I don't really care. I just don't want an organ playing sad music."

And Mary (and *Mary*) got just the kind of funeral she would have wanted. There was a lot of speculation as to

Anchormen: Ted meets Walter Cronkite

how they would actually end the show, what the final episode would be like. (One speculation had Mary and Lou getting married. They would turn off the lights and Mary would murmur, "Oh, Mr. Gra-ant!")

But that last mournful episode had the same ironic twist as the rest: a new owner buys the station and fires everybody—except Ted.

Everybody is bunched together in the newsroom, holding on to each other to literally hold themselves together. Lou whispers in a cracked voice that holds back his tears: "I treasure you people."

And then it's time for Mary's last words, which she speaks softly and simply: "I thought about something last night: what is a family. And I think I know. A family is people who make you feel less alone and really loved. Thank you for being my family."

And thank you, Mary, for being ours.

THE ODD COUPLE

On November thirtieth, Felix Unger was asked to remove himself from his place of residence. That request came from his wife. Deep down he knew she was right. But he also knew that someday he would return to her. With nowhere else to go, he appeared at the home of his childhood friend, Oscar Madison. Sometime earlier, Madison's wife had thrown him out, requesting that he never return. Can two divorced men share an apartment without driving each other crazy?

That's the way *The Odd Couple* began, week after week, for five years, and of course the answer each week was No.

Felix Unger and Oscar Madison lived together at 1049 Park Ave., Apartment 1002, in Manhattan. Theirs was the ultimate in mixed marriages. Oscar was dumpy and disorganized and oral. Felix was prissy and compulsively neat and anal-retentive. For Oscar's birthday one year, Felix bought him a lint brush. Felix and Oscar might have seemed like just roommates, but in fact they were as much husband and wife as Archie and Edith, Samantha and Darrin, Lucy and Ricky, and any of sitcomdom's other mismatched couples.

The show starred Tony Randall (Felix) and Jack Klugman (Oscar), both veterans of TV from the early days. Klugman had appeared in over 400 shows before this; he starred in the 1964–1965 *Harris Against the World* (part of the trio of ninety-minute comedies that made up *90 Bristol Court*). In 1963, he won an Emmy for his role in "The Black List," an episode of *The Defenders*. Although Randall had been a guest star on several series, his role as Felix was his first in fifteen years since he had played English teacher Harvey Weskitt on the popular *Mr. Peepers*.

The Odd Couple was interesting—not just because it was interesting, but because of the behind-the-scenes goings-on that occurred from 1970 until 1975, when Oscar and Felix were evicted by ABC. Randall and Klugman had a marvelous chemistry going between them, and they both felt the same way when they first saw Neil Simon's *The Odd Couple* on Broadway in 1965—they loved it.

The sitcom and the Broadway comedy shared the same name—but there were differences. Felix wasn't a photographer, as in the TV series; he was a TV newswriter. That was changed because it gave Felix more "movement" on the series, according to the producers, and put him in more active situations. Oscar was always a sportswriter for the New York *Herald*.

Also: in the play, both Felix and Oscar had children who lived with their wives. No way, ABC said. Added Randall: "The ABC Standards and Practices says that divorced people don't have children. In the play, the fact that the men had children placed the beam of heartache under the structure." But ABC stood firm; children were not to be in the show because they might, God forbid, be poignant, not funny. And so, no children.

It's interesting that, across the dial on CBS that same season, the producers of *The Mary Tyler Moore Show* had wanted their heroine to be a divorcée. "Audiences

Felix Unger	Tony Randall
Oscar Madison	Jack Klugman
Police Officer Murray Grechner	Al Molinaro
Speed	Gary Walberg (1970–1974)
Vinnie	Larry Gelman
Roy	Ryan McDonald (1970–1971)
Dr. Nancy Cunningham	Joan Hotchkiss (1970–1972)
Cecily Pigeon	Monica Evans (1970–1971)
Gwen Pigeon	Carol Shelley (1970–1971)
Miriam Welby	Elinor Donahue (1972–1974)
Myrna Turner	Penny Marshall (1971–1975)
Gloria Unger	Janice Hansen (1971–1975)
Edna Unger	Pamelyn Ferdin;
	Doney Oatman
Blanche Madison	Brett Somers Klugman

won't tune in to see a divorced woman," CBS told them. Apparently, ABC felt, audiences *would* tune in to see a divorced *man* or—better yet—two divorced men. Anyway, later in the series, Klugman and Randall did get their way, and the characters of Edna, Felix's daughter, and Leonard, his son, were eventually added.

Klugman and Randall were no strangers to the play. They were both buddies of Danny Simon, Neil's brother, about whom the play was written. (He was Oscar.) And both Klugman and Randall had been in the play. Randall had first played Felix opposite Mickey Rooney on stage in Las Vegas, and thereafter for two summers at the Drury Lane Theater in Chicago. Klugman had replaced Walter Matthau (who, along with Art Carney, had originated the roles) on Broadway in 1966. He also played Oscar in London for one year, winning several British acting awards.

The first episode on September 24, 1970—notable mainly for its exceedingly noisy laugh-track—was called "The Laundry Orgy," and was rather typical of the shows to follow for the next five years. Oscar has made a date with Gwendolyn and Cecily Pigeon (played by Carol Shelley and Monica Evans, who also played the roles of the two daffy upstairs neighbor English sisters in the stage and movie versions). Felix reminds Oscar that it's poker night, a weekly ritual. The players arrive and Felix and Oscar try unsuccessfully to break up the game. No luck. When the girls arrive, the players finally allow Oscar to take their dates out. Instead, Felix insists that they take the sisters downstairs and all do the laundry together.

Neil Simon wasn't wild about the series. After its premiere, he was quoted as saying that he hated the show, but felt the basic plot could sustain itself—"that is, provided they don't carry the fastidiousness of Felix too far. Belaboring that point could wear it out."

At midseason, low ratings prompted ABC to move the show to 9:30 on Friday nights, where it fared better. The show, however, was never a big success—in fact, it was always only marginally successful. It wasn't until reruns that it became the hit it is.

The first season, *The Odd Couple* garnered itself some publicity when Klugman and Randall started mouthing off about the show's overzealous canned laughter: "It's an atrocity!" Randall exclaimed. And so, in March of 1971, ABC let them conduct an experiment: there would be no laugh-track for one episode, and before it began, and afterward, Randall gave a short speech, asking for viewers' written comments about the lack of laughter. Mail response came in at twenty bags— 50,000 letters—voting 4 to 1 in favor of getting rid of the laugh-track altogether. ABC wasn't impressed; the executives said they had expected the people who didn't like laugh-tracks to be more highly motivated to write in than those who did. However, it wasn't totally ineffective. Starting during the show's second season, it was filmed—

à la *Mary Tyler Moore*—in front of a live audience, so at least the laughs got out of the can.

This episode shows the way things usually worked on *The Odd Couple*: Felix comes home and finds a pregnant girl sleeping on the sofa. He wakes her. "The doorman let me in. I'm looking for Oscar," she explains. Oh, Felix thinks—what trouble is Oscar in now? But it's really Oscar's niece Martha. Oscar comes in.

OSCAR: It's been a long time.
MARTHA: Ten years. *(She starts to laugh.)*
OSCAR: What's so funny?
MARTHA: You were wearing the same shirt.

She explains that her husband is in Germany. Oscar offers to let her stay in his room. "No, No!" Felix screams, "Don't even look at his room—it could affect your child!"

Martha explains that she's in New York because she wants to have her baby by natural childbirth in a motel in the Bronx "where Phil and I honeymooned—not in an antiseptic hospital." Oscar is upset. Not Felix, who simply stares at him. "I'm warning you, Felix," Oscar brays, "at least blink."

Oscar takes Martha to see his girlfriend, Dr. Nancy Cunningham, who says that "there are psychological factors that could make home delivery more desirable." "Home delivery," Oscar sputters, "is for newspapers— not for babies." He's just not wild about the idea of his niece giving birth in a hotel. "The first thing that baby sees is not gonna be a bellhop from the Bronx—it's gonna be a doctor."

After much havoc, Martha agrees to go to a hospital, but ends up giving birth in Oscar and Felix's living room. Felix, of course, goes through sympathetic labor pains; when the baby is finally born, he exclaims, "We did it!"

Klugman and Randall loved working together and often boasted about the "real ensemble feeling we have on the set." In an unusual arrangement, both were partners in the business end of the show (rare for stars), so they had somewhat more control over their show than most stars do. They both said that they spent the first day of rehearsals "repairing the script." Said Klugman: "We tear the script apart. We take out all the jokes and put in character. The only reason we put in any jokes is for that rotten canned laughter . . . I hate it. . . ."

"I repair the script," Randall said, "to make sure that I remain a kind of male Jewish Mother, manipulating others as hysterical people do." Klugman agreed: "In the play, Oscar is really a sensitive man. His sloppiness is merely neurotic." He wanted to get more of that sensitivity into the scripts. "Anyway," he added, "you ought to see the scripts—we tear them apart like we were doing *King Lear*."

Oscar and Felix buy a Japanese restaurant: Tony Randall and Jack Klugman

In the fall of 1972, producer Gary Marshall explained why so few guest stars were used on the show. "When you find two men who can really deliver material, you go with it." He was later to change his tune when a number of guest stars made their way through Apartment 1002.

And then they gave Felix a girlfriend, played by Elinor Donahue of *Father Knows Best* fame (strangely enough, on *The Odd Couple*, Donahue played Miriam Welby—as in Marcus Welby, her old TV dad's new name). After *FKB*, she played Andy Griffith's girlfriend on that show.

This episode led off the 1972–1973 season: Gloria (Felix's ex-wife, played by Janice Hansen), is paired with Oscar by a computer-dating service when he registers under the name of André la Plume. Felix is jealous, even though he has nothing in common with his ex-wife anymore (and has lovely Elinor as his girlfriend). It all—surprise, surprise—works out fine. (That same season saw the addition of Oscar's ex-wife, Blanche Madison, played by Brett Somers, Klugman's real wife. Klugman and Somers later split up because she didn't like his gambling. And life imitates art.)

That summer, when shooting the series was over for the season and episodes were being rerun, Klugman and Randall hit the road and went on a nationwide tour with the original stage version of *The Odd Couple*, as sort of a change of pace for them.

When they returned for the 1974–1975 season, the first show got rid of Penny Marshall, who had played Oscar's secretary, Myrna Turner. (Penny Marshall was the producer's sister and left for a part as a regular on *Paul Sand in Friends and Lovers* [she played a friend], which didn't score well in the ratings game. She later did better as Laverne on *Laverne and Shirley*.) They disposed of Myrna by marrying her off to her boyfriend, played by guest star Rob Reiner (they were married in

Real Life; Reiner was already at the time playing Mike on *All in the Family*.)

That was also the year of the Energy Crisis, when companies were going on four-day work weeks and the nation was turning off its lights to conserve electricity. *The Odd Couple* was no exception. In response to LA Mayor Tom Bradley's plea for energy conservation, the cameraman and the lighting supervisor cut the use of electricity in the show by 40 percent by reducing stage lighting by 100,000 kilowatt hours each week and compensating by lens adjustments. The system was then adapted to (and adopted by) other series.

Many viewers and critics thought the roles of Oscar and Felix were perfect typecasting. Klugman wouldn't disagree: "Oscar is me and I'm Oscar. All I gotta do is act natural. I could drink booze all afternoon, have a couple of beers with dinner, wash down the meal with wine—and still go onstage and handle the role of Oscar with no sweat. It's not like having to assume the role of some character who's totally unlike me in real life."

Randall loved—adored—opera and would actually sing Italian opera while shooting, "as a way of relieving tension, I guess." It would later be edited out. His love of opera extended to the scripts as well: Guest opera star Marilyn Horne played Jackie (Horne's real-life nickname), a shy singer/secretary who can't make herself sing in front of strangers. Randall had a field day as president of "the local opera company." Jackie/Horne falls in love with Oscar, who brushes her off by telling her he only has two weeks to live. Then he's honest with her and tries to instill her with confidence. He does, and she becomes a small-time prima donna.

The show often centered around the fellows' buddies, who'd convene for regular poker nights—Murray the cop, Speed the compulsive gambler, meek Vinnie.

Oscar stayed single, but Felix finally got married—not to Miriam, but to his ex-wife, Gloria. In the final season, they reconciled, and in the last episode Felix

Good Housekeeping: Oscar greets Felix's daughter, Edna.

moved out to remarry her. Oscar returned to his apartment—and burst out for joy in finally being able to live alone—and messy.

Said Klugman of his relationship with Randall: "We have our own interests—mine, horse racing; his, opera. When he finds a horse that can sing *La Traviata*, and I find a baritone who can run seven lengths in one-tenth of a second, then we'll have something of common interest."

They did have something of common interest: the load of money they both made from *The Odd Couple*. In syndication, the show has run in eighty-one cities and in over 100 overseas markets. Klugman and Randall made more money from the show in reruns than they did when it was first aired. In some cities, like New York, it has played as many as three times a day, with two episodes running back-to-back. They became rich men. "I began in television in the fifties," Klugman has said. "In those days, we got five dollars or ten dollars a show. We figured we were just doing somebody a favor. Now there are unions and the prices today are quite different."

Klugman, post-*Odd Couple*, vowed he'd never make

another sitcom—"Nothing could top what we did in *The Odd Couple*"—but did sell his own (unsuccessful) sitcom pilot at the end of 1977 (people change their minds). Before that, he starred in the TV drama *Quincy, M.E.* Randall tried his hand at a couple of versions of the funny and well-done *Tony Randall Show* in 1976–1978—in which he played a widowed judge—but the show didn't fare well with the audience.

One of the dilemmas of being in a successful sitcom, actors keep telling us, is that even when the shows aren't being filmed anymore, the actors are typecast for life. Who could think of Lucille Ball as anyone else but Lucy? Or Eve Arden as anyone but Miss Brooks? Dick Van Dyke will always be Rob Petrie. And Tony Randall and Jack Klugman—no matter what other parts they'll play—always seem to carry Felix and Oscar with them—especially since *The Odd Couple* is still playing daily (sometimes as many as three times a day) to remind us.

But look at it this way: if Randall and Klugman can't find anything else to do, they need only turn on their television sets and watch themselves on *The Odd Couple*. Why not? Everybody else watches it.

ALSO RANS

Arnie

Broadway star Herschel Bernardi (he'd originated the lead in the musical *Zorba*, and was one of many to replace Zero Mostel in *Fiddler on the Roof*) finally got a sitcom of his own. It was called *Arnie* and it wasn't half-bad. In fact, many felt it was half-good. Here was the premise: Arnie Nuvo was perfectly happy being a loading dock foreman at the Continental Flange Company. Then, one day, he found himself promoted—to the head of the Product Improvement Division. A definite change of collars for the man. And lots of new challenges, responsibilities, and problems. The networks, however, did give him one leftover blue-collar friend, Julius (Tom Pedi), but for the most part, Arnie stuck with his new own-kind, including his family (his wife Lillian was played by Sue Ann Langdon), his wonderful hefty secretary Felicia (Elaine Shore), and his boss and new contemporaries. The show ran on CBS for two seasons, at first preceding *The Mary Tyler Moore Show* on Saturday nights.

Arnie: Herschel Bernardi and Roger Bowen

Barefoot in the Park

Neil Simon's play and the movie that followed it spawned this series in blackface—in which Paul and Corie Bratter resume their struggles with the difficult first year of their Manhattan marriage. Paul (Scoey Mitchell), a young attorney with the firm of Kendricks, Kein and Klein, and his wife (Tracy Reed) survived for only half a season on ABC, proving once again that weekly coast-to-coast visitors in a small Greenwich Village apartment will put too much of a strain on any new marriage. Also on the show: Corie's busybody mother, Mabel (Thelma Carpenter) and her arduous suitor, Honey Robinson (Nipsey Russell); Paul's boss, Mr. Kendricks (Harry Holcombe); and the building's super, Mr. Velasquez (Vito Scotti).

From a Bird's Eye View

Coffee, tea, or . . . sitcom. Here we have the adventures of two young stewardesses—Millie Grover (played by British musical star Millicent Martin) and Maggie Ralston (Pat Finley)—who both worked for an international airline based in London. Millie—oh, that Millie—was always trying to help people; boy, was she good-natured. But, well, you know, every time she tried, something invariably went wrong. But, thank goodness, Maggie—her levelheaded American friend—would get Millie out of those terrible predicaments. NBC got them both out of their predicament as quickly as possible, and grounded them after a few months' test-fly.

The Headmaster

Hot off the success of *The Andy Griffith Show*, Mr. G. tried a new series—*The Headmaster*—which never got to the head of the class. It was expelled from CBS after only two and one-half months. Griffith played—albeit briefly—Andy Thompson, the headmaster of Concord, a small, private coed high school in California. The sitcom showed how he dealt with the personal and academic problems of the students in a tender way. Also in the show: Claudette Nevins as his wife, Margaret, and Jerry Van Dyke (Dick's brother) as Jerry Brownell, the athletic coach. The show's theme song, "Only a Man," was written by Dick Williams.

Make Room for Granddaddy

After Danny Thomas' supersuccessful *Make Room for Daddy* (1953–1964), they thought they'd try it again. This sitcom—sort of a footnote to the original—is most interesting as an update of the original characters. Here goes: Rusty (Rusty Hamer), now twenty-three, has just been discharged from the Army (honorably, of course) and is in medical school—and married to Susan MacAdams, a colonel's daughter. Linda (Angela Cartwright) is now seventeen. Terry (who originally had been married to Pat Hannegan) turns up here married to Bill Johnson. She has a six-year-old son, Michael—a terror—and she is planning to join her husband in Japan, where he is stationed. The kid is supposed to stay with Bill's parents, but Danny and Kathy connive to get him to stay with them. He does. Other cast members—Hans Conried, Sid Melton, and Roosevelt Grier as (respectively) Uncle Tonoose, "Uncle Charley" Helper, and Rosey the accompanist—are around for good measure. Guest stars included Lucille Ball, Frank Sinatra, Bob Hope, and Milton Berle. This ABC show, however, didn't fare so well, and the network made room for a new show when it knocked this one off the air in September 1971.

Nancy

This NBC sitcom—which lasted a half-season—took place in Center City, Iowa. Veterinarian Adam Hudson (played by John Fink) meets and falls in love with pretty Nancy Smith (Renne Jarrett), who just happens to be the daughter of the President of the United States. They get married on November 5, but their lives are more public than private, thanks to nonstop surveillance by Secret Service agents Turner (William Bassett) and Rodriguez (Ernesto Macias). Also in the show: Celeste Holm as Abby Townsend, Nancy's chaperone. The President (played by an actor named Lyndon Johnson) was never shown.

Nanny and the Professor

Remember *The Farmer's Daughter*? This was more of the same. On 10327 Oak St. in LA, Professor Harold Everett (Richard Long) lived with his children Hal, Butch, and Prudence, plus a sheepdog named Waldo, Myrtle the guinea pig, et al. Everett was a widower and taught math at Clinton College. Also living there: Phoebe Figalilly—"Nanny"—who mysteriously appeared when the professor needed help around the house. And a good thing too—she was his fifth housekeeper in a year; all the others had quit in frustration because of the chaos (Hal and his chemistry set; meddlesome Butch; piano prodigy Prudence and her one piece she played nonstop). Fortunately, Phoebe was an uncanny nanny. She seemed to cause all these happenings around the house although, like some of her TV sisters, she was neither a witch nor a magician; somehow she had the ability to spread love and joy. Not to ABC, apparently, who canceled the program in December of 1971.

The New Andy Griffith Show

He should have been satisfied with the old. But, no, Andy Griffith just kept persevering. After he retired from his classic *Andy Griffith Show*, he went into movies, and then into *The Headmaster*. When that bombed earlier in the season, he tried with this one playing . . . Andy Sawyer, mayor of a small rural Southern town—hey, does this sound familiar? It's true. Andy'd been working in a government job in the state capital when he got the word: the mayor of Greenwood was retiring and they wanted Andy to take his place. So he moved back, with his wife, Lee (Lee Meriwether), and their two children to take the job. Also on the show: their housekeeper, Nora (played by Ann Morgan Guilbert, who'd been Millie on the old *Dick Van Dyke Show*). *The New Andy Griffith Show* (which was a midseason entry on CBS's roster) was canceled after four months. What's ahead for us? *The Newer Andy Griffith Show*?

The Partridge Family

"Come On, Get Happy" was the theme song for this musical sitcom all about a show-biz pop music group who all shared the last name Partridge. They were: widow

The Partridge Family: *Shirley Jones surrounded by the kids*

Shirley Partridge (Shirley Jones), Keith Partridge (David Cassidy), Laurie Partridge (Susan Dey), Danny Partridge (Danny Bonaduce), Tracy Partridge (Suzanne Crough), and Chris Partridge (Jeremy Gelbwaks, later replaced by Brian Foster).

They were just an ordinary fatherless family until Danny, age ten, organized the family into a rock group, recorded a single and talked agent Reuben Kinkaid (Dave Madden) into hearing their demonstration tape of "I Think I Love You," which led to a recording contract. And fame. This well-scrubbed family traveled around the country in a colorful old painted school bus (very Mod), and the series took them on the road, as well as showed them at home in California.

Also in the cast: Ricky Segall as Ricky Stevens, the neighbor's four-year-old son, who joined the cast in song in 1973; Alan Bursky as Alan Kinkaid, Reuben's nephew; and Simon, the family dog. Besides singers David Cassidy (who went on to become a teen idol—soon replaced by his half-brother Shaun—soon replaced by . . . well, you know how that goes) and Shirley Jones (who was Cassidy's Real Life stepmother), there were four professional singers who supplied the background vocals on the Partridges' songs (both on the show and on record).

The show ran on ABC until September 7, 1974. There was a spin-off series—*Partridge Family: 2200 AD*—an animated cartoon series that ran on CBS from 1974 to 1975. The original *P.F.* was loosely based on the Cowsills, a real recording family.

1971–1972

The New Dick Van Dyke Show

Me and the Chimp

Sanford and Son

OFF-SCREEN

9/11 Nikita Sergeevich Khrushchev dies in Moscow at the age of seventy-seven.

9/13 Nine hostages and at least twenty-eight prisoners killed when about 1,000 state troopers, sheriff's deputies and guards regain control of Attica Prison in Attica, New York, held for four days by 1,200 inmates.

11/13 Mariner 9, an unmanned US spacecraft, goes into orbit around Mars; is the first man-made object to orbit another planet.

2/21 President Nixon arrives in Peking to begin a week-long visit to China.

3/12 The First National Black Political Convention ends after adopting a political agenda and voting to set up a permanent body to provide leadership for black political and social action.

3/13 Clifford Irving and his wife, Edith, plead guilty to selling publisher fake autobiography of billionaire Howard Hughes.

3/22 The US Senate completes congressional action on a constitutional amendment to be ratified by the states guaranteeing equal rights to women.

4/13 First players' strike in the history of baseball ends in its thirteenth day.

5/15 Governor George Wallace seriously wounded in an assassination attempt at a shopping center in Laurel, Maryland.

6/17 Five men seized while trying to install eavesdropping equipment in Democratic National Committee Headquarters in Washington, D.C.

FRONT RUNNER

SANFORD AND SON

> FRED: *I still want to sow some wild oats!*
> LAMONT: *At your age, you don't have no wild oats—you got shredded wheat!*

Poor Norman Lear. Well, *rich* Norman Lear, actually. He just couldn't create and produce a sitcom without its being heaped with criticism, controversy, and crisis. If he had produced *Ozzie and Harriet*, somehow, somewhere, some group of White Anglo-Saxon Protestants would have protested the show, alleging that *Ozzie and Harriet* was giving boring, bland Middle Americans a bad name (which it, of course, was, but that's another story).

Sanford and Son was no exception. It was the simple story of a man and his son—who happened to be black, who happened to live in the ghettos of LA, who happened to be junk dealers, who happened to argue, scream, and carry on with each other like crazy men. There was enough ammunition here to keep special interest groups, anxious networks, and the stars themselves in conflict for years.

Fred and Lamont Sanford were junk dealers—no, not in the narcotics sense, but in the collectible sense. Their house and front yard were littered with the leftovers from other people's lives: an old refrigerator, statues, old lampshades, vacuums, cushions, and other assorted debris, all carted around in a slow-starting pickup truck that said "Sanford and Son" on the side.

To the left of the front door was a sign that warned "Beware of Dog." That could have referred to only one thing: Fred Sanford, a sixty-five-year-old who would have spent his time *kvetching*, had he been of a different ethnic persuasion. Instead, he had to settle for *complaining*—about everything from Chinese food—"I can't eat that chink food; those people do their cooking and laundry in the same pot"—to being a second-class citizen—"Bet I wouldn't have to wait if I was white."

But the two things he loved to complain about the most were his son, Lamont, and his own health. And very often combinations of the two. Fred Sanford was known for his "arthuritis" and his hysterical—and hysterically funny—heart attacks. "Oooh, oooh," Fred would whine, reeling from the "pain." "This is *the* one—hear that, Lizabeth? I'm comin' to join you."

In the premiere episode, Lamont and Fred had a discussion about Fred's allegedly delicate health.

> FRED: If you'll just be patient, I'll be gone soon—and all this'll be yours.
> LAMONT: *(looks around junk in the house and laughs)*
> FRED: That's the way it usually happens—the wife dies, the husband follows—usually of a broken heart.
> LAMONT: Mother died twenty-three years ago.

Fred Sanford	Redd Foxx
Lamont Sanford	Demond Wilson
Melvin	Slappy White (1972)
Bubba	Don Bexley
Officer Swanhauser	Noam Pitlik (1972)
Officer Smith (Smitty)	Hal Williams (1972–1976)
Julio Fuentes	Gregory Sierra (1972–1975)
Rollo Larson	Nathaniel Taylor
Aunt Esther	LaWanda Page (1973–1977)
Grady Wilson	Whitman Mayo (1973–1977)
Donna Harris	Lynn Hamilton
Officer Hoppy	Howard Platt (1974–1976)
Ah Chew	Pat Morita (1974–1975)
Janet	Marlene Clark (1976–1977)
Woody	Raymond Allen (1976–1977)

FRED: Well, sometimes it takes a little longer. And to tell you the truth, I'm surprised I been around this long with this heart.

LAMONT: Yeah, me too. You know, you been complaining about your heart for as long as I can remember. And you know, they say if you have three heart attacks, you die. Now, Pop, you done had at least fifteen.

FRED: Ooh, ooh. Now you done it. You really got me upset! This is a bad one . . . oooh . . .

LAMONT: Is it a tight feeling across the chest?

FRED: Yes.

LAMONT: Pain in the back of the left shoulder?

FRED: Yes.

LAMONT: A little dizziness, kind of sick to your stomach?

FRED: Yes.

LAMONT: I guess you have Number 16 then. Now come on out and help me unload the truck. . . .

"I'm Comin' to Join You, Elizabeth": Fred flanked by Bubba and Lamont

Sanford and Son wasn't always about a black father and son team. In fact, *Sanford and Son* wasn't even always about Sanford and Son. Another Norman Lear English import (*All in the Family*, which had revolutionized television one season before, had been based on the British *Till Death Do Us Part*), in its former incarnation *S&S* had been called *Steptoe and Son*, which had been kicking around English telly for ten years before its American import. But it didn't become *Sanford and Son* right away. Earlier, American actors Lee Tracy—who had starred as *Martin Kane, Private Eye,* on television in 1952—and Aldo Ray had made a pilot based on the British series, but it never sold. Norman Lear bought the rights from Screen Gems and tried his own pilot, starring Barnard Hughes—who'd go on to star in *Doc*—and Paul Sorvino—who'd go on to star in two short-lived series: the sitcom *We'll Get By* in 1975 and *Bert D'Angelo/Superstar* in 1976. That *S&S* pilot failed to sell too. Then Lear got a bright idea: why not make it black? And so he did. And the show was a smash; debuting as a midseason insert show, it was the most popular first six weeks of any new midseason entry at that time.

Casting had a lot to do with it. Redd Foxx—who played the whining, domineering and indomitable Fred Sanford—was no slouch. Although he'd been known in show business for years, TV made him a star. "*Sanford and Son* made it in a few weeks," Foxx said. "Yet Redd Foxx has been around for thirty-three years. What took them so long?"

The son of a St. Louis electrician, Foxx ran away to New York when he was seventeen to break into show business. His first job: playing washtub on a street corner with a group called The Five Hip Cats. Eventually, Foxx got to work on the Chitlin Circuit, the trade name for black clubs and music halls around the country, but he still wasn't making it. So he got a gimmick: the dirty joke. He recorded his first "party" LP in 1956 and it was so

successful, he went on to record forty-eight more. Blue humor was his trademark then; it would change to black humor later.

Sometimes he appeared on television—"my clean appearances," he called them—and that, coupled with his albums, brought him to the attention of a Las Vegas manager who booked him into Hilton Hotels around the country. "I was doing two shows a night at the clubs—ninety minutes' work for grand-theft money," he said. But the money was nothing compared to what he'd make from his series.

Sometime in there, Foxx made a movie, *Cotton Comes to Harlem,* in which he played a junk dealer. Bud Yorkin (Lear's producing partner) saw the movie and asked Foxx to do the series. Foxx was leery at first; his TV break cost him more than $70,000 in forfeited pay from his Hilton contract. Plus, he had to move his wife and seven dogs from Vegas to Los Angeles. He was worried he wouldn't make it on TV.

They named their character "Sanford" because that had been Foxx's real name (in fact, he got his name from baseball great Jimmie Foxx, and the Redd from a name in a children's story).

For years and years, a close friend of Foxx's was a man named Lamont. That's what he wanted his son to be named on the sitcom. *Sanford and Lamont?* No. *Sanford and Sanford?* No. *Sanford and Son?* Yes.

For the role of Son, they found Demond Wilson, who'd been an actor since he was four years old and in a revival of *Green Pastures* on Broadway. That was just the beginning. He loved acting, and by the time he was twenty-five (when he started playing thirty-four-year-old Lamont) he'd been in several plays—including *The Boys in the Band* and *Ceremonies in Dark Old Men*—and two movies, *The Organization* and *Dealing*. He called himself a Serious Actor, and had no qualms about taking part in the sitcom. "I can fulfill my needs, both spiritually and materialistically with my job," he said. "If you're a true artist, you have to fulfill yourself."

Right from the start, sparks flew back and forth between Lamont and Fred Sanford.

LAMONT: I'm gettin' tired of your nagging and complaining and holding me back. If it wasn't for you, holding me back, I could be in an office.
FRED: Yeah—the welfare office.
LAMONT: You even made me quit high school in the tenth grade.
FRED: The only time you were Number One was when you were the first dropout, dummy.
LAMONT: Now why do you call me dummy?
FRED: The only reason I call you a dummy is that I call them as I see them—*dummy!*
LAMONT: I want to get a job where I can use my head as well as my hands.
FRED: That's easy—they'll put a cap on your head and a broom in your hands.
LAMONT: I can't stand it here. I can't stand being poor.
FRED: Poor? When I was a kid, we slept seven in one room—same bed, same underwear. When I was a youngster, I wore one pair of tennis shoes five years—wore them out up to the name on the ankle. Now *that's* poor. You're in the lap of luxury here.

But no matter what, Fred and Lamont stuck it out. And Lamont tried to get away, using any threat and tactic he could.

"If I stay here," he'd say, "I'll never get married, I'll never get anywhere. I'll just end up an old broken-down junk dealer like you. Now I've got to get out of here. The partnership is over."

And he would go away. And he would come back. Once, they split up and Lamont went to work for another junk dealer (but was fired) and Sanford hired a new Son, whom he started to browbeat just like he'd done with Lamont:

"Now you go to Supreme Salvage and pick up some bathtubs I ordered. Here's a check. Now, listen, if you try to run off with my truck and try to cash my check, I'll find you. It may take me a week, it may take me a month, it might take me years—but one day—maybe fifty years from now—you'll be walkin' down the street and, when you least expect it, a hundred-fifteen-year-old man gonna jump out of the alley with a two-by-four and cave your skull in."

Of course they didn't spend all their time fighting and insulting each other; sometimes they'd fight and insult *other* people.

FRED: Where's our truck?
LAMONT: Julio borrowed it.
FRED (*slamming fist on table*): Now you gone got Puerto Rican all over our truck!

Fred wasn't wild about whites either. Once, when he'd accidentally broken a piece of Lamont's prized porcelain, Fred claimed that they'd been stolen. "Who did it, Pop?" Lamont asked him.

"Four men . . . four *white* men. With stockings over their heads. I know they weren't black—you can't get a stocking over one of them naturals."

A white policeman came to ask Fred some questions about the burglars.

POLICEMAN: Were they colored?
FRED: Yeah . . . *white*.
POLICEMAN: Were you hurt? Do you want to go to the hospital.
FRED: I can't waste three days.
POLICEMAN: It only takes a few minutes . . .
FRED: It only takes *you* a few minutes—it takes *us* three days in the waiting room.

"Ug-leee!": Fred and his sister-in-law Esther

And so it went. Back on the set, the producers were waxing philosophical about the show. Said Yorkin: "People are beginning to approach comedy with more realism and more honesty than before. For years, TV networks and ad agencies said, 'We don't want to show anybody poor,' the theory being that people will be depressed if they see anyone lower down the economic ladder than themselves. Radio got away with it. I guess seeing it in front of you is what makes the difference. One of the major concerns about *Sanford and Son* was not to make it look too grim. We took great pains to make the set poor, but not depressing."

Meanwhile, Foxx was enjoying his new success, but not without difficulties: "The hardest thing for me to adjust to is sleeping at night. I used to sleep all day when I worked Vegas; you meet a whole different class of people when you sleep at night." He enjoyed playing Fred Sanford: "The character I'm playing is a natural, pretty much like me if I were sixty-five. Being the kind of comedian I am, I always try to become the part of the story I'm telling anyway, so doing the show falls into that same area. It's really not a whole new thing for me—but I didn't realize it until I'd done the first few shows."

Naturally, Foxx injected himself into the show—both with some of his comedy routines and some of his personal philosophy. "One line in a script referred to a sapphire ring. So in order to eliminate the word *sapphire*—which was a name on *Amos 'n' Andy*—I called it a red ruby. I just don't want the word *sapphire* on my show. I don't want the show to be *Amos 'n' Andy*."

Then things started happening. And not all of them good. Some critics—black ones—started accusing *Sanford and Son* of being an *Amos 'n' Andy* update. One critic said it should be "more political." Another said the producers should hire black writers (which they eventually did). Another said they should take the plots "out to the streets" for richer material. One critic said that "*Porgy sans Bess* with canned laughter is not enough."

On January 17, 1973, a review of the show by a black critic appeared in the New York *Times:* "Fred Sanford and his little boy Lamont, conceived by white minds and based upon a white value system, are not strong black men capable of achieving—or even understanding—liberation. They are merely two more American children-men. We—all of us—need to be surrounded by positive—and true—images of blackness based upon black realities, not upon white aberrations."

Well! Letters poured into the *Times*, pro-program, including one from twenty-three-year-old Memphis-born Ilunga Adell, a writer on the series who said he had "never spoken with a white person until I was eighteen years old." Redd Foxx was also livid: "I don't agree that our show is 'white to the core.' The success is what matters, not the color. The fact that we're doing a show that appeals to everybody, not just blacks, or whites or Mexicans, but everybody. It' entertainment. I personally thought it would be meaningful to have a black show that appeals to everyone. It's a fun show, about love and

most of all entertainment. There are incidents that happen with us that happen in every family, black or white. I don't think a show has to be all-black. Why, that's setting us back, not moving forward."

Meanwhile, while all the bickering was going on—which made Fred's arguings with Lamont sound like a tea party—*Sanford and Son* was making some breakthroughs: at inner-city New York schools, students were watching *Sanford and Son* during their classes and following the show's scripts at the same time. The result: kids seemed to be showing "high motivation" (according to the school report) to learn how to read, and were interested in taking writing and typing courses so they could learn to write *Sanford and Son* scripts themselves.

Better they should have taken acting classes so they could star in the show. Because, during the 1974–1975 season, it looked like *Sanford and Son* were splitting up.

First, Redd Foxx said he wouldn't come back to work unless they upped his salary from $25,000 per episode. Okay, Redd, they said. Then word came that Foxx had been diagnosed as having a "nervous condition as a result of overwork," and was "advised to leave the country for a rest." So the network shot two episodes in which Fred wasn't around, but at a funeral in St. Louis, and centered around his buddy Grady Wilson instead. Later, Foxx admitted that his "illness was a lie." He simply wanted a better salary and better treatment. He continued missing segments of the show.

In March, Foxx finally talked: "Money isn't the main consideration. I don't even want it under these conditions." He went on to enumerate a number of complaints that would have put Fred Sanford to shame: the "Uncle Tomisms" in the script, and physical discomforts. "After thirty-six years as a nightclub act, I can't adjust to working seven days a week, being holed up in a rehearsal room with no windows and no sunlight." And that wasn't all: "We only have two principal actors on the show. *All in the Family* has four principals. That makes less script for everyone to learn. But for me, fifty-one years old with forty or fifty pages of script to go over, that's hard. . . ." Foxx went on to complain how he'd broken out in hives several times while working at the studio, and had to be taken to the hospital when they discovered a spur on his spine. Also, he claimed he had two torn cartilages in his back from doing Fred's bent-over walk. Plus: "I object to all those jokes about coffins, people rolling their eyeballs, girls dressed like damn fools in rummage sale outfits. We don't all have to be raggedy just because it's set in a junkyard." But he did add that "when I watch the show, I miss myself." So did the viewers. It dropped from Number One to Number Seven.

Changes were made. Yorkin left as producer. Windows were put in Foxx's dressing room and the rehearsal hall. They bought him a golf cart to speed through NBC's long and winding corridors. And—most important—they raised his salary and gave him 25 percent of the producers' net profits.

Meanwhile, at the start of the 1975–1976 season,

TV Watches TV: Redd Foxx and Gregory Sierra

Lamont Wilson didn't show up. "Contractual differences," he claimed. He wanted more money. In fact, the only one who seemed content on the show was Ninny, the goat, who was happy with her carrot and didn't even want a dressing room.

It worked out for that season. But the next season would be the last. Foxx signed with ABC for his own variety show—*Redd Foxx*, a comedy-variety show which lasted four months—and Wilson wouldn't go it alone (*and Son?*) unless he got more than $25,000 an episode and an $85,000 Silver Cloud Rolls-Royce, as a token for signing a long-term agreement.

Forget it, the network said. And, finally—136 episodes later—Lamont got to move out of his father's house. (Wilson went on to star in the disastrous *Baby, I'm Back* in the 1977–1978 season.) But NBC, knowing that they'd lost a good thing, tried to get some mileage out of *Sanford and Son*, although now, with Foxx and Wilson gone, all that was left was the *and*, which might have made for an interesting sitcom title, but not an interesting sitcom.

And so they looked next door. Fred was always fussing and feuding with Aunt Esther, who ran the Sanford Arms, a run-down rooming house next to the junkyard. The new star was Theodore Wilson as Phil Wheeler, a widower with two teenage children. Supposedly, Sanford and Sanford had retired to Arizona, and Esther looked after their property. But the renovated rooming house—and the renovated program—were both failures and lasted less than two months. And, basically, all it did was to remind us how good *Sanford and Son* had been. All it did was to bring back memories . . .

. . . of the time when, taking a tour of the NBC studios, Fred bumped into Lena Horne and talked her into coming back home with him . . .

. . . of the time when Lamont took Fred to a Chinese restaurant for his birthday and Fred ordered "ham hocks and lima beans" . . .

. . . of the time when Fred's sister married a white man, whom Fred called "Mr. Intermarry," "Paleface," "Snow Whitey," "Honky," "Color Blind," and "White Tornado" . . .

. . . of the time when Fred's new girlfriend turned out to be Lamont's old one . . .

. . . of all the times Fred wanted to read something and he'd go rummaging through the bureau drawer (top right) to find a pair of glasses of the dozens stashed away there . . .

. . . of the time Lamont tried to put his father into a nursing home, and all the shouting and hollering that went on before Fred got out . . .

. . . of the time when Fred came back from a weekend at a posh hotel and took everything with him, including the lightbulbs—"I would've taken the lamp, but I couldn't fit it in my suitcase" . . .

. . . but most of all, we remember Fred Sanford's heart, whether it was attacking him or he was attacking someone else. He always kept $200 hidden away. "That's the money I was saving for my heart operation," he explained. "I was gonna get one of them heart transplants."

They said he moved to Arizona for his "arthur-itis." But we know better. At last, Fred Sanford finally joined Elizabeth.

Or had he? In 1980, Foxx returned to NBC starring in a sitcom called *Sanford*. *Sanford?* The story of a junkman who marries rich and moves to Beverly Hills. What was it that lured Foxx back to Sanford-land? Did he miss the part? Was it for artistic fulfillment? Was he anxious to get back to work? No. "It was money," Foxx said. "They made me an offer I couldn't refuse." Fred Sanford couldn't have put it better.

R.I.P.: Redd Foxx said goodbye to Fred Sanford forever—that is, until Sanford in 1980

ALSO RANS

The Chicago Teddy Bears

Dean Jones—alumnus of numerous Disney doodles and Broadway's *Company*—starred as Linc McCray, a partner with his uncle Latzi (John Banner) in a twenties Chicago speakeasy, which did good business and was covered by a small-time gangster, Big Nick Marr (Art Metrano). But Nick tried to muscle in on the business, which provided much of the show's action. It was all in the family anyway, because Linc and Nick were cousins and both were nephews of Uncle Latzi and—confused? It doesn't matter. The plot of this one takes longer to tell than the time it ran on CBS: three months. Footnote: Jamie Farr (*M*A*S*H*'s Klinger) played one of the club's bodyguards, Lefty.

The Chicago Teddy Bears: *Art Metrano with guest Sarah Fankboner*

The Corner Bar

This show had two incarnations. Number One: Gabriel Dell (a former Bowery Boy) played Harry Grant, who ran a New York tavern called Grant's Toomb. Into its portals came a number of crazies and zanies—stock homosexuals, stock boozers, stock stockbrokers. Number Two: In 1973, the place—and the sitcom—was taken over by Mae and Frank (Anne Meara and Eugene Roche) and Gabriel Dell went back, once again, to being a former Bowery Boy. But the clientele was mainly the same: a cabdriver named Fred; a lawyer named Phil; a gay set designer named Peter Panama; a flamboyant actor named Donald, not to mention the hired help: Joe, the liberated black cook; Meyer, the long-suffering Jewish waiter, and Mary Ann, the sexy, daft waitress. Alan King was executive producer of this ABC show, which ran from June 1972 through September 1973.

The Don Rickles Show

Before Rickles tickled the country with his *C.P.O. Sharkey* a few seasons later, he took a stab at this sitcom, in which he played an ad agency exec who fell flat on his frustrations week after week (but not too many weeks),

The Don Rickles Show *(from left): guest Joyce Van Patten Louise Sorel, Don Rickles*

spewing out insults, as his loving wife and doting daughter stood by and smiled. He played a guy named Don Robinson and he worked at Kingston, Cohen and Vanderpool, Inc. After four months, CBS fired Rickles, who went on unemployment until he joined the navy.

Funny Face

The myth went that anything—Durward Kirby reading the phone book—could get high ratings if it were placed between *All in the Family* and *Mary Tyler Moore* on the Saturday night lineup. *Funny Face* was the perfect example of this. It starred Sandy Duncan as Sandy Stockton, a pert and perky UCLA student majoring in education but working her way through college by acting in TV commercials. She came from a small town—Taylorville, Illinois—and the big city was a real challenge to her. Fortunately she had a complete cast of characters to help her along: her next-door neighbor and best friend Alice McRaven (played by Valorie Armstrong), and Mr. and Mrs. Harwell (Henry Beckman and Kathleen Freeman), her nosy landlords. The show went off the air—high ratings and all—because Duncan had to undergo eye surgery. When she finally did return the following season with a new show—*The Sandy Duncan Show*—she lasted only three months.

Getting Together

Once again, the music world meets the sitcom world. On a 1971 episode of *The Partridge Family*, the Partridges introduced a guy named Bobby Conway to a guy named Lionel Poindexter. They got together and started their own series: *Getting Together*. It was all about a struggling young songwriter (Bobby Sherman, in real life a recording artist) who worked with a tone-deaf lyricist. But there was more: Bobby was also the legal guardian of his freckle-faced twelve-year-old sister Jennifer (Susan Neher). The three lived in an antique shop, where the furniture was often sold out from under them. They had a motherly landlady, Rita Simon (Pat Carroll, a standard sitcom mother) and her policeman-boyfriend Rudy Colcheck (Jack Burns). Unfortunately, Sherman's recording career was not in high swing to begin with, and went even lower when the show went off the air after a thirteen-week run (although there was a minor hit single, "Jennifer," that came out of the show, as well as an LP called "Getting Together").

The Good Life

This show had a good cast of character actors familiar to the sitcommunity: Larry Hagman (from *I Dream of*

The Good Life: *Larry Hagman and Donna Mills*

Jeannie), Donna Mills, David Wayne, and Hermione Baddeley. Here was the premise: Albert and Jane Miller (Hagman and Mills) were middle-class and tired of their boring routine. Instead of dropping out, they dropped up—and got work as a butler and cook for a teddibly wealthy family, hoping they could share in some of the Good Life. Naturally, their new employer, industrialist Charles Dutton (Wayne), didn't know they were not a professional cook and butler. He just thought they were Pleasant. His wife, however, found the duo quite inexperienced, and was constantly looking for ways to have them fired. The Duttons' teenage son, Nick (Danny Goldman), discovered the truth about the Millers' identity, but he thought it was all great fun and helped them get through their Cross-Cultural Experience. After thirteen weeks, NBC sent the whole lot of them to the poorhouse.

The Jimmy Stewart Show

TV eventually gets 'em all—but not for long. Famed movie actor James Stewart was snared by sitcomland to play the part of an anthropology professor (James K. Howard) at Josiah Kessel College, founded by his grandfather. Naturally, he had a complicated home life: he had a twenty-nine-year-old son, Peter (Jonathan Daly), who with his wife and son was temporarily living with his parents after his own home burned down. Plus, James had another son, Teddy, who was eight years old, the same age as Peter's kid, which made James' eight-year-old son Peter's son's uncle. Or something like that.

The Jimmy Stewart Show (clockwise): Dennis Larson, Jonathan Daly, Jimmy Stewart, Julie Adams, Ellen Greer, Kirby Furlong

Anyway, none of it was particularly funny—or particularly interesting—and NBC called it quits after one season.

Me and the Chimp

This midseason CBS replacement quickly got its own summer replacement. The "me" was Mike Reynolds (played by Ted Bessell, who had been That Boy on *That Girl*) and the chimp was played by a chimp (whom he had obviously traded Marlo in for). Anyway, there was a story, and this is what it was: Reynolds was living happily with his wife, Liz (Anita Gillette), and two kids in their California home of San Pascal. Then they found the chimp, Buttons, in a local park and brought him home as a pet—and then he became a regular member of the family. (He was named Buttons because he pushed them all the time around the house). Naturally—as Marlo had before him—Buttons created all sorts of confusion and problems around the house—and, once again, Ted Bessell had to clean up the mess.

The New Dick Van Dyke Show

A year after his ex-wife, Mary Tyler Moore, changed identities, moved to Minneapolis, and got her own show, Dick Van Dyke decided to try sitcom life again too. He'd been a big CBS star in the sixties, and the network was eager to get him back again—eager enough to submit to his demands of having the show filmed near his home at Carefree, Arizona. For the three years this show tugged to make it in the ratings race, the format changed and changed. In fact, the only people who remained on the

show were Van Dyke as Dick Preston, Hope Lange (the ghost of *Mrs. Muir*) as his wife, Jenny, and Angela Powell, as their daughter, Annie.

During the first two seasons, Dick played the host of a local talk show in Phoenix. But mainly episodes revolved around his family life, with intrusions by his manager Bernie Davis (Marty Brill), his sister/secretary "Mike" (Fannie Flagg) and Bernie's wife, Carol (Nancy Dussault, who'd go on to co-anchor *Good Morning, America* for a while). *TNDVDS* wasn't terribly successful. So, for the third season, they moved the premise of the show, and this time Dick—*sans* Brill, Dussault, and Flagg—starred in a daytime soap opera, *Those Who Care*, with the new cast regulars including Dick Van Patten (as Max Mathias, the show's producer), Barry Gordon (as Dennis Whitehead, the soap's writer) and Henry Darrow (as Alex Montenez, the stage manager). The show went off the air when the network censored an episode in which the Prestons' daughter watches while her parents are having sex and asks them about it. Although handled quite tastefully, CBS thought America wasn't ready for parents talking to their kids about sex— at least not on television. But that wasn't the end of Dick Van Dyke—he went on to host his own unsuccessful variety show, *Van Dyke and Company*, and for a while, was a regular on *The Carol Burnett Show* during its last season. Who knows? Maybe there'll be a *New New Dick Van Dyke Show*. . . .

The Partners

Veteran sitcommer Don Adams (*Get Smart!*) and newcomer Rupert Crosse were Lennie Crooke and

The Partners: *Don Adams and Rupert Crosse*

George Robinson, a pair of loony detectives who were always getting into crazeee situations while trying to investigate crimes. Sometimes, in fact, they'd get into more trouble than the criminals they were chasing. And, of course, they had a frustrated boss, Captain Andrews (John Doucette). Dick Van Patten—a long-time television performer—played Sergeant Higgenbottom, who was constantly making fun of Lennie and George while trying to get in good with the captain. NBC canceled this show after one season.

Shirley's World

If you want to know the *real* poop about this disaster, read Shirley MacLaine's memoirs. But if you don't want to bother, here's the plot of the show: Shirley Logan was a mod young reporter-photographer who traveled around the world for her assignments on *World Illustrated Magazine* (the show was filmed in England, Scotland, Tokyo, Hong Kong, and other locales). Shirley always got involved with her subjects—queens, spies—but not for long: ABC sent her home after thirteen weeks.

Shirley's World: *Shirley MacLaine helps women break into an all-male club.*

The Super

Richard Castellano—who had gone through an ugly and painful death in *The Godfather* and later starred in a 1975 sitcom called *Joe and Sons* (he played Joe, not Sons), died another ugly and painful death when this summer replacement series was killed off by ABC. Actually, *The Super* was one of the more interesting sitcoms of its time. Castellano played Joe Girelli who, at 260 pounds, wanted only three things out of life: cold beer, hot pizza, and hot and cold running television. However, work sometimes got in the way; he was the superintendent of an old, walk-up apartment building in a poor section of New York; he always had tenants banging on his pipes (radiator pipes, that is, although it seemed they would have loved getting at some of his other pipes), and all the tenants complained about him and about each other and about everyone else. Naturally, the tenants were all Jews, blacks, Irish, Poles, Italians, Puerto Ricans, homosexuals, cops, radicals, social workers—what a motley crew. And his family would not leave him alone, including his wife, Francesca (Ardell Sheridan), and his disrespectful kids, Anthony (Bruce Kirby, Jr.) and Joanne (played by Castellano's daughter Margaret). As if that weren't enough, Joe also had a loudmouth lawyer brother, Frankie (Phil Mishkin). With all that aggravation, he was probably grateful when ABC canceled him.

The Trouble with Tracy

This single-season syndicated sitcom took place in Toronto and was all about the Young family—father Douglas (Steve Weston), an advertising executive with Hutton, Dutton, Sutton and Norris, and his scatterbrained wife, Tracy (Diane Nyland). Produced in Toronto, this was sort of an *I Love Lucy*, Canadian style.

1972–1973

The Bob Newhart Show

Maude

M*A*S*H

OFF-SCREEN

9/1 Bobby Fischer wins match vs. Boris Spassky of the USSR and becomes first US chess champion.

9/4 Champion swimmer Mark Spitz becomes first person ever to win seven Olympic gold medals.

9/5 Black September Palestinian terrorists in Munich shoot two Olympic team members, hold nine others as hostages several hours until taken to Munich airport, where hostages, four terrorists and one West German policeman die in shoot-out.

9/11 US Democratic Party, in suit seeking damages for Watergate break-in, accuse Maurice Stans and three others of conspiring to commit "political espionage."

11/7 Richard M. Nixon wins re-election to presidency.

12/26 Harry S Truman dies in Independence, Missouri.

1/22 US Supreme Court legalizes abortion during the first three months of pregnancy. Also that day: Lyndon Johnson dies of heart attack.

1/23 President Nixon announces agreement earlier that day in Paris to end Vietnam War.

1/30 G. Gordon Liddy and James W. McCord, Jr., found guilty of attempting to spy on Democratic National Committee Headquarters in Watergate building complex in Washington, D. C.

2/27 Wounded Knee, on Oglala Sioux reservation in South Dakota, occupied by members of the American Indian Movement, who demand an investigation of federal treatment of Indians.

FRONT RUNNERS

THE BOB NEWHART SHOW

Mrs. Bakerman: Dr. Hartley, if you're looking for a new member for our group, I know a nice schizophrenic.
Mr. Peterson: Or how about a manic-depressive? At least you know they'll be fun half the time.

On paper, all sitcoms look alike: the wacky neighbor, the bumbling husband, the sensible wife, the man-hungry secretary, the nutty clients. The token weddings, misunderstandings, mistaken identities, sight gags, and the substandard jokes. But somehow *The Bob Newhart Show* took an unexpected turn and created human beings, not beanbrains, and people who, season after season after season after season after season (six of them in all), we grew to care about. *Care* about. Not the way we tuned in to *Bilko* or the *Beaver*, but a different way: to visit our buddies. *Bob Newhart's* characters were so real, so lifelike, that, when they weren't on, we found ourselves thinking about them during the week, wondering how Bob and Emily were doing.

Bob and Emily Hartley, that is. He: a successful psychologist who bordered on the ineffectual (but always human and humane). She: a successful person (also school teacher), who was most often effectual, plus kind, warm, funny, understanding. They: lived in a Chicago high-rise apartment, loved each other—no, no—*loved* each other (many of the scenes took place in their king-sized bed).

And they argued—not the pulsating, pounding Edith/Archie, Maude/Walter kind of argument. Quieter arguments. But for real. But more often than argue, they were TV's first couple to be stubbornly hostile. They jabbed each other, but—because they loved each other—never punctured the skin.

Bob: Your mother wore black to our wedding.
Emily: That wasn't black, Bob, that was dark gray. Only her armband was black, Bob.
Bob: It rained on our wedding day. Your mother called it an omen.

And once, after looking at photos of them when they were younger:

Emily: Whoever thought that two ugly ducklings would turn into a swan—and a flabby psychologist.

It's not certain that Bob was flabby (we trusted enough to take Emily's word for it), but he certainly was a psychologist. Nothing fancy, mind you. Just the plain,

Robert (Bob) Hartley	Bob Newhart
Emily Hartley	Suzanne Pleshette
Howard Borden	Bill Daily
Jerry Robinson	Peter Bonerz
Carol Kester Bondurant	Marcia Wallace
Margaret Hoover	Patricia Smith (1972–1973)
Dr. Bernie Tupperman	Larry Gelman (1972–1977)
Ellen Hartley	Pat Finley (1974–1976)
Larry Bondurant	Will Mackenzie (1975–1977)
Elliott Carlin	Jack Riley
Mrs. Bakerman	Florida Friebus
Miss Larson	Penny Marshall (1972–1973)
Michelle Nardo	Renee Lippin (1973–1976)
Mr. Peterson	John Fielder (1973–1978)
Mr. Gianelli	Noam Pitlik (1972–1973)
Mr. Vickers	Lucien Scott (1974–1975)
Mr. Herd	Oliver Clark (1976–1977)

old, simple ordinary kind. He had respect for his patients, and sometimes they even had respect for him. The premise of the show was that Bob was a whiz at solving his patients' problems but a dud when it came to handling his own. That was the first season. As the years went on, the two—whiz and dud—were interchangeable. Oftentimes we weren't sure if the patients were crazier than the people at home.

Actually, it was daring for television to tackle a sitcom about neurotic people. Who in a sitcom isn't a little bit dizzy? (Okay, okay, maybe not Robert Young or June Cleaver—but they could have used some therapy to loosen up a little and stop being so . . . so *perfect*.) But in the history of sitcoms, everyone's crazy. If Lucy Ricardo were loose in your neighborhood, mightn't you at least suggest a little professional counseling? And what about a guy who talks to horses, or who talks to his mother, the car? So how do you differentiate the Crazies from the crazies? The producers were smart: they didn't make the patients much different from the nonpatients. They were the same. The patients just weren't as well adjusted. Often, Bob's friends and family seemed to have far worse problems than his patients, but—true to sitcom form—everything was worked out within the last seven minutes of each episode. Tune in next week for new problems, new solutions, new entertainment.

Of course it all had to do with Bob Newhart, who transplanted his first name (as so many well-known actors have done) to his character, and added a close-sounding last name: Hartley.

His Bob Hartley was one of the nicest, mildest fellows since Robinson Peepers. *The Bob Newhart Show* was, well, amiable, and so was Bob Newhart/Hartley. One of the producers described Newhart as "a reactor. He listens funny." Said another: "Strange thing about Bob—he works small but gets those big laughs. They come more out of attitude than lines."

Newhart first came to national attention as a stand-up comic of the Mort Sahl and Shelley Berman era. His LP, *The Button-Down Mind of Bob Newhart*, sold 1,500,000 copies (a lot for the early sixties), and made him a sudden star. His routines consisted mainly of monologues on the telephone, with Newhart ending conversations with "Same to you, fella" (the telephone also figured somewhat into his sitcom ten years later). Fame brought him a first *Bob Newhart Show*—this one of the variety-variety in 1961—and each telecast opened with Newhart on the phone, talking to an unseen and unheard adversary. There were no regulars on the show, but a group of semiregular guests—Mickey Manners, Joe Flynn, Kay Westfall—who showed up once in a while. The show won an Emmy. But the show also won low ratings. It went off the air in June of 1962. "It was like trying to fly a plane without knowing what makes it go," Newhart said about the first show. "I had this hang-up about perfection. But I knew nothing about my craft. I was raw funny, not polished funny. Deep down I guess I didn't feel entitled to all that success."

Between *The Bob Newhart Show* and *The Bob Newhart Show*, he recorded more albums, appeared in nightclubs, and made several movies, including *Cool Millions, Catch-22, On a Clear Day You Can See Forever*, and *Cold Turkey*, among others.

Then *The Mary Tyler Moore Show* people—who were scoring big with Mary, Rhoda, Phyllis, Ted, Lou, and the rest of the gang—approached Newhart about trying his hand—and his humor—at sitcom. It would be intelligent, they promised. It would be witty. It would be Him. "We're not trying to do Archie Bunker," the producers told him. "We're selling class and wit and charm." Good, Newhart said, "because I don't want to do *Father Knows Best* or daddy's-the-dummy-but-we-love-him."

He got what he wanted. According to one of the early reviews: "The characters are credible, each having an identity, each contributing to the overall comedy effect of the show. And one also finds a constant play between normalcy and idiosyncrasy. There are the conversations between the psychologist Bob and his patients in the inimitable Newhart style. And the supporting characters include so many recognizable traits that we can easily identify with their feelings and actions."

Like Mr. Carlin. He was one of Bob's patients—in group therapy, in solo sessions, any way he could get it. Carlin was a professional neurotic. For example, listen to this exchange between Bob's sassy secretary and Mr. Carlin:

CAROL: Hi, Mr. Carlin. How's the real estate business?
CARLIN: Couldn't be better.
CAROL: And how are you?
CARLIN: Couldn't be worse.
CAROL: Then everything's normal.

Father and son: Mr. Carlin and the kid who claims to be his son

In one session with Bob, Mr. Carlin had a breakthrough:

CARLIN: I think I'm overcoming my agoraphobia.
BOB: I didn't know you had a fear of open places.
CARLIN: I thought it was a fear of agricultural products. Anyway, wheat doesn't scare me anymore.

One of Bob's other patients—not a paying patient at all, just someone he has to have an inordinate amount of patience with—is the Hartleys' across-the-hall neighbor, Howard Borden. He's someone you have to hear to believe.

BOB: What do you say we take some orphans camping?
HOWARD: It's okay with me if it's okay with their parents.

Or:

EMILY: Bob and I are giving a Fourth of July party—would you like to come?
HOWARD: Oh, great! When is it?

Howard—a grown man, an airline pilot who often brought Bob and Emily teeny-tiny bottles of liquor, as souvenirs of his travels—is the Hartleys' child. And with him around, they don't need kids of their own. He's an innocent, much like his cousin, Ted Baxter, on *The Mary Tyler Moore Show*. But there's a difference: Howard is dumb, a semiincompetent. But he doesn't have the inflated ego Ted Baxter does, so we laugh at him in a different way.

BOB (*walks in and sees Emily sewing a button on Howard's shirt*):   Why are you sewing Howard's shirt?
EMILY: Howard says he's all thumbs when it comes to sewing.
BOB: Howard's all thumbs when it comes to living.

The show's hundreds of episodes developed the characters, something that differentiated the seventies sitcoms from those in the sixties. Carol, the husband-hungry secretary, satisfied her appetite when she got married in 1975. For a season or so, Bob's sister moved in with him and Emily, and even had an affair—no, a relationship—with Howard. But what stayed the same was Bob's regular group therapy meeting, before which he would drop the plaque on the outside of his door that said "In Session."

Once, the "core group"—made up of Mr. Carlin; squeaky-voiced, ineffectual Mr. Peterson; Mrs. Bakerman, a dizzy grocery clerk who's constantly knitting; overweight and lonely Michelle Nardo—is looking for a new member—"a mild neurotic with compulsive tendencies" would fit in fine, Bob thought. "Where's the new loon?" Mr. Carlin asks, and in walks the new member,

Office work: Jerry and Carol

who turns out to be a homosexual. Everyone is stunned. Except Mrs. Bakerman, who pauses and says, "Then maybe you know my nephew Kenny." The group is upset and they all quit until Bob talks them into tolerance.

In another episode, Howard, who's very dependent on the Hartleys (he has most of his meals there, and even slept in their bed with them when the heat went out) goes to a therapist to become more independent.

Bob has found him a psychologist, an old friend of Bob's who has new-fangled treatments of intensive in-house therapy.

DOCTOR: Why do you keep working in an office, Bob?
BOB: It's either work here or out of my car.
DOCTOR: The trouble with psychologists is that we're stuck in a rut. All we do is repeat ourselves.
BOB: Repeat ourselves?
DOCTOR: Repeat ourselves.
BOB: How?
DOCTOR: How?
BOB: Yeah—how?
DOCTOR: By using the same old methods, over and over and over again and again and again and again.
BOB: I see what you mean.

Bob and Emily are going on a vacation, and Howard's very upset: "Ten days? My plants will die in ten days. Who's going to water them? You always water my plants. You know I have a tendency to drown things. That's why I don't have any pets. How could you do this to me? I'll be all alone. Don't leave me."

They leave Howard with the fast-working psychologist. And when they return, Howard is transformed into a competent, responsible—boring—person. Upon entering their apartment, Bob and Emily notice that their sofa is piled with things—vacuum cleaners, golf clubs, clothing.

EMILY: Maybe we've been burglarized.

BOB: Burglars don't deliver, Emily.

Howard knocks on the door. He's cold, stodgy. Just like his therapist. He now watches William Buckley on television. "Thanks to the doctor," he tells them, "I'm not myself—I'm me."

Bob goes to talk to the doctor: "Howard used to have his own personality. Now he's got yours." The doctor says that he has "processed" Howard and plans to take him on a national tour with him. "Who's going to be your opening act—Jerry Vale?" Bob asks.

The Hartleys can't stand the new Howard. He won't even stay for dinner. Emily tries to bait him with roast beef, mashed potatoes, and broccoli.

HOWARD: I don't know what's going on here. First you want me to be independent. Then you want me to borrow things and stay for dinner.
BOB: Howard, are you happy?
HOWARD: No.
BOB: Are you hungry?
HOWARD: Yes.

He'll stay for dinner—"But can we have asparagus tips instead of broccoli?"—and then he re-borrows all the things he's returned. The old Howard is back.

The show had its own special brand of humor. Sort of straight-daffy. Some examples:

Goofy Jerry, the dentist in Bob's office and Bob's best friend, is off to Mexico, staying at the Hotel Smith, "where anybody caught stealing a towel will be forced to drink the water." He's staying in the "José Rivera Memorial Suite, named for a guy named José Rivera who was executed in your very own room." (When Howard hears that Jerry's staying at his old haunt, the Hotel Smith, he tells him: "They'll name a suite after you, but it's not worth it.")

JERRY: What do you want me to bring you back from south of the border, Bob?
BOB: Oh, one of those sombreros with the fringe . . .
JERRY: What color?
BOB: Oh, something that'll go with more than one suit.
JERRY: Howard, what do you want me to bring you from south of the border?
HOWARD: Some pant-and-coat hangers.
JERRY: Some pant-and-coat hangers? You can get them right here.
HOWARD: I don't care where you get them—just get them.

When Bob is going to take the orphans camping—"You don't have to worry about me, Emily. Just wind the compass"—he is afraid he won't be able to find a vacant campsite. "I'll just tip a bear and he'll let me in." Instead, however, he ends up taking the two boys camping in a parking lot.

BOB: Look up there—that's the North Star.
BOY: No, that's the Wrigley Building.
BOB: So it is . . .

Once Bob and Emily try to throw a Bicentennial party.

BOB: I invited Mr. Carlin.
EMILY: Why?
BOB: He says he gets lonely every Bicentennial.

Carol's Wedding (from left): Will Mackenzie, Bob Newhart, Marcia Wallace, Suzanne Pleshette.

Family Therapy: Bob Hartley and his sister, Ellen

While looking for their punch bowl, Emily locks them in the storage locker in the building's basement by mistake.

EMILY: Look, Bob—your barbells. You haven't lifted these in a long time.
BOB: Yeah, well it got to the point it was too easy.
EMILY: Yeah, I remember the day Jerry and Howard helped you carry them down here?

Later:

BOB: I can't even tell if it's day or night. How long have we been trapped down here?
EMILY: Fifteen minutes.
BOB: It seems more like twenty.

To pass the time:

BOB: Wanna tell jokes?
EMILY: Yeah, sure.
BOB: Here's a good one—why did the moron lock herself and her husband in the storage locker?
EMILY: Come off it, will you, Bob?

They begin to get a little philosophical.

EMILY: Do you think we're going to die?
BOB: Probably.
EMILY: That's a damn shame. Say, Bob, did you ever make a will?
BOB: I left everything to you.
EMILY: That's no good if we're both done for . . . but, Bob, if I die—would you remarry?
BOB: Sure.
EMILY: What kind of woman would you look for?
BOB: Someone different from you—someone big enough to break through that door over there. (pause) Emily, I would never remarry.

And he probably wouldn't. Although Bob's not very articulate about his affection for Emily—

EMILY: Bob, do you love me?
BOB: Sure.
EMILY: Why?
BOB: Why not?

—it's obvious that he's totally devoted to her. And that she's devoted to him.

Emily was cool. So was Suzanne Pleshette, the deep-voiced, dark-haired beauty who played the part. And perhaps it was no part at all. "At first," Pleshette said, "the writers were afraid to inject 'Suzannisms' into the scripts, but now I can pretty much play myself." Over

the years, Emily changed slightly. In the beginning, she was purely a domestic, with little concern for her career, teaching school. Later on, they showed her in action with her students, and even promoted her to vice-principal. The producers, however, had the good sense (and the good taste) not to promote her to Mother.

Oh, there were times when Emily and Bob talked about having children, as in this exchange:

EMILY: Bob, do you ever wish we had kids? Do you ever think about it?
BOB: Yeah, once in a while. Sometimes I wish we had a little girl.
EMILY: I think about a little boy. You know, that's nice—a girl for you, a boy for me. . . .

But they had to content themselves with Howard. Anyway, Bob Newhart insisted they remain childless. He didn't want to turn the show into a domestic comedy. And so it wasn't. And that was fine with Pleshette too.

She loved her role: "Bob is just like my husband, Tommy, letting me go bumbling and stumbling through life. And the way it's written, the part *is* me. There's the stream of non sequiturs by which I live. There are fights. I'm allowed to be demonstrative."

She was lucky to get the part. "Actresses with dark hair and deep voices always are cast as the bad girl or the bad-good girl. I rarely got the man in the end of the movie. Or if I did, he died in my arms." Some of those movies were *Rome Adventure, The Birds, Parrish, A Distant Trumpet,* and *Fate Is the Hunter*. It was on *The Tonight Show* that Pleshette was discovered for *Bob Newhart;* she was talking endlessly and seemed very honest, so the producers thought she'd be perfect for the part. "Frankly," said one of them, "we were surprised when she accepted." "Emily is not smarter than Bob," Pleshette said, "nor is she manipulative like most wives in television series. She is appreciative of Bob's idiosyncrasies, and he respects her desire for an identity of her own."

In 1977, Newhart announced that he was going to quit the series. He wanted to get back to nightclub work and, frankly, he'd had enough. But suddenly there was another announcement: he would film a final year. How come the switch? "Both MTM and CBS were so darned nice to me. I got to thinking, why not go ahead with another year? What's so tough about it? People were already starting to say I was quitting because I wouldn't have *The Mary Tyler Moore Show* as a lead-in." (*Newhart* always followed *Mary*, which was a wonderful security blanket for any show.) "So I said, hell, why not. One more year won't be so bad. So I said yes. And you wouldn't believe the number of people who bothered to sit down and write. People who said thank you for giving us so many good times and things like that. It almost made me cry."

Buddies: Jerry and Bob sing along with The Peepers (Tom Poston).

It almost made a lot of people cry when, a year later, Bob Hartley—and that other Bob—left the air. In the last episode, Bob gave up his Chicago psychology practice and became a professor at a small college in Oregon.

Said Newhart: "I could see what was coming in situation comedy, and I didn't want to be a part of it. If we'd gone another year, they'd have had a guy and two girls living in the apartment above us; a Martian living on the same floor next door to three girl detectives. That way we'd have had all the elements of what passes for a hit sitcom this year."

Is that really why he quit? "Well, I saw a slight slackening in the writing, which scared me a little bit. I didn't want to limp off the air with a show that didn't measure up to what it had been a few years earlier."

And so Newhart quit. Millions of Americans went through sudden withdrawal—after all, their psychologist had left town without a forwarding address or the number of a service to call in case of an anxiety attack that needed a shot of Bob and Emily.

And, what do you know, just as we were getting used to Bob's being gone—just as we were learning to go it alone—*The Bob Newhart Show* came back as reruns.

That means we still get to hear Bob's wonderful stories—those convoluted tales of his childhood, told to make a point, but rambling tales that lead nowhere.

BOB: Have I told you this story before?
EMILY: On our wedding night. You were stalling.
BOB: I wasn't stalling. *(Newhart pause)* I just didn't want to come on like an animal.

M*A*S*H

> HOT LIPS: *The army has no gratitude.*
> HAWKEYE: *Go talk to the owners . . .*

M*A*S*H was TV's first black sitcom. No, not like *Amos 'n' Andy* and *The Jeffersons* were black sitcoms. It was a sitcom about war. No, not like *Sergeant Bilko* and *Hogan's Heroes*. M*A*S*H was more than lovable lunks running around doing nutty things. This was comedy that showed war. Not like a John Wayne epic, but one of small-scale, more human dimensions. M*A*S*H showed the blood and violence of war without ever actually showing the blood and violence. It showed the inside and underside of battle. The loneliness, the fear, the emotional as well as physical casualties. It showed death.

And yet M*A*S*H was a lot of laughs.

Actually, M*A*S*H—maybe the most sophisticated sitcom of them all—was not a sitcom at all, but a minimovie with a laugh-track. If, say, *Midnight Cowboy* had had a laugh-track and been broken up into thirty-minute segments on television, it too might have qualified as a sitcom.

It was unusual in many ways. It took place in the early 1950s, during the Korean War—and it lasted four times as long as the Korean War. It had a daring sense of humor that took itself very seriously; and when it was serious, it always had a sense of humor about it. And, like Silly-Putty, it could change its form. One week it was a strictly-for-laughs sitcom. The next week there was hardly any comedy at all, just the horror of trying to put back together the young men of war—and lamenting those who didn't make it to the operating room. Often, there'd be no situation at all, just vignettes (sometimes in the guise of a letter home).

Once, in a classic episode, the principals of M*A*S*H changed the principles of M*A*S*H when, "interviewed" by a US TV reporter, they talked about their fears, anger, and horror at the war (like a fifties newsreel, this episode was filmed in black and white; in fact M*A*S*H, which took place in the fifties, was the other side of *Happy Days*. M*A*S*H was Sad Days and Scary Nights). Another relic episode showed the M*A*S*H unit as seen—at bedside level—through the eyes of a wounded soldier whose mouth had been wired shut. Very often there would be no resolution at the end of an episode. Just as there would be no resolutions at the

Captain Benjamin Franklin Pierce (Hawkeye)	Alan Alda
Captain John McIntyre (Trapper John)	Wayne Rogers (1972–1975)
Major Margaret Houlihan (Hot Lips)	Loretta Swit
Major Frank Burns	Larry Linville (1972–1977)
Corporal Walter O'Reilly (Radar)	Gary Burghoff (1972–1979)
Lieutenant Colonel Henry Blake	McLean Stevenson (1972–1975)
Father John Mulcahy	William Christopher
Corporal Maxwell Klinger	Jamie Farr (1973–)
Colonel Sherman Potter	Harry Morgan (1977–)
Captain B. J. Hunnicut	Mike Farrell (1975–)
Major Charles Emerson Winchester	David Ogden Stiers (1977–)
Lieutenant Maggie Dish	Karen Philipp (1972)
Spearchucker Jones	Timothy Brown (1972)
Ho-John	Patrick Adiarte (1972)
Ugly John	John Orchard (1972–1973)
Lieutenant Leslie Scorch	Linda Meiklejohn (1972–1973)
General Brandon Clayton	Herb Voland (1972–1973)
Lieutenant Ginger Ballis	Odessa Cleveland (1972–1974)
Nurse Margie Cutler	Marcia Strassman (1972–1973)
Nurse Louise Anderson	Kelly Jean Peters (1973)
Lieutenant Nancy Griffin	Lynette Mettey (1973)
Various nurses	Bobbie Mitchell (1973–1977)
General Mitchell	Robert F. Simon (1973–1974)
Nurse Kelly	Kellye Nakahara (1974–)
Various nurses	Patricia Stevens (1974–)
Various nurses	Judy Farrell (1976)
Igor	Jeff Mitchell (1976–1977)
Nurse Bigelow	Enid Kent (1977–)
Sergeant Zale	Johnny Haymer (1977–1978)
Colonel Flagg	Edward Winter

end of *our* episodes. And yet, no matter how it changed forms, *M*A*S*H* always managed to maintain its lightning humor, frightening reality, and enlightening insights. *M*A*S*H*'s* theme song—unlike the ditties of *Colonel Flack*, *Hogan's Heroes*, and *F Troop* before it—was a tune called "Suicide Is Painless."

* * *

HAWKEYE: I just don't know why they're shooting at us. All we want to bring them is democracy and white bread, to transplant the American Dream: freedom, achievement, hyperacidity, affluence, flatulence, technology, tension, the inalienable right to an early coronary sitting at your desk while plotting to stab your boss in the back.

* * *

*M*A*S*H* was a smash.

But to begin at the beginning. The characters were all members of the 4077th Mobile Army Surgical Hospital (M*A*S*H) unit, stationed behind the lines during the Korean War (sometimes things didn't work as planned, and the unit found itself stationed *on* the lines—but more on that later). Their job: to treat the wounded being sent from the front lines and try to save as many lives as possible. It was depressing—especially for the doctors who'd been drafted; they couldn't believe the conditions they were subjected to. Futility and insanity were the passwords in *M*A*S*H*. A sense of humor was the survival kit.

* * *

DOCTOR: *M*A*S*H*—the *M* stands for "Mobile."
HAWKEYE: Also *Meshuggah*.

* * *

More than any other sitcom, the characters who peopled the show were people, not caricatures.

Aiding the Enemy: B.J. and Hawkeye help two North Koreans.

Hawkeye, Trapper John, Hot Lips, Frank, Radar, Father Mulcahy, Klinger, Colonel Blake—and later Colonel Potter, B.J., Charles, and several others—were so real that they seemed interchangeable with the actors who portrayed them. Like its sitcom contemporaries—*Sanford and Son*, *Happy Days*, and *Kotter*—it had a proliferation of one-liners, but unlike the others, those jokes grew out of the characters' characters, and not just the networks' insistence on a laugh every twenty-eight seconds.

* * *

COLONEL POTTER: You too young to die, Pierce?
HAWKEYE: I was hoping to make it to Thursday.

* * *

Somehow the *M*A*S*H*ers* managed to create for us a real place out of a Hollywood backlot, the back yard of a raging war, a place with "hot and cold running rodents," a place that "received four stars from the International Hell Hole Society." The men and women lived in fear and tents, often under siege, always under pressure, overworked, overtired, overcome and overwrought. Everything was constructed in a hurry—the tents, Hawkeye's homemade still from army medical leftover parts—the gin was "strained through official GI underwear"—and there was always anxiety that the Big M—Mobile—would go into effect and the crew would have to move on. There was no place like home.

* * *

HAWKEYE: *(while the operating room is mistakenly under fire—by US troops):* We're safe as long as they keep aiming at us.

* * *

It was a place where, instead of Bob Hope, a troupe of performing dogs entertained the soldiers. A place where mail call was the only link to civilization, and special delivery was a wounded body delivered by copter, COD. A place where men went to Rosie's to get drunk and to the Pink Pagoda in Seoul to release other tensions. Where the Koreans sold everything—real estate, counterfeit money, people, watches that ran backward—"Try other wrist, soldier." A place where "bombs bursting in air" had no melody. Where the service was of no service to anybody.

* * *

COLONEL POTTER *(operating on an eight-year-old Korean girl):* Somebody dropped a bomb on her building from an airplane.
PILOT: Who did it?

HAWKEYE: He just dropped it. He didn't autograph it.
PILOT: Was it one of theirs or one of ours?
HAWKEYE: What difference does it make?
PILOT: A lot. It makes a lot of difference.
COLONEL POTTER: Not to her.

* * *

M*A*S*H started life as a novel written by an unidentified physician, an alumnus of the Korean War, who wanted to write his honest account—honest in every way except that he used a pseudonym—Richard Hooker—so as not to ruin his stateside medical practice. Years later, when the TV M*A*S*H became so successful, he revealed himself—Dr. J. Richard Hornberger—saying that "I'm not going to knock anything that pays me an extra gallbladder a week for no work" (he received $300 an episode in royalties, apparently about the same as he got for a gallbladder operation).

Movie director Robert Altman bought the book rights and made M*A*S*H, a hit movie starring Elliott Gould and Donald Sutherland. It was a financial and critical success. So, of course, television reared its rip-off head and, willing to cut a clone anywhere it could, bought the rights, and decided to sitcomize M*A*S*H. And, on Sunday night, September 17, 1972, CBS gave birth to M*A*S*H.

It wasn't an easy delivery. That first season, the ratings went up and down, and, at midseason, CBS strongly considered sending the M*A*S*H troops home and canceling the show. The network gave it a second chance and the second season—sandwiched between the hits All in the Family and The Mary Tyler Moore Show—it too became a hit.

Right from the start, the dialogue gave away that this show was going to be something different: "Hey, nurse, you wanna play doctor when we're finished with this operation?" "Captain, if you don't move, I'm going to have to cut around your B cups."

* * *

RADAR: How can I ever thank you?
HAWKEYE: Well, you can give us your firstborn.
B.J.: And an order of fries.

* * *

To understand the character of the show, you have to understand the characters. Alone, they were all interesting; together—interacting and reacting to one another—they were fascinating. Here's a Who's Who of the 4077th M*A*S*H unit, the aides, nurses, and doctors who kept us in stitches while stitching up the wounds of war:

● Captain Benjamin Franklin Pierce—a.k.a. Hawkeye—was the star of the show, the leader of the

Trouble: Radar and Colonel Blake

pack, the anchor of the unit. He was a terrific doctor and a terrific jokester. His problem: he couldn't adjust to life behind the lines, so he came up with funny lines. "Me, scared?!" he once exclaimed. "This whole body is one white knuckle."

In a sense, Hawkeye was a serious Mork, a spaceman from Earth who somehow landed in the war zone. Underneath his cynicism was a deep streak of optimism and devotion (once, when he was eligible to go back home, he refused because he was needed at the base). Hawkeye's words speak louder than actions, so here are some of them on a variety of subjects:

NURSE: I thought we were going to talk about Gray's Anatomy—not mine.
HAWKEYE: Gray has a fabulous personality, but no body whatsoever. You really want to talk about surgery? How 'bout if I just show you my appendix scar.

And when someone walked in on Hawkeye and a nurse, he explained: "We were just discussing the ups and downs of doctor/nurse relationships."

When caught wearing civilian underwear: "These are my mother's underwear. She said as long as I wore them, nothing would ever happen to me—she figured that, since nothing ever happened to her when she wore them . . ."

Hawkeye's cynicism ran deep and dark. It wasn't merely segregated in the barracks, but evident in the operating room too:

HAWKEYE: Do you realize what time it is? It's quarter to dead.

Once a doctor in the operating room pardoned himself to go to the bathroom. "Officers don't go to the toilet," Hawkeye said, "they just explode when they're fifty."

Another time, Hawkeye was helping out by performing surgery in a Korean hospital.

HAWKEYE (*after a Korean nurse hands him a dirty pair*

of scissors): What did you sterilize this in—egg drop soup?

KOREAN DOCTOR: We do the best we can, Captain, with the little we have.

HAWKEYE: Sorry, it's just that I'm opposed to germ warfare. *(Gunfire explodes.)* I'm not too crazy about *that* warfare either.

It seemed that Hawkeye would do anything. But the one thing he wouldn't do was carry a gun: "I'll treat their wounds, heal their wounds, bind their wounds—but I will not inflict their wounds."

Often, he and other M*A*S*H surgeons would work round the clock, then collapse from exhaustion. On one such occasion, he and Colonel Potter collapsed in a heap together.

COLONEL POTTER: By the way—what war *is* this?
HAWKEYE: The latest war to end all wars.

• Captain John McIntyre—a.k.a. Trapper John—was Hawkeye's buddy. Also a great surgeon, but he wasn't as humane; he was more brittle, more cynical and let it be known that he was a big-city boy. A macho type. He was married, but he thought nothing of sleeping around.

TRAPPER JOHN *(emerging from the operating room):* I'm taking ten minutes.
NURSE: I'm off for ten minutes.
TRAPPER JOHN: Between us, we've got twenty minutes—let's go.

But he had a serious side. Once, he contemplated deserting the M*A*S*H unit and the army: "If I don't like a movie," he explained to Hawkeye, "I get up and leave. I'm going. War—it doesn't end. It continues. When it's finished playing here, they'll take it on the road."

The behind-the-screen background of Wayne Rogers' exit from *M*A*S*H* is far more interesting than Trapper John's reason for leaving the unit (he was discharged). One day, it seems, Rogers simply didn't show up for work. And never came back. Explains his manager, Arthur Gregory: "He's not one of these young SOBs who just want more lines. He had an agreement originally, before they ever signed Alan Alda, that said he was to be the star. But when they signed Alda, they got an actor with a bigger name, and Alda got all the good stuff. Trapper John became subservient to the Hawkeye character. Soon all Wayne was saying was, 'Do you want a martini?' I've got the original memos stating that Rogers would be the star, and you can tell those SOB executives I'll shove the memos in their faces."

• When Trapper John left, B. J. Hunnicut took his place. He seemed very conservative—a real Army Man—but, of course, he wasn't. He was much like Hawkeye, but gentler, sweeter, more malleable and more of a conformist. When another doctor was speaking pessimistically about a patient in front of the patient, B.J. threatened him: "You make one more doomsday remark and you're going to need splints for your teeth."

As Hawkeye said about him: "B.J.'s clean-cut, even-tempered, a family man—and in spite of that, I really like the guy." B.J. was hopelessly devoted to his wife, Peg (even during the one brief moment he had a guilt-ridden affair), and was continually writing her letters that were the basis of some episodes. Whereas Trapper John was often Hawkeye's straight man, B.J. was right there next to Hawkeye, embellishing on his one-liners, like this instance in the operating room when they'd saved a wounded soldier's life:

HAWKEYE: This guy should be eternally grateful.
B.J.: And internally grateful . . .

• Lieutenant Colonel Henry Blake was an upper-middle-class AMA type—suburban, straight, and silly. "Oh, gosh," he always said as he wore his fishing hat and wondered what he should do. He loved and missed his wife, but slept around anyway. He was bumbling and leering and a dirty old man. Also wishy-washy and ineffectual. But likable. Really likable.

He was constantly and continually confused by the mess and mass of bureaucratic business, and was totally dependent on Radar to fix and figure things out for him,

Temptation: Colonel resists the advances of a career nurse who's fallen in love with him.

whether it was requisitioning for a new incubator or a pizza maker.

Once, however, he came through with some wise words about war: "All I know is what they taught me at command school. There are certain rules about a war, and Rule Number One is that young men die, and Rule Number Two is that doctors can't change rule Number One."

• When he was discharged, Colonel Sherman Potter took his place. "Why didn't I shoot my foot and stay in Honolulu?" he once said in frustration, but he didn't mean it. As the elder statesman of the M*A*S*H unit, he was a friend and counselor, an arbitrator and career man, surrounded by the artifacts of his long, traditional career. He was open to change. He loved his wife.

HOT LIPS: You've been away from Mrs. Potter a long time . . . surely you must feel . . . yearnings.
POTTER: Yes—she does make a helluva raisin cupcake.
HOT LIPS: You've forgotten what it's like to be young.
POTTER: Listen, missy—I don't take these cold showers just cause I'm dirty . . .

● Hot Lips—her real name and title were Major Margaret Houlihan—was a tough, feisty, humorless career woman. As head nurse of the M*A*S*H unit for years, she could barely tolerate the drafted doctors, but then she married and divorced Lieutenant Colonel Donald Penobscott (whom we rarely saw) and mellowed a bit. (Once, in gunfire, she even kissed Hawkeye—after her divorce, of course.) Before that, she'd had a long-standing (and other positions as well) affair with Major Burns, but always denied it. It was implied that she slept around with the Big Brass. She was a great nurse. But a tough cookie.

RADAR (interrupting a conversation between Hot Lips and Colonel Potter): Excuse me . . .
HOT LIPS: Will you butt out!!! This is man talk!!!
RADAR: I'm sorry, sir.

In one moving episode, Hot Lips was having difficulties with her nurses. She'd been hard on them and they didn't like her. By the episode's finale, we finally got a glimpse at her heart.

NURSE: Once, just once, couldn't you show a little compassion?
HOT LIPS: Why? Did you ever show me any kind of friendship? Ask my help with a personal problem? Include me in one of your bull sessions? Can you imagine what it feels like to walk by this tent and know I'm not welcome? And did you ever offer me a lousy cup of coffee?
NURSE: We didn't think you'd accept.
HOT LIPS: Well, you were wrong.

"I just don't let it get to me," she once explained about the war. "I don't feel a thing. I just won't permit it." And immediately after saying that, she learned that her husband had taken a honeymoon without her. She screamed and ranted and yelled—because an officer had left his jockstrap laying on his bed where she could see it. And then she'd straighten up again: "I won't accept pain. I just won't."

● Major Frank Burns once said of Hawkeye: "He has no respect for his superiors and seems almost deliberately kind to those beneath him." Once, after he'd tried to court-martial Hawkeye—for, among other things, writing "Know your enema" under Senator Joseph McCarthy's photo—the judge said to Frank: "If you hadn't been drafted as a doctor, I think you'd have been assigned as a pastry chef." Frankly, Frank was a lousy doctor. And a lousy person. And, since he shared a tent with B.J. and Hawkeye, he was the continual butt of their jokes:

HAWKEYE (when Frank wakes up): I thought the lump under the blanket was dirty laundry.
B.J. It is.

Often, Hawkeye had the unfortunate experience of teaming up with Frank on surgery:

HAWKEYE: While I'm cutting, Frank, you give him a manicure.

Although married (and plenty worried his wife would "change" by the time he returned home—"I'll kill her before I divorce her"), he was having a "clandestine" affair (that everyone knew about) with Hot Lips. He was greatly depressed when she got married, and kept hoping she'd "come to your senses" and come back to him.

As a little comic relief in a heavy-duty episode about Communists vs. Americans, Frank was kidnapped by Korean soldiers. Unable to put up any longer with his constant jabbering, they finally released him: "Go back to your camp—it's the best thing you could do for *our* side."

● When Frank left the M*A*S*H unit, his bunk was taken by Major Charles Emerson Winchester, a fine academic surgeon who'd been to all the right schools and hated anyone he thought was beneath him. Hawkeye and B.J. weren't too wild about him either. Said Hawkeye: "I recommend an evening with Charles. We don't get Milton Berle here, so we're trying Charles out. We think he can replace dysentery." Charles was a thoroughly competent surgeon and a thoroughly incompetent person.

*Newcomer: Charles joins the M*A*S*H unit.*

• Father John Mulcahy—or "our resident celibate," as Colonel Potter once called him—was a different kind of outsider to the war than the doctors. Once, when a soldier had been wounded, he refused to talk to Mulcahy because he didn't know about war at first hand. "No offense, Father, but we have nothing to talk about." So Mulcahy sneaked out on a mission with Radar to deliver a wounded soldier in order to see what the war was all about. Bombs blew up all around them, and Father Mulcahy was devastated. "Do you ever get used to it?" he asked a soldier. "You get used to never getting used to it," the soldier answered. On his private secret mission, Mulcahy had to perform an emergency tracheotomy, which he did with his Tom Mix pocket knife. It worked and he'd accomplished what he'd wanted to: he'd been part of the action of war.

He was gently dizzy. "Let us now pray for a speedy end to this war . . . uh, police action," he once recited in his daffy way. But he could be strangely and strongly articulate, as when he described the operating room battlefield to a visitor: "When the doctor cuts into a patient, and it's cold like it is now today, steam rises from the body, and the doctor will warm himself over the wound. Could anyone look on that and not feel changed?"

• Always around to lighten things up was Corporal Maxwell Klinger, a Lebanese operating room aide whose roots were in a Toledo mob family. He wanted a Section Eight more than anything: to be discharged because of insanity. His ploy: wearing women's clothes. As he once explained to a guest: "These are the outward trappings of my unfortunate insanity. I don't belong here. If two doctors will sign a form, I'll be able to go home. And, so far, I've got all but both of them."

So in the meantime, Klinger paraded around like a *Vogue* model, looking much more like Florence Nightingale than a M*A*S*H medic. "My uncle got out of World War Two this way," he explained. "He keeps sending me pieces of his wardrobe. What love that man has for me." Of course, when he assisted in surgery, Klinger wore a nurse's cap, and when on guard duty, he often had a pink chiffon scarf dangling from his rifle.

COLONEL POTTER: I wouldn't want an entire company of Klingers.
HAWKEYE: Unless, of course, Christian Dior attacks Pearl Harbor.

Once Klinger had this conversation with Radar:

KLINGER: I'm a GI all the way—I go by the book.
RADAR: In *dresses?*
KLINGER: But they're always in the best of taste.

Once, when all of Klinger's dresses disappeared, he looked at the one he was wearing and exclaimed: "I can't wear this every day—people will laugh." And always

Dressing Up: Hot Lips dresses down Klinger.

hanging out of the side of Klinger's mouth was "a Havana cigar made in Newark by Puerto Ricans." Klinger was the comic relief among the comic relief.

• Young Corporal Radar O'Reilly—aide first to Colonel Blake and then to Colonel Potter—was an avid collector of both comic books and animals. He would have liked being a lover of other things—such as women—but never had much luck (except—finally—once). When Frank was making an inspection of his bunk and discovered Radar's teddy bear, Radar murmured shyly that "I'm trying to do better, sir." He was a devoted son to his mother in Iowa. (When he won at poker, he'd say, "Now I can buy my mom some more electrolysis.") About the extent of his sexual experience was when "back home on Saturday night, we used to watch them undress the store window dummies." When a nurse, who lusted after his pudgy body, called him "stud," he nearly fainted.

Another time, Hawkeye tried to bribe Radar by telling him he'd get to be assistant at the nurses' annual physical. Radar's glasses dropped and his eyes popped: "Is that the *complete* physical?"

Radar got his name because he had a special "sense"—he knew what people were going to say before they'd say it, and he could hear choppers coming before anyone else could.

Most important, though, Radar was everybody's right arm. He kept the camp running efficiently, and without him, it seemed as though it would have fallen apart. Everyone adored him. More than any of the others, Radar absolutely idolized Hawkeye and B.J.

In one episode, it was nearly the end of his friendship with Hawkeye. It began when Radar told Hawkeye and B.J. that he was tired of holding on to his virginity. "I want to be a hot lover—or even a cold one. I'm the only one who's gonna leave this place younger than when I came in."

They told him to go to Seoul to the Pink Pagoda. He started off.

Then word—and the body—came back that Radar had been hit by mortar fire. Hawkeye felt stricken with guilt—"He's such a cute little guy, you know"—and wouldn't even joke in the operating room. When it was clear that Radar was okay, Hawkeye went out and got drunk—and became sick the next day in the operating room. "What's your explanation?" Colonel Potter demanded. "I screwed up," Hawkeye explained, "I socked another belt into my body because I didn't have anyone else to sock."

Hawkeye later went to visit Radar in the recovery room—but Radar was angry with him for walking out of an operation because he was sick from drinking too much. His idol had fallen. A recovering Radar asked Hawkeye how *could* he have gone out and gotten drunk, forsaking his responsibilities as a surgeon. "Don't you know how much this place stinks?" Hawkeye blurted out. "Don't you know what it's like to stand, day after day, in blood—and the blood of children. I hate this place."

But that wasn't good enough for Radar. His hero had not behaved perfectly, and so he told Hawkeye how angry he was with him.

Hawkeye became livid. "How dare you! To hell with your Iowa naiveté! To hell with your hero worship! And your teddy bear! And while I'm at it, to hell with you! Why don't you grow up, for cryin' out loud? I'm not here for you to admire . . . now cut it out—you *ninny!*" He stormed out. Radar was stunned, and everyone on the base was angry with Hawkeye for hurting Radar. When Hawkeye returned to apologize, Radar screamed at him: "The hell with you!"

Potter went in to talk to Radar, who reported bitterly that he no longer viewed Hawkeye as an idol. "You might like him better now that you can see more eye to eye," Potter told Radar. And he was right. When Hawkeye and Radar passed each other on the road, they just stopped and stared at one another. Hawkeye went into Rosey's and ordered a beer. At a separate table, Radar ordered a Grape Nehi soda. They talked—slowly and politely—about the weather and that day's breakfast. Finally, Hawkeye apologized again. They made up. The waitress brought Hawkeye his beer and Radar his Nehi. In a demonstration of friendship, the two traded bottles. And later, when Radar received the Purple Heart for his valor, Hawkeye did something he almost never did: he saluted Radar.

Strangely, as cast members came and left, the core of the show stayed the same—partly because the form of the show had a built-in format for change, so that new people could come and go without the writers having to write in another kooky-next-door-neighbor—as was usually done as part of the silly sitcom-syndrome.

In the spring of 1975, McLean Stevenson left the series after signing a long-term contract with NBC (that eventually led him to the dippy *McLean Stevenson Show* and the moderately successful—and even dippier—*Hello Larry*). The exit was handled like this: Henry Blake got his orders to ship out. He and the crew had an emotional farewell. During the final tag of the show, Radar entered the operating room—without surgical mask on—and told the doctors that "I have a message": the colonel's helicopter had just been shot down over the ocean. The camera did a slow pan across all the faces of the surgeons—who were waging war in the operating room, hunched over open bodies—as they all cried softly and silently upon hearing the news. (The actors didn't know Colonel Blake was going to get killed; Radar/Gary Burghoff was given the script just a moment before the scene was shot, so the cast's reactions would be fresh.) On the next episode, Colonel Henry Blake was replaced by Colonel Sherman Potter. (On a talk show once, the host asked Harry Morgan, the *Dragnet*, *December Bride*, and *Pete and Gladys* alumnus who played Potter, if there was anyone who didn't like *M*A*S*H*. "Yes," Morgan answered, "McLean Stevenson.")

When Wayne Rogers (who played Hawkeye's best buddy, Trapper John) left the show over contract disputes at the end of the 1974–1975 season (there were suits and countersuits flying for months), it was also handled sadly: Hawkeye was on a do-not-disturb R&R when Trapper John got his sudden orders to leave for home. When Hawkeye finally heard, he ran for the airport to say goodbye—but he was too late. Instead, he met a guy just arriving—a B.J. Hunnicut—whom Hawkeye was sure he wouldn't like at all. But they went out drinking—and thinking—and became fast friends. B.J. went on to take Trapper John's place in Hawkeye's life (and bunk).

When Hot Lips fell in love with and later married Lieutenant Colonel Penobscott (who once sent her a leather whip—"Oooh, that thoughtful darling. He knows I love fine leathers," she purred), Frank Burns burned. When actor Larry Linville left the show, the writers had Frank go AWOL (Linville wanted to leave and do other work, ending up as the silly buffoon, Major General Kevin Kelley, in the 1978–1979 one-seasoner *Grandpa Goes to Washington*). The spot that Frank Burns had in the M*A*S*H unit—as the butt of everyone's nasty jokes—was filled by pompous Major General Charles Emerson Winchester (played by David Ogden Stiers, who had once played the stuttering station manager at WJM-TV on *The Mary Tyler Moore Show*, and had appeared in the fall of 1976 as Dr. Stanley Moss, who ran the Westside Clinic on *Doc*).

In the course of the series, a number of nurses passed through the M*A*S*H unit (many of them played by the same actress, who was referred to by different names in different episodes, plus, a lot of nurses seemed to be called Nurse Baker or Nurse Able). Also a silly CIA agent (who fancied himself a "master of disguise") and Dr. Friedman, a poker-playing army psychiatrist, made occasional appearances.

During the 1978–1979 season, Gary Burghoff—who had played Radar since the show's start and had invented

Nuptials: Hot Lips marries her Colonel Donald Penobscott—but not for long.

the part in the motion picture—decided he'd had enough:

"Success can be the biggest bore in the world when it gets to the point that you have done everything you can do. I can't stand going to the set anymore and watching people play chess or do needlepoint in order to occupy themselves. At one time everybody talked and laughed, and the enthusiasm carried us along. You can't expect enthusiasm to last. I'm not bored with what you see on the screen, I'm bored with what I have to do to get it there. Sit around four hours, get up and do a short scene. If I'm an unhappy person, Radar will be unhappy on the screen. Listen, if I don't work in TV again I won't give a damn. M*A*S*H was the best show I could do."

Emergency Discharge: Hawkeye says goodbye to Radar, who leaves to run his family's farm.

Radar left Korea—in a two-part tearful good-bye—after returning from an R&R and finding out that his uncle had died and his mom had to tend the farm alone—making him the sole-surviving-son and eligible for discharge. Klinger—out of drag—went on to take over Radar's position.

The one actor who was the man for all seasons (all TV seasons, that is) was Alan Alda (his real name: Alphonso D'Abruzzo). Strangely enough, his father, actor Robert Alda, wanted Alan to be a doctor, not an actor. On M*A*S*H, he got to be both. Before going to Hollywood, Alda had appeared in many Broadway shows, including *The Apple Tree* and *The Owl and the Pussycat*. In college, he was in the ROTC, where he had to teach other students "how to kill. One time I got physically sick. That's when I learned I was a pacifist," he said.

A staunch feminist (he contributed material to the book, the record, and the TV versions of *Free to Be You and Me*), Alda was also a family person who commuted between Hollywood, where M*A*S*H was shot, and his home in the New Jersey suburbs, where his wife and daughters lived. (Not strangely at all, in the 1974–1975 season, Alda developed a sitcom called *We'll Get By*, all about a lovingly understanding family who lived in the New Jersey suburbs.)

"I admit," Alda said, "that there have been times when I've worked too much, too hard, especially during the *We'll Get By* period. For long stretches, weeks at a time, the only contact I had with my family was by phone. That's no longer true. I finally realized how absurd it was to be writing and coproducing a show about family solidarity when I was neglecting my own family."

In the summer of 1978, however, Alda did make three movies back-to-back: *California Suite*, *Same Time Next Year*, and *The Seduction of Joe Tynan*. He always kept busy, writing and directing many of the M*A*S*H episodes, and starring in them all.

But the real man behind M*A*S*H was Larry Gelbart, who was living in London back in 1972 when he got a call to make a TV version of the book and movie M*A*S*H—"without tearing yourself away from London, of course," he was told. Says Gelbart: "I wrote the pilot in London and then, just out of curiosity, I flew to Los Angeles for the first reading and rehearsal." He got interested, and packed up his wife and kids for a few months' stay in L.A.—which turned into four years, during which Gelbart wrote most of the M*A*S*Hes (his favorite is the Clete Mathews improvised interview show), directed many episodes, and shaped the series. In 1976, at the show's popularity peak, Gelbart suddenly quit. M*A*S*H had become my home away from home," he say, "and there were other creative juices flowing in me." He meant Broadway—*Sly Fox*—and movies—*Oh, God, Movie, Movie* and others—and didn't return to television until the 1979-1980 season with *United States*, a half-hour marital com-dram that many critics thought (and hoped) would change the course of sitcoms forever.

*   *   *

FRANK: Unless we each conform, unless we obey orders, unless we follow our leaders blindly—there is no possible way we can remain free.

*   *   *

Reams, chapters, books could be written about *M*A*S*H*. But *M*A*S*H* deserves it—not because it was "the best" (others might be better), but because *M*A*S*H* helped change the way we think about America. In *M*A*S*H* the "good guys"—the superpatriots, the gung-ho war people—were often the bad guys. Even more so, no one in *M*A*S*H* was totally good or bad; it was the first sitcom to paint its characters in varying shades of grays.

It was antiwar while remaining pro-life. "It's pro-sanity," Alan Alda once said. "Because war is obviously an insane institution . . . so we at *M*A*S*H* agree with a long line of American Presidents and generals and, um, other butchers. Everybody who's ever made war agrees it's a bad thing."

But the positive proof of *M*A*S*H*'s impact was in the spring of 1979 when Alan Alda was asked to give the commencement address at Harvard Medical School. (Years ago, Robert Young had given the commencement speech at another medical school—after he had played fantasy-figure *Marcus Welby, M.D.*—but it was part of a student protest because the speaker they had originally wanted wasn't approved by the faculty. As a joke they submitted Young's name. He was approved.) Alda, you can be certain, was never asked to speak at West Point.

Most of all, though, *M*A*S*H* improved on the history of "service sitcoms," as they were called. Bilko told us that War Is Fun. Hogan went a little deeper and said that, perhaps, War Is Heck. *M*A*S*H* just came out and said it: War Is Hell.

Perhaps *M*A*S*H* melded so well because it was a contradiction of terms: war is supposed to take away lives. And here were these doctors in the middle of a deathly war—trying to save lives—which made them subversives. Which meant that we—the millions and millions of Americans tuning into *M*A*S*H* each week—were harboring war criminals in our living rooms.

But how would *M*A*S*H* call it quits? Said Alda: "Well, I'd like to see the show end with the war being over and I'd like to see—I think that it would be a very

*Some of the M*A*S*Hers (from left): Front row: Frank, Colonel Potter, Radar. Second row: Hot Lips, Hawkeye, B.J. Back row: Klinger, Father Mulcahy*

powerful episode—I'd like to see a long piece, maybe an hour and a half, in which the people say goodbye to each other and to the experience and have it end, have it be over. I think that the audience and this story, this experience, deserve that kind of conclusion."

It's the eighties now. It's been thirty years since the *M*A*S*H* troupe fought for freedom in Korea.

One can only wonder where they are now. Perhaps Father Mulcahy left the priesthood. Maybe Klinger owns a successful chain of ladies' apparel stores. And, no doubt, B.J., in the late sixties, got involved in the peace movement and even marched on Washington with the Veterans Against Foreign Wars.

But Hawkeye. He's back in Maine—Crab Apple Cove—having taken over his father's practice. He's married, with two young children. He often tells them his war tales, just like Frank and Charles and the rest of them tell their war tales.

But Hawkeye's kids think he's exaggerating when he tells them about Corporal Klinger in his dresses, Radar's teddy bear, the still he and B.J. built in their tent, Hot Lips' whips . . . They don't believe his stories—"That's silly, daddy."

And then they go upstairs to watch reruns of *F Troop*.

MAUDE

Enterprising, socializing, everything but compromising—right on, Maude!

—*Maude* theme song

If, by some miracle of time and telecommunications, Maude and Walter Findlay had moved in next door to Harriet and Ozzie Nelson, you can be sure Ozzie and Harriet would have moved out—and taken all their friends with them: Jim and Margaret Anderson, June and Ward Cleaver, Donna and Alex Stone, the Partridges, the Bradys, everyone.

But, boy, were we lucky to have Maude in our neighborhood. She was rough and tough—also fragile and frail—and one of the first Real People to hit the small screen in sitcom history. She was yet another welcome example of the then new-school of sitcom-vérité, in which sitcoms imitated life (of course, the joke was on sitcoms, because life had been imitating sitcoms for years). *Maude*'s theme song compared her to other strong, sturdy ladies of history—Lady Godiva, Joan of Arc, Betsy Ross. But Maude had something that none of them had, something that made her more powerful than them all: she had her own weekly TV show. Plus, the Nielsen family (not to be confused with the Nelson family) loved her.

Maude imitated nobody, but *Maude* seemed to intimidate everybody—the network censors, easily threatened men, and reactionary and frightened Americans who tried to burn crosses on *Maude*'s screen. As a child of Norman Lear (along with her cousins the Sanfords, the Jeffersons, the Bunkers, and several others), Maude got herself in some R-rated antics, strictly seventies-style: a dab of politics, a nervous breakdown here, a little manic-depression there, a little wife-swapping, a bit of abortion, some alcoholism. She was giving *All in the Family* a nose-to-nose race for the Most Controversial Pageant. And neither Maude nor cousin Archie was a strong contender for Miss Congeniality.

Maude was the first child of *All in the Family*, the first spin-off that itself would beget a spin-off of its own (*Good Times*). Maude's roots crept back to a guest shot on *All in the Family*. Maude went sailing to the Bunkers' to care for her ailing cousin Edith. Maude was Archie's adversary. He was lower-middle class. She was upper-middle class. He was archconservative. She was an archliberal. But, you see—and this was the catch—they were really a lot alike: both were stubborn and pigheaded and outspoken. At that time, however, he had his own series; she didn't. Daddy Lear rectified that situation on Tuesday, September 12, 1972, when he gave Maude a show of her own.

Maude lived in suburban Tuckahoe, New York (years later—in Real Life—someone in Tuckahoe opened up a tavern called Maude's Bar), in a wonderful sitcom house that was just a little grander than the Bunkers': a flame-stitched, camelback sofa was the room's centerpiece (vying closely with a stand-up, halfmoon bar, around which a lot of the action and interaction took place). There was a bentwood coatrack near the front door, and a small dining area at the other end of the room. There was a den off toward the back, an angular set of stairs that led to the bedrooms, and swinging doors that led to the modern kitchen where Maude and Walter often argued and fought with food and dishes. It was in this house that all of the situations were situated.

It was a breakthrough show—most of Lear's were, of course—but it dealt with not only sex, but its side- (and after-) effects: birth control, unwanted pregnancy, menopause. It dealt with other moral issues—everything from the meaning of life to the meaning of death, and points in between. With humor, of course.

But more important than even breaking the barriers

Maude Findlay	Beatrice Arthur
Walter Findlay	Bill Macy
Carol	Adrienne Barbeau
Phillip	Brian Morrison (1972–1977); Kraig Metzinger (1977–1978)
Dr. Arthur Harmon	Conrad Bain
Vivian Cavender Harmon	Rue McClanahan
Florida Evans	Esther Rolle (1972–1974)
Henry Evans	John Amos (1973–1974)
Chris	Fred Grandy (1973–1974)
Mrs. Naugatuck	Hermione Baddeley (1974–1977)
Bert Beasley	J. Pat O'Malley (1975–1977)
Victoria Butterfield	Marlene Warfield (1977–1978)

The Family: Walter, Maude, Carol

of sex and the single sitcom (*All in the Family* had already done that), *Maude* was most significant in its exploration of the problems of upper-middle age. *Maude* had wrinkles. Most sitcom families were young and perky (Donna Reed and Margaret Anderson never aged from week to week, from season to season) and sitcom singles were usually forever young (*That Girl* never evolved into That Woman, and even Mary Richards canceled herself when she was nary thirty-seven). Maude Findlay was in her late forties, and every year she got older (and bolder). She was a grandmother. She went through menopause. She worried about aging. She had a facelift. She still looked her age. When she turned fifty, Maude's birthday celebration was a moving visit to a psychotherapist. "I'm fifty and nobody loves me," she cried, and then looked into the mirror: "Oh, God, if I could only repeal the law of gravity."

Since the show was a Lear creation, the subject matter was never the usual sitcom-style fare. In one of the most significant series of episodes, Maude discovered she was pregnant, and was going through great consternation about what to do. Viewers—used to Lucy Ricardo's not being able to even mention the word "pregnant"—probably assumed Maude would rid herself of an unwanted "expectancy" by having the baby and putting it up for adoption. But that would have been too easy. Instead, Maude—who always did things her own way—had an abortion.

Although the Supreme Court had legalized abortion, many CBS local affiliates tried to abort *Maude* from their airwaves. Those who ran the episodes received hundreds of letters and calls from irate and offended viewers. Stations and viewers went to court to battle the episodes being put on/pulled off, depending on their stance. "Pro-life" groups were pro-death for *Maude*; many mailed Norman Lear 8 X 10 glossies of aborted fetuses.

Of course, Maude didn't have abortions every week. No. Sometimes she had just the daily operations of her existence: Run-ins with John Wayne, trying to run Henry Fonda for President (of the US, not CBS), and working out the staples of everyday radical-chic sitcom life. Some examples:

☐ An acquaintance of Maude's died. Maude had lent her a beloved brooch, and there it was, on the dead friend's body in the casket. Maude hovered over the casket, crying hysterically, and then ripped it from the corpse. ☐

☐ Maude was arrested for speeding and, certain of her innocence, she contested and demanded her day in court. She won the battle but, as she was leaving, the bailiff demanded she pay up some delinquent parking fines. She'd gone to all the trouble to come down to court, but rather than wait in a long line at the cashiers', she offered the bailiff a $5 bribe. ☐

☐ Maude wanted to cheer up Walter on his birthday, and so arranged a reunion between Walter and an old friend—only to have the friend drop dead of a heart attack when he'd been reunited with Walter, whose depression sank to new depths. ☐

Maude was a ballsy bully who could—and would—rant and rave and roar like a lion (and purr like a kitten). The only one she ever listened to was husband Walter. "Maude—*sit!*" he would command. And Maude would obey.

Until her next outburst. "God'll get you for that!" she would bray at Walter, her fingers outstretched as though she were casting a spell or finger-painting an evil curse on his spirit, or simply ripping his heart out.

Beatrice Arthur, the dandy actress who played her, *was* Maude. Norman Lear had been trying to cajole her into sitcomland for years, but she resisted. Her husband at the time, writer/director Gene Saks, finally persuaded her. "Ambition didn't land me the role of Maude," Arthur said, "it was my husband nagging me to get off my butt and do something." Not that she'd been doing nothing before. An accomplished actress, she had appeared in the original New York productions of *Three Penny Opera*, as well as *Gentlemen Prefer Blondes* and *Mame* (for which she won a Tony as Vera Charles; she subsequently made the movie with Lucille Ball and, many believe, was the only bright spot in it). She appeared with Chita Rivera and Dody Goodman in *Shoestring Revue*, and understudied Tallulah Bankhead

Maude and Vivian: At the funeral of a "dear friend" they both hated.

in *The Follies*. (Bankhead used to call her "the Divine Beatrice.") Beatrice Arthur—whose real first name was Bernice—was born in New York on May 13, 1926. Both she and Maude were nearly 5'10" and weighed nearly 150 pounds. "My true inner self is a tiny blonde sex object," she once said.

Maude writer/executive producer Rod Parker had this to say about Arthur: "This lady's perfect timing and fantastic talent is just unbelievable. If she loves a line of dialogue or a bit of business and she wants to take a big laugh and make it into a big scream, she'll challenge the audience by holding off until the last possible second. Then, when she finally does it, they'll go bananas. That takes a lot of courage and it gives the writer a bonus. Jackie Gleason is about the only one I ever worked with who could do that same thing."

It's a good thing she made it. With her deep-deep voice (people who called the Findlay house always thought she was *Mr.* Findlay) and her tall build, she shunned drama school to study to become a laboratory technician. But she ultimately realized that she was a different sort of technician. "There is no one else like me," she once said.

Although it often seemed like a one-woman show (and on one occasion it actually was), *Maude* had quite a supporting cast of characters. Walter, her current husband, was played by Bill Macy, whose reputation painted him as childlike and faintly irresponsible. Before *Maude*'s Walter, Macy had an odd variety of acting roles: from poetry readings and small parts in movies (*A Thousand Clowns* and *The World of Henry Orient*), to the original cast of the "nudie-musical" *Oh! Calcutta*. He progressed. Back in 1973, his *Maude* salary was $10,000 a month.

Many episodes of the show focused around Walter, the voice of reason. He was sort of an inside-out version of Maude (kitten outside; tiger within). Once he and Maude split up ("It's either politics or me, Maude") and he went to live in a leopard-patterned singles palace, replete with swinging stewardesses and horny beer-guzzlers. Walter had troubles down at Findlay's Friendly Appliances (until it went bankrupt and he tried to commit suicide). And, of course, there was his nervous breakdown and his alcoholism (little things like that . . .) that gave his character some character. Mainly, though, Walter was on the receiving end of Maude's ploys and passions, and he often had a difficult time adjusting to her loud liberation. But we knew that in the bedroom, everything was equal.

Maude, of course, had friends—in this case, the token TV neighbors, her Fred and Ethel: Arthur and Vivian Harmon. Arthur was a conservative fathead (of a higher class, but not caliber, than Cousin Archie), a doctor who appeared faintly incompetent, which allowed for many jokes against the medical establishment. Vivian Harmon had been Vivian Cavender when we first met her. At that time, she was happily-ever-after married; she and her first husband were the Love Couple—until, after

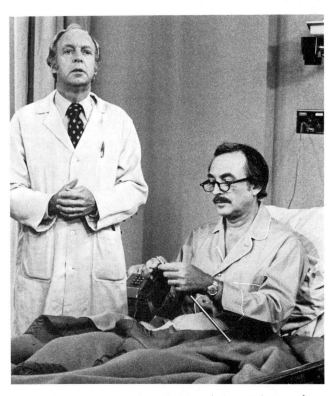

Bedside Manner: Arthur comes to Walter's hospital room after Walter has had a heart attack and refused to contact Maude.

an island vacation with the Findlays (who were envying their lovey-dovey demeanor), they suddenly and unexpectedly announced they were divorcing. And soon after, an ever-twittering Vivian met the widower next door and married him. Always slightly askew of true liberation, Viv worried about her hair and what to serve for dinner, whereas Maude, with her crusades and modern ways, served up only sacred cows over dinner.

Also involved—although peripherally—was Maude's divorced daughter Carol, who lived with Maude along with her son. Carol was the daughter from Maude's second marriage—or was it her first? (Maude had four in all.)

Marriage or the lack of it played a big part on the show. Everybody was always married or re-married (or re-re-re-married, as in Maude's case) or divorced or widowed or between marriages. For years (or seasons, anyway), Carol toyed with the idea of marrying her boyfriend Chris. Walter too had been married before. In fact, everyone had been married—everyone except Carol's son Phillip, who wasn't married once (but who did change personalities in 1977 when they hired a new actor to play the role, which must count for something).

Besides marriage, Maude had a sprightly succession of maids. Her first was Florida (who would later spin off to *Good Times*). Their initial meeting, back in 1972, is a good example of Maude's misdirected liberalism. When Florida came for her initial interview, Maude made it clear—loud and clear—that she didn't want this black woman to be a traditional maid. She insisted that Florida use the front, not the back door. She wanted Florida to

Florida Comes to New York: Maude meets her new maid.

eat her meals with the family as well as join them for cocktails each day. Florida expressed her outrage: she'd rather use the back door because it was easier to get the groceries in that way; she'd prefer to eat alone and didn't like drinking martinis in the middle of the afternoon.

FLORIDA: Now, the first week'll be on a trial basis.
MAUDE: Oh, Florida, don't be ridiculous—you're not on trial.
FLORIDA: I know—*you* are.

Florida's departure at the end of the next season was a tearful one. There had developed a loving bond between the two women. When Florida—whose husband didn't want her to work as a maid anymore—was about to leave and go back to her home in Harlem, she and Maude quietly faced each other. "Oh, we'll visit," they

promised each other. Then Florida stopped. "Mrs. Findlay, you know we'll never visit each other." Said Maude quietly, "I know." A very tender moment.

Things were not so tender between Maude and her next maid, a cynical, hard-drinking Englishwoman, Mrs. Naugatuck, played by Hermione Baddeley, a veteran British stage actress. Baddeley had trouble with the role (in many ways), especially with the American English and lines like "Mrs. Findlay struck out," so she switched to an accent that was half-American, half-Cockney. In time, Baddeley became disgruntled with the show—in any

Underground Courtship: Bert finally proposes to Mrs. Naugatuck.

Maude Turns Fifty: Beatrice Arthur in a one-woman episode

accent. "My parts were getting smaller and smaller," she said. "I didn't want it to get to the 'Yes, mum, no, mum' thing." Mrs. Naugatuck exited in 1976 when she married Bert Beasley and returned to England. Her replacement was Victoria Butterfield (played by Marlene Warfield), who joined the household in the fall of 1977. But none of them ever achieved the popularity of Florida.

Like all Norman Lear sitcoms, there were some classic *Maude* episodes, just as there were classic *I Love Lucy* episodes (such as Lucy stomping grapes in Italy and stuffing chocolates down her blouse on an assembly line). But there's a difference between those classics and *Maude*'s; Lucy's episodes became classics because viewers loved them. *Maude*'s—and the other Norman Lear shows—were classics by design, as though the writers and producers got together in conference and tried to figure out what subjects would become "classics." Here's what they came up with: A stirring episode in which Walter, revealed as an alcoholic, hits Maude across the face and then undergoes rehabilitation; Maude, upon discovering she's a manic-depressive, starts taking Lithium (a medication that "evens out" moods); another in which Maude tries, unsuccessfully, to get Henry

Fonda to run for President. In an early episode, Maude refuses to let Carol and her boyfriend sleep at the house in the same room; of course, the abortion episode; and one in which Maude gives a party at which John Wayne shows up. (Maude refers to him as "Mr. Conservative" and promises to give him "a piece of my mind" only, of course, to melt when he arrives. He calls her "the little woman," and says, "I'm sorry, ma'am, I can't discuss politics with a woman.")

Speaking of politics: when the ratings on the show started to decline in 1978, *Maude* was going to be transplanted to Washington, D.C. (the thinking was that the viewers were tired of the old setting and the old characters); only Walter would remain on the show. By that time, all three maids had left, and Adrienne Barbeau (Carol) was tired of having so little to do on the show. And the other characters had pretty much played out their roles. But Beatrice Arthur had a change of heart. "One can only live with the same character for so long, and it is time for both of us to take a rest," she said in 1978. The fact that the show was sixty-sixth in the ratings and sinking didn't encourage her.

And so Maude retired. Lear sold the shows in an unusual manner—only a year at a time—to a newly formed syndication. Many fans eagerly awaited seeing the 142 episodes of *Maude* over and over again.

Said Beatrice Arthur: "We've accomplished what we set out to accomplish. We brought good theater to television. I may be kidding myself, but I think we gave quality shows to television. Also, for the very first time, we presented somebody who wasn't just a bubblehead out to get laughs. For the first time, issues were dealt with, thoughts were exchanged. I think we made television a little more adult, I really do."

In one of the early episodes, Maude was groaning and griping—nothing unusual—until a friend asked her what it was, exactly, that she wanted. Maude deliberated a moment before answering. "I want it *all*."

And that, of course, was the point of Maude and *Maude*. She wanted it all, and when she got it she handed it on to us. Maude made waves: with one hand she unbuttoned the stuffed shirts of convention, and with the other she gave the finger to authority.

And, no doubt, God'll get her for it.

ALSO RANS

Anna and the King

In Real Life—which, of course, has nothing to do with television—Anna lived with the king of Siam's family for a long time. On the Broadway stage, they danced together for many years. In the movies, they're still singing on late-night TV. But in sitcomland, their relationship lasted less than three months. CBS got the bright idea (and it was a good one) to bring the bald Yul Brynner (he had first shaved his head back in 1951 for his original role in the Rodgers and Hammerstein musical) together with Samantha Eggar to recreate this 1860s story of a school-teacher widow and her twelve-year-old son who pop off to Siam to live with the King and teach his dozens of children (by his dozens of wives). There was conflict, there was affection. There was no music. There was no one watching.

The Little People/The Brian Keith Show

This one started life under the title of *The Little People*, and was another of those heartwarming comedies about a father and daughter team—of pediatricians—who ran a free clinic (as well as a private practice on the side) on the Hawaiian island of Oahu. The Jamisons—as Dr. Sean (Brian Keith) and Dr. Anne (Shelley Fabares, in yet another sitcom comeback-back-back) were called—had only great concern for the little people, and the show was sort of a cross between *Family Affair* and *Hawaii Five-O*, the former also starring Keith. The second season, the situation—and the title—changed. A Dr. Austin Chaffee—a proper physician played by Roger Bowen—shared the office space with Keith; Chaffee's formality and Jamison's informality created many conflicts and—

The Little People / The Brian Keith Show: *Brian Keith, Shelley Fabares and unidentified patient*

well, you know the rest by heart. Then there was Wealthy Widow Mrs. Gruber (played by Nancy Kulp, alumna of *Love That Bob,* and *Beverly Hillbillies'* Miss Jane, who, on this show, had gotten as far as having once been married), who provided problems for the doctor and his daughter. The show ran two seasons on NBC before it was sued for malpractice.

Bridget Loves Bernie

The priests were kvetching. The rabbis were hollering. Never before—except, possibly, when Lucy got pregnant—had there been so much ecumenical commotion over a sitcom. Because Bridget, you see, was Catholic. And Bernie, you see, was Jewish. And because Bridget, you see, loved Bernie, and Bernie, you see, loved Bridget, and the problem, you see, was that nobody

Bridget Loves Bernie: *David Birney and Meredith Baxter (later Meredith Baxter-Birney)*

seemed to love *Bridget Loves Bernie.* Anyway this ethnic show (in which none of the actors, it seems, were even Jewish or Catholic or very good) followed *All in the Family* on Saturday nights, acting as a bridge to get to *Mary Tyler Moore.* The story went something like this: Bridget's parents (David Doyle and Audra Lindley) were wealthy Irish. Bernie's parents (Harold J. Stone and Bibi Osterwald) owned a delicatessen, over which the young married couple lived. The four parents weren't too wild about the union either, and spent many an episode trying to be nice to one another. Sort of an *Abie's Irish Rose,* sitcom-style. The show seemed to condone intermarriage between religious faiths and—God forbid—this is what so many faithful people protested. All right already, CBS said, and canceled the show after one season, even though its ratings were good. David Birney (Bernie) and Meredith Baxter (Bridget) showed them, though, and shortly afterward were married themselves. So there.

Here We Go Again

Larry Hagman—apparently no longer dreaming of Jeannie—got reinvolved in a sitcom about divorce. This one was about a newly married couple, Richard and Susan Evans (Hagman and Diane Baker) who, it turned out, lived right nearby their former mates. Susan's first husband was the owner of Jerry's Polynesian Paradise, Jerry Standish (Dick Gautier). Richard's ex was a domineering magazine editor, Judy Evans (Nita Talbot). Plus there were several children—too many and too confusing to account for here. Anyway, apparently America did not think musical divorce was particularly funny, and so ABC canceled this midseason replacement at the end of the season, proving that Larry should have stuck it out with Jeannie—until, that is, he moved to *Dallas.*

Love Thy Neighbor

This ABC summer replacement show was what was called "an integrated comedy"—which did not mean there were equal parts of laughs and drama, but that it was about a friendship between black people and their all-white neighbors. Charlie Wilson (Ron Masak) was somewhat taken aback when he found out that his new neighbor was *black* (that's the way things were on Friar Tuck Lane in the LA suburb of Sherwood Forest Estates), and then—double whammy!—discovered that the black guy was the new efficiency expert at Turner Electronics, where he was union shop steward. The idea came from the English hit sitcom *Love Thy Neighbor.*

The Paul Lynde Show

It seemed like such a logical thing, to star TV comedian Paul Lynde in his own sitcom. And this show had a lot of fans—people who liked Lynde's sour-prune style of humor. Here was the situation: Lynde played a respectable attorney, Paul Simms, who was living with his wife,

The Paul Lynde Show: *Paul Lynde and Elizabeth Allen*

Martha (Elizabeth Allen), and two daughters in a small California town, Ocean Grove. And then—enter Howie Dickerson (John Calvin), Paul's new son-in-law—wearing blue jeans, long hair, and, most important, wearing an IQ of 185. And they were moving in to Paul's place. Howie was a whiz, but he couldn't hold a job. Which drove Paul crazy. Occasionally seen were Howie's parents, played by Jerry Stiller and Anne Meara. The show lasted one year on ABC.

The Sandy Duncan Show

When Sandy Duncan had to duck out of her successful *Funny Face* because of an eye injury, she reappeared as the same character—Sandy Stockton—in this sitcom. Once again, she was a cute young perky girl, but this time she worked in a small ad agency called Quinn and Cohen. Her close pals were her two neighbors in her apartment building: Kay Fox (Marian Mercer) and Alex Lembeck (M. Emmet Walsh), an overprotective cop who was worried about Sandy being single and living all alone. He shouldn't have worried; she moved out of sitcom city three months later.

The Sandy Duncan Show: *Sandy Duncan*

Temperatures Rising

This medical sitcom had three different casts in two different years, as well as two different titles. Here's how it started and here's how it ended:

During the first season, the show was set at Capital General Hospital in Washington, D.C., where a no-nonsense chief of surgery, Dr. Vincent Campanelli (James Whitmore), presided over his staff—which seemed to be all-nonsense. Here's who created some of the havoc: prankster Jerry Noland (Cleavon Little), a ghetto guy who was also the hospital's chief bookie; sexy nursy Annie Carlisle (Joan Van Ark) and her mischief-maker of a buddy Mildred MacInerny (Reva Rose); and Dr. David Amherst (David Bailey), the handsome young doctor who was adored (among other things) by every nurse in the place. Then there were the patients, who made the staff look like saints, such as an old man who'd drag-race in his wheelchair and a paranoid who wanted all his medication pre-tasted and then slipped under the door.

During its second season, the show got a title alteration: it was now *The New Temperatures Rising Show*, and it had a new set of producers and almost a totally new cast (Cleavon Little was the only one who stayed put). This time around, though, Capital General was a private hospital (a better class of loonies) and it was run by penny-pinching Dr. Paul Mercy (played by Paul Lynde), and owned by his meddlesome mom, Martha (Sudie Bond). She was constantly there and called her son by using a beeper on his belt. There was also an efficient accountant, Miss Tillis (Barbara Cason); a roman-

Temperatures Rising *(from left): James Whitmore, Nancy Fox, Joan Van Ark, Reva Rose, Cleavon Little*

tically inclined nurse, Nurse "Windy" Winchester (Jennifer Darling); and Dr. Axton (Jeff Morrow), a quack who had published two books, *Profit in Healing* and *Malpractice and Its Defense*. This version was no more successful than the first, and lasted only through midseason. But the show did come back again during the summer of 1974 with several new episodes (this time Mom was gone and Paul Lynde's character's sister (played by Alice Ghostley) was there, as was the Cleavon Little character. It didn't help. *Temperatures Rising*—new or old—died on the operating table.

Thicker Than Water

Julie Harris—the great lady of the American stage—tried hard to be the great gal of the American sitcom with this ABC summer replacement series (with hopes that it would run forever). She played Nellie Paine, a staid spinster who was battling her swinging brother Ernie (Richard Long) for their father's $75,000 inheritance. Not that he was dead yet. It's just that he'd told them if they could both live at his home and together run the family pickle factory—"Paine's Pure Pickles"—then they could

have the loot. The old coot, Jonas (Malcolm Atterbury), never died, but hung around to watch them bicker, week after week (fortunately, there were only four of them in all). Based on the English TV series *Nearest and Dearest*.

A Touch of Grace

Jews, Poles, blacks, Puerto Ricans, Italians, young people, middle-aged suburbanites—they'd all made it on sitcoms, so why not a sitcom about old people? Here's why: *A Touch of Grace*, an ABC sitcom designed to be touching, but that was really just touched. It starred Shirley Booth (without her *Hazel* uniform) and J. Patrick O'Malley (who would later turn up as another oldie-but-goodie and marry Mrs. Naugatuck right off *Maude*), who got together on *ATOG* for some steady dating. He was a gravedigger who proposed to Grace finally (but in the final episode, when it was too late to do anything about it). Grace Simpson lived with her conservative daughter, Myra Bradley (Marian Mercer), and Myra's square husband, Walter (Warren Berlinger). Based on the British series *For the Love of Ada*, *A Touch of Grace* died of young age after only thirteen episodes.

1973–1974

Good Times

Happy Days

OFF-SCREEN

9/20   Billie Jean King defeats Bobby Riggs in $100,000 "battle of the sexes" tennis match.

10/10   Vice President Spiro T. Agnew resigns and pleads no contest to one count of income tax evasion. Justice Department drops all pending charges against him. He is fined $10,000 and placed on three years' probation.

10/21   Kuwait, Bahrain, Qatar and Dubai announce boycott of oil shipments to US, completing the Arab oil embargo, imposed in retaliation for American support of Israel.

11/26   Rose Mary Woods, President Nixon's personal secretary, testifies she had accidentally erased five minutes of one of nine Watergate tapes.

12/6   Gerald R. Ford takes office as the fortieth Vice President of US.

12/28   Comet Kohoutek makes closest approach to the sun, having failed to appear as spectacular as predicted.

2/5   Patricia Hearst kidnapped by group connected with radical-terrorist Symbionese Liberation Army.

3/1   Seven former White House and Nixon campaign officials—including former Attorney General Mitchell and former White House advisers Ehrlichman and Haldeman—indicted on charges including conspiracy, obstruction of justice, and making false statements to investigators.

4/8   Hank Aaron of Atlanta Braves hits his 715th career home run, surpassing Babe Ruth's total of 714.

4/11   House Judiciary Committee issues subpoena ordering President Nixon to turn over tapes and other Presidential materials relating to forty-two White House conversations.

FRONT RUNNERS

GOOD TIMES

Dyn-O-Mite!
—J.J.

Oh, boy. Florida Evans should have never left the Findlay household. She never knew how good she had it there.

You see, Florida used to be *Maude*'s maid. That was way back in 1972. But her husband, Henry, didn't want her to work as a maid. He wanted Florida to have a sitcom of her own.

And so, in February of 1973, Florida got a sitcom of her own—*Good Times*—on which, most of the time, times were not so good. The joke was this: here was a ghetto family living in a housing project of Chicago, struggling-struggling-struggling, but because there was so much love-love-love between them, these were good times for them. But the real joke was that there were so many bad times going on among the cast and producers of the show—no love-love-love at all, just struggling-struggling-struggling—that they should have renamed the show *Bad Times*.

It started out with good intentions until—five years later—it became yet another footnote in TV comedy series history. First, the good times of *Good Times*. Later, the bad times.

Florida and her husband, James (that's right, they changed actor John Amos' name from Henry to James when he crossed the Illinois state line), lived in a housing project in Chicago with their three kids: a ten-year-old named Michael; a sixteen-year-old named Thelma, and seventeen-year-old James Evans, Jr., a.k.a. J.J., played by the then-twenty-five-year-old comic Jimmie Walker.

Actually, they lived in Role Model City; there was so much love in the family, somehow they managed to feed and clothe themselves on it. Father James had an erratic income (which somehow led to an erotic outcome with his everlovin' wife, Florida). The kids—of your Basically Good Variety—loved and respected their parents and only good-naturedly teased one another.

To help his family out, J.J. spent a lot of time looking for get-rich-quick schemes (some rather shady) to get his family out of the ghettos (could it be back to Tuckahoe, New York, near the Findlays?). Once he tried to form a rock group. Another time he tried to manage a young comedian. He was very popular with The Girls, which both pleased and displeased his mother.

It was actually very heartwarming at times. James would come back from yet another day of job hunting. "I lost out on the last one by only four years of college, four years of high school, and two years of grade school."

There were parent-child interactions like this one:

THELMA: Mama, if the President made two hundred thousand dollars, how come he only paid seven hundred dollars in taxes?
FLORIDA: Maybe he took Israel to lunch.

Naturally, there was a goodhearted and lovable next-door neighbor, Willona Woods, who doubled as Florida's best friend and said things like: "Make my coffee like I like my men: hot, black and strong."

Florida Evans	Esther Rolle (1974–1977, 1978–1979)
James Evans	John Amos (1974–1976)
James Evans, Jr. (J.J.)	Jimmie Walker
Willona Woods	Ja'net DuBois
Michael Evans	Ralph Carter
Thelma Evans Anderson	BerNadette Stanis
Carl Dixon	Moses Gunn (1977)
Nathan Bookman	Johnny Brown (1977–1979)
Penny Gordon Woods	Janet Jackson (1977–1979)
Keith Anderson	Ben Powers (1978–1979)

Good Times' Roots: "Henry" tells Florida he doesn't want her working for Maude anymore.

(Willona's character had changed considerably from the way she was originally written. Said actress Ja'net DuBois: "When they gave me Willona, she was a mother of three kids who loved to bake and cook. I said, 'No way!' The days of the black mammy are over." Apparently the producers agreed, and transformed her into a hip, independent foxy female.)

The show did swell in the ratings and well with the black viewers, who seemed to like the image of a stable black family on television—realistic, but where the affection outweighs the affliction.

The comic security blanket of the show was Jimmie Walker, who only had to open his mouth and the studio audience laugh-meter erupted. On the second show of the season, he uttered his most celebrated phrase. After a brush with the police, the scrawny, chicken-breasted J.J. boasted: "They knew they were in trouble once they realized they were dealing with Kid Dyn-O-Mite."

Things were going great for the show—high ratings, high accolades, even a British version called *The Fosters* (an unusual switch, since normally Norman Lear, *Good Times*'s producer, got his inspiration from British series that he transformed to Americana—*All in the Family (Till Death Do Us Part)* and *Sanford and Son (Steptoe and Son)*. *Good Times* soon became a hit.

But then, the hit . . . hit the fan. At the start of the 1975–1976 season, John Amos (who played James) had contractual differences with the producers (mainly money), but they were settled. Then the controversy—and confusion—began. An article in *Ebony* came out entitled "Bad Times on *Good Times*." In it, both Amos and Esther Rolle (Florida) complained about the show and the producers and writers in particular. Apparently Master Norman Lear wasn't happy about the article. Effective September 1976, John Amos was released from

his contract, after saying that he didn't feel he was being used enough on the show. Others say Lear wrote him out of the script "to try a new story line." They got a new story line, all right.

Amos said a mouthful: "The only regrets I would have about leaving *Good Times* is that it might mean the show would revert to the matriarchal thing—the fatherless black family. TV is the most powerful medium we have, and there just are not enough positive black male images—which I think James Evans is—on TV. What bothers me, too, is that they seem to be trying to project an image of jealousy among the cast. It's an ensemble company. The emphasis may be on anybody. The show's longevity is not counted on how long any individual is on the camera."

Very politic. But the "individual" whom Amos was referring to was Jimmie Walker, who was emerging as the biggest star in the show—every kid in the country seemed to be sashaying around shouting "Dyn-O-Mite!"—and Esther Rolle was the loudest protester:

"I resent the imagery that says to black kids that you can make it by standing on the corner saying 'Dyn-O-Mite!' He's eighteen and he doesn't work. He can't read or write. He doesn't think. The show didn't start out to be that. Little by little . . . they have made J.J. more stupid, and enlarged the role. Negative images have been quietly slipped in on us through the character of the oldest child."

Things got worse when, with John Amos out of the show, J.J. became the male head of the family. What happened was that father James got a job working at a garage in Mississippi. The family was all excited and set to move there to start a new life. Then they got word: James had been killed in an auto accident. (Amos, who had been Gordy the Weatherman on *The Mary Tyler Moore Show*, went on to play the adult Toby/Kunta Kinte on the hit miniseries *Roots*.)

With Father gone, there were new protests—this time from groups like the National Black Media Coalition, a Washington-based organization that was concerned with black representation on television. They demanded that Norman Lear make casting changes in the family, which they felt was giving "new roots" to the stereotype of the fatherless black family.

Meanwhile, back on the set: Jimmie Walker was complaining that he wasn't happy on the series, that there was no fun on the show anymore. Florida, in the meantime, had been given a new husband—Carl Dixon (played, albeit briefly, by Moses Gunn), the owner of a small appliance shop. They were married during the summer of 1977 (the wedding was not seen), and the plan was that, beginning in the 1977–1978 season, the Evans family would be complete again.

Not quite.

Esther Rolle quit the show before taping for the 1977–1978 season even began. "It's a matter of black pride, not pique," she said. She said she wasn't returning to the series because of the way the J.J. character was written and the image he projected.

Jimmie Walker was stunned: "I don't know how it all started. The series is in its fifth year and all of a sudden these people are finding fault with my character. Where have they been all these years? He's not supposed to be a genius. And he's not supposed to be dumb. All I do is deliver the lines the writers turn out for the series. They seem to be acceptable to most people or we wouldn't be in the top twenty in the Neilsen ratings. I mean, is The Fonz on *Happy Days* representative of white teenagers? Are the sweathogs in *Welcome Back, Kotter* a reflection of young whites? I surely don't feel guilty or apologize for the character I portray. Many of the scripts deal with real-life topics such as my hatred of narcotics, which I think is healthy for my young viewers."

But they didn't kill Florida off, hoping someday she'd be back. Just as Archie Bunker was "missing" at a convention when Carroll O'Connor was going through contractual disputes on *All in the Family*, the writers simply sent Florida off on her honeymoon until Rolle

returned to the show. But she never returned, leaving her three kids to fend for themselves. Esther Rolle was incensed with the way the split was handled: "A mother just wouldn't do that. It's wrong, terribly wrong." The story line explained it this way: Florida, you see, had been ill and that's why she had left; she was living with her new husband in the South for health reasons.

But Rolle's leaving defeated her protest: J.J. was now firmly ensconced as head of the household. Meanwhile: Willona (the lady next door) became surrogate mother, and, in fact, adopted Little Penny Gordon, a victim of child abuse. Esther Rolle—who seemed to be watching the show's every move—said she couldn't understand Willona's adopting a child when she was never home. "This is a reflection on Social Service!" Rolle roared.

But to keep themselves busy, Thelma got married to Keith Anderson—a.k.a. Kool Aid—a football star. J.J. got himself a job with a small ad agency. And they introduced a new character: Nathan Bookman, the obese young superintendent of the building, who was the butt of many

Argument (from left): BerNadette Stanis, guest Chip Fields, Jimmie Walker, Ja'net DuBois

fat jokes and became a more prominent cast member. And the ratings dropped from 26 to 53.

And—guess who's coming to dinner?—Florida came home.

Esther Rolle had a lot to say about her return to the show: "There were a lot of things that I was dissatisfied with. Well, CBS fixed the things that were troubling me the most. They agreed to my terms. Having gotten all those concessions, how could I turn them down?" Her demands were to have the producers replaced, to give herself a voice in "script consultation," and to put J.J. into the background.

"I must admit," she said, "there was a bit of practicality behind my decision to come back. Having been off regular salary for a year, my funds were getting depleted." She went on. "They are supposed to make J.J. a more meaningful character. They say they'll take some of that junk off him and dress him a little differently. They say they'll try to make him more intelligent. Personally, I don't know how intelligent they can make him. After all, you can't get blood from a turnip. But we're sure gonna try. Basically, we hope to put the show back on the foundation it started on. Instead of using me as a stage prop, the show will revolve around me.

"I just hope," she said, "it isn't too late to make the show work."

It was too late.

The ratings went down, down and down. The last show of the series tied up all the ends, and was typical of all the others.

It began with banter between J.J. and sister Thelma, who were just continuing the argument they'd started five years before.

J.J.: You made sponge cake the other night and used a real sponge.

THELMA: But you ate all of it.

J.J.: Yeah—but it was the best thing you ever cooked.

After a joke like that, the hoot-track (which seemed to be a special on black sitcoms) hoots. The laugh-track laughs. And the sigh-track sighs. Willona comes in and announces that she's moving to another part of town. *Sighs.* Thelma and Keith kiss long and passionately—*hoots*—and then he has an announcement to make: he's joining the Chicago Bears, with a starting salary of $60,000, and has bought a house for himself and Thelma. *Hoots.* "I just hope it's got an extra bedroom for the

Mother and Sons: Florida with J.J. and Michael

baby," Thelma says. Says Keith: "Sure, it's got three bedrooms and a sundeck—a baby!!!" *Hoots and laughs.* And J.J. has an announcement: He's just sold a cartoon strip—"Dyn-O-Woman," a big-breasted version of Thelma—*laughs*—and he's moving out of the house and into the college dormitory. *Yeah!* And that leaves Florida. *Sigh.* But, of course!—Thelma and Keith want Florida to move in with them (she gets her choice of the extra bedroom or the sundeck). *Sighs and cheers.* And, guess what? What a coincidence: Willona lives downstairs from Keith and Thelma in the new house. They'll all still be together. *Hoots and sighs and laughs.*

End of episode.

End of series.

And then there was a beer commercial.

HAPPY DAYS

*Sometimes I just wish I were Ozzie Nelson. He'd just say,
"Go to college"—and that would be the end of that.*
—MR. CUNNINGHAM, *counseling his son Richie*

In January of 1974, the comic strip arrived on television. Sure, there had been *Blondie*—two incarnations, in fact—and *Hazel* and *Superman* and *Batman* and several others. But *Happy Days*, which did not have its antecedents in the funnies, was a cartoon strip. Animated. With real actors. The only things that were missing were ads for miniature "teacup" monkeys and whoopee cushions on the back pages. *Happy Days* was TV's first electronic funnies. And it wasn't even that funny.

When it became a hit—after a slow start—in the 1976 season—and when ABC started spinning it off—*Laverne and Shirley* and *Mork and Mindy* were both children of *Happy Days*—ABC got a nickname: Acne Broadcasting Company.

Not that *Happy Days* gave you pimples or anything like that; you didn't need a dermatologist after each episode. It was about and for adolescents. It *was* adolescent. Each week it seemed to burst into puberty.

Happy Days' roots—bleached and thinning, to be sure—were not so much in the fifties (it was allegedly about life in the mid-fifties), but in the mid-seventies' vision and version of the fifties: innocent, carefree, fun. Happy days.

Even the nights were happy in the Cunningham household. They were the Ozzie and Harriet—or the Andersons or the Cleavers—of a generation that was just getting used to the Bunkers—or the Findlays or the Jeffersons. But where Harriet Nelson was shown making

out recipe cards, *Happy Days* showed making out. While Ward Cleaver brought the Beaver along when he shopped for a new Ford, Richie and Potsie and the rest of the *Happy Days* crowd were necking in the back seat of those fifties Fords. Where *Father Knows Best* worried about Betty dropping out of the glee club, *Happy Days* dealt with dropping out of school.

Nothing heavy, mind you. In fact, while watching the show, viewers went into sort of a *Happy Days* daze: here was television—usually ten years behind the Real World—giving us a version of the fifties—which really were ten years behind the Real World—in the seventies, which, social scientists said, were a throwback to the fifties anyway. . . . All very confusing.

But on with the show.

Each week, *Happy Days* began with a 45-rpm record spinning around and the music coming out: "Sundays, Monday, Happy Days . . ." (The song eventually went on to become a hit single on the seventies charts.) In the beginning—that first season—the show revolved around two students at Jefferson High School in Milwaukee: Richie Cunningham and his worldly pal, Potsie Weber. Richie had a father, Howard, who ran a hardware store; a mother, Marion, who ran around in circles; a thirteen-year-old kid sister named Joanie and an older brother, Chuck, who was quickly headed for college (not to mention oblivion; although two different actors played the part, the producers eventually got rid of the character

Richie Cunningham	Ron Howard
Arthur "Fonzie" Fonzarelli	Henry Winkler
Howard Cunningham	Tom Bosley
Marion Cunningham	Marion Ross
Potsie Weber	Anson Williams
Ralph Malph	Donny Most
Joanie Cunningham	Erin Moran
Chuck Cunningham	Gavan O'Herlihy (1974); Randolph Roberts (1974–1975)
Marsha	Beatrice Colen (1974–1976)
Gloria	Linda Purl (1974–1975)
Wendy	Misty Rowe (1974–1975)
Trudy	Tita Bell (1974–1975)
Bill "Sticks" Downey	John Anthony Bailey (1975–1976)
Arnold	Pat Morita (1975–1976)
Alfred Delvecchio	Al Molinaro (1976–)
Chachi Arcola	Scott Baio (1977–)
Lori Beth	Lynda Goodfriend (1977–)

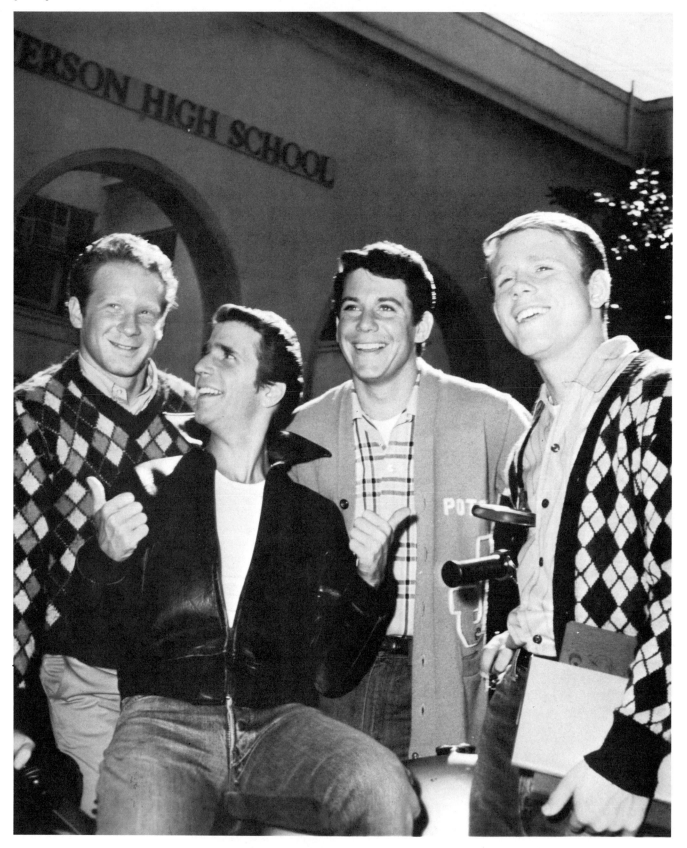

altogether and never even referred to him again). Richie and Potsie hung out at a malt shop near school called Arnold's Drive-In (run by Arnold, played by Pat Morita, who left in 1976 for his own series *Mr. T. and Tina;* actor Al Molinaro, who had played the sad-sack cop, Murray, on *The Odd Couple,* played Alfred Delvecchio, the man who bought the diner in 1976).

It seemed *Happy Days* were pretty boring days. And so the producers added some seasoning to the show: A leather-jacketed greaser named Arthur Fonzarelli. On the first episode, when he gave his soon-to-be-famous thumbs-up gesture and whined his smartass *aaayyh!,* "Fonzie" became the real star of the show (not to mention Henry Winkler, the actor who played him). Soon the show switched emphasis and centered on the relationship between the straitlaced Richie and the unlaced Fonzie, a cool-cat dropout motorcycle rider. Most important, though, Fonz was the only character on the show who had more than one dimension; Winkler infused him with life and—even more difficult—with vulnerability. By the second season, 10,000 of the 15,000 fan letters to *Happy Days* had been addressed to "The Fonz."

The Fonz cared about three things: girls, cars, and the Cunninghams. He had no family—once his father, having long abandoned the family, returned to town to meet his son; Fonzie refused to see him. One of the classic episodes of the show was at Christmastime, and showed Fonz's dingy, cluttered pad—motorcycle in the middle of the floor—with a tiny, pathetic Christmas tree. Of course, he was too proud to admit he was alone for Christmas. Eventually, though, he joined the Cunningham family to celebrate with them. (This episode was so popular, it was rerun each year.)

As Fonz's popularity rose—he went from fifth billing to third, and ended up second right behind Ronnie Howard, who played Richie—viewers wanted more and more of him. So the producers moved him into a small apartment over the Cunninghams' garage. And he was always turning up everywhere—popping out of lockers, coming around corners, keeping irregular hours in his "office" in the boys' room at Arnold's, working as a mechanic at the garage. Fonzie was the tough guy in town, the person *everyone* respected.

And loved. In one episode, when The Authorities were going to have him thrown out of town for being a hood (although a harmless hood), the entire community—including Richie and his sister and mother—came into Arnold's dressed just like Fonzie, with black leather coats and greased-back hair (The Fonz never parted with his black-leather coat. You got the idea he even slept in it. In one episode they even showed him waterskiing while wearing it).

He and Richie didn't get along at first. Richie's Lone Ranger lunchpail didn't help matters much. They even had a small confrontation in a dark alley one night. Then they became best buddies. Fonz was Richie's protector. When some toughies were after Richie, Fonzie threat-

ened them with: "Let him go—unless you want to make medical history. . . ." Sometimes Richie and Fonzie would fight, like the time Richie called The Fonz a "nerd."

Said Henry Winkler: "I sometimes get to play the dark side of Fonzie, but you have to tone it down for TV. I sometimes have the fantasy of wiping the Fonz out of everyone's imagination—and then coming back and doing a feature film, an adult film, with the Fonz—because I know him so well."

Well, Winkler never did get his own Fonz film, but there was talk of a TV spin-off. The producers decided against it, though; they were smart enough to realize that without the Richie/Fonzie contrast, it wouldn't be interesting.

Not that the regular show was always so interesting. This 1978 episode is typical of the show:

Fifties' music blares from Arnold's, where The Guys—who are now in college (this is several years later)—talk about how they have to take out visiting baton twirlers for their fraternity dance. Richie is scared. He doesn't know what to tell his girlfriend Lori Beth (who calls him "sizzle-lips"). And so he lies and tells her that he's driving around in a police car on a journalism assignment (he's a journalism major now at the University of Wisconsin in Milwaukee, but nothing's changed).

The Original Family (from left): Ron Howard, Tom Bosley, Erin Moran, Randolph Roberts, Marion Ross

"Hey, Rich," his friend Ralph yells, "does a police car twirl a baton?" Richie feels plenty guilty.

He feels even worse when Lori Beth bakes him oatmeal cookies to take with him. His parents ask him where he's going, and he says in a police car. Finally he confesses. His mother is shocked: "You're going to cheat on a girl who made you oatmeal cookies?" But his father —who himself was Young Once—thinks it's okay he told "a little white lie" to protect himself.

"What could happen?" Richie asks. "She's a baton twirler. Her arms are probably tired. You know—life's tough." And then he adds, "Yowsa, yowsa, yowsa."

He and his date end up at Arnold's, where she calls him "Richie-kins" and where he's still feeling guilty. She starts kissing and hugging him. He lets her "take" him.

When the baton twirler leaves, Richie remembers he's supposed to meet Lori Beth at Arnold's at 11 P.M. He's worried. He should be. Although he doesn't know it, he has lipstick smeared all over his face. "She's gonna find out," he says, "It's probably written all over my face."

Enter The Fonz: "Oh, Coral Pink, number Five," he says, identifying the species of lipstick. Then he gives Richie a lecture: "*You* cheated? A former Eagle Scout? Is there no end to life's disillusionments? The next thing you know, I'm gonna find out that Tonto hated the Lone Ranger."

The Fonz leaves and Richie heads for the bathroom to try to get the baton twirler's perfume off his clothes. He can't. Lori Beth calls for him, and Richie leaves the bathroom and tries to avoid being close to her. "Let's go outside and talk in the wind," he says. But finally— because he is a decent, upright, and moral type—he confesses all.

"I can forgive you for kissing," Lori Beth says, "But tonight you lied. I can't forgive you for that. Goodbye, Richie." And they part. Never to see each other again. The End.

Of course not The End. In the next scene, Potsie and Ralph—who claim they run a dating service (their motto: "You want a hunk, we sift out the junk")—try to fix Lori Beth up with a new guy in town: "He's got red hair

and freckles," they tell her. But she's no dummy—she graduated from Jefferson High School, you know—so she's on to their scheme to fix her up with Richie. Meanwhile, Richie is so depressed, he's spent three solid days in front of the TV set watching *Divorce Court*. "It's the only program I can identify with," he explains.

Finally—at last—The Fonz intervenes and talks Richie into seeing Lori Beth. "I should have had more faith in our relationship," Richie says (about his relationship with Lori Beth, not his relationship with The Fonz). So Richie approaches Lori Beth, who says that they should try to "start all over again." They re-enact the day they met, when Richie told her he was in a fraternity called Mama, Papa, Sister (because he lived at home), and they laugh. And they kiss. And that really is the end.

As innocuous as it was, *Happy Days* spawned a whole movement of sitcoms known as kidcoms or kidvid—shows tailored for kids. Shows that seemed to go through an assembly line to reach a mass audience. Very predictable. Very profitable.

Actually, shows like *Happy Days*—and *Laverne and Shirley* and *Three's Company*, and *Mork and Mindy* and all the other bits of juvenilia that made ABC the Clearasil of the video crowd—were not created to appeal to everyone. In fact, they were designed to appeal to the minority of US TV watchers, those people who watch seven to ten hours of programs a day. In the industry these people are referred to as "the heavy-viewing center," "the wad," and "Billy and Mary Six-Pack." An NBC programmer said it best: "Most TV watchers are like a kid with candy, who eats and eats. They're nice people. They have good jobs. But they don't want to think. *Dummies,* I call them."

Whatever, each week, 50,000,000 people tuned into *Happy Days*. Not at first, of course, when the ratings were merely "marginal" (another TV term). It wasn't until The Fonz became a family member—living over the garage—that the show became Number One. Said the show's creator, Garry Marshall: "I knew that if I could get him over the garage, I could get him into the kitchen; he could 'become' a member of the family." When The Fonz became a folk hero, *Happy Days* dawned.

There was some talk that Ron Howard—who played Richie and who played Opie on the mega-successful *Andy Griffith Show*—was being eclipsed by Henry Winkler. Howard said, indeed, he did once feel threatened by the Fonz character overtaking his own. "Before the third season we were on the air," he said, "seventy-five percent of the stories centered around Richie, and then the percentage dropped to thirty-five percent. I was still in every scene, and my parts were the same, but I felt awkward.

"The emphasis changed because the Fonzie character began getting a lot of attention and fan mail, so the network decided to promote him. All of a sudden the episodes started dealing with Fonzie's problems rather than mine. Maybe if Henry Winkler and I hadn't liked

Masquerade (from left): Donny Most, guest Eileen Coch, Henry Winkler, Anson Williams, Ron Howard

Cousin Chachi (above):
Scott Baio; Heavy Metal:
The Fonz and the Pinky

each other, and if we were two different people, there would have been problems. But we're all on the series to make it as successful as possible, and it benefits us all that Fonzie is tremendously popular."

Howard got his part after he'd been in George Lucas' *American Graffiti* as an apple-pie fifties' kid. In fact, *Happy Days* was not based on the film, but on a segment of TV's *Love, American Style*, in which Howard and Anson Williams (he played Potsie) starred in a skit called "Love and the Happy Day" in February of 1972.

Apparently, Ron Howard was a lot like Richie Cunningham. Both said "Gee" a lot. Both ate cheeseburgers. "Yeah, I eat french fries and drink beer," he once said. "I eat junk food all the time. I've never smoked dope, but I've been drunk three times. I've also had a speeding ticket. And I've seen some porno movies. But, basically, I make a big effort to try to be healthy, and as a result, people think I'm dull sometimes. I'm always falling asleep at ten o'clock."

Henry Winkler—known as "a nice Jewish boy from New York"—was, of course, nothing like The Fonz. He'd been in several Broadway shows and movies (*Crazy Joe* and *The Lords of Flatbush*) as well as bit parts on several TV shows (he was once Rhoda Morgenstern's date on *The Mary Tyler Moore Show*). Then he hit it big with The Fonz. A graduate of the Yale School of Drama, Winkler had his worries. "I spent nine long years training for my craft. I don't want to see it suffer. It's difficult trying to remain unaffected by such devotion. My head does get inflated once in a while, I admit, but then I tell myself that it's all unrealistic. I can't ever start thinking I'm more than I really am."

According to Marion Ross (who played mother Marion Cunningham): "When Henry feels crowded, he'll make cutting, rude, sarcastic remarks. When he directs them to me, I say, 'I don't like that. I don't like you, Henry.' Most of the time, I like him, though. I'm watching a young actor who's going to be famous." Winkler tried becoming even more famous when he made two movies—*The One and Only* and *Heroes*—but both bombed. (At the start of the 1977–1978 season, Winkler wouldn't sign his *Happy Days* contract because he was waiting to see how well his movies did at the box office. Needless to say, he ended up signing.) "Henry Winkler," he once said, "is my reality. Fonzie is my fantasy." His fantasy, however, did earn him at least $80,000 an episode (he was making $750 an episode when the show began), plus a large chunk of the show's profits, plus residuals, plus . . .

Over the years, there were several cast changes and additions and just-passing-throughs: Laverne and Shirley got their start on *Happy Days* in late 1975 when they went on a double date with Richie and Fonzie (who made occasional visits to *Laverne and Shirley*, and once, when Fonzie was presumed dead, L&S paid their respects at his funeral). In 1977, Chachi Arcola—played by teen idol Scott Baio—arrived on the scene, playing a mouthy kid (who happened to be Fonzie's young cousin). He was accompanied by Lori Beth (played by Lynda Goodfriend; both she and Baio got second jobs on NBC's short-lived *Who's Watching the Kids?*). "Sticks" Downey was a black student who appeared briefly—during the 1975–1976 season—and played the drums and added "an ethnic element" (which was de-elemented the next season and left to the shows of Norman Lear). *Happy Days* remained, for the most part, white, Anglo-Saxon, Protestant. Maybe that's why they were all so happy).

Fonzie met his match when Roz Kelly appeared as Pinky Tuscadero. And she was even *cooler* than The Fonz. She was an old girlfriend who, coming back into town, wrapped The Fonz around her little finger and even joined him in a demolition derby (she was always accompanied by her girls, Tina and Lola, collectively known as The Pinkettes). She didn't last long. Said Ron Howard: "Roz Kelly would come on the set doing her 'Fonzie' imitations. No one really appreciated that. She was undercutting the Fonzie character and the only way the character works is if the others show respect." Kelly and Winkler clashed almost immediately. Pinky was soon off the show.

But not her sister. A season later Leather Tuscadero (played by rock star Suzi Quatro) arrived on the scene and did a couple of episodes with her rock group The Suedes (in one episode, she even "got all dressed up like a real girl" and went to the Prom with Ralph "the Mouth" Malph).

There were also guest stars on the show—appropriately of fifties vintage—like *Howdy Doody*'s Buffalo Bob Smith, and *You Asked For It*'s emcee Jack Smith (he played the host of *Happy Days*' "You Wanted to See It," in which Fonzie tried to set a new world's record by

leaping his cycle over fourteen trash cans behind Arnold's, on national TV).

One classic episode showed the essence and humanity of *Happy Days*. The Fonz—who is the Big Guy in Town—gets a chance to go to Hollywood and make a movie. Naturally, Richie goes with him. Back in Milwaukee, The Fonz can do anything, it seems. In Hollywood, he just doesn't fit in. Oh, Richie fits in. Not The Fonz. They quickly go back to Milwaukee.

The Fonz would never take a chance. He was all image. Underneath, he was scared. He tried to finish high school, but he couldn't cut it. It was too much of a defeat for him (he finally did surprise everyone when he went to night school and got his high school diploma, although he remained working at Happy's Garage while Richie and the crew went to college in the city. Still, though, Fonzie advised and counseled them on life and love).

The years—seasons—went on and *Happy Days* just became *Happier Days*. Richie went to journalism school. Potsie took psychology courses (and Anson Williams sang a lot on the show). Ralph—who really wanted to become a comedian—"I still got it," he'd always say, referring to his sense of humor—became an eye doctor, just like his father.

Possibly, much of *Happy Days'* success was because it took place in the fifties. Said producer Garry Marshall: "I couldn't figure out how I could do a realistic comedy about young people today and avoid drugs and avoid the sexual revolution, because I know they wouldn't put that on television. So I said—what's the use—it's not real, people are gonna watch it and say: 'Baloney, that isn't life.' Then it crossed my mind—how can I beat this? I can do it if I push it back in time—to the fifties. If I'm not doing drugs, and I'm not doing sex things, then the audience will buy it and they'll say: 'That's right—it's not today, but that's the way it was.'"

Marshall was right, although the show wasn't exactly a television version of fifties' memorabilia. Except for an occasional bit of dialogue like "Al, I bet you're the type who would have told Elvis not to wiggle," and Richie saying things like "That's the way the burger burns," *Happy Days* didn't take place in the fifties any more than it actually took place in Milwaukee. What the fifties gave to it—and to us—was an excuse for the show's innocence. *Happy Days* masqueraded as the Good Old Days. Although, what was so happy about the fifties? Apparently, any time is happy, depending on what you don't look at.

But *Happy Days* almost got caught. Mork—who made his debut appearance on *Happy Days* in 1977—returned the following year after his own sitcom, *Mork and Mindy,* had beaten its father in the ratings. Ostensibly he went back to the fifties to learn something about relationships. When he met Richie, the questions flew:

RICHIE: What's it like in 1979?
MORK: The air is thicker. Birds wake up in the morning and go *cough*.
RICHIE: Who's President?
MORK: Do you like peanuts?
RICHIE: I can take them or leave them.
MORK: Then you'll love Jimmy. Say, do you remember Nixon?
RICHIE: Whatever happened to him?
MORK: Don't ask.

But it was the end of *Happy Days* when Mork did his traditional *Mork and Mindy* finale of conjuring up Orson in his head via brain waves, and we finally found out the truth about those allegedly *Happy Days*.

MORK (*sung to an old Ronettes tune*):   Mork calling Orson, Mork calling Orson, Come in, Orson . . .
VOICE OF ORSON: This isn't your day to report . . .
MORK: I know that, sir. I'm doing a spin-*on* to pay back for my spin-*off*. That's why I went back to the fifties. You know: "One, two, three o'clock, four o'clock . . ." "Wow, Tommy, that's a really boss car, what a drag . . ."
VOICE OF ORSON: Mork, you seem to like the fifties.
MORK: Yes, sir. It's a wonderful, naive, and romantic time. I went back to visit the Cunninghams and their friends. They're really nice people, but a little mondo-mundane. . . . I'm talkin' white bread and mayonnaise. . . . But, you know, they all seem to block out one thing: Senator McCarthy.
VOICE OF ORSON: Ah, yes—those were sad days.
MORK: I guess that's why it's so romantic—they never remember the sad things.

ALSO RANS

Adam's Rib

Blythe Danner and Ken Howard played Amanda and Adam Bonner, two lawyers—he, the assistant DA; she, a junior partner in a law firm. Therefore—get it—they were often on opposite sides of the courtroom. Also the bedroom. The show had a "women's rights" theme (half the show's writers were women), and Amanda spent a lot of time crusading for women's rights. Not enough time, unfortunately; the show was canceled by ABC after only three months. Based on the Katherine Hepburn/Spencer Tracy movie.

Adam's Rib: *Ken Howard and Blythe Danner*

Bob & Carol & Ted & Alice

Once again, television went to the movies in search of situations. This time, TV found *B&C&T&A*, and quickly sitcomized it. Here was the TV plot: there were two couples living in LA, see, and they were close friends, but shared different moral values. Couple One: Filmmaker Bob Sanders (Robert Urich) and his wife, Carol (Anne Archer), twentyish, aware, and hip. Lawyer Ted Henderson (David Spielberg) and his wife, Alice (Anita Gillette), were in their thirties and conservative. They got together and—well, what resulted could have been—and in fact was—shown on The Family Hour: cutesy-pie stories about extramarital sex, nude swimming parties, and unmarried people living together. None of it mattered anyway, because ABC sent the show to Sitcom Heaven after little more than a month.

Calucci's Department

Funnyman James Coco portrayed the supervisor of a branch of the New York State Unemployment Office, where he dealt with the unemployed (of which he was soon to be one) and his own multiethnic staff. He also had

Calucci's Dept.: *James Coco and guest Jim Starey*

to deal with government red tape. Plus he was in love with his secretary Shirley—played by Candy Azzara—who possibly did or did not return his affections. We'll never know. CBS canceled the show after only three months of foreplay.

Bob & Carol & Ted & Alice *(clockwise): Bob Urich, Anne Archer, Anita Gillette, David Speilberg*

Diana

Everybody was waiting for this one: English import Diana Rigg, known to TV viewers for her highfalutin' acting as Emma Peel on the British spy series, *The Avengers,* was coming to sitcom land in her very own show. Here is how the NBC press kit described her: "Diana Smythe, a divorcée seeking a new life in America working as a fashion coordinator assigned to the merchandising and advertising of Butley's, a fashionable Fifth Avenue department store . . . each week, she finds herself in amusing situations with her co-workers and a variety of her brother's friends who hold keys to the apartment he has rented for her. . . ." Of course the show was peopled by a bunch-of-lovable-nuts (as they are called in sitcom lingo) who included: commercial model Holly Green (Carol Androsky); Norman Brodnik, president of Butley's (David Sheiner); his wife, Norma (Barbara Barrie); Howard Tolbrook (Richard B. Shull), a cranky copywriter who shared an office with Diana; and Marshall Tyler (Robert Moore), a window dresser. None of them could save this series, and four months later NBC sent Diana packing back to England where, apparently, she got a job at Harrods.

Dusty's Trail

Westerns were big moneymakers for the TV producers, and so were sitcoms. So some guy got the bright idea to combine the two. The result: *Dusty's Trail,* a Western comedy set in the 1880s on a wagon train headed for California. The wagon master, Mr. Callahan (Forrest Tucker), had to put up with his dumbbell scout, Dusty (Bob Denver, post-*Gilligan*) who somehow separated a stage and a wagon from the main part of the wagon train. So Callahan spent his time—actually only thirteen weeks over syndicated TV—trying to deliver his passengers safely. His horse, incidentally, was named Blarney, while Dusty's horse was named Freckles.

The Girl with Something Extra

Before Sally Field had begun to be thought of as a serious actress (thanks, mostly, to her role in *Norma*

The Girl with Something Extra: *Sally Field and John Davidson*

Rae), she had been thought of as a most unserious actress, thanks to things like *The Flying Nun, Gidget,* and this show, in which she played a newlywed with ESP (wonder if she could sense the fast demise of this show?). On her wedding night, Sally (playing Sally Burton), tells her husband, John Burton (played by John Davidson, possibly the only male on television who would be called "perky"), that she can read people's minds (shades of *Bewitched*). Anyway, naturally, John decides that love is more important than the minor inconvenience of his wife being a freak, and so they settle in for a one-season marriage—full of ESP adventures—courtesy of NBC. Also on the show: Sally's single friend Anne (Zohra Lampert) and John's brother Jerry (played by Jack Sheldon, alumnus of both *The Cara Williams Show* and *Run, Buddy, Run*—he'd played Buddy).

Lotsa Luck

This show needed more luck than it apparently got. It starred Dom DeLuise as bachelor Stanley Belmont, the custodian of the New York City bus company's lost and found department. (Blue-collar workers—post-Ralph

Lotsa Luck: *Dom DeLuise surrounded by (from left) Kathleen Freeman, Wynn Irwin, Beverly Sanders*

Kramden—were beginning to make a comeback on sitcoms, thanks to Archie Bunker.) His problems came from his home life—he lived with his bossy, bitchy mother (Kathleen Freeman), his klutzy sister Olive (Beverly Sanders, later on *CPO Sharkey*), and her unemployed husband, Arthur (Wynn Irwin). They all lived off Stanley's earnings and didn't seem to be in any rush to move out of his house (this sounds like the first sitcom written by Tennessee Williams). Jack Knight played Stanley's buddy and co-worker, Bummy, which could have also been the nickname for this show, borrowed from the British series *On the Busses*. *Lotsa Luck* lasted a short NBC season.

Needles and Pins

This one—starring Norman Fell (later Stanley Roper on *Three's Company* and *The Ropers*) and Louis Nye (alumnus of *Private Secretary* and *The Steve Allen Show*, on which he was the suave-yet-smug Gordon Hathaway)—brought Hollywood to New York's garment district. Nathan Davidson (Fell) owned the Lorelei Fashion House, which manufactured women's clothing. He worked side by side with his brother and partner, Harry (Nye), and his new designer, Wendy (Deirdre Lenihan), a transplanted Nebraskan. Also on hand were the requisite cast of kooks: Sonia, the bookkeeper and secretary;

Needles and Pins: *Deirdre Lenihan and Norman Fell*

Charlie, the firm's salesman; Max, the fabric cutter; Myron, the patternmaker; and Singer, the competition. NBC discontinued the line after half a season.

Ozzie's Girls

What were the Nelsons without Ricky and David? Not much. But when the boys moved out (and *The Adventures of Ozzie and Harriet* got mercilessly canceled after all those years), Ozzie and Harriet took in boarders. Two girls: one white, one black. They were called Ozzie's Girls (guess they weren't Harriet's Girls), and they moved right into David and Rick's old room. Their names: Susan Hamilton (Susan Sennett) and Brenda Mackenzie (Brenda Sykes). Three sample episodes: (1) Harriet, Brenda, and Susie gang up on Ozzie when they think he is interested in a sexy new neighbor who has just moved in next door. (2) Brenda and Susie's popularity becomes a problem for Ozzie and Harriet when the phones never stop ringing and the Nelsons find themselves acting as an overworked dating service. (3) Once, Ozzie and Harriet have to work overtime when Brenda seems to be receiving more than her share of attention and Susie begins to feel left out. End of three sample episodes. And, after 11 more filmed and syndicated episodes, end of *Ozzie's Girls*.

Roll Out

A program called *M*A*S*H* had been on TV for one season. And then came *Roll Out*, sort of a half-grown clone that didn't quite make it on its own. Set in France during the Second World War, it was the story of the men on the 5050th Trucking Company—a.k.a. the "Red Ball Express"—an army trucking unit that gets supplies to the troops at the front. Like the *M*A*S*H* unit, discipline meant little to these rowdy men; all they wanted to do was get the supplies in, no matter how they did it. The difference between this unit and *M*A*S*H*'s, though, is that the *Roll Outs* were mostly black, led by Captain Rocco Calvelli (Val Bisoglio). The two best drivers were Sweet (Stu Gilliam) and Jed (Hilly Hicks), who were sort of the Hawkeye and Trapper John of the trucking set. When they weren't working, they'd hang out at the nightclub near their base camp, run by Madame Delacort (Penny Santon). *Roll Out* was based on the story of a real World War II transportation unit. CBS sent them all trucking after three months.

1974–1975

Barney Miller

Chico and the Man

Rhoda

OFF-SCREEN

9/8 President Gerald Ford grants a full pardon to ex-President Nixon for all federal crimes he "committed or may have committed or taken part in" while in office.

9/16 President Ford signs proclamation offering conditional clemency to thousands of Vietnam deserters and draft dodgers.

10/1 The Watergate cover-up trial opens in Washington, D.C., before US District Court Judge John J. Sirica.

11/8 Eight former Ohio National Guardsmen acquitted of violating rights of students at May 4, 1970 demonstration at Kent State University, in which four students were killed and nine wounded.

12/3 US space vehicle Pioneer 11 heads toward Saturn after surviving pass within 26,000 miles of Jupiter; due to arrive in vicinity of Saturn in 1979.

12/10 Representative Wilbur D. Mills (Democrat, Arkansas) resigns as Chairman of the House of Representatives' Ways and Means Committee after ridicule and scorn because of his indiscreet association with strip-tease dancer Fanne Foxe.

12/19 Nelson Aldrich Rockefeller sworn in as Vice-President of US, marking first time neither a president nor his vice president is elected to office.

3/9 Work starts on 789-mile Alaskan oil pipeline, largest private construction project in US history.

4/18 Two-hundredth anniversary of Paul Revere's ride; President Ford officially kicks off year-long American Revolution Bicentennial celebration.

4/29 American military involvement in Vietnam ends, with departure of last remaining Americans from Saigon embassy 7:52 P.M. Saigon time.

FRONT RUNNERS

Barney Miller

That man robbed me! Robbed me! I had revenge in my heart! Revenge! *Revenge is sweet . . . but I'm trying to cut down. . . .*
—an irate New Yorker running into the precinct station

When *Barney Miller* premiered on ABC as a midseason replacement, like a bad marriage it was given six months. *Tops*. The diagnosis was terminal. The prognosis was a quick mercy-killing.

But *Barney Miller*—like the spritely group of police detectives who inhabited the 12th Precinct in Greenwich Village—stuck it out.

Justice triumphed, and *Barney Miller* not only polevaulted to the top of the ratings, but picked up a slew of awards on the way, including an honorary membership award to the cast from the New York City Police Department, a "Barney Miller Week" in Los Angeles, and a Congressional tribute. And it was only twelve years before that the same police departments were screaming about the bimbos portraying New York City policemen on *Car 54, Where Are You?*

Well, Barney's police didn't have cars. In fact, they didn't even have uniforms; they were plainclothes policemen and policewomen, who weren't that much different from the people they picked up. Said star Hal Linden: "There are no dumb cops in this series. Our relationship with one another will be warm and real. Barney Miller knows there are forces that cast people on one side of the desk or the other. So he does his job as effectively as possible."

And so each week, Barney and his crew would drag in at least three loonies per episode (there seemed to be a quota). The wide assortment of public (and private) offenders who marched through the station included men who snatched purses, men who carried purses, hookers, bookies, crooks and conmen, outlaws, in-laws, men who were bombed, men who carried bombs, muggers, sluggers, buggers, pushers, obscene callers . . .

VISITOR: You guys must have a lot of fun around here . . .
DIETRICH: We manage to have a laugh or two at humanity's expense.

Like the WJM newsroom, like the M*A*S*H operating room, like *Taxi*'s garage, the detectives' squad room was yet another sitcom microcosm of what television executives seemed to think might be the Real World. Actually, in *Barney*'s case, they weren't too far off. But they were smart and went that one step beyond: rather than simply make the criminals the crazies, they made the detectives themselves a little loony too. Not incompetent. Just a little off. Not like Toody and Muldoon, not like Bilko's brigade, not like Maxwell Smart. Just a little neurotic. Some examples: Detective Wojohowicz—the

Captain Barney Miller	Hal Linden
Detective Phil Fish	Abe Vigoda (1975–1977)
Detective Sergeant Chano Amenguale	Gregory Sierra (1975–1976)
Detective Wojohowicz ("Wojo")	Maxwell Gail
Detective Nick Yemana	Jack Soo (1975–1979)
Detective Ron Harris	Ron Glass
Elizabeth Miller	Barbara Barrie (1975–1976)
Rachael Miller	Anne Wyndham (1975)
David Miller	Michael Tessier (1975)
Bernice Fish	Florence Stanley (1975–1977)
Detective Janice Wentworth	Linda Lavin (1975–1976)
Inspector Luger	James Gregory
Officer Carl Levitt	Ron Carey (1976–)
Detective Baptista	June Gable (1976–1977)
Detective Arthur Dietrich	Steve Landesberg (1976–)

1974–1975

token Pole—was naive, trusting, and often said the wrong thing. He continually fell in love with the hookers he picked up for soliciting. Harris—the token black—was the erudite literate detective who was always working on a novel (until he finished it, that is, and it became successful). Fish—the token Jew—was continually complaining about everything from the toilet in the station house to his wife, Bernice. Yemana—the token Oriental—was constantly making coffee, bets, and wisecracks. The police upstairs didn't like him because they thought Orientals ruined the looks of the St. Patrick's Day Parade. Dietrich—the token German-American—was a closet psychologist and was always coming up with a psychiatric diagnosis for everything.

Quite a crew. And quite an ethnic mix (there was also a token Puerto Rican, a token WASP, and so on—the show was both praised and damned for its tokens). But at the helm stands Barney Miller, their humane and humorous captain. In his white shirt and tie, Barney is always there—a little exasperated at times, but always sensitive and kind, and generous about the foibles of his crew.

On most sitcoms you could show a sample day; on *Barney Miller* you can also show a sample night. The graveyard shift, which the detectives are often sentenced to, is a good indication of life in the precinct office.

First, a woman comes in. She's an out-of-towner, and her luggage has been stolen at knifepoint in front of her hotel. "You know," she says, looking through the police dossier of photos, "I watched all those 'I Love New York' commercials back in Youngstown—with all the Broadway actors singing and dancing—they're so exciting and colorful. But they never mention the people with knives." Responds Harris: "Well, they only have a minute."

In the meantime, the phone rings. Someone's calling in a bomb threat—right in the station. Everyone evacuates. They come back later, realizing it was a false alarm.

Just then a man is dragged in. He'd been caught stealing sleeping pills from a drugstore. Why? Because, he claims, every night he is plagued by a female demon who creates sexual havoc in his sleep. "I've considered going to a sex therapist," he says, "but she won't go."

As if things weren't complicated enough, Inspector Luger—in hat and bow tie—comes in to chat. He has nothing better to do, and wants to talk to Barney, who doesn't want to be bothered. Luger's a pest.

Then: Another bomb threat ("That last one was a test one"). They trace the call and find out it's a fellow named Leon who lives right next door to the station. When they haul him in, he is still dressed in his pajamas and robe. Why did he do it?

LEON: All day long—hookers and deviates in front of my apartment. All night long—sirens howling, people screaming, shouting. It's like a wild party. And all you people are always in a hurry in your squad cars, shooting down the street at sixty or seventy miles an hour. You killed three of my cats!
BARNEY: Just what is it you were trying to accomplish with this bomb threat?
LEON: I thought you'd move.
BARNEY: It's the only neighborhood we can afford.
LEON: When I moved here fifteen years ago, I thought: beautiful, live right next to the police station, rest easy, feel secure. I've been robbed seven times—and it took you people twenty minutes to come over—and I live next door to the police station, for God's sake!

They lock him up in the same cell with the guy and his "lady demon." Finally, the out-of-town woman finds her photo and gets ready to leave.

BARNEY: I'm sure getting robbed at knifepoint and spending half the night up here wasn't exactly what you had in mind when you decided to visit New York.
LADY: Well, it was better than seeing *Annie*.

End of a long night on the graveyard shift. End of the episode.

Somehow *Barney Miller* managed not to be silly. Although it dealt in humor—some of which was pretty heavyhanded (such as when the gay purse-snatcher said, "Kleptomania is a disease, not a crime. I've thrown away better purses than this"), *Barney Miller* always had respect for itself. Just as *M*A*S*H* knew that the army was stupid, *Barney Miller* knew that the American judicial system was far from fair. Once a prisoner, whose sentence was being decided in Barney's office by his probation officer and Barney, asked: "How long are they going to be in there?" Responded Dietrich: "Discussing procedures doesn't usually take too long, but deciding the fate of a human being—give them a couple of minutes."

When a man wanted to prosecute a woman he claimed had supernatural powers and had put a curse on him, one of the detectives told him that "She could do a lot more punishment with her powers than New York City could do with its."

And of course, there were lots of other loonies. Once a man is caught embezzling a half-million dollars from his securities company.

HIS BOSS: Have you no remorse?
EMBEZZLER: No—just the half-million.

His boss, however, doesn't want to prosecute because he knows the publicity will hurt the company. So he tells the employee that if he gives back the money and submits his resignation, he won't press charges. Knowing he's got him, the embezzler holds out and demands a substantial raise, a new title, a big office, and the right to call his boss by his first name.

Often the detectives weren't much brighter than their prey. Consider this phone call, in which Detective Wojohowicz—a.k.a. Wojo—is talking on the phone to a police officer: "Harris and Dietrich were shot at?! Are they all right? Okay, so they were checking out a disturbance—who cares! Are they all right? They are. Well, why didn't you say so in the first place? Well, think a minute—that shoulda been the first words out of your mouth."

Barney enters.

BARNEY: What's going on?
WOJO: Harris and Dietrich were shot at.
BARNEY: Are they all right?!
WOJO: They were checking out a disturbance.
BARNEY: *WOJO!!!*
WOJO: Yeah, they're fine.

Bomb Threat: Guest William Windom dons dynamite as Barney, Yemana and Wojo look on (the man behind bars is Washburn, a fake priest—played by Steve Landesberg, one season before he became Dietrich)

Barney Miller was all about trouble—the Human Condition, as it was often called by the social scientists. And *Barney Miller*, for a while, had nothing but trouble.

First, ABC—having pitted it against *The* unbeatable *Waltons*—wanted to knock it off the air. They hadn't been happy about casting Broadway musical actor Hal Linden as the squad-room captain in the first place, and in the second place there were no major stars and all these *minorities* and . . .

But the producer, Danny Arnold, begged ABC to cool it for a while and wait for the nation to get used to Barney and the other characters. It wasn't a long wait. Apparently the TV intelligentsia—those people who watched *Masterpiece Theater* and *M*A*S*H, Agronsky & Company*, and *Mary Tyler Moore*—took up the calling and turned to *Barney Miller* for comic relief. Even New Yorkers, living in *Miller*'s Manhattan, who got a busy signal when they dialed 911 and to whom muggings were often a monthly occurrence, tuned in in order to tune out. Said one Manhattanite: "Watching *Barney Miller* in the middle of the police chaos and cutbacks here didn't give me more sympathy for the cops. But it made me laugh at—and with—them, which helped relieve some of my anxiety. Made me realize that the cops aren't any better off or better protected than the rest of us out here."

Ironically, the police on *Barney Miller* were themselves constantly policed—by network censors. First, the show, like many others of its era, was the casualty of an "innovation" called "Family Viewing Hour," which was really the first two hours of prime time TV. In 1975, the National Association of Broadcasters deemed that nothing "inappropriate for viewing by general family audiences" could be on the air. That meant that *Barney Miller*—which dealt with everything from prostitution to constipation, from indecent exposure to assorted perversions—was in big trouble. And yet, somehow the show managed to get away with a lot. How did they do it? Said

Hal Linden: "We fought to get away with those subjects. Tremendous concessions had to be made on lines and situations. For example, a show we did about two homosexuals got on the air only because the gay community put pressure on the network. What the network was saying in effect was that a homosexual was not fit viewing for The Family Hour, and they were forced to backtrack from totally eliminating the subject."

Also, at that time, ABC was prudish about language, and words like "damn" and "hell" weren't permitted on that network (although they were used on NBC and CBS) because they were supposedly "religious." Said *Barney*'s producer: "How can you have a policeman in an urban area say, 'What the heck was that?' and 'Darn you'? But it wasn't just words, it was themes. In 1974, Wojo fell in love with a prostitute, and the network went crazy. In 1976, though, *Barney Miller* was able to win a battle with network censors over a hooker who was selling Bicentennial buttons as a ploy for $75. The network wanted her to sell them for $1.25, which, of course, would have killed the joke. Another time, the network didn't want the word "diarrhea" used on the show.

Said Linden: "We've had to change scripts and film scenes over again, and sometimes, when we think we've got everything letter perfect, word comes down that we have to make more changes. It's hard to believe, but we lost a station in Omaha because we had a hooker as a character one week. What did they want—a librarian?"

But eventually times changed—including the Family Viewing Hour (apparently they realized that what goes on in real families is much worse than what goes on in television), and *Barney Miller* was able to go on with its business: comedy.

WOJO: Another outburst like this and I'm gonna handcuff your lips together.

* * *

HARRIS: I don't care if you have psychotic episodes—but for God's sake, don't whine about it.

* * *

WOMAN: That man took my shoe. Have I been violated?
HARRIS: Metaphorically, yes.

The man behind *Barney Miller* was Danny Arnold (and in many ways *Barney Miller* was more *Danny Arnold* than *Barney Miller*). Arnold, the dynamo executive-producer, had lived on New York's Lower East Side before coming to Hollywood in the fifties. "Compromise is a disease" was his motto. He had a pal back in New York named Barney Ruditsky, and that's where Barney got his name. Plus, Arnold had once been arrested (a film crew of his was throwing pennies for some reason), and he was hauled into the station. He modeled *Barney's* squad room after that one, and each of the characters on *Barney Miller* was really a part of Danny Arnold.

Said one associate: "Barney himself was Danny's ideal—the compassionate, understanding supercop. With the Yemana character, it was Danny's love for horses—he owns more than twenty. With Harris, it was Danny's sense of the luxurious—the clothes, the Rolls Corniche worth over eighty thousand dollars. Chano was Danny the street kid. Fish's wife, Bernice, was really Danny's wife, Donna. Fish always complained about Bernice, but he couldn't do without her. Danny's the same way."

Barney Miller was written and filmed much differently from most other sitcoms—not in terms of technique, but the behind-the-scenes scenario. Arnold would write most of the scripts (and heavily rewrite the rest). He was involved in every aspect of the show, and, in 1979, after running himself ragged, ended up in the hospital for quadruple-bypass surgery (another master-builder of sitcoms, Nat Hiken, was totally involved in his cop show—*Car 54, Where Are You?*—and also had to slow down for health reasons; he too was fearful of a heart attack). Anyway, on most sitcoms, the cast has the weekend to look at the script before Monday's rehearsal; *Barney's* cast was lucky to get the script on Monday morning. Plus, while most half-hour sitcoms tape their shows within four hours, *Barney's* sessions were like marathon tapings—they'd begin at 8 A.M. on a Friday and continue on until about 6 A.M. the next day. "What is this —*Gone With the Wind*?" asked one crew member.

Said Arnold: "The actors never knew how the show was going to end, or even what the next scene would be. While this terrified them, to a certain extent it was stimulating as hell. It kept their interest alive to the last second. It also never produced any sense of familiarity with what had happened in the past. They'd see these shows and couldn't remember half the things they did."

Of course, all that "familiarity" created some problems. Twenty writers and ten directors came and went. Plus, as production costs rocketed, Arnold's finances swept toward bankruptcy and the network had to bail him out. And, finally, the cast began complaining that they were working too hard.

The first cast casualty was Abe Vigoda, who'd played the favorite, Phil Fish. The crusty, broken-down Fish didn't verbalize much, but kept his anger hidden inside. He could show his frustration but couldn't bring it out enough to fight.

Vigoda had been in show business for twenty-five years and had appeared in eighty plays. But it was his role as the ruthless Mafia leader Tessio in *The Godfather* (a role much unlike Fish) that brought him recognition. And Vigoda wanted more recognition on *Barney Miller*. He even told Arnold that he'd like the show's title changed to *Fish and Barney* (not even *Barney and Fish*). In June of 1977, a rift developed when for the second season in a row Vigoda's agent booked him into another project that delayed *Barney's* shooting. Arnold insisted that Abe come to work. Abe sued. Arnold countersued. But by the time Vigoda returned on the set—just to be careful, they'd written in a new character, Arthur Dietrich (who could, they figured, be Fish's replacement if Vigoda didn't come back). But both actors stayed in the cast—until Vigoda was spun off into his own series—*Fish*—something he and the network had wanted. When *Fish* flopped, Vigoda wanted back in. Arnold thought he asked for too much money. The answer was no.

Another regular, Greg Sierra (who played Chano Amenguale) left the show for his own series, *AES Hudson Street*, which might be considered one of the Great TV Flops (if there hadn't been so many other Great TV Flops in the late seventies). Instead of replacing Sierra, they simply enlarged Ron Carey's role as Carl Levitt, a nebbish, a bumbling uniformed policeman who longed to be a plainclothes detective (although his clothes were always tacky; he constantly apologized for the way he looked).

Welcome Back, Barney: *Barney and Fish lock up the Sweathogs.*

Next to producer Arnold, it was star Hal Linden who made Barney Miller *Barney Miller*. Linden started life in New York as Harold Lipshitz, but changed it while driving through Linden, New Jersey (point of interest: shortly thereafter, Hal's older brother Bernard changed his name to Linden too). For business purposes.

And Linden had a lot of business. He started out playing saxophone in big bands and after serving in Korea, he turned to acting "because I got tired of carrying around a sax." By 1958, he was getting featured roles on Broadway, including parts in *Wildcat* (with Lucille Ball), *On a Clear Day You Can See Forever*, *Subways Are for Sleeping*, and *The Rothschilds*, for which he won a Tony. Linden, for all his success, was feeling trapped by Broadway musicals and thought that TV might change his image. He made two unsuccessful pilots—*Mr. Inside, Mr. Outside*, and another that was a spoof on *Peyton Place*, which went off the air before the spoof could get on. Then he met Barney.

In the pilot episode (which was part of a 1974 ABC summer anthology called *Just for Laughs*), the show revolved around not only Barney's precinct problems, but his problems at home. He had a wife, Elizabeth (portrayed by Abby Dalton), and two kids. When the sitcom made it to the big time (prime time) the next year, the family (with Barbara Barrie as Elizabeth this time around) played a smaller part—soon to get even smaller when the couple separated and the emphasis totally shifted away from domestic comedy to situation comedy (although Barney and Elizabeth got back together during the 1978–1979 season—not in person, as far as we were concerned—but on the phone, which was enough. We wanted Barney to stay a cop, not become Robert Young).

Another firm foundation upon which *Barney Miller* was built was Jack Soo, who had appeared for one season in *Valentine's Day*, the Tony Franciosa sitcom in which Soo played Rockwell "Rocky" Sin, Valentine Farrow's con-man, poker-playing valet. Said Soo: "I've quit this business a hundred times, and as soon as I do, the phone rings. Maybe it's because I am, seriously, one of a kind in this industry. That's not braggadocio; there's no one of my race who's doing what I do—making people laugh without using either dirty or heavily ethnic routines."

As Nick Yemana, Soo was the senior member of the squad room (after Fish left), and he would sit around and comment on the goings-on with his swift one-liners. On January 11, 1979, after a long illness, Soo died of cancer. Said Steve Landesberg (Dietrich): "Jack was always making jokes, no self-pity. One of the last things he said to me was, 'Enjoy your time.'" After Soo's death, when it was time to reshoot the group photo for PR purposes, producer Arnold said No Way: "Nothing goes out without Jack. Use the old shots," he insisted. (The following year, though, they did take new group photos.)

What about replacing Soo? "It's pretty late to add new people," said Arnold. "I think we're heading down the road to that final sunset." Translated: *Barney Miller*

Mr. and Mrs. Miller: Barbara Barrie and Hal Linden

was about to retire. The 1979–1980 season would be his last—the actors' contracts were up then and they wanted to do other things. But it wasn't an unhappy ending: when the show went into syndication, it was expected to make at least $400 million. Not bad for a show that nearly went bankrupt.

One of the worries about *Barney Miller* at the beginning was that it was "too New York," that the rest of America wouldn't relate to it. As it became successful, there were worries that it couldn't possibly appeal to anyone outside of the US. But in January, there was an announcement that *Barney Miller* was being transferred (and translated) to Israel. Seems that some Israeli students there were making a version in Hebrew for Israeli TV. With a few changes, of course: instead of Yemana, there'd be Yeheil the Yemenite. There'd be no more ever-present cups of coffee but, instead, tiny cups of muddy Turkish brew. Harris would be replaced by Motti, whose heart's still back on the kibbutz. Fish would still be there, but instead of being sixty-five years old, he'd be nearly ninety.

But back to English: *Barney Miller* didn't make any great inroads in terms of understanding the real plights of detectives in a big, bad city (the way, for example, *M*A*S*H* showed us the underside of a big, bad war). It didn't make any headway in terms of language and permissiveness on television (Archie Bunker had already taken care of that four years before). And it didn't really tell us much more about life in the precinct station any more than *Mary Tyler Moore* showed us a true picture of life in the TV newsroom. What *Barney Miller* did do, though, was make us laugh. But in contrast to its peers *Happy Days* down the block and *Chico and the Man* down the dial, *Barney Miller* had more than respect for its characters. It had respect for us, its audience. *Barney Miller* was the logical conclusion to a very illogical entertainment form: the TV sitcom.

DIETRICH: You could point to every item in the Sears catalog and somebody, somewhere, wants to sleep with it.

CHICO AND THE MAN

Lookin' Go-o-o-d.
—CHICO

They say the music business has its casualties of sudden success. And of course, there are the self-defeating Hollywood movie stars, with too many pills and ills. But the cliché is also true for the small screen; the same kids who spent their youths transfixed in front of their TV screens, gazing at the stars, grew up to become TV stars. Sitcoms, like their big sister, movies, made speedy stars—and chewed them up and spat them out and destroyed them. There is, unfortunately, no better example than *Chico and the Man,* a sad saga of self-fulfillment and self-destruction, triumph, trouble, and tragedy.

But back to the beginning: sitcoms created stars; stars did not create sitcoms. Some of those homegrown stars from the recent sitcommunity include John Travolta, Henry Winkler, Jimmie "J.J." Walker, *Taxi*'s Andy Kaufman, Gary Coleman, Robin Williams (interestingly, all men). But none took TV by more storm or surprise than Freddie Prinze, who made *Chico* chic and himself a household word, like Cuisinart.

When *Chico* checked into the sitcom neighborhood, moving right next door to the Sanfords on Friday the 13th of September—a lucky day, indeed—it was one of the most shining examples of a show that was built around the unique talents of someone whom most of America had never heard of. Freddie Prinze, complete with the beat of the New York streets, was unknown to most of America; on Saturday, the 14th of September—a lucky day indeed—Prinze was known to most of America.

Not since Desi Arnaz played Ricky Ricardo had TV audiences had a Latin lover. And America was certainly having a love affair with Prinze. For those of us who might have been scared by streetwise, tough Puerto Ricans, Prinze won us over with his benign sense of humor. "Tha's not my job," he would protest. Network officials thought: A-*ha!* Here, at last, was a Puerto Rican you didn't have to be frightened of. And so—as some sort

of reward for being benign—they had given him his own show. They hadn't counted on the nightmare that would follow.

Chico and the Man hardly had a unique premise—it was an ethnic variation on the *Sanford and Son* theme of the ultimate conflict (which of course was a racial variation on *All in the Family*), all about a crotchety WASP owner of a garage and the Chicano kid who had moved in on his life. The show would change and evolve over its four seasons on NBC, but its initial format is the one most people remember:

It was set in the barrio in East Los Angeles, and there was Ed Brown—the Man—who was the cranky, feisty, cynical and sarcastic owner of a deteriorating one-man garage. He just wants to be left alone with his bottle. Enter Chico Rodriguez—an enterprising, determined, fast-talking, smart-mouthed young Chicano who was determined to go into partnership with the Man. God knows why. Ed's garage was shabby and run-down, and so was he. He spent all his time complaining and alienating people. Although he seemed only interested in making his business work, he was really touched that Chico was genuinely interested in him. And—although he kept kvetching (WASP-style)—he begrudgingly let Chico clean up the place, move into a beat-up old truck in the garage—and bring in business. Each of them alleviated the other's loneliness.

Chico must have had the magic touch, because he brought in lots of business to the NBC sitcom too. (It became the Number One show immediately.) Just as the sparks flew between Mike Stivic and Archie Bunker—and Alice and Ralph Kramden, and a bunch of other sitcom bickerers—the nation watched, fascinated and amused, at the verbal warfare that went on between the two of them. "Get out of here and take your flies with you!" Ed would holler at Chico.

But not for long. It was remarks like that—coupled

Ed Brown (the Man)	Jack Albertson
Chico Rodriguez	Freddie Prinze (1974–1977)
Louie	Scatman Crothers
Mable	Bonnie Boland (1974–1975)
Mondo	Isaac Ruiz (1974–1975)
Reverend Bemis	Ronny Graham (1975–1976)
Della Rogers	Della Reese (1976–1978)
Raul Garcia	Gabriel Melgar (1977–1978)
Aunt Charo	Charo (1977–1978)

with a few other factors—that got *Chico and the Man* in a lot of trouble with the Men. There were picket lines outside of the studio. There were protests of all forms. And—horrors!—people were beginning to boycott the show's sponsor, McDonald's. Here's what happened:

"I've never seen anything like it," complained Jack "the Man" Albertson during rehearsals. "Here's a brand-new show that's Number One in the ratings this week. It's a miracle. So why is it like a funeral in here?" The answer: because of the pressure special-interest groups were putting on the producers of the show to clean up their act. Their gripe: that the show was, basically, insulting to all Americans of Mexican descent. Mental Flashback: *Bridget Loves Bernie* . . . Flash-back-back-back: *Amos 'n' Andy*. It could only mean trouble.

It only meant trouble. Their specific complaints were that: (1) The name of the main character, Chico, was demeaning because it meant "boy," a word also offensive to blacks. (2) They didn't like the theme song by José Feliciano because it was flamenco and, according to one expert, "Flamenco music is as foreign to the Chicano, or Mexican-American, as bagpipe music." (3) Though Chico was supposed to be high school educated and a Vietnam veteran, they felt Prinze delivered some of his lines in the comedic accents of an illiterate wetback who has just swum the Rio Grande—via New York-street overtones. (4) But it was the ethnic insults—the "get out of here and take your flies with you"—that the groups most objected to, and they cited "the overused stereotype of the simplistic, bumbling Mexican who must inevitably commit his dishonesties and stupidities only to be saved from himself by the condescending Anglo-American." (5) They thought Prinze was wrong for the role because he was not a red-blooded Chicano (Mexican-American), but of Puerto Rican/Hungarian heritage.

In short, what they seemed to want was not a sitcom but a documentary.

Plus, it didn't help when the show's own associate producer—a Mexican-American war hero named Ray Andrade—called the Chico character "cheap, demeaning and offensive."

What to do . . .

What they did—a first for network people and producers—was to hold meetings and try to resolve the problem. Said a producer later: "We listened, which is an activity network officials unfortunately don't indulge in too often." They pulled a half-dozen already filmed episodes and did some surgery. They removed the offensive lines and inserted ethnic explanations—when another character asked Chico why he talked funny, Chico answered: Because "I have a Puerto Rican mother and a Hungarian grandmother," and so he was no longer posing as a bona fide Chicano.

Most important, though: the relationship between Chico and the Man changed. Instead of only fighting and biting humor, things mellowed a bit.

The turning point was an October 4 episode called

"The New Suit," in which Chico, out of love for the still-bitter Ed, bought him a new suit in order to persuade him to emerge into the world again and attend a reunion of his wartime army unit. All very funny and touching. And so, the relationship between Chico and Ed evolved from master-and-slave to father-and-son. Chico started to speak what the producers called "normal English" (not realizing, of course, that, unfortunately, the kind of English Prinze had been speaking as Chico is considered "normal English" by most people). And there were some interior design changes: the curtains from Chico's truck—made from the green, white, and red Mexican flag—were removed. They added a few new real-life Chicanos to the cast—including Isaac Ruiz as Chico's best friend, Mondo (Ruiz originally had been beaten out by Prinze for the part of Chico). Everything was changed—except one thing: Jose Feliciano's theme song.

"Nobody's going to make me a bigot against Puerto Ricans," Feliciano announced, but later in the first season the show introduced two Mexican youngsters, eight and nine years old, who played mariachi music.

End of crisis. On with the show. For a while, anyway.

Here are a few samples illustrating what the episodes were like during the first few seasons:

● When Chico joins the Garage Mechanics Union (during the 1975–1976 season), the union organizer forces him to strike—because Ed refuses to abide by the union contract. Trouble.

● Ed merited newspaper coverage as a good samaritan when he gave $20 to an inept mugger and refused to press charges against him. Of course, soon every mugger in town pays the garage a visit. Trouble.

● When Ed's former secret love, Violette Baynes, comes into the garage to have her car repaired, Chico suddenly finds that his life is disrupted since Ed becomes mesmerized by the lady. Trouble.

● A new neighbor, Della Rogers—played by singer Della Reese—moves in. She is Ed's landlady, and also owns a diner across the street. After arguing with the cantankerous Ed, she informs him that his thirty-year lease is about to expire. Trouble.

Running out of pithy exchanges between Chico and the Man, the producers added Reese to the cast in 1976 as somebody new for Ed to argue with, and to set up a "battle of the sexes," as it was called back then. Comedian/actor Franklyn Ajaye was added to the cast in 1977 as her son Woody.

Although it was clearly Chico's show, Albertson brought a lot to his part—certainly a lot of experience. Although he was called an "overnight star" because of *Chico and the Man*, this was hardly true for him, as it was true for Prinze. Albertson had been in show business for forty-five years before *Chico*; he'd worked in vaudeville, burlesque, opera, stage, movies, and television (including his role as Lieutenant Commander Virgil Stoner, executive officer of the *Appleby* on the sitcom *Ensign*

O'Toole, from 1962 through 1964). Albertson always suffered from stage fright, and it was no wonder—he worked with Phil Silvers as his first partner, then as a straight man for Milton Berle and Bert Lahr. He won a Tony for his role of the father in Broadway's *The Subject Was Roses*, and an Oscar for the movie version. About *Chico* he said: "One good thing about hitting it in show business this late is that you get a shorter time left to be a has-been." After *Chico* went off the air, Albertson tried again with *Grandpa Goes to Washington* (he played Grandpa, not Washington), which lasted one season in 1978.

Freddie Prinze's career went a bit differently. He was an overnight star, bursting into that sitcom-superstar phenomenon. At the High School of Performing Arts in Manhattan, Prinze did his "act" in the boys' room during lunch hour, moving, after classes, to the Improvisation Club in Manhattan. He got a lot of laughs onstage—in school as well, which he never completed because he flunked economics. It didn't matter, though, because Prinze's personal economics would soon zoom sky-high, and he could afford to hire people to study his economics for him.

Prinze was truly a child of the ghettos. Because he was part Puerto Rican, part Hungarian, he called himself a "Hungarican." He was born in New York's Hell's Kitchen, and was a switchblade-carrying member of the Royal Lords. A religious Catholic, Prinze worshiped God and his mother, the latter often credited by him for steering him away from a life of crime. Prinze worked hard, doing street theater and studying ballet, and often said he wanted to be "the complete performer."

Celebrity hit him hard, and even at the start of *Chico*, when Prinze was first becoming a star, people commented that his success was going to his head. At the beginning, however, he managed to keep things in perspective. In 1975, Prinze commented: "I remember I used to write letters to David Janssen on *The Fugitive* when I was in high school. It was such a thrill when he

Two-on-the-Floor: Jack Albertson and Freddie Prinze

answered me back. I promised myself that when I became a celebrity, I would answer all my mail too. The first couple of months, I was able to do it. But then, when I started getting ten thousand letters a week, it became impossible. I still read the personal ones, though. They're the ones from kids in the street who are happy because I've made it. I tell you, I cry like a baby when I read them. I hope I'm providing them with a good example." And for a while, he was.

Prinze seemed to have everything: money, fame, love, and a hit show. But he also had pills. And a gun. On January 28, 1977—halfway into the third season—twenty-two-year-old Freddie Prinze shot himself in the head and, after a thirty-three hour fight for his life at the UCLA Medical Center, he died. He had been despondent over his shattered marriage to Katherine Elaine, who had sued him for divorce the previous month after only fifteen months of marriage, as well as the ugly lawsuit brought against him by his former manager.

The night of the shooting, Prinze had called his wife and parents, telling them of his intended suicide, and then reached under his pillow for a pistol he'd hidden there and shot himself. If he had not died, he would have lived out his life as a vegetable.

There was great controversy—and sadness—surrounding his death. "He did not mean to kill himself," his mother insisted, "he was just playing with that silly gun, just showing off. If anyone killed him, it was Hollywood. He became a product, a piece of merchandise."

His close friend, singer Tony Orlando, had a lot to say about Prinze's death: "He planned it. In his backyard, Freddie came to me one day after a year of practicing suicide with an empty pistol. He didn't have a bullet in there, but what he would do was click the gun off at his temples and, sometimes, as gruesomely, in his mouth. Sometimes he would shoot a pistol off to show how . . . how ill he was. If his secretary was in the next room, she thought he shot himself. He would be lying on the floor and get up laughing.

"He was ill," Orlando said. "You read about not being able to cope with success at a young age—that was part of it—you read about a young marriage that was not working out—yes, that was part of it. But the ultimate part of it was that he found glory in suicide. He said he wanted to be a legend; he wanted to be like James Dean." According to Orlando, Prinze had even told him the pallbearers he had wanted—Johnny Carson, Richard Pryor, David Brenner, Paul Williams, "and any other big star you can find." He said Prinze had taken nine Quaaludes "plus some Courvoisier on the night he killed himself. So that alone, you know, could have put him into a comatose state."

"Hollywood did not destroy Freddie and neither did drugs," said *Chico* producer James Komack, another close friend of Prinze's. "The seeds of destruction were in him since childhood. He brought it all with him the day he got off the plane from New York in 1974."

Although Prinze died, *Chico and the Man* did not. They had filmed four episodes with Prinze, before his death, and these had not aired yet. Plus, the next episode scheduled had Prinze/Chico talking about death. Many people thought that they should have dropped the series for good. But the producers simply switched episodes and televised a different episode of *Chico* with Prinze, and the death-reference episode later.

The producers decided to "write out" Chico for the rest of the season rather than replace him, and they expressed hopes of keeping the show running the following season. Shortly after Prinze's death, Komack read the following tribute on the air before a telecast in which Prinze was featured:

"We can honor his contribution to all our lives by remembering his dedication to entertain a world that needs laughter. The following program is part of the legacy he leaves toward that."

There was a lot of talk and chatter that it was totally tasteless of Komack to have continued *Chico* at all after Prinze's suicide. A year after that event, Komack finally addressed himself to the charge: "People have asked me: Why did I continue the series after his death? Did I put making money ahead of my concern for another human being? All of this is insane, of course, and wherever Freddie is right now, he's looking down and laughing at me. 'Hey man,' he's saying, 'don't you know what a waste of time this is? People won't understand. They think you didn't care about me because you continued the series; that you got personal happiness and monetary rewards from somebody else's misery.' I loved Freddie. I didn't continue *Chico and the Man* strictly for selfish reasons. Besides protecting other people in the production, I didn't want the country to become eternal mourners.

"What people don't understand," Komack said, "is that the show's ratings were slipping. When we first started out, within five weeks we were Number One in the country. The second year we were in the Top Ten. Then we started to slip. Let's be honest—my life would have been a lot easier without *Chico and the Man* and the problems with Freddie."

Komack paused. "I remember the night he left my home—it was the last time I saw him. He talked about doing *Chico and the Man* for another year and how much he loved me. Walking out the door, he turned to me and said, 'When you see Jack Albertson tomorrow, tell him I love him.' I said: 'You'll see him yourself tomorrow.' Freddie replied: 'That's right, but just in case I'm late, tell him.'"

When the Prinze episodes ran out, Komack started shooting *Chico* as a solo show for Albertson. But it didn't work well. "Without Prinze," said *Variety*, "Jack Albertson is the sound of one hand clapping."

They needed Chico. But they couldn't have him. And then they remembered something from back in the protest days: "Chico" means "boy"—not any one, specific boy, but *any* boy. And so they found a new Chico, a cute

Chico and the New Man: Jack Albertson with (clockwise) Della Reese, Scatman Crothers, Gabriel Melgar

twelve-year-old, Gabriel Melgar, who played Raul, a cheeky Chico who debuted on the fourth season opener. Melgar was spotted in LA by a talent scout—not sitting on a stool at a drugstore (that's the old-fashioned way)—but playing the marimbas for *turistas*. But the relationship between Albertson and Melgar just wasn't the same; the affection seemed to have been replaced by affectation.

Albertson, however, liked Melgar: "You work with so many precocious kids over the years that you come to hate them. But this one—he combines maturity and an independence, and yet he's warm and charming and genuine. And that's why everyone loves him."

There were problems. Some viewers actually didn't realize that Prinze had died and, in fact, the producers had received hundreds of letters from people who wanted to know "what happened to Chico." And so they filmed an hour-long show in which the characters mentioned that Chico is dead. According to the producers, it was the only way they could stop all those letters. Of course there was even more protest, claiming that the producers were exploiting Prinze's death, especially since the telecast came close to the one-year anniversary of his suicide. In the episode, Raul discovered that there had been a previous Chico, left a poignant note to Ed, and then ran away. The episode contained flashback film footage of Prinze on the early shows, which were intercut into the hour.

It didn't matter. It just wasn't the same show. And NBC killed off this *Chico*, content to let the old one live on via TV reruns. Even now, looking at them, Freddie Prinze seems so vibrant, so fresh, so alive, that it's hard to believe he took himself away from us so soon. The real tragedy is that Chico never allowed himself to become the Man.

THE JEFFERSONS

> BANKER: *Before I give you the money, Mr. Jefferson,*
> *I'll need your John Hancock.*
> GEORGE: *What do you want with my life insurance?*

It seems that Television Land has become Spin-off City. As soon as a character on a show becomes successful— i.e., if the polls say that viewers are "responding favorably"—the network gives that character his own show. *Lou Grant, Betty White, Phyllis* and *Rhoda,* were graduates of *Mary Tyler Moore* and were rewarded with shows of their own. *Happy Days* begat the good-time Charlies *Laverne and Shirley* and *Mork and Mindy.* Flo didn't live here anymore when *Alice* gave her a show. *Trapper John,* transplanted in time from the Korean to the Vietnam War, came out of *M*A*S*H.* *Three's Company* gave us *The Ropers,* and *Barney Miller* delivered *Fish.*

But nobody has spun off more, and more successfully, than the granddaddy of the new-wave sitcom, *All in the Family,* which waved goodbye to its cousin *Maude* (who in turn waved goodbye to her maid Florida for more *Good Times*) and said farewell to the Bunkers' neighbors, the Jeffersons, who became *The Jeffersons.*

Of all the spin-offs, none had a more interesting evolution than George and Louise and Lionel Jefferson, an up-up-upwardly mobile black family who, after a tearful goodbye to Edith (and a good-riddance to and from Archie), bid adieu to Queens for the life of a king on New York's Upper East Side.

George Jefferson was a black Archie Bunker—except for one crucial difference: Archie was struggling, George was a tycoon. Newly rich. And the prejudices and persuasions that came along with being a rich black man were much different from those sitting at home eating up poor, white Archie.

At the series' start, George Jefferson was probably television's most unsympathetic character. Until later episodes he had no redeeming warmth. He was verbally abusive to his wife and his son. He was a snob and a social climber. He was a bigot (he called white people "honkies"). He tried to exploit his black maid. He was uppity, pushy, conniving (in fact, George Jefferson was much more a Jewish stereotype than a black one). Probably George wanted to be white (and, if he had been, you can be sure he would have hated blacks).

Perhaps part of it was an adjustment problem. George had had a small dry-cleaning business back home in Queens, and he'd worked himself up to middle class (which is what brought him to Archie's neighborhood as the blockbusting black). Then he went on to bust better and better blocks when he opened a chain of stores and moved to an elegant building in Manhattan.

The Jeffersons was sort of *The Beverly Hillbillies* in blackface, except that, unlike the Clampetts, George didn't want to continue living his old way; he wanted to move up in the world, to rub shoulders with the erudite, to become a rich-white-man. But he couldn't pull it off.

> GUEST: Those are beautiful occasional tables.
> GEORGE: Yeah, but we're gonna use them all the time, not just occasionally.

And:

> NEIGHBOR: George, your office has that certain *je ne sais quoi* . . .
> GEORGE: Not anymore—I just had it exterminated yesterday.

George was also the type who, when a guest asked for a glass of "Scotch—neat," takes offense and retorts with "Don't worry, you'll get a clean glass."

George Jefferson	Sherman Hemsley
Louise Jefferson	Isabel Sanford
Lionel Jefferson	Mike Evans (1975, 1978–); Damon Evans (1975–1978)
Helen Willis	Roxie Roker
Tom Willis	Franklin Cover
Jenny Willis Jefferson	Berlinda Tolbert
Harry Bentley	Paul Benedict
Mother Jefferson	Zara Cully (1975–1978)
Ralph the Doorman	Ned Wertimer
Florence	Marla Gibbs
Marcus Garvey	Ernest Harden, Jr. (1977–)
Allan Willis	Jay Hammer (1978–)

He wasn't kidding. George flailed through life—or at least our weekly half-hour sessions with him—as though his very existence depended on it. When he moved up in the world, his blood pressure galloped right along.

Fortunately there was Louise to try to smooth things out. Louise was a wise owl to Edith's dingbat. Whenever George would go off the deep end with his self-involvement and narcissism and delusions of grandeur, Louise—or "Weesie," as he called her—would remind him of his roots.

GEORGE: It's the American dream come true. Ten years ago I was this little guy with one store. And now look at me—
LOUISE: Now you're the little guy with seven stores.

Even in their high-rise, Louise was down-to-earth. She worked hard before they had money, and now, even though she could luxuriate in wealth, she was still practical and humble. "How do you do, Mrs. Jefferson?" someone asked her, and George responded: "Oh, she does fine—as long as she's married to me." Louise was a saint. "Where's my breakfast, woman?" he'd often ask her. And she'd tell him.

What kept George human—and somewhat humane—was the fact that underneath his obnoxiousness there was a great deal of sadness. He had struggled all his life, thinking that money was the key—and when he got it, he found out that the key didn't open all the doors. He was afraid to express his love for fear he'd be hurt, and later in the series, when he did loosen up, it was truly touching. *The Jeffersons* was all about the bittersweet American Dream and the silly side of success.

Because the Jeffersons lived in sitcomland (as well as the Upper East Side), they had the requisite wacky neighbors. Harry Bentley, a hopelessly square English eccentric who lost things (like his pants) and was always crying to the Jeffersons for help, lived right next door. He was, at best, a little dense. When George received a strange phone call, a guest asked, "What kind of person would make a crank call like that?" and Bentley responded: "A crank." And he meant it. Often his back would go out, and he'd come hobbling over to ask George to walk all over him—blatant sitcom symbolism. But funny.

On the show's premiere—Saturday, January 18, 1975—we met another set of neighbors: Helen and Tom Willis. She was black. He was white. George was appalled.

HELEN (*after an argument*): George—no one's wrong, no one's right. Everything is not black and white.
GEORGE: It is in *your* family.

Because of Louise's pressure, George began to tolerate the couple (although it didn't help matters when his only son, Lionel, married the Willis' daughter).

Weesie and George: Isabel Sanford and Sherman Hemsley

GEORGE: Want a drink? How 'bout a white mule?
TOM: What's a white mule?
GEORGE: A honky donkey . . .

For, worst of all, George was a racist. He wanted to impress some whites, but disdained most of them (although he was ever eager to make it and be accepted in their world).

NEIGHBOR (*after George has hung up the phone*): How do you know he's white?
GEORGE: Because he had a white accent.

But besides "Weesie's" soothing reprimands, George had another important adversary—his maid, Florence, who called him "Shorty." In the opening episode she wasn't written in as a permanent character, but her tag line—"How come we overcame and nobody told me?"—brought the house down. And so she became a regular.

Good thing, too. She was a terror, taking jabs at and jibes from George. She was uneducated, but she knew all the answers. George thought she was lazy and shiftless. She thought he was just what he was.

Sometimes he zinged her:

FLORENCE: Is there something you don't like about my cooking?
GEORGE: Yeah—eating it.

Or:

FLORENCE (*wearing a bright-red dress*): Do you think this color suits me?
GEORGE: Sure—it's loud, isn't it?

Or:

LOUISE: I'm afraid there's something wrong with Florence.
GEORGE: Why? Did you see her cleaning something?

And:

FLORENCE: My fiancé Buzz has such high standards.
GEORGE: Then what's he doing with you?

And Florence zapped him right back:

GEORGE: Get away from the mirror—you don't need any more bad luck!
FLORENCE: I know. I already got you.

Or:

GEORGE: If I paid you to think, you could cash your check at the penny arcade.
FLORENCE: Where do you think I cash it now?

And:

FLORENCE: I ain't got no money.
GEORGE: I just paid you a full week's salary.
FLORENCE: I know. I blew it all on a pay toilet.

Everybody liked Louise except one person—George's cranky, nasty mother, a heavy-drinking snip of a woman who would not pass up any opportunity to say anything rotten about Louise. For example, when Louise was supposedly kidnapped:

MOTHER JEFFERSON: It's a good thing they kidnapped Louise.
GEORGE: What are you talking about, Mama?
MOTHER JEFFERSON: Just think how much money they'd be asking for if they kidnapped *me*.

And later, when Louise is home:

LOUISE: You thought *I* was kidnapped. Why would anybody want me?
MOTHER JEFFERSON: That's what I've been asking myself for years.
GEORGE: Louise, you're worth your weight in gold.
MOTHER JEFFERSON: I don't think there's that much gold in Fort Knox.

At the beginning, Louise didn't fight back. Then she would slip it in slowly. Like when Mother Jefferson showed her a photo of herself: "Oh," Louise purrs, "is this the one taken during the Civil War?"

That's the Jefferson's com. Here is some of their sit:

Once George wanted Florence to "act like a real maid," and so she dressed up in a "mammy" outfit, wearing a bandana and saying: "No, Masta, please don't be angry with me . . ." George became so sick of her that he wanted the old Florence back. And that's what he got. Another time, George gave a tenants' party in his apartment to show off and impress a white banker he was trying to cultivate (naturally, everything went wrong). There were several episodes with George, who was a high school dropout, scheming to get Lionel to finish college and go into the family business; Lionel earned an engineering degree and refused to do it. Then, of course, there was the time Lionel married Jenny, Tom and Helen's daughter. Or when Bentley next door had an unwanted houseguest whom he was too chicken to remove. Another time, Florence fell for a psychiatrist, pretended she was "many women" to appeal to him, and he thought she was schizophrenic and tried to have her committed. On one episode, Louise was allegedly kidnapped, but it turned out to be Florence, who managed to give out clues to the hideaway and be rescued without George having to part with the $100,000 ransom.

Very often *The Jeffersons* was sophomoric slapstick, very back-to-burlesque. Like many other sitcoms, its

Neighbors: George and Bentley

humor was predominantly insult (and often insulting), plus the usual mistaken identities and dumb remarks, and expected people doing expected unexpected things, as in this exchange between Bentley and George when Bentley is afraid to tell a woman he doesn't want to marry her.

BENTLEY: I can't be there when you break the news. I hate it when grown-ups cry.
GEORGE: Oh, she won't cry.
BENTLEY: Not her—me!

Early in 1977, another character was added to the cast: a young, streetwise black named Marcus Garvey, who was an employee of George's store, which was located in the lobby of the Jeffersons' apartment building. In 1978, they added the white brother of black Jenny (Lionel's wife, who was Helen and Tom's daughter). He was a source of annoyance to both George and Tom.

The character of Lionel took an interesting turn. Originally Mike Stivic's buddy on *All in the Family*, he continually bickered with his father, but moved in with them when they went to Manhattan. After one season on *The Jeffersons*, Mike Evans, who played Lionel, wanted out. Said Norman Lear: "There was no question of money. He was unhappy and, speaking for myself, he was not alone. It was by mutual agreement." But Lionel "left home" only to return for visits—in the slightly altered personage of Damon Evans (no relation to Mike) as Lionel. He left the show at the end of the 1977–1978 season, and was only referred to thereafter. During the 1979–1980 season, Lionel returned as a regular—played by the original Lionel, Mike Evans. *The Jeffersons* meets *The Twilight Zone*.

Sherman Hemsley—from his smug expressions to his chicken walk—let himself become George Jefferson. As a kid in Philadelphia, he'd been in a gang, but taught himself dance steps on the sly. After four years in the air force, he worked for the postal service and enrolled in the Philadelphia Academy of Dramatic Arts. He arrived in New York in 1967 and opened up a chain of cleaning stores—no (that's what happens when an actor is so closely associated with his character), he performed Off-Broadway (he played the Mad Hatter in an all-black *Alice in Wonderland*) and on Broadway in *Purlie*, where Lear saw him and years later remembered him when he was casting George.

Louise was played by Isabel Sanford, the lovable, nice, warm wife of George. Sanford was known for her strange line-readings of the part (she seemed to speak slowly and then rapidly, with strange emphases on words), but her husky voice and pleasant manner made her beloved. As a kid in New York, Sanford did nightclub acts, against her mother's wishes. Then she joined the American Negro Theater and acted anywhere and everywhere she could, including Broadway. She married a housepainter and worked as a keypunch operator. In 1960, she loaded her family on a bus and moved to California, where she appeared in a number of movies, including *Guess Who's Coming to Dinner*. Said Sanford: "There are no black comediennes today. I'm gonna break that mold. I have wanted to be a comedienne, the one who gets all the laughs, all my life. What *The Jeffersons* is for me is a beautiful stepping-stone."

Marla Gibbs (Florence) had grown up in Chicago, dreaming of becoming a star. After a divorce, she worked as an airline clerk and telephone solicitor, and then came to Hollywood, where she studied singing and acting. She appeared on *Barney Miller* and *Doc* before she became a *Jeffersons* regular. Some people felt her role as Florence is the stereotypical lazy and shiftless maid. "I feel we break out of stereotypes," she says. "I don't take any guff. If Mrs. Jefferson is standing close to the door when the bell rings and tells me to answer it, I say, 'You're closer, you answer it.'" (Gibbs was known to joke on the set, and if Sanford, in Real Life, invited her to a party, she would say: "Now, Miz Jefferson, you know I don't like to work on my day off.") "I see Florence as part of the black heritage of this country. All blacks began in a servant capacity. There's not a black person who didn't come from that heritage," Gibbs said.

She was also known for adding lines to the script: "The lines just came up. I'd suggest them and the writers put them in the script. Florence's dialogue is fed right out of my memory bank."

Probably the most interesting case history of all of *The Jeffersons'* clan was that of Paul Benedict, who played the family's klutzy but well-intentioned neighbor, Bentley. He had a strange look about him—an over-loose walk plus a distorted face; a large nose and a huge jaw, making him look more like a race horse than a TV actor. Benedict was lucky to look that way at all.

In 1965, while performing with the Theatre Company of Boston, a radiologist in the audience sent him a note. Said Benedict: "The man wrote that he suspected I might be the victim of a bizarre glandular disorder, acromegaly [which enlarges the hands, feet and face]. The note said, 'If you'd like to talk to me, I'll wait for you outside the lobby.' Of course I rushed out and grabbed him by the lapels—and his diagnosis turned out to be correct. He sent me to an endocrine specialist and I underwent a twenty-minute operation. And that was that. Actually, it would've killed me if it hadn't been caught at that time. My headaches had grown worse and I was completely exhausted. There's been no recurrence. The only thing is, the ailment changed my casting possibilities. It turned me into a character actor."

That was fine with Norman Lear, *The Jeffersons'* producer. "We wanted something different for a neighbor and liked the idea of an Englishman. Oddly enough, we interviewed some British actors, but they were *too* British. When Paul auditioned, he had just the right kind of level."

The Jeffersons was a popular show. But it was also a

significant one because more than any other program it helped open the way toward racial tolerance. That probably sounds like a lot of garbage now—sitcoms about blacks being Significant—but TV (and sitcoms in particular) have always been light-years behind reality. For example: in 1968, on a Petula Clark TV special, the singer touched the hand of her guest star, Harry Belafonte. Viewers, stations, and sponsors went crazy, turning a simple touch into an Incident. And here, just seven years later, *The Jeffersons* had an interracial couple living in their building.

Once again, the credit goes to Norman Lear, who brought minorities into our living rooms, and, more importantly, took us into their living rooms—and kitchens and bedrooms. Sure, it was often masked in silly situations and banal banter. But perhaps that was not by mistake; perhaps Lear was on to something: Perhaps the same people who respond to stupid situations and puerile humor are the same ones who are prejudiced. The tactic: lure them in with the jokes and then throw a little Relevance at them.

Sure, George Jefferson was often mean and nasty and unfeeling. But you have to delve deep into television history to see how far he'd come. There is another George in the sitcom archives—George Stevens, a.k.a. the Kingfish on *Amos 'n' Andy*—who was a distant cousin to George Jefferson. The difference—and this is the key to how far we've come in thirty years of sitcoms—is that George Stevens said "Yes'm, boss," and George Jefferson *was* the boss.

Cheek-to-Cheek: Mother Jefferson dances with Harry Bentley at his birthday party.

RHODA

My name is Rhoda Morgenstern. I was born in The Bronx, New York, in December of 1941. I've always felt responsible for World War II. The first thing that I remember liking that liked me back was food. I had a bad puberty; it lasted seventeen years. I'm a high school graduate. I went to art school. My entrance exam was on a book of matches. I decided to move out of the house when I was twenty-four. My mother still refers to this as the time I ran away from home. Eventually I ran to Minneapolis where it's cold and I figured I'd keep better. Now I'm back in Manhattan. New York—this is your last chance.

—the opening of *Rhoda*, 1974

Whatever happened to Rhoda Morgenstern?

That is one of the most confusing sitcom mysteries of all time. Here's her case history: She started life as Mary Richards' upstairs neighbor—and foe—on *The Mary Tyler Moore Show*. By the second episode, they had become friends. Best friends. Rhoda was short and heavy and schleppy and amusingly self-deprecating, a New York Jew. Not only was she an oddity on Waverly Street in Minneapolis, where she lived, she was a freak in the TV neighborhood of Ozzie-and-Harriet ranch homes with white-bread inhabitants. Rhoda was television's first single-Jewish-goil-looking-to-snatch-a-catch. She had a big heart and a mouth to match. Audiences—some of whom had Nielsen boxes fused to their sets—loved Rhoda. They soon had a chance to love *Rhoda*.

On September 9, 1974, Rhoda moved back to New York. Even though we'd never actually seen Rhoda in New York (except once on a *Mary Tyler Moore* episode where Rhoda and Mary weekended in New York for Rhoda's younger sister Debbie's wedding—definitely pre-Brenda, Rhoda's little sister on her own series), we knew a lot about Rhoda's roots. First, we had met and laughed at and identified against (as opposed to identified with) her parents, Ida and Martin Morgenstern—or "Ma" and "Pa," as Rhoda called them. Like the rest of us, Rhoda carried her parents around with her in a little pocket in her psyche, usually with acres of wiseacre remarks about them. Plus, we already knew a lot about Rhoda's relationship with her hometown: "I moved to Minneapolis because I couldn't find an apartment in New York."

So, by the time Rhoda moved back to New York, we pretty much knew what everybody and everything looked like, right down to the see-through plastic slipcovers on her mother's upholstery.

But what we mainly knew was that we loved Rhoda—and, frankly, it couldn't happen to a nicer person: to get a show of her own.

So what happened then? Why did Rhoda the Soaring turn into Rhoda the Boring? She went from being *That Nice Jewish Girl* to *That Girl*.

The answer is Trust. Rhoda's creators didn't trust her to be Rhoda anymore. It was *The Invasion of the Body Snatchers*—sitcom-style. Oh, Rhoda looked the

Rhoda Morgenstern Gerard	Valerie Harper
Brenda Morgenstern	Julie Kavner
Joe Gerard	David Groh (1974–1977)
Ida Morgenstern	Nancy Walker (1974–1976, 1977–1978)
Martin Morgenstern	Harold Gould (1974–1976, 1977–1978)
Carlton the Doorman (voice only)	Lorenzo Music
Mae	Cara Williams (1974–1975)
Alice Barth	Candy Azzara (1974–1975)
Myrna Morgenstern	Barbara Sharma (1974–1976)
Justin Culp	Scoey Mitchell (1975–1976)
Gary Levy	Ron Silver (1976–1978)
Sally Gallagher	Anne Meara (1976–1977)
Johnny Venture	Michael Delano (1977–1978)
Benny Goodwin	Ray Buktenica (1977–1978)
Jack Doyle	Ken McMillan (1977–1978)
Ramon Diaz, Jr.	Rafael Campos (1977–1978)
Tina	Nancy Lane (1978)

"Ma, you're driving me crazy!": Rhoda tries moving back home.

same. The accent was the same. She still dressed in the same fashionably offbeat garb. But something was missing—Rhoda's spirit, her energy, her soul. They had taken it away—in the middle of the night—and had replaced it with a look-alike corpse.

Or maybe it was the format. *Rhoda* went through more changes of life than all the women in her mother's Bronx apartment building put together. First, Rhoda was single, visiting New York. Then she met a guy and they dated. Then they got married. They stayed married for a while. She got bored and started a window-dressing business. Then she and her husband got separated and saw each other only occasionally. Then they got divorced. Then Rhoda tried to make it on her own. Then she started dating again. Then she got a job, then she . . . then she got canceled.

It's the old sitcom rule that characters who are neurotic—people with minor-league hang-ups and who can laugh about them—are more interesting than ones who are Normal. Rhoda got normal.

It started back in the early seventies when Valerie Harper—the gifted comedienne who played Rhoda on *MTM*—came back from vacation . . . twenty-two pounds thinner, thanks to Weight Watchers. And so, the writers made Rhoda thinner. And, gradually, she got more and more "together"—like she was just hatched and was learning how to walk. So *MTM*'s Rhoda took baby steps. She was still insecure and self-deprecating, but she just looked different.

Then Rhoda moved to New York. For a while all was terrific. She moved in with her parents but couldn't stand it, and instead moved into a Greenwich Village apartment with her little sister Brenda who was—overweight, insecure, and self-deprecating. In fact, she was Rhoda to Rhoda's Mary. (We expected, any minute, a spin-off called *Brenda*.) In fact, as Rhoda got thinner, so did *Rhoda*.

Said the show's producer: "We're going to let Rhoda

be what she wants to be. She's still going to wear the same crazy things. She told us she wouldn't be comfortable being a glamour girl. Maybe she's kidding and maybe she isn't."

The highlight of *Rhoda* came just eight weeks after its debut—Rhoda's wedding. She had met handsome Joe Gerard—divorced, and owner of the New York Wrecking Company and a ten-year-old son. He was clearly Catholic. She was genuinely Jewish. Oh, there was no *Bridget Loves Bernie* problem (TV had learned better). Just love and laughter. On October 28, 1974, *Rhoda* blossomed into a full-hour telecast when the husband-hunter finally snared her prey.

The episode is still a classic. Fifty million people stayed home—and some actually threw parties for Rhoda's wedding. It was a TV phenomenon, unlike anything since Lucy had her baby on television. Here was the ultimate triumph: the ugly duckling-turned-swan marrying Prince Charming, seventies-style. It was cause for celebration. It was a funny sequence. Most of the old clan had flown in from Minneapolis for the wedding—Lou, Phyllis, Mary. Phyllis had promised to give Rhoda a lift to The Bronx for the wedding in her parents' apartment, but she forgot. And so Rhoda—dressed in her long-lacy white gown—ended up taking a subway to her own wedding. "Some guy tried to write graffiti on me!" she exclaimed. The episode drew strong acclaim: "Television may finally have devised the electronic equivalent of the hash brownie," said the New York *Times* about the episode.

Unfortunately, after that the show settled down to domestic comedy, routine husband-and-wife entanglements—Joe sees his ex-wife, Rhoda has to lend a proud Joe money for a failing company while Rhoda's own business is flourishing, Rhoda counsels Brenda . . .

But when the show worked, it was wonderful. There was a running gag on it that grew into a galloping gag. During rehearsals, they couldn't find anyone to be the voice of Rhoda's inebriated doorman, Carlton, so writer/producer Lorenzo Music subbed. But he was so successful at it that he retained the job for the show's entire run. In an early episode, Rhoda's mother tells Rhoda that "there's a drunk in the lobby, so you'd better tell the doorman." "Ma," Rhoda replies, "that *is* the doorman."

During her first season, Rhoda seemed as surprised as we were that her life had turned out so swell. Fortunately she had a reservoir of loser-memories to draw from, and there were still those not-so-fond fat memories: "My first dress size was toddler stout."

Although *Rhoda* seemed like the logical conclusion to Valerie Harper's character on *The Mary Tyler Moore Show*, it wasn't an easy transition at all. Here's the story, itself enough sustenance for a sitcom:

In the spring of 1970—four months before the start of the TV season—the producers were shopping for someone to play Mary Richards' upstairs neighbor on her show. In walked Valerie Harper, whose credentials were not incredible—no TV, small parts in Broadway shows, and some improvisation work. But: "She croaked out one line," said the producer, "and we had what we'd been looking for. We didn't even bother to interview anyone else." When Harper lost all the weight before the third season, there were rumblings that she'd get a series of her own. The diet did it, people insisted.

"Untrue," claimed former CBS programming chief Fred Silverman. "I looked at her very first piece of film in the first show, way back in 1970. And from that moment, we knew we were going to star her in her own series. We liked her as much when she was fat and gorgeous as when she became skinny and gorgeous."

Actually, during *MTM*'s second season, there was talk—small talk—about a Rhoda show. But the producers thought that Moore's show wasn't strong enough yet to risk taking the Emmy-winning Harper away yet. When Harper came back streamlined for the third season, things started happening. The *MTM* producers had not been very happy at CBS (who'd been turning down their pilots for other shows), so they went to ABC with the idea for a Rhoda spin-off. CBS got wind and wooed them back, agreeing to air *Rhoda* without even seeing a pilot.

It was all chaotic. "We didn't even know if we could deliver Valerie," said one of the producers, "who had won three Emmys by then and was getting restless. She was making noises like she wanted to switch to movies. A lot of movie producers were talking to her." Harper says it was Mary Tyler Moore who talked her in to taking *Rhoda*, which she was on the verge of turning down. Said Harper: "I told Mary maybe I should spend another year on her show and go out on my own later. 'Fool!' Mary snapped at me, 'CBS is offering you a show. Take it!'

"When I heard the idea for my own show, I thought, 'Why rock the boat?' I was happy working with Mary. But Mary said if I left to do my own series, she'd feel like a proud mother sending one of her children off to college."

But who was Valerie Harper? All we had heard over the years was that Valerie Harper *was* Rhoda Morgenstern. And, indeed, it would seem that Valerie Harper—being Jewish and a New Yorker—was born to play Rhoda. In fact, Harper was neither Jewish nor a New Yorker. She was a Protestant-Catholic mixture of Spanish-English-Scottish-Welsh-French-Canadian. Harper had said that she based her characterization of Rhoda on her best friend, Penny Almog, a New Yorker who moved to Virginia, and her Italian aunt. And rather than New York, Harper grew up in Oregon, Michigan, and Jersey City. "I was a ballet dancer," she said, "but the world of dancing is a world of emaciation. I was always too round. But I was a ballet girl behind the Radio City Rockettes. There I was with tambourines and flower

The Beginning of the End: Rhoda and Joe fight.

umbrellas, spelling out the names of Presidents." When she gave herself an injection of inflection, she made it seem like she and Rhoda were the same person. "No," Harper said. "I call a lot on my own life. But I guess I'm not as funny as Rhoda—or as free. I'm working on it, but Rhoda is very easy. That's what I like about her—she's the person who says the unsayable. I'm getting better, but I must admit I am a little more uptight than Rhoda. Otherwise, I guess it's me. I too have a weight problem. But then I lost thirty pounds. . . ."

Weight had always been on her mind. "I was pretty round. It never showed in my face, but it did in the caboose. I'm five-six, and I used to be one hundred and fifty pounds. I had a real hang-up with food. I could eat one cake or a dozen brownies at a time. It was crazy. When I lost ten pounds during the first year of *The Mary Tyler Moore Show*, there was a little worry about the fat jokes. So I'd continue to wear sweatshirts—you can look fat even when you're not—and I'd make sure my hair was always a little messed up. Rhoda was just a girl who didn't take care of herself very much. . . ."

Apparently, so was Valerie Harper, who once described herself as "totally neurotic." When she became less neurotic, so did Rhoda—later in the series when Harper became a strong advocate of est—Erhard Seminar Training—even going so far as to thank est guru Werner Erhard when she won an Emmy for *Rhoda*.

Harper's other spiritual ties were to Mary Tyler Moore. When she got her own show, Harper tried to emulate Moore's behavior, such as supplying fresh bowls of fruit for the cast and crew. According to an article in the New York *Times*: "With Valerie, it doesn't quite work. She *starts* the day with a full fruit bowl, but by midafternoon the bowl will contain perhaps a half-eaten apple core turning brown. She simply forgets to order up new apples, peaches, and bananas."

That was Valerie. Back to Rhoda. And *Rhoda*.

Although it seemed inevitable that the network would send Rhoda back to New York—where she belonged—that's not at all the way it happened. In fact, Rhoda almost ended up in Wyoming.

The network had just flopped hard with *Calucci's Department*—with James Coco in a New York unemployment office—and didn't want to risk another New York-based sitcom. Said producer Allan Burns: "Some of the network people were positively violent about moving Rhoda Morgenstern out of Mary Tyler Moore's Minneapolis and back to her native Manhattan and The Bronx. I got the feeling they would have liked her to settle on a ranch in Wyoming somewhere—until we asked them if they wanted *Green Acres* all over again. They argued that Rhoda in Minneapolis was so successful because it was the fish-out-of-water bit, one of those favorite network clichés. We argued that New York was the most fertile background for a returning Rhoda, and that basically it was the human being people were interested in, not where she lived."

Engaged: Brenda agrees to marry Benny.

That wasn't all. There were other questions: should Rhoda marry or remain single? Harper answered that one: "Do you want me to be Corliss Archer with a eunuch for a boyfriend?" Everyone agreed that Rhoda should get married on the air. It was great for ratings for a while; it was disastrous for *Rhoda* after a while.

The producers knew that there would be more and more flak if they stuck around and waited for CBS's phone calls of caution—so they all took vacations from the arguments and started casting the show.

The only transplant from *Mary Tyler Moore* along with Rhoda would be her mother, Ida Morgenstern, who was not a regular on *MTM*, but a favorite drop-in guest—plus, Rhoda referred to her mother so much, it was almost as if she were there, constantly hovering over her daughter. And of course there was no question that Nancy Walker would continue on with her role of smother-mother Ida. And Rhoda's father, Martin, would still be played by Harold Gould, who had made occasional visits to *MTM* as Rhoda's pa.

Besides Ida, Walker had been known to TV audiences as Mildred the housekeeper on NBC's *McMillan and Wife*, but she was most famous for a paper towel commercial and for one line in particular: "Bounty—it's the quicker-picker-upper." But somehow, when she was Mrs. M., you could forget all about Mildred and Rosie and her paper towels.

At 4'11", she was no tall, raving beauty—"She's put together funny," said her husband, who added that "She's not a funny lady. She's not amusing at all"—but became a comedienne when in her first Broadway appearance she came onstage and delivered her one serious line: "Where do the aliens go to register?" The audience howled with laughter. And so she became a comic, appearing in numerous musicals and movies. Surprisingly, Walker—who was best known for playing the quintessential Jewish Mother—wasn't Jewish. "I don't dislike Ida Morgenstern," she once said. "I know who she is. I've met her eight million times. But she has no life away from her children." But Walker liked being on *Rhoda*. "If I belch in one episode of *Rhoda*, fifty million people see it. That's more than all the people I played to in thirty years of theater put together."

Two down. Two to go. They had to find Rhoda a sister. They found Brenda—as she was to be called—the same way they had found Rhoda on *MTM*: Julie Kavner auditioned and got the part. That was that.

Before playing innocent and insecure Brenda—a younger version of the old Rhoda—Kavner had been a theater student at California State University in San Diego, and had done no professional acting before Brenda, a winning, whining Sara Lee addict, whose dates are always blind ones. Said Valerie Harper about Julie Kavner: "Julie is a woman. Brenda is a girl. Julie's much more self-assured than Brenda. She operates on a much less naive level." Said Kavner: "Brenda is an innocent. She isn't liberated. Just because there's an occasional hint of sexual activity on her part doesn't make her liberated. She's still struggling for her independence." The big Bronx accent of Brenda's was a put-on; Kavner's was strictly Southern California.

Since they decided that Rhoda was going to get married, they had to find her a husband. Harper was in New York, right before shooting on the series was about to begin, and they still hadn't cast a husband for her. "I was leaning out of cabs in New York, staring at men I thought might be Rhoda's type," Harper later said. "I was going to march right up and ask, 'Will you marry Rhoda?'—waiting for them to refuse." Meanwhile, back in LA, the producers discovered David Groh, a former Rhodes Scholar, to play the building-wrecker who becomes Rhoda's husband (and eventually ex-husband). Groh, however, wasn't selected until the Sunday before the series' Monday-morning start.

Said Groh: "I headed for the Coast when my friends said I'd clean up on cop shows. It was two and a half months later that I read for *Rhoda*—me and a hundred and forty-nine other Joes. But it was like magic. You walk in and your height is right and your voice quality, your ethnic character. . . . The fact that I looked older than Valerie Harper . . . if I had looked three months younger, forget it! It was like one shot in a million. You walk in and everything is right."

And so they had found Rhoda a family. They still had to find her a job. They finally settled on having her work in a publishing house (she'd been a window-dresser back in Minneapolis and had once threatened Mary that she was moving back to New York to take a job in Bloomingdale's windows, but it was a false alarm). Said the

Reunion: Martin tries to make it up to Ida after running away from home.

Carlton's Mother: Valerie Harper with guest Ruth Gordon

producers: "By show number five, we realized publishing wouldn't work. It was too much like the Mary Tyler Moore character, with an office life and a home life that intermeshed. So while the show was already in production, we broke our tails to rewriting the ending. We had Rhoda fired from her publishing job, and just to make sure we wouldn't be tempted to reverse ourselves, we fired Rhoda's boss too. We then sent our heroine back to window-dressing."

When *Rhoda* first premiered, there was a lot of talk that Harper had become temperamental, that her ego had gone way out of control. Harper later explained it this way: "A few people might have gotten their noses bent out of shape that first season when our director, Bob Moore, decided to close the set and I backed him up. When you're putting a show together, the first three days is not a spectator sport. I didn't want tourists coming through when we were rehearsing. Fortunately the people I work with are stage-trained, and they all felt the same way. There's no way you can maintain your concentration when people are sitting up there in the bleachers, eating their lunches and talking."

On-screen, however, all looked terrific for *Rhoda*. When the show finally debuted on Monday, September 9, 1974, vying with the formidable Monday-night football game, it won first place in the Nielsens—the only time in TV history that a new show accomplished such a feat in its premiere. No wonder, though: we'd grown up with Rhoda and she'd grown up with us. We'd seen her transformation from schlepper to a stunning, competent woman. Rhoda was like the rest of us: insecure, bruised around the edges (and in the middle too). We hoped she'd stay that way even after she got married. No such luck.

Joe Gerard and the situations that came up with him were as much a problem for the writers as for the viewers. In 1976, one of the show's producers made this statement: "We all suddenly realized we were getting bored with our show. Maybe the audience wasn't bored—yet—but we figured that at some time in the future it was inevitable the way we were going. Everything was so nice for Rhoda in her happily married life. She had no vulnerability; she wasn't the underdog anymore. When in doubt, we'd go to Brenda for a script idea. Sometimes we'd sit around for days thinking up a single story with some conflict that could focus on Rhoda. . . ." A different *Rhoda* producer said: "The real problem was that we had saddled ourselves with a lousy actor playing Rhoda's husband."

Soon after the start of the 1976–1977 season, Joe and Rhoda separated. Groh was still on the show, but he didn't live there anymore. Letters flooded the *Rhoda* offices. Groh himself received more than 1,000 letters, and nearly 100 percent of them begged him to reconcile with Rhoda. Viewers began to wonder why the love couple of the seventies was separating anyway. At last, late in November of 1976, Joe finally answered the question: he had married Rhoda because otherwise she wouldn't live with him. Occasionally after that Rhoda and Joe spent an uneventful episode together, but for the most part Rhoda was single.

Also motherless. Nancy Walker had left *Rhoda* to hit the road over to ABC to star in her own series, *The Nancy Walker Show*, all about a talent agent. The show was canceled after only three months. Walker tried again the following February with *Blansky's Beauties*, in which she played den mother to a flock of Las Vegas showgirls. That one lasted three months.

While Ida was gone—ostensibly on a year-long world cruise—Rhoda became involved with some new folks: thirty-nine-year-old divorced airline stewardess Sally Gallagher (played by Anne Meara) and upstairs neighbor Gary Levy (played by Ron Silver).

In the fall of 1977, all kinds of new things happened to Rhoda: her mother returned; Brenda got a new boyfriend, Benny Goodwin (played by Ray Buktenica, who would go on to become *Three's Company's* Joyce DeWitt's live-in boyfriend in Real Life); Rhoda started dating the egocentric lecherous lounge lizard Johnny Venture (Michael Delano), who wooed her in a number of extravagant ways; and Rhoda got a new job at the Doyle Costume Company, working side-by-side with frumpy Jack Doyle (Ken McMillan, who became her Lou Grant), and his assistant Ramón Diaz, Jr. (Rafael Campos). By this time the show was totally convoluted. Ida would pop in and pester Rhoda at work. Brenda suddenly got engaged to Benny—another wedding to improve the ratings? Rhoda had adventures in singles bars and Rhoda's father left his wife. Rhoda got a permanent. The situations were contrived and the humor was becoming silly. Rhoda was now part Mary Richards, part Marlo Thomas, part Gidget, part Maude, part—well, that was the problem. She wasn't Rhoda anymore.

Plus, something else happened those last two seasons, something bizarre that only television can do. *The Mary Tyler Moore Show* had gone into syndication. And so, at, say, 4 P.M. on any given afternoon, you could see Rhoda—shlumpy, dumpy, and full of life—in Minneapolis competing with herself as Rhoda on *Rhoda* at night—the svelte swan with everything going for her. Guess which one people preferred?

When *Rhoda* was canceled—even though the last two years of shows had been less than interesting—it was a sad event for people who had hailed the fact that TV had gone from silly to satisfying. That *Rhoda* couldn't make it seemed to mean that maybe a woman who was not wacky, who did not have a sensible husband, and who did not get herself into prickly predicaments—maybe she couldn't make it on television. The problem was that *Rhoda* had started out as television and ended up being TV. And Rhoda had gone from someone we cared about to someone we had lost interest in.

But cheer up: Rhoda isn't dead. She's alive and swell and rerunning in Minneapolis, the way she should always have been. Because the best way to see *Rhoda* is on *The Mary Tyler Moore Show*.

ALSO RANS

Karen

*R*oom 222's Alice Johnson dropped out and got With-It when Karen Valentine got her own series called—strangely enough—*Karen*. Remember, this was the TV era of *Mary Tyler Moore*'s phenomenal success as a single-woman-making-it-in-the-working-world, and other networks—including ABC, which presented this one—followed suit. Karen Angelo was single, bright, and young. She was involved in a citizen's action group called Open America, headquartered in Washington, D.C. Her job: to uncover crooked politicians and to fight for citizens' rights. Helping her were crusty Dale Busch (played by Denver Pyle on the first episode, thereafter replaced by Charles Lane); the group's cynical office manager, Dena Madison (Dena Dietrich); a young student working for the organization, Adam Cooperman (Will Seltzer); and Karen's roommate Cissy Peterson (Aldine King). Naturally, Karen had neighbors: Jerry and Cheryl Siegel (Oliver Clark and Alix Elias). She also had rating troubles. This midseason replacement ran only thirteen weeks.

Love Nest

*A*fter a pilot the previous season, this syndicated sitcom got under way, but briefly. Florida Friebus (she'd been Dobie's mama on *Dobie Gillis*, and Bob Newhart's everknitting Mrs. Bakerman on his show) played elderly Jenny Ludlow, who lived in a Florida trailer camp. Others in the show: Charles Lane as Ned Cooper, Alice Nunn as Mary Francis, Burt Mustin as Dickie Ewing, Dana Elcar as Mort, and Dee Carroll as Dorothy.

Love Nest: *Florida Friebus and Charles Lane*

Karen: *Karen Valentine*

Paper Moon: *Jodie Foster and Chris Connelly*

Paper Moon

Joe David Brown wrote a novel called *Addie Pray*. Peter Bogdanovich made it into a movie called *Paper Moon*, starring Ryan O'Neal and O'Neal's daughter Tatum. That was 1973. Not wasting any time, the following year ABC quickly bought out all the rights and brought it to the small screen. Big mistake. This time Christopher Connelly and Jodie Foster played Moses (Moze) Pray and his daughter, Addie. The story—once again—was all about an itinerant Bible salesman (who dabbled in con artistry) and his smartass eleven-year-old daughter, both of them traveling across Kansas (where the sitcom was actually shot) during the Depression. They got by through scheming and staying one step ahead of the law. But they had each other. Not for long, though; it was only a *Paper Moon*, and it fell into the cardboard sea in January of 1975.

Paul Sand in Friends and Lovers

Paul Sand first came to public attention when he played on Broadway in Paul Sills' *Story Theater*, in which his greatest creation was an itching dog. Then he guested on

The Carol Burnett Show. And played a dizzy tax auditor who fell for Mary on *The Mary Tyler Moore Show*. The MTM people were so impressed with Sand and his ever-amazing talents that they gave him his own show: this one. He played Robert Dreyfuss, a bassist with the Boston Symphony Orchestra. He was sort of schleppy, unaggressive—almost a male Rhoda—and he always had a tough time with women (also, unfortunately, ratings; this was a funny show). However, he fell in love with nearly every pretty woman he met. And spent time with his brother Charlie (Michael Pataki), who was loud and aggressive. Charlie had a wife, Janice (played by Penny Marshall, who'd go on to achieve fame as *Laverne*), who was always making fun of Robert. Not enough fun, evidently, for CBS dumped the show in January of 1975. Pity.

Paul Sand in Friends and Lovers: *Paul Sand with friend/lover guest Andrea Marcovicci*

Sunshine

John Denver wrote a song called "Sunshine on My Shoulder," which was the theme of this show, and also the dead wife's favorite song (which is how the show became *Sunshine*) and—well, basically, this was one of TV's first (and perhaps last) sobcoms. It was all about a brave young widower, living in Vancouver, who was trying to raise his daughter and make ends meet. His name was Sam Hayden (played by singer Cliff DeYoung), and his wife had died of cancer, leaving him with Jill (Elizabeth Cheshire), her five-year-old daughter by a previous marriage (are you following this?). Anyway, Sam was a composer and along with his two buddies, Weaver (Bill Mumy) and Givits (Corey Fischer), he was a member of a singing trio. Sam and Jill had a very easygoing "lifestyle" (as it was called back then), and neighbors and friends were worried about the kid's welfare. Jill was always trying to find someone to marry her father so she'd have a mother and her daddy would be happy again. Helping Sam out was a friend and neighbor named Nora (Meg Foster). But what Sam did not realize was that his sitcom too had a terminal disease; NBC sent this late-season entry straight to the emergency room. The *Sunshine* series of books, however, did quite well. Based on a TV Movie-of-the-Week.

The Texas Wheelers

This sitcom is notable mostly in that it featured Mark Hamill—later of *Star Wars* fame—and Gary Busey—later of *The Buddy Holly Story*—as two of the four Wheeler children, led by a crotchety (but with-a-heart-of-gold, natch) father, Zack (Jack Elam). They lived in rural Texas, and didn't have a lot of money. Or a lot of viewers, either. ABC canceled the show at the end of the season.

That's My Mama

What could be more heartwarming than the story of a boy and his mother? Well, maybe the story of a boy and his dog. Anyway, in this one, the Mama was Eloise Curtis (Theresa Merritt) and the Boy was Clifton Curtis (Clifton Davis), a hip young black barber in a middle-class Washington, D.C., neighborhood. He'd inherited the

That's My Mama: *Theresa Merritt beats the hell out of Clifton Davis.*

family barbershop, "Oscar's," when his dad died. He also seemed to inherit his mother, who wanted to see him married to a Nice Black Girl, instead of all the running around he was doing. His sister Tracy (played by Lynn Moody, later by Joan Pringle) had a conservative husband Leonard (Lisle Wilson), and Cliff had a mailman buddy, Earl (played by Ed Bernard on the first two telecasts, later by Theodore Wilson, who was playing another role on the show back then). Other buddies stopped over for jokes and talk and checkers and advice. In the fall of 1975, for its second season, there were a few cast changes, and then they sent *Mama* to the home in December.

We'll Get By

Alan Alda—Hawkeye on *M*A*S*H*—worked hard creating this show, based somewhat on his own family life. It was all about the Platt family, a middle-class group living in the suburbs of New Jersey (which was where Alda lived). George (Paul Sorvino) worked as a lawyer in New York. He and Liz (Mitzi Hoag) had three kids: Muff (Jerry Houser), Kenny (Willie Aames), and Andrea (Devon Scott). There were conflicts, but there was also support and understanding. Not on CBS's part, however; they canceled the show after two months. When he got word of *WGB*'s cancellation, Alda—who said he'd been working all the time and sleeping only four hours a night—was "somewhat relieved."

We'll Get By: *Paul Sorvino and Mitzi Hoag surrounded by their children (clockwise), Jerry Houser, Willie Aames, Devon Scott*

1975–1976

Laverne and Shirley

One Day at a Time

Welcome Back, Kotter

OFF-SCREEN

9/5 Lynette ("Squeaky") Fromme, twenty-six, follower of Charles Manson, unsuccessfully attemps to assassinate President Ford in Sacramento, California. On September 22, activist Sara Jane Moore, forty-five, makes another attempt on the president's life with a .38 as he leaves San Francisco hotel, but ex-Marine Oliver Sipple pounces on Moore.

9/18 Patricia Hearst is taken into custody by FBI in San Francisco along with SLA members William and Emily Harris.

12/29 Deadly bomb kills eleven and injures seventy at LaGuardia Airport in New York.

1/19 Former Governor Jimmy Carter of Georgia emerges as leading contender for Democratic Presidential nomination after winning 27.6 percent of vote in Iowa's precinct caucuses.

3/19 After sixteen years of marriage, Princess Margaret of Britain and Lord Snowdon announce separation.

3/31 New Jersey State Supreme Court rules unanimously that Karen Ann Quinlan's father can request she be removed from respirator that has kept her alive for almost a year.

4/28 Senate Select Committee on Intelligence says FBI and other national intelligence agencies have violated constitutional rights of hundreds of thousands of US citizens by investigating their political activities.

5/24 Supersonic Concorde jets begin regular flights to Dulles International Airport near Washington, D.C., from London and Paris; trip takes less than four hours.

6/3 Representative Wayne L. Hays of Ohio draws condemnation of his congressional colleagues after charges made that his mistress, Elizabeth Ray, is on payroll of a House committee.

6/5 New dam on Teton River in Idaho bursts, flooding area, killing eight and leaving 30,000 homeless.

FRONT RUNNERS

LAVERNE AND SHIRLEY

If in heaven we don't meet
Hand in hand we'll bear the heat
And if it ever gets too hot
Pepsi-Cola hits
the spot
—What Shirley wrote in Laverne's high school yearbook.

The time: any afternoon.

The place: your television set.

The station: any that can afford to rerun a program like this (about $50,000 per episode).

The show: *Laverne and Shirley,* the story of two single girls who work at a Milwaukee brewery in the early fifties.

The premise (according to *TV Guide):* Laverne has a crush on a mortician.

Here goes: Shirley walks in to find her landlady, Mrs. Babish, and her dance instructor-boyfriend, Carmine, dancing together in her apartment. Carmine exits. Mrs. B. asks where Laverne is.

SHIRLEY: I always get home early when Laverne doesn't drive.
MRS. BABISH: Why?
SHIRLEY: We circle Pfister Park three times and watch the athletes sweat.

Meanwhile, Laverne—who is boy-crazy—has followed a man named Stanley home on a bus. Only he's not going home, he's going to work—which turns out to be a mortuary. She follows him in and coyly drops her bracelet. He picks it up and notices that it's a charm bracelet with little metal cows on it.

LAVERNE: Yeah, it's a souvenir from the Chicago stockyards.

STANLEY: I didn't know they had a gift shop.
LAVERNE: It's right behind where they slaughter the cows—you really gotta look for it. . . .

She says she's interested in looking at some urns and caskets. He shows her some and then has to leave to take care of another customer. She drops her bracelet in an urn, then blows in it as the ashes fly in her face. "Excuse me, sir," she says, talking to the ashes inside the urn. Then she puts her hand in and it sticks. She tries to pry the urn off, but no luck. She puts it between her legs, but still can't get it off. "I got a dead person on my arm—I think I even got it on my hair. . . ."

Stanley returns and sees her in peril. "Oh, Laverne—that model's been discontinued. We use it as an ashtray." "Oh," Laverne says, "so that's why I felt gum in it."

Finally, Stanley asks her why she's there. Laverne's too embarrassed to tell him that she wants to go out with him, so she stammers and says that her friend is dying: Shirley. He sends her into the waiting room to read some burial literature. Lenny and Squiggy—the girls' screwball neighbors—enter, delivering a keg of beer to the mortuary. They see Laverne in the waiting room, and ask the mortician why she's there. "Because," Stanley responds, "her friend Shirley is dying." They are in shock.

Back home, Shirley is reading aloud to her stuffed animal when Laverne enters. Laverne tells Shirley that

Laverne De Fazio	Penny Marshall
Shirley Feeney	Cindy Williams
Carmine Ragusa	Eddie Mekka
Frank De Fazio	Phil Foster
Andrew "Squiggy" Squiggman	David L. Lander
Lenny Kolowski	Michael McKean
Mrs. Edna Babish	Betty Garrett
Rosie Greenbaum	Carole Ita White (1976–1977)

she's fallen for a wonderful man—a mortician. Shirley is appalled.

Laverne stammers. "I told him all about you, Shirl. He wants to meet you. There's just one little thing—you're gonna die laughing when I tell you this." And she tells Shirley that she told the mortician that her friend Shirley is dying. Shirley is not amused. And will not take part in it.

SHIRLEY: No, no, no. Never, never, never, never, never.
LAVERNE: Do you remember Alan Sheckler?
SHIRLEY: Please don't do this.
LAVERNE: Alan Sheckler—a guy who chewed his socks. Do you know what it's like makin' out with a guy who chews his socks? It's like kissin' a hamper. You made me go out with him.
SHIRLEY (offering a glass to Laverne): Kool-Aid?
LAVERNE: And why? Because you wanted to go out with his pal, Von Blish the pharmacist.
SHIRLEY: Yes, but you didn't have to pretend you were dying.
LAVERNE: No—I only wished I were dying. And do you know why I went out with Alan Sheckler?
SHIRLEY: Because I made ugly threats.
LAVERNE: No—because I was your friend and (sings) "If you're ever in a jam, here I am . . ."

Laverne leaves and Lenny and Squiggy come to pay Shirley a condolence call in advance. "Not now, guys," she tells them, "I haven't got the time." They break down crying and give her a gift. "Oh," Shirley coos, "A lifetime subscription to *Confidential* Magazine—but it's only for six weeks!"

Finally, Shirley agrees to go see the caskets. It turns out that Laverne has bought her—"on layaway"—an ugly, beatup casket. Says Shirley: "Why didn't you just get me a great big carton from Pence's Grocery Store?"

Stanley the mortician feels sorry for Shirley, and holds her in his arms. Laverne is jealous and says: "Oh, Shirl, I meant to tell you—the doctor called and said you're not dying. They found a vaccine. Yippee."

"Wooo," Shirley exclaims, "is *that* a load off my mind!"

But Stanley knows they've been pulling his leg. "This is no place for practical jokes. Death is not funny."

And so they confess. First Shirley: "Laverne didn't mean to do anything low and disgusting—it only turned out that way, that's all."

Then the warm and soothing music rises.

LAVERNE: I just wanted to go out with you.
STANLEY: Then why didn't you just ask me out?
LAVERNE: Because if I did, you woulda thought I was cheap.
STANLEY: That's not true.

LAVERNE: No?
STANLEY: Well . . . maybe. Let's start all over. Can I call you next week?

Laverne says yes and the girls exit, debating whether it's better to be considered cheap or disgusting.

And the episode's over.

But there were others. Once the girls were both wooed by the same spoiled playboy (they straightened *him* out, all right). Another time, they discovered a German spy who was trying to steal the secret formula for the Shotz Beer diet beer that they were testing. One episode showed Shirley planning a high school reunion (this was the fourth she'd planned in the three years since they'd graduated).

Once, Laverne's father arranged a marriage for her (the generation clash caused some laughs, but no nuptials). You can imagine what happened when FBI agents used the girls' apartment to stake out counterfeiters. Or when, after a small fire in their bedroom, both Laverne and Shirley fell in love with the handsome young fireman. And the time when Shirley became friends with a rich older man—Carmine was jealous, and the man's daughter thought Shirley was just a golddigger. Or when Lenny invited Laverne to a debutante ball . . . or when the girls tried to become high-fashion models . . . or the time when Laverne and Shirley were imprisoned in a run-down mansion. Or . . .

Enough already?

That's what a lot of the critics said. "Perhaps their shouting is due to playing before a live audience—the idea may be to drown out their groans, or possibly to wake them up." And that was *TV Guide*. Some of the others were much less kind. Other critics—including some of the country's most respected—proclaimed *Laverne and Shirley* to be a breath of fresh air—"as good as the *Laurel and Hardy* shorts."

But it didn't matter. A spin-off from *Happy Days* (Laverne De Fazio and Shirley Feeney had been brief visitors to that show, and still in fact lived in Milwaukee—and the fifties—which were both inhabited by the *Happy Days* clan), *Laverne and Shirley* was an instant success. Executive producer Garry Marshall espoused his philosophy this way when he explained how to get to the young TV viewers: "You have to do something silly to get their attention. Then I like to knock them off their chairs with laughter. I go for the gut. I want them to laugh *hard*. I don't want them quietly staring at a bright, witty show."

Laverne and Shirley was hardly bright and witty. It was a farce with a formula. Its message was: There is no message here. Relax. Have a good time. Watch us. It was entertainment for entertainment's sake. *Laverne and Shirley* had absolutely nothing to say except what it had to say.

Frequently the humor wasn't oral at all, but physical. In one extraordinarily funny episode, Shirley—who hasn't eaten for days because she's been part of a laboratory experiment—goes to a posh cocktail party and spots a shrimp a guest has dropped on the floor. She stares at it for a few moments, takes a few dainty steps toward it, and then pounces, lands on the floor on all fours and picks up the shrimp doggie-style. Then, suddenly poised again, she turns to Laverne and says, "I feel worlds better." Laverne has spent the weekend at the same lab, but she wasn't allowed to sleep. At the party, she sits in a chair, falls asleep, falls forward, and lands on the floor after a broad somersault. (Penny Marshall and Cindy Williams, who played Laverne and Shirley, were never injured in their many stunts, except once when Marshall hurt her neck on a trampoline.)

Laverne and Shirley—bosom buddies for life (they even got kicked out of the Brownies together)—were really quite different from each other. Shirley Feeney was naive, trusting, a sucker for a sad story. She was Mary Richards crossed with Lucy Ricardo. She was virginal and prudish (although much attention was focused on the fact that she wore falsies), but she could sling a loopy line along with the rest, such as when she said about her relationship with her boyfriend: "Carmine and I have an understanding—I'm allowed to date other men and he's allowed to date ugly women." She was constantly concerned about keeping her virginity for as long as possible.

SHIRLEY: Laverne, I promised myself I would stay intact till my wedding night, if you read me.
LAVERNE: Shirl—guys don't care if you lose your appendix.

But while Shirley was sentimental, Laverne was "mental" (a term of semiendearment popular in the

"Bye, Mom": Laverne visits her mother's grave.

fifties). With a strangely thick Bronx accent (which seemed to come more with the actress than the character), Laverne was the loudmouth, the coarse member of the duo. They lived at 730 Knapp Ave., and Laverne pronounced the *K*. And, speaking of letters, she always wore a curly *L* on every piece of her clothing. It was her trademark. So were off-the-wall comments. "A cemetery's a creepy place," she once said. "Everybody there is dead." Her mother had died when she was young and "I had to learn all that women's stuff by myself—like how far up to shave your legs." She picked everything else up on the street (and the implication was that she spent a lot of time out on the streets, although she probably did little more than heavy-duty petting . . . and yet . . .).

Of course it was the actresses who played the parts who made the characters. Cindy Williams (Shirley) was best known as Ron Howard's girlfriend in the movie *American Graffiti*. This is what she had to say about *Laverne and Shirley*: "I'm high-strung, just like any other actress. I'd be a liar if I said that I was calm, cool, and collected all the time. I've never been under so much strain, doing a weekly series. It's the most brutal work I've done since working the midnight shift at the House of Pancakes." She wasn't wild about doing a sitcom, worried that it would halt her budding movie career. "I thought I would have regrets after agreeing to do the show, but I haven't found a single one. The series has opened a lot of doors, and I'd be a fool if I didn't admit it was the best move I ever made."

However. The show almost became *Laverne and Laverne*. Williams felt that Laverne was getting all the good lines and the good laughs. The producers said they would try to work it out. That was back in 1976. It didn't work out. In October, Williams walked off the set in tears and returned two days later when promised that changes would be made in her character—by firing the two head writers, who were replaced by a *Mary Tyler Moore Show*

writer who said: ". . . the place was in chaos. I couldn't work that way. I needed an organization and a staff." Two days later the writer quit. Changes were made and Shirley lived on.

Penny Marshall was no newcomer to sitcoms. She had been a regular on *The Odd Couple* and *Paul Sand in Friends and Lovers*, and an irregular regular on *The Bob Newhart Show* and Mary Richards' neighbor in her second apartment on *The Mary Tyler Moore Show*. She had also been up for the part of Gloria on *All in the Family*, but lost out to Sally Struthers. Her husband at the time, Rob Reiner, got the part of Mike. "It's better that I didn't get the role or we'd be killing each other," she later said. "It's hard to work at the studio all day with someone and then go home with him."

Marshall seemed to be a bundle of insecurities. "I'm insecure, mostly because of my looks. I keep thinking that they'll comb my hair, put on makeup and lipstick, and I'll turn out to be Liz Taylor. I just cannot bring myself to accept that the homely person on the screen is me. After I saw myself on *Love, American Style*, I cried for three days. I've had braces put on my teeth twice, but they did no good. Rob (Reiner) tells me that I don't look bad, but I've got a pretty good idea what I look like standing next to Cindy, who's cute, little, has dimples and a high voice. I was in analysis for about four years. It

helped, but not enough. I'm still constantly seeking approval. I hate bad reviews. I hated *Time* for saying that I was doing a lousy impersonation of Judy Holliday. I didn't care what they said about the show, but why did they have to single me out that way? I'm constantly asking Rob if he likes me, if I'm nice, if I'm happy. At parties, I ask him if I'm having a good time. No, I am definitely not the most secure person in the world."

Her insecurities didn't end there. It didn't help her ego that her brother and father were the producers of *Odd Couple* and *Laverne and Shirley*. "I always thought I wasn't any good when I appeared on *The Odd Couple*. I always felt my brother and father were carrying me. And then of course Jack Klugman and Tony Randall kidded me unmercifully. They never let me forget that my family was all over the place. Finally I told my brother: 'Garry, I think I'm getting work on this show just because you're trying to be nice to me.' He laughed and said, 'Penny, nobody is that nice. I gave you one break. That was nice. But the fact that I've had you back several times means that you're good.'"

Of course, Laverne and Shirley weren't all there was to *Laverne and Shirley*. Naturally there was the nutty set of neighbors—except in this case there were a couple of sets. Laverne's father (a harassed, confused, but likable

Dream Sequence: Eighty-year-old Laverne and Shirley get ready to marry—not each other—Lenny and Squiggy.

Laverne and Shirley and friends: Laverne and Shirley (center) flanked by (from bottom right, clockwise) Squiggy, Lenny, Rosie Greenbaum, Frank, Carmine, Mrs. Babish

man who owned the Pizza Bowl) lived in the building, as did his woman friend, the sardonic Edna Babish, who was also the landlady.

Lenny Kolowski and Andrew "Squiggy" Squiggman were the two crazy neighbors, who were stupid and literal minded. When Shirley asked Laverne: "Are you upset or is that nature calling?" the phone rang and Squiggy said, "That's nature calling."

Once, Laverne was talking about "rancid yeast and rotten hops" and—right on cue—in walked Lenny and Squiggy (an old ploy from *Dobie Gillis* that would get Maynard G. Krebs on-screen whenever Mr. Gillis said anything was "lowdown, disgusting, rotten" and Maynard would reply, "You rang?"). "When God was handin' out brains," Shirley once said to "the boys," as she called them, "he mistook you for a cactus."

Here's what Lenny and Squiggy had to say about each other:

Squiggy on Lenny: "When you've known a person as long as I've known Leonard Kolowski, you can easily describe him as being a guy whose weight is one hundred fifty-five pounds, about six feet tall, and also has kind of sandy beige hair. When we first met we was having a fistfight in the schoolyard. I guess it was fate or something, but we've stayed together for the rest of our lives (so far). If I had to put Lenny on kind of a macho scale from one to a hundred, I'd probably give him an eighty-three; I'd probably be a ninety-four, but that's what makes us different. His favorite drink is beer. And he's great at making funny noises with his skin. He's got many interests but spends most of his time at his hobby."

Lenny on Squiggy: "Squiggy was born in either Newark, New Jersey, or Flushing, New York. His ma is

okay, but strict, which is why Squig has earaches. Him and his old lady moved to Milwaukee to be with some Germans, and that's where he met me. We got to be best friends before you know it. We grew up a lot together and got a job driving a truck together. He's a short guy with strawberry-black hair and pink skin. He's cute-looking to girls, or at least he can usually scrape up something on a Saturday night. He always wanted to go to Canada and he once pushed my sister in a hole."

Michael McKean (Lenny) and David Lander (Squiggy) created their greaser characters in 1966 while they were in college. They were first hired as writers/consultants for *Laverne and Shirley* and quickly wrote themselves into the premiere as Lenny and Squiggy. Said Cindy Williams: "They are the only two people in the world who can make Laverne and Shirley look classy."

No one expected *Laverne and Shirley* to be a hit. It wasn't a hit—it was a tornado, speeding up and up in the ratings until it was a firm Number One. But it really wasn't surprising. *Laverne and Shirley* were really just retreads of Lucy and Ethel, back there in the fifties, but this time with their collars blue and, instead of playing around in vats of grapes in Italy (as Lucy did in a classic episode), Laverne and Shirley played around in vats of beer in Milwaukee (they actually did this on one classic episode). Some say the difference between the two shows is the difference between beer and wine, between Italy and Milwaukee.

Said Garry Marshall: "No one else on TV is doing early *Lucy*. The other ladies on sitcoms are classy—they're well-off, smart, and they dress well. Laverne and Shirley are definitely not classy. They're blue-collar workers who went to work right after high school. They're decent people."

They were crazy people. The sitcom characters of the seventies were, for the most part, like the seventies: they took themselves seriously and became involved in problems big and small—from abortions to child rearing, from the death of a friend to making a new friend. Not Laverne and Shirley. They had *adventures*. Like the time when Lenny (or was it Squiggy?) had written their names and phone numbers on the men's room wall, so the girls dressed up as guys and sneaked in to erase them. You'd never have caught Mary Richards doing that. Or Edith Bunker.

Laverne and Shirley did that and much more. The proof of their success is not their popularity in this country—we know all about that—but how well they, like Lucy, translated to other countries. How their broad humor worked abroad.

Although there was almost a problem in Thailand. Seems that the Thai people don't like "fresh" women. And so, before each episode was aired on Thai TV, this blurb flashed across the screen:

THESE WOMEN ARE FROM AN INSANE ASYLUM.

ONE DAY AT A TIME

MAN: *Mrs. Romano . . .*
ANN: *Ms.*

Women hit television in the seventies. Before that, there were only girls—from Lucy and Ethel, who always referred to themselves as "the girls," to *That Girl,* who would have referred to herself as Bat Woman before she'd have called herself That Woman.

Mary Richards, Edith Bunker, Maude—those were television's first Women. And then—because they were so successful and popular, and because times had indeed changed—there came an onslaught of Women's· Programs—not shows *for* women, but shows *about* women—women on their own (mostly interpreted, however, by men). *One Day at a Time* was TV's first success story in which the leading lady was a leading woman, but with a twist: she was divorced, living in Indianapolis; she was raising two daughters—she even retained her own name after her divorce—and, most important, she wasn't a flighty bimbo. Ann Romano was more than one of TV's first women; she was one of televisions first persons.

And—surprise-surprise—Norman Lear brought her to us. By this time he'd already shot us with massive doses of Archie and Edith, *Maude, The Jeffersons, Good Times, Sanford and Son,* and was on his way to *Mary Hartman, Mary Hartman,* so we were all prepared for *One Day at a Time.* He'd already brought us abortion, menopause, sodomy, death, manic depression, mental retardation—so a divorced mother who kept her own name was not much of a shock.

In fact, *One Day at a Time* was no shock at all. It was not another Norman Lear "breakthrough comedy," except that it was fairly forthright in its treatment of its subject matter. In fact, the most surprising thing about the show was how successful it came to be.

Lear himself had said that with *One Day at a Time,* he was trying to do for the divorced woman what *All in the Family* had done for the bigot—make her comically respectable (although the question still exists—should bigots be treated with respect, comical or not?—but that's speculation for another book).

One Day at Time wasn't just another generation gap/generation yap show like *All in the Family.* If there was any valley between the generations, it was that mother Ann was often more independent than her kids. Ann was having affairs and having careers.

Ann Romano was also TV's first feminist—not a liberated loudmouth like Maude, but a reasonable feminist. She didn't burn her bra and stop shaving her armpits, but Ann lived out the principles of feminism. In a sense, she was Donna Reed—updated: liberated, without Alex, confused and together, wary and insecure, plugging away at independence.

Said the show's creator: "Our divorcée isn't a chicly turned out woman of the world. She is vulnerable and scared." That's right. Ann was struggling. After marriage at seventeen, and then the next seventeen years as a wife, she was finally on her own, trying to make her own decisions and her own living.

Some of the problems Ann and her daughters, Julie and Barbara, faced bore out the premise: Julie wanted to drop out of school; Ann's ex-husband was having financial problems and could no longer afford child support, so, after a bitter feud, Ann got a job at a public relations firm; Julie went out protesting increased Arab oil prices; Barbara wanted to be "popular," so she wouldn't date a nice boy who was interested in her; Julie got involved with a forty-two-year-old man; Ann's boss "doesn't appreciate her," so she took another job; Schneider, their building's super, had designs on Ann; Ann broke up with her fiancé . . .

. . . and on and on like that. All with the typical mature Norman Lear subject matter. But somehow different. Somehow on *One Day at a Time,* the studio audience's laughter isn't quite so deafening. In fact, *One Day*'s audiences added a new sound to the small screen—the "awwww" sighed when, for example, Ann would receive a long kiss from one of her beaus.

But like the other Lear shows, *One Day at a Time*

Ann Romano	Bonnie Franklin
Julie Cooper	Mackenzie Phillips (1975–1980)
Barbara Cooper	Valerie Bertinelli
Dwayne Schneider	Pat Harrington
David Kane	Richard Masur (1975–1976)
Ginny Wrobliki	Mary Louise Wilson (1976–1977)
Mr. Davenport	Charles Siebert (1976–)
Max (Julie's husband)	Michael Lembeck (1979–1980)

was still a member in good standing of the Crisis-of-the-Week Club. It was always Big Dilemmas that were being tackled (should Ann let Barbara date Julie's boyfriend behind her back?), but they were solved and resolved much more calmly and quietly than on *All in the Family* or *The Jeffersons;* more discussions than outbursts of emotion.

Unlike most other Lear ventures, there was little controversy surrounding the show. Not that it was bland. Just that it was sensible.

A classic example was a three-part show (*One Day* often took two or three nights to tell its story) in which Ann—long committed to noncommitment—fell in love with Neal—who turned out to be married. Ann was shocked but decided to go on seeing him. "It may not be proper," she told her daughters, "but you can't tell me what's right. I don't expect you to understand . . . I only hope that you will."

The girls tried to understand.

JULIE: But you were all enthused with mother's new man.
BARBARA: That's when I thought she was getting a *new* man—how did I know she was getting a used one?

When Ann and her used man go out to a restaurant, they run into an old friend of her beau's who's hard of hearing and thinks Ann's the guy's wife. The next day Ann tells her lover: "Last night I felt like I had the starring role in a dirty joke."

But she insists he's "a terrific guy."

"Some terrific guy!" Schneider the super says. "He cheats on his wife and lies to his mistress."

Ann is ready to break the relationship off, when Neal comes in and tells her that he's left his wife. A neat ending, right?

Wrong. Seems that the guy now feels obligated to Ann and just doesn't want to make a commitment to her. Says Ann: "We happened too fast." And, with tears in both of their eyes, he leaves. And that's that.

Interesting because it ends the right—"proper"—way, but for unexpected reasons. Not because Ann took a moral stand, but because of circumstances. We can never be sure how our heroine would have ended up, except that probably television viewers would have become bored with her dating a married man week after week (or even a single man; in 1975, they gave Ann a boyfriend, David Kane, who was younger than her and wanted to marry her. The courtship got boring, so they quickly wrote him out of the show).

Over the seasons, other regulars—or near regulars—came and went. Mary Louise Wilson, during the 1976 season, played "the wacky neighbor" (they just couldn't do without one), who was outspoken and brassy. (They quickly decided that they could do without one.) Ann's mother (Nanette Fabray—who'd also been Mary Richards' mom) stopped in occasionally.

But basically the cast revolved around Ann, Julie, Barbara, and Schneider, played by Pat Harrington. He'd been around. He had played Pat Hannigan on *The Danny Thomas Show* and during 1959 had courted Thomas' TV daughter Terry until they were married and written out. He was also Monte Markham's "best friend and confidant," Tony Lawrence, on 1969's *Mr. Deeds Goes to Town*. He's possibly best known, though, as Italian golf pro Guido Panzini on both the Steve Allen and Jack Paar shows in the late fifties. Harrington was, for three months, the host of the 1962 quiz show *Stump the Stars*, and Jackie Gleason's *You're in the Picture*, which ran only one episode (the next episode consisted of Gleason apologizing for the last episode).

So Harrington was experienced. "Schneider was a big break for me," he said. "Everyone should have a chance like that." He said he was much more like Ozzie Nelson than Schneider, who was a self-proclaimed macho-pig, who went around in a too-tight vest, a white T-shirt (with cigarettes rolled up under the right sleeve)— "The ladies in this building don't call me *super* for nothing." As the girls' self-appointed Dutch uncle, Schneider sputtered forth his philosophies. "Please always remember and don't ever forget—It is better not to have been in love than to never have loved at all," Schneider once mused.

Schneider seems to have been Lear's throwback to Archie Bunker, but over the seasons he became more seasoned and softened. He started off as a romance-obsessed character (he'd been married once, for a week)

Runaway: Schneider tries to locate Julie on his C.B. radio.

who had the hots for Ann. Then he became the friend of the family, Uncle Schneider.

Ann's daughters grew and developed as the show went on. Mainly, they became less obnoxious and more supportive. Still, they sniped at each other.

JULIE: Try some of my pancakes.
BARBARA: Oh, they're pancakes? I thought they were Frisbees with syrup on them.

And sometimes they'd give Ann the business, as when Barbara said to her thirty-six-year-old mother: "Mom, now you're going steady—or whatever you in the geriatric crowd call it."

A far shot from *Leave It to Beaver*, which had kids speaking in comic-strip versions of little-life—"Aw shucks, Mom, do I *have* to?" Ann Romano dispensed with the milk and cookies of former sitcom mommies, and instead dispensed good advice to and respect for her separate-but-equal daughters. In turn, the kids on *One Day* spoke more like real kids do talk—well, as much as sitcoms allow their adults to speak like real people do. Examples:

ANN: What were you watching?
BARBARA: A special on the human body.
ANN: Oh, who was on it?
BARBARA: A doctor, a physiologist, and Suzanne Somers. She got up to do a demonstration and the TV went dead.
JULIE: The TV went dead? How will I fall asleep tonight?

And:

JULIE: I took care of dinner—I picked up three submarine sandwiches on my way home from work.
ANN: You're trying to kill me for the insurance, aren't you?

Divorced: Ann and her ex-husband Ed Cooper (played by guest Joe Campanella)

Off-screen, Barbara and Julie—well, really Valerie Bertinelli and Mackenzie Phillips—had their share of troubles with growing up. Bertinelli's problems were just those of the typical teenager who went from a fat, flat brat to sex symbol (all teenagers should have such troubles). Phillips had—and caused—quite a bit more aggravation: her alleged on-going problems with drugs (she had been found unconscious on a Hollywood street and was arrested for disorderly conduct while under the influence of drugs and alcohol in 1978), difficulties on the set (she was often overtired and overwrought), and her unhappiness on the show all caused the twenty-year-old to be fired during the 1979-1980 season. Said one of the production company's executives: "I consider this firing a step toward saving a child's life." Julie's absence on the show was explained away easily—she'd just gotten married, and she and her husband had moved to Texas. And that was the *finis* of Phillips.

Insiders on and off the set said it was Bonnie Franklin who held the show together. Once, she refused to do a scene, saying that she, Bonnie Franklin, would never do that. Someone had to remind her that she was playing Ann Romano, not Bonnie Franklin. Even so, Franklin's politics—a gentle, at-ease sense of feminism—permeated the script and the show.

The Answer Is No: David proposes to Ann.

Mothers: Ann, Barbara and Grandma Romano (played by guest Nanette Fabray)

Franklin was a show-business baby. At nine years old, she was a chubby little dancer on the Donald O'Connor show. While in high school and college, she made several TV appearances as an actress and dancer. She was definitely considered to be an eager over-achiever, of the Dale Carnegie variety.

As Ann, Franklin showed great spirit, more than anything else. She didn't have Mary Tyler Moore's vulnerability, but she did have a strong will and determination not seen elsewhere on television until that time. And—rather than being a joke, as so many sitcom heroines and heros are—she could make the jokes. (If anyone was the joke on the show, it was Schneider, but he was a beloved joke, like an amusing family anecdote.) Franklin/Romano's humor often saved the day (or at least the episode). She learned to match her daughters' barbs, and occasionally beat them at it. She eventually even came up with some rejoinders to the running jokes about dyeing her hair red.

In the sitcoms of the fifties, the mother raised the kids and the father raised the mother. Ann Romano brought up both her kids and herself. It was mother-knows-best without being *Mother Knows Best* . . . or *Father Knows Best*, for that matter. When Julie ran away from home, we were reminded of when, twenty years earlier, Bud Anderson had done the same. Sister Betty simply pretended that she needed Bud to fix a radio or something to let him know that he really was an important part of the household (at least as important as the radio, anyway). Julie ran away because she didn't like the rules of her mother's house. When Ann finally found her, she said that she would really like her daughter to come home—but only if she followed the rules of the house. Otherwise she should stay away. Julie came back. It wasn't that Ann knew best—or even better. She simply knew what she wanted for herself.

The key to the program, though, shows up in one bit of dialogue—a little schmaltzy, to be sure, but sitcom-sophisticated. Ann had just broken up with her married lover and was explaining to him why she had to do it.

"There is something that matters more than you do," she tells him. "My self-respect."

Because if *One Day at a Time* had anything, it had self-respect.

Coronary Care: Barbara and Julie visit their mother after Ann's suffered a heart attack.

WELCOME BACK, KOTTER

Did I ever tell you about my Uncle Bernie, who never took a bath?
    —GABE KOTTER talking to wife Julie at the end of an episode

One day, stand-up comic Gabriel Kaplan sat down and came up with a great idea: a comedy routine all about his Brooklyn high school days, when he was a "slow" student in Miss Shepard's remedial class, and all about the tough but funny classmates of his. When he stood up to deliver his monologue—on *The Tonight Show* and on a best-selling comedy album—it became Kaplan's own personal comedy anthem that kept people pledging their laughter for years.

It was all true, too. Kaplan—a smart and savvy guy—really had been a badnik back in his Brooklyn days. Then, on September 9, 1975—a Tuesday night, immediately following *Happy Days*—his comedy routine turned into a sitcom, *Welcome Back, Kotter,* and he returned to the high school of his youth—this time as the teacher. This is how Kaplan described it: "The show is based on my act. They're all the same kids. Epstein the animal is there. Horshack . . . all of them. Except this time they're not my classmates—they're my students. All the characters are based on real students, the kids I grew up with. And a lot of the shows are based on real experience. If Kaplan became a teacher instead of a comedian, he'd be Kotter. . . ."

And so, for four years—seasons—semesters—he was.

As Kotter, Kaplan was as hip as his students—well, almost as hip. There wasn't so much a generation gap as a degeneration gap. And what a troop of remedials he had:
• Juan Luis Pedro Phillipo de Huevos Epstein: a Puerto Rican Jew (or, more appropriately, a Jewish Puerto Rican), who was voted "Most Likely to Take a Life" in school, and said things like: "Tie yourself up with some chick and pretty soon she's gonna be having you eat with a knife and fork." Juan had dozens of brothers and sisters. Said Epstein: "Half of my brothers were out stealin' pants—the other half were altering them." The worst of both the Jewish and Puerto Rican stereotypes, Juan would steal hubcaps—and then try to sell them. He spoke Yiddish with a Puerto Rican accent.
• Freddie "Boom Boom" Washington was the hip black of the crew, who at one point was hooked on uppers and downers. Very often he'd start to get very tough—and then he'd back down. He was not too bright, but very *cooool*.
• Arnold Horshack was the class yo-yo, the class nerd. He was the stupidest of the bunch, and looked and talked as though he came from another planet. He wheezed out a laugh that sounded like he was gasping for air—pre-Heimlich Method. If television had allowed it, he would have picked his nose.
• Vinnie Barbarino was the undisputed swaggering leader of the pack—"This is *my* place and these are *my* people," he announced. Dumb-Italian-Macho was the stereotype he fitted into, and he began most sentences with a "heeey." Underneath, of course, he was sweet and vulnerable. Whenever he walked onto the set, young girls in the television audience would squeal. "A woman's place is in the car," said Barbarino, except, of course, for his mother: "That woman is completely holy."

They called themselves the Sweathogs, a gang of benign hoodlums who were street-wise but not living-room-wise. They were unable—or unwilling—to make it

Gabe Kotter	Gabriel Kaplan
Julie Kotter	Marcia Strassman
Vinnie Barbarino	John Travolta
Juan Luis Pedro Phillipo de Huevos Epstein	Robert Hegyes
Freddie "Boom Boom" Washington	Lawrence-Hilton Jacobs
Arnold Horshack	Ron Palillo
Mr. Michael Woodman	John Sylvester White
Rosalie Totzie	Debralee Scott (1975–1977)
Verna Jean	Vernee Watson (1975–1977)
Judy Borden	Helaine Lembeck (1975–1977)
Todd Ludlow	Dennis Bowen (1975–1977)
Maria	Catarina Cellino (1975–1976)
Angie	Melonie Haller (1978)
Beau De Labarre	Stephen Shortridge (1978–1979)
Carvelli	Charles Fleischer (1978–1979)

in the normal classes at James Buchanan High School in Bensonhurst, Brooklyn (ironically, near where Ralph and Alice Kramden lived some years before; one can imagine Ralph howling if he'd run into the Sweathogs on his bus . . . or, better yet: if Ralph and Alice had had a son, and he had grown up to be . . . Horshack).

It was an interesting time in educational history for *Welcome Back, Kotter*. A far throw from Miss Brooks and Mr. Peepers, Our Mr. Kotter was definitely permissive. Which might have been even funnier (it was funny) if the country hadn't been emerging from the permissive-classroom period when Kotter debuted. Experimental school and open classrooms were just fading, and here was a classroom full of jokers, and many parents—and teachers—were concerned that their smartalecky routines were going to be mimicked in cross-country classrooms the next day. And they were.

Said Robert Hegyes (who played Juan): "Originally the concept of the program was an upbeat *Blackboard Jungle*. But after the network saw the pilot, they thought it should be lightened up. I suggested that the Marx Brothers had a certain style, so they decided to incorporate some of their routines into the show. Our concept became taking ridiculous situations and turning them into chaos. We're not doing reality."

Of course, like any even slightly innovative sitcom in the seventies, controversy surrounded *Kotter*. Right from the start it was banned from Boston, which since has come to represent a compliment for being progressive, but back then meant many lost dollars for ABC. The ABC affiliate refused to air the series—they feared the program might aggravate Boston's strife over schoolbusing—and, instead, it aired on a low-powered UHF channel in the area. For the premiere, the network even edited the episode—and deleted a minor "crime" committed by the Sweathogs—but the Boston station wouldn't budge.

Schoolteachers weren't too pleased with the character of Kotter, who was lenient with his students. And so the National Education Association planted an "adviser" on the show "in order to protect the image of school-

teachers," they said. As a guest of *The Tonight Show*, Kaplan quipped: "Would you believe—a technical adviser on *Sanford and Son* to protect the image of junk dealers!"

Many indeed thought that *Kotter* was a junk dealer—in that the show was junk, and that it would be promoting the use of "junk"—i.e., drugs. Some people thought the story of potential hoods and pushers was no laughing matter. And that was just the beginning of the show's troubles.

There were problems even before *Kotter* got on the air, ones that nearly prevented its being broadcast at all. Executive producer James Komack quit the series three times before he actually set up the deal with ABC. He said that he hated the concept, was indifferent to Kaplan's brand of humor, and wasn't that wild about Kaplan himself. Apparently he changed his tune, because he went on to become one of Kaplan's "few friends," as he put it.

Kaplan was difficult; but a good comic—glib, articulate, funny and clever. One night in 1974, producer Alan Sacks dropped by The Comedy Store, a comedy club on Sunset Boulevard, to hear Freddie Prinze's stand-up comedy act. Kaplan was on the same bill. "When Gabe did his routine about those Brooklyn kids I love and know so well," remembers Sacks, a former Brooklynite, "he killed me."

And so, the next logical step: they had lunch. Said Kaplan at the restaurant: "It's too bad I'm not a kid anymore. I could do a *Happy Days* and be one of the kids." And then Sacks said: "Let's do a show about those kids with you as their teacher."

Kaplan quickly overcame any problems he may have had in the transition from comic to actor. "I had to learn how to react to other people on the stage, instead of just responding to the audience," he later said. "At the beginning I would play to the audience. If they would laugh, I'd make some gesture in response. You're not supposed to do that. You're not supposed to acknowledge the presence of the audience other than by waiting for the laughter to subside. But other members of the cast were accomplished Broadway and Off-Broadway actors. They helped me with the acting, and I helped them with the timing on their comedy lines." As soon as he learned the tricks of his new trade, Kaplan became a star.

Welcome Back, Kotter made a lot of people stars. For a brief moment it even regenerated singer/songwriter John Sebastian's waning career when his Kotter theme song, "Welcome Back," shot up to the top of the pop charts. Of course the show transformed Kaplan into Kotter and made him a star. But the biggest of them all was the swaggering Sweathog, Vinnie Barbarino, played by John Travolta.

Right from the start, viewers knew they were in for something special. There had been speculation that Travolta's character would merely be a seventies' version of Henry Winkler's fifties' Fonzie. Not so. Travolta had

The Crew (from left): Arnold, Vinnie, "Boom Boom," Juan, Mr. Woodman, Kotter

an energy, a glow, that permeated his character. There was a star bursting and beaming beneath the character of Vinnie.

Travolta, of course, went on to become a major movie star, first receiving glorious accolades for his role of the disco dance king/hardware store clerk Tony Manero in *Saturday Night Fever*, as well as the fifties cool-cat Danny Zucko in *Grease* (which he had appeared in on Broadway), and as a mean teen in *Carrie*. Few realize that Travolta's first film, pre-*Kotter*, was the 1975 low-low-budget horror movie *The Devil's Rain*, in which he wore a mask and yelled: "Blasphemer! Get him, he is a blasphemer!"

Travolta's Vinnie changed as he grew as an actor. Said the executive producer, Komack: "Originally Vinnie was very slick and very tough. He was a bully and a con artist. But Johnny has a very likable, sweet, and even soulful personality. He has a very spiritual attitude, so we made Vinnie a devout Catholic. Because Johnny can play against Barbarino's conceits, he makes him an extremely vulnerable character." An example of this was, after Vinnie had dropped out of school and gotten a job as an orderly in a hospital, he tried to talk the other Sweathogs into doing the same, saying that his job would soon enable him to become a doctor. Kotter came and talked to him and Vinnie ended up telling the guys that they should stay in school.

Said Travolta about himself and Vinnie: "When I was in Englewood (New Jersey, where he grew up and dropped out of high school at sixteen), I was a dumb clown, not a cool clown like Barbarino. I was the sort of fool who'd do anything dumb for a laugh. But now I'm regarded as a hero at that school. They want to hold a John Travolta Day. I'm just trying not to let all this make me crazy. Like I've met Henry Winkler, and each time he asks me how I'm dealing with it. We're trying to keep our heads together. That's what my old actor friends in New York can't seem to understand. They think I don't phone or see them as often as I used to because I've gone Hollywood, but it's just that I'm so busy. But how do you convince people you haven't gone Hollywood?"

In truth, Hollywood—right along with the rest of the country—had gone Travolta. But on a show like *Kotter*, with its string of young male starlets, one star wasn't always easy to take. Especially when the star was supposed to be the star—Gabe Kaplan. There'd been a lot of talk that Kaplan and Travolta didn't get along, that they'd been feuding. Said Kaplan: "I think John is a terrific actor and has helped the show immensely. If there is anybody on the show I'm close to, it's John."

It certainly wasn't Marcia Strassman, who played his wife, Julie Kotter. "I'm miserable," said Strassman in 1978. "Gabe runs hot and cold, one day your best friend, the next day not speaking. Even blatant hostility would be easier to deal with. It has always been hard to act with him, especially in intimate scenes. I hate the series. I pray every day for a cancellation."

Bathroom Humor: Gabe and Julie lock Juan in the john.

Strassman continually tried to break her contract, with no luck. "When I came back on the set (after a summer break), the other guys on the show stood in a circle around me to protect me from Gabe. We joked that I should be wearing a bulletproof vest. But the man never said a word. Not a word." The cast—which used to play softball together—soon started playing tug-of-war. Apparently Travolta and Jacobs ("Boom Boom") stayed out of the fights, but Robert Hegyes (Juan) sided with Kaplan, and Palillo (Horshack) was Strassman's main ally. Kaplan's response to Strassman's antagonism: "I think Marcia is a good serious actress and perfect for the role, but I was shocked that she had such hostility." She went on to complain that she was irritated that her part consisted mainly of "And what happened, honey?" when Kotter came home. "I had the feeling Marcia thought of me as a square," Kaplan said, "compared to most of her friends. But I always thought there was mutual respect. Obviously, I was wrong."

When the show's ratings sagged during the 1977–1978 season, the network switched it to a better time slot. When Strassman heard that, she was hardly happy. "Oh, God. The network is going to make us a hit again. There's only one thing I want to hear: 'You're fired.'"

The Strassman story was not the only one that upset the Kotter clan. For some time, Kaplan was involved in a power struggle with his "good friend" James Komack. Kotter lost. Komack fired nearly twenty Kaplanites from the show—writers, directors, etc.—and brought in Carol Burnett's old producing and writing team. The result: more one-liners and less ambitious situations.

It also brought around other changes: Kaplan was far less involved with the show (he only appeared in several episodes during its final, 1978–1979 season), and Marcia Strassman suddenly went from nothing to do, to the vice-principal of the school. And Travolta—who was by this time a super-super-star—made only occasional appearances. As a *special* guest star.

On one of the last episodes of *Kotter*, the Sweathogs—getting a little long in the tooth by this time—were still up to their old antics, although it seemed they were just walking through the antics this time around. For example, when Mr. Woodman (who was now principal) asked Horshack if he knew something, Horshack said: "Search me," and Mr. Woodman said: "I wouldn't touch your body; how do I know where it's been?"

Anyway, it turns out that Juan has brought an X-rated movie to school. Says ditzy Horshack: "An X-rated movie—where they really show the Xs?"

Naturally, confusion abounds and the X-rated movie is mixed up with the school's sex-education film, leading to obvious one-liners such as Mr. Woodman saying: "I never had any sex education and look how I turned out . . ."

Meanwhile, Mrs. Kotter meets with the parents to talk to them about sex education.

MRS. KOTTER: We're trying to teach kids that sex is not disgusting.
MRS. ZUGLER: I've been married for twenty-seven years—don't tell *me* what's disgusting!

Welcome, Mrs. Kotter: Marcia Strassman takes over for Gabriel Kaplan.

To prove that sex is not disgusting, she tries to show the sex-ed film to the parents—only instead it turns out to be the film the gang brought in, *The Passionate Plumber*. The parents view the X-rated movie, are upset, and want her fired. Mrs. Kotter is angry with Epstein, who has been the head of audiovisuals at school. "I made one very big mistake," she tells him. "I trusted you."

Of course it all works out when Juan confesses to the parents that it was he who, by mistake, switched the films—but Mrs. Kotter steps in to say that *she* did it, in order to prove the difference between sex education and pornography. They believe her. She and Epstein make up. The students burn the porno film, announcing that "The movie was elected to the hall of flame—now it's hotter than ever."

That year—without the full-time seasoning of Travolta and Kaplan—the show did rottenly in the ratings and was laid to rest. Since it had run only four years, there was fear that no syndicate would want to buy it, since there were only about 100 episodes to be aired. But at least in the late seventies and early eighties there was little to worry about, since Travolta was still a big star and people would flock around their sets to watch his TV roots.

It had been a long haul for the *Kotter* gang, a long four years of tears and sweat for the Sweathogs. When Freddie Prinze killed himself early in 1977, there was panic on the set—a set that had created its own instant stars, as *Chico and the Man* had created Prinze's stardom. Hegyes, Palillo, and Travolta immediately made a pact—an antisuicide pact—that if one of them ever became that depressed, he'd call on the others for aid. "We recognized that what happened to Freddie could happen to us," one of them said.

More than anything else in the history of television, *Welcome Back, Kotter* proved how a sitcom could make stars and break shows. When the power plays began offstage, the power in front of the camera seemed to dwindle. At the beginning, Kotter was less *The Three Stooges* and more comedy of substance (for example, episodes on teenage alcoholism and suicide).

It was a good idea: Kaplan coming back as Kotter, overseeing a group of seventies'-style Kaplans. And what do we have to look forward to besides Welcome Back *Welcome Back, Kotter* in reruns? Who knows, maybe in twenty years there'll be a sitcom called *Welcome Back, Barbarino*.

ALSO RANS

Big Eddie

Big Eddie was not a big hit. It ran—walked, really—three months on CBS and starred Sheldon Leonard (TV sitcom producer and former movie heavy) as Eddie Smith, a reformed gambler trying to make it big as a sports promoter. He had a thick Brooklyn accent and was a rough guy, but underneath, of course, he had a heart of gold and tried to become more intellectual. Unfortunately there wasn't much he could do about it in three months. But he did have an unusual family: a wife, Honey (played by Sheree North of *Bachelor Father's* daughter days), who was an ex-stripper, his granddaughter, Ginger (played by *Goodbye Girl's* and *Family's* Quinn Cummings), as well as a brother. There were other characters—a cook and a jive-talking black man. The show was a summer tryout that made it and then quickly died when pitted against *Sanford and Son* on Friday nights.

The Bob Crane Show

*B*ob Crane emigrated to TV from radio and played parts on *Dick Van Dyke*, *Donna Reed* (he was good neighbor Dave Kelsey) and, of course, his big show, *Hogan's Heroes*. So there was high hope for his own show—under his own name—in which he played an insurance exec in his forties who unexpectedly quit his job and enrolled in medical school. Oh, the family pitched in to help with the finances—they always do on TV, you know—but there were a lot of problems in being twice the age of the other medical students and . . . well, it's not easy when you become dependent on your working wife for your income, nor if you live in a place with a lot of resident nuts, as well as situations like this one: Bob's wife wins a real estate sales award, only emphasizing the fact that she's become the breadwinner of the family. Bob refuses to attend the awards banquet and, in fact, moves out of the house and into a coed dorm. Fortunately he runs into the medical school psychiatrist, who puts things back in their proper perspective for him. NBC put things in their even more proper perspective for Bob when they canceled his show after only three months. A few years later, Crane was brutally murdered in a hotel.

The Cop and the Kid

*T*he seventies were full of ethnic comedies (among other things), and this was one of them. Here's how this one happened: Through a freak set of circumstances a stout, middle-aged Irish cop, Frank Murphy (Charles Durning), is assigned custody of Lucas, a young, black, streetwise orphan (Tierre Turner)—sort of a *Diff'rent Strokes* before it happened. Apparently Lucas had been shoplifting and Murphy had had an asthma attack, for which he could have been dismissed from the force. Lucas blackmailed Murphy into asking for leniency at Lucas' trial. And so—the court made Murphy Lucas' guardian. Ha ha. The efforts of Murphy and his mother (former hoofer Patsy Kelly) to reform Lucas provided the comedy. But only for three months, at which time NBC relinquished custody.

Doc

*I*t began as a summer replacement series and ended up with a life all its own, albeit a short one. Barnard Hughes—who went on to grab a Tony in Broadway's *Da* —starred as the lovable, soft-spoken Doc Joe Bogert, who was much more concerned about his patients' welfare than about his fees (a pleasant switch from Real Life). He was married to a toughie named Annie (Elizabeth Wilson), and he had a daughter, Laurie (Judy Kahan), and a son-in-law, Fred (John Harkins), whom

Doc: Elizabeth Wilson and Barnard Hughes

Doc didn't much like at all. The children rented the apartment above Mr. and Mrs. Doc's apartment (which happened so much on TV; does that ever happen in the Real World?). When things got tough, Doc often spent time with his cronies Ben (Herbie Faye) and Happy (Irwin Corey). The first season's ratings were not terrific, and so a little surgery was performed on *Doc*. First, they—CBS Hospital—did away with his wife and kids. They moved him to the Westside Clinic, run by Stanley Moss (David Ogden Stiers, later Charles on *M*A*S*H*). They even fired his nurse (the wonderful Mary Wickes) and hired a new one (Audra Lindley, soon to become Mrs. Roper on *Three's Company*). Even mouth-to-mouth couldn't have resuscitated this show, and in its new format it lasted only two months.

The Dumplings

Norman Lear. He brought us bigots, blacks, liberals. With *The Dumplings*, Lear brought us Fat. The message was that fat people could be good and kind and hardworking and lovable (just as he had told us that black people could be industrious and not at all shiftless). The Dumplings were Joe and Angela (James Coco and Geraldine Brooks), who ran a lunch counter in a large Manhattan office building. As the NBC press release said: "Joe and Angela aren't at all afraid to hug and kiss in public, and they often dance around their living room just for the love of it." Sort of the *Donna Reed Show* of the Weight Watchers set. Except they weren't watching weight and, actually, nobody was watching this show. It was sent to the fat farm after only a few episodes.

Far Out Space Nuts

Someday Bob Denver will play Hamlet—well, maybe Ophelia—but his career on television was strictly sappy dimwits. On this one he played Junior who, along with Barney (Chuck McCann) was a ground crewman for NASA. They were loading food aboard a spaceship, PXL 1236, when they accidentally launched the moon rocket into outer space. Each week—and there weren't many of them—they would meet people like Honk, a pet space creature (played by Patty Maloney) and Crakor, a robot (played by Stan Jenson). CBS soon brought them back down to earth.

Fay

This show is one of TV's Famous Flops, mainly because its star—Lee Grant—went on a talk show and lambasted NBC for not giving it a chance, because they placed this "risqué" comedy in The Family Hour, and for canceling it after only a month. So, during summer reruns, the network ran it again—and immediately canceled it after a month due to lack of interest. So much for *Fay*'s broadcast history. This was the story, riding on the crest of single-liberated-woman Mary Tyler Moore's success: Fay Stewart is a forty-three-year-old woman who's "searching for identity" (that's what the NBC press release said, anyway) after raising two children and divorcing her unfaithful husband (whom she always seems to be running into). She leaves the suburbs, moves into an apartment, and becomes a legal secretary. Here were some of the complications: her ex-husband thought that she should quit her foolishness and come home; her twenty-three-year-old conservative and traditional-thinking daughter didn't approve of her mother's actions; Fay's best friend, Lillian, lived vicariously through Fay because she lacked the courage to leave a similar marital situation. Fay had affairs. But only four weeks' worth.

Fay: *Lee Grant*

The Ghost Busters

Kong (Forrest Tucker) and Eddie Spencer (Larry Storch) were ghost-busters who, with their assistant, Tracy (a gorilla played by Bob Burns), tried to battle the ghosts of legendary fiends—Frankenstein's monster, Dracula, the Mummy, the Werewolf. CBS busted this ghost of a show after a single season.

Good Heavens

Carl Reiner used to be known as Alan Brady on *The Dick Van Dyke Show,* of which he was the writer-producer-director. Now, mainly, he's known as Rob Reiner's father (although Reiner, Sr., has been active in a number of TV and film projects, including George Burns' *Oh, God!,* which was itself like a big-screen sitcom). In 1975, Reiner resurfaced on TV, playing a funny angel, Mr. Angel, who dressed in a business suit. It was *The Millionaire* in heavenly drag. Each week, Mr. A. would pop down to earth to give a mortal one wish. On an early episode (actually they were all early episodes; the show was canceled by ABC after three months), Rob Reiner and then-wife, Penny Marshall, were a young couple— Rob a sporting-goods salesman who wanted to be a big-league baseball player. In another episode, a woman, who couldn't decide between suitors, got a brand new one who combined the best of both. An unsuccessful author finally got everyone to publish his book. Unfortunately, Mr. Angel needed a Mr. Angel of his own to answer his one wish—to keep the show on the air. *Good Heavens* died and went to heaven on June 26, 1976.

Grady

This spin-off of *Sanford and Son* lasted only three months. It centered around Grady Wilson (Whitman Mayo), who had been one of Fred Sanford's cronies. Here he was transplanted out of Watts and into a racially mixed, middle-class neighborhood in LA, along with his daughter, Ellie Wilson Marshall (played by Carole Cole), and her family. A sample episode: Grady came to grips with bureaucracy when the Social Security Administration owed him several checks. And when his daughter and son-in-law owed the IRS money, Grady settled the account his own way. NBC also settled accounts their own way: cancellation.

Hot l Baltimore

Many affiliates refused to air this show. They thought it was lewd and racy. Norman Lear—riding high with *All in the Family* and *Maude*—believed in the show and, in fact, was the one who had produced it after seeing the award-winning Off-Broadway play of the same name by Lanford Wilson. There was so much commotion about this show that by the time it actually aired, it seemed to be no big deal. Here was the story line: The setting was the dilapidated Hot l Baltimore (the letter "e" in the sign had burned out and never been replaced), which was inhabited by a bunch of crazies: the desk clerk Bill Lewis (James Cromwell) and his girlfriend April Green (Conchata Ferrell); the harried manager Clifford Ainsley (Richard Masur, who would also pop up as the love interest on *One Day at a Time);* the philosophical Charles Bingham (Al Freeman, Jr.); a Colombian hooker named Suzy Marta Rocket (Jeannie Linero); an unemployed waitress named Millie (Gloria Le Roy); a tomboy named Jackie (Robin Wilson); an old man who was always on the brink of dying, Mr. Morse (Stan Gottlieb); a homosexual couple, George (Lee Bergere) and Gordon (Henry Calvert); and the eccentric Mrs. Bellotti (Charlotte Rae, later the housekeeper on *Diff'rent Strokes).* In addition, there was a crazy kid—never seen, but always heard— named Moose Bellotti who was up to such tricks as buttering the hallways and staging *The Poseidon Adventure* in the bathtub. ABC threw the whole mess overboard after trying to keep the show afloat for four months.

Ivan the Terrible

This was a summer five-week limited series on CBS about a contemporary Russian named Ivan (Lou Jacobi) who was the headwaiter at Moscow's Hotel Metropole. There was great congestion in his three-and-one-half room apartment, because in it lived nine people and a dog (which we never saw) named Rasputin. Inhabitants included: his wife, Olga (Maria Karnilova); their children, Sonya (Caroline Kava), Nikolai (Alan Cauldwell), and Sascha (Matthew Barry); Olga's first husband, Vladimir (Phil Leeds), and her mother, Tatiana (Despo); Nikolai's wife, Svetlana (Nana Tucker); and a Cuban named Raoul (Manuel Martinez).

Joe and Sons *(from left): Barry Miller and Richard Castellano*

Joe and Sons

After *All in the Family* debuted in 1970, there began a huge onslaught of blue-collar sitcoms. Not since *The Honeymooners* and *The Life of Riley* had the Little Man been so glorified on the small screen. Joe Vitale was yet another of blue-collar persuasion to have his own sitcom. As played by Richard Castellano (whom viewers might have remembered if they looked quickly enough from three seasons ago when he tried to play yet another Italian-American working class hero, Joe Girelli, on *The Super*), Joe Vitale was a widower who lived with his two teenage sons—Mark (Barry Miller, who'd pop up again two seasons later in *Szysznyk*) and Nick (Jimmy Baio, who'd go on to play bratty Billy on *Soap*)—in Hoboken. His best buddy, who worked with him at the Hoboken Sheet and Tube Company, was Gus Duzik (played by Jerry Stiller, half of the comedy team Stiller and Meara—former members of the 1972 *Paul Lynde Show*). Anyway, Joe didn't have it easy, working hard, raising his boys, and trying to tend house. Helping him out with the latter, fortunately, was Estelle (Bobbi Jordan, who'd played Tootsie Woodley on the 1968 version of *Blondie*), a cocktail waitress who lived in the apartment across the hall. Joe lasted in the building—and on the airwaves—only thirteen episodes before CBS married him off to obscurity.

The Montefuscos

And yet another sitcom about an ethnic minority: this time Italians. A big fat boisterous middle-class family living in Connecticut. The show ran on NBC Thursday nights, but the sitcom took place Sunday nights, when

the entire family came over for dinner. The subjects they came up with provided the stories of the series. The entire cast was Tony and Rose, their three sons and a daughter and their families (there was a token WASP who had married the daughter). Indigestion set in and the show was given a large bottle of Pepto-Bismol after one month of meals.

On the Rocks

This fall entry—which lasted one season on ABC—was all about a minimum security prison (i.e., the prisoners could sit around and tell bad jokes) that had a hatful of minorities as prisoners: Hector Fuentes (Jose Perez), a resourceful Latin; his pal DeMott (Hal Williams); Cleaver (Rick Hurst), who was sure that everything was going to turn out fine; Nicky Palik (Bobby Sandler), a young con; and Gabby (Pat Cranshaw), the old, toothless inmate. Their strict correction officer was Mr. Gibson (Mel Stewart) and their guard was the easygoing Mr. Sullivan (Tom Poston, who'd go on to sitcom success in *Mork and Mindy*). Probably the most interesting thing about this loudmouthed sitcom is that it followed TV's leading cop show, *Barney Miller*. Ah-*ha*! So that's where they sent the criminals . . .

On the Rocks: *Jose Perez surrounded by (from left) Leonard Stone, Hal Williams, Rick Hurst, Jay Gerber, Bobby Sandler*

Phyllis

Oh, the sorrow of the spin-off. Okay, so *Mork and Mindy* and *Laverne and Shirley* made it (maybe you have to have two names in the title to make it as a spin-off), but it didn't always work (unless you were a magician like Norman Lear, who could produce successful sitcom spin-offs like *Maude* and *Good Times* and *The Jeffersons* out of a hat). Anyway, Cloris Leachman, an actress of super

Phyllis: *Mary Tyler Moore pays a surprise visit to Cloris Leachman.*

talents, had played boorish busybody Phyllis Lindstrom, Mary Richards' neighbor, friend, and landlady on *The Mary Tyler Moore Show*. Phyllis was funny, and a truly obnoxious character. When they gave her her own show, they tried to "warm her up" a bit—to make her more human, more humane and, frankly, more boring. *Phyllis* simply wasn't Phyllis. It was the same name, the same actress, but a different character. Anyway, supposedly Phyllis' husband, Lars, had died, and Phyllis was leaving Minneapolis to return to her native San Francisco. She was in her mid-forties and had a teenage daughter with her, Bess (Lisa Gerritsen). So she moved in with her scatterbrained mother-in-law, Audrey Dexter (Jane Rose), and her husband, Judge John Dexter (Henry Jones). Phyllis got a job immediately as an assistant to Julie Erskine at a commercial photography studio. Tragedy struck the show immediately when Barbara Colby, who played Julie in the show's first episode, was murdered; Liz Torres took her place for the remaining episodes. But only for the first season, after which Phyllis—still self-centered and oblivious, but without the *oomph* she had had back in Minneapolis—got a job as an administrative assistant to Dan Valenti (Carmini Cardidi), a member of the San Francisco Board of Supervisors. She worked with another supervisor, Leonard Marsh (John

Lawlor) and his assistant, Harriet (Garn Stephens). Back at home, Judge Jonathan's eighty-seven-year-old mother—who could put Phyllis down better than anyone—married ninety-two-year-old Arthur Lanson (Burt Mustin). Again tragedy struck: Judith Lowry (who played Mother Dexter) died before the episode aired and Mustin, who was too ill to see it, died shortly after. Then they tried to marry Bess off to Phyllis' boss' nephew, Mark (Craig Wasson), and the couple sneaked off to Las Vegas for the ceremony. Nothing helped, and *Phyllis* went off the air at the end of the 1976–1977 season.

Popi

This one lasted five episodes on CBS as a midseason replacement show. Here's the story: Abraham Rodriguez (Hector Elizondo) was a poor Puerto Rican immigrant who had three part-time jobs he worked at to support his habit—his two small sons. He was a widower and lived in a small New York apartment building, where Lupe (Edith Diaz), a woman he was dating, also lived. During the summer of 1976, *Popi* was rerun, and the remaining episodes that had been filmed but not aired from the first time around finally saw the light of the TV screen. But still, no luck. Now *Popi*'s just a memory. Based on the movie starring Alan Arkin.

The Practice

This sharp sitcom lasted much less time than it should have—it started out as a midseason January 1976 replacement on NBC and died the following January. Here's what it was all about while the patient lived: Danny Thomas played grouchy/warm, absentminded/concerned Dr. Jules Bedford, who wanted to help people as much as he could. He wasn't interested in money, just his patients on New York's West Side. On the other side of town was his son, David Bedford (David Spielberg), a Park Avenue doctor who was making money and trouble when he pestered his dad to join him on his East Side practice. But how could Jules leave? He had a terrific nurse, Molly (Dena Dietrich), who'd been with him for years and had a crush on the widowed physician; then there was Helen, the dizzy receptionist played by Didi Conn. All Dr. David had was a wife (played by sitcom regular Shelley Fabares) and a couple of kids. Mike Evans (who'd played Lionel on *All in the Family* and for a time on *The Jeffersons*) played Lenny.

Viva Valdez

ABC decided that it was time for a sitcom about noisy Mexican-Americans who lived in East Los Angeles (apparently *Chico and the Man*, across the dial on NBC, wasn't enough for them). This, however, was a family show—all about Luis Valdez (Rodolfo Hoyos) who ran a plumbing business with his eldest son, Victor (James Victor). Also on hand: Mama Sophia (Carmen Zapata); Ernesto (Nelson D. Cuevas), who was training with the phone company; Connie (Lisa Mordente), a teenager; Pepe (Claudio Martinez), a baseball fanatic; and Jerry (Jorge Cervera, Jr.), a newly arrived cousin from Mexico. Valdez didn't Viva very long, when ABC canceled it after four months.

What's Happening

This ethnic show—in which the g in *Happening* was never pronounced—was an ABC summer replacement that was given a spot on the fall schedule during the 1976–1977 season. It was loosely based on the movie *Cooley High*. Here's the story:

It was all about three spirited black kids in a large American city: Raj (Ernest Thomas) wanted to be a writer and studied and dreamed about it; Rerun (Fred Berry) was the jolly, fat clown who always said the wrong thing; Dwayne (Haywood Nelson) was the shy tag-along who wanted to be a cool cat. They were always involved in some sort of mess, which they often discussed at the soda shop near the school, where Shirley (Shirley Hemphill, who got her own sitcom, *One in a Million*, in 1980) was the overweight and overwrought waitress. Plus there were family problems: Raj often clashed with his no-kidding-around mother (Mabel King), who worked as a maid. He also had a pesky little sister, Dee (Danielle Spencer). Seen in several episodes were Bill, the kids' father (played by Thalmus Rasulala) who'd run out on the family; and Marvin (Bryan O'Dell), the gossipy reporter for the high school paper. The show lasted through the 1977–1978 season.

When Things Were Rotten

Movie maven Mel Brooks created this sitcom for TV, and a lot of people seemed to think the title was a more than apt way to describe the show, a wild and zany satire (so what else?) all about Robin Hood and his Merry Men in Sherwood Forest during the twelfth century. But the catch was this: instead of history's boldly heroic Robin, this one was a total nincompoop (as played by Dick Gautier). Also in the case were Dick Van Patten as Friar Tuck, Bernie Kopell as Alan-a-Dale, and Jane A. Johnston as Princess Isabelle. Robin Hood's Merry Band of Men were total incompetents, getting by only because the evil Prince John and the rotten Sheriff of Nottingham were even more stupid.

The comedy was like Brooks' movies—fast-paced and based on silly non sequiturs and historical anachronisms—like the time when Prince John hired the four fastest woodcutters to chop down the entire Sherwood Forest to make way for a new housing development for wealthy burghers. Once the men disguised themselves as a traveling conga band and rescued Robin. Critics seemed to love this show, but for some reason no one was watching. It lasted only four months on ABC.

When Things Were Rotten: *Dick Gautier*

1976–1977

Alice

Holmes and Yoyo

A Year at the Top

OFF-SCREEN

9/3 Viking 2 spacecraft lands on Mars.

9/9 Mao Tse-tung, leader of Chinese Communist revolution and founder of People's Republic of China in 1949, dies at age of eighty-two.

9/16 Episcopal Church approves the ordination of women to be priests and bishops; Indianapolis woman becomes first to take advantage of new ruling.

9/30 California first state to give terminally ill right to authorize withdrawal of life-sustaining procedures when death believed imminent.

10/21 Cincinnati Reds win World Series, against New York Yankees, thus becoming first National League team in fifty-four years to win two consecutive Series.

11/30 Utah Board of Pardons grants Gary Mark Gilmore's plea for death by firing squad rather than life imprisonment.

1/20 Jimmy Carter sworn in as thirty-ninth President.

1/30 TV mini-series *Roots* sets new records: viewed by more Americans than had watched any show in television history; 35 percent of all US households tune in.

5/11 Chlorofluorocarbons to be outlawed as propellants in spray cans; studies show rise in cancer risks when ozone layer is depleted by increased amounts of the compounds.

6/20 First oil from Alaska's frozen North Slope begins flowing into trans-Alaska pipeline.

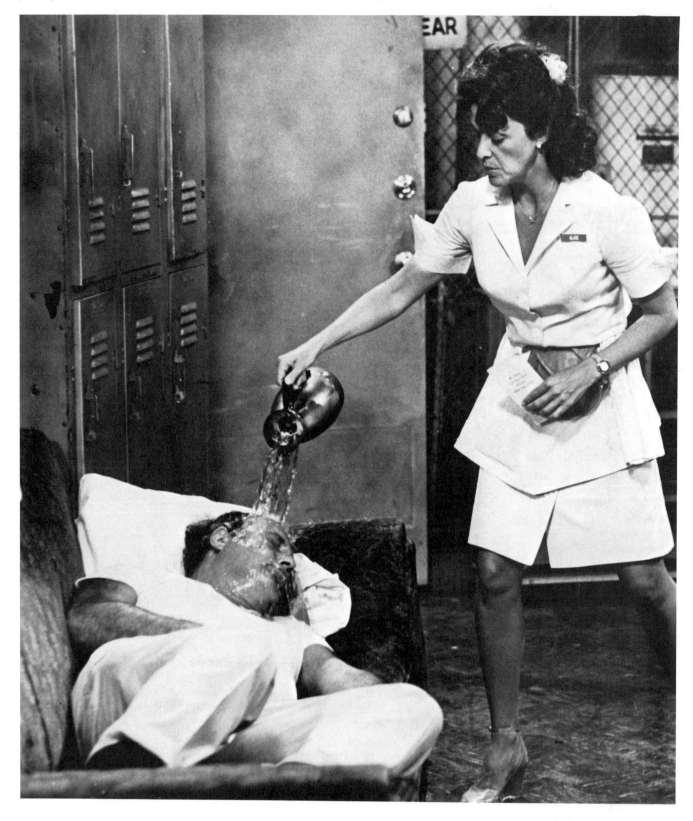

FRONT RUNNER

ALICE

FLO: Hi, handsome. What would you like?
CUSTOMER: Well, what have you got in mind?
*FLO: If it's the same thing you have in mind, you ain't
gonna find it on the menu.*

*A*lice was one of those shows where, if the main
character had gotten what she wanted, if she'd been able
to fulfill her dream, then there wouldn't have been any
more show. Alice Hyatt wanted to be a singer. But, in
the meantime, she worked as a waitress in Mel's Diner.
She was a good singer—oh, how did we know? Well, we
heard her performing the show's title tune each week:
There's a new world out there . . .

But still, what made Alice different from her long-
lost sitcom sisters is that Alice had a job, but longed for a
career. The others in the TV job market—Suzie
McNamara, Miss Brooks, Schultzy, et al.—all held jobs
until they could find a man to hold.

Still, in many ways, *Alice* was just like everything
else on television during the late seventies. It had the
sight gags and the slight gags and the silly jokes and the
sassy allusions to sex—low humor—but it had two things
that made it a hit: good acting and a good concept.
Whether the American public realized it or not, the
subliminal message of *Alice* was that Sisterhood Is
Powerful. It was Flo and Vera and Alice all the way.
There was a loyalty that existed between them, a support
system that, week after week, no matter what the trial,
no matter what the tribulation, couldn't be shaken.
Although their personalities were all different (and sometimes bizarre), they always stuck together—through loneliness, through crises, and through their ill-fated
relationships with men. There was a true affection among
the three of them. They were sort of the women's
auxiliary of the *M*A*S*H* doctors, only their battlefield
was Mel's Diner, run by the tough (but tender), cranky
Mel.

It all came from a movie (which was not a comedy)
called *Alice Doesn't Live Here Anymore*, all about a New
Mexico widow who takes her son and moves to Phoenix
in search of a singing career. What she finds instead is a
job at a diner, a job at raising her son, and a job at
working out a relationship with a guy she's met (Ellen
Burstyn and Kris Kristofferson played Alice and her
beau.)

Alice was as abbreviated from the concept of the
movie as its title was. The premise was basically the
same—she landed in Phoenix, but came from New Jersey
(and sounded like it)—but she never met Kris Kristofferson, although she had lots of other mismatched relationships.

Her two co-workers consisted of a loudmouthed,
raunchy, softy of an old-hand waitress named Flo, and a
dingdong, timid waitress named Vera. The premiere
dialogue went like this:

ALICE: My husband's been dead six months and some
life insurance company is still trying to sell him a policy.
VERA: When was his birthday?
ALICE: September seventeenth.
VERA: Oh, a Virgo. That's a good sign. Robust and
healthy. Ooops. Sorry, Alice.
MEL: You mean he never had a policy?
ALICE: Never. Don didn't believe in insurance.
MEL: How come?
ALICE: It didn't come in a six-pack.
FLO *(to Mel)*: If it did, you'd be the most overinsured
man in the world.
MEL: Keep it up, Flo, and you're gonna get one from
column A and one from column B.
FLO: Mel—kiss mah grits!

Alice Hyatt	Linda Lavin
Tommy Hyatt	Philip McKeon
Mel	Vic Tayback
Flo	Polly Holliday (1976–1980)
Vera	Beth Howland
Henry	Marvin Kaplan (1977–)
Belle	Diane Ladd (1980–)

Of the three, Flo was the most colorful. What came out of her brain came out of her mouth. Some examples:

FLO:　If Mel doesn't give us a raise soon, I'm gonna have to swallow my pride and marry that Texas millionaire.
ALICE:　What Texas millionaire?
FLO:　The first one that asks me.

And when one of her gentleman friends comes into the diner for breakfast:

FLO:　Earl, honey, what would you like this morning?
EARL:　The same thing I had last night.

Brassy and sassy, her favorite expressions were "Kiss mah grits," "When donkeys fly," and "You bet your sweet patoot." But it was her blue humor—baby blue, to be sure—that got her the most laughs. "You ought to see my new bikini," she once announced. "It came in a plain brown wrapper."

Once Mel asked her to carry in a sack of sugar. "If I'm gonna get a bad back," Flo caws, "it's not gonna be from lifting sugar."

Vera, on the other hand, probably would get a bad back from lifting sugar. But the real question is: where did she get such a bad brain?

MEL:　I'm gonna live on easy street.
VERA:　You mean you're giving up your apartment?

Or:

MEL:　I'm a humanitarian.
VERA:　Mel, you've never been in church a day of your life.

And:

HENRY:　We love the ambience of Mel's Diner.
CUSTOMER:　What's ambience?
VERA:　That's what they pick you up in after you've eaten Mel's food.

And she wasn't kidding.

Later in the series, Vera became less stupid and more innocent (i.e., she said the same idiotic things, but the motivations were different. So she became dizzy instead of dumb).

Besides Vera's lame brain and Flo's sex life, Mel's cooking was the main source of jokes on the show. Here are some of the bad food jokes (that is, good jokes about bad food . . . and sometimes bad jokes about bad food; the bad food remained the constant on *Alice*):

MEL (*about to retire*):　One more hour and my cooking days are over.
FLO:　Your cooking days were over the day that you attacked that stove.
MEL:　Stow it, Flo.

***Kiss Their Grits** (from left): Tommy, Vera, Flo, Mel, Alice*

FLO:　You know, Mel, the doctors of Phoenix oughta get together and stop you from retiring—they're going to lose a fortune.

When the jokes subsided, it was Linda Lavin, as Alice, who kept the show together. She was part of a new breed of sitcom heroines. Not the silly ones who did wacky things like Lucy or Margie or Gracie. Nor was she like the sitcom mommies of the fifties and early sixties—Margaret Anderson, Donna Stone, Harriet Nelson. Plus, she wasn't an Edith Bunker or a Maude Findlay, one of the larger-than-life ladies. She was somewhere between Mary Richards and Ann Romano; she was a reactor. She didn't do dumb things. She was sensible and calm; Lavin was generous enough as an actress to bring out the humor in the people around her. Sort of the litmus-paper performer.

Lavin was a little anxious about taking the part of Alice, at first, because Ellen Burstyn, who'd won an Academy Award for the movie version, was so firmly embedded in audiences' minds. But she turned Alice into her own character—warm and witty and knowing. Her Broadway experience and her guest shots on other sitcoms (as well as a year as detective Janice Wentworth on *Barney Miller* in 1975) all paid off on *Alice*, which could have been a thankless acting job. Alice went about solving everybody else's problems—it could have been retitled *Go Ask Alice*—and intervening in their crises. Plus sitting back and smiling while other people around her got the big laughs.

But not always. Sometimes Alice did say some funny things herself (though different from the mindless mouthings of the other characters).

TOMMY (*Alice's son, who wants her to take a job singing*): If you didn't have me, I bet you'd say "Yes" just like that.
ALICE:　That's why I have you—because I said "Yes" just like that.

Very often, *Alice*—like so many other sitcoms of the era—was guilty of that school of sitcom writing called Fill-in-the-Blank Dialogue. Pick a subject, any subject, and the writers could come up with predictable jokes. The subject for the week, one week, was: Marriage. Flo, who'd been married three times, was going to marry Mel's brother Al, who'd also been married three times. Here is some of the dialogue that took place on that episode:

CUSTOMER: I didn't know you had a brother, Mel.
MEL: Yeah—he's a little younger than me.
VERA: That's because Mel was born before him.
MEL: My brother's coming here to forget his alimony. He's doing so well in the used car business, he can afford all three of his divorces.
ALICE: That's success.

Al comes and he and Flo hit it off; she asks Mel if she can take the day off to go swimming with Al.

MEL: Nobody swims on a workday.
VERA: Except a salmon. A salmon goes upstream to lay her eggs, so she's certainly swimming on a workday.
MEL: Well, if Flo wants to swim upstream to lay her eggs—fine. Otherwise, forget it.
FLO: Mel—kiss mah grits!

The next day, Flo and Al announce they're going to be married. Bubba, one of Flo's beaus, overhears the announcement and is hurt.

BUBBA: I didn't even get a Dear John letter.
VERA: That's because your name is Bubba.
BUBBA *(to Flo)*: I've known you so many years—it may take me a minute or two to get over you.
FLO: We're planning to have our wedding on Sunday.
BUBBA: Does that mean our date next Saturday night is off?

They talk about the wedding. Flo wants a preacher. "No more justice of the peace. I had three of them quickies—they don't seem to take." When asked about her dress, Flo announces that "I'm gonna be a vision in white." All the men in the diner turn around and cry in unison: *"White??!!!"*
Flo asks Alice and Vera to be her bridesmaids.

VERA: You know me—always a bridesmaid but never a bridegroom.

Flo asks Bubba if he'll give her away. "Don't worry," he tells her, "I'll keep my mouth shut."
When Flo and Al fly off to make their plans, Mel turns to Alice:

MEL: What do you think?
ALICE: Did you see the *Poseidon Adventure?* This is a bigger disaster.

The day of the wedding (taking place in the diner, of course). Flo is scared. "I'm as nervous as a long-tail cat in a roomful of rockers." Two male guests talk:

GUEST #1: A wedding can't start without the bride.
GUEST #2: I wish mine had.

The preacher calls for "the hapless—I mean, the happy—couple—who will be united in holy deadlock—uh, wedlock . . ." But Flo has something to say to Al first:

FLO: I've got cold feet.
AL: Oh, I can get used to that.

Suddenly the episode takes a turn for the serious:

FLO: Al, I've been thinkin' . . .
AL: Honey, this is no time to be thinkin' . . . we're about to be married.
FLO: You just said the story of my life in two sentences. I never did think before I got married. The first time I was just a wild kid. The second time I was on the rebound, and the third time I was tryin' to recapture my lost youth. You and I are good friends, and I'd hate for our marriage to get between us.

Meanwhile, the preacher is getting nervous: "We really must get started. I have a disco lesson at two P.M."
But Flo and Al are gone. "We're calling off the wedding," reads the note they left, "and going on the honeymoon instead."
Everyone celebrates and the credits roll over the picture as Flo and Al peek in the window to make sure everyone's having a good time at their wedding.
Wisecracking, man-chasing Flo was clearly the fa-

Visitation Rights: Mel's mother (played by guest Martha Raye) comes to stay with Alice and Tommy.

Smack!: Mel dares Flo to hit him.

vorite on the show and in fact was rewarded with a sitcom of her own, a midseason replacement during the 1979–1980 season. Actress Polly Holliday, who played Flo, was delighted with her sudden stardom. Hers was a slow road to success, after more than ten years of regional and Off-Broadway work and occasional movie roles (Dustin Hoffman, who directed her in *All Over Town* on Broadway in 1970, later remembered her when he was filming *All the President's Men*, in which she appeared.)

Flo changed Holliday's life. Until *Alice*, there'd never been much demand for her Southern accent, which she'd worked hard at losing during her drama school days. But when she auditioned for Flo, she put the accent back on—and got the part. She said that she was rarely recognized because she never wore her Flo wig (Flo was a redhead; Holliday was a blonde).

When Flo left Mel's Diner for the show of her own, the producers were looking for a new character to take up the comedic slack left by Holliday's absence—and they hired Diane Ladd, the actress who played Flo in the movie *Alice Doesn't Live Here Anymore*. (Vic Tayback also carried over his role of Mel from the film.) Said Holliday: "I have every intention of making *Flo* work as a long-running series. But even if it doesn't succeed, I won't want to return to *Alice*. It's like leaving the nest. Once you do, you don't go back."

One of the things Lavin missed about the difference between the sitcom and the film was that, well, Alice doesn't sing here anymore (except for the show's theme song). Said Lavin: "The original concept of the show was that Alice would do some singing, play the local Ramada Inn, but concepts changed. The network thought the singing dream was too frustrating to work on, and that

people wouldn't want to sit and listen to somebody in a sitcom sing for five minutes. But John Rich, one of the writers on the series, told me that 'So you won't sing on the show. You'll sing on other people's shows.' And he's right."

Alice was always predictable. We knew exactly what kind of jokes were coming and whom they'd be coming from (the nature of the sitcom game, unfortunately). But that could be overlooked on *Alice*, whereas it couldn't be ignored on some of her contemporaries like *Happy Days* and *Three's Company*, where the cheap jokes and pokes were said for their own sake. *Alice's* humor didn't strive for the high of a *M*A*S*H* or a *Taxi*, where every one-liner told you ten things about the person who said it. But underneath *Alice's* sometimes corny jokes and slapstick routines (one of the show's writers, incidentally, was Arthur Marx, Groucho's son), there was something on the show that was missing from so many sitcoms: compassion. *Alice* shows us how Mel, a guy from Brooklyn, and Flo, a gal from cowtown, and Alice, a woman from New Jersey, and Vera, a girl from—outer space?—could get together and—well, be each other's *families*. And that was the important underlying message of *Alice*—that friends are the new family. And what a long step that was from *Ozzie and Harriet*, which told us (without ever telling us) to be kind and respectful and considerate of the people whom we were sentenced to live with by birth (even if we didn't like them). Shows like *All in the Family* (which would have—and possibly did—give old Ozzie a coronary) went on to upset the sitcom structure of family life. But *Alice* went one step beyond: that you can feel warm and familial with someone who'd tell you to . . . well, to *kiss mah grits!*

ALSO RANS

All's Fair

This show had everything going for it—and against it. It was trendy and it was produced by Norman Lear (some say the two are synonymous). The plot: all about a forty-nine-year-old political columnist (conservative) and a twenty-three-year-old freelance photographer (liberal). The age difference, the political difference—all was conflict on this show. Unfortunately there was some conflict between the show and the audience (apparently they weren't watching), and so CBS canceled *All's Fair* after one season. Richard Barrington was played by Richard Crenna (of *Real McCoys* and *Our Miss Brooks* fame); Charlotte Drake—a.k.a. Charley—was played by

All's Fair: *Richard Crenna and Bernadette Peters*

perky Bernadette Peters (who had once attempted to seduce Mike on an episode of *All in the Family*). When Jimmy Carter was elected President, Norman Lear sent Barrington to work for him as a special assistant. Even that couldn't save the show. Or Carter.

Ball Four

Strike Three should have been the title of this turkey—it lasted only about three episodes, and that was about three too many. But here's the plot anyway: Jim Barton (played by Jim Bouton, a former major league pitcher

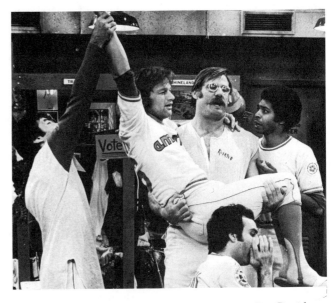

Ball Four *(from left): Jaime Tirelli, Jim Bouton, Ben Davidson, Sam Wright and (seated) unidentified extra*

who wrote a book called *Ball Four*), played a pitcher who was informed—in the locker room, of course; it all seemed to take place in the locker room and smelled like it too—that he was going to write a series of articles on baseball life off the field. The manager and other players weren't exactly wild about the idea, and bla and bla and bla. Bouton also had the distinction of being one of the writers on the show. CBS had the distinction of dropping it.

Blansky's Beauties

Nancy Walker was such a hit as Rhoda's mother (on both CBS's *The Mary Tyler Moore Show* and *Rhoda*) that ABC gave her a contract of her own. And so, she was written out of *Rhoda*—"Ma's taking a trip around the world"—and somehow, she reappeared in February of 1977 as Nancy Blansky, den mother to a bunch of beautiful Las Vegas show girls in a swinging apartment complex. Rhoda should only have known. Two of the girls were Nancy's roommates—Bambi Benton (Caren Kaye) and Ethel "Sunshine" Akalino (Lynda Goodfriend), both of whom took their personas to the sitcom *Who's Watching the Kids* when *BB* folded after three months.

But things weren't all bad. Nancy got to stage the girls' big numbers at the Oasis Hotel, where she saw a lot of her boss, Horace Wilmington (George Pentecost). And Nancy did have a boyfriend, maitre d' Emilio (singer Johnny Desmond). And then there were the kids who lived with Nancy too: her nephews, choreographer Joey DeLuca (Eddie Mekka—on loan from *Laverne and Shirley*, where he played Carmine) and the dirty-young-boy Anthony DeLuca (played by Scott Baio, on loan from

Happy Days), who was constantly trying to "make it" with Bambi, even though he was only twelve years old ("but going on twenty-eight," he would say). As if that weren't enough: also living in the apartment was a rather large Great Dane named Black Jack. Later added to the cast was Pat Morita—he'd been on *Happy Days* as Arnold (owner of the drive-in where the Happy Dayers hung out) and then got his own series *Mr. T. and Tina* (he'd played Mr. T). When that show flopped, he joined Blansky—as the same character with the same name he'd had on *Happy Days*. Talk about musical sitcoms. . . . Several months later, Caren Kaye, Lynda Goodfriend, and Scott Baio would go on to star in another ABC sitcom—about Las Vegas show girls living with young kids: *Who's Watching the Kids*. And, of course, Walker had—five months before she became Blansky—starred in yet another ABC sitcom, *The Nancy Walker Show*, which had been a terrible failure. And so, at the start of the 1977–1978 season, Ida Morgenstern came home. came home.

Busting Loose

Adam Arkin—son of Alan—starred in this sitcom about a nice Jewish engineering school graduate named Lenny Markowitz, who moved away from his overprotective parents (played by Jack Kruschen and Pat Carroll). Lenny moved into a run-down apartment, and his next-door neighbor was Melody, a curvaceous woman who worked for an escort service. There was much chuckling about his apartment—how he didn't have enough money to cover up the ducks on the wallpaper left by the previous tenant. To make money, Lenny got a job as a shoe salesman and worked with a hip black dude named Raymond, and he had lots of buddies, with names like Lester, Allan, Woody, and Vinnie. Eventually he even got a girlfriend, with the strange name of Jackie Gleason. Before she entered the show, though, all the boys left New York for the Catskills to hunt girls. The show was a CBS midseason replacement that itself busted loose after a few short months.

CPO Sharkey

Don Rickles—insult master—scrounged around for years to find the successful sitcom format for his talents. He found it here, for two seasons, anyway. Sort of a *Bilko Goes Bonkers*. Rickles played Otto Sharkey, a twenty-four-year navy veteran, stationed in San Diego. His

CPO Sharkey: *Don Rickles (second from right) is locked in a Tijuana jail.*

company of new recruits—many ethnic types (of course—this was the mid-seventies, after all)—and he tried to "make sailors" out of them. He used his verbal barbs and nasties but, naturally, a softie lurked beneath. Jonathan Daly played Sharkey's immediate supervisor, the long-winded, overbearing Lieutenant Whipple (no relation to the "do-not-squeeze-the-Charmin" Whipple); the base commander was a nice-looking woman named Captain Quinlan (Elizabeth Allen). For its second season (replacing *Sanford Arms*), Sharkey had a new commanding officer, Captain "Buck" Buckner (Richard X. Slattery). The show went off the NBC air in July 1978.

Fish

This was an unusual spin-off—of the hit series *Barney Miller*—because not only did Abe Vigoda play Detective

Fish: *Abe Vigoda and Florence Stanley*

Phil Fish on his own series, for many months he continued playing the dilapidated cop on the *Barney Miller* series. There was a difference, though: *Fish* showed the home life of the detective, and *Barney Miller* was nearly all On The Job. Here was the premise: Fish and his wife, Bernice (Florence Stanley), decided to move out of their New York apartment and into a run-down house, so they could become foster parents to five racially mixed street kids who were, of course, always causing problems. Loomis (Todd Bridges) was the funny guy, a preteen hipster who made friends with a dead cat in Fish's basement. Mike (Lenny Bari) was the oldest, charming and streetwise. Victor Kreutzer (John Cassisi) was a tough guy. Jilly (Denise Miller) was an angelic con artist, and Diane (Sarah Natoli) was a TV addict—not much different from the people who were watching the show. It was all sort of *Welcome Back, Fish*. Psychologist Charlie Harrison (played by one-time child star Barry Gordon) tried to help, but didn't; Fish and the nonstop talker, Bernice, had to deal with everything. But only until June 1978, when ABC evicted them all.

Holmes and Yoyo

Here is the rundown on this ABC sitcom: Alexander Holmes (Richard B. Shull) was an accident-prone policeman who never got hurt himself, but kept sending his partners to the hospital. So, not knowing what to do, the police department assigned him a robot as a partner—Yoyo (named after its inventor, Gregory Yoyonovich), played by John Schuck. Now, Holmes wasn't supposed to know that Yoyo was a computer, but he did. In fact, few on the police force knew it, including Officer Maxine Moon (Andrea Howard) who kept making advances at Yoyo. But Yoyo did have his positive qualities as well as his drawbacks: he weighed 427 pounds, but he had a photographic memory, an independent power source, a silent track compressor, and he could produce color prints. He was sort of the ultimate Xerox machine. He couldn't be injured, although once a bullet hit him, shorting out his rhythm system, causing him to tap dance during a chase. The producer of the program had this to say before its debut: "For over thirty years, we had the marvelous antics of Laurel and Hardy, Abbott and Costello, Hope and Crosby, Martin and Lewis, Gleason and Carney—and then came an unexplainable gap. But now, hopefully, Schuck and Shull will fill the comedy void." They didn't. ABC bumped and dumped the show after only three months.

The Kallikaks

Describing this NBC sitcom will take longer than the show ran, but here goes: Jasper T. Kallikak (David Huddleston) hoped to find fortune. So he moved his family from their native Appalachia (where he'd been a coal miner) to Nowhere, California, a very small town. He'd inherited a two-pump gas station and figured he could improve his economic standing by being his own boss. He was always looking for a way to beat the system (the series' theme song, incidentally, was "Beat the System," sung by Roy Clark) and, actually, Jasper was pretty greedy and conniving. He had an oversexed wife, Venus (Edie McClurg); a social climbing teenage daughter, Bobbi Lou (Bonnie Ebsen, daughter of Buddy, who was Jed Clampett on *The Beverly Hillbillies*); a preteen son, Junior (Patrick J. Peterson), who was a mechanical genius; and a German hired hand named Oscar (Peter Palmer, once Abner in the Broadway *Li'l Abner*).

The Kallikaks: *David Huddleston and Bonnie Ebsen*

Loves Me, Loves Me Not

Okay, here are the details. Dick dated Jane. They weren't sure about their feelings for each other. Neither was the audience. CBS canceled after one month. The end.

The McLean Stevenson Show

Hot off the *M*A*S*H* trail (he had played Lieutenant Colonel Henry Blake), Stevenson changed decades and identities and became Mac Ferguson, a middle-class family man who owned a hardware store in Evanston, Illinois. His two grown kids were living with him and his wife. Here's why: daughter Janet had separated from her husband and moved in along with her two young kids, David and Jason. Son Chris, after not being able to "find himself," bummed around Hawaii and then came back home to return to college part-time, holing up in the basement, which he turned into a bachelor pad. And guess who else lived there? Mac's mother-in-law. The show—which was eagerly awaited to see what Stevenson would do next—lasted only three months on NBC. Soon after, though, it was Goodbye, Mac and *Hello Larry*.

Mr. T. and Tina

Mr. T. was Taro Takahashi (Pat Morita) and Tina was Tina Kelly (Susan Blanchard) and this was their relation-

Mr. T. and Tina: *Susan Blanchard and Pat Morita*

ship: Mr. T. was a hotshot Japanese inventor who had been transferred by his firm from Tokyo to Chicago. Culture shock. But that's not all—he also had to cope with a nutty, Nebraska-born housekeeper named Tina (sort of a *Farmer's Daughter* reversal). Tina was, quite naturally, well-intentioned, but often her ideas clashed with the traditional, male-dominated Japanese society that Mr. T.—and the rest of his entourage—came from. There were other characters too—but to name them would take as long as this show lasted on ABC: one month.

The Nancy Walker Show

This Norman Lear show should have worked. It even had a theme song written by Marvin Hamlisch. And—best of all—it had Nancy Walker (recently transplanted to ABC sitcom via CBS's *Rhoda*) playing Nancy Kitteridge, part-time wife (her husband was in the navy and came home only two months each year) and full-time talent agent, head of her own Nancy Kitteridge Talent Agency, which she ran out of her Hollywood apartment. Then her husband, Lieutenant Commander Kenneth Kitteridge (William Daniels), came home for good and tried to instill order into Nancy's chaotic household. Plus, he wasn't too happy about Nancy's gay male secretary, Terry Folson (Ken Olfson), who lived in the house. Plus, the lieutenant commander thought Nancy should give up her business. As if that weren't enough craziness, Nancy also had a neurotic daughter, Lorraine (played by Beverly Archer, who'd be rewarded with her own sitcom, *We've Got Each Other*), her husband Glen, (James Cromwell), plus Michael (Sparky Marcus, who'd later be on *Grandpa Goes to Washington*), and his daddy, Teddy Futterman

The Nancy Walker Show: *Nancy Walker and Beverly Archer*

(William Schallert)—"boy wonder network TV executive"—modeled, no doubt, after Fred Silverman, his real-life counterpart. The show, however, lasted only three months, and then Walker went on to try again with *Blansky's Beauties* (she played Blansky, not the Beauties) before she returned to The Bronx, where she belonged, as Mother Morgenstern.

Sirota's Court

Michael Constantine—who'd sitcommed it before in the 1966 *Hey, Landlord!* and had played principal Seymour Kaufman on *Room 222* beginning in 1969—got a sitcom of his own with this one. He played Matthew J. Sirota, a night-court judge in a big city. He was different from other judges: he was funny, he was more concerned with practical considerations than legal ones, and he was a "character." (But then, if he hadn't been a character, this would have been a courtroom drama, not a sitcom.) He also seemed to have a sexual appetite—he'd been having an on-again, off-again affair with court clerk Maureen O'Connor (Cynthia Harris) and sometimes it even seemed as though they'd get married. Others who hung around the courtroom: Gail Goodman (Kathleen Miller), a superliberal lawyer who had ideals but not always ideas; DA Bud Nugent (Fred Willard, Martin Mull's partner on *Fernwood*—and later *America— Tonite*), who was vain and incompetent; Sawyer Dabney (Ted Ross), who'd handle any case if there was enough money in it for him; and bailiff John (Owen Bush), who adored the judge. After four months on the bench, *Sirota's Court* was sentenced by NBC to the dead sitcom morgue.

Sugar Time!

This summer comedy series was about three beautiful girls—Maggie (Marianne Black), Diane (Didi Carr), and Maxx (Barbi Benton, *Playboy* centerfold [*sans* staples] who went on to become Hugh Hefner's live-in girlfriend and a regular *Hee Haw*er)—who were trying to make it as rock singers. (They got little help from composer Paul Williams, who wrote original songs for this show.) The trio called themselves Sugar, and shared an apartment in California where they were trying to launch their act— without pay—at a place called Al Marks' Tryout Room. But they all had other jobs to see them through: Maxx was a hatcheck girl; Bronx-born, wiseacre Diane was a dental hygienist, who continually worried whether or not to marry her dentist; practical Maggie taught dancing to

Sugar Time! *(from top): Didi Carr, Barbi Benton and Marianne Black*

children. *Sugar Time!*—which should have been titled *Saccharine Time!*—ran from August to September in 1977, and again in April and May of 1978, both times on ABC.

Szysznyk

This is an example of a summer replacement show that did so well it was renewed for the fall—and then bombed miserably, only to be recalled by CBS two months later. It was the story of Nick Szysznyk (Ned Beatty, the well-

Szysznyk *(from left): Susan Lanier, Olivia Cole, Ned Beatty and Leonard Barr*

regarded movie character actor), a retired marine who was used to discipline and order. Naturally—this being sitcomland—he wasn't getting any of either. Especially not on his job as a playground supervisor at the Northeast Community Center in a poor Washington, D.C., neighborhood. He spent his days coping with government bureaucracy, street kids, and chaos—which all proved challenging to him.

The Tony Randall Show

After years of sitcomming with *Mr. Peepers* and then with Oscar on *The Odd Couple,* Tony Randall finally got his own show, playing a middle-aged, often-stuffy, always-kind Court of Common Pleas judge. As a widower of two years, Walter Franklin was ready for some romance, but he was always worried about being dignified about it. He dated around a bit, but his main Love Interest (as they are called in sitcoms) was Judge Eleanor Hooper (Diana Muldaur). Walter also had a long-time, superaccurate court reporter, Jack Terwilliger (Barney

The Tony Randall Show: *Tony Randall and Brad Savage*

Martin); a sharp, obnoxious secretary, Miss Reubner (Allyn Ann McLerie); another obnoxious person, the ingratiating Mario Lanzo (Zane Lasky); and a nutty housekeeper, Mrs. Bonnie McClellan (Rachael Roberts). Walter also had a family: eighteen-year-old Bobby (Devon Scott the first season, then played by Penny Peyser), and a precocious eleven-year-old son, Oliver (Brad Savage). When the show returned the second season (having been transplanted from ABC to CBS), Hans Conried (once Uncle Tonoose on *The Danny Thomas Show*) played Walter's dad, Wyatt, who thought his son was sort of a stuffed shirt (they didn't get along), but that didn't stop him from moving in. CBS canceled this very funny show in March of 1978.

A Year at the Top

Sitcom mogul Norman Lear and music maven Don (*Rock Concert*) Kirshner teamed up on this sitcom all about the music business (well, not *all* about the music business—how much could you fit in in just five weeks?). Anyway, this was a summer series that kept being delayed and delayed because of production and conceptual troubles (it was originally supposed to have run in January with a totally different cast). It was about two young pop singers who were looking for fame and fortune. Greg (Greg Evigan) and Paul (Paul Shaffer) moved to LA from Boise, Idaho, and were looking for an agent to help them get their Big Break (which, as it turned out, was certainly not being on this show). They did manage to find Frederick J. Hanover (played by Gabriel Dell, who'd been the original owner of *The Corner Bar*), who was sort of Kirshneresque in that he was known for discovering and creating music stars. He offered them a contract—but there was a catch: Hanover was the son of the devil (no reflection on Kirshner) and if they wanted a year at the top as stars, they had to sign away their souls (not to mention all royalties). Greg and Paul never actually signed. CBS quickly renamed this show *Five Weeks at the Bottom.*

1977–1978

Three's Company

The Roller Girls

The Sanford Arms

OFF-SCREEN

9/7 President Carter and Panamanian leader Brigadier General Omar Torrijos Herrera sign accord that gives Panama eventual control over Canal and Canal Zone in 2000.

9/26 Laker Airways completes first transoceanic daily low-fare ($102) flight from London to New York.

10/17 After nineteen months of legal battles, a Supreme Court ruling finally allows supersonic Concorde plane to begin test flights into Kennedy Airport.

10/18 New York Yankees beat Los Angeles Dodgers to capture World Series.

11/21 National Women's Conference in Houston approves twenty-five proposals, including abortion, lesbian rights and the Equal Rights Amendment.

12/27 Prime Minister Menachem Begin returns to Israel after two days of discussion with President Anwar el Sadat at Ismailia, Egypt, aimed at a peace treaty.

1/13 Former Vice President Hubert H. Humphrey dies of cancer at the age of sixty-six.

5/8 David "Son of Sam" Berkowitz, New York City's notorious ".44-calibre killer," pleads guilty to murder charges.

5/26 Legalized gambling begins in Atlantic City, New Jersey.

6/28 Supreme Court rules in the case of *University of California Regents* vs. *Alan P. Bakke* that some affirmative action by college admissions officers to redress past discrimination is constitutional.

FRONT RUNNER

THREE'S COMPANY

> CHRISSY: *I have a two-part question: Why?*
> JACK: *How's that a two-part question?*
> CHRISSY: *We both want to know.*

There are three schools of thought about *Three's Company*. First, that it is, quite simply, the worst piece of sitcom trash that's ever been on television. Second, that it is, quite simply, the worst piece of trash that's ever been on television. Third, that it is, quite simply, the worst piece of trash that's ever been on the face of the earth.

There are, of course, those who feel that the show is some of the above or all of the above. Those who opt for none of the above are usually those people who watch the program—the millions and millions and millions (times fifty) of folks who each week tuned into *Three's Company* and made it one of the most popular shows in the history of television. Popularity-schmopularity. It was also popularity, people argue, that elected Nixon President, that kept the Vietnam war going, and that made *Grease* the longest-running Broadway musical and biggest money-making movie. *Three's Company* was the Pet Rock of sitcoms.

Here's the premise: Two girls—one blonde, one brunette—are looking for a roommate. They discover a boy—a holdout from the going-away party of the last tenants—sleeping in their bathtub. He wants to move in with them. They're leery. He tells them that he's harmless, that he's a homosexual and not interested in sleeping with them. They say okay. Naturally, he isn't a homosexual and is interested in them. But it's all Strictly Platonic (and moronic). The subplot revolves around their impotent landlord and his sexually aggressive wife.

The producers turned their backs on the sensitive sitcom heritage that they'd had over the years with *All in the Family* and *One Day at a Time*; they turned their backs on Norman Lear in favor of abnormal leers. *Three's Company* became a three-ring circus: sex, sexism, and sniggering. It had poor taste, poor writing, and great ratings. Well, there's no accounting for tastelessness. The show was insulting to gays, to office workers (the dumb blonde character was a typist), to florists (the brunette worked in a flower shop), to landlords, to cooks (the boy was in cooking school), and to television viewers in general. *Three's Company* made *Laverne and Shirley* look like *Masterpiece Theatre*.

But enough with the commentary. On with the show (and then, of course, back to the commentary).

First, the cast of characters:
- *Jack Tripper*, a student at a cooking school, is interested mainly in women—specifically, getting them into bed with him. He's sort of a seventies version of Bob Collins (from *Love That Bob*).
- *Janet Wood* is the attractive-but-down-to-earth roommate, who acts as den mother to her two roommates. She's a sensible girl who's just slightly man-crazy. When a woman comes to the door and says she's looking for a man, Janet answers: "Who isn't?"
- *Chrissy Snow* is blonde and pretty and dizzy—sort of a spaced-out cheerleader who, when she decorates a cake, gets it all over her face. When someone says that "I'll take a raincheck on that," Chrissy says something like "I can't wait till it rains . . ." Her father is a preacher and she personifies the old joke about the preacher's daughter.
- *Stanley Roper*, who lives downstairs from them, is their landlord. Also impotent. That's all you have to know.
- *Helen Roper* is Stanley's wife and would very much like to get into his pants. He's got a headache.

Jack Tripper	John Ritter
Janet Wood	Joyce DeWitt
Chrissy Snow	Suzanne Somers
Helen Roper	Audra Lindley (1977–1979)
Stanley Roper	Norman Fell (1977–1979)
Larry	Richard Kline (1978–)
Ralph Furley	Don Knotts (1979–)

• *Ralph Furley* (who replaced the Ropers when they became *The Ropers*) was a sex-starved old-maid-man, whose prurient interests lie in the apartment upstairs.

The show often begins in the landlords'—the Ropers'—apartment underneath the company of three. In their living room, Helen makes jokes about Stanley's lack of sexual prowess. Try this episode on for size:

STANLEY: This house means a lot to me.
HELEN: How come you never say that about *me?*
STANLEY: You're not in a rising market.
HELEN *(after a long pause)*: Neither are you.
(Noise is heard from upstairs.)
STANLEY: There goes that banging again.
HELEN: A little of that never hurt anybody.
STANLEY: Well, it gives me a headache . . .

Mrs. Roper explains that "We tried and tried and tried to have children. I'd have tried a fourth time, but Stanley had a headache . . ." And yet another time they have this exchange:

HELEN: I had a wonderful present for you on your last birthday—I never understood why you didn't want it.
STANLEY: I had a headache . . .

(On the opening credits, Mrs. Roper jumps into bed, leering, and Mr. Roper quickly fakes being fast asleep.)
So Stanley Roper goes upstairs to check on the noise. As he walks in, Jack Tripper, the young stud about the house, whom Roper thinks is gay, has hurt his wrist on the coffee table and is flexing it back and forth.

STANLEY: What are you doing?
JACK: I'm loosening up my wrist.
STANLEY: I didn't know you guys had to practice.

There follows a few minutes more of homosexual jokes. When Chrissy tries to pretend to seduce Jack, she tells Stanley that "I acted as sexy as I could," and he responds with "What do you expect when you send a woman to do a man's job?"
What follows is approximately twenty-two minutes of jokes (followed by wild laughs, leers, and hoots) that mainly concern parts of women's anatomy (especially breasts) and men's pursuit of those parts. For example, when Jack's interested in a girl student in one of his classes, his roommates give him a hard time.

JACK: She happens to be a great cook. No one can touch her pasta.
CHRISSY: I'm sure you'll try.
JACK: She's pure and wholesome and virtuous. Whatever happened to girls like that?
JANET: They all go out with guys like you.

The student comes to cook and asks to see his bedroom.

Roomies: Chrissy helps Jack with his limp wrist.

JACK: Right now the bedroom's dirty.
DEBBY: Will I get to see the bedroom later?
JACK: I'm counting on it . . .

Chrissy's father visits and wants to know where Jack and Debby are.

JANET: Jack's doing a project in the kitchen with this girl.
CHRISSY: Yeah, and they're in there right now, making it . . . oops.

Later, on the sofa with Jack, the girl turns to him:

DEBBY: Jack, shouldn't we be cooking?
JACK: That's what I say *(embraces her)*.

And yet later, when Chrissy asks Jack to help her clean up the apartment:

JACK: I'm entitled to a little rest; I've been working all day over a hot dish.
CHRISSY: Yeah—Debby.

Janet tells Jack she's got to get ready for her date.

JANET: When you take a girl out and you go to get her, don't you like it if she's dressed and ready?
JACK: No . . . just ready.

You want more? You got it.
Once, Janet is passed over for a promotion because, she thinks, the woman who got the job had a better figure.

CHRISSY: What's she got that you haven't got?
JANET: *(spreads her fingers in front of her chest to indicate breasts)*
CHRISSY: Arthritis?

Neighbors: Mrs. Roper and Janet strip off their clothes to protest the closing of a nude beach.

JACK: Stop exaggerating, Janet. You're making mountains out of molehills.

Janet tells the history of her problem: "Once in class the teacher asked the class to locate the great American flatlands. Every single boy pointed to me."

In another episode, Jack talks about geography—hills and valleys—while leering at a girl's breasts and cleavage.

And so forth . . .

It's hard to believe, but *Three's Company*—like *All in the Family* and *Sanford and Son*—was a transatlantic transplant. Over the British Thames network it was called *A Man About the House,* and ran for a long time. The differences: *A Man About the House* was raunchier and the girls weren't as attractive, which somehow made it funnier.

A little history: On March 15—a Thursday night—in 1977, ABC presented a trial four-week run of *Three's Company* following *Happy Days.* It was a happy night for ABC; both shows did very well. So the network ordered a whole batch of *Three's Companys* for the following season. The show had great impact. Not only did it set journalists' typewriters in motion all over the country—"mindless," "instantly disposable," "the dirtiest show on the air," were some of the names they called it—but it created a whirlwind of controversy. Not about quality television programming, unfortunately, but about smut on the small screen. The network didn't pay much attention, since TV was getting heat to cut down on violence; they cut down on violence, all right, and replaced it with sex. Said the program vice-president over at ABC: "Admittedly the subject matter is spicy, but the program passes all our standards and practices criteria and therefore we find it acceptable."

Most noticeable, though, was that the show created new TV stars (as evidenced by weekly blaring headlines of the covers of the *National Star* and *National Enquirer*).

John Ritter, son of Tex, "the Singing Cowboy," played Jack, and he himself admitted he was a "ladies' man" before he married and settled down. Before *Three's Company,* he had played the small role of—of all things—the minister on *The Waltons.* He also had been the neophyte minister who married Ted and Georgette on *MTM.* Said Ritter: "I'm interested in laughter, real laughter. I give to the people and they give to me. But—me, a TV star? It's all pretty funny. Imagine having an audience for what I do. I know a lot of burning geniuses with no one to listen to them but their wives. I've got to be the luckiest guy in the world."

Joyce DeWitt (Janet) went to graduate school at UCLA and acted in every play she could get into. She graduated to parts on *Baretta* and, she said, the turning point was getting a permanent on her hair. "It was the best thing that ever happened to me. Because it took me out of the category of the long-haired lovelies, where I could never get a part, and into the category of the short, jerky girl." She got the part of the smart girl on *Three's Company* when she was twenty-eight. Said DeWitt: "I think of my ability as a gift, a precious commodity of which I am the custodian. I won't do something if I don't love it. I am an actress."

When asked how the "actress" could justify working on something as fluffy as *Three's Company,* she said, "I make my own choices; I'm helping to make America laugh. There's a lot of physical comedy in *Three's Company,* and I don't begin to say we're as good as Chaplin and some of his contemporaries, but we *are* in that tradition. People are turned on by what we do. I mean, what's to be ashamed of if you can make America laugh?"

The true luminary of the show, however, was sizzling sex-kitten Suzanne Somers, who played the dumb but sexy Chrissy. With posters, T-shirts, lunchpails, and dolls with her face on it, she was one of the biggest biodegradable products of television since Farrah Fawcett-Majors. In fact, she was the "product" of starmaker Jay Bernstein, who had also plotted and manufactured the careers of Farrah Fawcett and Susan St. James. Married for the second time to Alan Hamel, a Canadian talk show host, and the mother of a son she had when she was married at seventeen, Somers supported herself by doing some modeling and lightweight acting (she played the blonde in the Thunderbird in the film *American Graffiti*), and had made nine unsold TV pilots. She was one of 250 young women who auditioned for the part of Chrissy. Said Somers: "I have a sexy quality about me that often makes people not take me seriously. I always have to overcome the dumb blonde stereotype." And so she wrote two books of "how to get more out of life" poetry, as well as a novel called *Some People Live More Than Others.* About the series she said: "When I see the crazy faces I make in the show and the way I hold my hands sometimes, I begin to wonder how I got anywhere at all." But just in case, she wrote a cookbook for something to fall back on.

Just-Good-Friends: Mr. Roper wakes up to find himself in bed with Jack.

There was a lot of talk about rivalry between DeWitt and Somers on the set (Somers was easily the winner in the popularity pageant). DeWitt denied it: "There was a magazine article that said Suzanne and I wouldn't speak to each other except through a third person. Well, the day we heard that, I think she was rubbing my feet at the time. Suzanne is a very nice girl. She has wonderful taste. If she compliments something I'm wearing, I feel good all day about it. But it's fair to say we are different people. She started in modeling. I'm a dramatic actress. That's not against her, that's not against me. There's a difference in the way we're going about things. I want to be careful. It's different with Suzanne. If Suzanne is anything at all, it's smart. She's goodhearted and intelligent and she knows there's a new blonde in town every year. She knows that shooting down last year's sex goddess is the nature of the business. So that's why she has every right to do her things the way she's doing them. I love it when she comes on the set and she's thrilled about one of her new posters."

Hmmm . . .

But it doesn't matter anyway. Because the program—with lines like "I married you for better or worse—when's it gonna start getting better?"—topped the rating polls. In fact, the British returned the compliment and soon after began airing *Three's Company*. And the Ropers—who should have enrolled at Masters and Johnson—soon got their own series, *The Ropers* (in Britain, there was a Roperesque spin-off called *George and Mildred*).

STANLEY: You gay?
JACK: Well . . . sometimes I'm quite depressed.

It was dialogue like that one that sent the critics crawling to their typewriters (not all of them; *McCall's* ran a cover story on whether *Three's Company* was the reason so many men were living with two women; another publication linked *The Ropers'* success to the enormous number of impotent men in this country). But mainly, writers hadn't much nice to say about the series because of the writing. "Why can't the writing be as good as *All in the Family*?"

Guess what? The same writers who wrote *All in the Family* were responsible for *Three's Company*. Which, in a sense, isn't surprising at all. *All in the Family* broke boundaries and barriers and gave TV sitcoms permission for permissiveness. *Three's Company* was like a little kid who'd learned a few dirty words and couldn't keep his mouth shut; *All in the Family* was the permissive parent whose child grew up to abuse the freedom its parents fought so hard for. Because Archie Bunker is the true parent of *Three's Company;* if he'd been smart, he'd have told them to "stifle yourself" . . . three times.

ALSO RANS

Baby, I'm Back

Demond Wilson—formerly the "son" in *Sanford and Son*—came back in *Baby, I'm Back*, all about a man who reunites with his family seven years after deserting his wife. Funny, huh? Well, the viewers didn't think so either, and the show popped off the air seven months after it popped on as a midseason CBS replacement. Wilson played Raymond Ellis, who not only tried to rekindle a romance with his ex-wife (played by Denise Nicholas), after she had had him declared legally dead, but he had to contend with a mother-in-law who hadn't much liked him when he was alive the first time around. Plus, a sitcomesque hitch: his wife was now engaged to a Pentagon official. And then—have you had enough yet?—Ray was continually trying to have himself legally declared alive. Which was more than CBS could do with this show.

The Betty White Show

Oh, Lou! Oh, Mary! Oh, Ted! Where were you when Betty White—formerly Sue Ann Nivens from the *Mary Tyler Moore* years—needed you? Working on your own shows, probably. And you might have been better off. But in case you missed *The Betty White Show*, here's the story: Bitchy-sweet Joyce Whitman (White) and dizzy Mitzi Maloney (Georgia Engel, née Georgette Franklin Baxter) were roommates on this spoof of—once again—television and the people who worked on it. White played a fortyish movie actress whose career had hit the skids. Then she was offered the starring role in a new series, *Undercover Woman* (a spoof on Angie Dickinson's *Police Woman* that reportedly didn't much please Ms. Dickinson). But—naturally—the director turned out to be her sardonic, antagonistic ex-husband, John Elliot (John Hillerman). And there were other characters who were, of course, real characters: Tracy Garrett (Caren Kaye), Joyce's co-worker on the TV show's TV show, who was young and sexy and ambitious; Fletcher Huff (Barney Phillips), a flaky actor who played the police chief on *Undercover Woman*; Hugo Muncy (Charles Cyphers), who was Joyce's stunt "woman," and Doug Porterfield (played by Alex Henteloff), who was the censor from the network (the show actually said that this goofy idiot was

The Betty White Show *(from left): John Hillerman, Betty White and Georgia Engel*

from CBS, the show's real network). *The Betty White Show*, produced by the MTM stable of terrific writers, was several notches above run-of-the-mill sitcoms of the time. A very funny show—and another example of a show "too good" to run too long. CBS gave it the ax after only half a season, which many feel was only half a chance.

Carter Country

Carter Country was Jimmy's home and, for a while anyway, the country was Carter country. The situation: a racial comedy set in the small Georgia town of Clinton

Carter Country *(from left): Harvey Vernon and Kene Holliday*

Corners (right down the lane from Plains). Chief Roy Mobey (Victor French) was the lovable redneck police chief (it was Archie Bunker who made it possible for "lovable" and "redneck" *not* to be a contradiction in terms). He had a sharp black deputy, Sergeant Curtis Baker (Kene Holliday), who had been trained in big-time police tactics in New York. There were conflicts—racial, and urban vs. rural—but the two had a basic respect for each other. Others on the force: Cloris Phebus (Barbara Cason), a man-hungry policeperson; Deputy Harley Puckett (Guich Koock); and Deputy Jasper DeWitt, Jr. (Harvey Vernon), a "good ole boy." There was also a mayor—chubby Teddy Burnside (Richard Paul), a mama's boy who was elected because nobody else wanted the job. Curtis' girlfriend, Lucille (Vernee Watson), was the mayor's secretary. Some thought this sitcom was funny. But not quite as funny as the Carter administration. All courtesy of ABC.

The Harvey Korman Show: *Harvey Korman and Susan Lawrence*

Free Country

We were all expecting big things from Rob Reiner. First, he was the son of creative genius Carl Reiner, who brought us, among other things, *The Dick Van Dyke Show*. Plus, he was an intelligent alumnus of *All in the Family*. So when he announced he was going to quit that series for some very "special projects," we all expected them to be special. The first one was called *Free Country*, in which Reiner played a dual role, that of a Lithuanian immigrant at a young age, and then at age eighty-nine. Reiner opened each series as the elderly Joseph Bresner, recalling his days when he was a new immigrant. Then—flash—the scene would shift to the Lower East Side in New York in the early 1900s, where we would meet his wife, Anna (Judy Kahan), and watch them struggle to adapt and adjust to their new homeland. There were many articles in magazines and newspapers about how Reiner—who also co-produced and co-wrote the series—took hours to put on his old-man makeup. Fortunately for us all, he only had to do it five times.

Reiner, however, was left with bitter feelings about the experience. "I gave them a show that was, in terms of situation comedy, the most unique thing ABC had ever done. I told them, 'You are dealing with a strange animal here. It's not *Mork and Mindy*. It's got to be handled carefully.' I was doing a real look at life through the eyes of an immigrant." He said that ABC was "scared of it. They put it on in the summer. And they put on only five segments. I asked to do thirteen. *All in the Family* didn't click until its sixteenth episode." After *Free Country*, Reiner went into directing, writing and producing feature films.

The Harvey Korman Show

Comedy wonderman Harvey Korman slipped on his own second banana on *The Carol Burnett Show* and decided to go it on his own (to be replaced by Dick Van Dyke, after which Burnett's variety show fell apart.) Korman's first sitcom vehicle on ABC was this series, in which he played an out-of-work actor looking for a job. But not just any actor—an out-and-out ham named Harvey Kavanaugh, who lived in an old house with his daughter. Things happened to him. For example, once he answered an ad for a leading man and ended up being an escort. Another time he refused to learn to drive, and started hitchhiking. Once, he helped foil a bank robbery by cosigning a loan for a bungling bandit. Then there was the time he guest-starred on a kids' TV show—playing a carrot. Well, not great situations, but Korman, as always, was wonderful. Unfortunately, we only got about four episodes of the program before Harvey, once again, went looking for other work. The real Harvey found it—in the movies. Said Korman in 1979 about his series: "It didn't work, so I retired from the TV business. There doesn't seem to be anything around on TV that's fun."

Husbands, Wives and Lovers

Comedienne Joan Rivers got the bright idea for this one. *H,W&L* followed the lives of five couples—all friends—who lived in the San Fernando Valley suburbs outside of LA. Murray Zuckerman (Stephen Pearlman) was a traveling salesman with a pharmaceutical company and spent much of his time out of town; Harry Bellini (Eddie Barth) was a self-taught garbage truck tycoon with a young and naive second wife, Joy (Lynne Marie Stewart). Lennie (Mark Lonow) was Harry's younger brother, who was living with Rita DeLatorre (Randee Heller), and together they ran a stylish boutique; Ron Willis (Ron Rifkin) was a dentist who had a friendly relationship with his estranged wife, Helene (Jesse Welles); Dixon Carter Fielding (Charles Siebert) was Ron's best friend, who had represented Helene in the separation proceedings; his wife, Courtney (Claudette Nevins), shopped and shopped and shopped. Confusing? Well, it was for a lot of viewers too; the show ran three months on CBS. But, once again, it proved that a sitcom that's an hour long—as this one was—just doesn't seem to be able to make it.

Joe and Valerie

After *Saturday Night Fever* became such a big movie hit, TV took the hint and started its own disco sitcom: *Joe and Valerie*, which did not have John Travolta (that was another show), but, instead, starred Paul Regina and Char Fontane, as two kids who fall in love at a New York City disco. They were clearly In Love, but they clearly had problems, mainly because of their nutty friends: Joe shared an apartment with the macho Frankie Berganski (Bill Beyers) and simpleminded Paulie Barone (David Elliott); Valerie lived at home with her divorced mom, Stella (Pat Benson), and had a man-hungry friend, Thelma Medina (Donna Ponterotto). Then, by day, Joe worked at his father Vincent's plumbing store (Travolta had worked in a hardware store), and Valerie was a clerk at a cosmetics counter. At night they both went out dancing. So, apparently, did the viewers; NBC canceled this show after only a few episodes.

On Our Own

This sitcom had the distinction of being the first one produced in New York since—well, perhaps since *Car 54, Where Are You?* was filmed in The Bronx in the early sixties. When David Susskind, the show's producer, announced *On Our Own*, TV insiders predicted a renaissance of TV production in New York (especially on the tail of live-from-New York's *Saturday Night Live*). Unfortunately it didn't work out that way and New York television production remained limited mainly to some syndicated game shows and soap operas. But *On Our*

On Our Own: *Michael Tucci and (second row, from left) Georgann Johnson, Bess Armstrong, Dixie Carter and (foreground) Lynnie Greene*

Own—the story of two young working women trying to make it in Manhattan—showed real promise: it was better written and better acted than most of its contemporaries. But it remained marginal in the ratings.

On Our Own was the story of Maria Teresa Bonino (Lynnie Greene), a Nice Catholic Girl, and Julia Peters (Bess Armstrong), a nice WASP, who were both promoted from secretarial positions they'd held at an ad agency to Real Jobs: Maria was art director, Julia was a copywriter. Sure, they were green behind the ears, but they were really eager to Make It in Manhattan (and they certainly went about it with more vigor and passion than their sitcom predecessor Ann Marie, who'd tried to Make It in Manhattan on *That Girl*). Naturally, though, they had the requisite loonies to contend with: A worldly, sexy secretary named April Baxter (Dixie Carter), TV commercial producer Eddie Barnes (John Christopher Jones), and the head of the agency, Toni McBain (Gretchen Wyler), who had to report to her boss, the dumb J. M. Bedford (Bob Randall). The show lasted a solitary season . . . and that was that for New York TV sitcom production. For a while.

Operation Petticoat

Operation Petticoat

No: Operation Mind-Change. This show—which sank in the ratings and should have sunk at sea—was another example of a total cast change, midshow, but with the title staying the same. Anyway, here's what it was about: During World War II, in the Pacific, Lieutenant Commander Matthew Sherman (John Astin, formerly Gomez on *The Addams Family*) wanted to see some of the action before it was over. So he was assigned to command a submarine, *Sea Tiger*, that, much to his dismay, was sunk at seaside when he arrived to find it. He started painting it—first with pink undercoating—and then, before he could apply the second coat, was called out to sea to avoid an air raid. And so, the navy's first pink sub. Along for the ride were five army nurses whom he'd rescued, and a wheeler-dealer supply officer, Lieutenant Nick Holden (Richard Gilliland), who wanted to avoid action as much as Sherman wanted to find it. So much for Situation One.

The following fall, they were all gone. There was a new skipper—Lieutenant Commander Haller (Robert Hogan) and a bunch of new (and not necessarily improved) zanies. This time, *Sea Tiger* was assigned to patrol the Pacific for downed airmen and sailors. Sort of a *M*A*S*H* afloat. It sank, and the new situation comedy with the old name was canceled after four episodes. An interesting note, though: the show was based on the 1959 movie starring Cary Grant and Tony Curtis; Curtis' daughter Jamie Lee played one of the nurses.

Quark

This is another of those sitcoms that takes longer to tell than it ran (which was less than two months on NBC, starting in late February 1978 as a midseason replacement). Anyway, here's the poop: *Quark* was a parody on all those space adventure epics, so popular because of the great success of *Star Wars*. This, however, was no *Star Wars*. It took place in the year 2222 A.D. on a giant space station called Perma 1. It was there that Adam Quark (played by Richard Benjamin, who played He in *He and She* on that sitcom ten years before) was given command of an important mission: to clean up all the trash in outer space. His assignments came from The Head—no, not a toilet, but a disembodied head that governed the universe and was seen only on a TV screen (not unlike *Quark* . . . ah, how TV imitates . . . TV). Anyway, Quark also received assignments from Otto Palindrome (Conrad Janis, who'd later play Mindy's father for one season on yet another outer-spaced-out show, *Mork and Mindy*), who was the fussy head architect of Perma 1. Quark's crew consisted of first officer Jean/Gene (a transmute who was both fish and foul, sexually speaking); a humanoid vegetable named Ficus; two cute clones, Betty 1 and Betty 2 (no one was sure which one was cloned from which); and Andy the Robot, a walking junkpile. Naturally, Quark had other adventures (although obviously not too many of them), and the program blended four qualities: sex, jokes, slapstick—and bad ratings.

The Roller Girls

It was just a matter of time. When planning situation comedies, network officials and producers would go anywhere for situations (hoping the comedy would fall in place later). This time they went too far: The Roller Girls were . . . well, roller girls. The Pittsburgh Pitts was an all-women's roller derby team, owned and managed by the crafty and conniving Don Mitchell (played by Terry Kiser), who was always trying to bail his team (and his money) out of bad times. In the TV era of sexy-looking girls (*Charlie's Angels* and *Three's Company*), the roller girls were more of the same—but inept. They were an ethnically-mixed crew, consisting of a black girl, a dizzy blonde, an Eskimo-American (possibly sitcom's first), and several others. Howie Devine (James Murtaugh), a down-and-out opera commentator, was the team's announcer. The Pittsburgh Pitts was a good name for this show—because, as they said back then, it was "the pits."

NBC thought so too, and rolled the crew out of town after only three episodes.

The Sanford Arms

No, this one wasn't about Sanford and Son finally reaching out and embracing each other. Just the opposite. Redd Foxx and Demond Wilson had split *Sanford and Son* for more money and more freedom. That left the producers with a show, but no stars. So they went across the street to the rooming house owned by Sanfords' Aunt Esther (LaWanda Page) and kept the supporting players to become this show's stars. The new lead was a guy named Phil Wheeler (Theodore Wilson), a widower with two teenaged kids. So he put a down payment on the Sanford property—the house, junkyard, and the rooming house—and tried to convert it to a nice residential hotel. Also on the show: Esther's husband, Woody (Raymond Allen); Fred's friend Grady (Whitman Mayo), and his wife, Dolly (Norma Miller); and several others. Neither the rooming house nor the show was very successful, and NBC decided to forget the whole thing after less than one month.

The San Pedro Beach Bums

Our Boat—a houseboat in California—was the locale of this sitcom, all about five beach bums, buddies since high school (it's a wonder they ever graduated—but then, the show never actually said they did). Here's who they were: confident Buddy (Christopher Murney), the group's leader; shy and nervous Dancer (John Mark Robinson), who couldn't sit still; Stuf (Stuart Pankin),

San Pedro Beach Bums *(from left, standing): Jeffry Druce, Chris Murney, Darryl McCullough; (sitting): Stuart Pankin and John Mark Robinson*

who was a compulsive eater; muscular-but-gentle Moose (Darryl McCullough); and Boychick (Chris De Rose), the heartthrob of the bunch. Exactly three months after the show's debut, ABC told them to stop loitering and sent them into the water for a long, long swim.

Soap

Soap: *Katherine Helmond and Robert Guillaume*

Soap—that's what some people thought this sitcom should have its mouth washed out with. Even before its debut on September 13, 1977, there was more controversy surrounding this spoof on soap operas than all the Norman Lear shows put together. In fact, ABC received 22,000 letters about the show (before it had even aired) and only four were in favor of it. That wasn't all: ABC affiliates were being picketed for planning to run *Soap*, and some sponsors were being urged to boycott the show (some even did). Some affiliates refused to air it, and many ran it late at night. The biggest opposition to *Soap* came from religious groups (including the all-powerful National Council of Churches). Reverend Everett Parker, a longtime critic of television, had this to say about *Soap:* "It's a deliberate effort to break down any resistance to whatever the industry wants to put into prime time. . . . Who else besides the churches is going to stand against the effort of television to tear down our moral values and make all of us into mere consumers?" ABC retaliated, calling the show a "breakthrough in TV comedy." Others thought that *Soap* was just an ongoing dirty joke. Which of course it was.

But morality aside, here's the story of *Soap:* It was all about two families—the wealthy Tates and the lower-middle-class Campbells. Chester Tate (Robert Mandan) was a stuffed-shirt businessman who liked sleeping with women who weren't his wife, Jessica (Katherine Helmond), who was a stupid idiot. They had three children: Corrine (Diana Canova), who was curvy and used her body to get what she wanted; quiet and conservative Eunice (Jennifer Salt); and Billy (Jimmy Baio), a fourteen-year-old brat. Also living with them was Jessica's father, the Major (Arthur Peterson), who crawled around on the floor wearing his old army uniform (he thought he was still fighting the great war). They also had an insolent and obnoxious black servant and cook named Benson (Robert Guillaume), who commented on what was going on (during the 1979–1980 season, he got a spin-off of his own called *Benson*).

Across town was Jessica's sister, Mary Dallas Campbell (Cathryn Damon), and her working-class husband, Burt (Richard Mulligan), who didn't know what to do about his two sons: Danny (Ted Wass), who was part of the Mafia) and Jodie (who was gay). Everyone had sex on the mind (and the body). But then, 1977–1978 was the Season of Sex (witness the success of *Three's Company*, a silly sex farce, also on ABC that season).

The truth is that after watching some of the daytime soaps (which are certainly in The Family Hour), the goings-on there are much more detrimental to the mental health. At least in *Soap* the sex is a joke; on the real soaps it's all serious. The real immorality of *Soap*, many people thought, was not its subject matter, but how stupid it was. Still, others thought that *Soap* was superb.

Tabitha

As hard as it is to believe, *Tabitha* was a rip-off of *The Mary Tyler Moore Show*—but in this case, Mary was a witch. That's right: witch. You see, Tabitha (Lisa Hartman) was the daughter of Darrin and Samantha Stevens of *Bewitched*, the product of a very mixed marriage. In November of 1977, she spun off and got a job as a television production assistant at station KLXA in California. She worked for producer Marvin Decker (Mel Stewart) and Paul Thurston (Robert Urich), an ineptly dumb but handsome newscaster. (Sound familiar?) Also there was her brother Adam (David Ankrum), who was a fellow employee. Her meddlesome Aunt Minerva (Karen Morrow) would pop in for a little witchcraft. Like her mother before her, if Tabitha wanted to get her own way, all she had to do was twitch her nose. Unfortunately, all the twitching in the world couldn't help the show's ratings, and it was thrown into the caldron at the end of the season.

The Ted Knight Show

It was the WJM-TV reunion in Minneapolis and everybody was there. Let's see now: Mary was getting ready to

unveil what would become two unsuccessful variety shows. Betty White and Georgia Engel had tried it for a while with *The Betty White Show* and failed. Gavin MacLeod was now happily ensconced on *Love Boat*. Cloris Leachman had fizzled on *Phyllis*. Valerie Harper was still trying with *Rhoda*. Ed Asner was still *Lou Grant*. But *Ted*—where was Ted?

The answer came on April 8, 1978, when Ted Knight starred in *The Ted Knight Show*, in which he played Roger Dennis, head of Dennis Escorts, a posh dating service in Manhattan, staffed by shapely young ladies. Ted clucked over them like a mother hen. Also on hand: his no-nonsense brother Burt (Normann Burton), who had financed the operation and saddled it with his wise-cracking wife, Dottie (Iris Adrian), as receptionist. Others in the cast: Roger's college-age son, Winston (Thomas Leopold), who was trying to make time with girls and make it in the business (one and the same, perhaps). There was also a mailman, Hobart (Claude Stroud) who had designs on Dottie. Unfortunately for Ted, the whole thing—the dating service, his sitcom, everything—bombed after one month on CBS.

And that, gang, is what happened to Ted.

We've Got Each Other

This one had an interesting premise: that two plain-jane people could fall in love and have an interesting relationship—hopefully, interesting enough to the millions of viewers CBS hoped to attract. Also, their marriage was a reversal of roles: Stuart Hibbard (Oliver Clark, who'd been one of Bob Hartley's groupie neurotics on *The Bob Newhart Show*) worked at home as a copywriter for the "Herman Gutman Mail Order Catalogue" (which was chock full of useless gadgets) and did most of the cooking. His wife, Judy (Beverly Archer, once Nancy Walker's whining daughter on *The Nancy Walker Show*), commuted each day to LA, where she was assistant to professional photographer Damon Jerome (Tom Poston, who'd also been on *Newhart* as Bob's buddy the Peeper, and later went on to play the cranky neighbor on *Mork and Mindy*), who was a great cameraman, but a lousy businessman, and so was totally dependent on Judy. Naturally, Stuart and Judy had the nutty neighbor at home (Ken Redford, played by Martin Kove) and at work (self-centered model Dee Dee Baldwin, played by Joan Van Ark). The office secretary, Donna (Red Woods), tried to keep peace. CBS canceled the show after thirteen weeks.

1978–1979

Mork and Mindy

Delta House

Taxi

OFF-SCREEN

9/7 Presidents Sadat and Prime Minister Begin sign accords providing for negotiation of full peace treaty between Israel and Egypt within three months.

9/28 Pope John Paul I dies of heart attack after only thirty-four days as Pontiff, the shortest reign in nearly 400 years; replaced by Polish Pope John Paul II.

10/6 Senate votes to extend the states' ratification deadline for Equal Rights Amendment thirty-nine months from the original March 22, 1979, date.

11/20 In Jonestown, 911 men, women and children apparently commit suicide by drinking a mixture of Kool-Aid and cyanide on the orders of cult leader Reverend Jim Jones.

12/9 Golda Meir, former Prime Minister of Israel, dies at age of eighty, after suffering from leukemia for twelve years.

12/16 President Carter announces an "historic agreement" under which US and China would establish diplomatic relations on January 1.

3/26 Prime Minister Begin and President Sadat sign formal peace treaty at White House to end state of war existing between Israel and Egypt for more than thirty years.

3/28 An accident at Three Mile Island Nuclear Power Plant near Harrisburg, Pennsylvania, releases above-normal levels of radiation into the atmosphere.

5/13 The New York *Times* reports that summer plans for millions of American motorists are in turmoil because of falling supplies and rising prices of gasoline.

5/25 All 272 passengers and crew members aboard are killed as an American Airlines DC-10 bound for Los Angeles crashes shortly after takeoff from Chicago—the crash is worst disaster in US aviation history.

FRONT RUNNERS

MORK AND MINDY

MINDY: *Walk faster, Mork.*
MORK: *Oh—you want the Evelyn Wood version.*

It's a common misconception that TV producers would like everyone in the country—the world—to watch their sitcoms. Not so. Actually, each sitcom—even if it is watched by 21,000,000 viewers—is designed to appeal to a specific part of the TV audience. There's a giant computer up there that tangos and tap dances around with the ratings, trying to determine what kind of shows will appeal to what kind of viewer (and therefore sell more Twinkies, feminine hygiene spray, or cornflakes). That doesn't mean, for example, that *Chico and the Man* was designed just to appeal to Chicanos, or that *Alice* was manufactured to get the waitress audience in Phoenix. It's not that specific. But there is a definite design to some sitcoms. For example, *Happy Days* was pieced together to appeal to the big, glutted, beer-filled potbelly of Middle America. *The Mary Tyler Moore Show* had hoped (and succeeded) in appealing to a more sophisticated, educated audience. *Three's Company*, of course, was designed to appeal to cretins and mental mutants.

But for some reason—no, for *one* reason—*Mork and Mindy* appealed to everybody. And the reason wasn't Mindy. In fact, many contended, the show should have been retitled *Mork and Mork* (not that Mindy was so bad or anything; it's just hard to play straight girl to TV's Jesus). The reason wasn't even Mork—it was Robin Williams.

Robin Williams was the star of the moment, truly an overnight sensation. That "overnight" was the evening of Thursday, September 14. By Friday, Williams was the hottest thing since John Travolta . . . Henry Winkler . . . Archie Bunker . . . *Lucy*. He was hot.

The show's premise? Oh, yeah. It was about an alien from a planet called Ork who came to earth—specifically, Boulder, Colorado—because he was a misfit on his own planet. (Why? Because he had a sense of humor and Orkians were supposed to be emotionless.) So they sent him here to study earthlings, whose crazy customs they had never been able to understand.

It was really a spin-off of *Happy Days*, in which Mork, in February 1978, landed—in Milwaukee, in the fifties, of all places and times—to kidnap Richie. The episode was so popular that they gave Mork—and Williams—their own show.

And it was Williams' own show. He was a human yo-yo, a spinning top that would not stop, a dazzling, dizzying mimic and mime whose inspired insanity and cockeyed outlook exploded in fast, furious routines, pratfalls, and bursts of foreign and unknown languages. Although *Mork and Mindy* was part of the same sitcom factory that churned and turned out *Happy Days* and *Laverne and Shirley*, Williams insisted that he improvise much of his role, and so he did. He'd draw from popular culture—he was a sponge—and he'd throw in references to Eastern religion and est, the gas crisis and old surf movies, "surfs up" and "gusto." Before he landed on earth, Mork—who was hundreds of years old—must have spent most of his adult life watching American television.

He arrived in a giant egg, carrying with him an absurd language he was never to part with: *Nanoo-nanoo* (which meant hello), *nimnul* (which meant jerk), *shazbot*, *grebble* and a grabbag of other Orkania. *"Toad-tush,"* he'd call someone he wanted to insult.

Mork	Robin Williams
Mindy	Pam Dawber
Frederick McConnel	Conrad Janis (1978–1979)
Cora Hudson	Elizabeth Kerr (1978–1979)
Eugene	Jeffrey Jacquet
Bickley	Tom Poston
Remo DaVinci	Jay Thomas (1979–)
Jean DaVinci	Gina Hecht (1979–)
Nelson Flavor	Jim Staahl (1979–)
Voice of Orson	Ralph James

Special Delivery: Mork's luggage arrives from Ork.

After he walked out of the egg, he got tired and later went to sleep—hanging by his feet in Mindy's closet. He sat on his head. He drank orange juice through his fingers, which of course could burp. "My father was an eyedropper and my mother was a sterile dish," he once explained. Soon, though, he became domesticated and learned to sleep in Mindy's dark, dusty attic instead of her closet (she needed it for her clothes, after all).

Mork had been sent from Ork—his home planet—to learn about earth culture, and he was a quick study. He was a pop-culture sponge. When things got eerie, he'd hum the theme from *Twilight Zone*. When Mindy's grandmother talked about loving others, Mork looked at her in awe: "What a McKuen-like thing to say." In order to learn about earth behavior, Mork would talk to anyone—and anything. He'd been known to converse with a moose head for hours, and to discuss the state of the world with his space suit. He was a commentator, a barometer on how well we earth-types were doing (not very well, apparently). He couldn't understand, for example, how we can make love *and* war, how we're slaves to our emotions and yet we're afraid to say how we feel. Maybe he didn't understand why people argue. He didn't get the point of locking people up when they'd committed crimes.

MORK: I know about jail. It's when you get free food, free clothes, and no rent.
PRISONER: It sounds better the way you say it. I got caught shoplifting.
MORK: Wow, you must be strong!

His innocence, his naiveté, played a big part in his appeal. And because he was basically a child, a fully grown earth-infant, he was always learning things we thought everybody knew. "The garbage man told me never to lie on the curb on pickup days," Mork said one morning. "I was watching some ants mug a grasshopper."

And the next morning, someone asked what he'd done on a date last night. "We went to a big parking lot with a big TV in the front." When asked what he brought his date, he said, "Five dollars and some vegetation."

DATE: I think I'd like a little wine.
MORK: All right, if you insist—WAAAAA.

A typical Orkian Joke:
Q.: How many Martians does it take to screw in a lightbulb?
A.: Eight-point-two.

At the end of each episode, Mork would conjure up the spirit of Orson—"Your Immenseness" or "Your Fattitude," Mork would call him—to report on his week's learnings. Out of his civvies—which consisted of a striped shirt, baggy pants, and luminous suspenders—and into his red space suit with silver boots—Mork and Orson would wax philosophical. Shades of George Burns stepping aside and talking to us. It was here that the laugh-track quieted down and the writers started working on our emotions.

In one early classic episode, Mork lets his emotions out (a *nanoo* no-no for Orkians). "Something happened last night that's going to affect the rest of my life, if I live that long," he tells Mindy. "I had talking pictures in my sleep." Mindy: "You mean you had a *dream*." Mork: "Well, I know it wasn't a movie, because when I woke up, there was no gum under my seat."

Orkians are not supposed to have any emotions or dreams, "but sometimes I let them slip out, flashing them in the raincoat of my mind," Mork confesses. Mindy cajoles him into letting his emotions out—"you're dead to me without them"—and he gets ready: "Mindy, run for your life—the emotions are coming!"

And do they ever come—in a frenetic, frantic, split-second change of facial expressions and voices, ranging from Peter Lawford to Peter Lorre to Peter Pan. "I've done things that would embarrass Idi Amin," Mork confesses "the morning after" he and his emotions ran wild. Finally, Mindy realizes she has prompted him to go too far, and she says: "Mork, you'd better get your emotions under control or you're going to be scooped up by a net." Mork smiles and answers: "Frankie Avalon didn't mind in all those movies when he was scooped up by Annette—har har *har* har." Soon he is back to normal—or abnormal.

Mork, Mork, Mork. What about Mindy? Although the critics were kind to her—the way one would be polite to a visiting relative—Mindy wasn't paid much attention to. And so, neither was Pam Dawber, the young actress who held the part. Unfortunately, Mindy was nice and straight and cute and . . . and boring. "I have to admit," Dawber said during the first season's filming, "that I'm getting a bad taste in my mouth about the way things are going. It bothers me that I'm being pushed into the background. I keep telling myself that I shouldn't be annoyed, that it's just my ego being hurt. But the facts are certainly there. Robin is really unique, and I wouldn't dare try matching him joke for joke. But nobody could. I'm not a comedienne anyway. The way I see my Mindy role is that I'm sort of an anchor—someone to give the show breathing room as Robin goes through his antics. I haven't felt overshadowed by him even though I have a thankless role on the show."

An alumna of commercials—on the Neet advertisements she grimaced and said, "Razor stubble"—Dawber got a lot of help on the set from Williams. At first, when Mork would say things like, "Sorry, kids, we can't go to the zoo—Mindy ate all the endangered species," Mindy was given no snappy rejoinder except to sit there and giggle or say, "Oh, Mork . . ." Then Williams would be helpful in coming up with funny lines for her. (About the only funny thing Mindy said on the first season was when she announced that a couple she knew was going on separate honeymoons. "They've been living together so long," she explained, "they want a little time alone.")

Robin Williams never did depilatory commercials. He came from a posh Detroit suburb by way of Chicago, and spent lonely times in his house making up his characters. "My imagination was my friend, my companion," he said. His father—a Ford Motor vice-president—wanted him to study welding. But then Williams won an acting scholarship and ended up at the Juilliard School in New York, where he was most memorable for his panhandling whiteface mime performances in front of the Metropolitan Museum. After moving to LA, he got work on TV on the second incarnation of *Laugh-In* and *The Richard Pryor Show*, which led to his celebrated guest shot on *Happy Days*.

The story goes that *Happy Days* executive producer Garry Marshall was talking to his nine-year-old son, who wanted Daddy to bring *Star Wars* to the land of The Fonz. Marshall took the kid's advice and put out a call for actors to audition for the role of Mork from Ork. When Williams arrived for the audition, he was told to sit down—and so he sat on his head. "He was the only Martian who applied," so he got the job, and the following year his own show—watched by 57,000,000 viewers—was the hit sitcom of the season. ("When the show became Number One," said a CBS vice-president, "into my office came an avalanche of concepts about funny three-headed people from Jupiter and Mars.")

Marshall worked hard at making *Mork and Mindy* popular: "You've got to bust through the competition," he said. "We had Mork drink with his finger so children would put their finger in their orange juice and parents would say, 'What are you doing?' And the kid'll say, 'Mork does that,' and the parents'll take a look at *Mork and Mindy*." Apparently it worked.

Robin Williams worked hard at making the show a hit too. Because the level of humor on *Mork and Mindy* was practically a carbon copy of every other sitcom on ABC at the time, Williams tried to improve it, mainly through improvisation. "Sometimes I have an idea I want to go with—like Mork falling in love with a manikin and then breaking up with her," he explained. "I don't know what I'm going to do or say until I do it. I improvise about one-third of my dialogue. The director gives me a time slot and I fill it. I walk all over the script. I pick up a verbal shotgun and go berserk. Otherwise you end up giving in to TV. The pressures on TV writers are so great they'll do the silliest things over and over. My job is to fight that voodoo repetition."

But he added a warning to himself: "You can *nanoo* your heart out. It would be very easy to do that. So I try to work on several levels at once, to slip in tiny innuendos. It's a game I play with the censors called 'Getting Shit Through the Radar.' Yiddish is good because the censor is Spanish. She knows what *putz* (penis) means though."

It was also Williams who came up with Mork's costume. Explains Williams: "When they asked about my wardrobe for the show, I suggested I wear my usual clothes. They're simple and comfortable. Who knows what they wear on Ork? But now I can't wear my outfit in public, because people shout, 'That's him!'" In a 1979 benefit auction for "Actors and Others for Animals," one pair of Williams' red-striped suspenders went for $235. At the same time, though, wrapped-in-plastic approximations were sold in novelty stores for under $10.

During *Mork and Mindy's* second season, Williams' salary doubled—to $30,000 an episode (although there were rumors that it went as high as $80,000). Said one ABC honcho: "Williams can get exactly what he wants because his popularity with the public is enormous. I'm surprised he didn't ask us to triple his pay instead of merely doubling it."

All finances aside, Williams often said that success wasn't so wonderful. "There are things you're afraid to do—you feel like a freak of nature. Like you stop to make a phone call at a phone booth and there are fifty people watching." Early in 1979, when the sitcom was going strong, Williams performed at small clubs to keep his stand-up routines in shape. At one point in his act, he asked the audience for the name of someone in the news. "Robin Williams!" they answered. "No," he said. So they called out, "Mork!" "I'm free from that now, massa Bob," Williams said to the audience. "Don't have to *nanoo* fo' a while." But they persisted, so he broke into a role he rarely plays: himself. "I have to explain one thing. I ain't doin' the Mork, because this is why I perform here—to do something different."

There were other changes during the second season besides Williams' salary. Gone were Mindy's conservative music-store-owning father and swinging grandmother—"they were stuck into the stories and became a writing problem," said one of the writers—and replaced by three new characters: Remo DaVinci, operator of the New York Delicatessen in Boulder (where the show's supposed to take place); his sister Jean, a medical student who helps out at the deli; and Mindy's cousin Nelson Flavor, an uptight sexist social climber with grandiose political ambitions.

The part of Mork's guardian, Orkan Orson—well, actually, only the voice, since we never saw him—was played by veteran actor-impersonator Ralph James. "I don't mind being just a voice on the show," he said. "I like being mysterious, and it adds to the interest of the show. The strength of the character is letting people imagine what Orson looks like." James was one of fifty actors who auditioned for the role. "I sat down with the coproducer, and as he talked about the concept of the character, I went through a range of voices for him, from high to low. I told him I saw Orson as a big man with a very theatrical, resonant voice coming from the chest. And to make him both human and mechanical I decided to be pedantic on words—like a robot."

The first season offered a few touching episodes, like the one in which Mork and Mindy get involved with black market babies. In another one, Mork said that after botching things up for Mindy and her father, "I feel like a light bulb in Buckingham Palace—a royal screw-up," and vanished to see what life would be like without him. Not good. (But then, life without Mork on TV that season

Spin-on: Mork travels back in time to visit The Fonz in Milwaukee.

wouldn't have been too good either.) He learned that his presence on earth was an important one. At the show's end, Orson told him that "one can learn that only from one's self." "Oh, wow, what a Werner-like thing to say," Mork responded, referring to est founder Werner Erhard.

Mork and Mindy's second season began with an hour-long episode called "The Incredible Shrinking Mork," a send-up on *The Incredible Shrinking Man, Alice in Wonderland*, and even *The Wizard of Oz*. In the episode, Mindy gave Mork a cold tablet that shrank his membranes—and since he was all membranes anyway, he shrank to nothing and fell into a parallel universe where there was no gas shortage, but there was an electricity crisis. This new world was made up of animals who wore pants and who had outlawed humor.

Mork and Mindy will never become dated. Partly because its concept—a little *My Favorite Martian* crossed with *I Dream of Jeannie*, cloned from *Bewitched*, by way of *Topper*—is already so dated it hasn't far to go. But mainly because Robin Williams has become TV sitcom's Charlie Chaplin. And what he does—the tricks, the hijinx—is timeless.

At the close of Williams' nightclub act, he portrays Grandpa Funk, a television has-been who recalls his days of glory. "Ninny, *nanoo*," he slurs. "Remember me? I was on every damn magazine cover except *Ebony* and *Popular Mechanics*. I used to play an alien."

Pause. "Of course, that was before the real aliens landed . . . and it wasn't so funny any more."

TAXI

9:30 p.m. Taxi: *The woman who services the garage's candy machine goes sweet on sour Louie—who takes her out, then brags about their sexual adventures.*
—1979 *TV Guide* listing

When *The Mary Tyler Moore Show* went off the air in 1977, a lot of die-hard viewers packed their television sets in mothballs and put them in the attic. Sure, *Bob Newhart*, *M*A*S*H*, and *Barney Miller* offered some sophisticated laughs, but nothing as good as *Mary* could ever be on TV again . . .

And then, on a Tuesday night in September—two seasons after *MTM* had been laid to rest—*Taxi* drove onto the screen. There was something hauntingly familiar about it—no, Lou and Mary and Murray were not there; they were all on other shows and other networks. The familiarity was *behind* the scenes. It was the writing and producing and directing. As it turned out, *Taxi*'s creators and writers were defectors from *MTM* who had started their own production company. *Taxi* was their first show. *Taxi* was terrific.

The situation: six lovable, loony cabbies and one tyrant of a dispatcher and their adventures.

The comedy: plenty.

Actually, the situation does sound like any other sitcom, whether it's a Norman Lear production with a multiracial cast of cabbies, a taxi company in Boulder with a resident Martian, or just another bunch of inept cabdrivers who can't find their cars. *Taxi* was a little all- (and yet none-) of-the-above.

The characterizations of the characters were what made the show.
• Bobby Wheeler is a forgetful, scatterbrained would-be actor who's driving cabs because he's not willing to take a risk; he constantly in conflict over being an actor and making money.
• Tony Banta is a tough—like oatmeal—part-time prize fighter who spends most of his career on the canvas listening to the countdown.
• John Burns, the new arrival in Manhattan, has been

jilted in love, and uses hacking to forget his problems. After one season, he left the taxi fleet.
• Elaine Nardo, an unmarried mother, is an artist and the token woman driver on the crew. She is liberated without being cloying about it.
• Latka Gravas is the chief mechanic, who's from an unidentified fourth-world country. He's the token immigrant and speaks in an indeterminate foreign tongue—he's sort of quasi-lingual and is the comic relief within the comic relief (which is what the show is).
• Louie De Palma is the pint-sized gnome of a tyrannical dispatcher who bellows to his own mother, who's honking for him in her car: "Keep your pants on, crazy lady."
• Dour-faced Alex Rieger holds the ensemble together. Unlike the others, he enjoys being a professional taxi-driver and has no other aspirations. He's the father of the family.

They're all losers of one sort or another, and they all get on one another's nerves. But when there's trouble—just as in any other kind of family—they all rally together to help out. In one episode, for example, all the cabbies take turns taking care of Elaine's son, Jason, during the weekend he has to prepare for a big spelling bee. They each take him for a couple of hours, and before long he is lined up to see the Knicks, to go to a wrestling match and to the movies, as the cabbies vie for his time. As a result, Jason loses the spelling bee. Everyone feels terrible, but Jason accepts full responsibility for not studying, and his mother realizes this was a much more valuable lesson than winning.

Sound a bit like something out of *Father Knows Best*? The lesson might be the same, but the route of arrival is quite different.

So is the writing. Not just fast-flying gags, great sight-jokes, or insult exchanges—although they're all

Alex Rieger	Judd Hirsch
Bobby Wheeler	Jeff Conaway
Louie De Palma	Danny De Vito
Elaine Nardo	Marilu Henner
Tony Banta	Tony Danza
John Burns	Randall Carver (1978–1979)
Latka Gravas	Andy Kaufman
Reverend Jim	Christopher Lloyd (1979–)

there—but the fact that each word of each episode shows us what's going on inside the character's heart as well as his mouth. For example, what can tell you more about the tyrant Louie than when we overhear this conversation on the phone: "Ma'am, you say one of our drivers was rude to you? . . . What is it he said to you? . . . I see . . . well, how fat *are* you? . . . I want you to know that we expect our cabdrivers to be kind and courteous to our passengers—especially to you blimpos." Dimwitted John had this to say about his wife: "Suzanne and I've talked about kids, but we decided to wait till we find out how . . . I mean, how to raise them."

Even in its first season on television, when most sitcoms are still growing up and trying TV on for size, the *Taxi* people came up with a slew of winners. In one episode, an eccentric old lady (played by Ruth Gordon) latches on to Alex to drive her around and around, each night, for a lot of money. (She is convinced she can buy anything—"nice food, nice clothes, nice people.") Alex becomes increasingly more uncomfortable about being "kept" in his cab. At a ballroom serving older customers, he meets a gigolo with his shirt unbuttoned to his waist. "I like your tie," says the gigolo. "Thanks," Alex responds, "I like your ribs." It all ends when Alex says to the lady that he has qualms about this new and unusual relationship and wants to end it. Then he pauses: "Why do I sound like Joan Crawford?"

Another episode, called "Friends," involves the childlike boxer, Tony, who leaves his prized pet fish with Bobby, who becomes preoccupied and forgets to feed him. "I guess it was just their time," he explains to Tony. "It was one of those murder-suicide things." Their friendship is threatened and Alex is recruited to mediate. "Why should I sit down and talk?" Tony asks. "Your fish would want it that way," Alex says. Finally there is a reconciliation over steaks and Löwenbräu—"Just like in the commercials," one of them comments.

Still another rift occurs when Latka's mother comes to visit from the Old Country. "Louie gave me the day off so I could show her around the Big Banana," Latka explains, but then Louie changes his mind and tells Latka he has to work. "I'm not doing this because I enjoy it," Louie tells him. "I *do* enjoy it, but that's not the reason." And so Alex is relegated to take Latka's mother—a young widowed beauty who was married when she was fifteen—around the town. That's not the only place he takes her.

Meanwhile Louie talks about his mother: "My mother's good-looking, if she'd just stop wearing those black dresses all the time—if she'd shed a few pounds—get rid of the warts and the mustache. . . ."

Alex tells Elaine he feels guilty about how "shockingly friendly" he became with Latka's mother.

ALEX: She flew in yesterday from the Old Country.
ELAINE: Just for *that?*
ALEX: I couldn't help it—after we were alone for a while, she turned into an animal—a *great* one. . . .

LATKA: *(calling out his name)* Alex . . . Alex Rieger . . . I must talk to you man-to-face. . . . Last night Mama came home very late and I ask her where she been and she did not want to tell me, but I make her. She told me everything.
ALEX: Latka, I can explain . . .
LATKA: You no need to explain . . . *Daddy!*

Latka, of course, expects his mother to marry Alex. "Mama, if you play *nik-nik* with Alex, you must marry—it's the only way to save the family honor." "Oh, goat droppings," she says, and explains to Latka—in their strange convoluted foreign tongue—that she's been lonely since his father died. He forgives her, "but you, Mr. Rieger, you I never forgive—we're no longer friends."

Louie intervenes and talks to Alex: "Look, I don't know what's going on here; I don't know who's right and who's wrong, but I just want you to remember one thing: my mother's off-limits."

Alex tries to patch things up with Latka.

ALEX: What your mother and I did was indiscreet.
LATKA: You mean not even indoors?!

But there's no way out. It's Latka's honor and he won't budge. Then he thinks of a way to patch things up: "You and I could *globnik*," which means that they could pretend the incident between Alex and Latka's mother never took place.

ALEX: Do you think that would do it—to pretend that it never happened?
LATKA: *What* never happened?
ALEX: Beats me.
LATKA: Me too.

And so it all ends happily when they bump rumps—which is Latka's homeland's special "handshake."

Coffee Break: Alex and Elaine talk in the garage.

The* Taxi Crew *(from left, seated): Elaine, Bobby, Louie, (standing) John, Latka, Alex and Tony

Taxi shot up to the top of the ratings almost immediately—a feather in ABC's cap (or whoopee-cushion—since the network was constantly barraged with criticism for cramming the airwaves with junky juvenilia like Laverne and *Happy Days* and *Three's Company*). *Taxi* redeemed the network, not only on the cocktail party circuit, but in the ratings war.

There were other ways that *Taxi* outrated some of ABC's other shows. Now, *Happy Days* and *Laverne and Shirley* both took place in Milwaukee; *Mork and Mindy* took place in Boulder. But all three might just as well have taken place in Hilldale, USA, or Springfield, USA, where, respectively (but not respectfully) *The Donna Reed Show* and *Father Knows Best* hung their hats and called home. But *Taxi* took place in New York. Manhattan. It just couldn't have—and wouldn't have—worked anywhere else. *Taxi* looked and sounded—everything but smelled—like New York. Even with outdoor locations of Alex and Co. riding around and picking up fares, just driving around the streets.

So how did New York cabdrivers feel about the show? Early in 1979, when the show was becoming one of the most popular on TV, the New York *Daily News*—probably read by more taxi drivers than any other paper

in the world—asked some local cabbies how they felt about *Taxi*. Here are some of the responses:

"It's a cute show, but I don't see where they get off calling it *Taxi*. The ones I seen, they got those cabs just to lean against, all the time they're chewing the fat in a garage. . . ."

"You know why they always show an actual customer in a cab at night? Because they don't want you to see the whole thing is done in a studio. God forbid they should film on Lexington Avenue. They might catch a disease."

"The show needs more realism? No. Realism is crazy. Realism is stuck empty behind a bus on Seventh Avenue and nobody's gonna take a cab because they can get there faster walking backwards—that's realism. Would you watch that for half an hour?"

"*Taxi*? I'm too busy driving cabs to watch TV shows."

Well, so the cabbies didn't like *Taxi;* they weren't judging it on artistic merit anyway, but on the realism of the situation rather than the realism of the comedy.

Judd Hirsch—alumnus of such TV dramas as *The Law* and *Delvecchio*—was known primarily as a stage actor before he hit it big on *Taxi* (he had headed the original cast of Neil Simon's *Chapter Two*). As Alex, he was the anchor of the *Taxi* crew, the professional-forever-after driver who was the glue that held everything together. As an actor, his actions were good, but his reactions were what made him so fine—just as Mary Tyler Moore's shrugs, grimaces, and small gestures gave her sitcom its substance. In the following exchanges between Alex and Latka's Old World mother, you can almost picture how his reactions were punctuation marks to her funny lines.

ALEX: What do you want to see in New York?
MRS. GRAVAS: I want to see all the sights—the garbage strike, the blackout, urban blight.
ALEX: I'll find out when the next tour is. You know, you talk very good English.
MRS. GRAVAS: So do you. (*Her hamburger arrives.*)
ALEX (*passes her the ketchup*): Try this.
MRS. GRAVAS: No thirsty.

Later . . .

MRS. GRAVAS: My husband, he died and struggle for liberty and freedom . . .
ALEX: Oh, he was a freedom fighter shot by the police . . .
MRS. GRAVAS: No, he was a police shot by freedom fighter . . .

And so on.
The other two important characters on the show were Latka and dispatcher Louie. Stand-up (and often sit-down) comic Andy Kaufman played Latka as an innocent, a childlike semilingual who often said things like "*Betya balasja buttya sallabak,*" but somehow we understood everything he meant. "*Abi, dabi, icky, bicky, sabi,*" he would say, and we knew that he was counting. In concert, Kaufman's comedy expanded from Latka's illegal-alien accent to a series of conceptual routines in which he'd wrestle any woman in the audience (and pay her $500 if she won), to reading *The Great Gatsby*—in its entirety—to an audience he didn't particularly like. His Latka wouldn't—and couldn't—do such a thing. When he was dressed up one day, Bobby told him: "Latka, nice threads." "Thank you," Latka said, and picked up a loose thread from his collar and handed it to Bobby. "You like? You can keep."

Danny De Vito auditioned for his role of Louie De Palma, the nasty dispatcher—"Louie's got a crusty exterior, but underneath there's a heart of granite," said one of the *Taxi* producers—by walking into the audition room and glaring at the producers. "One thing I wanna know before we start—who wrote this junk?" He was kidding, of course. And got the part. One of the producers said De Vito was "the nicest man in the world."

Standing a full five feet tall and weighing a paunchy 155, Louie is the prototypical little big man. Once he snarled: "Only one guy ever made it out of this garage. That was James Caan . . . and *he'll* be back."

The entire cast formed another fine television repertory company that worked well together. They were caustic yet caring, and got one another out of jams—traffic and otherwise.

Strangely enough, TV viewers knew that *Taxi* was—well, *real class*, as one of the drivers might say—on the premiere episode of the series. Alex accepted a blind date with a telephone operator who, it turns out, was fat and defensive. When he knocked at the door she said, "You wanta come in? You got guts." The other cabbies gave Alex a hard time about his fat date, but his big heart got to him and he just had to see her again. He told her he wanted to be her friend even though she was obnoxious. The episode ended when they hugged.

The 1978–1979 season proved that with shows like *Taxi* and more people watching them, the Golden Age of Sitcoms—long considered to be lost in the fifties during nights of Lucy and Ethel, *Our Miss Brooks*, and *Burns and Allen*—might be right now.

Blind Date: Alex picks up guest Suzanne Kent's apartment number that fell off her door.

ALSO RANS

A.E.S. Hudson Street

This one-month-only ABC series was, basically, a sitcom about a city hospital and its wacky staff. A.E.S. stood for Adult Emergency Services, and some of those adults were as down and out as the neighborhood. Gregory Sierra starred as Dr. Antonio—everyone called him Tony—Menzies, the harried chief resident. A sample episode: a deceased patient sprang back to life and Dr. M. had to tell his not-so-grieving widow.

Angie

ABC was riding high this year and, in fact, the network was home to most of the sitcom hits. *Angie*—along with *Mork and Mindy, Laverne and Shirley,* and the by now perennial *Happy Days*—came off the Miller-Milkis assembly line. It was the story of a lovable-warm-understanding-honest Italian waitress who marries a pediatrician—only to discover that he comes from a millionaire family (her family's hardcore poor). It took place in Philadelphia (it could have taken place in Rangoon) and starred Donna Prescow as Angie Falco (Pescow had made her movie mark as the girl-who-chased-Travolta in *Saturday Night Fever*). Also in the cast: Doris Roberts as her mother, and Debralee Scott as her sister (Scott had before been Mary Hartman's sister Kathy, and Rosalie Totzie on *Welcome Back, Kotter*). As sung by Maureen McGovern, *Angie's* theme song became a hit single.

Angie: *Donna Pescow and Robert Hays*

Another Day

Poor Rhoda's husband. He keeps getting dropped. First, his marriage with Ms. Morgenstern ended in TV's first landmark divorce. Then he played a struggling businessman on this series that barely made it "another day" before it was dumped by CBS after only a few episodes. David Groh played Don Gardner. His wife was played by Joan Hackett. They had two kids—an introverted boy and an extroverted girl. He also had the bonus of a kvetchy mother, played by Hope Summers.

Apple Pie

One week—and one episode—only did this silly sitcom last. But the premise was interesting. On paper, anyway. A lonely hairdresser, Ginger-Nell Hollyhock (played by *Maude's* neighbor, Rue McClanahan) placed ads in local papers for a family. What she ended up with was "Fast

Apple Pie *(from left, seated): Jack Gilford, Dabney Coleman, Rue McClanahan, Caitlin O'Heaney and (standing) Mike Binder and Dick Libertini*

Eddie" Murtaugh (played by Dabney Coleman, *Mary Hartman*'s Merle Jeeters), a daughter who tap danced, a son who wanted to fly like a bird, and a tottering old grandfather (played by the great Jack Gilford, who was wasted here). The setting was Kansas City, Missouri, and the time was 1933. ABC performed a greatly appreciated mercy killing on this show.

The Bad News Bears

Tatum O'Neal and Walter Matthau had—literally—a field day with the movie version of *The Bad News Bears*. When it was transplanted to TV, Jack Warden and a corps of little folks took over all the roles and it proved to be a moderate success on CBS, lasting more than one season. The star of the show was Warden, who was known to movie audiences for his role as the trainer in *Heaven Can Wait*, as well as for his role as Frank Whip on the sitcom *Mr. Peepers*. Warden played Morris Buttermaker, the "volunteer" coach of the Hoover Junior High School baseball team, the Hoover Bears, a.k.a. the Bad News Bears. Here's how he got the job (as we learned on the show's premiere episode): He was first seen in his professional occupation as a swimming pool cleaner. When a fast-talking client refuses to pay his bill, Buttermaker—a former minor-league ballplayer—drives the man's car into his own swimming pool. Buttermaker is hauled into court and given a choice—jail or coaching the team at Hoover Junior High (a special school for kids with behavioral problems). He meets the kids—and opts for jail. However, the Hoover principal, Dr. Emily Rappant (Catherine Hicks) persuades him to take the job—and the sitcom. Tatum's role of Amanda was played by Tricia Cast, although there was considerably less emphasis placed on it.

The Bad News Bears: *Jack Warden*

Billy

This midseason entry on CBS—the network was hoping for anything to pull it out of its ratings slump—was all about a young guy's incredible fantasy world (actually, not quite as incredible as a generation of kids sitting in front of their television sets watching shows like this). Anyway, Billy Fisher (played by Steve Guttenberg) is a mortuary employee whose fantasies keep getting tangled up with his realities. He does things like imagine his family rolling in money, fantasizes himself to be an executive, once pictures using a machine gun shortly before facing a firing squad. Viewers found it much easier to turn their dials and tune in to one of the real-fantasy shows, *Mork and Mindy*, that was debuting that season.

Also on the show: James Gallery as Billy's father, who would call him a "liar"; Peggy Pope (alumna of *Calucci's Department* in 1973) as Billy's mother, who said "he exaggerates a little"; and Paula Trueman as his grandmother, who calls Billy "a nut."

Brothers and Sisters/Coed Fever/Delta House

When the *National Lampoon's Animal House* was such an unexpected success in the summer of 1978, each network immediately got to work creating its own TV version. They learned well when *American Graffiti*'s producers didn't want to bring out a TV version, and then a knock-off, something called *Happy Days*, became a huge success. Said *The Wall Street Journal*: "Remember the 1950s fraternity competition of stuffing phone booths? Well, the three major networks are about to embark on their own version to answer the question: How many TV series based on fraternity life can be stuffed into the nation's homes?" The answer: None. All three were flops, perhaps mainly because the movie depended on raunchy humor and a lot of sex, and the TV shows were cleaned up considerably. Said an ABC vice-president: "For the television series we had to replace some of the outrageousness in the movie with lovability." Perhaps it was that lovability that killed the shows. John Belushi's Bluto character was not very lovable.

However, just for the record, here's the stories: NBC's *Brothers and Sisters* revolved around three irreverent college fraternity buddies—Miles "Checko" Sabolcic (played by Chris Lemmon, son of Jack), Stanley Zipper (Jon Cutler), and Ronald Holmes (Randy Brooks)—who were always up to mischief, like betting their entire tuition money that they can get a girl up in their room by midnight (in this case, the sorority girl was Suzi Cooper (played by Mary Crosby—Bing's daughter; conservative Bing must have been rolling over in his grave). Another time, Zipper is kidnapped by the angry sisters of Gamma Delta, who think he's been stealing their diaries. Yet another episode had Zipper revealing that he hiccupped every time he became sexually excited, a condition which the entire college soon finds out about. And once—well, you've got the picture.

Coed Fever was CBS's entry into the fraternity rush. Jane Rose (formerly of *Phyllis*) played the housemother of a swinging coed dorm, and had her hands full at Baxter College. There was Gobo (Michael Pasternak), as the typical offbeat brother; blonde sex bomb Sandi (Heather Thomas); the romantic Tuck (David Keith—no, not Brian's son); and Mousie (Alexa Kenin), a compulsive eater with a crush on Tuck, who she mistakenly thinks is in love with her too. One sample situation: In one of the coed dorms, everyone wants to find a boyfriend for Mousie. Everyone wants Tuck for Mousie, but Tuck is more interested in a religious girl. Ho hum.

Meanwhile, on ABC: *Delta House*, written and produced by the *Animal House* people (although it didn't seem to help much). Bluto/Blutarsky—played in the movie by Belushi—was here played by Josh Mostel (son of Zero), who was supposed to be Bluto's younger brother. Peter Fox played Otter, Bruce McGill played D-Day, Stephen Furst was Flounder, James Widdoes was Hoover, and Dean Wormer was played by John Vernon (Furst, Widdoes, and Wormer had also been in the movie). In the first episode, Dean Wormer threatens to expel the Delta "animals" from Faber College unless they convince Blotto to play on the school's disastrous football team. In another episode, the Deltas take some photos of Dean Wormer in a compromising position with a shapely coed, and then use them to try to get him fired—but change their minds at the last minute. And one more: The Deltas pull a con job and switch houses with the Omegas for the annual Parents' Visit. Their parents are delighted, but the stuffy Omega parents, marooned in the Delta House, are a bit bewildered.

And that, brothers and sisters, was the story of Fraternity Fever.

Detective School

Originally called *Detective School—One Flight Up*, and then later shortened to a simple *Detective School* when it was renewed the next season, this ABC summer entry was about a strange assortment of students who went to night school, trying to learn how to become detectives. Naturally, as novice private investigators, they got into a lot of trouble and had a variety of

misadventures. Take the premiere episode, for example. The students at Nick Hannigan's Detective Academy (Nick was played by James Gregory) had to search for a missing classmate in a nearby funeral home when they discovered that there was more than dead bodies in cold storage. It all began when student sleuth Eddie Dawkins (Randolph Mantooth) suspected foul play at the funeral home and tried to talk Nick into checking it out, which he eventually agreed to do. One of the students' names was Robert Redford, which always allowed for a few chuckles. The show was canceled in the middle of the 1979-1980 season.

Diff'rent Strokes

This show made a star of eleven-year-old Gary Coleman, a young precocious kid who could hold his own with Johnny Carson and Conrad Bain, the latter of whom starred in this show; the other had another show of his own. Here's the plot: Bain (playing New York millionaire Phillip Drummond) adopts two orphaned black brothers (real brothers, not the vernacular) and gives them a Park Avenue home. How come? Well, it seems that Drummond, a concerned and tender man (not at all like Bain's former incarnation—Arthur Harmon on *Maude*), had promised his dying housekeeper that he would raise her two sons, Arnold (Coleman) and Willis (Todd Bridges). They move in and share his penthouse with his thirteen-year-old daughter, Kimberly (Dana Plato), and their funny live-in housekeeper, Mrs. Garrett (Charlotte Rae).

Arnold loves his new world of limos, expensive toys, and other of the Finer Things. Willis, more streetwise than penthousewise, is more skeptical and misses his Harlem home.

Some sample episodes:

• Phillip's socialite mother comes to visit and is quite surprised to find two black ghetto kids—whose parents were domestics—living with her son. Since Drummond had advised his new sons to "always say what's on your mind," they do. But it ends happily.

• Willis misses his old buddies from Harlem, but when they come to visit, he goes a little overboard in trying to impress them with his new wealth. He insists that because he is rich, he is better. But it ends happily.

• Arnold becomes such a pest that Willis divides the bedroom in half . . . and then moves out for a while. But it all ends . . . well, you know.

In July of 1979, dumpling-cheeked, pudgy prodigy Gary Coleman held up shooting on the show because, it was reported, he wanted "more money, added benefits, and a bodyguard." Specifically, he wanted $15,000 per episode (as opposed to the $1,600 he'd been getting). The suit was settled and Coleman went on to continue his wisecracking and his sitcom sass.

Dorothy

Dorothy was Dorothy Banks (really Dorothy Loudon, who'd been a Broadway star, her career rejuvenated thanks to her role in *Annie*), and, during the sitcom summer, she had a show of her own, in which she played a showgirl-turned-music teacher in a stuffy girls' school. The series had a limited run, but it did allow Loudon to knock off a song each week (which meant four songs, because that's how many weeks there were). Added for spice were a pompous headmaster, Foley (played by Russell Nype, another Broadway musical exile), and two other teachers: the young Jack Landis (Kenneth Gilman) and the ditzy Lorna Cathcart (played by Priscilla Morrill, who'd been much more mature as Lou's wife, Edie, on *Mary Tyler Moore*), and a hardboiled city student, Frankie (played by Linda Manz, who'd made a brief burst of recognition in the film *Days of Heaven*). But the ratings weren't very good, and so CBS did not invite them back for more.

Flatbush

There was much uproar in New York because citizens of the Brooklyn neighborhood were afraid that America would think Flatbush was really like the Flatbush presented in *Flatbush* on CBS. They needn't have worried;

Flatbush *(from left, top row): Adrian Zmed, Joseph Cali, Sandy Helberg (in center): Randy Stumpf and (sitting): Vincent Bufano*

no one was watching the show anyway, and it only lasted one month. Basically, it was yet another of those sitcoms about "young men emerging from their teens into the adult world . . ." Here, they were called the Fungos—sort of a gang, but benign. In the first episode, for example, their car, the Fungomobile, became the victim of a gang of car thieves. So the Fungos start stealing cars in retaliation. Funny, eh? The unofficial leader of the group was Presto Prestopopolos, played by John Cali, who had acted with John Travolta in *Saturday Night Fever*. Other members of the Fungos had names like Socks Palermo, Turtle Romero, Joey Dee, and Figgy Figueroa.

Grandpa Goes to Washington

An offbeat politician: he wasn't crooked, he drove a Volkswagen, he played the drums for relaxation, and he said that his chief political asset was a circle of "friends in low places." This was the vehicle for Jack Albertson after the disappointing demise of *Chico and the Man*, in which he played the Man. This time, Albertson was Senator Joe Kelley, a maverick freshman Senator who did things his own way; he had been forcibly retired from teaching political science, so he quickly got himself elected to the US Senate when both of the regular candidates were exposed as crooks. (And so, yet another sitcom was made possible by the Nixon administration . . .) He lived with his son ("My son, the fathead," he'd say) played by Larry Linville (formerly Frank on *M*A*S*H*), who was married to Rosie (Sue Ane Langdon, who was once married to *Arnie* and who, years ago, had a tryout stint as Alice Kramden). Madge Sinclair played his trusty secretary, Madge. The show was unusual in that it was a sitcom that ran a full hour—although it only ran one season on NBC.

Hanging In

Bill Macy—who'd been Maude's husband, Walter (as in "God'll get you for that, Walter")—was now Louis Harper, a former football hero turned university president. He soon learned that life off the football field was tougher than life on. Greeting him on his arrival were Maggie Gallager (Barbara Rhoades), a high-pressure idealistic dean of faculty whom Harper initially fired and then of course rehired; Sam Dickey (Dennis Burkley), the fast-talking PR man; and Pinky Nolan (Nedra Volz), Lou's spunky, wisecracking little housekeeper. But

Harper and Braddock U didn't make a big impression on the viewers (much less the students), and this summer sitcom series was expelled from CBS U after only a few weeks.

Hello, Larry

M*A*S*H graduate McLean Stevenson played Larry Aldler, divorced radio talk show host and throwback to bumbling fathers of twenty-odd (with the emphasis on "odd") years ago. After his divorce, Larry takes his daughters (precocious, naturally)—fourteen-year-old Ruthie (Kim Richards) and sixteen-year-old Diane (Donna Wilkes)—to Portland. The show's situations revolve around Larry keeping up with his "hip" daughters and dealing with the loonies who call in to his talk show for advice. Others on the show: his ambitious producer, Morgan Winslow (Joanna Gleason), and the cheerful engineer, Earl (George Memmoli). When the show returned for its second season, it had two new additions: jazz singer Ruth Brown playing Larry's neighbor Leona, and former Harlem Globetrotter Meadowlark Lemon playing—well, himself, but this time owning a sporting goods store. In addition, Shelley Fabares (who's been in about every fifth sitcom in TV history) played Larry's ex-wife. The show ran on NBC and was produced by TAT Communications Co. (i.e., Norman Lear).

Highcliffe Manor

Consider Shelley Fabares. Like Elinor Donahue and several others in her sorority, Shelley made the rounds, from sitcom to sitcom to sitcom. Her comedy series habit began when she played daughter Mary on *The Donna Reed Show*. Later, she'd play daughter Ann on *The Brian Keith Show* (a.k.a. *The Little People*), and daughter-in-law Jenny on Danny Thomas' *The Practice*. As well as *Hello, Larry* (see above). In this sitcom, she got her first crack at playing a grown-up—albeit a widow. Here was her story in this NBC "multipart gothic comedy," as the network called it. As Helen Blacke, Shelley inherits her dead husband's castle off the coast of Massachusetts, his "think tank" which is housed there, and the foundation that supports it. The board members want to unseat her, but she's naive and doesn't realize it. Meanwhile, the Reverend Ian Glenville (Stephen McHattie) arrives from South Africa with his valet, Smythe (Ernie Hudson), to work on his theory that blacks are really natives of the US, and only went to Africa to keep warm. In the basement, the eccentric Frances Kiskadden (Eugenie Ross-Leming) is trying to replace the missing limbs of Bram (Christian Marlowe), who's lost his memory, among other things. Frances' silent servant, Cheng (Harold Sakata), gets her replacement parts from the graveyard each night. And so forth.

Hizzonner

David Huddleston starred as the mayor of a Midwestern town in this "limited run" sitcom (limited, that is, by the network, not the ratings—yet). A former sitcom star in the short-short-lived *The Kallikaks*, Huddleston here played Mayor Cooper, who did things like issue a parade permit to a visiting dictator, much to the consternation of his liberal daughter (who vowed she'd throw herself on the street to stop the event), and appointed a girl runaway (in an episode entitled "Mizzoner") mayor-for-a-day in an attempt "to teach her responsibility." Others in the case included the mayor's secretary, Ginny (played by Diana Muldaur), who once dated his son James (Will Seltzer); the mayor's daughter Annie (Kathy Cronkite, daughter of Walter); and several other "lovable characters" played by several other lovable character actors. The whole point was that the mayor adored his city and his city adored him. The viewers, however, weren't so enamored, and the mayor retired from NBC soon after he arrived.

In the Beginning

Going My Way, seventies-style. The conflict here was between the pompous, traditionalist Father Daniel M. Cleary (McLean Stevenson, of *M*A*S*H* fame, pre-*Hello, Larry*) and the streetwise nun assigned to him, Sister Agnes (Priscilla Lopez, alumna of the Broadway musical *A Chorus Line*). They worked in a storefront, community center/mission in the inner city of Baltimore—Aggie's home neighborhood. She loved being there; he hated the hookers, the hustlers, and the winos—also Sister Agnes, whom he called "Attila the Nun." Also in the cast as Sister Lillian was Priscilla Morrill, who had played Lou Grant's wife (and ex-wife) on *The Mary Tyler Moore Show*. The show lasted a month on CBS before it changed its title to *In the End*.

Makin' It

Garry Marshall, the kidcom creator who brought us *Happy Days*, *Laverne and Shirley*, *Odd Couple*, and *Mork and Mindy* (although not necessarily in that order), made mistakes too. One of them was this show that,

Makin' It: *David Naughton*

although it gave us a Top 20 hit single (star David Naughton singing the theme song), gave us little else except a few interesting statistics. What the show was, you see, was a sitcom version of *Saturday Night Fever*, a movie that promoted disco frenzy around the country. Interestingly, it costarred Ellen Travolta (sister of John), who had appeared briefly in the movie, and here played the star Billy's mother. Anyway, here's what it was all about: Billy, hot to follow in his older brother Tony's footsteps (Tony was the king of Saturday-night disco), is torn between his disco fever and his college career. Should he study or dance at the Inferno? The sitcom's music was written by the Bee Gees (who had also written much of *Saturday Night Fever*) and, in fact, the premiere episode was entitled "Staying Alive," the name of a hit song from *SNF*. However, after only about seven episodes on ABC, the show was canceled.

Miss Winslow & Son

This CBS show could have been a landmark sitcomedy if so much hadn't happened before it (abortion, rape, and other family fare). It was about an unmarried woman who, rather than marry a man she doesn't love, becomes an "unmarried mother." That was the show's premise, based on the British series *Miss Jones & Son*. Darleen

Carr starred as Miss Winslow, and her next-door neighbor was Harold Neistadter (Roscoe Lee Browne), who swore that he hated kids. Miss W. also had a boss (William Bogert), who cared only about his job security. And she had a set of parents—a mother (Sarah Marshall) who was not too sympathetic to her unmarried daughter, and a father (Elliot Reid) who was. The baby, however, never grew up (at least not on TV), because the show was canceled after only about eight episodes.

Stockard Channing in Just Friends

When Bette Midler bumped (or dumped) the lead in the movie *The Fortune*, the role went to Stockard Channing, who was supposed to become a star from it, but didn't. She got several other movie chances, but the real break was her role of Rizzo in *Grease*. It was then that CBS gave her a long-long-term contract. One of the terms was a starring stint on this sitcom, into which she had much input. A midseason entry, *Just Friends* (but always officially called *Stockard Channing in Just Friends*) was the saga of Susan Hughes, an unhappy recent divorcée who moved to LA (her first mistake) and found a job working at a health club. Her husband, for the first couple of episodes, anyway, followed her there and tried to control her with his authoritarian ways. It

Stockard Channing in Just Friends: *Stockard Channing*

didn't work. She stayed put, even though her snobby sister Victoria (Mimi Kennedy), gave her a lot of grief. She found a new family at The Fountain of Youth, the Beverly Hills health spa where she worked, mainly because of people like Milt D'Angelo (Lou Criscuolo), her boss, and Coral (Sydney Goldsmith), a beautiful but dim co-worker. At home, she hooked up with Leonard (Gerrit Graham), an offbeat neighbor. Although the show did well in the ratings, Channing et al. decided to wait until the middle of the following 1979–1980 season before airing it again to work out "production problems."

13 Queens Blvd.

ABC called this a "limited series"—and indeed it was limited, although not in the way they meant it to be. They were hoping it would be such a success that they could revive it the next season, but they didn't even get the chance to revise it. Here's what the show was all about: "a hilarious group of tenants in a garden complex in Queens, New York," is how the network described it. Others characterized it somewhat differently. This is what happened in the premiere episode. Felicia Winters (Eileen Brennan), a housewife, decides to have a class reunion—class of '59—and invites, among others, her best friend, Elaine, and Elaine's ex-husband. They haven't seen each other for several years. She also invited Fat Hughie, the class sexpot, and the class photographer. Jerry Van Dyke—brother of Dick and alumnus of many sitcoms—played Steven Winter, who lived in the building.

Turnabout

This was a fantasycom with a gimmick: a husband and wife become each other. That simple. Strangely enough, the switch was just one of those things one of them had casually hoped for, and suddenly their wish was granted. Sam Alston (played by John Schuck) is a sports reporter. Penny Alston (played by Sharon Gless) is a cosmetics executive. Or maybe he's the cosmetics exec and she's the sportswriter—well, since they both looked like each other, it was hard to tell. It was easy to tell, however, that this show wasn't successful. It lasted only a few weeks on NBC.

The Waverly Wonders

Somebody up there decided that it would be a good idea to star former pro football quarterback Joe Namath in a TV sitcom—all about a pro basketball player-turned-history teacher at Waverly High in Eastfield, Wisconsin. Joe Casey was not exactly a terrific history teacher. In fact, he was lousy. And his basketball team, the Waverly Wonders, wasn't exactly great. In fact, they were lousy. In fact, this show was lousy. Linda Harris (Gwynne Gilford) was the attractive principal, and George "Old Prune Face" Benton (Ben Piazza) was the stodgy former coach. NBC expelled them all after two episodes.

The Waverly Wonders: *Joe Namath*

Who's Watching the Kids

The pilot for this ABC sitcom—under the strange name *Legs*—was aired in May 1978, and was popular enough to warrant a second chance and a name change. The kids who needed watching were fifteen-year-old Frankie "the Fox" Vitola (played by *Happy Days'* Scott Baio, a teen

Who's Watching the Kids *(from left): Jim Belushi and Larry Breeding*

idol of the time), and his hyperactive sister, Melissa (Tammy Lauren). Both of them lived with their older sisters, who were showgirls in Las Vegas (that's why it used to be called *Legs,* get it?). Anyway, Angie (Lynda Goodfriend) and Stacy (Caren Kaye) spent a lot of time performing at a third-rate local nightspot, The Club Sand Pile, so they asked—nicely, of course—their neighbor Christopher Day (Larry Breeding) to—well, watch the kids. Tough, streetwise, Frankie and know-it-all Melissa were too much for Christopher, a reporter who wanted to become a hardcore investigative journalist, but had to be content reading the weather and garden news on a local station. Also on the show: Mitzi (Marcia Lewis), the obese emcee at the club (she was also the girls' landlady); and Bert Gunkel (played by *Saturday Night Live*'s John Belushi's brother Jim). The show—by any name—did not last long.

WKRP in Cincinnati

This show had a shaky, slow start (it was actually yanked off the air by CBS, and then came back later in the season), but went on to become an endurable hit. The premise was that a new program director, Andy Travis

(Gary Sandy), had come to a radio station that had been losing money by playing sedate music. And so there was a format switch—it became a rock 'n' roll station, which alienated its elderly audience and sponsors (such as the Shady Rest Home, and Barry's Fashions for the Short and Portly). It also created some tough times for Arthur Carlson (Gordon Jump), whose mom owned the station—that's the only reason he got the job; he was totally inept. His mother, who had her eye out for the buck, was willing to try rock music if it would make money. And so a new staff was hired: Les Nessman (Richard Sanders), the naive and gullible news director; Jennifer Marlowe (Loni Anderson), a curvaceous receptionist whose brain was also curvy; Herb Tarlek (Frank Bonner), the married high-pressure salesman who was always after Jennifer; and Bailey Quarters (Jan Smithers), Andy's young assistant. There were also two jive-talkin' DJs—Venus Flytrap (Tim Reid) and Dr. Johnny Fever (Howard Hesseman).

Although basically a farce, *WKRP* sometimes touched upon some serious issues. For example, in one episode a sportswriter remarked that the timid news director, Les, was a homosexual, which nearly caused a suicide before the matter was cleared up. In another, a desperate young mother left her baby in a basket on the doorstep of the station because she felt that Dr. Johnny Fever was the only person in town she really knew. Another episode focused on punk rock vs. hoodlum rock as Andy arranged for WKRP to sponsor a concert by a British rock group, Scum of the Earth, and almost lost his job.

WKRP in Cincinnati: *(from left) Gordon Jump and Gary Sandy*

1979–1980

WHATEVER HAPPENED TO 1979–1980?

This season was the beginning of the end. Oh, it's been said before—the sixties looked pretty barren, sitcomly speaking. But here it was, happening again in the seventies, when we should have known better. There were many more misses than hits this season. No, change that—there were no *real hits*. Real hits are the like of *All in the Family* and *Laverne and Shirley*—shows that people talked about and loved and lived with and ran home to see each week. In fact, the last show that TV had like that was *Mork and Mindy* (which, by this season, was falling apart).

So let's take an inventory. In 1979–1980, besides the new shows, the returning shows were from another era: *One Day at a Time*, *The Jeffersons* and Archie Bunker—the Sunday Night Norman Lear Museum—plus long-runners like *Alice*, *Happy Days*, *Laverne and Shirley*, *Three's Company*, *Mork and Mindy*, *Taxi* and *Barney Miller*. Getting ready to say good-bye were *Hello, Larry*, *The Ropers*, *Angie*, *The Bad News Bears* and—unfortunately—most of the new shows. Better luck next season . . .

OFF-SCREEN

9/10 Violence erupts in El Salvador.
10/17 Mother Theresa wins Nobel Peace Prize.
2/2 FBI snares corrupt congressman in Abscam Scandal.
3/27 Mt. St. Helens erupts, leaving 66 dead or missing.

ALSO RANS

Archie Bunker's Place

For in-depth information about *Archie Bunker's Place* and its roots, look in the 1970–1971 season under *All in the Family*. But here are the developments that took place at Archie Bunker's bar—where the show takes place—in recent seasons:

Archie's Jewish partner, Murray Klein (Martin Balsam), quits, and is replaced by another Jew (Archie's attorney and business partner, Gary Rabinowitz, played by Barry Gordon). Other new and old characters in Archie's bar include his longtime buddy and steady customer (who never pays his tab) Barney Hefner (Allan Melvin). Old friend Harry Snowden (Jason Wingreen) is the bartender,

Archie Bunker's Place *(from left): Denise Miller, Carroll O'Connor, Jason Wingreen, Marianne Muellerleile and Allan Melvin*

and blind (but keenly insightful) Mr. Van Ranseleer (Bill Quinn) is a perennial patron. And then there are two behind-the-bar helpers: Jose (Abraham Alvarez) and Raoul (Joe Rosario), who are Spanish-speaking and hard-working. Comedienne Anne Meara played the sardonic Irish cook Veronica Rooney for several seasons.

At home, in addition to niece Stephanie (Danielle Brisebois), Archie now has custody of Billie Bunker (Denise Miller), who is growing up and—horrors—is having a relationship with Archie's Jewish attorney. And after Edith's death, Archie hired a black housekeeper (my, how things change), Ellen Canby (Barbara Meek), sister-in-law of one of his neighbors, Polly Swanson (Janet MacLachlan).

Other things changed too. Archie started dating, and so did others on the show, like Barney, who found a girlfriend, Laura (Marianne Muellerleile). Plus, Archie isn't as prejudiced as he used to be; the kids have worn him down. After all, he even hired a *black* housekeeper and has a Jewish partner. What's next for Archie Bunker? Rumor has it that, after he gives up his bar, he'll become head of the American Civil Liberties Union and dedicate his life to fighting prejudice in America. Or not.

The Associates

One of the most highly-touted—albeit short-lived—shows of the season, *The Associates* was the baby of the *Taxi* creators, and it had the same bent, unexpected humor, as well as intelligent writing and a rich set of genuinely likable characters. Why it didn't last . . . well, you'll have to ask the Nielsen families that one.

The premise: It was about a hotshot Wall Street law firm and the people who worked there. That's it. (Maybe that was its problem—no real premise.) But as *Taxi* was set in a garage, this show was set in the law firm. Heading the cast was the distinguished British actor Wilfrid Hyde-White, who played eighty-year-old, absentminded babbler Emerson Marshall (sole surviving partner of the fifty-year-old, staid and stodgy Bass & Marshall), but it was the three recent law school grads—the associates—who were at the core of the show: Leslie Dunn (Alley Mills), who kept reminding everyone that she came from a poor family and wanted to work with the oppressed (although the only oppressed this law firm worked with were the first year lawyers); Tucker Kerwin (Martin Short), the naive, charming midwesterner who was slightly out of step with his Harvard-Yale-Columbia colleagues; and beautiful, brainy—and calculating—Sara James (Shelley Smith), who was descended from a long line of Boston blueblood attorneys.

Others in the cast included Joe Regalbuto as Eliot Streeter, the simpy, self-serving junior partner who longed to take over the firm; and Tim Thomerson as

The Associates

Johnny Danko, the twenty-one-year-old mailboy who was far less concerned with making good than with making out.

The Los Angeles *Times* called *The Associates* the "can't-miss comedy of the season." They were wrong. Critically, it didn't miss; but in terms of people watching, it missed by a mile. ABC—which was having a success with *Taxi* at the time—found the faith to give the show a second chance. After a premiere in September of 1979, it had a second premiere in March of 1980, but still it didn't fare well. A month later it was off the air for good.

Benson

This spin-off—which ran longer than its daddy, *Soap*—is proof that the butler did it. Benson, who had been the sole sane member of the Tate household, was assigned by ABC to Jessica Tate's widowed cousin, Gov. Gene Gatling (yet another loon). Well, at least he was honest, not to mention bumbling and inept.

Benson's nemesis in the household was the frightening German maid with a heart of iron, Gretchen, played by Inga Swenson. Also present were the Governor's precocious (are TV tots ever any other way?) daughter Katie, played by Missy Gold; and Marcy, the Gov's secretary, played by Caroline McWilliams. For one season, Benson also had to deal with Taylor, Gatling's political aide (played by Lewis J. Stadlen), who was replaced by Clayton in 1980 (René Auberjonois), who brought along with him Pete the press assistant (Ethan Phillips) and Frankie the messenger boy (Jerry Seinfeld).

On the debut episode—which aired Thursday, Sept. 13—when Benson arrives at the executive mansion, he is searched by guards, soaked by sprinklers, attacked by dogs, mistaken for the Rev. Jesse Jackson, and insulted by both Gretchen and a political aide.

Naturally, Benson was much more than a butler (in fact, we rarely saw him buttle). He made important decisions for the Governor, raised little Katie, fought a lot with Gretchen and ran the household. As funny and slapsticky as the show was, *Benson* sometimes even got serious, like the 1981 episode in which Benson's mother, visiting him, dies.

The man behind—or in front of—Benson was actor Robert Guillaume, who—pre-*Soap*—had starred in Broadway musicals, and was generally considered to be a fine comic actor. During the 1982–1983 season, Guillaume—well, Benson really—was promoted from butler to state budget director, and Gretchen took over his old job. Didi Conn—who lit up our lives in that movie—was brought in as Benson's assistant when Marcy left the show to start a business with her husband (whom she had married in a February 1981 episode). It's all so complicated.

The Facts of Life

This show—a spin-off of *Diff'rent Strokes*—was never a monster hit, but a moderate hit. It wasn't really about anything, nor was there ever any one major star of the show—a Gary Coleman or a Henry Winkler. There were, in fact, many little stars of this NBC show. The first season (*The Facts of Life* had its premiere on Friday, August 24, 1979), Edna Garrett (Charlotte Rae), who had been the Drummonds' housekeeper on *Diff'rent Strokes*, moved to the Eastland School for young women, where she became housemother and eventually dietician. In her charge were several girls: Blair Warner (Lisa Whelchel), fifteen, who was wealthy, snobby, snotty, attractive and spoiled; Tootie Ramsey (Kim Fields), the eleven-year-old resident gossip; Natalie (Mindy Cohn), age (and, apparently, last name) unknown, who was fat and impressionable and bursting with energy. Also on the show (but later written out to simplify things) were other girls: Nancy (Felice Schachter), fourteen years old and well-rounded; Sue Ann (Julie Piecarski), also fourteen, who was cute and boy-crazy. The headmaster at Eastland that first season was Steven Bradley (John Lawlor); later, Mr. Harris (Kenneth Mars) joined as headmaster. During the tryout run of *The Facts of Life*, Jenny O'Hara played teacher Miss Mahoney. When the show returned in the fall of 1980, there were two new additions to the cast: Howard (Hugh Gillin), the Eastland cook; and Jo Polniazek (Nancy

The Facts of Life *(from left, top row): Nancy McKeon, Charlotte Rae, Lisa Whelchel; (bottom row): Kim Fields, Mindy Cohn*

McKeon), a tough-but-tender sixteen-year-old student from New York. Comedienne Geri Jewell joined the show in 1980 as Blair's handicapped (she has cerebral palsy) Cousin Geri, who was a stand-up comic.

Although many felt the show was a comic book for kids, it did deal with many important subjects (during irrelevant television times when thoughtful subject matter was no longer on the sitcom menu): suicide, teenage marriage, handicaps, shoplifting, pregnancy, self-defense, the aged, runaways, prostitution, book banning, cancer and libel.

The show was always popular and, in fact, in the fall of 1982, an unusual one-time spin-off was made: *The Facts of Life Goes to Paris*, a two-hour TV movie that swept the ratings (though not necessarily the hearts of the critics).

The Facts of Life *meets* Diff'rent Strokes: *Gary Coleman delivers dinner to (from left) Charlotte Rae, Mindy Cohn, Lisa Whelchel and Kim Fields.*

Flo

After her grits had been kissed week after week (see *Alice*), the network decided to give Polly Holliday a show of her own. Unfortunately, CBS had not learned from its neighbor ABC, when, years before, they decided *not* to spin off the Fonz to his own show because they realized that the character was not a leading man, but an integral supporting player. Flo—who wasn't good at kissing other people's grits—should have stayed in Arizona instead of transplanting to Texas. She would have had a better life expectancy in Phoenix.

Here was the new premise: Florence Jean "Flo" Castleberry was on her way to a hostess job in Houston when she spotted a run-down old roadhouse in Cowtown, Texas, her home town. She bought it and it became Flo's Yellow Rose. But she needed a boss (i.e., a Mel), so she hired Earl Tucker (Geoffrey Lewis) as her bartender; he hated the thought of working for a woman. The man who held the mortgage (if *one* crotchety Mel had worked on *Alice*, let's not take any chances; let's have *two* on *Flo* . . .) was obnoxious skinflint Farley Waters (Jim B. Baker), who was always breathing down Flo's neck. Also on hand: Les Kincaid (Stephen Keep), the resident piano player; Randy Stumphill (Leo Burmester), the mechanic who worked in the garage next door. Plus Flo's family: Mama Velma Castleberry (Sudie Bond); her introverted klutzy sister Fran (Lucy Lee Flippin). Then there was Flo's long lost buddy Miriam Willoughby (Joyce Bulifant).

As a midseason replacement, the show was a hit; following immediately after *M*A*S*H* didn't hurt. The following season, it moved to Monday nights, playing against *Little House on the Prairie* and *Monday Night Football*. Its ratings plummeted. So the network moved it to Saturday nights opposite *The Love Boat*, changed its time slot once again, and then moved it to Tuesday night, where it died down, down, down in the ratings. Many involved with the show thought that moving it around so much didn't give *Flo* a chance to capture an audience.

Said Polly Holliday about Flo's demise: "We knew it was coming. The ratings tell you. But you sort of keep hoping. I felt sad. I cried a bit. Once it becomes official, you feel it. I hated saying good-bye to Flo. She was a good character, like a sister. I hated to let her go. She was a good ole girl."

Jim B. Baker, who played Farley, had this to add concerning *Flo*'s cancellation: "Oh, hell . . . fifty years from now, nobody will know the difference anyway."

Goodtime Girls

This was the first sitcom in a long time that didn't take place Right Now. *M*A*S*H* was in the fifties, as were *Happy Days* and *Laverne and Shirley*, but this was the first sitcom that took place in the forties—1942, to be exact—during World War II. The premise: Three young women ended up living in the same one-room attic apartment in Washington, D.C. They were: Edith Bedelmeyer (Annie Potts), the leader of the group who was working at the Office of Price Administration; Betty Crandall (Lorna Patterson, later TV's *Private Benjamin*), from Sioux City, Iowa, who was working in a Baltimore defense plant; and Loretta Smoot (Georgia Engel, previously *The Mary Tyler Moore Show*'s ditzy Georgette), who was shy and worked for Gen. Culpepper, a Pentagon bureaucrat. The room became even more crowded when snobbish Camille Rittenhouse (Francine Tacker), who was doing a magazine article on the apartment shortage, found out she'd lost her

Goodtime Girls (from left, top row): Annie Potts, Lorna Patterson, Merwin Goldsmith, Georgia Engel and Marcia Lewis; (bottom row): Adrian Zmed, Francine Tacker and Peter Scolari

apartment—and had to move in with the other three. Proprietors of the Coolidge Boarding House, where they lived, were Irma and George Coolidge (Marcia Lewis and Merwin Goldsmith), who ran a tight ship. The hustling cabbie who brought the girls there—and lived downstairs—was the Fonz-like Frankie Millardo (Adrian Zmed). Others in the cast included Sparky Marcus as Skeeter, and Peter Scolari (who would go on the following season to become a Bosom Buddy) as Benny Loman.

The opening episode dealt not only with the girls moving in and in and in and in . . . but the discovery that married Loretta never spent her wedding night with her sailor husband . . . who's arriving shortly on a two-hour pass. The subtext of all the episodes—and there were only a few of them—was the nostalgia of the forties: jitterbugging, ration stamps, big bands and—most important—lack of men.

Goodtime Girls began as a midseason replacement in

January of 1980. It ran about a month on ABC, was yanked off the air, was brought back in April, then yanked again, then returned for a few episodes in August. Then the "Goodtimes" were over.

Good Time Harry

Ted Bessell—alumnus of such mediocre sitcom fare as *That Girl* and *Me and the Chimp*—finally got a crack at a quality show. This one. Naturally, it went right off the air. No thanks to the network that put it on Saturday nights—in the middle of the summer—at 10:30 P.M., a time period usually reserved for midget wrestling and *Fantasy Island*. And so *Good Time Harry* died. Oh, not without outcries from the critics. But it didn't do any good. Today, it's just one of those shows people talk about fondly with a do-you-by-any-chance-remember-a-great-show-called . . . ?

This was the premise: Harry Jenkins (Bessell) was a sportswriter for the San Francisco *Sentinel* who should only have chased stories the way he chased women. This didn't exactly please his editor, Jimmy Hughes (Eugene Roche), who had once fired Harry before he charmed his way back into the fold. And there were, of course, others: Sally (Ruth Manning) was Hughes' secretary; Carol Younger (Marcia Strassman, a *Welcome Back, Kotter* alumna) was Harry's fellow worker; Billie Howard (Jesse Welles) was a cocktail waitress Harry played around with; Stan (Barry Gordon, who would go on to become Archie Bunker's Jewish business partner) was Harry's Woody Al-lenesque insurance agent neighbor who was always trying to get Harry to fix him up with some of his leftover dates. Off duty, from both writing and romancing, Harry hung out at a San Francisco writers' watering hole, Danny's Bar, presided over by Lenny the bartender (Richard Karron).

The sitcom, a summer trial show, had a one-hour pilot (the producers expanded it from the original half-hour pilot), that aired on July 19, 1980. The limited series finished its run on September 13, just in time to not be invited back for the following season. There are a lot of theories about why the show failed, besides the network's loss of interest. One of these is that the show—in the words of the network, NBC—"didn't test well." Testing today means that they preview the show for a large group of people—usually off the street (some of whom, the story goes, don't speak English; unfortunately, *Good Time Harry* was in English). The testers judge why they like the show—and why not. In *Harry's* case, the testers said they didn't find Harry "likable"—and, indeed, he wasn't always. But he wasn't *supposed* to be. Harry Jenkins was egocentric, often obnoxious. Harry—in the words of the Jolson theme song—was just wild about Harry.

Good Time Harry was the dreamchild of the late Steve Gordon, who went on to make people laugh in movie theaters with *Arthur*. Wonder how *Arthur* would have fared in testing. . . .

House Calls

Based on the Walter Matthau-Glenda Jackson movie of the same name, written by Max Shulman (who was the wonder behind the classic *Dobie Gillis*), *House Calls*-The Sitcom was usually more interesting offscreen than it was on.

Like the movie, it was the story of nonconformist surgeon Charley Michaels (Wayne Rogers, post-*M*A*S*H*), and his relationship with the hospital's new administrative assistant, Ann Anderson (Lynn Redgrave). She was committed to making sure the hospital ran efficiently; he didn't care about rules or order. So there was that conflict when his concern for his patients ran up against her concern for the hospital. Not to mention the pressures of dating someone you work with. All this took place at Kensington Memorial Hospital in San Francisco. Also on CBS.

Others in the cast were the neurotic young obstetrician, Norman Solomon (Ray Buktenica, late of *Rhoda*); the doddering (but brilliant) chief of surgery Amos Weatherby (David Wayne); Ann's stodgy boss Conrad Peckler (Marc L. Taylor); not to mention Mrs. Phipps (Deedy Peters), the ditzy hospital volunteer who provided the patients with books and candy.

That was *on* screen. Behind the screen, the cast of characters interacted somewhat differently. In a greatly publicized dispute in the summer of 1981, it was Redgrave against Universal TV, the show's production company. Neither side seemed to agree even on what the dispute was about. According to Universal, Redgrave wanted more money. According to Redgrave, it was a dispute over whether she would be allowed to breast-feed her infant baby on the Universal lot. Then Universal said that it was Redgrave who wanted to be released from her contract because Universal wouldn't guarantee her a deal to develop and produce her own properties—and, once again: money. Whatever the truth—or the "real truth," as they say out west—Redgrave was off the show, replaced by Sharon Gless, who, upon the show's demise, went on to replace Meg Foster in the dramatic series *Cagney and Lacey* (which is yet another story about controversy and disputes—but that's another book). So the show continued another season without Redgrave, and then was canceled, supposedly—according to the network—when Rogers walked off the set after demanding, and being turned down for, much more money and a bigger cut in the program's profits. In November of 1981, Universal workers struck the *House Calls* set, even though the show was still doing well in the ratings.

Joe's World

This midseason replacement was a family show about a family man—of the old-fashioned variety. An interesting switch for 1979–1980, where the only traditional values seemed to take place around the Waltons' pond or in that little house. But fleshy Joe Wabash (Ramon Bieri, who looked blue-collar, but actually started out acting Shakespeare) was a tough disciplinarian trying to cope with the quickly changing social and economic world around him. He was a not-so-distant cousin of Archie Bunker's—he drank beer and looked chagrined a lot. He was a house painter living in Detroit with his wife Katie (K Callan) and his five kids: eighteen-year-old Steve (Christopher Knight, formerly Peter on *The Brady Bunch*), an apprentice painter on Joe's crew who feels the aggravating pressure to take over the family business; attractive sixteen-year-old Maggie (Melissa Sherman), whose dating gave her parents a bit of anxiety; and the three young ones: twelve-year-old Jimmy (Michael Sharrett), ten-year-old Rick (Ari Zeltner) and six-year-old Linda (Missy Francis). On the job, Joe worked with his assistant Brad Hopkins (Russ Banham), a self-titled stud; Judy Wilson (Misty Rowe of *Hee Haw*), a sexy blonde who nursed her baby during lunch breaks; and Andy (Frank Coppola), Joe's longtime buddy.

Some sample storylines of the show: (1) Joe insists that his son Steve follow in his footsteps, which nearly costs him Steve's respect; (2) Kate thinks she's pregnant—and they can't afford it; (3) Maggie's nearly expelled from school because she can't take the pressure from Joe to be the best in her class and win a scholarship; (4) Kate and Joe are worried that Steve is becoming an alcoholic—especially since the family has a history of alcoholism.

Joe's World collapsed when it was canceled by NBC after only eleven episodes.

The Last Resort

MTM—the production company that gave the airways such sitcoms as *Bob Newhart, Mary Tyler Moore, Rhoda,* and others—temporarily gave up comedies and became the classiest producer of dramatic series (*Lou Grant, Hill Street Blues*) around. *The Last Resort* was their last entry into the comedy fold for several seasons to come. It was about a resort (surprise!) in the Catskill Mountains in upstate New York. And about the bunch of college students who worked there: Michael Lerner (Larry Breeding, formerly of last season's *Who's Watching the Kids?*), a romantic, bright premed; bookworm Duane Kaminsky (Zane Lasky, who had played Mario Lanza on *The Tony Randall Show*); snobby Jeffrey Barron (Ray Underwood); and fat, bumbling Zach Comstock (Walter Olkewicz), who once said to a fat customer, "What's an attractive woman like you dieting for anyway—when surgery's available?" Also on the staff: pastry chef Gail Collins (Stephanie Faracy), who had left her rich husband to pursue a career in baking, about which she knew not much (in the premiere episode, we met her husband, Dexter, and his chauffeur, Armando, who tried to pursue her); the samurai-style Japanese chef Kevin (John Fujioka), who conveniently didn't understand English when it suited him; and dim and easily tricked Murray the maitre d' (Robert Costanzo), who ran the kitchen like a drill sergeant.

The Last Resort was a ratings failure, and CBS pulled it off the air after only three episodes. They resurrected it in December, 1979, and it ran through March, when it was permanently canceled.

Me and Maxx

On the heels of *Kramer vs. Kramer* came *Me and Maxx,* all about a little girl who comes to live with her swinging-single father, thus cramping his lifestyle (as they were called back in 1979). Joe Santos (formerly of *The Rockford Files*) played Norman Davis, a guy who'd left his wife and child years earlier. Now, it seems that mom too wants to "spread her wings"—and the kid, eleven-year-old Maxx ("My mother says I have two x's in my name because I was double-crossed."), played by Melissa Michaelsen, unexpectedly moves in with dad. Maxx was—of course—precocious and sensitive, with a huge vocabulary she picked up from watching soap operas. At first, she had a negative attitude toward her heel-father, but she worked hard—thanks to her incredible sensitivity—and by the end of the first episode, she was licking her wounds and purring at pa. Dad, meanwhile, was irked that he had to adjust his bachelor life to accommodate a young daughter. But every week they made up—tenderly.

Also in the series: Barbara (Jenny Sullivan), Norman's business partner in the ticket brokering business (and his occasional date); the mandatory swinger-next-door Mitch (Jim Weston); and the inept elevator operator Gary (Denny Evans).

Critics seemed to despise the show. Said the Los Angeles *Times,* "*Me and Maxx* is abominable, and that's giving it the benefit of the doubt . . . a low-energy, low-witted sitcom whose one relief is that it's only thirty minutes long." Many critics noted that it seemed that the show was trying to be reminiscent of its producer-creator James Komack's sitcom, *The Courtship of Eddie's Father.* Previous to *Me and Maxx,* Komack also did *Chico and the Man* as well as *Welcome Back, Kotter.*

He and Maxx went off to live somewhere else when NBC canceled this replacement show by the end of the season.

A New Kind of Family

The title told the offscreen story as well as the onscreen story. According to the Los Angeles *Times*, this show was created by the wives of two of television's most powerful executives—a former ABC executive (the show was on ABC) and the president of Paramount who was also a former ABC executive. Plus, the *Times* said, these women (novices in television), at reported salaries together totaling $6,000 a week, were made executive producers instead of just given the standard "created by" credit. Plus (you thought that wasn't enough?), the head of prime time series at the network had worked for the Paramount prez when he was at ABC. Cries of nepotism were heard in Hollywood.

Not that it mattered anyway, because the show they all created, produced and nursed—*A New Kind of Family*—was a dismal failure. And not even Mrs. Freddie Silverman could have saved this one. Critics called it "vapid," among other insulting things.

Here's the premise: Recently widowed Kit Flanagan (Eileen Brennan, pre-*Private Benjamin*) decided to move from New York to L.A. with her three kids: Andy (David Hollander), Hillary (Lauri Hendler), and Tony (Rob Lowe). When they got to the house they had rented, they found out that someone else had rented it too: Abby Stone (Gwynne Gilford) and her daughter Jill (Connie Ann Hearn). So, because neither family could afford the place themselves anyway, they all moved in together. What resulted, of course, was a clash of life-styles: Kit was free-wheeling and cynical; Abby was conservative and careful. In other words, it was *The Odd Couple* with women and children. There was also clownish landlord Harold Zimmerman (Chuck McCann) and a dog named Heinz played by O.J. (or was it a dog named O.J. played by Heinz?).

The story lines revolved around such plausible plots as the time Andy finds a runaway lion cub, thinks it's a kitten and takes it home for a pet; the time Jill wants to try out for the cheerleading team, and her mom thinks it's ridiculous; and the time the two women argue about an overcharge on the electric bill.

The show was an instant flop and was pulled from the schedule after only a few weeks. It returned briefly in December and January with new episodes—and new changes: the Stones had been replaced by Jess Ashton (Telma Hopkins) and her daughter Jojo (Janet Jackson). No luck. ABC pulled the plug on the whole thing and went hunting for a new kind of show. Now, what they should have done was do a sitcom about these two executives' wives who produce their own sitcom . . .

Nobody's Perfect

This show, when previewed for the critics, was regarded as one of the best new shows on the fall schedule. And then, fall came . . . and *Nobody's Perfect* didn't. The reason, the network explained, was that the show wasn't developing as well as they had hoped, and it wasn't until the following summer that *Nobody's Perfect* hit the small screen and lasted only seven weeks as a summer replacement for *Soap*.

British farceur Ron Moody (best known as Fagin in the movie *Oliver!*) played Detective Inspector Roger Hart, an elegant Pink Pantherish Scotland Yard detective on loan to the San Francisco police department where he worked with more down-to-earth cops than he'd been used to: his boss, Lieutenant Vince de Gennaro (Michael Durrell), who teamed him with Detective Jennifer Dempsey (Cassie Yates). Others on the force: Detective Jacobi (Victor Brandt), Detective Grauer (Tom Williams) and Detective Ramsey (Renny Roker).

The tall grinning Hart (the original title of the sitcom was *Hart in San Francisco*, by the way) was a bumbler—klutzy and accident-prone; but he was also a master of disguises, pilot, swordsman, and bomb expert. As inept as he seemed to be, he always solved the problem at hand (although there was that one time he so startled a would-be suicide on the Golden Gate Bridge that the man actually jumped). Once, he stripped all his clothes off to talk a highjacker off a plane.

One in a Million

Shirley Hemphill—who played the overweight, overwrought, overpowering waitress in *What's Happening!!*—got a show of her own, all about a down-to-earth cabbie named Shirley Simmons (Hemphill) who inherited a multimillion-dollar conglomerate, Grayson Enterprises, when one of her fares died. Oh, yeah: the company was all-white and Shirley was all-black. Naturally, Shirley—who was of The People—had her own way of running the company, and making sure the big, bad industrialists started looking out for the little guy.

The new cast of characters in her life included: bald, scowling Mr. Cushing (Keene Curtis), who had planned to take over the company himself; Barton Stone (Richard Paul), the naive nephew of Grayson, the man who left the company to Shirley; Grayson's secretary, Nancy Boyer (Dorothy Fielding), who was Shirley's ally; the owner of the deli where Shirley hung out, Max Kellerman (Carl Ballantine); and Edna and Raymond Simmons (Ann Weldon and Mel Stewart), Shirley's parents.

The show had its debut as a midseason replacement on January 8, 1980. Moderately successful, it finally ran its course during the following season.

Out of the Blue

Stand-up comic Jimmy Brogan (his trademark was wearing a cardigan, carrying books and trading remarks with his audience—*he* heckled *them*) got a shot at sitcomdom with this one, which was sort of *Mork and Mindy and Mindy and Mindy and Mindy* . . . Well, not exactly. But sort of.

On ABC's *Out of the Blue*, Brogan played Random, an inept angel who was dispatched to live earthside with a harried Chicago woman, Marion Richards (Dixie Carter) and her batch of inherited nieces and nephews (their parents had been killed in a plane crash and left to Marion): sixteen-year-old Chris Richards (Clark Brandon), a sports-loving cynic who was not too crazy about Random; thirteen-year-old Laura Richards (Olivia Barash), a TV and movie addict; ten-year-old Stacey Richards (Tammy Lauren), a tomboy who idolized Chris; and, of course, The Twins—eight-year-old Jason Richards (Jason Keller) and eight-year-old Shane Richards (Shane Keller), who both loved fooling people about who's who and which one is which. Gladys (Hannah Dean) was the housekeeper, and

Out of the Blue: *Jimmy Brogan meets Hannah Dean.*

Boss Angel (Eileen Heckart) was Random's own personal guardian angel. Since Aunt Marion was looking for a boarder (because she didn't have enough people living in the house, right?), Random moved in. But only the kids knew he was an angel with magic powers.

Now Random, of course, wasn't your average brand-name angel. He loved the Chicago Cubs, told one-liners and played a guitar instead of a harp ("The music's just as good and it's easier to carry," he explained). He could "twinkle" and move things—and people—around. And with all his powers, he could teach the kids little lessons about growing up. In the premiere episode—aided by fellow ABCer Robin Williams playing Mork (*Out of the Blue* wasn't exactly a spin-off, but a spin-on), Random tries to talk Chris into buckling down in school or quit. Chris chooses to quit—and Random's almost recalled to heaven for giving out bad advice, until he can show Chris the long-range consequences of leaving school. Said the Los Angeles *Times*, "The resolution makes *The Brady Bunch* look like a model of subtlety and sensitivity . . ." But for all of Random's magic, it was not within his powers to improve the ratings on this show, which soon "twinkled" its way into the toilet.

Phyl and Mikhy

This was yet another situation comedy that had more interesting situations offscreen than on. The show, about two track stars who wanted to get married (no, they weren't both men—one was a man, one was a woman; but one was also a Russian and the other was an American), had originally been intended as a topical series to be broadcast prior to the coverage of the 1980 Summer Olympics from Moscow. But then Russia invaded Afghanistan, and the United States withdrew its team, and Olympic coverage was canceled—and so, almost, was this show. But CBS figured with all the time and money (especially money) invested in the show, they might as well run the six episodes that had been made as a summer replacement for *The Stockard Channing Show*. They needn't have bothered.

Here, in greater detail—for those who are dying to hear it—is the story of *Phyl and Mikhy:* Phyllis "Phyl" Wilson (Murphy Cross) is a female track star who falls in love with Mikhail "Mikhy" Orlov (Rick Lohman, transplanted from the daytime soap *Search for Tomorrow*). There were, of course, complications. Since he was a Russian, he had to defect to the United States. And since they had no money, they had to move in with Phyl's father, Max Wilson (Larry Haines, who had played Lohman's grandfather on *Search for Tomorrow*). Max, of course, was a bit dubious about his new Russian son-in-law. Meanwhile, Mikhy had to cope with life, American-style—from kitchen appliances to language (he pronounced "dad" like "dead," which got him in some trouble). Meanwhile, Vladimir Gimenko (Michael Pataki), the requisite Mad Russian who worked at the fictitious L.A. Consulate, was always on their tails, trying to get Mikhy to return to Mamma Russia. Edgar "Truck" Morley (Jack Dodson) played Max's boss. Rae Allen played Max's girlfriend, who was always talking about orgies.

Sanford

After all the disputes on the set of *Sanford and Son* (see 1971–1972 for the in-depth dirt), who would have ever thought that Redd Foxx would've tried to become Fred Sanford again? But he did.

This midseason CBS show debuted on March 15. Here was the revived—no, the resurrected—format: Lamont was gone—working on the Alaskan pipeline—which left Fred all alone to run his Watts junkyard. Helping him were two new partners: down-trodden, jive-talkin' Rollo Larson (Nathaniel Taylor, who'd also played Rollo on the original *Sanford and Son*) and Cal Pettie (Dennis Burkley), a fat white southerner who'd invested a couple of thousand dollars to claim part ownership in Fred's "semi-precious recyclables," as Fred called them. Also living with Fred was Aunt Esther's son Cliff (Clinton Derricks-Carroll), who was enrolled at a nearby college. Even Aunt Esther (LaWanda Page) stopped by for occasional visits.

Fred also had a full-time girlfriend, Evelyn Lewis (Marguerite Ray), who was a wealthy Beverly Hills widow.

Sanford

Her freeloading, status-conscious brother Winston (Percy Rodrigues) was always trying to break up the relationship. Even her maid Clara (Cathy Cooper), was not crazy about Fred (nor he about her). The only one who seemed to like Fred was Evelyn's daughter Cissy (Suzanne Stone), who thought Fred was a relief from all the stuffy suitors and friends her mother had. Evelyn, meanwhile, wanted to marry Fred. He was not so sure. But he finally did it (though only as a ploy to improve the ratings) in January of 1981.

The show had one of those schizophrenic broadcast histories on NBC. It started out on Saturday nights at 9 P.M. from March to July. Then, for August and September, it was moved to Wednesday nights at 9:30. Then, Friday nights at 8:30 in January of 1981. It was then off the air for four months and finally resurfaced—and died—in May on Friday nights at 8:30. And you wondered why you couldn't find it.

Semi-Tough

This sitcom—borrowed from the movie of the same name, which was borrowed from the book of the same name—lasted almost less time than it took to write this sentence. It had its premiere on May 29, 1979, and by the middle of June it was off the air. All courtesy of ABC.

The slapstick story—for those who haven't seen/read/seen it before: two macho members of the New York Bulls (a team that always loses)—Billy Clyde Pucket (Bruce McGill) and Shake Tiller (David Hasselhoff)—are roommates who take in a pretty young woman named Barbara Jane Bookman (Markie Post), and they live platonically ever-after. Sort of *Three's Company*, sports-style.

According to the trade paper *The Hollywood Reporter*, "*Semi-Tough* isn't even semi-funny, and so far the concept is limited, the characters are limited, the acting is limited and the prospect for survival limited . . ."

Others in the cast included Hugh Gillin as Big Ed Bookman, Mary Jo Catlett as Big Barb, Jim McKrell as Burt Danby, Ed Peck as Coach Cooper, Bubba Smith as Puddin, and Freeman King as Story Time.

The Six O'Clock Follies

This adventurous sitcom about the military personnel assigned to a U.S. Army TV station in Vietnam during the war, started (and ended) its life as a limited-run six-episode summer replacement series on NBC. The show attempted to deal with the serious aspects of the Vietnam War, and the people whose lives revolved around it.

Those included black anchorman-soldier Corporal Don (Robby) Robinson (played by Larry Fishburne, who, at age 15, had been cast in *Apocalypse Now*); newscaster Sam (A.C. Weary); weather-girl Candi (Aarika Wells); scrounging entrepreneur Nick "Midas" Metkovich (Philip Charles MacKenzie); nincompoop assistant Lieutenant J.G. Vaughan Beuhler III (Randall Carver); their beleaguered commanding officer, Colonel Harvey Marvin (Joby Baker); and Corporal Percy Wiggins (Dave Hubbard).

In one episode, Robinson encounters problems because he's black. In another, Robinson craves the action of the front lines. One week, Candi draws the ire of a visiting congressman who insists she's been too ribald on the air and wants her fired. President Johnson eventually intervenes, and the day is saved—but not the series.

Struck by Lightning

Sometimes a silly show seems even sillier if you read about it, rather than watch it. If you want to know about a silly show that's going to sound sillier, read on.

Struck by Lightning—which debuted on CBS in the fall—was about a guy named Frank (Jack Elam), who was caretaker of the run-down Brightwater Inn on the Old Boston Post Road in rural Massachusetts, circa 1979. Enter Ted Stein (Jeffrey Kramer), a young science teacher who had recently inherited the inn and was planning to sell it. But then Ted discovered that Frank was really the

Struck by Lightning *(from right): Frank (Jack Elam) 'n' Stein (Jeffrey Kramer)*

231-year-old Frankenstein monster and that he, Ted, was the great-great-grandson of the original Dr. Frankenstein (Ted and Frank—Frank 'n' Stein—get it?). So each week (and there weren't many of them), they set out to keep the inn open and recreate Ted's ancestor's life-sustaining formula so that Frank could remain alive. Now, Frank—as opposed to the monster on the midnight movies—was a kind and gentle, even clumsy, monster, no doubt thought to be lovable by the show's creators.

But Frank 'n' Stein didn't have the run of the inn to themselves. Also in the inn were a longtime, left-over boarder, Glenn (Bill Erwin); Nora (Millie Slavin), the lady who'd managed the inn before Ted's arrival; her boy, Brian (played by Jeff Cotler); and hot-to-sell real estate agent Walt Calvin (Richard Stahl, who'd been an irregular on *Mork and Mindy*).

Does it all sound silly? Well, try this one: There is this space alien named Mork—from a planet called Ork—and he drops in to visit this girl named Mindy (Mork and Mindy—cute, huh?)—and . . .

Struck by Lightning was canceled by CBS after three episodes.

United States

RICHARD: It's no thrill lying next to you like I'm some accident the dog had in bed.
LIBBY: You've got enough nastiness in you to be a one-man show.
RICHARD: I'm sorry.
LIBBY: Sorry doesn't make it anymore . . . not after you're ten.
RICHARD: I never mean to be rotten.
LIBBY: I know, it's just a gift. . . . We've had this fight so many times I think it goes on when we're not here.

So Edward Albee wrote his first sitcom. No. This isn't a scene from the "Virginia Woolf" sequel, but the most-talked-about (and perhaps the least-watched) show of the season. Created by Larry Gelbart (he had given television *M*A*S*H*), it was heralded as the first "eighties sitcom." It lasted less than eight episodes.

If the show was a failure, it was an honorable—albeit controversial—one. Some critics praised it to the sky, saying it was the new wave of television comedy; others said that it was plodding and ponderous. Whatever, there'd never been anything like it on TV. Nor will there be for some time.

The title *United States* referred not to the country, but to marriage—the state of being united. The show centered around Richard and Libby Chapin (Beau Bridges and Helen Shaver) who lived in the Los Angeles suburbs and had two sons: Dylan (Rossie Harris) and Nicky (Justin Dana). The stories included problems about a dinner party guest list, their young son's dyslexia, Libby's reunion with an old family friend who may have molested her when she was a girl, their different attitudes about sex, their admission that each had been unfaithful—and not one of the stories ever got solved. Kind of like real life. Not only were there no happy endings, there was no theme music and—horrors!—no laugh track. Not even a studio audience to provide real laughs. And sometimes there were no laughs, like when the characters talked about death, infidelity and divorce.

"Everybody keeps talking about the twelve-year-old audience," Gelbart said before *United States* premiered. "I believe there are a lot of thirty-two- and forty-two-year-olds out there who are hungry for thinking and feeling, and who are willing to work with what they're watching." Gelbart also said he thought that the show's time slot—10:30 P.M.. opposite the middle of one-hour dramas—was "insulting" on the part of the network. When the show died, Gelbart said he had had it with television. "I've had the best of it and I've had the worst of it. I'd rather just watch it now."

Working Stiffs: *Michael Keaton and Jim Belushi*

Working Stiffs

Jim Belushi (forever to be known as brother-of-John, but also star of *Who's Watching the Kids?*) and Michael Keaton (who'd been in *All's Fair* and who went on to become a movie star in 1982's *Night Shift*) teamed up together as two young brothers, Ernie and Mike O'Rourke, who wanted to make it in the business world. They were ambitious—but also klutzy—janitors who wanted to work their way from the bottom of the building to the top of the building management field. It seemed that slapstick was their ticket to the top. Or at least CBS thought so.

Also on this extra-short-lived (three episodes) show: Val Bisoglio played Al Steckler, their uncle who owned the building where they worked; Phil Rubinstein played Frank Falzone, their immediate supervisor; Allan Arbus (he had played Major Sidney Friedman on *M*A*S*H*) was Mitch Hannigan, who owned the Playland Cafe which the boys lived over; Lorna Patterson (later Private Benjamin on TV) played waitress Nikki Evashevsky, their friend and confidante.

1980–1981

WHATEVER HAPPENED TO 1980–1981?

Good question. Here's the lineup: A little *M*A*S*H* (which would be kicking around for two more seasons), *Mork and Mindy* (which was on its last "nanoo"), and the old standbys: *One Day at a Time, Alice, Archie Bunker's Place, The Jeffersons, Laverne and Shirley, Happy Days, Three's Company*, etc., etc., etc.—you probably know it by heart now. Nothing exciting. Nothing risky. Nothing tube-shattering. Just the same old fare. But meanwhile, according to statistical reports, people were having these boxes—and not Nielsen boxes—surgically attached to their TV sets that let them watch movies, uncut and uncensored. And they started attaching other boxes to their sets—called video games. Finally, there was an alternative to the three networks. Network officials were pooh-poohing this new technology. But look at what they gave us as an alternative to the alternative: Spun-out spin-offs, trendy cute-coms, and more movie rip-offs. Well, at least they finally canceled *Hello, Larry*. Read on.

OFF-SCREEN

9/17 War rages in Middle East between Iraq and Iran.
11/2 US and Iran bargain for release of Iranian-held American hostages.
11/12 Voyager I spacecraft discovers new moons of Saturn and Jupiter.
1/20 On 444th day of captivity, American hostages released from Iran.
3/30 President Reagan survives would-be assassin's bullet.
5/13 Pope John Paul II shot in Vatican Square.
7/29 Prince Charles marries Lady Diana Spencer.

ALSO RANS

Bosom Buddies

Pre-*Tootsie*—the Dustin Hoffman movie in which he masqueraded as a woman to get work in show business—copywriter Henry Desmond (Peter Scolari) and commercial artist Kip Wilson (Tom Hanks) dressed up like women (Hildegarde and Buffy) to get a place to live. You see, when their apartment building was demolished, the only place they could afford to move to was the for-women-only Susan B. Anthony Hotel. The ironic part of *Bosom Buddies* was that the best part of the show was when the two guys were two guys; often, when they were in drag, the show became a drag.

As in *Some Like It Hot* (which many reviewers believed to be the inspiration of *Bosom Buddies*), the two guys had a brotherly bond and got into a lot of weird predicaments. Kip was in love with dizzy-but-beautiful nurse Sonny Lumet ("Sonny, Sonny, Sonny," he used to sigh), played by Donna Dixon. But Sonny was only interested in being friends with Buffy, who lived across the hall from her in the hotel, although she did occasionally date Kip, who was Buffy's "brother." Following so far? Now, Sonny's roommate, Amy Cassidy (Wendie Jo Sperber)—the only one who knew Hildy and Buffy's real identity—was the chunky receptionist at the ad agency where the guys

Bosom Buddies: *Tom Hanks and Peter Scolari*

Some sample storylines from *Bosom Buddies:* (1) Kip quits his job over an ad campaign, sure that best pal Henry will join him in resigning. Wrong; (2) Henry's scared he's losing Kip as a friend when Kip starts palling around with an old buddy who's now a big rock star; (3) Henry joins a video dating service where he meets a woman who claims she keeps company . . . with the devil; (4) Kip gets crazy-jealous when nurse Sonny gets the hots for a blind patient, as Kip and Henry—dressed up as Buffy and Hildegarde—watch while working as candy stripers; (5) Henry's mad at Kip, who's offered to let Sonny move into their apartment after Amy's thrown her out.

In 1982, ABC tried again—and this time succeeded. *Bosom Buddies* was canceled.

Checking In

Marla Gibbs, who was beloved as the Jeffersons' maid Florence on that hit show, got a shot at her own hit show. Unfortunately for her—and fortunately for *The Jeffersons*—it missed, and she spun back onto her old show. (This didn't often happen with spun-out spin-offs. Flo never returned to *Alice*. *Rhoda* never moved back to *Mary Tyler Moore*. And the Ropers never went back to reclaim *Three's Company*.)

Checking In transported wiseacre Florence from "a deluxe apartment in the sky" to a New York hotel, the St. Frederick, where she was head housekeeper. Instead of George, there was an aggravating—and snobbish—manager, Lyle Block (played by Larry Linville). In fact, Block

Checking In

worked. She, incidentally, had the hots for Henry, who was mainly interested in writing. At the office, Amy, Kip and Henry's hard-edged boss was the conniving Ruth Dunbar (Holland Taylor), who wasn't above appropriating their ideas.

It all sounds rather complicated in print, but the real comedy behind *Bosom Buddies* was the freshness with which it was written and acted. There was a contemporary hipness to the show, an easy camaraderie between the characters that made these sitcom people seem almost realistic. The references bandied about on the show—to *Laverne and Shirley, Urban Cowboy, Underdog, Twilight Zone,* champion wrestling, and Joan Crawford "hurt-me pumps"—illustrate this.

Naturally, a show with this much wit was—what else?—canceled by the network. Such cynical publications as the *Village Voice* adored the show and printed articles of protest, urging readers to write letters to ABC to demand the show's reinstatement. Whether or not people actually wrote in, the network had a change of heart, and brought the show back the following season for a limited run. The second-season opening took the air out of the title: Buffy and Hildy finally revealed themselves to their hotel-mates as Kip and Henry (right in the middle of a big political party). From then on, the premise was only pulled out occasionally. *Bosom Buddies* became another gang comedy—or "ensemble comedy," as the more refined networks like to call them.

wasn't at all unlike Major Frank Burns, Linville's character on *M*A*S*H*.

By this time Florence wasn't just working *for* people; she had people working for *her*. Among them were her efficient assistant Elena Beltran (Liz Torres), and Betty, one of the floor supervisors (Ruth Brown). There were also the subcompetent house detective, Earl Bellamy (Patrick Collins); the big-bodied heating/air conditioning/ plumbing supervisor, Hank Sabatino (Robert Costanzo); as well as the bellboy, Dennis (Jordan Gibbs).

The show was greeted with negatives from the reviewers. And not many viewers. CBS pulled it off the air within a matter of weeks. And Florence was back with the Jeffersons where she belonged.

I'm a Big Girl Now

Diane Canova—daughter of Judy and alumna of *Soap* (where she played Corinne Tate Flotsky for three seasons)—teamed up with Danny Thomas (playing her father, Benjamin Douglass) in this rather drab show—according to the critics, anyway—about a divorced woman named Diana Cassidy, who comes home to live with her suddenly-single father, a dentist. Naturally, he was cantankerous because his wife has run off to Spain with Ira, his partner (she was obviously into teeth). The point of the show—well, the title tells the tale.

To add some comic relief to the comic relief were Diana's daughter Rebecca (though everyone called her Becky), played by Rori King; Benjamin's neurotic son (and therefore Diana's neurotic brother), Walter, played by Michael Durrell; Edie, the ultratense boss at the research center where Diana worked (played by Sheree North, Lou Grant's occasional girl on *The Mary Tyler Moore Show*). Actor/comic Martin Short (hot off the previous season's *The Associates*, and before he went on to *SCTV*) played a character named Neal Stryker.

A sample plot line: After a crank call, Edie moves in with Diana. Meanwhile, Neal installs a security system that has the two women scared to go into the house.

ABC canceled the show midseason, proving that you can't go home again.

Harper Valley P.T.A./Harper Valley

It started its life as a 1968 hit song by Jeannie C. Riley—all about a widowed mother, with a teenage daughter, who's been branded a loose woman by the oh-so-respectable members of the Harper Valley P.T.A. Respectable is not the word. Mrs. Johnson, at the P.T.A. meeting that afternoon, wreaks justifiable revenge and wrecks the P.T.A.'s starched attitudes by showing the members to be what they thought she was: adulterous, drunken, and hypocritical. The song became a sitcom, starring Barbara Eden (formerly the dreamt-of Jeannie) as Stella Johnson, the looked-down-upon mother. It started out as an hour-long series; then was trimmed to half an hour. "We just couldn't lick it in the hour form," explained a network executive. Said Eden: "I think we can do better, even though the first season was acceptable to the audience, as horrid as it was . . ."

The versions had one thing in common (besides the music): they were about hypocrisy in a small Southern town, with liberated Stella fighting the hypocrites. Sort of *Green Acres* meets Norman Lear. Stella, a widow, had a thirteen-year-old daughter, Dee (Jenn Thompson). Both of them lived in—where else?—Harper Valley, which appeared to be upright, but was filled with adulterers, drunks and assorted creeps. Stella drove the P.T.A. crazy (she had been elected a board member), because she did as she liked: she wore miniskirts (!), she flirted (!), and the board members thought she was a rotten role model for kids . . . and their fathers (naturally, they all lusted after Eden's body, just like "Master" before them). So all those lady board members tried to get Stella ousted. But Stella fought back, and won every time.

Her leading adversary was rich society-lady Flora Simpson Reilly (Anne Francine), whose entire family was just as bad: daughter Wanda Reilly Taylor (Bridget Hanley), leading attorney and son-in-law Bobby Taylor (Rod McCary), Dee's classmate Scarlett Taylor (Suzi Dean), and assorted others. Stella did have one buddy in town—beauty parlor proprietor Cassie Bowman (Fannie Flagg—remember her from *The New Dick Van Dyke Show*?). Oh, yeah—Stella didn't just sit home and collect her pension checks. No, she went right out there into the city that hated her and sold Angelglow cosmetics, door to door.

Hard as they tried, the show never really caught on. In fact, most of the critics hated it. (This from the *Hollywood Reporter*: "Eden's style of acting is strictly lightweight . . . the series is juvenile and relentlessly callow . . .").

The show began as a midseason replacement, debuting on January 16, 1981. It finally went off the air the following season.

It's a Living/Making a Living

This is a show that started out good and ended up not-so-good. It was another "gang comedy"—this time the gang was a bunch of waitresses in a ritzy Los Angeles restaurant. During the first, and best, season, this was the gang: knowingly wise Lois Adams (Susan Sullivan); sweet, forthright Dot Higgins (Gail Edwards); innocent Vicki Allen (Wendy Schaal); sassy, sexy Cassie Cranston (Ann Jillian); and sharp, savvy Jan Hoffmeyer (Barrie Young-fellow). They were ruled by their affected supervisor Nancy Beebe (Marian Mercer), and they ruled their always-on-the-make narcissistic piano player Sonny Mann (Paul Kreppel). Plus there was the dictatorial chef Mario (Bert Remsen).

The women talked about sex, wore skimpy uniforms, laughed a lot and chatted a lot. None of this pleased the Religious Right, who labeled the show Unfit and Immoral in their list of objectionable programs. ABC didn't dump the show, but it did insist on a title change (that way, the same show—with the new title—wouldn't be on the hit list).

In the fall of 1981, *Making a Living* had its debut with a pared-down cast. Gone were Remsen (whose character was replaced by frustrated, sarcastic gourmet chef Dennis Hubner, played by Earl Boen), Schaal and Sullivan. The new arrival was Louise Lasser—who had previously guested on several sitcoms before becoming *Mary Hartman, Mary Hartman*, and had played Alex's wife on *Taxi* the year before. Her character, Maggie McBurney, was an extension of sorts of Mary; Maggie was a guileless, vulnerable woman who was often tactless. A cross between Gracie Allen and Mary Hartman.

Some sample story lines from the resurrected *Making a Living:* (1) "Of Mace and Men": Maggie is victimized by a purse snatcher, so the waitresses sign up for a self-defense course; (2) "The Boys of Summer": Minor league players hang out at the restaurant, and Maggie, Dot, Cassie and Jan get baseball fever. Especially Jan, who falls for a third baseman, Stan (played by Larry Breeding)—who, she finds out, is married and a father.

Critics were not exactly enchanted by the revival of the show. Said the *Soho Weekly News:* "*It's a Living* last season dealt with a group of waitresses and particularly the problems of two single parents among them. It had low-key sympathetic characters and realistic plotlines (cf. *Taxi*). It did not do well. Now, remade . . . it is moving rapidly towards a low, broad and silly style. I trust it will do even worse."

It did. ABC canceled *Making a Living*—without any help at all from the Religious Right—after thirteen weeks.

Ladies' Man

Lawrence Pressman (who played Lou Grant's philandering son-in-law on *The Mary Tyler Moore Show*) got a show of his own. It seemed like a promising premise: he's the only guy working on an all-women's magazine. Trouble

was, it was just too hard to tell all those ladies apart. Let's see. There was his acid-tongued boss Elaine Holstein (Louise Sorel), plus the other garden varieties of gals-at-the-office: Gretchen (Simone Griffeth), Susan (Allison Argo), and Andrea (Betty Kennedy). One of them—no one could expect to remember which—was once asked: "What do you wear to bed?" Her answer: "A little perfume behind each ear."

Then—to fill out the premise—there were all women at home: Alan Thackeray (Pressman's character) had custody of his very, very, very precocious (what else?) daughter Amy (played by Natasha Ryan), and living next door was his wisecracking (what else?) neighbor-lady Betty (Karen Morrow). The only semi-regular man on the show (not to imply he wasn't a "regular man," but only that he didn't appear regularly) was Herb Edelman as Reggie, "Women's Life's" crazed bookkeeper.

In the first episode, Alan is assigned to write an article entitled "Sexual Harassment and the Working Woman"—which he is supposed to investigate firsthand.

Plagued by petered-out ratings, CBS canceled *Ladies' Man* after it had run out its 13 weeks.

Park Place

This little-known—and seldom-watched—sitcom aired on CBS for just a few weeks in April of 1981. The premise: a bunch of lawyers, working in a New York legal aid clinic . . . well, that's the premise. *Park Place* was what is called in the trade a "gang comedy"—much like *Barney Miller* and *Taxi*—it wasn't really *about* anything; it just *was*.

The loonies on the Park Place Division of the New York City Legal Assistance Bureau included senior attorney David Ross (played by Harold Gould, who had once been Rhoda's father), and the five young lawyers who comprised his staff: feminist Joel "Jo" Keene (Mary Elaine Monti); status-seeker and opportunist Howie Beech (Don Calfa); naive and eager Jeff O'Neil (David Clennon); a black, wheelchair-bound Vietnam vet, Aaron "Mac" Mac-Rae (Lionel Smith); and a Harvard grad who was trying to fit in, Brad Lincoln (James Widdoes). But those weren't even the real loonies. The true crazies were the tired, the poor, the obnoxious—all trying for free legal assistance. And then there was the born-again (and again and again) secretary Frances (Alice Drummond), and the male receptionist who was always frazzled, Ernie Rice (Cal Gibson).

Although the viewers didn't respond, some of the reviewers did. The *New York Times* called *Park Place* one of the "most promising" of the new shows, but with only four episodes aired, viewers didn't get much of a chance to see for themselves.

Private Benjamin

From the 1980 hit Goldie Hawn movie all about the adventures of a Jewish American Princess who joins the military, *Private Benjamin* hit the small screen in the spring of 1981. It did well enough on CBS to be renewed for the following season—where it didn't do well enough to be picked up for the rest of the year. CBS canceled *Private Benjamin* at halftime of 1982.

The sitcom, like the movie, was about Judy Benjamin (Lorna Patterson), a rich, spoiled young woman who is seeking security in the US Army. (The network was seeking security, too, so they made sure that Judy's religion was never divulged.) Judy and buddies were stationed at Fort Travis, outside Biloxi, Mississippi. Recreating their movie roles were Eileen Brennan as the mean-spirited Captain Doreen Lewis, and Hal Williams as the no-nonsense drill sergeant Ted Ross. Judy's fellow recruits were street-wise Maria Gianelli (Lisa Raggio), who picked the army over jail; Rayleen White (Joyce Little), a smart, ambitious former resident of the Detroit ghetto; Barbara Ann Glass (Joan Roberts), a country girl who sang strange country songs; and Carol Winter (Ann Ryerson), an obnoxious, brown-nose brat.

Eileen Brennan, of course, had been in sitcoms before, including the doomed *A New Kind of Family*. Lorna Patterson, who'd co-starred in *Working Stiffs* and *Goodtime Girls*, had played the female lead in the *Sidney Schorr* TV movie on which *Love, Sidney* was based. She had said she felt pressure following in Goldie Hawn's role: "I know people are going to compare us and that's fine. But we're not doing the same words or the same action."

According to gossip columnist Marilyn Beck, "A not-so-private war has broken out on the *Private Benjamin* set between leading ladies Lorna Patterson and Eileen Brennan. Actually, the matter of just who is *the* leading lady on the show seems to be the root of the trouble between the two actresses. I'm told things have gotten so bad that Lorna and Eileen are simply not talking to one another—except when the script demands it." (Said Brennan two months prior: "Lorna's a joy to work with. I wish we could do more good scenes together.")

For the 1982–1983 season, *Private Benjamin* was back on the air with new writers and producers, and some new members of the cast, including *Bosom Buddies* alumna Wendie Jo Sperber as Stacy Kouchalakas, a new (but insecure) staff photographer whom Judy met when she was transferred out of the infantry and into Army public affairs. And—coincidence of coincidences—Captain Lewis happened to be the head of public affairs. The supporting cast consisted of Private Gianelli as an MP, and Private Sims (Damito Jo Freeman).

Also that year, Brennan was injured in an automobile accident, and Polly Holliday (formerly of *Flo*) was brought in—not to replace her, but just to fill in as a new character, with the understanding that she'd exit when Brennan was well enough to return. Unfortunately, they never had the chance. *Private Benjamin* was canceled after 13 weeks of the 1982–1983 season.

Too Close for Comfort

Viewers who loved *Three's Company* were bound to adore *Too Close for Comfort*, which dealt with sex as something dirty, demeaning and to be constantly and continually lusted after (but never fulfilled). The premise (borrowed from the British *Keep It in the Family*) centered around two parents who agree to let their curvy young daughters move out of their San Francisco apartment and live together—in the vacant apartment right below theirs. The previous tenant—who had died—was a transvestite (he couldn't have been just an accountant,

Too Close for Comfort: *Ted Knight*

right?) and, during the first season, there were a lot of sex-switch jokes. That's the kind of humor that kept the audiences loving this show. Said the L.A. *Times*: "The popularity of this show has to rank right up there with such other unexplained phenomena as Billy Carter, pet rocks and French Lick, Ind. . . . You have to wonder whether a nation that gets jollies watching *Too Close for Comfort* can be trusted to tie its own shoes, let alone elect a president."

But *Too Close for Comfort* never became a monster hit, although it had every chance. Located immediately following the hit *Three's Company, Too Close* couldn't have been closer and, lucky for it—it picked up the follow-through audience.

Starring was Ted Knight playing Henry Rush, a professional cartoonist (he drew the "Cosmic Cow" kids' comic strip) who was middle-aged, conservative and orderly. Knight, of course, had created the legendary Ted Baxter on *The Mary Tyler Moore Show*. Playing his wife Muriel was Nancy Dussault, former Broadway musical star and regular on *The New Dick Van Dyke Show*. In a 1982 *TV Guide* cover story, she publicly lamented *Too Close's* scripts under a banner headline that beamed "I hate dealing with these people"—meaning the writers and caliber of actors she had to work with. An insider with the show claimed this was a publicity move to improve sagging ratings, but those close to Dussault said she meant it.

There were others on the show too. Deborah Van Valkenburgh played their brunette daughter, Jackie Rush, who worked in a bank. But it was Jackie's sister, Sara—a blonde, bubbly, nubile freshman at San Francisco State College—who personified the term "jiggle comedy," and it seemed the writers and producers took every opportunity they got to get Sara (played by Lydia Cornell) jumping around and shaking her mammaries. So much for responsible television.

At the start of the second season, Muriel—upon turning 52—discovers she's pregnant. Her pregnancy was good for 12 months (a new record) of jokes, finally erupting into birth in the third season.

The humor on the show was definitely broad—in all senses of the word. This exchange, for example: Sara: "I just happen to be a 10!" Jackie: "You just happen to be a 36C!" More than breast size, the humor revolved around father Henry fretting about his daughters' virginity, or loss of it. On *Too Close for Comfort,* there wasn't a laugh track, but a snigger track.

The Two of Us

Critics praised this midseason replacement—which went on to become a regular show the following season—for the intelligence of the writing and the terrific ensemble acting. Based on the English *Two's Company, The Two of Us* had an interesting premise: What happens when an English butler goes to work for a modern American household—especially when the proper servant is working for a free-wheeling TV talk show host who happens to be a single parent.

Comic actress Mimi Kennedy played Nan Gallagher, who was as sloppy as her manservant Robert Brentwood was neat. *The Two of Us* was a cross-cultural *Odd Couple.* Playing Brentwood was Peter Cook who, with Dudley

Moore, had been part of *Beyond the Fringe* in the sixties. This was his American series debut. Said the *New York Times,* "Together, Mr. Cook and Miss Kennedy are one of the best teams to hit television since Lucy and Desi."

Oliver Clark played Nan's agent Cubby Royce and—as an added treat—the wonderful young Dana Hill played daughter Gabrielle "Gabby" Gallagher.

In the first episode of the show, the idea of working for a woman with a child nauseates overbearing, sarcastic, pompous Brentwood. But the idea also intrigues him, and he takes the job. And since Nan is always entertaining a diverse group of people, all of his skills—the many languages he knows, the gourmet cooking—come in handy. He puts order in her disorderly household, while she goes off to work (her co-host on "Midmorning Manhattan" is the unseen Reggie Philbis—a parody of real-life gab host Regis Philbin).

The Two of Us: *Peter Cook*

The story lines support the premise. Once, the plumbing breaks down and Brentwood has to share his bathroom with Nan and Gabby, which repulses him. Then he finds out that Gabby is having a slumber party. When Nan reels off the menu for the evening—potato chips, Cheezits, Mallomars and hot dogs—without blinking, Brentwood asks, "Might I suggest a red wine?"

The show aired only a few episodes, and then returned the next year on CBS. This time, however, it was less successful—for some reason it didn't work as well, and those first episodes will always remain the best. It was finally canceled due to low ratings in 1982.

1981–1982

WHATEVER HAPPENED TO 1981–1982?

Remember 1969–1970? That was the TV season when we had such fascinating programs as *Green Acres, To Rome with Love, That Girl, The Flying Nun,* and *The Brady Bunch*. Well, this season—1981–1982—made 1969–1970 seem like the Golden Age of Television. It's not that the shows were worse (some, like *Love, Sidney,* were even better). It's just that, for the most part, they were the same. They were just like the shows we had hated last year, which were retreads of the shows we had hated the year before, and which would be renovated into next year's shows. Instant nostalgia. The best that can be said for 1981–1982 is that it was the TV season that taught millions of Americans what that funny-looking little button on the front of the cabinet is for: to turn the set *off*.

OFF-SCREEN

9/25 First woman, Sandra Day O'Connor, appointed to serve as associate justice of US Supreme Court.
10/6 Egypt's President Anwar Al-Sadat assassinated while reviewing military parade.
10/26 Soviet submarine *Whisky*, reportedly carrying nuclear warheads, runs aground in restricted Swedish naval zone.
12/13 Martial law declared in Poland in response to Solidarity strikes.
1/13 An Air Florida jetliner crashes into the 14th Street bridge in Washington, D.C., killing 78.
4/2 Argentina seizes British Falkland Islands.
6/6 Israel, attempting to destroy PLO strongholds, invades Lebanon.
6/25 US Secretary of State, Alexander M. Haig, resigns.
6/30 Deadline for ratification of the Equal Rights Amendment expires.

ALSO RANS

Bakers Dozen

Ron Silver (who had played Rhoda and Brenda Morgenstern's buddy on *Rhoda* and Stockard Channing's boss on the second incarnation of her show) got a show of his own. This cop show (they called it a comedy-drama) was a *Barney Miller*-like ensemble sitcom about Mike Lacosale (Silver) and Terry Munson (Cindy Weintraub), who are undercover cops . . . and just plain undercover (they're lovers).

The most interesting thing about the show was that it was created by Salvatore (Sonny) Grosso, a local New York cop for 20 years who, with his partner, found $3.5 million in heroin in a French TV personality's car (this event was later chronicled in the movie *The French Connection*). Talking about *Bakers Dozen*, Grosso said: "I based this show on my own experiences. It's about people who have a very difficult, pressured, tense job being cops and how the pressure of the job enables them to release their humor." The show was filmed on location in New York City's Little Italy. The title, incidentally, referred to the special anticrime unit under the command of Captain Baker (Doris Belak).

Others in the show (which debuted on CBS in March of 1982 and was off the air soon after) included Alan Weeks as O.J. Kelly, Sam MacMurray as Harve Shoendorf, and Thomas Quinn as Martin.

Best of the West

This show—because it came from the creators of *Taxi*—had high expectations attached to it. It was one thing that the Nielsen Families never discovered (according to one legend, they never do discover the good stuff). But it was another thing when the critics (who, according to their own legend, always discover the good stuff) didn't like *Best of the West* a whole lot. The New York *Daily News* dubbed it "the Worst of the West."

Best of the West: *Carlene Watkins, Tom Ewell and Joel Higgins*

Here's what it was about: Sam Best (Joel Higgins, who would go on to co-star in the next season's *Silver Spoons*), a widower with a 10-year-old son, Daniel (Meeno Peluce), left Philadelphia for a fresh start out west in the corrupt town of Copper Creek. Along with him was his rattlebrained new wife Elvira (Carlene Watkins). They met while Sam's fellow Union soldiers burned down her plantation (oh, yeah—this show took place in the *old* west). Anyway, Elvira's father (Andy Griffith) couldn't forgive her for marrying a Yankee (at least not until the third episode). The Bests opened up a general store and Sam became the town's totally inept marshal as a result of a bumbled gunfight. Also on the show: Tom Ewell who played Jerome Kullens.

Perhaps the best of *Best of the West* was the show's villains. In the tradition of *Taxi's* Louie De Palma was deliciously mean Parker Tillman (Leonard Frey), who was the owner of the Square Deal Saloon. His thick-witted Quasimodo was named Frog (Tracey Walter). In episode two, the Calico Kid turned up. "You can call me Calico or you can call me Kid . . . I'm easy," he said. He gave up gunfighting to become a cook at the Square Deal Saloon.

Best of the West was a broad spoof of the old west that proved that viewers liked their old west narrow and serious.

Filthy Rich

This summer spoof on *Dallas* was an instant hit. And an almost-as-instant flop. When CBS aired several episodes of the sitcom during the summer of 1981, the ratings went through the roof. Number One on the Nielsens. Reviewers were aghast because they thought the show was so dreadful and so many people were watching it; they got their retribution when they still thought the show was dreadful during the 1982–1983 season, but few enough people were watching it to jeopardize its existence.

Here's what all the fuss was about: An old southern codger (Slim Pickens) dies and leaves his fortune to his illegitimate son, Wild Bill Westchester (Jerry Hardin) and his harebrained wife Bootsie (Anne Wedgeworth, formerly of *Three's Company*). Prior to his death, the old goat had videotaped his will, and we got to see all his loony heirs gather at his Memphis mansion and bicker about the loot. Naturally, the family doesn't get along, but the deceased stipulated that they must get along—or no dough. His widow Kathleen (Delta Burke) is not amused by any of this (especially the fact that Wild Bill got the money). That night, Bill and Bootsie are celebrating in their bedroom lustily whooping it up. Carlotta—the head vamp and money-grubber played by Dixie Carter—says "I'm going to call the animal shelter and have them taken away." Carlotta also has no time for Kathleen's complaints and says: "Spare us the hysterics—if sex were fast food, you'd have an arch over your head."

Said the *New York Times*, "*Filthy Rich* has the distinction of being the most vulgar and raunchy new show of the season." But not for long; keep reading.

Gimme a Break

That's what the critics said about this show when they got a look at it. The creator of the show had promised that *Gimme a Break* would be "significant and deep, but it's not going to offend anybody. And it's going to be wildly funny." Critics claimed that he had broken all three promises. Said the *New York Post:* "The show is unspeakably smutty. These aren't cheap laughs, this is a fire sale. As the maid and cook of the household, Nell's principal duty is drinking coffee and telling her boss he's old and stupid." Said Nell in one episode, "The man's brain is so small you could suck it through a straw and never touch the sides."

In this show, Nell was the black maid who worked for a white police captain, Carl Kanisky (Dolph Sweet) and his three daughters. Once, the grouchy captain fired Nell for having her boyfriend in her room. She bustled off to stay with a girlfriend while he tried to run the household.

When the youngest daughter wanted lunch for school, he tossed her a loaf of bread and a jar of peanut butter. "What's this?" she asked. The captain answered, "Sandwiches. It's a kit."

Nell Carter (the bombastic Tony Award winner from *Ain't Misbehavin'*) was given a show of her own after the cancellation of *Lobo* (where she'd played Hildy). She had a lot of problems on the show, as she herself explained: "You become known as a bitch if you know what you want. You don't yell at people, but you start asking for things. I got a reputation as being hard to work with. And all of a sudden, people write things about you. Friends think you've changed." Carter took off nine months from work: "I was crazy! I had to get myself together; I had to see doctors. I mean, I was really wacko. And I'm not ashamed to say it. I realized I did not like Nell, and I had to go through a period of accepting myself."

The show was renewed by NBC the following season, when it switched from Thursday nights to Saturday nights and then back to Thursday nights—breaking up, many thought, NBC's "class lineup" because it was sandwiched in between *Fame* and *Cheers*, replacing *Taxi*.

Joanie Loves Chachi

There was no way in the world that this show was going to fail. First, it had two well-known characters, Chachi and Joanie, who viewers had grown up with for years on *Happy Days*. They were young. They were in love. She was played by Erin Moran—you know, Richie Cunningham's little sister. And he was played by teen idol Scott Baio. How could it miss?

It missed.

But not until the next season. During the 1981–1982 season, America seemed to love Joanie and Chachi as much as they loved each other. As a midseason replacement on ABC, *Joanie Loves Chachi* hit the ratings roof. But then, it was playing on Tuesday nights, right after its godparent, *Happy Days*.

Here's what it was about: Chachi Arcola had left Milwaukee and moved with his parents to Chicago, where he ended up singing in their restaurant and nightclub. Joanie turns up from Milwaukee and sees all the attention Chachi is getting from the girls in the club where he's performing, so she starts singing bubble-gum tunes with Chachi. In no time at all, she's talking her parents into letting her move to Chicago and enroll at Northwestern University—not to get an education of course, but to be near Chachi.

Also on the show: Al Molinaro (the owner of Arnold's from *Happy Days*) played Chachi's new stepfather, restaurateur Al Delvecchio; Chachi's mother Louisa was played by Ellen Travolta. Art Metrano played Chachi's

Joanie Loves Chachi: *Scott Baio, Art Metrano and Erin Moran*

patriarchal Uncle Rico, who helped Joanie and Chachi advance their careers.

Each week, Joanie and Chachi spent a lot of time—our time—singing and quarreling and holding hands and breaking up and making up and out. Not unlike real life. Baio once admitted that he and Moran were actually romantically involved at one time: "Now, we're very, very good friends. We dated years ago, but when you work with a person all day and then go out at night, it gets a little tense."

The major theme of the show, if a show such as this actually has a theme, was jealousy. When Joanie was wearing a low-cut outfit and wiggling her way through a song, sitting on customers' laps, Chachi was outraged. He once almost got into a fight with a fraternity kid when Joanie started hanging out with a college crowd and saying words like "marvy." But there was always that happy reconciliation at the end. If it hadn't been for those damned Nielsens, Joanie and Chachi could have lived happily ever after. Scheduled as the lead-in show on ABC's Thursday night in the fall of 1982, *Joanie Loves Chachi* went from being the biggest hit to the biggest disappointment. It was taken off the air at the end of 1982.

Lewis and Clark

This could have been called *Welcome Back, Kaplan*—

since it heralded Gabe Kaplan's return to network TV after the demise of his hit sitcom, 1975's *Welcome Back, Kotter*. This time around, he wasn't so lucky.

The show centered around Stewart Lewis (Kaplan), a New Yorker fed up with the city who moves his wife and two kids to a rural Texas town where he becomes a saloon owner. His first task: to fire the manager, Roscoe Clark (Guich Koock)—but when Clark prevents a beer salesman from cheating the new owner, Lewis decides not to let him go after all.

Also in the cast: Ilene Graff as Alicia Clark; Amy Linker as Kelly Clark; David Hollander as Keith Clark; Mike McManus as John (the bartender); Wendy Holcomb as Wendy (the waitress); and Aaron Fletcher as Lester.

Said Kaplan: "There is a big movement of people who are trying to simplify their lifestyles, and I think that New Yorkers will be able to relate to this show because it's about a New York family adjusting to the country atmosphere in Texas."

Kaplan resurrected an interesting device in the show: he talked directly to the camera as narrator and protagonist (à la George Burns on *The Burns and Allen Show*).

The show was a major ratings failure, and NBC took it off the air before Lewis and/or Clark could make it back to New York.

Love, Sidney

Love, Sidney star Tony Randall once described his role on the show like this: "I play your typical middle-aged Jewish homosexual who lives in a huge apartment in New York City."

It was true. Where homosexuals (Sidney Shorr could hardly be called gay) had only had guest-role parts or small humorous roles on *The Nancy Walker Show* or *The Bob Crane Show*, this was the first time America was asked to take a homosexual seriously. As a sympathetic—and funny—leading man. No kidding.

Naturally, there was an outcry. When NBC announced that it was airing a TV movie, *Sidney Shorr*, that was going to be spun off into a sitcom about a homosexual man living platonically with a young woman—*Love, Sidney*—the Moral Majority (which, as the bumper stickers say, is neither) was up in arms (among other parts of the anatomy). Naturally, those groups that were raising fire and brimstone and evangelizing that *Love, Sidney* was ruining the morals of everybody in the U.S.A. had never even seen the show. How could they? It hadn't been on the air yet. Tony Randall had this to say about the so-called religious organizations who were protesting the show: "Ambitious political oportunists. They say they're interested in moral issues, but they are really out to promote themselves. They've actually done us the biggest favor anyone

could do. They attacked something they hadn't seen, and they got us more space in the papers and more talk than we ever could have gotten on our own. For that, I say they're wonderful."

NBC, however, didn't think they were so wonderful, and after the protesting began, Sidney Shorr was never again referred to—on screen or off—as a homosexual. He simply became an older, unmarried man. Said Randall: "No, there've been no changes. I'm still playing a homosexual. *Love, Sidney* is about how a lonely soul finds a family. And the homosexuality is there to explain his loneliness. To show how he's cut off from society."

But enough behind-the-scenes. Here's what happened in front of them: *Love, Sidney* centered around the relationship between lonely Sidney Shorr, his roommate Laurie (Swoosie Kurtz) and her daughter Patti (Kaleena Kiff). It was, in the true sense of the phrase, a new kind of family. Patti's father—well, no one really knew where he was (or even who he was). Sidney had always lived with his mother—"that terrible woman," he called her—until her death. So Sidney, Laurie and Patti became each other's real family.

In the premiere episode of the sitcom, Sidney is united with six-and-a-half-year-old Patti and her mother Laurie, whom he then persuades to move in with him. (It works out fine, because Laurie has landed a part as Gloria, the town tramp who was the only survivor of a plane crash that killed 275 people, on a soap called "As Thus We Are." "You don't love her," Gloria snaps. "She's only tryin' to use her brain tumor to hang on to you.") In another episode, the head writer on Laurie's soap (played by guest Betty White) takes a romantic interest in Sidney, and unless she has her way with him, Laurie will be written out of the show.

There were touching and tender moments on the show too, such as the time Sidney finally made peace with his mother on the anniversary of her death. Or the time Laurie made peace with her parents when, thanks to Sidney, she was reunited with them.

Wisecracking Laurie was played by Broadway actress Swoosie Kurtz, who had once wandered into television as a regular on the short-short-lived Mary Tyler Moore variety show called *Mary*.

Tony Randall (who, of course, had been in *Mister Peepers* and had starred in *The Odd Couple* and *The Tony Randall Show*) was an ardent New Yorker. He signed with NBC as Sidney when that network's strategy was to get big-name TV stars to return to the small screen (James Arness, Angie Dickinson, Rock Hudson and James Garner were others with whom they tried and failed). Randall said he'd do it if the show could be shot in New York (as opposed to Los Angeles, where nearly all sitcoms are made). The other part of his deal was that NBC had to put up $50,000 a year toward a repertory company Randall wanted to form in New York. Halfway through the first season, *Love, Sidney* was ousted from its production studio in New York because the space had been committed to *Sesame Street* ("BIG BIRD KICKS 'SIDNEY' OUTTA N.Y.," the *Variety* headline screamed). Randall screamed too, but reluctantly packed up and went west. When the show got renewed for the 1982–1983 season, production moved back to New York.

In its second season, new producers were brought in (the people who'd produced and directed *Maude*), but they stayed true to the flavor of the show, which was now aired on Saturday nights. Chip Zien, who had been an irregular the first season, was added full-time to play Sidney's boss, Jason, a hard-driving adman.

But *Love, Sidney's* ratings got worse and worse and finally, midseason of 1982–1983, the network said it was putting the show on the shelf 'til a later date.

Maggie

This show—marking the sitcom debut of the American housewife's answer to Dorothy Parker, Erma Bombeck—was the first flop of the season. Ranking 65th in the Nielsens (68 was as low as you could go), *Maggie* just didn't make it.

Maggie was a light domestic comedy—sort of an Erma Bombeck column brought to life (which was exactly the idea)—all about a housewife and her husband and kids.

But even though she wrote and produced the shows, the cry kept coming that there wasn't enough Erma Bombeck in the show. Miriam Flynn played Maggie, but the character wasn't really as perceptive as Bombeck is, nor as self-critical nor as . . . face it—funny. She seemed to spend all her time at the beauty parlor or in her new car—always gossiping. Also in her cast: James Hampton as her husband Len; Christian Jacobs and Bill Jacoby as their children. (There was another son, L.J., we never saw. Maggie: "L.J.'s after me to teach him to drive." Len: "You talked to our son L.J.?" Maggie: "Well, just under the bathroom door.") Doris Roberts and Marcia Rodd were also in the cast.

Bombeck has been called a republican humorist, but none of the risks she usually takes—nor the keen observations—were here. What emerged in *Maggie* was just a string of semi-amusing jokes in search of a story. Apparently audiences thought so too, and ABC axed the show after about four episodes.

Making the Grade: *James Naughton*

CBS, *Making the Grade* debuted on Monday, April 5, 1982 and impressed the critics.

The series was about a group of teachers at Franklin High School in St. Louis, an inner-city school with rowdy kids and a variety of problems, from apathy and absenteeism to vandalism and violence. It wasn't a broad, slapstick comedy, but a serious, sophisticated comedy. These lines of dialogue indicate the flavor of the show:

Teacher (on a Monday morning): "Five more days to the weekend . . ."

Upon finding a student drinking something out of a brown paper bag in the hall, a teacher says: "Six years and you haven't learned anything—it's white wine with Hershey bars."

Heading up the cast was James Naughton as teacher Harry Barnes. Graham Jarvis ("Baby Boy" Haggers in *Mary Hartman, Mary Hartman*) played the nervous principal Jack Felspar. Other teachers were played by Alley Mills, Steven Peterman, Zane Lasky, George Wendt, Philip Charles MacKenzie, Veronica Redd and John Vargas.

Making the Grade

This was one of the finer shows of the season and, naturally, it didn't last long. A midseason replacement on

Mr. Merlin

In this short-lived sitcom, Barnard Hughes (he had played the title role on *Doc*) starred as a garage mechanic who also happened to be the reincarnation of Merlin, the magician from King Arthur's court. That's right—there's nothing wrong with your set—you read it right.

Mr. Merlin (or "Max," as he was also known) had a youthful assistant/apprentice, Zac. (Sort of *Chico and the Man* meets *The Twilight Zone*.) Their mission from CBS: to use their magic to do good deeds and come to the aid of people in distress, not for personal gain. The conflict: Max wanted Zac to use his magic powers reasonably; Zac much preferred to learn about love potions. (Incidentally, with a show held together by sheer fantasy, one would have anticipated a lot of special effects and tricks. The producer announced that this wouldn't be the case—all the tricks were just too expensive.)

Also in the cast were Elaine Joyce, playing the messenger for the sorcery business; Jonathan Price as Leo; Mallie Jackson; De Anna Robbins, and Vincent Bufano. It was Clark Brandon, who co-starred with Hughes as Zac, who was supposed to be the big attraction to the teenybopper set. "I want to be respected by my peers," said the twenty-two-year-old Brandon. "I am aware of being a teen idol and I love being one. But I want to be accepted for what I do on TV and the screen, especially by my fellow actors."

He didn't get much of a chance—not on this show, anyway. *Mr. Merlin* was canceled almost before the network could whimper "Abracadabra."

9 to 5

The rollicking Dolly Parton themesong and the basic plot were about the only things left over from the funny feminist movie when it made the transformation to a prime-time TV sitcom. Coproduced by Jane Fonda (who had produced and starred in the movie original), *9 to 5* got off to a shaky start during the 1981–1982 season on ABC. At that time actor Jeff Tambor played sexist boss Franklin Hart (the part played by Dabney Coleman in the movie). During its second season, a toned-down Mr. Hart was played by Peter Bonerz (Jerry the dentist from *The Bob Newhart Show*), who was more eccentric than sexist.

As the three secretaries, Valerie Curtin, Rachel Dennison and Rita Moreno took over the parts of Judy, Dora Lee and Violet which Fonda, Parton and Lily Tomlin had originated in the movie. Also in the TV cast was Jean Marsh (famous from *Upstairs, Downstairs*) as the office snoop, Roz.

The plots ranged from lingerie parties, to Dora Lee and Mr. Hart being trapped in his office during a storm, to Judy being fired because Hart wanted a man in the job (so she dressed up like a man and got the job). Jane Fonda made a guest appearance at the start of the second season, playing a tough security guard who thought that a secretary's lot was an easy one; through a series of flash-backs, they gained her respect.

No Soap Radio

This show had nothing to do with either soap or radio. It wasn't even a sitcom as much as it was a skitcom, filled with sight gags and silliness. *No Soap Radio* was about the goings-on at the run-down Pelican Hotel—a formerly elegant place in Atlantic City that's become seedy because it has no casino license. The hotel has leaky plumbing and decaying ceilings and is a hazard for any guests who might stay there. The hotel owner, Roger (Steve Guttenberg), is pressed by an unscrupulous lawyer to sell the Pelican to the unseen Tarantula Brothers, Joey and Nick.

The show—which lasted thirteen episodes on ABC—was a hybrid between *Monty Python's Flying Circus*, *Laugh-In*, the Marx Brothers and the Three Stooges. The opening credits—in a send-up of public television—noted that the program was being underwritten by "Trans National Petroleum and Rico's Boom Boom Room." In the middle of the plot, there was a "Special Report" announcing that Mr. Potato is missing. Then there might be a news flash that the president has asked American families to put a French fry in their windows. In one interview conducted in non sequiturs, the cartoon character Elmer Fudd confesses that "cartoon characters aren't weal." The interviewer chokes: "You mean you can't tie your head into a knot?" Then there's a flashy blonde who is roughed up and contemptuously thrown money by a puppet called Harry the Hippo (the voice of Sheldon Leonard); a mean young guy who's head is transformed into a basketball; a doctor who seems to show signs of hard-core psychosis after offering a tribute to the "health and happiness of the American family."

In the pilot, Sharon was played by Brianne Leary (later replaced by Hillary Bailey). Also in the cast were Bill Dana and Fran Ryan (as two beleaguered occupants of the hotel), Jerry Maren, Stuart Pankin and Johnny Haymer.

One of the Boys

Mickey Rooney tried making it on television again (see the index for his various other efforts), but this one didn't work out for him either.

The premise: Rooney plays feisty sixty-six-year-old Oliver Nugent, who is rescued from a nursing home by his grandson, Adam Shields (Dana Carvey), a college student who lets Oliver move in with him and his uptight roommate, Jonathan Burns (Nathan Lane). In the premiere episode, Oliver goes looking for a job that will keep him out of his nursing home roommate's hair. He didn't find work, but he did make a friend (played by Scatman Crothers). The two of them went to a restaurant, started singing together, and were offered a part-time job entertaining there.

Also in the cast: Francine Beers, Brandon Maggart, Marilyn Cooper, Joseph Bova.

Said Rooney before the first show aired: "Gosh, I love TV, and this show is perfect for it. It's in good taste, flamboyantly. Its writing and scripts are justified by tremendous performances. It has the quality of an *Andy Hardy* and the frivolity of a *Sanford and Son*."

The show started swell in the Nielsens—Number 18. That was in January. But within a month, it was in 68th place, where it stayed for some time until NBC killed the show. Rooney wasn't too pleased about that: "The show never stood a chance. It was placed on Saturday nights at 8 P.M. when everybody is out to dinner. Besides, nobody knew it was on. NBC kept saying, 'Our Pride Is Showing.' It's more like 'Our Idiocy Is Showing.' Let them put Tony Randall or Gary Coleman in that spot and see what happens to them." (Actually, NBC did put Gary Coleman's *Diff'rent Strokes* in that exact spot the following season, followed, ninety minutes later, by Randall's *Love, Sidney*. Coleman survived; Randall didn't.)

But Rooney had more to say: "I'm through with NBC. They'll never get another chance. *One of the Boys* had to be a flop because it was [NBC president] Fred Silverman's last order before he was fired. So Grant Tinker had to see it fall. I don't care for myself. It's the rest of the cast and crew I feel sorry for. They put so much good work and effort into the show. It's too bad those guys at NBC don't know anything about programming. They seem to thrive on being the third place network. I think they stink."

Open All Night

This show was one of the highlights of the 1981–1982 sitcom season. It was well written and had bright, funny performances. Unfortunately for the show, it wasn't really *about* anything—just the trials and tribulations of a family that runs a 7-Eleven–type store.

It was about Gordon Feester (George Dzundza), a community college dropout who'd been a mediocre soldier, a short-order cook and a used-car salesman (the opening theme song told us all this about him). He attempted to redeem himself by being the proprietor of a "364" store—a twenty-four-hour shop in Los Angeles. Along with him was a daffy wife (Susan Tyrrell), and a wimped-out spacecadet stepson (Sam Whipple in one of the best sitcom performances of all time). There were also two inept

neighborhood cops named Steve and Edie (Jay Tarsis and Bever-Leigh Banfield), who can't locate the night manager who ripped them off, even though they had some helpful clues: he had one eye and one leg. But along came mountain-sized Robin (Bubba Smith), who was the answer to Gordon's prayers.

ABC put the show on Saturday nights, where it died swiftly. Perhaps *Open All Night* was ahead of its time (the son was a Valley Boy months before anyone knew what that meant), or just given a bad time (after the *Mary Tyler Moore* days, Saturday night sitcoms faced an ugly death).

Police Squad!

After *Airplane!* swept from the sky and captured America's hearts at the box office, TV tried to cash in. They signed the movie's creators to come up with a sitcom. *Police Squad!* was just that, filled with the same bent, loopy humor, and starring *Airplane*'s own Leslie Nielsen (here he played Lieutenant Frank Drebin). One time, he calmly told a murder victim's widow: "Sorry to bother you at such a time. We would have come earlier, but your husband wasn't dead then." Also on the show were Alan North, Rex Hamilton, Ed Williams, William Duell, Barbara Tarbuck, Terry Wills, Terence Beasor, Russell Shannon, Jimmy Briscoe and Kathryn Leigh Scott.

A parody of the sixties' TV police shows, the series was

Police Squad: *Leslie Nielsen*

scheduled to be on for just six episodes, with the hope that it would be successful enough to warrant becoming a full-time series. It never did. It was sharp, wicked, brittle, at times brilliant. Perhaps too brilliant. There are many theories as to why it failed: No laugh track or live studio audience at all (so you had to figure out for yourself what was funny and what wasn't, since there was no Greek Chorus yukking it up in the background to guide you). Also, there were no characters on the show to care about; only caricatures. Plus, you had to pay attention to the show, especially since so much of the humor was visual. (Once, when the cops were driving through New York's Little Italy, there was a shot of the Coliseum behind them.) You couldn't walk into the other room or read *TV Guide* or do your homework while it was on. You had to either watch or not watch. Most Americans chose the latter.

Initially, *Police Squad!* did okay—Number 26 in the ratings—but it started slipping, and by the fourth week the show was Number 57. Plus there were other problems. Each week, in the opening credit sequence, a celebrity would get murdered, and that would be that—you'd never see him or hear about him again. It was just a loony non sequitur. One episode opened with John Belushi being killed—and was scheduled to air just days after he died from a drug overdose. That episode had to be shelved. Eventually, so was the whole series. ABC didn't even let it run out its six-show commitment. But when *Taxi* was canceled by ABC (and picked up by NBC), ABC replaced it during the summer with reruns of *Police Squad!* and the two unaired episodes, but it never picked up an audience. There was talk of all the episodes being edited together for a European theatrical film, but that never worked out, either.

Report to Murphy

From the title, it didn't sound like a sitcom, but it was. *Report to Murphy* was a midseason replacement starring Michael Keaton (who went on to win fans in the movie *Night Shift*) as a trusting parole officer—Murphy—who had unorthodox approaches to handling ex-cons. His superior (played by Olivia Cole) let him have his way, much to the amusement of his cynical co-parole officer (played by Donnelly Rhodes). Assistant District Attorney Baker (played by Margot Rose) was his main love interest in the show.

Also in the cast: Donna Ponterotto, Dan Hedaya, Woodrow Parfrey, Ken Foree and Howard Dayton.

Forget the situations. Here are some of the jokes from the show: "Murphy," says his girlfriend, "I never move in with anyone on the first date."

Murphy on the phone to a woman: "Cathy, you're too kinky for me . . . I feel so vulnerable when I'm tied up like that."

Murphy asks a parolee why he stole a tape deck and the guy replies: "I dunno . . . who can fathom the criminal mind?"

Well, maybe you had to be there. Few were, and the show was thrown into the CBS slammer with no hope of rehabilitation.

Teachers Only

When Lynn Redgrave left *House Calls* on doctors' orders (see 1980 for specifics), she rebounded with this series—a limited midseason replacement debuting in April on NBC.

Here's the story: Redgrave played Diana Swanson, an idealistic teacher who takes a personal interest in her students and their problems. She was spoon-fed wisdom by Principal Cooper (Norman Fell, formerly Stanley Roper on, and then off, *Three's Company*), who said to her on the pilot: "You're paid to be a teacher, not a psychiatrist." Other teachers: Dreyfuss (Adam Arkin), who seemed to be only interested in scoring a date; Lois (Kit McDonough), who was dizzy but sweet; wisecracking Gwen (Vanessa Clark); and Pafko (Richard Karron), the school custodian.

Although the show did okay in the ratings, the critics weren't too wild about the first few episodes. Said the *New York Times:* "Lynn Redgrave departed from *House Calls* reportedly because the producers would not allow her to breast-feed her new baby on the set. She's now in another sitcom, *Teachers Only,* and it would seem that she should come up with another unusual excuse to get out of this one."

CBS renewed *Teachers Only*—and then held it back for major renovations. When the show returned in January of 1983, it occupied the spot where *Love, Sidney* once lived on Saturday nights. All the regulars—except for Redgrave and Fell—had been dismissed. Whereas the first time around the school was a middle-class, white-bread school, now they were working in a downtrodden Brooklyn school. Said the new producer: "We feel it's not fair in a half-hour show to be showing affluence of this kind in a rough economy." Another change: Redgrave's character was no longer a teacher, but a guidance counselor. And Fell's character changed too: whereas before he was weak and powerless, he had become dynamic and had more authority. The other major change: They tried to make Redgrave's character more vulnerable—assertive at work, but lacking in confidence with men and social situations. New cast members included Teresa Ganzel as Sam, Jean Smart as Shari, Steve Ryan as Spud and Tim Reid as Michael.

1982–1983

WHATEVER HAPPENED TO 1982–1983?

It's too early to tell the fate of this season. No true hits have emerged—except for a few critical raves. And, once again, there are still no shows that anyone seems to be rushing home to see (or even bothering to set the VCR for).

And the networks are in trouble. Viewership is way down as more and more people are switching to cable, switching to video games, or just plain switching off. The networks are worried. Oh, not worried enough to try new and innovative programs. Naturally not. In fact, most of the 1982–1983 shows are tired recycles of other shows: *Gloria* (spin-off of *All in the Family*), *Silver Spoons* (inspired by the movie *Arthur*), *Newhart* (*The Bob Newhart Show*), *Amanda's* (from the British sitcom *Fawlty Towers*), *Mama's Family* (*The Carol Burnett Show*), *The New Odd Couple* (the old *Odd Couple*) and *Filthy Rich* (a spoof of *Dallas*). In fact, the only new shows that are really *new*, with no previous television antecedents, are *Square Pegs*, *Cheers* and a couple of others. Nonetheless, the networks were still hoping we'd watch.

ALSO RANS

Cheers

Probably the most highly touted show of the season was *Cheers*, the name of a neighborhood bar in Boston. The owner and chief bartender, young, handsome Sam Malone (Ted Danson), is an ex-baseball player and recovered alcoholic (he explains that he quit the Red Sox because of "elbow problems," but that he's now fully cured of his "injuries"). Sam has hired his ditsy former coach, Ernie Pantusso (Nicholas Colasanto), to help him tend bar, although Ernie claims he's been working on a book for six years ("You're writing a novel?" someone asks. "No, reading one," Ernie explains). And there are others, of course: the pretty, over-intellectual former Boston University teaching-assistant-turned-cocktail waitress Diane Chambers (Shelley Long), who was jilted by her academic intended ("He has an article in the current *Harper's*") and ends up coming to work at Cheers—"And what better place is there in which to study life in all its many facets than here?" Another waitress is tough and tiny Carla Tortelli (Rhea Perlman), who claims her TV repairman ex-

Cheers *(from left, in rear): Nicholas Colasanto, Shelley Long, Ted Danson; (front): Rhea Perlman and George Wendt*

husband "isn't all bad . . . he left me with four kids, but still fixes my set and only bills me for the parts." The show's other regular is sports strategist and steady customer Norm (George Wendt), who comes in every day for one beer and stays for too many. Asked if his wife wonders where he is, he replied, "She wonders—she doesn't care, but she wonders."

Created by some of the writers and producers of *Taxi*, *Cheers* did awfully in the ratings in the first half of the season, but—in an act of faith on the part of NBC—the show was renewed and moved to a later time slot on Thursday nights.

Family Ties

*F*amily Ties is another intelligent comedy that managed to hold its own. The premise is simple: It's about parents who are liberal, and their kids who aren't. But the gimmick never got in the way of the show, which carried the comedy to logical—rather than illogical—conclusions. In the premiere episode, Elyse and Steven Keaton (Meredith Baxter–Birney and Michael Gross) are showing their three children slides of their good old days—the sixties. The scene is a peace rally, and the person on screen has long hair and a headband. "Oh, Mommy, you look so pretty. Like an Indian princess," says nine-year-old Jennifer (Tina Yothers). "That's your father, dear," Elyse replies.

The Keaton kids are throwbacks. Seventeen-year-old Alex (Michael J. Fox) is a young Young Republican who's hung a poster of William F. Buckley over his bed, reads the *Wall Street Journal* and dresses for success. Fifteen-year-old Mallory (Justine Bateman) suffers from chronic embarrassment at almost everything her parents say or do. She is far more interested in designer jeans than politics, and picks sprouts out of her school lunches. The

Family Ties *(from left, in rear): Justine Bateman, Michael Gross, Meredith Baxter–Birney, Michael J. Fox; (front): Tina Yothers*

youngest Keaton, Jennifer, has both feet firmly on the ground and her ear to the phone.

It's the parents who hold it all together. Elyse and Steven, former sixties activists, both have careers—she's an architect, he runs the local PBS station. They're open-minded, caring and still very much in love (in fact, their constant smooching grosses Mallory out). To their amazement—and dismay—their kids are growing up to resemble the generation against which they rebelled.

Gloria

*W*hen in doubt . . . spin off. That's what the creators of *All in the Family* did with *Gloria*, the bucolic adventures

Gloria: *Lou Richards, Sally Struthers, Christian Jacobs, Burgess Meredith and Jo de Winter*

of Ms. Bunker Stivic. It could have been called "Is there life after Meathead?"

Apparently so, for although the show received mixed reviews, it certainly did well in the ratings (of course, directly following the ratings winners *Sixty Minutes* and *Archie Bunker's Place* didn't hurt a bit).

The story was this: Abandoned by husband Michael, who ran off to a commune with a student named Muffy (we thought he'd gotten over the sixties mentality in the late seventies), Gloria (Sally Struthers) is anxious to carve out a new life for herself: she's going to study to become a veterinarian. Gloria goes off to upstate New York to study with crusty Dr. Willard Adams (Burgess Meredith), to learn about veterinary medicine. She and her eight-year-old son Joey (Christian Jacobs) learn to live with Adams' partner, a semiliberated vet named Maggie Lawrence (Jo de Winter), and his assistant, a semiliterate named Clark Uhley (Lou Richards).

Reviews of the show were mixed. Said the *New York Times:* "Miss Struthers is, as usual, a problem. She is terribly earnest, but then smothers her just-folks characterization in a hairdo that could have been left over from last night's most fashionable discotheque opening. When in doubt, she has a tendency to overact, resorting to Paul Lynde reaction bits or, in two instances, vulgar Bronx cheers. Two years of washing those cages would seem, from this vantage point, interminable." *Variety,* on the other hand, called *Gloria* "the biggest new comedy of the season . . . it has a lot going for it . . . the show looks like a winner."

It Takes Two

This is a show about equal rights. Dr. Sam Quinn (Richard Crenna, veteran of so many sitcoms that if you want to know what they are, head for the index) is a chief of surgery at a Chicago hospital, and he is concerned about progress. His wife's progress. Molly (Patty Duke Astin; again, see the index), after years as a doting mother and devoted wife, finished law school and is now an assistant district attorney. Sam was proud of her at first. Then he started saying things like: "Do you know in the last two months this bed has been used solely for the purpose of sleeping?" So it's feminism vs. chauvinism . . . not to mention the children: eighteen-year-old Andy (Anthony Edwards), and sixteen-year-old Lisa (Helen Hunt). Plus a dippy live-in mother (hers, played by Billie Bird).

Says Molly, about a psychopathic kid she's prosecuting: "Says it's because he comes from a broken home. Of course he comes from a broken home—he killed his father." *It Takes Two* ran on ABC on Thursday nights.

Mama's Family

We've had crazy spin-offs before: Movies had become sitcoms; sitcoms had been translated into dramatic shows. But not since *The Honeymooners*—which began as a segment of Jackie Gleason's variety show—had a variety show spun-off into a sitcom.

Several seasons after *The Carol Burnett Show* laid itself to rest, one of its beloved segments—"The Family"— became a weekly sitcom. True, Carol Burnett's Eunice and Harvey Korman's Ed were no longer regulars (they made guest visits), but Vicki Lawrence was still running around in that curly gray wig playing matriarch to that bickering southern family.

Also on this NBC show, which had its debut at the halfway point of the 1982–1983 season, were Ken Berry, playing Mama's ne'er-do-well son, Vint, who moves back home when his own house is repossessed; Eric Brown and Karin Argoud, as Vint's kids; Rue McClanahan (formerly neighbor Vivien on *Maude*), playing Mama's bickering sister, Fran; and Betty White (SueAnn Nivens on *The Mary Tyler Moore Show* in another life) as Mama's daughter, Ellen.

The New Odd Couple

Shortly after ABC announced they were remaking the sitcom *The Odd Couple* with a black Oscar and Felix, the playwright Neil Simon announced he was reviving the stage version of *The Odd Couple* with a female duo. What can we expect next? An all-gay/Hispanic/quadraplegic/diabetic/one of the above/all of the above/cast?

The New Odd Couple: *Ron Glass and Demond Wilson*

At any rate, this *Odd Couple* was just like the 1970–1971 season *Odd Couple*. Except in blackface. In fact, some of the scripts and stories were the same. The changes: Felix (Ron Glass, formerly of *Barney Miller*) is less persnickety and does more fashion photography and fewer bar mitzvahs and weddings. Oscar (Demond Wilson, formerly *son* in *Sanford and Son*) is the same: a sportswriter and a slob. And the year is now 1982, not 1970.

Newhart

Following *M*A*S*H* on Monday nights, *Newhart*—or anyone else for that matter—couldn't help but succeed. But if you like Bob Newhart (and millions did on the good old *Bob Newhart Show*), then you'd probably like *Newhart*, with or without Hawkeye as a lead-in.

This time around, Bob Newhart played Dick Loudon, a how-to book writer who, with his wife Joanna (Mary Frann), bought the Stratford Inn, a dusty—albeit historic (1774)—place in Vermont. It seems a strange choice, since they know no one in Vermont—nor do they know anything about running an inn. First, they hired a nitwit incompetent caretaker (Tom Poston, who had played Bob's friend The Peeper on the old show). They had a compulsively lying neighbor, Kirk Devana (Steven Kampmann). They threw in a maid, Leslie Vanderkellen (Jennifer Holmes), who was studying for her master's in Renaissance theology.

Occasionally, they even managed to have a customer or two. When they got their first guest, Bob said: "Just give me your John Hancock." "Where?" asked the guest. "Right there, under John Hancock." When the same guest asked how much the rooms were, Bob had to look it up in the ledger: "Rooms, ah, here we are . . . that'll be a farthing."

Silver Spoons

There are two schools of thought about *Silver Spoons*. Take your pick:

The *Los Angeles Herald Examiner:* "Viewers are going to have to search their memories to remember a more charming half-hour than *Silver Spoons*, a thoroughly de-

Silver Spoons: *Son (Ricky Schroder) and father (Joel Higgins)*

lightful new series. Any way you look at it—the cast, writing, premise—you've got a freshness here that is unique and appealing.

The *Washington Post:* "If Norman Lear were dead, he'd be spinning in his grave; this is perhaps the worst show yet to come out of Embassy Television, formerly Tandem Productions, the company Lear co-founded but which is now managed by others. The humor is simpering and the heart-tugs appalling in this wretched sitcom . . . there's something here for everyone to hate."

So much for the reviews. Here's what all the fuss was about: Edward Stratton III (Joel Higgins, formerly Best in *Best of the West*) is a childlike adult. He likes Pac-Man, pinball machines, and riding on his toy train. His son Ricky (Ricky Schroder, star of such movies as *The Champ*) is an adultlike child. He is twelve years old and light years more mature than Edward is. As *TV Guide* said: "Edward is very rich. He also talks like Goofy, has the brains of a speed bump and lives in a mansion furnished by Santa Claus." What they failed to mention is that Edward is also kind and trusting and innocent. Ricky is considerably more cautious, analytical and responsible.

Others in the cast: Edward's lawyer, Leonard Rollins (Leonard Lightfoot), Edward's reasonable secretary (and later fiancée) Kate Summers (Erin Gray, who had been in the TV series *Buck Rogers*), and Derek Taylor (Jason Bateman, formerly on *Little House*), Ricky's Eddie Haskell-like school friend. John Houseman guested as Edward's straitlaced and snobby father, Edward Stratton II.

Square Pegs

This vividly unique sitcom—which had a pace, style and language all its own—had some of the most fascinating characters ever to grace the small screen.

Patty Greene (Sarah Jessica Parker) and Lauren Hutchinson (Amy Linker) are freshmen at Weemawee High School, where they vow to become popular—"even

Square Pegs *(from left, top row): Jon Caliri, Claudette Wells, Jami Gertz; (middle row): Tracy Nelson, John Femia, Merritt Butrick; (bottom row): Amy Linker and Sarah Jessica Parker*

if it kills us." They never do become popular, but they keep trying, week after week after week. What they are up against is Jennifer DeNuccio (Tracy Nelson, daughter of Rick), the class beauty who was born with the Jordache Look, and whose every sentence begins with the word "like" and ends with "you know"; handsome and tough Vinnie Pasetta (Jon Caliri), Jennifer's guy who drives his own van; and LaDonna Fredericks (Claudette Wells), Jennifer's best friend who is black, brassy and cool. Then there is Muffy Tepperman (Jami Gertz), who is majoring in pep, and organizes fundraisers for "Rosarita," her Guatemalan pen pal. That leaves two other peglets to be Lauren and Patty's friends: Marshall Blechtman (John Femia), who longs to stand up and be funny; and Johnny Slash (Merritt Butrick), totally New Wave in his blond braid and car, the "Slashmobile."

But it's really Patty and Lauren's show. Each has her own particular curse. Patty has glasses and is skinny and tall. Lauren is fat and has braces. She constantly prods Patty—mostly about boys and ploys to become popular.

Square Pegs—which is sort of the *Dobie Gillis* of the eighties—had its supporters and detractors. Many critics and viewers, because it was so different, and often lacking in form and structure, thought it didn't hold up; others, because it was so different and often lacking in form and structure, thought it held up fine.

Star of the Family

EDITOR'S NOTE: Although he didn't actually work on or contribute to *Star of the Family*, the author was co-creator of this show. This means that he came up with the idea upon which *Star of the Family* was based.

Once again, it all depends on who you talk to. The *Los Angeles Times*'s critic claimed that he had "hangovers that were more fun than *Star of the Family*." Other publications—the *Milwaukee Journal*, for example—thought *Star of the Family* was refreshing and promising.

It's too late now, since the show was an early 1982–1983 casualty, being canceled by ABC halfway into its run. But for memory lane's sake, here's the story of *Star of the Family*:

Overprotective Buddy Krebs (Brian Dennehy) has a sixteen-year-old daughter Jennie Lee (Kathy Maisnik) who is just starting to make it big as a country singer. But he doesn't know how to deal with the young star who wears low-cut costumes, goes on things called "gigs"—out-of-town yet—and has a blonde Amazon road manager named Moose (Judy Pioli)—"a person named after venison," Buddy cries. And it's all gotten worse since his wife has run off with a hotel manager (who he refers to as a bellhop), and his dim seventeen-year-old son Douggie

Star of the Family: *Kathy Maisnik, Michael Dudikoff and Brian Dennehy*

(Michael Dudikoff) eats chili dogs at 7 A.M. Then there are the guys at the firehouse where Buddy is captain: Feldman (Todd Susman), who writes to his mother that he's really a cardiologist; Rosetti (George Deloy), who, Buddy's convinced, has got the hots for his daughter; and Maximilian (Danny Mora), a street-wise and sharp-tongued Chicano.

THE TAGS

The Emmies: Who Won What

Each year the National Academy of Television Arts and Sciences gives its version of the Oscar, which is called the Emmy (short for Academy). Here is a brief list of the sitcoms that won Emmies over the years. Notice how the Academy seems to change the categories each year.

1949
The Life of Riley (with Jackie Gleason)—Best Film Made for and Viewed on Television

1950
Gertrude Berg *(The Goldbergs)*—Best Actress

1952
I Love Lucy—Best Situation Comedy
Lucille Ball *(I Love Lucy)*—Best Comedienne

1953
I Love Lucy—Best Situation Comedy
Make Room for Daddy—Best New Program
Eve Arden *(Our Miss Brooks)*—Best Female of a Regular Series
Vivian Vance *(I Love Lucy)*—Best Series Supporting Actress

1954
Danny Thomas *(Make Room for Daddy)*—Best Actor Starring in a Regular Series
Make Room for Daddy—Best Situation Comedy Series

1955
The Phil Silvers Show—Best Comedy Series
Phil Silvers *(The Phil Silvers Show)*—Best Actor (Continued Performance)
Lucille Ball *(I Love Lucy)*—Best Actress (Continued Performance)
Phil Silvers *(The Phil Silvers Show)*—Best Comedian
Nat Hiken *(The Phil Silvers Show)*—Best Director (Film Series)

1956
The Phil Silvers Show—Best Series (Half Hour or Less)
Robert Young *(Father Knows Best)*—Best Continued Performance by an Actor in a Dramatic Series
Sheldon Leonard, "Danny's Comeback" *(The Danny Thomas Show)*—Best Direction (Half Hour or Less)

1957
The Phil Silvers Show—Best Comedy Series
Robert Young *(Father Knows Best)*—Best Continued Performance by an Actor in a Dramatic or Comedy Series
Jane Wyatt *(Father Knows Best)*—Best Continued Performance by an Actress in a Dramatic or Comedy Series
Ann B. Davis *(The Bob Cummings Show)*—Best Continued Performance by an Actress in a Dramatic or Comedy Series

Nat Hiken et al. *(The Phil Silvers Show)*—Best Comedy Writing

1958–1959
(the year television "seasons" began)
Jane Wyatt *(Father Knows Best)*—Best Actress in a Leading Role (Continuing Character) in a Comedy Series
Ann B. Davis *(The Bob Cummings Show)*—Best Supporting Actress (Continuing Character) in a Comedy Series
Peter Tewksbury, "Medal for Margaret" *(Father Knows Best)*—Best Direction of a Single Program of a Comedy Series

1959–1960
Jane Wyatt *(Father Knows Best)*—Outstanding Performance by an Actress in a Series (Lead or Support)

1960–1961
Don Knotts *(The Andy Griffith Show)*—Outstanding Performance in a Supporting Role by an Actor or Actress in a Series
Sheldon Leonard *(The Danny Thomas Show)*—Outstanding Directorial Achievement in Comedy

1961–1962
Shirley Booth *(Hazel)*—Outstanding Continued Performance by an Actress in a Series (Lead)
Don Knotts *(The Andy Griffith Show)*—Outstanding Performance in a Supporting Role by an Actor
Carl Reiner *(The Dick Van Dyke Show)*—Outstanding Writing Achievement in Comedy
Nat Hiken *(Car 54, Where Are You?)*—Outstanding Directorial Achievement in Comedy

1962–1963
The Dick Van Dyke Show—Outstanding Program Achievement in the Field of Humor
Shirley Booth *(Hazel)*—Outstanding Continued Performance by an Actress in a Series (Lead)
Don Knotts *(The Andy Griffith Show)*—Outstanding Performance in a Supporting Role by an Actor
Carl Reiner *(The Dick Van Dyke Show)*—Outstanding Writing Achievement in Comedy
John Rich *(The Dick Van Dyke Show)*—Outstanding Directorial Achievement in Comedy

1963–1964
The Dick Van Dyke Show—Outstanding Program Achievement in the Field of Comedy
Dick Van Dyke *(The Dick Van Dyke Show)*—Outstanding Continued Performance by an Actor in a Series (Lead)
Mary Tyler Moore *(The Dick Van Dyke Show)*—Outstanding Continued Performance by an Actress in a Series (Lead)
Carl Reiner et al *(The Dick Van Dyke Show)*—Outstanding Writing Achievement in Comedy or Variety
Jerry Paris *(The Dick Van Dyke Show)*—Outstanding Directorial Achievement in Comedy

1964–1965

The Dick Van Dyke Show—Outstanding Program Achievement in Entertainment

Dick Van Dyke (*The Dick Van Dyke Show*)—Outstanding Individual Achievement in Entertainment

1965–1966

The Dick Van Dyke Show—Outstanding Comedy Series

Dick Van Dyke (*The Dick Van Dyke Show*)—Outstanding Continued Performance by an Actor in a Leading Role in a Comedy Series

Mary Tyler Moore (*The Dick Van Dyke Show*)—Outstanding Continued Performance by an Actress in a Leading Role in a Comedy Series

Don Knotts, "The Return of Barney Fife" (*The Andy Griffith Show*)—Outstanding Performance by an Actor in a Supporting Role in a Comedy

Alice Pearce (*Bewitched*)—Outstanding Performance by an Actress in a Supporting Role in a Comedy

Bill Persky and Sam Denoff, "Coast to Coast Big Mouth" (*The Dick Van Dyke Show*)—Outstanding Writing Achievement in Comedy

William Asher (*Bewitched*)—Outstanding Directorial Achievement in Comedy

1966–1967

The Monkees—Outstanding Comedy Series

Don Adams (*Get Smart!*)—Outstanding Continued Performance by an Actor in a Leading Role in a Comedy Series

Lucille Ball (*The Lucy Show*)—Outstanding Continued Performance by an Actress in a Leading Role in a Comedy Series

Don Knotts, "Barney Comes to Mayberry" (*The Andy Griffith Show*)—Outstanding Performance by an Actor in a Supporting Role in a Comedy

Frances Bavier (*The Andy Griffith Show*)—Outstanding Performance by an Actress in a Supporting Role in a Comedy

Buck Henry and Leonard Stern, "Ship of Spies" (*Get Smart!*)—Outstanding Writing Achievement in Comedy

James Frawley, "Royal Flush" (*The Monkees*)—Outstanding Directorial Achievement in Comedy

1967–1968

Get Smart!—Outstanding Comedy Series

Don Adams (*Get Smart!*)—Outstanding Continued Performance by an Actor in a Leading Role in a Comedy Series

Lucille Ball (*The Lucy Show*)—Outstanding Continued Performance by an Actress in a Leading Role in a Comedy Series

Werner Klemperer (*Hogan's Heroes*)—Outstanding Performance by an Actor in a Supporting Role in a Comedy

Marion Lorne (*Bewitched*)—Outstanding Performance by an Actress in a Supporting Role in a Comedy

Allan Burns and Chris Hayward, "The Coming-Out Party" (*He and She*)—Outstanding Writing Achievement in Comedy

Bruce Bilson, "Maxwell Smart, Private Eye" (*Get Smart!*)—Outstanding Directorial Achievement in Comedy

1968–1969

Get Smart!—Outstanding Comedy Series

Don Adams (*Get Smart!*)—Outstanding Continued Performance by an Actor in a Leading Role in a Comedy Series

Hope Lange (*The Ghost and Mrs. Muir*)—Outstanding Continued Performance by an Actress in a Leading Role in a Comedy Series

Werner Klemperer (*Hogan's Heroes*)—Outstanding Continued Performance by an Actor in a Supporting Role in a Series

1969–1970

My World and Welcome to It—Outstanding Comedy Series

William Windom (*My World and Welcome to It*)—Outstanding Continued Performance by an Actor in a Leading Role in a Comedy Series

Hope Lange (*The Ghost and Mrs. Muir*)—Outstanding Continued Performance by an Actress in a Leading Role in a Comedy Series

1970–1971

All in the Family—Outstanding Series, Comedy

All in the Family—Outstanding New Series

Jack Klugman (*The Odd Couple*)—Outstanding Performance by an Actor in a Leading Role in a Comedy Series

Edward Asner (*The Mary Tyler Moore Show*)—Outstanding Performance by an Actor in a Supporting Role in a Comedy

Valerie Harper (*The Mary Tyler Moore Show*)—Outstanding Performance by an Actress in a Supporting Role in a Comedy

Jay Sandrich, "Toulouse-Lautrec is One of my Favorite Artists" (*The Mary Tyler Moore Show*)—Outstanding Directorial Achievement in Comedy (Series)

James L. Brooks and Allan Burns, "Support Your Local Mother" (*The Mary Tyler Moore Show*)—Outstanding Writing Achievement in a Comedy (Series)

1971–1972

All in the Family—Outstanding Series (Comedy)

Carroll O'Connor (*All in the Family*)—Outstanding Continued Performance by an Actor in a Leading Role in a Comedy Series

Jean Stapleton (*All in the Family*)—Outstanding Continued Performance by an Actress in a Leading Role in a Comedy Series

Edward Asner (*The Mary Tyler Moore Show*)—Outstanding Performance by an Actor in a Supporting Role in Comedy

Valerie Harper (*The Mary Tyler Moore Show*)—Outstanding Performance by an Actress in a Supporting Role in Comedy

John Rich, "Sammy's Visit" (*All in the Family*)—Outstanding Writing Achievement in Comedy (Series)

Burt Styler, "Edith's Problem" (*All in the Family*)—Outstanding Writing Achievement in Comedy (Series)

1972–1973

All in the Family—Outstanding Comedy Series

Jack Klugman (*The Odd Couple*)—Outstanding Continued Performance by an Actor in a Leading Role in a Comedy Series

Mary Tyler Moore (*The Mary Tyler Moore Show*)—Outstanding Continued Performance by an Actress in a Leading Role in a Comedy Series

Ted Knight (*The Mary Tyler Moore Show*)—Outstanding Performance by an Actor in a Supporting Role in Comedy

Valerie Harper (*The Mary Tyler Moore Show*)—Outstanding Performance by an Actress in a Supporting Role in Comedy

Jay Sandrich, "It's Whether You Win or Lose" (*The Mary Tyler Moore Show*)—Outstanding Directorial Achievement in Comedy (Series)

Michael Ross, Bernie West, and Lee Kalcheim, "The Bunkers and the Swingers" (*All in the Family*)—Outstanding Writing Achievement in Comedy (Series)

1973–1974

M*A*S*H—Outstanding Comedy Series

Alan Alda (*M*A*S*H*)—Best Lead Actor in a Comedy Series, also Actor of the Year (Series)

Mary Tyler Moore (*The Mary Tyler Moore Show*)—Best Lead Actress in a Comedy Series, also Actress of the Year (Series)

Rob Reiner (*All in the Family*)—Best Supporting Actor in Comedy (For a Special Program, a One-time Appearance, or a Continuing Role)

Cloris Leachman, "The Lars Affair" (*The Mary Tyler Moore Show*)—Best Supporting Actress in Comedy (For a Special Program, a One-time Appearance in a Series, or a Continuing Role)

Jackie Cooper, "Carry on Hawkeye" (*M*A*S*H*)—Best Directing in Comedy (A Single Program of a Series with Continuing Characters and/or Theme)

Treva Silverman, "The Lou and Edie Story" (*The Mary Tyler Moore Show*)—Best Writing in Comedy (A Single Program of a Series with Continuing Characters and/or Theme), also Writer of the Year (Series)

1974–1975

The Mary Tyler Moore Show—Outstanding Comedy Series

Tony Randall (*The Odd Couple*)—Outstanding Lead Actor in a Comedy Series

Valerie Harper (*Rhoda*)—Outstanding Lead Actress in a Comedy Series

Ed Asner (*The Mary Tyler Moore Show*)—Outstanding Continued Performance by a Supporting Actor in a Comedy Series

Betty White (*The Mary Tyler Moore Show*)—Outstanding Continued Performance by a Supporting Actress in a Comedy Series

Cloris Leachman, "Phyllis Whips Inflation" (*The Mary Tyler Moore Show*)—Outstanding Single Performance by a Supporting Actress in a Comedy or Drama Series (for a One-time Appearance in a Regular or Limited Series)

Gene Reynolds (*M*A*S*H*)—Outstanding Directing in a Comedy Series (A Single Episode of a Regular or Limited Series with Continuing Characters and/or Theme)

Ed Weinberger and Stan Daniels, "Mary Goes to Jail" (*The Mary Tyler Moore Show*)—Outstanding Writing in a Comedy Series (a Single Episode of a Regular or Limited Series with Continuing Characters and/or Theme)

1975–1976

The Mary Tyler Moore Show—Outstanding Comedy Series

Jack Albertson (*Chico and the Man*)—Outstanding Lead Actor in a Comedy Series

Mary Tyler Moore (*The Mary Tyler Moore Show*)—Outstanding Lead Actress in a Comedy Series

Ted Knight (*The Mary Tyler Moore Show*)—Outstanding Continued Performance by a Supporting Actor in a Comedy Series

Betty White (*The Mary Tyler Moore Show*)—Outstanding Continued Performance by a Supporting Actress in a Comedy Series

Gene Reynolds, "Welcome to Korea" (*M*A*S*H*)—Outstanding Directing in a Comedy Series (A Single Episode of a Regular or Limited Series with Continuing Characters and/or Theme)

David Lloyd, "Chuckles Bites the Dust" (*The Mary Tyler Moore Show*)—Outstanding Writing in a Comedy Series (a Single Episode of a Regular or Limited Series with Continuing Characters and/or Theme)

1976–1977

The Mary Tyler Moore Show—Outstanding Comedy Series

Carroll O'Connor (*All in the Family*)—Outstanding Lead Actor in a Comedy Series

Beatrice Arthur (*Maude*)—Outstanding Lead Actress in a Comedy Series

Gary Burghoff (*M*A*S*H*)—Best Continued Performance by a Supporting Actor in a Comedy Series

Alan Alda, "Dear Sigmund" (*M*A*S*H*)—Outstanding Directing in a Comedy Series (a Single Episode of a Regular or Limited Series with Continuing Characters and/or Theme)

Allan Burns et al, "The Final Show" (*The Mary Tyler Moore Show*)—Outstanding Writing in a Comedy Series (a Single Episode of a Regular or Limited Series with Continuing Characters and/or Theme)

1977–1978

All in the Family—Outstanding Comedy Series

Carroll O'Connor (*All in the Family*)—Outstanding Lead Actor in a Comedy Series

Jean Stapleton (*All in the Family*)—Outstanding Lead Actress in a Comedy Series

Rob Reiner (*All in the Family*)—Outstanding Continued Performance by a Supporting Actor in a Comedy Series

Julie Kavner (*Rhoda*)—Outstanding Continued Performance by a Supporting Actress in a Comedy Series

Paul Bogart, "Edith's 50th Birthday" (*All in the Family*)—Outstanding Directing in a Comedy Series (a Single Episode of a Regular or Limited Series with Continuing Characters and/or Theme)

Bob Weiskopf and Bob Schiller, teleplay; Barry Harman and Harve Brosten, story, "Cousin Liz" (*All in the Family*)—Outstanding Writing in a Comedy Series

1978–1979

Carroll O'Connor (*All in the Family*)—Outstanding Lead in a Comedy Series for a Continued or Single Performance in a Regular Series

Sally Struthers, "California, Here We Are" (*All in the Family*)—Outstanding Supporting Actress in a Comedy or Comedy-Variety or Music Series for a Continued or Single Performance in a Regular Series

Alan Alda, "Inga" (*M*A*S*H*)—Outstanding Writing in a Comedy or Comedy-Variety or Music Series for a Single Episode of a Regular Series

Andy Zall, pilot (*Stockard Channing in Just Friends*)—Outstanding Video Tape Editing for a Series for a Single Episode of a Regular Series

Taxi—Outstanding Comedy Series

Ruth Gordon, "Sugar Mama" (*Taxi*)—Outstanding Lead Actress in a Comedy Series for a Continued or Single Performance in a Regular Series

Robert Guillaume (*Soap*)—Outstanding Supporting Actor in a Comedy or Comedy-Variety or Music Series for a Continued or Single Performance in a Regular Series

M. Pam Blumenthal, "Paper Marriage" (*Taxi*)—Outstanding Film Editing for a Series for a Single Episode of a Regular Series

1979–1980

Taxi—Outstanding Comedy Series

Richard Mulligan (*Soap*)—Outstanding Lead Actor in a Comedy Series

Cathryn Damon (*Soap*)—Outstanding Lead Actress in a Comedy Series

Harry Morgan (*M*A*S*H*)—Outstanding Supporting Actor in a Comedy Series

Loretta Swit (*M*A*S*H*)—Outstanding Supporting Actress in a Comedy Series

James Burrows, "Louie and the Nice Girl" (*Taxi*)—Outstanding Directing in a Comedy Series (a Single Episode of a Regular Series)

Bob Colleary, "Photographer" (*Barney Miller*)—Outstanding Writing in a Comedy Series (a Single Episode of a Regular Series)

M. Pam Blumenthal, "Louie and the Nice Girl" (*Taxi*)—Outstanding Achievement in Film Editing for a Series for a Single Episode of a Regular Series

1980–1981
Taxi—Outstanding Comedy Series
Judd Hirsch (*Taxi*)—Outstanding Lead Actor in a Comedy Series
Isabel Sanford (*The Jeffersons*)—Outstanding Lead Actress in a Comedy Series
Danny De Vito (*Taxi*)—Outstanding Supporting Actor in a Comedy Series
Eileen Brennan (*Private Benjamin*)—Outstanding Supporting Actress in a Comedy Series
James Burrows, "Elaine's Strange Triangle" (*Taxi*)—Outstanding Directing in a Comedy Series (a Single Episode in a Regular Series)
Michael Leeson, "Tony's Sister and Jim" (*Taxi*)—Outstanding Writing in a Comedy Series (a Single Episode in a Regular Series)

M. Pam Blumenthal, Jack Michon, "Elaine's Strange Triangle" (*Taxi*)—Outstanding Achievement in Film Editing for a Series for a Single Episode of a Regular Series

Andy Ackerman, "Bah, Humbug" (*WKRP in Cincinnati*)—Outstanding Video Tape Editing for a Series for a Single Episode of a Regular Series

1981–1982
Barney Miller—Outstanding Comedy Series
Alan Alda (*M*A*S*H*)—Outstanding Lead Actor in a Comedy Series
Carol Kane, "Simka Returns" (*Taxi*)—Outstanding Lead Actress in a Comedy Series
Christopher Lloyd (*Taxi*)—Outstanding Supporting Actor in a Comedy Series
Loretta Swit (*M*A*S*H*)—Outstanding Supporting Actress in a Comedy Series
Alan Rafkin, "Barbara's Crisis" (*One Day at a Time*)—Outstanding Directing in a Comedy Series (a Single Episode of a Regular Series)
Ken Estin, "Elegant Iggy" (*Taxi*)—Outstanding Writing in a Comedy Series (a Single Episode of a Regular Series)

The Ratings: Who Won What

The following were the top-rated sitcoms of their seasons, ranked according to their standing in the over-all television ratings for each year.

1950–1951
10. *Mama*

1951–1952
 3. *I Love Lucy*
11. *Mama*
13. *Amos 'n' Andy*

1952–1953
 1. *I Love Lucy*

1953–1954
 1. *I Love Lucy*
14. *The Life of Riley*
15. *Our Miss Brooks*

1954–1955
 1. *I Love Lucy*
12. *December Bride*

1955–1956
 2. *I Love Lucy*
 6. *December Bride*
12. *Private Secretary*

1956–1957
 1. *I Love Lucy*
 5. *December Bride*

1957–1958
 2. *The Danny Thomas Show*
 9. *December Bride*
16. *The Gale Storm Show*
15. *Father Knows Best*

1958–1959
 5. *The Danny Thomas Show*
 8. *The Real McCoys*
14. *Father Knows Best*
22. *The Ann Sothern Show*

1959–1960
 4. *The Danny Thomas Show*
 6. *Father Knows Best*
11. *The Real McCoys*
13. *The Bing Crosby Show*
17. *Dennis the Menace*
25. *The Ann Sothern Show*

1960–1961
 4. *The Andy Griffith Show*
 5. *The Real McCoys*
11. *Dennis the Menace*
12. *The Danny Thomas Show*
13. *My Three Sons*
25. *The Many Loves of Dobie Gillis*

1961–1962
 4. *Hazel*
 7. *The Andy Griffith Show*
 8. *The Danny Thomas Show*
11. *My Three Sons*
14. *The Real McCoys*

17. *Dennis the Menace*
21. *Car 54, Where Are You?*
23. *The Many Loves of Dobie Gillis*
25. *The Joey Bishop Show*

1962–1963
 1. *The Beverly Hillbillies*
 5. *The Lucy Show*
 6. *The Andy Griffith Show*
 8. *The Danny Thomas Show*
 9. *The Dick Van Dyke Show*
15. *Hazel*

1963–1964
 1. *The Beverly Hillbillies*
 3. *The Dick Van Dyke Show*
 4. *Petticoat Junction*
 5. *The Andy Griffith Show*
 6. *The Lucy Show*
 9. *The Danny Thomas Show*
10. *My Favorite Martian*
16. *The Donna Reed Show*
18. *The Patty Duke Show*
22. *Hazel*
23. *McHale's Navy*

1964–1965
 2. *Bewitched*
 3. *Gomer Pyle, USMC*
 4. *The Andy Griffith Show*
 7. *The Dick Van Dyke Show*
 8. *The Lucy Show*
12. *The Beverly Hillbillies*
13. *My Three Sons*
15. *Petticoat Junction*
18. *The Munsters*
19. *Gilligan's Island*
23. *The Addams Family*
24. *My Favorite Martian*

1965–1966
 2. *Gomer Pyle, USMC*
 3. *The Lucy Show*
 6. *The Andy Griffith Show*
 7. *Bewitched*
 8. *The Beverly Hillbillies*
 9. *Hogan's Heroes*
11. *Green Acres*
12. *Get Smart!*
15. *My Three Sons*
16. *The Dick Van Dyke Show*
21. *Petticoat Junction*
22. *Gilligan's Island*

1966–1967
 3. *The Andy Griffith Show*
 4. *The Lucy Show*
 6. *Green Acres*
 8. *Bewitched*
 9. *The Beverly Hillbillies*
10. *Gomer Pyle, USMC*

15. *Family Affair*
18. *Hogan's Heroes*
22. *Get Smart!*
23. *Petticoat Junction*

1967–1968
 1. *The Andy Griffith Show*
 2. *The Lucy Show*
 3. *Gomer Pyle, USMC*
 5. *Family Affair*
11. *Bewitched*
12. *The Beverly Hillbillies*
16. *Green Acres*
24. *My Three Sons*

1968–1969
 2. *Gomer Pyle, USMC*
 4. *Mayberry, RFD*
 5. *Family Affair*
 7. *Julia*
 9. *Here's Lucy*
10. *The Beverly Hillbillies*
12. *Bewitched*
14. *My Three Sons*
19. *Green Acres*

1969–1970
 4. *Mayberry, RFD*
 5. *Family Affair*
 6. *Here's Lucy*
10. *The Doris Day Show*
11. *The Bill Cosby Show*
15. *My Three Sons*
18. *The Beverly Hillbillies*
25. *Bewitched*

1970–1971
 3. *Here's Lucy*
15. *Mayberry, RFD*
19. *My Three Sons*
20. *The Doris Day Show*
22. *The Mary Tyler Moore Show*

1971–1972
 1. *All in the Family*
 6. *Sanford and Son*
 8. *Funny Face*
10. *The Mary Tyler Moore Show*
11. *Here's Lucy*
16. *The Partridge Family*
18. *The New Dick Van Dyke Show*
24. *The Doris Day Show*

1972–1973
 1. *All in the Family*
 2. *Sanford and Son*
 4. *Maude*
 5. *Bridget Loves Bernie*
 7. *The Mary Tyler Moore Show*
15. *Here's Lucy*
16. *The Bob Newhart Show*
19. *The Partridge Family*

1973–1974
1. *All in the Family*
3. *Sanford and Son*
4. *M*A*S*H*
6. *Maude*
9. *The Mary Tyler Moore Show*
12. *The Bob Newhart Show*
16. *Happy Days*
17. *Good Times*

1974–1975
1. *All in the Family*
2. *Sanford and Son*
3. *Chico and the Man*
4. *The Jeffersons*
5. *M*A*S*H*
6. *Rhoda*
7. *Good Times*
9. *Maude*
11. *The Mary Tyler Moore Show*
17. *The Bob Newhart Show*
25. *Paul Sand in Friends and Lovers*

1975–1976
1. *All in the Family*
3. *Laverne and Shirley*
4. *Maude*
6. *Phyllis*
7. *Sanford and Son*
8. *Rhoda*
11. *Happy Days*
12. *One Day at a Time*
15. *M*A*S*H*
17. *Good Heavens*
18. *Welcome Back, Kotter*
19. *The Mary Tyler Moore Show*
21. *The Jeffersons*
24. *Good Times*
25. *Chico and the Man*

1976–1977
1. *Happy Days*
2. *Laverne and Shirley*
4. *M*A*S*H*

10. *One Day at a Time*
11. *Three's Company*
12. *All in the Family*
13. *Welcome Back, Kotter*
17. *Barney Miller*
24. *The Jeffersons*
25. *What's Happening*

1977–1978
1. *Laverne and Shirley*
2. *Happy Days*
3. *Three's Company*
6. *All in the Family*
8. *Alice*
9. *M*A*S*H*
10. *One Day at a Time*
13. *Soap*
18. *Barney Miller*

1978–1979
1. *Laverne and Shirley*
2. *Three's Company*
3. *Happy Days*
4. *Mork and Mindy*
5. *Angie*
6. *M*A*S*H*
8. *All in the Family*
9. *The Ropers*
10. *Taxi*
13. *Alice*
15. *One Day at a Time*
19. *Barney Miller*
23. *WKRP in Cincinnati*
25. *Soap*

1979–1980
2. *Three's Company*
4. *M*A*S*H*
5. *Alice*
7. *Flo*
8. *The Jeffersons*
10. *One Day at a Time*
11. *WKRP in Cincinnati*
12. *Goodtime Girls*

13. *Archie Bunker's Place*
14. *Taxi*
17. *House Calls*
20. *Happy Days*
24. *Barney Miller*

1980–1981
4. *M*A*S*H*
6. *Private Benjamin*
7. *The Jeffersons*
8. *Alice*
9. *Three's Company*
10. *House Calls*
13. *One Day at a Time*
14. *The Two of Us*
15. *Archie Bunker's Place*
19. *Too Close for Comfort*
20. *Happy Days*
23. *Diff'rent Strokes*
24. *Laverne and Shirley*

1981–1982
3. *Three's Company*
4. *The Jeffersons*
5. *Joanie Loves Chachi*
7. *Alice*
9. *Too Close for Comfort*
10. *M*A*S*H*
11. *One Day at a Time*
14. *Archie Bunker's Place*
19. *Happy Days*
21. *Laverne and Shirley*

1982–1983
3. *M*A*S*H*
6. *Three's Company*
11. *The Jeffersons*
13. *Newhart*
16. *9 to 5*
17. *One Day at a Time*
19. *Gloria*
20. *Goodnight, Beantown*
23. *Archie Bunker's Place*

The Seasons: Who Ran the Longest

The following are the longest-running sitcoms (through January 1983):

1. *The Honeymooners* (on *The Jackie Gleason Show*)—15 seasons
2. *The Adventures of Ozzie and Harriet*—14 seasons
3. *All in the Family* (and *Archie Bunker's Place*)—13 seasons (so far)
4. *The Danny Thomas Show* (*Make Room for Daddy* and *Make Room for Granddaddy*)—13 seasons
5. *The Lucy Show, Here's Lucy*—12 seasons
6. *My Three Sons*—12 seasons
7. *M*A*S*H*—11 seasons
8. *Happy Days*—10 seasons (so far)
9. *Barney Miller*—9 seasons
10. *The Beverly Hillbillies*—9 seasons
11. *Father Knows Best*—9 seasons
12. *The Jeffersons*—9 seasons (so far)
13. *The Andy Griffith Show*—8 seasons
14. *Bewitched*—8 seasons
15. *The Donna Reed Show*—8 seasons
16. *Laverne and Shirley*—8 seasons (so far)
17. *One Day at a Time*—8 seasons (so far)
18. *The George Burns and Gracie Allen Show*—8 seasons
19. *I Love Lucy* (including *The Sunday Lucy Show* and *The Lucy Show*)—8 seasons
20. *Mama*—8 seasons
21. *Alice*—7 seasons (so far)
22. *The Bob Newhart Show*—7 seasons
23. *The Life of Riley*—7 seasons
24. *The Mary Tyler Moore Show*—7 seasons
25. *Petticoat Junction*—7 seasons
26. *December Bride*—6 seasons
27. *The Goldbergs*—6 seasons
28. *Gomer Pyle, USMC*—6 seasons
29. *Good Times*—6 seasons
30. *Green Acres*—6 seasons
31. *Hogan's Heroes*—6 seasons
32. *Leave It to Beaver*—6 seasons
33. *Maude*—6 seasons
34. *The Real McCoys*—6 seasons
35. *Sanford and Son*—6 seasons
36. *Three's Company*—6 seasons

INDEX

Index

Index